THE OXFORD HANDBOO

RELIGION
AND
AMERICAN
POLITICS

THE OXFORD HANDBOOK OF

RELIGION AND AMERICAN POLITICS

Edited by

CORWIN E. SMIDT
LYMAN A. KELLSTEDT
JAMES L. GUTH

OXFORD
UNIVERSITY PRESS
2009

OXFORD
UNIVERSITY PRESS

Oxford University Press, Inc., publishes works that further
Oxford University's objective of excellence
in research, scholarship, and education.

Oxford   New York
Auckland   Cape Town   Dar es Salaam   Hong Kong   Karachi
Kuala Lumpur   Madrid   Melbourne   Mexico City   Nairobi
New Delhi   Shanghai   Taipei   Toronto

With offices in
Argentina   Austria   Brazil   Chile   Czech Republic   France   Greece
Guatemala   Hungary   Italy   Japan   Poland   Portugal   Singapore
South Korea   Switzerland   Thailand   Turkey   Ukraine   Vietnam

Copyright © 2009 by Oxford University Press, Inc.

Published by Oxford University Press, Inc.
198 Madison Avenue, New York, New York 10016
www.oup.com

Oxford is a registered trademark of Oxford University Press

Library of Congress Cataloging-in-Publication Data

The Oxford handbook of religion and American politics / edited by Corwin E. Smidt,
Lyman A. Kellstedt, and James L. Guth.
p.   cm.
Includes index.
ISBN 978-0-19-532652-9
1. Religion and politics—United States. I. Smidt, Corwin E., 1946–
II. Kellstedt, Lyman A. III. Guth, James L.
BL2525.O94 2009
322'.10973—dc22   2008049920

1 3 5 7 9 8 6 4 2

 l States of America
ʒe paper

CONTENTS

....

CONTRIBUTORS

....

Harold F. (Hal) Bass (Ph.D., Vanderbilt University) is Professor of Political Science and Dean of the School of Social Sciences at Ouachita Baptist University in Arkadelphia, Arkansas. His primary scholarly interest has been presidential party leadership. He is the author of numerous journal articles and book chapters addressing the presidency and political parties.

Marie A. Eisenstein (Ph.D., Purdue University) is Assistant Professor of Political Science at Indiana University Northwest in the School of Public and Environmental Affairs. Her research focuses on the intersection of religion and political tolerance, and includes articles in *Political Behavior* and the *Interdisciplinary Journal of Research on Religion*. She is also the author of *Religion and the Politics of Tolerance* (2008).

Gregory Fortelny is a Ph.D. student in government at Georgetown University. He holds an undergraduate degree in both psychology and philosophy from the California State Polytechnic University, Pomona. His other research interests include political psychology, lobbying, and campaign finance.

James G. Gimpel (Ph.D., University Chicago) is Professor of Government at the University of Maryland, where he has been on the faculty since 1992. His interests lie in the areas of political behavior, political socialization, and the political geography of American politics. He currently serves as editor of *American Politics Research.*

James L. Guth (Ph.D., Harvard University) is William R. Kenan, Jr., Professor of Political Science at Furman University. He is the coauthor or coeditor of several books, and his work has appeared in numerous scholarly journals and edited volumes.

Allen Hertzke (Ph.D., University of Wisconsin) is Presidential Professor of Political Science and Director of Religious Studies at the University of Oklahoma. He is the author of *Representing God in Washington* (1988), an award-winning analysis of religious lobbies; *Echoes of Discontent* (1992), an account of church-rooted populist movements; and coauthor of *Religion and Politics in America* (2004), a comprehensive text now in its third edition. His latest book is titled *Freeing God's Children: The Unlikely Alliance for Global Human Rights* (2004).

TED G. JELEN (Ph.D., The Ohio State University) is Professor of Political Science at the University of Nevada, Las Vegas. He has published extensively in the areas of public opinion, church–state relations, and the politics of such social issues as abortion and same-sex marriage. He is currently the coeditor of the journal *Politics and Religion*.

LYMAN A. KELLSTEDT (Ph.D., University of Illinois) is Professor of Political Science (emeritus) at Wheaton College, Illinois. He has authored or coauthored numerous articles, book chapters, and books in the field of religion and politics, including *Religion and the Culture Wars* (1996) and *The Bully Pulpit* (1997). He is currently working on a series of articles on religion and political behavior.

DOUGLAS L. KOOPMAN (Ph.D., Catholic University of America) is Professor of Political Science at Calvin College. He is the author or coauthor of three books— *Of Little Faith: The Politics of George W. Bush's Faith-Based Initiatives* (2004), *Serving the Claims of Justice: The Thoughts of Paul B. Henry* (2001), and *Hostile Takeover: The House Republican Party, 1980–1995* (1996)—and has written extensively on Congress, social policy, and religious faith and American politics.

GEOFFREY C. LAYMAN (Ph.D., Indiana University) is Associate Professor of Government and Politics at the University of Maryland, College Park. He is the author of *The Great Divide: Religious and Cultural Conflict in American Party Politics* (2001) and has published numerous journal articles on party politics, electoral behavior, public opinion, and religion and politics.

DAVID C. LEEGE (Ph.D., Indiana University) is Professor of Government and International Studies (emeritus). He is coauthor of *The Politics of Cultural Differences: Social Change and Voter Mobilization Strategies in the Post-New Deal Period* (2002) and coeditor of *Rediscovering the Religious Factor in American Politics* (1993). Leege has chaired the Board of Overseers of the American National Election Studies, and he is associated with the development of many of its current measures of religiosity.

MICHAEL LIENESCH (Ph.D., University of California, Berkeley) is Professor of Political Science at the University of North Carolina at Chapel Hill. His research focuses on religion and American political thought, and much of his recent work has been on contemporary Christian conservatism. His most recent book is *In the Beginning: Fundamentalism, the Scopes Trial, and the Making of the Antievolution Movement* (2007).

JOHN MICHAEL McTAGUE is a graduate student in the Department of Government and Politics at the University of Maryland, College Park. In addition to an interest in the role of religion in American politics, he has coauthored articles on the role of geography in shaping electoral competition in American statewide elections that were published in *State Politics & Policy Quarterly* and *Political Geography*. He is currently working on a dissertation that investigates the political behavior of the white working class.

MARK A. NOLL (Ph.D., Vanderbilt University) is the Francis A. McAnaney Professor of History at the University of Notre Dame. Among his books are *The Civil War as a Theological Crisis* (2006) and *God and Race in American Politics: A Short History* (2008).

ELIZABETH A. OLDMIXON (Ph.D., University of Florida) is Associate Professor of Political Science at the University of North Texas. Her research investigates the effects of religion on legislative policy making. Oldmixon is the author of *Uncompromising Positions: God, Sex, and the U.S. House of Representatives* (2005). She served as an APSA Congressional Fellow (2001–2002) and has chaired the APSA section on religion and politics.

LAURA R. OLSON (Ph.D., University of Wisconsin) is Professor of Political Science at Clemson University. She is the author, coauthor, or coeditor of nine books, including *Religious Interests in Community Conflict: Beyond the Culture Wars* (2007) and *Women with a Mission: Religion, Gender, and the Politics of Women Clergy* (2005).

SHANNA PEARSON-MERKOWITZ is a Ph.D. student in government at the University of Maryland. Her interests are in the areas of political behavior, elections, political socialization, and ethnic minority politics. Her work has appeared in several political science journals, including *State Politics and Policy Quarterly,* the *American Journal of Political Science,* and the *Journal of Politics.*

MARK J. ROZELL (Ph.D., University of Virginia) is Professor of Public Policy at George Mason University. He is coauthor of *Power and Prudence: The Presidency of George H. W. Bush* (2004); *Executive Privilege: Presidential Power, Secrecy, and Accountability* (2002); as well as the author of numerous studies on the intersection of religion and politics.

CORWIN E. SMIDT (Ph.D., University of Iowa) is the Paul B. Henry Professor of Political Science and Director of the Henry Institute for the Study of Christianity and Politics at Calvin College. He is coauthor and editor of *Evangelicalism: The Next Generation* (2002)*; Religion as Social Capital: Producing the Common Good* (2003)*;* and *Pews, Prayers, and Participation: The Role of Religion in Fostering Civic Responsibility* (2008).

ROBERT P. SWIERENGA (Ph.D., University of Iowa) is Professor of History (emeritus) at Kent State University and A. C. Van Raalte Research Professor at the A. C. Van Raalte Institute of Hope College. He is the author of a number of books, including

Faith and Family: Dutch Immigration and Settlement in the United States, 1820–1920 (2000) and *Dutch Chicago: A History of Hollanders in the Windy City* (2005).

C. DANIELLE VINSON (Ph.D., Duke University) is Associate Professor of Political Science at Furman University. She is the author of the book *Local Media Coverage of Congress and Its Members* (2003) and has authored or coauthored articles on media and the courts, and campaign finance. She has also done research on communication in political campaigns and communication in Congress.

PAUL J. WAHLBECK (Ph.D., Washington University; J.D., University of Illinois) is Professor of Political Science at George Washington University. He offers classes in judicial politics and research methods. His research explores legal change and argumentation, strategic interaction among justices, and institutional development. He is coauthor of *Crafting Law on the Supreme Court: The Collegial Game* (2000). His work has appeared in several journals, including the *American Political Science Review, American Journal of Political Science, Journal of Politics*, and *Political Research Quarterly*.

KENNETH D. WALD (Ph.D., Washington University, St. Louis) is Distinguished Professor of Political Science at the University of Florida. A specialist on religion in American politics, his most recent books include *Religion and Politics in the United States* (5th ed., 2006) and *The Politics of Cultural Differences: Social Change and Voter Mobilization Strategies in the Post-New Deal Period* (2002). Wald has held Fulbright fellowships to Israel and Germany, as well as visiting appointments at Harvard, the University of Haifa, and the University of Strathclyde in Glasgow (Scotland).

PETER W. WIELHOUWER (Ph.D., University of Georgia) is Associate Professor of Political Science at Western Michigan University, and has taught at Spelman College and Regent University, where he directed the graduate program in campaign management and the university's nonpartisan Center for Grassroots Politics. His research has appeared in *American Journal of Political Science, Journal of Politics, American Politics Research*, and *Social Science Quarterly*, and in recent edited volumes on campaigns and elections and African American representation.

CLYDE WILCOX (Ph.D., The Ohio State University) is Professor of Government at Georgetown University. He is author and coauthor of several books related to religion and politics, including *God's Warriors: The Christian Right in the Twentieth Century* (1992), *Public Attitudes on Church and State* (1995), and *Second Coming: The New Christian Right in Virginia Politics* (1996). In addition to religion and politics, he writes on gender politics, campaign finance, interest groups, and science fiction and politics.

J. Matthew Wilson (Ph.D., Duke University) is Associate Professor of Political Science at Southern Methodist University, where he has taught since 1999. Wilson's research, which has appeared in a range of top scholarly journals, focuses on public opinion, elections, representation, and religion and politics, both in the United States and abroad. He is editor of *From Pews to Polling Places: Faith and Politics in the American Religious Mosaic* (2007).

THE OXFORD HANDBOOK OF

RELIGION AND AMERICAN POLITICS

THE ROLE OF RELIGION IN AMERICAN POLITICS: EXPLANATORY THEORIES AND ASSOCIATED ANALYTICAL AND MEASUREMENT ISSUES

CORWIN E. SMIDT, LYMAN A. KELLSTEDT, AND JAMES L. GUTH

DURING the past three decades, there has been growing recognition that religion plays a vital role in American politics. As a result, the study of religion and politics has mushroomed from occasional analyses, largely ignored by the scholarly community, to a major subfield of study. This research has been dominated by studies of the mass public, but has included some examination of political activists and elites as well. The time has come to step back from this considerable body of work and assess what has been learned, what remains unsettled, and what important questions are still unaddressed. This volume seeks to accomplish just that, as each chapter summarizes the state of the art in a particular area of study; reviews important findings, insights, and theoretical advances; outlines current debates that engage scholarly attention; and proposes new avenues for research.

This chapter provides an overview of the major perspectives that seek to explain the linkage between religion and American politics. We begin with a brief discussion of how scholars have conceptualized religion itself and then turn to the theories advanced to explain the relationship of religion to American politics. Here we focus primarily on efforts to account for issue and electoral differences within the public—a major focus of research in American politics.[1] We then identify some basic problems with the conceptualization and measurement of the religious variables emphasized by each theoretical approach. Although our discussion focuses on the mass public, many of our observations apply to studies of activists and political elites as well, because their political attitudes and behaviors are shaped in comparable ways by religion.

What Constitutes Religion?

What is religion and how should it be defined? Most scholars have adopted a *substantive*, rather than a *functional*, approach, viewing religion as that related to the supernatural.[2] According to Stark and Finke (2000, pp. 91–92), "[r]eligion consists of very general explanations of existence . . . [and] religious explanations specify the fundamental meaning of life: how we got here and where we are going (if anywhere)." In a similar vein, Queen (2002, p. 91) argues that religions promote particular interpretations of "why the universe is the way it is, how it ought to function, and the individual's role and obligations in that universe." Although the core of religion—the realm of the transcendent, supreme beings, and direct communications with the divine—is beyond the realm of social science (Wald and Smidt 1993, pp. 31–32), research can show how the beliefs, behaviors, and organizations associated with religion shape individual political attitudes and behavior, as well as institutional structures and processes.

No matter how religion is defined, it is a multifaceted phenomenon. Scholars, however, have not always agreed on the number or nature of those dimensions. Nearly four decades ago, Stark and Glock (1968) identified five: beliefs, ritual practice, private devotionalism, religious knowledge, and a consequential or ethical dimension.[3] More recently, Stark and Finke (2000, p. 103) specified that religious organization and two aspects of religious commitment—objective (behavior) and subjective (beliefs)—serve as the primary components of religion. Similarly, Layman (2001, p. 55) found "three major components of religion that are potentially important for politics: believing, behaving, and belonging." For Layman (2001, p. 57), the substantive content of a faith is embodied in religious beliefs,[4] the practice of a faith is reflected in behavior, and belonging is revealed by affiliation with a religious community, reflecting "conscious recognition of membership in a social group." Although we think that believing, behaving, and belonging provide a useful schema for analyzing the political influence of religion, theories connecting religion to American political life put varying emphases on these three dimensions.

PERSPECTIVES ON THE RELATIONSHIP OF RELIGION TO AMERICAN POLITICS

How does religion relate to American politics? Historically, two competing theoretical perspectives have sought to explain that linkage: the *ethnoreligious* perspective and the *theological restructuring* perspective. The ethnoreligious perspective adopts Emile Durkheim's (1915) focus on religion as a social phenomenon, emphasizing affiliation with religious groups as the means by which religion shapes political responses. The restructuring perspective traces its roots to Max Weber ([1930] 1992), who saw religion embodied in beliefs, emphasizing their role in shaping political attitudes and behavior. More recently, something of a synthesis has emerged—a perspective that views religion as embodying belonging, beliefs, and behavior, with all three influencing political life. We will consider each in turn.

THE ETHNORELIGIOUS PERSPECTIVE: THE CENTRALITY OF RELIGIOUS BELONGING

Pollsters, pundits, and politicians have relied implicitly on an ethnoreligious interpretation of American politics. As developed by historians, this theory identifies the key religious groups as the historic denominations born in Europe and later multiplying on America's shores. Presbyterians, Lutherans, Baptists, Episcopalians, Methodists, and a myriad of other Protestants combined distinct religious worldviews with other cultural attributes, such as ethnicity, race, or regional location. They were soon joined by other traditions, including Catholics, Jews, Eastern Orthodox, and other religious "minorities." All these religious groups developed their own political cultures (often in conflict with neighboring groups), cultures fostered by religious leaders, houses of worship, and ethnic communities. During the 19th and early 20th centuries, American party politics involved competing alliances of ethnoreligious groups (Kleppner 1970; Jensen 1971; Kleppner 1979; Formisano 1983; Swierenga 1990).

For these historians, religion shaped American politics primarily through religious belonging, with partisan affiliations and voting behavior reflecting "political expressions of shared values derived from the voter's membership in, and commitment to, ethnic and religious groups" (Kleppner 1970, p. 35). Given a two-party system and great religious diversity, specific religious groups naturally sought like-minded allies to influence American politics, as each group, no matter how large, needed allies if it wished to affect electoral politics. During the 19th century, a coalition of "pietists" (primarily Whig and Republican) faced an alliance of "liturgicals" (primarily Democratic), later joined by southern white Protestants as a result of the Civil War (Kleppner 1970; Jensen 1971; Kleppner 1979). By the mid 20th century, these coalitions had reorganized, but ethnoreligious loyalties remained at their base. Mainline Protestants provided much of the leadership for the Republican Party as well as its most faithful voters, whereas Catholics, Jews, black Protestants and other religious minorities—including out-groups such as southern evangelicals—constituted the bedrock of the Democratic Party. As a result, early social science research in the 1940s found substantial partisan differences pitting most Protestants against Catholics, Jews and southern evangelical Protestants, even in the context of the supposed dominance of class-based New Deal politics (Lazarsfeld, Berelson, and Gaudet 1944; Berelson, Lazarsfeld, and McPhee 1954).[5]

Despite the historical value of the ethnoreligious model, many observers argue that it has lost relevance in contemporary politics. The underlying bases for ethnoreligious politics have largely vanished: the powerful social integration within religious traditions, the social isolation of those traditions, and the strong tensions among traditions (Kleppner 1979). Nevertheless, the political behavior of certain close-knit religious groups like black Protestants, Latino Catholics, Jews, and Latter-day Saints suggests that the model may still have relevance.[6] Indeed, even affiliation with a church in the historic evangelical, mainline Protestant or Catholic traditions may still matter politically, in part because such membership is elective today, allowing believers to choose a congenial religious—and political—environment (Green and Guth 1993).

RELIGIOUS RESTRUCTURING AND "TRADITIONALISM–MODERNISM"

Although many analysts still focus on religious tradition, variously defined (Manza and Brooks 1999; Steensland, Park, Regnerus, Robinson, Wilcox, and Woodberry 2000; Layman 2001; Leege, Wald, Krueger, and Mueller 2002), some sociologists argue that the ethnoreligious description of religious life and its implications for politics has less utility than previously. As ascriptive affiliations break down and geographic mobility increases, Americans move freely among religious settings, ignoring historical ties of doctrine, denomination, ethnicity, region, and even family (Ammerman 1997; Pew Forum, 2008). As people re-sort themselves into congenial theological environments, religion has been restructured into two camps with opposing worldviews, fostered by competing religious institutions and leaders. As Robert Wuthnow (1988) and James Davison Hunter (1991) have argued, old religious traditions have been polarized by theological, social, and cultural conflicts into a *conservative, orthodox,* or *traditionalist* faction on one side, and a *liberal, progressive,* or *modernist* one on the other. And for some theorists, the growing number of secular Americans represents a natural extension of the liberal or progressive side—and perhaps the product of struggles over restructuring (Hout and Fischer 2002). Wuthnow (1988) saw such developments splitting religious institutions, but Hunter's (1991) apocalyptic title, *Culture Wars,* projected the divisions into the polity as a threat to social stability.

Although scholarly reaction to the "culture wars" thesis has often focused on these purported political manifestations (Williams 1997; Fiorina 2005; Nivoli and Brady 2006), Wuthnow and Hunter's original formulations were rooted in theological developments, especially the emergence of opposing worldviews: The competing camps were characterized by alternative belief systems, different religious practices, and adherence to rival religious movements. Indeed, identification of these competing forces probably constitutes the most valuable insight of the restructuring perspective.

Although critics are rightly skeptical about extreme statements of the restructuring theory, evidence for a milder version is convincing, especially in "old-line" American religious institutions. The religious press reports continual battles between traditionalists and modernists in almost every major Protestant body, as well as in the American Catholic church. Although rooted in theology and practice, these struggles also produce opposing moral, social, economic, and political perspectives. True, culture war theorists do overstate the consequent polarization, both within religious institutions and the mass public: There are *centrists* in the religious wars, and *moderates* in the political wars. However, the religious divisions they identify may well influence politics, if only because both religious and political elites are polarized, thus shaping the cues presented to the public (Guth, Green, Smidt, Kellstedt, and Poloma 1997; Fiorina 2005).

RELIGIOUS CLASSIFICATION: RELIGION AS BELONGING, BELIEF, AND BEHAVIOR

A third formulation builds on the insights of the two previous explanations, arguing that both religious affiliation and religious beliefs, along with religious behavior, help to explain how religion shapes American politics (Layman 1997, 2001; Guth, Green, Kellstedt, and Smidt 1999; Kohut, Green, Keeter, and Toth 2000; Guth, Kellstedt, Smidt, and Green 2006b; Green 2007; Green, Kellstedt, Smidt, and

Guth 2007). According to this perspective, some groups behave as the ethnoreligious model would suggest, whereas others respond on the basis of contemporary divisions over beliefs, perhaps with religious behavior added to the mix. Accordingly, a hybrid model is appropriate, emphasizing the study of belonging, believing, and behaving, as well as their interactions, as the best means to understand the relationship between religion and American politics.

For the three largest religious traditions—evangelical and mainline Protestantism and Catholicism—the interaction of these three components of religion provides the best explanation for adherents' political choices and behavior. These historical traditions have not only had the longest experience in American politics, but also are the primary battlegrounds for the theological quarrels identified by restructuring theorists. Each includes many *traditionalists,* an apt term for believers who self-consciously seek to preserve their tradition against encroachments of the modern world. On the other side are *modernists,* who want to adapt beliefs and behaviors to modernity. Still other members (*centrists*) retain the beliefs and practices central to their tradition, but with less consistency and commitment than traditionalists, and are often puzzled by the conflicts between traditionalists and modernists. Finally, each tradition has *nominal* members who claim to belong but place little importance on their faith tradition. As a result, they seldom behave politically according to tradition norms, more often resembling the religiously unaffiliated or secular population.

Both religious affiliation (or its absence) and the traditionalism of one's beliefs and practices connect people to politics (Layman and Green 2005). The evidence suggests that religious belonging is still a potent influence on the American public: In recent years, evangelicals have trended strongly in a Republican direction, whereas mainline Protestants, the former centerpiece of the Grand Old Party (GOP) coalition, have moved toward the center. Meanwhile, white Catholics have abandoned their old Democratic ties, and have become a swing group (Guth et al. 2006; Green 2007; Green et al. 2007; Kellstedt, Smidt, Green, and Guth 2007).

Such trends, however, are not the end of the story. In each of the largest religious traditions, traditionalist beliefs push individuals toward the Republican Party, whereas modernist beliefs work in the opposite direction. Moreover, faithful church attendance also moves people toward the GOP, whereas the less observant tend to be Democratic (Green 2007). Other religious practices have the same effect.[7] How belief and behavior dimensions of religion interact remains to be examined, but a hybrid model—combining affiliation, belief, and practice—has some resonance with contemporary political developments.

This quick review suggests that scholars must consider several dimensions of religion to determine its impact on political behavior of the mass public, activists, and elites. Ethnoreligious theory focuses on religious affiliation or belonging almost exclusively, although it often carries the assumption that denominations or traditions share fundamental theological worldviews and, often, social and political values (McCormick 1974). In addition, the American religious traditions extant today have been powerfully shaped by past religious movements, which may have continued relevance. For example, contemporary evangelical Protestantism reflects the confluence of fundamentalist, holiness, Pentecostal, and neo-evangelical movements of the past. On the other hand, the restructuring perspective assumes that old ethnoreligious alignments have yielded to new religious formations, characterized by distinctive beliefs and practices, and expressed in contemporary religious movements.

In the following pages we examine the theoretical bases for emphasizing religious belonging, religious beliefs, and religious behavior, and then suggest strategies best suited to capturing the political impact of these concepts. The goal is to provide some guidance through the minefields of measurement, considering problems faced by researchers and possible solutions to them. Still, most analysts must rely on surveys that use a small and haphazard selection of religious measures. Therefore, the discussion is geared toward scholars thinking about generating their own surveys as well as those doing secondary analysis of existing data; in other words, we will be shifting between the ideal and real worlds, trying to make the best use of available data.

Religion as Belonging: Denominations, Traditions, and Movements

As a social phenomenon, religion is expressed through affiliation with a local church, a specific denomination, or a religious tradition. Individuals thereby share experiences that derive from their group affiliations. Through patterns of association and interaction, as well as exposure to varied teachings about the way religion is linked to politics, members of different religious groups exhibit divergent political traits. They may experience distinctive patterns of communication, receive different kinds of information, be exposed to varying interpretations of political events, and be subject to different patterns of political recruitment and mobilization. As a result, citizens respond to political stimuli as a function of differences in religious affiliation. As one analysis has it, "[b]elonging can matter in politics by providing a forum in which religion can be linked to political issues, parties, candidates and activities" (Kohut et al. 2000, p. 13). In this sense, religious groups function like other social groups.

The key question, then, is what is the most useful way to classify religious affiliation? There are many types of religious groups to which a person can claim attachment: a local church, a denomination (the Southern Baptist Convention, the Disciples of Christ), a religious family (Baptist, Lutheran, Methodist), or a religious movement (charismatic renewal or the fundamentalist movement). Moreover, affiliation has both objective and subjective components; one can be a formal member of a religious congregation and a denomination, but can also claim affiliation with, or identify with, such organizations without actually "joining."

Thus, scholars have classified religious affiliations in various ways, usually based on assumptions about the critical unit of analysis—and the availability of data. For example, early surveys focused on broad faith traditions, asking respondents whether they were "Protestant, Catholic, Jewish, something else, or nothing in particular." This formulation may have reflected pollsters' frustration with the complexity of American religion—or perhaps acceptance of Will Herberg's (1955) arguments about the relevant faith groupings. Even if one ignores the growing pluralism of faith traditions, the great diversity of Protestantism itself argues against this approach. As Stark and Glock (1968, p. 56) noted years ago, "when we speak of 'Protestants,' as we often do in the social sciences, we spin statistical fiction."[8]

Other scholars (Gaustad 1976) have used "religious families" (e.g., Baptists, Methodists, Presbyterians, Lutherans) as the unit of analysis. Although an improvement on more global classifications—and perhaps useful for a few theoretical purposes—the utilization of religious families is rarely justified in survey research, given the major theological, cultural, social, and racial differences that separate specific denominations within the same family. Indeed, significant theological and political differences often divide denominational "kin": Members of the Presbyterian Church in America, the Free Methodist Church, and the Lutheran Church–Missouri Synod tend to be theologically traditionalist, politically conservative and Republican, whereas adherents to the Presbyterian Church USA, the United Methodist Church, and the Evangelical Lutheran Church in America are theologically modernist and more centrist or even liberal politically. Such vital differences are obscured by family classifications.

As a result, other scholars prefer the concept of religious tradition to classify adherents. A religious tradition comprises religious denominations, movements, and congregations with similar beliefs and behaviors, all interrelated in some historical and organizational fashion (Kellstedt and Green 1993; Kellstedt, Green, Guth, and Smidt 1996). Such traditions exhibit several defining characteristics (Smidt 2007). First, they have a legacy rooted in specific histories, and they develop and change slowly.[9] They "place limits on what any given individual or groups of individuals can do within the tradition and still remain within it," and, as a result, religious traditions "shape and construct individuals and cultures" and "are not merely constructed by them" (Queen 2002, p. 91). Members of a religious tradition exhibit a characteristic way of interpreting the world, based on common beliefs and practices, although not all members necessarily hold these beliefs or exhibit these behaviors.[10] Conscious identification with a tradition is not necessary for inclusion. Many Southern Baptists, for example, do not identify as "evangelical," although they share religious beliefs and practices with members of denominations more comfortable with the label.[11] As Geoffrey Layman (2001, p. 60) has observed, religious traditions constitute "a useful and increasingly popular conceptualization of religious belonging." The concept has proved to be to be a powerful predictor of political attitudes and behavior (Kellstedt and Green 1993; Green, Guth, Smidt, and Kellstedt 1996; Kellstedt, Green, Guth, and Smidt 1997; Kohut et al. 2000; Layman and Green 2005; Guth et al. 2006b; Green 2007; Green et al. 2007; Kellstedt et al. 2007).

Which specific denominations and faiths should then be included in particular religious traditions? Within America's overwhelmingly Christian population, one can differentiate among evangelical, mainline, and black Protestant[12] traditions;

the Roman Catholic tradition; and the Eastern Orthodox tradition. Adding in ethnoreligious factors, one should also consider Latino Protestants and Latino Catholics as distinct traditions, or at least subtraditions. In addition, there are other "conservative" religious groups (Latter-day Saints, Jehovah's Witnesses) and other "liberal" religious groups (Unitarians and New Age groups). And, with growing religious pluralism, surveys discover Americans of non-Christian traditions (Judaism, Islam, Buddhism, Hinduism), although usually in numbers too small for extensive analysis (Pew Forum 2008). Finally, the unaffiliated population (Hout and Fischer 2002) can be regarded as a tradition in its own right, although it includes several types, such as *unaffiliated believers* (unattached to a church or denomination but exhibiting at least modest levels of religiosity), the *nonreligious unaffiliated*, and finally, the *antireligious*—agnostics and atheists. Each unaffiliated group differs in political attitudes and behavior (Green et al. 2007; Kellstedt 2008).

Some analysts use "conservative Protestantism" (Woodberry and Smith 1998; Greeley and Hout 2006) to designate a religious tradition (usually instead of "evangelical" Protestantism). Woodberry and Smith (1998, p. 26) argue that "evangelical" should not be used because many "conservative" Protestants do not identify with that label. However, affiliation and identification are analytically distinct phenomena; we should not expect that all, or even most, affiliates of an "evangelical" tradition (a sociological phenomenon) would identify with a religious movement label (a psychological phenomenon), just as most members of mainline Protestant denominations do not identify as "mainliners" despite scholarly use of that designation. In addition, Woodberry and Smith (1998) argue that "evangelical" itself is confusing, and we agree. The problem emerges because evangelicalism is both an ongoing religious tradition with historical roots and organizational ties, and a religious movement that can be traced to the creation of the National Association of Evangelicals in 1942. Rather than dropping "evangelical," it might be better to use "neo-evangelical" to describe the religious movement. What does seem clear, however, is that "conservative Protestantism" is even more problematic. Not only is it uncertain whether "conservative" is a theological or a political designation (the two are often conflated), but the term is ahistorical, suggesting current characteristics rather than a historical religious tradition. Moreover, "conservative Protestant" too easily encompasses groups such as Latter-day Saints and Jehovah's Witnesses who, although conservative in some sense, fall outside the evangelical Protestant tradition on almost every social, theological, and organizational indicator.

Another questionable analytical strategy is to assign denominations along a continuum comprising "fundamentalist," "moderate," and "liberal" categories (Smith 1990). This approach has neither a clear theological rationale nor any historical or organizational foundation. Not only does such classification fail to distinguish between black Protestants and other traditions, but it places a distinct religious tradition, Roman Catholicism, in the moderate category, and inappropriately classifies the growing number of nondenominational Protestants as "fundamentalist" (Kellstedt et al. 1996, p. 176; Steensland et al. 2000). As a result, this procedure classifies about one third of Americans as "fundamentalists," far more than warranted by any historical approach. Even more problematic is the assumption that "all respondents can be categorized along a single continuum based on the fundamentalist/modernist split of the 1920s, which is questionable even among Protestants and Catholics, let alone Buddhists and Hindus" (Woodberry and Smith 1998, pp. 34–35). Despite a strong critique by Steensland et al. (2000), assignment of denominations into fundamentalist, moderate, and liberal categories continues in the General Social Survey (GSS) time series and is used in study after study.[13]

ASSIGNMENT TO RELIGIOUS TRADITIONS

If affiliation is as important as we claim, it must be measured much more precisely than most surveys do. Identifying the respondent's basic faith tradition (Christian, Jew, Muslim) is the first step: Do you think of yourself as part of a religious tradition? For example, do you consider yourself as Christian, Jewish, Muslim, other non-Christian, agnostic or atheist, nothing in particular, or something else? Options such as "agnostic or atheist" and "nothing in particular" legitimize these choices, making them more acceptable to individuals in a highly religious society and avoiding "false positives" in religious affiliation. Indeed, many surveys simply assume a religious affiliation; for instance, the GSS asks: "What is your religious preference?" This may encourage respondents to give a religious preference when they have none.

After ascertaining respondents' broad faith tradition (Christianity, Judaism, and so forth), the researcher should probe for a more specific affiliation.[14] For example, Christians should be asked: "Which specific church or denomination is that?" Respondents may name a religious tradition (Roman Catholic), a denominational family (Baptist), a denomination (the Southern Baptist Convention), some nondenominational affiliation ("I attend a nondenominational evangelical church"), an identification with a religious movement ("I'm a fundamentalist"), a generic response ("I'm just a Christian"), or no affiliation at all. Depending on the response, follow-up questions should be added. For example, a "Baptist" can be given the choice of major (and minor) Baptist denominations, or simply asked to name a specific denomination. At the end of a series of probes, about 70 percent of respondents provide specific denominational affiliations.[15]

Precise affiliation data, then, are essential to accurate assignment of respondents to religious traditions. We recommend the following procedures for classification. At the outset, black and Latino Protestants and Catholics should be placed into four separate categories based on race and ethnicity.[16] This strategy reflects the ethnoreligious approach to religious belonging, as most black and many Latino Protestants attend churches with little or no racial diversity,[17] and the exceptions generally express political attitudes and display voting patterns like those who attend racially exclusive churches. In addition, this strategy obviates some chronic problems of measurement error. For example, many African American Baptists living in southern states report that they are "Southern Baptists." This is true geographically, but is only rarely the case in denominational affiliation. Hence, the ethnic assignment procedure recommended here makes sense empirically and avoids serious—and frequently made—errors.

The next major task is allocating white Protestants to either the evangelical or mainline tradition. As a starting point, those affiliated with denominations belonging to the National Council of Churches are classified as mainline, whereas those linked to the National Association of Evangelicals are placed in the evangelical category.[18] Not all Protestant denominations, however, belong to one of these organizations, necessitating assignment on another basis.[19] The analyst can usually make the appropriate choice after consulting religious encyclopedias (Mead and Hill 2005; Melton 2005) or examining a denomination's Web site to learn about its history and doctrinal stands. Although these resources usually provide information needed for classification, for some denominations they may provide mixed messages. Familiarity with American religious history—not always common among social scientists—is a great asset in making "close calls."

Three additional problems remain. First, if surveys do not probe beyond denominational family responses (Baptist, Lutheran, Methodist, Presbyterian), classification options are less than optimal. Under such circumstances, all white Baptists would have to be assigned to the evangelical tradition, because most Baptists belong to evangelical denominations. On the other hand, Lutheran, Methodist, and Presbyterian respondents would all count as mainline, because the largest denominations in these families are affiliates of the National Council of Churches.[20]

Second, the growing number of "nondenominational" respondents must be assigned.[21] Success here is dependent on clear understanding—and additional data. Assignment choices can be critical. For example, working with the GSS, Greeley and Hout (2006, p. 8) classify all Protestant "no denomination" respondents as mainline Protestants, artificially increasing the number of mainliners. In contrast, Steensland et al. (2000) classify frequent church attenders in the non-denominational group as evangelicals, with the less observant assigned elsewhere,[22] thereby arbitrarily increasing the religiosity of the evangelical tradition. Fortunately, when other religious questions are available, such assign difficulties can be mitigated, because belief items and religious identifications can be used to assign the nondenominationals to the evangelical and mainline traditions, and "closet" seculars to the appropriate location (see our discussion in the last section of this chapter).

We can illustrate the importance of detailed affiliation measures and accurate placement in religious traditions by drawing on the fourth National Survey of Religion and Politics (NSRP), conducted in 2004. The 2004 NSRP had a large sample (4000 preelection and 2730 postelection respondents), and a series of affiliation questions and probes that permit precise assignments. Table 1.1 compares this classification with several cruder affiliation schemes often used by pollsters and even some academic studies, using four political variables: the Bush vote in 2004, party identification, pro-life attitudes, and ideological self-identification. A quick perusal table confirms the

Table 1.1 Measures of Belonging and Their Relationships with Political Variables (measured as a percentage)

	Bush Vote 2004	Party Identification		Political Ideology		Pro-Life on Abortion	Size of Group
		GOP	Democratic	Conservative	Liberal		
All respondents	*51*	*38*	*42*	*40*	*28*	*48*	*100*
Protestant	*59*	*48*	*39*	*47*	*22*	*56*	*(53.4)*
Evangelical	78	58	26	58	16	70	25.1
Mainline	50	44	40	41	30	35	16.4
Black	17	11	71	31	26	54	9.3
Latino	63	38	44	35	25	63	2.6
Catholic	*50*	*36*	*47*	*39*	*31*	*50*	*(22.0)*
Anglo	53	41	44	40	29	48	17.5
Latino	31	15	62	35	36	56	4.5
Jewish	*26*	*22*	*68*	*22*	*57*	*16*	*1.9*
Other	*52*	*27*	*38*	*28*	*32*	*46*	*(5.4)*
Other Christian	79	42	21	41	15	72	2.8
Liberal faiths	25	15	55	8	60	15	1.2
Other non-Christians	19	9	54	19	40	23	1.4
Unaffiliated	*28*	*26*	*43*	*25*	*39*	*27*	*(17.3)*
Religious unaffiliated	36	29	34	26	32	47	4.8
Nonreligious unaffiliated	29	27	43	27	37	22	9.0
Atheist/agnostic	20	20	52	19	53	12	3.5
Nominals from all groups	*33*	*33*	*50*	*31*	*46*	*18*	*(4.5)*

The groups in parentheses do *not* count toward the 100 percent total in the column.
Source: National Survey of Religion and Politics 2004.

superiority of detailed religious tradition classification over the "Protestant, Catholic, Jewish, or Something Else" approach. Although "Protestants" are solidly Republican in vote and identification in 2004 and on the pro-life side, there are massive differences among evangelical, mainline, black, and Latino Protestants on almost all the political variables, with evangelicals much more Republican and conservative, and black Protestants very Democratic. A similar large gap appears between white and Latino Catholics. Even detailed breakdowns of the "Other" and "None" categories produce advances in predicting political choices, despite the general Democratic and liberal leanings of these groups. Note also that "nominals" (individuals who gave an affiliation but showed few or no signs of religiosity) closely resemble the "unaffiliated," and that atheists and agnostics take the most liberal political positions in the latter category.

One other comparison is especially telling. Table 1.1 shows that classification into evangelical and mainline Protestant traditions using precise denominational affiliation reveals far more political distinctions than other expedients. The Pew Research Center for the People and the Press, some exit polls, and many other surveys define evangelicals as "born-again" white Protestants, and mainliners as "nonborn-again." The precise affiliation strategy used by the NSRP reveals a 28 percent gap between evangelical and mainline Protestants in the Bush vote in 2004 (78 percent to 50 percent), whereas the Pew research group's strategy shows a 16 percent margin (66 percent to 50 percent). Clearly, measurement shortcuts sacrifice explanatory power. No doubt future research will refine strategies for determining precise affiliations and how to use this information in religious classification, but such procedures are clearly vital to understanding religion's influence on American politics. (For the assignment of denominations and religious groups to religious traditions, and their relative proportions within each, see Appendix A.)

Born Again: Conceptual and Measurement Pitfalls

We noted earlier that scholars often use a "born-again" measure to identify evangelicals. The strategy is tempting, because it is so simple. Instead of employing time-consuming probes of affiliation, the researcher simply asks Protestants, and perhaps others, if they identify as "born-again Christians" or if they have had such an experience. In this section we assess the conceptual status of the born-again phenomenon and conclude with tentative recommendations about the use of such measures.

Conceptually, "born again" could connote an *identification*, an *experience*, or both.[23] The born-again experience can be of two types: an identifiable point in time when an individual recognized his or her shortcomings and asked Jesus for forgiveness and future direction, or a gradual change in which the individual is unable to point to a specific time for the transformation. Still, both specific and gradual born-again experiences can signify an important transformation.[24] In contrast, "born again" could connote an identification with a religious movement or with a group of people—the "born-again crowd." Whether this term reflects an experience or an identification has not been addressed by scholars, although it should be, because the choice will determine the manner in which a born-again question is asked.

The GSS, following the approach of Gallup, has asked a born-again question on three occasions (1988, 1991, and 1998): "Would you say you have been 'born again' or have had a 'born-again' experience—that is, a turning point in your life when you committed yourself to Christ?" Evangelical, black, and Latino Protestants tend to respond similarly, with about two thirds of each group answering in the affirmative. In contrast, only about one third of mainline Protestants and one sixth of Catholics (Anglo and Latino) claim a born-again experience.

The NSRP has used an identification question: "Do you consider yourself a 'born-again' Christian?" Despite the different question wordings, responses in the 1992 and 1996 NSRP surveys are similar to those of the GSS. However, for all four Protestant groups (evangelical, mainline, black, and Latino), the percent claiming a born-again identification jumped to between 75 percent to 85 percent in 2000 and 2004 in the NSRP. In both GSS and NSRP surveys, the born-again variable was related to partisan identification and presidential voting—in particular for evangelical Protestants, but also, to a lesser extent, for mainline Protestants. The born again were more likely to identify as Republicans and to vote accordingly.

Finally, it should be noted that born-again questions are poor measures even for capturing evangelical respondents. Although many (although not all) evangelical Protestants claim to be born again, so do some members of other faith traditions (regardless of whether the variable is assessed in terms of an experience or an identity). Sometimes in an effort to identify evangelical respondents, the question is posed as: "Do you consider yourself to be a born-again or evangelical Christian?" But this too is problematic, for two distinct phenomena are being assessed in one question.[25]

Several conclusions can be drawn from these reflections. First, from a theoretical perspective, group identities (regardless of whether they are based in religion) are more likely to have greater political relevance than religious experiences. Second, given the similar findings regardless of the measurement strategy, it is likely that people who report a born-again experience also claim it as an identity. And, finally, born-again questions constitute a poor measurement approach to capturing evangelical respondents.

Thus, this brief discussion reveals that both the conceptual status and the measurement status of the widely used born-again variable are unclear. Moreover, when measures of religious affiliation, belief, and practice are included, the born-again question exhibits little independent impact in multivariate analyses.[26] Despite these findings, the survey research community is likely to continue asking such questions. The problem then for scholars is to provide explanations for their findings related to the born-again variable, taking us right back to the conceptual and measurement concerns just discussed.

Religious Movement Affiliation

In addition to affiliation with local churches, denominations, and religious traditions, some individuals identify with religious movements. Sociologists have been preoccupied with religious movements almost from the origins of their discipline, as they sought to distinguish and characterize *church* and *sect* (Troeltsch [1912] 1931; Niebuhr 1929). Modern sociologists have argued that movements are generally of two types—those calling for a return to traditional elements of religion (*sectarian* or *traditionalist*) versus those favoring adjustments or adaptations to modernity (*nonsectarian* or *modernist*). Examples of traditionalist movements include evangelicalism (or neo-evangelicalism), fundamentalism, Pentecostalism, and the charismatic movement.[27] Modernist movements are harder to pinpoint, although a liberal–progressive movement, neo-orthodoxy, ecumenism, the social gospel movement, and even a mainline movement may fit. Precise identification of modernist movements is difficult, in part, because they often originate in seminaries and have been the province of elites, rather than being mass based, like most sectarian movements. As we noted earlier, religious movements during the late 19th and early 20th centuries shaped the modern evangelical and mainline Protestant traditions, and contemporary movements have helped to restructure American religion along theological lines. Religious movements often cross denominational boundaries and, on occasion, even cross religious traditions (the charismatic movement, for example, includes both Protestants and Catholics). For Catholics, some Protestant movement terms may apply (Welch and Leege 1991), but other language may be better suited to capture the ebb and flow of Catholic movements.[28]

Historians (e.g., Marsden 1980; Carpenter 1997) and political scientists (e.g., Wilcox, Jelen, and Leege 1993) have paid some attention to religious movements. And sociologist Christian Smith (1998) used identification with religious movements as the conceptual and measurement centerpiece for his work on contemporary evangelicalism. The efforts of political scientists followed the insights of Pamela Conover (1984), who showed that group identifications were significant predictors of political behavior. Still, the work of political scientists has been sporadic, for the most part, and not well grounded in the theoretical work of sociologists and psychologists.

Religious movement identification is primarily a psychological phenomenon, whereas religious affiliation is primarily sociological, as affiliation has a much more objective foundation and social basis undergirding the concept. At times, both affiliation and movement identification are conceptualized as religious identities (Alwin, Felson, Walker, and Tufis 2006), and it is certainly possible that some claims of affiliation may reflect little more than identification. Nevertheless, most respondents who claim an affiliation also report some worship attendance. Hence, we believe that it is better to conceptualize affiliation as a sociological phenomenon, similar to gender or race, rather than a psychological one (although obviously there are psychological aspects related to these types of variables).

Assessing Religious Movement Identification Measures

The lack of a clear theoretical basis for using movement identifications has resulted in a confusing variety of measurement approaches and specific items. The American National Election Studies (ANES) arguably mixed Protestant movement identifications with theological postures in a forced-choice question asked of all Christians from 1990 to 1998: "Which one of these words BEST describes your kind of Christianity: Fundamentalist, Evangelical, Charismatic or Spirit-Filled, Moderate to Liberal." This wording implies that at least one term fits. In contrast, in 1996 and 1998 the GSS asked: "When it comes to your religious identity, would you say you are a fundamentalist, evangelical, mainline, or liberal Protestant, or do none of these describe you?[29] Thus, the GSS item acknowledges the possibility that none of the terms fits.

Other formats have also been used. For example, Christian Smith (1998) proceeds very differently, asking: "Thinking about your religious faith, would you describe yourself as: a fundamentalist, an evangelical, a mainline Protestant, a theologically liberal Christian," followed by the inquiry: "Which of those would you say best describes your religious identity?" If a respondent could not choose, another question was posed: "If you had to choose, would any of these describe you at all?"[30] However, Smith's religious identification questions were asked only of churchgoing Protestants (attending two or three times per month or more) or of those Protestants for whom religion was highly salient.

This diversity in format reveals little agreement on how to proceed in measurement. As a result, there are several problems in using movement identifications. First, the diversity of question format and wording noted earlier means that findings are likely to be method dependent—"what you get depends entirely on what you ask" (Alwin et al. 2006, p. 543), or, we might add, to whom you ask the questions. For example, churchgoing Protestants should have greater recognition of the terms than Protestants who rarely attend church or those from other traditions.[31]

Second, religious movements do not have formal memberships per se.[32] As a result, individuals can identify with these movements, but many do not, and, when asked, some are unaware of them, and others give confused responses.[33] Why do these difficulties emerge? It may be because the meaning of movement identities to respondents is less clear than a denominational response (for example, "charismat-ic" is less concrete than "Southern Baptist" or "Bethel United Methodist Church"). As a result, there is greater potential for measurement error in responses to movement labels than to denominational affiliation.

Third, when respondents are given the option to choose multiple identities, and do so, ranking them becomes a problem. One approach is to group all respondents who choose only sectarian or traditionalist religious labels and then combine those who choose only nonsectarian or modernist ones, leaving in the middle all who select mixed identities or none at all. Even though some studies attempt to solve this problem by asking respondents to choose the "best" identifi-cation, difficulties still arise: How do you classify two individuals who choose "evangelical" as their primary identity, but select very different secondary identities (e.g., "liberal" or "progressive")?

Fourth, the identities used in the ANES, GSS, and Smith surveys apply to Protestants only, and may not fit minority Protestants. Trying to apply Protestant movement terms to Catholics and other religious traditions ignores the movements within these other traditions that have little or nothing to do with fundamentalism, neo-evangelicalism, or liberal–progressive movements among Protestants. Clearly, much greater effort is needed to explore movement identifications for non-Protestant traditions.

Despite the pitfalls to using movement identifications, some results suggest their utility. For example, identification with Protestant and Catholic sectarian (or tradi-tionalist) movements pushes individuals toward political conservatism and the Republican Party, whereas identification with nonsectarian (or modernist) move-ments is linked with political liberalism and the Democratic Party. Nevertheless, religious identifications are more meaningful predictors of political attitudes and behaviors when religious traditions and movement identifications are congruent.[34] Thus, members of the evangelical tradition who identify with a sectarian movement exhibit more conservative political attitudes than those who do not. In contrast, mainline Protestants who accept a nonsectarian label hold more liberal attitudes. Consequently, scholars using movement identifications should regard them as supple-ments to religious tradition and not replacements. They provide valuable information on evangelical and mainline Protestants who are familiar with movement terms.

There may be a more efficient way in future research to tap respondents' prefer-ences for sectarian and modernizing movements. In the 2004 NSRP, respondents were asked whether their church or denomination should preserve traditional beliefs and practices, adjust these selectively, or modernize, with a second question asking if the respondent took sides in such arguments, and, if so, which side. The responses formed a reliable scale that behaved in much the same way across religious traditions, correlated quite well with existing Protestant and Catholic movement identifications, and often worked as well or better in predicting political variables. This approach has several advantages over traditional measurements of movement identifications: (1) the questions can be asked of respondents in every religious tradition (leaving out the "unaffiliated") and (2) it avoids using movement identifications that really apply to white Protestants only. In sum, religious movement identifications lead to complicated data analysis, and this explain in part why so little progress has been made in linking these measures to political behavior. Future research might experiment further in attempting to measure directly believers' location on the traditionalist–modernist movement dimension.[35]

APPROACHES TO RELIGIOUS BELIEFS

Beliefs are central to any understanding of religion. As Stark and Glock (1968, p. 16) put it, "theology, or religious belief, is at the heart of the faith." Such emphasis assumes that human behavior is governed by cognitive processes and that individuals relate to the world in atomistic rather than organic fashion. Thus, religion embodies the "fundamental beliefs, ideas, ethical codes, and symbols associated with a religious tradition, including what others call a theology or belief system" (Wald and Calhoun-Brown 2007, p. 26). These beliefs have social consequences, as "people act politically, economically, and socially in keeping with their ultimate beliefs," in that "their values, mores, and actions . . . are an outgrowth of the god or gods they hold at the center of their being" (Swierenga 1990, p. 154). As a result, religious beliefs should serve either as a constraint on, or a generator of, political beliefs, attitudes, and behavior.

Because beliefs are viewed as the critical link between religion and political variables, their effects are understood to be more "immediate" and direct, the product of internal psychology (Wald and Smidt 1993, p. 32). According to theories of cognitive consistency, those for whom religious beliefs are highly salient should feel greater pressure to bring their political attitudes into congruence with their religious convictions than those for whom such beliefs are less salient (Hoge and de Zulueta 1985).

If beliefs provide the critical link between religion and politics, which beliefs are central? Analysts have relied on a bewildering array of concepts and measures, but neither of the most popular social science data sources (i.e., the GSS and ANES) has asked many belief questions. The most commonly used measure taps beliefs about biblical authority (Jelen 1989; Kellstedt and Smidt 1993; Clydesdale 1999). Unfortunately, most Bible items are plagued by response options that put Americans into a very few categories, often suggesting very high views of biblical authority.[36] Although highly skewed distributions may reveal the high regard that Americans have for the Bible, they also limit the use of such items for explanatory purposes.

When several belief measures are available, scholars frequently combine them in a scale tapping religious traditionalism. For example, the Christian faith has historically held that Jesus was born of a virgin, rose from the dead, and will return to earth someday; such items can be used to create an index of Christian traditionalism. This illustration reveals, of course, that such measures are tied to particular faith traditions—what constitutes Jewish or Muslim traditionalism will differ from that for Christians. Nevertheless, because Christianity is the dominant American faith, most items assessing traditionalism draw from Christian tenets (Stark and Foster 1970; Driedger 1974; Davis and Robinson 1996).

This raises the thorny issue of whether traditionalism should be measured by items that are tradition specific or ones that apply to all or most traditions. Religious traditions have different foundational beliefs and normative practices that constitute traditional belief and behavior for their members (Green 2000). Catholic and Jewish traditionalists should exhibit some beliefs and practices distinct from those of evangelical or mainline Protestant traditionalists. Indeed, there are even facets of traditionalism that may be unique, whether beliefs (e.g., that priests should not marry, that females should not be permitted to be rabbis) or behavior (e.g., going to confession, keeping kosher).

If restructuring theorists are correct, however, current theological disputes cross the lines of religious traditions. Thus, in principle, it may be possible to identify certain beliefs and behaviors that are characteristic of most, if not all, religious traditionalists. For example, one might expect that traditionalists, regardless of specific location, would hold that there is a God and believe in an afterlife. In addition, traditionalists should agree that "there are absolute standards of right and wrong" determined by transcendent authority, not by human convention (Hunter 1991). Finding such commonalities may be important to ascertaining whether traditionalists from various religious faiths are coalescing politically, as the restructuring model predicts. Much more conceptual and measurement work will be required to identify and tap such pan-tradition beliefs.

Although scholars often focus on beliefs located on the religious dimension that we have called *traditionalism–modernism* (and we will show later that such measures have powerful predictive ability), other kinds of religious beliefs have been used as well, as dictated by theoretical interests or a particular research problem. For example, scholars have examined eschatological beliefs (about the "end times"), which are important facets of some evangelical theologies and a growing presence in popular writings. These beliefs influence public attitudes about conflict in the Middle East (Guth, Fraser, Green, Kellstedt, and Smidt 1996), but also affect environmental attitudes (Guth, Kellstedt, Green, and Smidt 1993; Guth, Green, Kellstedt, and Smidt 1995).

Other approaches have shown some promise in connecting religious beliefs to political behavior. Some researchers have examined *social theology*, or views on how one's religious faith relates to politics. Such analysts see specific faith traditions and religious beliefs fostering broader social perspectives, incorporating individualistic or communitarian worldviews that provide responses to core human questions and shape political values (Leege 1988; Leege and Kellstedt 1993, pp. 216–231; Guth et al. 1997), although other researchers use somewhat different language. Finally, conceptually, social theology can also entail attitudes toward church–state separation, the role of religion in election campaigns, and the role of the church in civic life (Guth 2007).

In addition, some social scientists have examined how images of God may influence social and political attitudes and behavior (Welch and Leege 1988).

People not only differ about the existence of a transcendent being, but have vastly different understandings of the nature of such an authority—and such differences can have political consequences. During the early 1980s, sociologist Andrew Greeley helped develop GSS items to tap different images of God using paired comparisons.[37] He found Americans with "maternal" and "gracious" conceptions of God tended to be political liberals and Democrats (Greeley 1988), support environmental protection (Greeley 1993), and oppose the death penalty (Greeley 1989, p. 98).[38] Similarly, Stark (2001) has argued that conceptions of God will affect moral attitudes but only to the extent that God is seen to judge human activities.

Recent efforts have built on the earlier work, using multivariate analyses, controlling for sociodemographic variables as well as other religious factors (church attendance, affiliation, and beliefs about biblical authority). Even with controls, the image-of-God variable[39] was a significant predictor of attitudes on sexual morality, abortion, and partisan identification. Moreover, images of God differ among religious groups, and such differences serve as a significant predictor of political attitudes among their members (Bader and Froese 2005). Finally, the Baylor Religion Survey of 2005 (www.baylor.edu/isreligion.org), using a somewhat different battery, found four conceptions of God (authoritarian, benevolent, critical, and distant) that explained variation in attitudes on social issues and the role of government.

Other scholars have attempted to measure American civil religion. Although civil religion can assume different meanings, it frequently is viewed as "an attempt by citizens to imbue their nation with a transcendent value" (Wald and Calhoun-Brown 2007, p. 54). Although some have examined civil religion through content analyses of public rhetoric (Bellah 1974; Hart 1977; Hart and Pauley 2004), there have also been a few surveys examining such perspectives among the mass public and among clergy (Wimberley 1976, 1979; Smidt 1980, 1982; see also Guth, chapter 9, in this volume).

Thus, scholars have explored a varied range of religious belief items in surveys. Even when defensible belief items are included, however, they are often used in problematic ways. Sometimes beliefs are mistakenly used as surrogates for religious group membership. For example, analysts may classify those with a literal view of scripture as "fundamentalists." In this case, a Bible item could be used more legitimately either (1) to tap fundamentalism as a belief system and its effects on other attitudes or behavior, or (2) as a means of discriminating among those in a religious group (to what extent do evangelical Protestants subscribe to biblical literalism?).[40]

In this vein, some widely publicized surveys produce findings for "religious groups" that are really categorical groups produced by arbitrary definitions. Thus, when the Barna Research Group specifies that "evangelicals" must be born again,[41] state that their faith is very important, and adhere to six additional beliefs,[42] it creates a categorical group without clear historical or conceptual meaning. All respondents (including Roman Catholics, Eastern Orthodox, or Latter-day Saints) who meet such criteria are placed in an "evangelical" subgroup. However, religious groups are *not* defined by all members holding the same beliefs; rather, they are defined by patterns of affiliation and social interaction. In this instance, Barna's "evangelicals" are unlikely to recognize each other as fellow believers, or exhibit any social cohesion. Religious beliefs should be analyzed for what they represent (beliefs)—and not as surrogates for religious affiliation.

A similar problem arises in reverse when analysts use denominational affiliation as a surrogate for religious beliefs, ordering affiliation with denominations or religious traditions along some hypothetical "high" to "low" traditionalism belief score (see, for example, Layman 2001, pp. 78–87). This expedient is particularly tempting when belief items are unavailable. Such an ordinal scale may seem to have advantages over nominal measures in multivariate analyses, producing a single measure rather than numerous dummy variables for traditions. However, such a surrogate will be correlated with various other religious measures (e.g., church attendance and religious salience), and therefore any statistical results using such a measure will be difficult to interpret, because one cannot be certain whether belief, belonging, or behavior drives the findings.[43]

Scholars have just begun to explore the political impact of religious belief. The relative utility of these (and other) belief items can be determined only through further research and analytical comparisons. Unfortunately, relatively few surveys include enough belief items to allow a thorough comparative examination of how different kinds of beliefs influence political attitudes and choices. Given the paucity of belief questions in the large surveys like ANES and GSS, smaller surveys may be necessary to ascertain the type of belief items needed for political behavior research. Special attention should be given to beliefs that are central to the many religious traditions that make up the American religious landscape. What evidence we have suggests that deeply held theological beliefs are often related to political attitudes and behavior, either directly or indirectly. Indeed, because religious beliefs are central to many Americans and are at the core of their worldviews, it would be surprising if this were not the case.

APPROACHES TO RELIGIOUS BEHAVIOR AND SALIENCE

All religions assume the importance of religious practice or behavior. Two aspects of religious practice can be distinguished: public ritual observance (such as attendance at worship services) and private devotional practices (such as prayer or Bible reading) (Stark and Glock 1968). Like beliefs, religious practices vary by tradition. Although attendance at worship services is usually normative, some traditions put a greater emphasis on such participation, and expectations on the conduct of corporate worship may vary as well.[44] Some religious practices are tradition specific: The rite of confession is not normative for Protestants, but once was and still may be for Catholics.[45] Just as variation in beliefs causes problems for researchers, so, too, does the variety in normative religious practices. Limited survey space precludes asking many questions about religious practice, and structuring surveys to tap tradition-specific religious practices may be technically difficult and costly. Nevertheless, at a minimum, items on ritual observance and private devotionalism should be asked, because both help ascertain the way in which an individual is religious.[46]

In addition, the salience or importance of religion to the individual is frequently used as a measure of "religiosity," although it is technically not a religious practice item. Many surveys allow respondents to choose a point on an ordinal scale to reflect how important religion is in their lives. The ANES uses a two-part question, asking first whether religion is important to the individual, and if so, whether religion provides "some," "quite a lot," or "a great deal" of guidance, producing a four-point scale. Although salience is technically attitudinal, it provides a good indication of an individual's religious commitment, and thus the likelihood of engaging in religious activities. Empirically, religious salience is highly correlated with measures of both public and private religious behavior.[47] Consequently, many scholars conceptualize religious behavior in terms of religious commitment (Layman 2001, p. 57), combining the frequency of public ritual practice, private devotionalism, and religious salience in a scale (Kellstedt et al. 1996). With a paucity of religious measures, this approach makes sense, but it does mask the individual impact that conceptually distinct religious measures—practice versus salience—have on political variables.

When not used as a component of a religiosity measure, salience may serve other purposes. For example, it can be used to weed out the nominally affiliated—in other words, those who claim a religious affiliation, but say that religion is not important in their lives. In the same vein, it may be used to differentiate among the religiously unaffiliated. Unaffiliated believers have no affiliation, but exhibit at least a modicum of religious belief and practice, suggesting that religion is of some importance to them. Unaffiliated nonbelievers have no religious affiliation and say religion is unimportant in their lives. Among them is a subset of the antireligious: the agnostics or atheists. Each group is different politically (Kellstedt 2008). Despite the growth in the unaffiliated population, such differences are usually ignored in social science research (see, for example, Hout and Fischer 2002). Salience measures may help sort out these subgroups.

ASSIGNING RESPONDENTS
ON THE BASIS OF THE THREE Bs

After this review of the religious variables used by social scientists, we can now combine the insights of the ethnoreligious and restructuring perspectives. As we have seen, the evidence suggests that religious traditions still matter. In particular, evangelicals are more conservative and Republican than either mainline Protestants or white Catholics, whereas black Protestants remain firmly Democratic, as do Jews and Latino Catholics. However, restructuring theorists also have a point: The old disputes *between* religious traditions are now overlain by divisions *within* them, making it important to assess differences within religious traditions and alliances across them. Some research has used church attendance to tap these divisions, by dividing active adherents within traditions from those less involved. However, this fails to get at the belief distinctions between traditionalists and modernists that are central to the restructuring model. To produce the most useful classification of American religious groups, we must draw from both theoretical perspectives.

In the following illustrative procedure we use the 2004 NSRP. As mentioned earlier, the NSRP has a large sample (4,000 preelection and 2,730 postelection), a precise affiliation measure, and includes multiple religious belief and behavior items. Some measures, such as church attendance, are similar to items in other surveys, but some, like belief in God, life after death, and biblical authority, have been improved by expanding response options.[48] All told, the religious batteries permit construction of a classification combining the ethnoreligious and restructuring perspectives with much greater confidence than is possible using the ANES or GSS.

As we argued earlier, the most difficult problems in assigning individuals to religious traditions include differentiating evangelical and mainline Protestants (see Appendix A), assigning nondenominational respondents, and classifying those who name a religious family but can give no further specifics. Some nondenominational respondents provide some information on the type of church they attend (fundamentalist, Pentecostal, charismatic, or evangelical)[49] and can be assigned to the evangelical tradition with some confidence. We allocated other nondenominational respondents to the evangelical tradition if they identified as sectarian Christians *or* claimed a born-again identification, and assigned those identifying as nonsectarian (liberal–progressive, mainline, or ecumenical) Christians or not born again to the mainline tradition. Nonattenders and those with low religious salience are placed in the "nominally religious" category. These procedures produced satisfying results: For nondenominational respondents, those assigned as evangelicals gave Bush 79 percent of the vote in 2004, compared with 40 percent of those assigned to the mainline and 31 percent for the nominally religious. Respondents in denominational families who name an unknown denomination or give no further specific information beyond "Lutheran" or "Presbyterian" were assigned to Protestant traditions using the same criteria as for nondenominationals.[50]

The second step in creating our combined classification is to calculate a composite measure of religious beliefs, because the theological or restructuring model argues that traditionalist and modernist factions will differ dramatically in political choices. Restructuring theory suggests that these divisions will be most developed and politically potent among members of the three largest American religious traditions: white evangelical and mainline Protestants, and white Catholics. We used five beliefs relevant to the religious traditions of most Americans: in God, life after death, the Bible, the devil, and the theory of evolution. The average inter-item correlation is a very healthy .54, demonstrating that such beliefs are highly constrained. For operational purposes, we used a factor score of these items.[51] Again, we stress that other beliefs could be used. Experimentation shows that alternative specifications are almost equally powerful, suggesting that many belief items are highly correlated with traditionalism–modernism, although this may vary somewhat by religious tradition.

Next we add a "behavior" measure to the restructuring analysis, as traditionalists should be more active in traditional religious practices than modernists are. Ideally, multiple indicators of religious behavior should be chosen, including both public ritual and private devotional items. We included items on church attendance, Bible reading, prayer, financial giving to religious causes, and small-group involvement. The average intercorrelation among these items was .55—again, very high.[52] Once again, we used a factor score to tap the underlying religious behavior dimension.

Finally, a second-order factor analysis of the belief and behavior factor scores produced a "traditionalism" score. We divided this measure into four categories for each of the three large white religious traditions, using religious salience to determine the size of the traditionalist, centrist, modernist, and nominal categories for evangelicals, the mainline, and white Catholics.[53] Although it is also possible to divide members of the smaller religious traditions in this way, we do not typically report findings for such divisions. In most instances, the respondents are too few, and our theory suggests—usually correctly—that the ethnoreligious model still provides a better description of their political behavior. Nevertheless, there is tantalizing evidence that restructuring has begun in some of these traditions (Guth et al. 2005).

Does our combined scheme have merit empirically? Table 1.2 examines the nation's three largest religious traditions on several political variables: presidential vote in 2004, party identification, abortion attitudes, and self-identification as a liberal or conservative. The table reveals massive *internal* variations for the evangelical, mainline, and white Catholic traditions based on traditionalism. Although differences continue to exist *across* the three largest traditions (see table 1.1), within-group variation by theological division is even greater. For example, the range for the Bush vote between evangelical traditionalists and nominals is from 88 percent to 55 percent; among mainline Protestants, from 65 percent to 31 percent; and among white Catholics, from 74 percent to 28 percent. Theological restructuring is obviously a vital political force.

In sum, this "Three Bs" measure not only captures the reality of contemporary links between religion and presidential voting, but also those between religion and party identification, abortion attitudes, and political ideology (Guth et al. 2006; Green et al. 2007).[54] Differences within the three largest white religious traditions are truly impressive. The results comport nicely with media reports of conflicts raging within many denominations and religious traditions today. The differences between traditionalists and the modernists and their "nominal" allies seem so pervasive that conflict within religious traditions is likely for years to come. The task for social scientists is to capture these differences with more sophisticated measurement strategies than have been the norm in the past.[55]

Future research can be planned using appropriate items, but is it possible to examine within-tradition differences in the past using available data sources? The

Table 1.2 The Three Bs and Political Variables (measured as a percentage)

	Bush Vote 2004	Party Identification		Political Ideology		Pro-Life on Abortion	Size of Group
		GOP	Democrat	Conservative	Liberal		
All respondents	*51*	*38*	*42*	*40*	*28*	*48*	*100.0*
Evangelical	*78*	*58*	*26*	*58*	*16*	*70*	*25.1*
Traditionalist	83	66	21	64	13	79	18.1
Centrist	56	34	41	47	19	58	3.4
Modernist	52	45	32	37	22	45	2.3
Nominal	56	33	40	40	28	27	1.3
Mainline	*50*	*44*	*40*	*41*	*30*	*35*	*16.4*
Traditionalist	63	57	32	54	21	52	5.1
Centrist	55	39	43	44	31	32	3.2
Modernist	39	38	42	32	32	31	5.1
Nominal	36	34	48	31	44	12	2.9
White Catholic	*53*	*41*	*44*	*40*	*29*	*48*	*17.5*
Traditionalist	73	56	29	56	16	80	5.0
Centrist	54	34	50	40	27	51	4.7
Modernist	38	30	50	29	38	30	4.9
Nominal	33	44	49	32	41	19	2.9

Source: National Survey of Religion and Politics 2004.
Numbers in bold italics represent findings for the entire sample, and for all members of the three religious traditions.

answer is yes, but with some limitations. In the ANES, the standard three-option Bible item was asked in both 1964 and 1968, and again in 1980 through 2004; a church attendance item has been asked regularly. Assignments to the Three Bs categories can be made as follows: traditionalists are biblical literalists who attend church regularly, modernists hold a "low" view of the Bible and rarely or never attend, and centrists fall in the middle on one or both measures. Using this strategy shows that the traditionalist–modernist split had no effect in the 1960s, a modest influence on evangelicals only in the 1980s (when traditionalists became more Republican), and a strong impact on evangelicals, mainliners, and white Catholics from 1992 through 2004 (Kellstedt et al. 2007; McTague and Layman, chapter 12, this volume). A similar procedure using GSS data produces similar findings: Presidential voting was largely unrelated to traditionalism–modernism in the 1980s, but was clearly affected in the 1990s.

A final important point should be made about the religious variables in our conceptual scheme. Although we have illustrated the impact of belonging, believing, and behaving variables in combination, each can be used individually in multivariate analyses. It may well be that religious tradition is what really matters for some dependent variables, whereas religious beliefs are the best predictor of others, and religious practice may influence yet other aspects of politics. For example, traditionalism in belief seems to have a powerful impact on political attitudes and ideology, whereas religious behavior is a much better predictor of political behaviors, such as voting. Carefully specified multivariate models can often disentangle the distinct influence of each type of religious influence.

CONCLUSIONS

This chapter has argued that neither the ethnoreligious nor the restructuring model is a complete explanation for the links between religion and American politics. The ethnoreligious model focuses on religious affiliation as the driving force in the political behavior of the American public. This explanation is the impetus behind the historical argument that religious affiliation was (and is) central to understanding the pietist/liturgical differences during the 19th century, the Protestant–Catholic divide during the 20th century, and the evangelical/mainline/Catholic divisions today. The model also accounts for the contemporary political behavior of Latino Catholics, black Protestants, Jews, and assorted minority religions. At the same time, the restructuring model seems to explain newer divisions within the large white traditions, and increasingly, some other groups as well. Currently, then, our argument suggests that the restructuring model fits best the largest white traditions, whereas the ethnoreligious model continues to hold sway among most minority traditions. In sum, both explanations have at least a degree of empirical validity. Belonging, believing, and behaving all matter in understanding American political behavior.

Clear theory and quality measurements are central to adequate tests of these models. This means that each dimension of religion should be carefully measured. Progress has been made during the past two decades in measuring religious belonging, but the investigation of religious beliefs lags seriously behind, and that of religious behavior is not much further advanced. In the case of the former, scholarship is uncertain about which beliefs are central to understanding political behavior. Our argument is that the conceptualization and measurement of traditionalist–modernist beliefs, couched within the context of religious traditions, is the direction in which research should go. In the case of religious practices, again, research should focus on behaviors central to religious traditions, including both ritual practice and private devotion. As for religious movement affiliations, a focus on the church–sect distinction in the sociology of religion may prove to be a fruitful conceptual starting point from which careful measurement strategies can follow. As the chapters in this volume show, much has been learned about religion and American politics during the past three decades. We are optimistic that the best is yet to come.

Appendix A

Table A.1 Protestant Denominations Classified into Religious Traditions (measured as a percentage)

	Evangelical Protestant	Mainline Protestant	Latino Protestant	Black Protestant
All nondenominationals	26.9	22.7	38.7	21.9
Adventists	0.6		2.7	0.9
Southern Baptist Convention	21.6		13.4	12.9
Other Baptist (all but American)	9.2		4.0	22.9
American Baptists		7.9	12.5	7.2
Sectarian Baptists	6.0		2.0	6.6
Nonsectarian Baptists		2.0		3.1
Brethren		0.7		
Christian church	2.8		1.7	0.4
Churches of Christ	3.1		2.7	0.4
Disciples of Christ		2.0		1.1

continued

Table A.1 Continued

	Evangelical Protestant	Mainline Protestant	Latino Protestant	Black Protestant
Sectarian churches of Christ	2.0			0.7
Nonsectarian churches of Christ		1.3	1.1	0.3
United Church of Christ		2.3		
Nonsectarian Congregationalist		0.1	0.9	
Sectarian Congregationalist	1.0			
Episcopalian		8.2		1.4
Nonsectarian Anglican		0.5		
Sectarian Anglican	0.1			
Evangelical covenant	0.1			0.2
Evangelical free	0.6			
Sectarian Friends	0.1			0.1
Nonsectarian Friends		0.5		0.7
Church of the Nazarene	2.3		1.1	0.4
Holiness Churches of God*	1.3			0.5
Other holiness denominations	2.1		1.6	2.5
Missouri Synod Lutheran	4.2		1.8	0.7
ELCA Lutheran		9.8	1.5	0.2
Sectarian Lutheran	2.0		0.9	0.4
Nonsectarian Lutheran		4.1		0.9
Mennonite	0.5			
United Methodist		27.2	1.2	2.6
Sectarian Methodist	1.1			0.2
Nonsectarian Methodist		1.7		2.5
Assemblies of God	4.1		3.5	
Pentecostal Churches of God*	2.5		1.9	6.0
Other Pentecostals	2.6		3.6	1.5
Presbyterian Church USA		7.5		0.4
Presbyterian Church in America	2.0		1.8	0.3
Sectarian Presbyterian	0.6			
Nonsectarian Presbyterian		1.3		
Christian Reformed Church	0.5		1.4	
Reformed sectarian	0.2			
Reformed nonsectarian		0.2		
Percent of total sample	25.1	16.4	2.6	9.3

*Includes numerous small denominations associated with the Holiness and Pentecostal families with Church of God in their denominational name. Percents in each column add up to 100, with deviations resulting from rounding.

Table A.2 Other Religious Groups Classified into Religious Traditions (measured as a percentage)

	Other Christians	Liberal Faiths	Jewish	Other Non-Christians	Unaffiliated
Mormons	51.8				
Jehovah's Witnesses	29.4				
Christian Science	1.0				
Eastern Orthodox	14.1				
Russian Orthodox	1.4				
Serbian Orthodox	1.3				
Other Orthodox	1.1				
Liberal Catholic church		1.7			
Unitarian-Universalists		17.1			
Unity		4.8			
New Age groups		68.0			
Other liberal faiths		8.4			
Reform Jewish			44.6		
Conservative Jewish			31.6		
Orthodox Jewish			10.6		
Other Jewish			13.2		
Sunni Muslims				13.6	
Shia Muslims				8.2	
Other Muslims				16.4	
Bahai				1.1	
Buddhist				15.7	
Hindu				21.3	
Native American religions				21.3	
Other non-Christians				2.5	
Unaffiliated believers					27.9
Unaffiliated nonbelievers					52.0
Atheists or agnostics					20.2
Percent of total sample	2.8	1.2	1.9	1.4	17.3

NOTES

1. Consequently, the theoretical approaches discussed here should not be viewed as the only ways to analyze the linkage between religion and public life.

2. The substantive approach views religion in terms of beliefs concerning the supernatural or in "those systems of thought embodied in social organizations that posit the existence of the supernatural" (Stark and Bainbridge 1985, p. 3). However, other analysts contend that it is the function that beliefs play in the life of the individual (or society) that is important, regardless of whether they embody supernatural beliefs.

3. Although these authors were cognizant of the belonging component of religion, their efforts in this study focused on religious commitment or religiosity.

4. Religious beliefs not only capture the basic worldview of adherents, but provide a basis for both religious belonging and behaving.

5. The ethnoreligious pattern was captured well in the famous book by Will Herberg (1955) titled *Protestant–Catholic–Jew*.

6. It is possible for religious subcultures to form in an increasingly urban setting that foster distinct patterns of association and social interaction, that create alternative educational institutions, and that are attentive to different media of communication (see, for example, Smith [1998, chap. 4]).

7. Drawing from data in the Fourth National Survey of Religion and Politics (NSRP), this finding also holds for Bible reading, frequency of prayer, small-group involvement, and financial giving to the church.

8. As Stark and Glock (1968, p. 56) note, "Protestantism [in contrast to Catholicism] includes many separately constituted groups and the only possible ground for treating them collectively would be if they shared in a common vision. [But] this is clearly not the case."

9. Despite the relatively static nature of religious traditions, it is possible for denominations and local churches to move from one tradition to another, although such changes are rare and occur very gradually. For example, during the past several decades, the American Baptist Churches USA appear to have moved from their evangelical roots into the American mainline, although not without internal dissent. The membership of this denomination in the National Council of Churches is evidence that mainline Protestantism is the appropriate location.

10. For example, although evangelical Protestants are more prone than members of other Christian traditions to hold that believers should share their religious faith with others, not all evangelicals necessarily hold this position. And many in other traditions believe strongly in evangelism efforts.

11. For example, in Christian Smith's study of churchgoing evangelicals (1998, p. 241), only 19 percent of Southern Baptists chose to identify as "evangelical," another 22 percent chose "fundamentalist," whereas a larger 28 percent selected "mainline" and another 22 percent opted for "liberal" in describing their primary identification. In fact, many Baptists do not even claim the label "Protestant," applying that label only to denominations more closely linked in time to the Reformation.

12. Given the historical experience of African Americans, and the unique theological interpretation of that experience, black Protestantism should be viewed as a distinct religious tradition (Sernett 1991).

13. The fundamentalist, moderate, liberal classification also has empirical difficulties. If you create a religious tradition variable using the GSS, following the suggestions of

Green, Guth, Smidt, and Kellstedt (1996, pp. 188–189) and Steensland et al. (2000), and then cross-tabulate that variable with the GSS classification, you find that 90 percent of evangelical Protestants are placed in the fundamentalist category with all but one of the remaining evangelicals classified as moderate. Yet those moderates were more likely than the fundamentalists to vote for Bush in 2000 (69 percent to 57 percent) and to identify as Republicans (52 percent to 42 percent). Mainline Protestants, classified by religious tradition, fell into moderate and liberal categories using the GSS classification (26 percent were moderate and 74 percent were liberal). The "liberals" gave Bush 60 percent of their votes, the "moderates," 55 percent. In addition, the liberals were more likely to identify as Republican than the moderates. As these results are for whites only, they are not a function of race. These findings are counterintuitive and suggest great caution in the use of the GSS classification.

14. In the 2004 NSRP survey, 74 percent claimed a "Christian" affiliation.

15. This figure is based on responses to questions across NSRP studies over the past four presidential elections (1992–2004).

16. Black Catholics are few in most surveys; the limited evidence suggests that they resemble other blacks politically.

17. We estimate that 75 percent of black Protestants and 43 percent of Latino Protestants attend churches predominantly of their ethnic group. These estimates are based on questions in the NSRP about the racial composition of the congregation one attends, asked during presidential elections from 1992 to 2004.

18. The Web site for the National Association of Evangelicals is www.nae.net; for the National Council of Churches, the Web site is www.ncccusa.org.

19. The following distinctions may be helpful in making these assignments. Generally speaking, evangelicals take a particularistic approach to how life after death is obtained (belief in Jesus as savior is the *only* way to salvation), whereas mainliners tend to be more universalistic (belief in Jesus is *one* way to salvation, but there may be other ways). For evangelicals, the Bible is inspired by God, often to be interpreted literally, and is viewed as the ultimate source of authority, whereas mainline Protestants, in contrast, are more likely to view the Bible as a book inspired by God, but not to be taken literally, as a source of authority, but not necessarily more important than human reason. "Membership" in an evangelical context occurs more frequently by means of personal conversion (in other words, being born again), whereas in mainline circles membership usually comes through infant baptism and participation in traditional faith communities. Evangelism and missions tend to be more important for evangelicals than for mainliners. Relationships with the world outside the church also differ, with evangelicals favoring strategies of personal conversion and mainliners favoring programs of social justice. Worship styles also tend to differ, with evangelicals favoring the informal and experiential, and mainliners leaning toward the formal and liturgical.

20. These assignments have serious political implications. American Baptists, the mainline group, gave Bush 64 percent of their votes, whereas evangelical Southern Baptists gave him 80 percent. Members of the Evangelical Lutheran Church in America, the mainline denomination, supported Bush with 59 percent, whereas Missouri Synod Lutherans gave him 71 percent. The mainline Presbyterian Church USA supported Bush with 55 percent, whereas the evangelical Presbyterian Church in America gave him 83 percent. The moral of the story: Specificity in responses is essential. These data are drawn from the 2004 NSRP.

21. In the 2004 NSRP, 16 percent of the national sample did not provide a specific denominational response.

22. Low-attending "nondenominational" and "no-denominational" respondents were assigned to "missing values."

23. Analytically, "born again" could also be viewed as a status—in other words, that I am born again in the sight of God. Such recognition of one's standing before God need not reflect some religious experience nor constitute some broader social identity with others. However, we are unaware of any research effort that measures being born again in this fashion.

24. Analysis reveals that when examining answers to questions as to whether one has had a powerful religious experience, whether one has had an identifiable religious turning point, and whether one has made a commitment to Jesus Christ, it is having made a commitment to Christ, rather than some powerful religious experience per se, that characterizes the "born again" (see Smidt 1989). In the 1992 and 1996 NSRP surveys, those who identified themselves as born again were asked: "By 'born again' do you mean a specific, one-time conversion experience or a gradual development of faith over time?" Most Protestants said that the experience had been "gradual," except for evangelicals, who were evenly divided. Among evangelicals, those who gave a "sudden" response were much more likely to identify as Republicans and to vote for GOP presidential candidates than those who chose the "gradual" alternative.

25. Although related, these two movement identification labels should not be equated, because many Americans understand these terms differently. For example, the *Exploring Religious America Survey* (PBS/U.S. News & World Report 2002) asked Christians in two separate questions whether they would describe themselves as evangelicals and as born again. Among those who labeled themselves born again, less than half (38 percent) also described themselves as "evangelical Christians." And, although "evangelical" and "born again" are frequently treated as identical concepts, more than one in four (27 percent) self-identified evangelical Christians did not describe themselves as born again. The comparable figure from the 2004 NSRP survey was 16 percent.

26. In the 2004 NSRP survey, for example, Protestants were asked a born-again item. At the bivariate level, born-again respondents (whether evangelical, mainline, black, or Latino) were more likely to identify as Republicans and to vote for Bush, to hold pro-life positions on abortion, and to identify themselves as "conservative" than nonborn-again religionists. Nonetheless, in a logistic regression model predicting the 2004 vote for Bush, the born-again variable washed out completely, whereas the religious belief, religious practice, religious movement, and religious affiliation measures all were significant predictors of the Bush vote (data not shown). This analysis does not suggest that a born-again item should be dropped from future surveys, but does imply that there is likely to be greater payoff in the alternative religious measures just noted.

27. One might also treat born-again identifications as a possible measure of identification with a sectarian movement.

28. "Traditional" versus "progressive" may also work for Catholics, with traditionalists believing in papal infallibility, going to confession, and praying the rosary, whereas progressives are less attached to traditional Catholic doctrines and practices. In NSRP data, the "traditional" versus "progressive" distinction among Catholics also has political implications. Traditional Catholics tend to identify as Republican and vote for the GOP, whereas progressives tend to support Democrats.

29. In 2000, the GSS added "Pentecostal" to the list of religious identities.

30. Smith (1998) also asked: "Do you consider yourself a charismatic Christian or involved in the charismatic movement, or not?" This item was not used much in the subsequent analysis, however.

31. Thus, it is not surprising that Smith (1998, p. 234) found that his respondents were able "to locate themselves accurately on a Protestant identity map."

32. Many who see themselves as a part of a movement are not formal members of any particular movement organization, whereas others may be members. Movements, however, are made up of many individuals and organizations; no single organization can encapsulate a movement.

33. For an example that illustrates some of the confusion in response to these identity questions, Gallup asked respondents in a 1979 national survey whether they were a "Pentecostal or charismatic Christian." Among those who responded affirmatively, approximately 3 percent said they did not believe in God, 6 percent reported that they did not believe that Jesus was God or the Son of God, and 13 percent said they did not believe in the devil (Smidt 1989). As an illustration of the nonresponse given to movement items asked in a forced-choice format, Alwin et al. (2006) found, using GSS religious identity measures, that significant percentages of respondents failed to identify with any of the options presented: One third of Protestants failed to identify with any of the movement terms (fundamentalist, evangelical, mainline, and liberal) in 1996 and 1998, with the percentage reaching 45 percent in 2000 (even with Pentecostal added to the list in 2000). Additional Protestants gave "other," "don't know," or "no answer" responses that brought the percentages of "nonresponse" among Protestants to about half.

34. Evangelicals by religious tradition gave Bush 78 percent of their votes in 2004, but evangelicals who identified with sectarian movements gave him 88 percent. The mainliners gave Bush 50 percent of their votes, but nonsectarian mainliners gave him 37 percent. Source: 2004 National Survey of Religion and Politics.

35. For a detailed discussion of this new religious movement measure, see Guth, Kellstedt, Smidt, and Green (2005); Guth et al. (2006b); and chapter 9, this volume The new measure had higher interitem correlations with religious measures (beliefs, behaviors, and salience) than a five-point sectarian/nonsectarian measure using religious movement identifications, and that included a traditionalist/liberal–progressive distinction for Catholics. We think the reason for this is that respondents have difficulty comprehending movement identification terms. There is almost no nonresponse on this new measure, and it can be asked of respondents in every religious tradition.

36. For example, the ANES Bible question provides the response options of "The Bible is the actual word of God and is to be taken literally word for word," "The Bible is the word of God but not everything in it should be taken literally," and "The Bible is a book written by men." In 1964, only 15 percent of the American people chose the last option; in 2004, 16 percent did so. "Literal" beliefs decline over time from approximately 50 percent during the 1960s to about 35 percent during the 21st century.

37. Respondents were asked to place themselves along a continuum in which the following four pairings served as the end points: (1) friend and king, (2) judge and lover, (3) master and spouse, and (4) mother and father.

38. These God–image items were later included in the 1998 International Social Survey Program in which nearly 40,000 respondents across 32 countries were surveyed. Using these data, Froese and Bader (2008) differentiate between an active and authoritarian image of God, and find that both images of God have a powerful effect on moral attitudes in the United States, whereas only those with active images of God are more likely to support policies of greater economic equality.

39. Based on six GSS items, the image-of-God variable is scored along a single dimension where, at the one end, God is viewed as a partner or friend who is relatively

distant from earthly affairs and, at the other end, God is viewed in more authoritarian terms and as one who takes an active interest in the world and in people personally.

40. Evangelicals as a social group do not, by definition, subscribe to biblical literalism. Empirically, in the 2004 NSRP, two thirds of evangelicals do so compared with just more than one third of the sample as a whole.

41. The Barna Research Group defines a born-again Christian in terms of two criteria. First, the respondent must have made a personal commitment to Jesus Christ that continues to be important in his or her life today. Second, the individual must acknowledge that, after death, he or she will go to heaven because sins have been confessed and Jesus Christ has been accepted as savior (see Hackett and Lindsay 2008).

42. Individuals must believe that (1) they have a responsibility to share their faith in Christ with non-Christians; (2) Satan really exists; (3) eternal salvation is gained through God's grace alone, not through human efforts; (4) Jesus Christ lived a sinless life while on earth; (5) the Bible is accurate in all that it teaches; and (6) God is an omnipotent, omniscient, and perfect creator of the universe who rules the world today. Such a definition has no relationship to affiliation or belonging.

43. Using the 2004 NSRP, we created a surrogate "traditionalist belief" measure by ordering religious traditions as follows: evangelical Protestant, black Protestant, Latino Protestant, other Christian traditions (Mormon, Jehovah's Witness, Eastern Orthodox), unaffiliated believers, Latino Catholic, mainline Protestants, Anglo-Catholics, other non-Christians (Muslims, Buddhists, and so forth), liberal faiths (Unitarians, New Age groups), Jews, unaffiliated nonbelievers, and atheists/agnostics. The order was based on factor scores of five religious belief items with the mean factor score for each group assigned to the surrogate measure. The measure was highly correlated with a religious behavior factor (.57), with religious salience (.52), and with a sectarian/nonsectarian movement measure (.64). Yet, in a logistic regression, it predicted only 58.5 percent of the Bush vote correctly, whereas dummy variables for the religious traditions predicted 67.6 percent accurately. (The dummy variables for religious traditions also had more than double the pseudo R^2 value of the surrogate belief measure.)

44. For example, in white Protestant churches, services rarely go beyond an hour, whereas in the black Protestant tradition, services may simply be getting started at that point. In addition, the style of service differs dramatically from tradition to tradition. Some follow a set liturgy or order of worship, whereas others are much more experiential and change "as the Spirit leads."

45. Thus, tradition-specific behaviors need only be asked of those affiliated with that religious tradition.

46. Using a measure that taps the public religiosity (e.g., church attendance) and a private religiosity (e.g., private prayer), one can ascertain four distinct ways in which religiosity might be expressed: diminished (low in terms of both), privatized (high in terms of private, low in terms of public), public (low in terms of private, high in terms of public), and integrated (high in terms of both) (see, for example, Smidt [2006]). One's form of religious expression shapes civic and political engagement even when controlling for standard sociodemographic variables as well as religious tradition (see also Smidt, den Dulk, Penning, Monsma, and Koopman 2008).

47. Guth and Green (1993, p. 158) note that scholars have used the concept of religious salience in two distinct ways: general salience, the importance that religion has in a person's life, and religious relevance, "the perceived relevance of faith to an individual's specific attitudes or decisions."

48. For example, our Bible measure has five categories rather than the usual three: the Bible is (1) inspired by God and interpreted literally, (2) inspired by God but not to be interpreted literally, (3) inspired by God but with human error, (4) a great book of wisdom and history, or a (5) book of myths and legends. The Bush vote in 2004 varied in linear fashion from 20 percent for the "myths and legends" response category to 71 percent for the "literalists." Using the standard threefold categorization, the Bush vote ranged from 37 percent for the least orthodox response to 71 percent for the literalists.

49. We think it is a good idea to ask these respondents for the name and address of their church, allowing the researcher to get at specific denominational affiliations. This procedure is followed by the Baylor researchers (Dougherty, Johnson, and Polson 2007).

50. Using these assignment criteria in NSRP 2004 data, respondents were divided into sectarian and nonsectarian categories. Sectarian Baptists, for example, were much more likely to vote for Bush than their nonsectarian counterparts (67 percent to 19 percent). For Lutherans, the figure for sectarians was 92 percent versus 49 percent for nonsectarians. Sample numbers were not large in all cases.

51. Factor loadings range from .73 to .84, with one factor explaining 61 percent of the variance, whereas the coefficient alpha for the five items is .84.

52. The items loaded on a single factor (variance explained 64 percent) and had a coefficient alpha of .86.

53. In the sample as a whole, salience percentages varied from the highest to lowest as follows: 41 percent, 18 percent, 21 percent, and 21 percent. These percentages were used as the cut points in the belief-behavior factor to determine traditionalist, centrist, modernist, and nominal subgroups among evangelical Protestants, mainline Protestants, and white Roman Catholics.

54. We have found that the measure works for numerous measures of political behavior, including foreign policy, church–state questions, and "moral" issues (Guth 2006, 2007).

55. In previous work (Guth et al. 2005, 2006), we used a measure of religious movement identification, in addition to the religious belief and behavior measures, in producing the traditionalism score. This involved two questions tapping directly respondents' preference for traditionalist or modernist movements within their denominations. Elaborating the traditionalism measure in this way only enhances the explanatory power of our classification. We have not used this measure here because the requisite questions are not available in other data sets in the 1992 to 2004 time series.

REFERENCES

Alwin, Duane, Jacob Felson, Edward Walker, and Paula Tufis. 2006. "Measuring Religious Identities in Surveys." *Public Opinion Quarterly* 70: 530–564.

Ammerman, Nancy. 1997. *Congregation & Community.* New Brunswick, N.J.: Rutgers University Press.

Bader, Christopher, and Paul Froese. 2005. "Images of God: The Effect of Personal Theologies on Moral Attitudes, Political Affiliation, and Religious Behavior.: *Interdisciplinary Journal of Research on Religion* 1, article 11, http://www.religjournal.com.

Bellah, Robert. 1974. "Civil Religion in America." In *American Civil Religion,* ed. Russell Richey and Donald Jones, 21–44. New York: Harper & Row.

Berelson, Bernard, Paul Lazarsfeld, and William McPhee. 1954. *Voting: A Study of Opinion Formation in a Presidential Campaign.* Chicago, Ill.: University of Chicago Press.

Carpenter, Joel. 1997. *Revive Us Again: The Reawakening of American Fundamentalism.* New York: Oxford University Press.

Clydesdale, Timothy. 1999. "Toward Understanding the Role of Bible Beliefs and Higher Education in American Attitudes toward Eradicating Poverty, 1964–1996." *Journal for the Scientific Study of Religion* 38: 103–118.

Conover, Pamela Johnson. 1984. "The Influence of Group Identification of Political Perception and Evaluation." *Journal of Politics* 46: 760–785.

Davis, Nancy, and Robert Robinson. 1996. "Are the Rumors of War Exaggerated? Religious Orthodoxy and Moral Progressivism in America." *American Journal of Sociology* 102: 756–878.

Dougherty, Kevin D., Byron R. Johnson, and Edwin C. Polson. 2007. "Recovering the Lost: Remeasuring U.S. Religious Affiliation." *Journal for the Scientific Study of Religion* 46: 483–500.

Driedger, Leo. 1974. "Doctrinal Belief: A Major Factor in the Differential Perception of Social Issues." *Sociological Quarterly* 15: 66–80.

Durkheim, Emile. 1915. *The Elementary Forms of Religious Life.* London: George Allen & Urwin.

Fiorina, Morris. 2005. *Culture War? The Myth of a Polarized America.* New York: Pearson Longman.

Formisano, Ronald. 1983. *The Transformation of Political Culture: Massachusetts Parties, 1790s–1840s.* New York: Oxford University Press.

Froese, Paul, and Christopher Bader. 2008. "Unraveling Religious Worldviews: The Relationship between Images of God and Political Ideology in a Cross-Cultural Analysis." *Sociological Quarterly* 49: 689–718.

Gaustad, Edwin C. 1976. *Historical Atlas of Religion in America.* rev. ed. New York: Harper and Row.

Green, John C. 2000. "Religion and Politics in the 1990s: Confrontations and Coalitions." In *Religion and American Politics: The 2000 Election in Context,* ed. Mark Silk, 19–40. Hartford, Conn.: Center for the Study of Religion in Public Life.

Green, John C. 2007. *The Faith Factor: How Religion Influences American Elections.* Westport, Conn.: Praeger.

Green, John C., and James L. Guth. 1993. "From Lambs to Sheep: Denominational Change and Political Behavior." In *Rediscovering the Religious Factor in American Politics,* ed. David C. Leege and Lyman A. Kellstedt, 100–117. Armonk, N.Y.: M. E. Sharpe.

Green, John C., James L. Guth, Corwin E. Smidt, and Lyman A. Kellstedt, eds. 1996. *Religion and the Culture Wars.* Lanham, Md.: Rowman and Littlefield.

Green, John C., Lyman A. Kellstedt, Corwin E. Smidt, and James L. Guth. 2007. "How the Faithful Voted: Religious Communities and the Presidential Vote." In *A Matter of Faith: Religion in the 2004 Presidential Election,* ed. David Campbell, 15–36. Washington, D.C.: Brookings Institution Press.

Greeley, Andrew. 1988. "Evidence That a Maternal Image of God Correlates with Liberal Politics." *Sociology and Social Research* 71: 150–154.

Greeley, Andrew. 1989. *Religious Change in America.* Cambridge, Mass.: Harvard University Press.

Greeley, Andrew. 1993. "Religion and Attitudes toward the Environment." *Journal for the Scientific Study of Religion* 32 (1): 19–28.

Greeley, Andrew, and Michael Hout. 2006. *The Truth about Conservative Christians.* Chicago, Ill.: University of Chicago Press.

Guth, James L. 2006. "Religion and Foreign Policy Attitudes: The Case of the Bush Doctrine." Presented at the annual meeting of the Midwest Political Science Association, Chicago, Illinois, April 20–22.

Guth, James L. 2007. "Political Religion and Church–State Issues." Presented at the Oxford Round Table on Separation of Church and State, Oxford, England, July 22–27.

Guth, James L., Cleveland Fraser, John C. Green, Lyman A. Kellstedt, and Corwin E. Smidt. 1996. "Religion and Foreign Policy Attitudes: The Case of Christian Zionism." In *Rediscovering the Religious Factor in American Politics,* ed. David C. Leege and Lyman A. Kellstedt, 330–360. Armonk, N.Y.: M. E. Sharpe.

Guth, James L., and John Green. 1993. "Salience: The Core Concept." In *Rediscovering the Religious Factor in American Politics,* ed. David C. Leege and Lyman A. Kellstedt, 154–174. Armonk, N.Y.: M. E. Sharpe.

Guth, James L., John C. Green, Lyman Kellstedt, and Corwin E. Smidt. 1995. "Faith and the Environment: Religious Beliefs and Attitudes on Environmental Policy." *American Journal of Political Science* 39: 364–382.

Guth, James L., John C. Green, Lyman A. Kellstedt, and Corwin E. Smidt. 1999. "Faith and the Vote: The Role of Religion in Electoral Politics." Presented at the annual meeting of the American Political Science Association, Atlanta, Georgia, September 2–5.

Guth, James L., John C. Green, Corwin E. Smidt, Lyman A. Kellstedt, and Margaret M. Poloma. 1997. *The Bully Pulpit: The Politics of Protestant Clergy.* Lawrence, Kans.: University Press of Kansas.

Guth, James L., Lyman A. Kellstedt, John C. Green, and Corwin E. Smidt. 1993. "The Theological Perspective and Environmentalism among Religious Activists." *Journal for the Scientific Study of Religion* 32: 373–382.

Guth, James L., Lyman A. Kellstedt, Corwin E. Smidt, and John C. Green. 2005. "Religious Mobilization in the 2004 Presidential Election." Presented at the annual meeting of the American Political Science Association, Washington, DC, September 1–4.

Guth, James L., Lyman A. Kellstedt, Corwin E. Smidt, and John C. Green. 2006. "Religious Influences in the 2004 Presidential Election." *Presidential Studies Quarterly* 36: 223–242.

Hackett, Conrad, and D. Michael Lindsay. 2008. "Measuring Evangelicalism: Consequences of Different Operationalization Strategies." *Journal for the Scientific Study of Religion* 47: 499–514.

Hart, Roderick. 1977. *The Political Pulpit.* West Lafayette, Ind.: Purdue University Press.

Hart, Roderick, and John Pauley, II, eds. 2004. *The Political Pulpit, Revisited.* West Lafayette, Ind.: Purdue University Press.

Herberg, Will. 1955. *Protestant–Catholic–Jew: An Essay in American Religious Sociology.* Garden City, N.Y.: Doubleday.

Hoge, Dean, and Ernesto de Zulueta. 1985. "Salience as a Condition for Various Social Consequences of Religious Commitment." *Journal for the Scientific Study of Religion* 24: 21–38.

Hout, Michael, and Claude Fischer. 2002. "Why Americans Have No Religious Preference." *American Sociological Review* 67: 165–190.

Hunter, James D. 1991. *Culture Wars: The Struggle to Define America.* New York: Basic Books.

Jelen, Ted. 1989. "Biblical Literalism and Inerrancy: Does the Difference Make a Difference?" *Sociological Analysis* 49: 421–429.

Jensen, Richard. 1971. *The Winning of the Midwest: Social and Political Conflict, 1888–1896.* Chicago, Ill.: University of Chicago Press.

Kellstedt, Lyman A. 2008. "Seculars and the American Presidency." In *Religion, Race, and the American Presidency,* ed. Gaston Espinosa, 81–99. Lanham, Md.: Rowman & Littlefield.

Kellstedt, Lyman A., and John C. Green. 1993. "Knowing God's Many People: Denominational Preference and Political Behavior." In *Rediscovering the Religious Factor in American Politics,* ed. David C. Leege and Lyman A. Kellstedt, 53–71. Armonk, N.Y.: M. E. Sharpe.

Kellstedt, Lyman A., John C. Green, James L. Guth, and Corwin E. Smidt. 1996. "Grasping the Essentials: The Social Embodiment of Religion and Political Behavior." In *Religion and the Culture Wars,* ed. John C. Green, James L. Guth, Corwin E. Smidt, and Lyman A. Kellstedt, 174–192. Lanham, Md.: Rowman & Littlefield.

Kellstedt, Lyman A., John C. Green, James L. Guth, and Corwin E. Smidt. 1997. "Is There a Culture War? Religion and the 1996 Election." Presented at the annual meeting of the American Political Science Association. Washington, DC, September.

Kellstedt, Lyman A., and Corwin E. Smidt. 1993. "Doctrinal Beliefs and Political Behavior: Views of the Bible." In *Rediscovering the Religious Factor in American Politics,* ed. David C. Leege and Lyman A. Kellstedt, 177–198. Armonk, N.Y.: M. E. Sharpe.

Kellstedt, Lyman A., Corwin E. Smidt, John C. Green, and James L. Guth. 2007. "Faith Transformed: Religion and American Politics from FDR to G.W. Bush." In *Religion and American Politics.* 2nd ed., ed. Mark Noll and Luke Harlow, 270–295. New York: Oxford University Press.

Kleppner, Paul. 1970. *The Cross of Culture: A Social Analysis of Midwestern Politics 1850–1900.* New York: The Free Press.

Kleppner, Paul. 1979. *The Third Electoral System, 1853–1892.* Chapel Hill, N.C.: University of North Carolina Press.

Kohut, Andrew, John C. Green, Scott Keeter, and Robert Toth. 2000. *The Diminishing Divide: Religion's Changing Role in American Politics.* Washington, D.C.: Brookings Institution Press.

Layman, Geoffrey. 1997. "Religion and Political Behavior in the United States: The Impact of Beliefs, Affiliation, and Commitment from 1980 to 1994." *Public Opinion Quarterly* 61: 288–316.

Layman, Geoffrey. 2001. *The Great Divide: Religious and Cultural Conflict in American Party Politics.* New York: Columbia University Press.

Layman, Geoffrey, and John C. Green. 2005. "Wars and Rumors of Wars: The Contexts of Cultural Conflict in American Political Behavior." *British Journal of Political Science* 36: 61–89.

Lazarsfeld, Paul, Bernard Berelson, and Hazel Gaudet. 1944. *The People's Choice.* New York: Columbia University Press.

Leege, David. C. 1988. "Catholics and the Civic Order: Parish Participation, Politics, and Civic Participation. *Review of Politics* 50: 704–736.

Leege, David C., and Lyman A. Kellstedt, eds. 1993. *Rediscovering the Religious Factor in American Politics.* Armonk, N.Y.: M. E. Sharpe.

Leege, David. C., Kenneth D. Wald, Brian S. Krueger, and Paul D. Mueller. 2002. *The Politics of Cultural Differences*. Princeton, N.J.: Princeton University Press.

Manza, Jeff, and Clem Brooks. 1999. *Social Cleavages and Political Change: Voter Alignments and U.S. Party Coalitions*. New York: Oxford University Press.

Marsden, George. 1980. *Fundamentalism and American Culture: The Shaping of American Evangelicalism, 1870–1925*. New York: Oxford University Press.

McCormick, Richard. 1974. "Ethno-Cultural Interpretations of Nineteenth-Century American Voting Behavior." *Political Science Quarterly* 89: 351–377.

Mead, Frank S., and Samuel S. Hill. 2005. *Handbook of Denominations in the United States*. 12th ed. Nashville, Tenn.: Abingdon Press.

Melton, J. Gordon. 2005. *Encyclopedia of American Religions*. Detroit, Mich.: Gale.

Niebuhr, H. Richard. 1929. *The Social Sources of Denominationalism*. New York: Holt.

Nivoli, Pietro S., and David W. Brady, eds. 2006. *Red and Blue Nation, Volume 1*. Washington, D.C.: Brookings Institute Press.

PBS/U.S. News & World Report. 2002. "Exploring Religious America Survey." http://www.pbs. org/wnet/religionandethics/week534/specialreport.html (accessed May 27, 2008).

Pew Forum on Religion and Public Life. 2008. *U.S. Religious Landscape Survey: Religious Beliefs and Practices, Diverse and Politically Relevant*. Washington, D.C.: Pew Research Center.

Queen, Edward. 2002. "Public Religion and Voluntary Associations." In *Religion, Politics, and the American Experience: Reflections on Religion and American Public Life*, ed. Edith L. Blumhofer, 86–102. Tuscaloosa, Ala.: University of Alabama Press.

Sernett, Milton. 1991. "Black Religions and the Question of Evangelical Identity." In *The Variety of American Evangelicalism*, ed. Donald Dayton and Robert Johnson, 135–147. Knoxville, Tenn.: The University of Tennessee Press.

Smidt, Corwin E. 1980. "Civil Religious Orientations among Elementary School Children." *Sociological Analysis* 41: 25–40.

Smidt, Corwin E. 1982. "Civil Religious Orientations and Children's Perceptions of Political Authority." *Political Behavior* 4: 147–162.

Smidt, Corwin E. 1989. " 'Praise the Lord' Politics: A Comparative Study of the Social Characteristics and Political Views of American Evangelical and Charismatic Christians." *Sociological Analysis* 50: 53–72.

Smidt, Corwin E. 2006. "Religion, Civic Engagement, and Political Participation." Presented at the annual meeting of the American Political Science Association, Philadelphia, Pennsylvania, August 30—September 3.

Smidt, Corwin E. 2007. "Evangelical and Mainline Protestants at the Turn of the Millennium: Taking Stock and Looking Forward." In *From Pews to Polling Places: Faith and Politics in the American Religious Mosaic*, ed. Matthew Wilson, 29–51. Washington, D.C.: Georgetown University Press.

Smidt, Corwin, Kevin den Dulk, James Penning, Stephen Monsma, and Douglas Koopman. 2008. *Pews, Prayers, and Participation: Religion and Civic Responsibility in America*. Washington, D.C.: Georgetown University Press.

Smith, Christian. 1998. *American Evangelicalism: Embattled and Thriving*. Chicago, Ill.: University of Chicago Press.

Smith, Tom. 1990. "Classifying Protestant Denominations." *Review of Religious Research* 31 (3): 224–245.

Stark, Rodney. 2001. "Gods, Rituals, and the Moral Order." *Journal for the Scientific Study of Religion* 40 (4): 619–636.

Stark, Rodney, and William Bainbridge. 1985. *The Future of Religion.* Berkeley, Calif.: University of California Press.

Stark, Rodney, and Roger Finke. 2000. *Acts of Faith: Explaining the Human Side of Religion.* Berkeley, Calif.: University of California Press.

Stark, Rodney, and Bruce Foster. 1970. "In Defense of Orthodoxy: Notes on the Validity of an Index." *Social Forces* 48: 383–393.

Stark, Rodney, and Charles Glock. 1968. *American Piety: The Nature of Religious Commitment.* Berkeley, Calif.: University of California Press.

Steensland, Brian, Jerry Park, Mark Regnerus, Lynn Robinson, W. Bradford Wilcox, and Robert Woodberry. 2000. "The Measure of American Religion." *Social Forces* 79 (1): 291–318.

Swierenga, Robert. 1990. "Ethno-Religious Political Behavior in the Mid-Nineteenth Century: Voting, Values, Cultures." In *Religion & American Politics: From the Colonial Period to the 1980s,* ed. Mark Noll, 146–171. New York: Oxford University Press.

Troeltsch, Ernst. [1912] 1931. *The Social Teaching of the Christian Churches,* 2 vols. New York: Macmillan.

Wald, Kenneth D., and Allison Calhoun-Brown. 2007. *Religion and Politics in the United States.* 5th ed. Lanham, Md.: Rowman & Littlefield.

Wald, Kenneth D., and Corwin E. Smidt. 1993. "Measurement Strategies in the Study of Religion and Politics." In *Rediscovering the Religious Factor in American Politics,* ed. David C. Leege and Lyman A. Kellstedt, 26–49. Armonk, N.Y.: M. E. Sharpe.

Weber, Max. [1930] 1992. *The Protestant Ethic and the Spirit of Capitalism,* trans. Talcott Parsons. New York: Routledge.

Welch, Michael, and David C. Leege. 1988. "Catholic Parishioners' Sociopolitical Attitudes." *Journal for the Scientific Study of Religion* 27: 536–552.

Welch, Michael, and David C. Leege. 1991. "Dual Reference Groups and Political Orientations: An Examination of Evangelically Oriented Catholics." *American Journal of Political Science* 35: 28–56.

Williams, Rhys, ed. 1997. *Cultural Wars in American Politics: Critical Reviews of a Popular Myth.* New York: Aldine DeGruyter.

Wilcox, Clyde, Ted G. Jelen, and David Leege. 1993. "Religious Group Identifications: Toward a Cognitive Theory of Religious Mobilization." In *Rediscovering the Religious Factor in American Politics,* ed. David C. Leege and Lyman A. Kellstedt, 72–99. Armonk, N.Y.: M. E. Sharpe.

Wimberley, Ronald. 1976. "Testing the Civil Religious Hypothesis." *Sociological Analysis* 37: 341–352.

Wimberley, Ronald. 1979. "Continuity in the Measurement of Civil Religion." *Sociological Analysis* 40: 59–62.

Woodberry, Robert, and Christian Smith. 1998. "Fundamentalism et al.: Conservative Protestants in America." *Annual Review of Sociology* 24: 25–56.

Wuthnow, Robert. 1988. *The Restructuring of American Religion.* Princeton, N.J.: Princeton University Press.

CHAPTER 2

RELIGION AND THE AMERICAN FOUNDING

MARK A. NOLL

CHRONOLOGICAL and conceptual precision are necessary for understanding the place of religion in the politics of the American founding era. Political–religious interaction was constant throughout the entire period, but the nature of that interaction varied greatly depending on contingent forces and events. These were years when politics underwent rapid metamorphoses as a result of imperial tensions and revolutionary war—then through uncertainties under the Articles of Confederation and conflicts over implementing a strong national Constitution—and on to new conflicts and tensions during the tenures of the nation's first presidents.

The period's religious history witnessed a similar series of jolting changes from the 1760s to the early 19th century. During the late colonial period, the dominant religious groups remained European-derived churches established by law: Congregationalists in New England and Anglicans in the southern colonies, which were tax supported; and Presbyterians with Anglicans and Quakers in the middle colonies, where the churches did not enjoy formal government support but acted as if they should. By 1810, the church–state dynamic had shifted fundamentally away from inherited establishments to self-directed voluntarism. While upstart Methodists, Baptists, and "Christians" (Disciples of Christ) were taking the lead, the older colonial churches struggled to catch up.

To sort out the political–religious interactions of such a dynamic period, it is useful to examine first the much-debated question of religion and the ideology of the American Revolution, then two issues that have received relatively less attention—religion during the War for Independence itself and religion and the Constitution—before indicating how changes in religion during the founding era were intimately related to the era's political history. As a preliminary note, it is important to remember that for this stage of American history, organized "religion" was mostly limited to Protestants, with the most influential derived from Britain. Protestant churches made up at least 98 percent of all religious bodies through the 1790s, with only a handful of Jewish synagogues and only slightly more Catholic churches (50 in 1770, 65 in 1790) sprinkling the landscape. Among the Protestants, churches of British origin dominated statistically (more than 80 percent of all churches [2,481] in 1770 and also in 1790 [4,696 churches]), but even more in public visibility, as the new nation's numerous Lutherans, German Reformed, Dutch Reformed, Mennonites, and Moravians were restricted in general influence by their use of European languages (Gaustad 1976; Marini n.d.). Although forms and forces were certainly put in place during this era that anticipated the flourishing religious pluralism of later American history, the actual appearance of that pluralism would wait the surges of immigration that began in the 1830s.

RELIGION AND THE IDEOLOGY OF REVOLUTION

Recent historical scholarship has made it abundantly clear that the multivalent, tumultuous, and often extraordinarily fluid ideas of America's founding era cannot be described simplistically. Heated debates during the past half century have mostly concerned the relative weight of republican and liberal ideologies, but one of the gratifying by-products of that debate has been new attention to how religious ideas functioned in the mix.

After World War II, the process began with a Lockean school of political scientists who saw a timeless set of liberal principles as central for all political developments. In the widely noticed phrase of Louis Hartz (1955, p. 60), the American founding drew especially on John Locke's "basic social norm, the concept of free individuals in a state of nature." The republican response to this liberal interpretation claimed that ancient conceptions of public justice and historically conditioned standards of public virtue were much more important than Lockean liberalism. In the influential view of Bernard Bailyn (1967, p. 34), the writers who "dominated the colonists' miscellaneous learning and shaped it into a coherent whole" reflected "the radical social and political thought of the English Civil War and of the Commonwealth period." What these commonwealth or country theorists advocated was a stance that Gordon Wood (1969, p. 53) identified as distinctly republican: "The sacrifice of individual interests to the greater good of the whole formed the essence of republicanism and comprehended for Americans the idealistic goal of their Revolution."

The thesis that the new American nation rested on these civic humanist, Real Whig, and republican foundations soon generated a sharply argued antithesis reasserting the central place of a more sophisticated, more democratic, and more historically conditioned liberalism. In revisions proposed especially by Joyce Appleby (1992) and Isaac Kramnick (1990), the liberalism of the Revolutionary War era was viewed as incorporating some of the republican emphases stressed by Bailyn (1967), Wood (1969), and several others (see especially Pocock [1975] and Rahe [1992]), but it was defined primarily by concern for personal interests in the new commercial, protocapitalist contingencies of the late 18th century (Kramnick 1990; Appleby 1992). Eventually, debates settled on trying to discern how much of the various ideological positions were in play and when different emphases came to the fore.

The historians' recognition that neither an air-tight republicanism nor an equally hegemonic liberalism dominated public intellectual life has led at least some historians to reevaluate the place of religion (e.g., Engeman and Zuckert 2004). John Murrin (2007, p. 30), for instance, has contended that along with civic humanism and Lockean liberalism, four other "discernible value systems" were being put to use by those who formed the American nation: "Calvinist orthodoxy," "Anglican moralism," "Tom Paine radicalism," and "Scottish moral sense . . . philosophy." The important point underscored by Murrin (2007) is that religious thought was fully active in the ideological clearinghouse that created the United States. With this historiographical opening, a number of studies have begun to flesh out the picture for how religion affected the founding, but also how, in turn, the politics of the era exerted an influence on religious convictions (see especially Bloch 1985; Bonomi 2003; Grasso 1999; and Noll 2002).

The beginnings of the ideological interchange that led directly to the Revolutionary era's political religion first took place during the colonial wars of the 1740s. Before that time, Protestant ideology in the colonies featured an almost exclusive concentration on God's direct providential control over events and opinions. It also was inclined to view republican accounts of politics as heterodox substitutes for reliance on divine providence. The complaint against Real Whig or republican thought was that it made human self-reliance rather than divine grace the key to human flourishing, and that it put an Enlightenment confidence in human perception and human action in the place historically reserved for the orthodox reliance on God's all-seeing and all-knowing power (see Clark 1994, 2000). The great change of the 1740s was to align historical Protestant doctrines of providence with heretofore suspect principles of republicanism.

To be sure, important New England pastors like Cotton Mather of Boston and John Wise of Ipswich had anticipated a merger of providential and civic humanist perspectives. In addition, the heritage of Protestant Dissent, which constituted the colonies' main ecclesiastical tradition, had always featured what Edmund Burke (1960, p. 208) would later point out in 1775 when he urged Parliament to consider that the colonists were "protestants; and of that kind, which is the most adverse to all implicit submission of mind and opinion." Moreover, in his view, "this averseness in the dissenting churches from all that looks like absolute government" was a fundamental reality of "their history." Yet in that history, dissenting wariness about British power only occasionally drew on specifically civic humanist, republican, Real Whig—or Lockean—thinking. Much stronger among all colonial religious traditions, and especially among the New England Puritans, was attention to divine revelation, concern for eternal life, and a belief in God's direct control of quotidian existence.

Well into the 1740s, religious commentary in the colonies on public events maintained the traditional Protestant emphases. Yet with King George's War (1744–1748), which for the colonies featured New England's miraculously successful assault on the French fortress at Louisbourg, Cape Breton Island, there appeared the first hints of what would become the standard religious politics of the Revolutionary era. The guise under which republican convictions marched into the fortress of Protestant thought was the familiar cloak of anti-Catholicism.

During this imperial struggle with France, a number of colonial ministers from across the theological spectrum began to link the fate of genuine Christianity to hopes for the future of liberty. The Presbyterian Gilbert Tennent (1745, pp. 7, 37) in New Jersey, for instance, hailed the reduction of Louisbourg as the rescue "of our civil and religious Liberties" from an enemy "who unweariedly labours to rob us of our civil and religious Liberties, and bring us into the most wretched vassalage to arbitrary Power and Church Tyranny." The liberal Charles Chauncy (1745, p. 11) of Boston also started to mix once-separated categories by referring to the "Salvation" that God had secured for the colonies in the defeat of the French. The theological moderate Nathaniel Walter (1745) of Roxbury went even further by finding biblical prototypes for the "good Commonwealth's Man" of New England who had fought so valiantly at Louisbourg. Even more strikingly, to Walter, Jesus was one who had carried "every Virtue to the highest Pitch," including "that Devotedness to the publick Service, and those other Virtues which render Antiquity venerable" (1745, pp. 17, 18).

Real Whig ideology had obviously arrived in America, yet it was being driven by an inflamed expression of traditionally Protestant anti-Catholicism. Phrases from Massachusetts ministers Charles Chauncy (1745, p. 22) and Joseph Sewall (1745, pp. 32–33) revived that spirit by referring to the pope as "Antichrist" and "the Man of Sin" as they rejoiced over the defeat of the French. If the American colonists were now beginning to rely on a republican picture of the world that their spiritual predecessors (as well as religious contemporaries outside the colonies) associated with heresy, the colonists' vigorous anti-Catholicism may have obscured innovations taking place in the use of a new political vocabulary.

It is important to stress that the timing of these innovations was critical. Besides war with France, the other great colonial event of the 1740s was revival (see Noll 2003; Kidd 2007). The affective preaching of George Whitefield and his many imitators produced spectacular results—from crowds of unprecedented size gathering to hear traveling preachers to unusually large additions to church membership rolls and a new sense of shared religious commitment linking partisans of the revival from Savannah, Georgia, to Portland, Maine. For political history, one of the most significant consequences of this colonial Great Awakening was the collapse of New England's Puritan churches as the all-encompassing guardians of public ideology. In the wake of the revivals, New England's church–state establishments were drastically weakened. Substantial ecclesiastical parties—differentiated by degrees of enthusiasm for the Awakening—were now competing vigorously against each other. Despite holding on for nearly a century more in Massachusetts, and almost that long in Connecticut and New Hampshire, the Puritan establishments would never recover their once nearly complete—and once welcomed—control of public life and thought. Republican discourse, in other words, became a significant influence in colonial religious discourse only after the grand experiment of the Puritans' godly commonwealths had suffered an irrevocable setback. Alasdair MacIntyre (1984, p. 236) was not thinking of colonial American politics when he wrote about radical political thought in the age of Enlightenment, but his words nevertheless apply directly to the American setting *in* war and *after* revival: "Republicanism in the eighteenth century *is* the project of restoring a community of virtue."

The ideological transformation of colonial religious usage in 1745 and 1746 provides the necessary context for understanding why Jonathan Mayhew's sermon of January 30, 1749–1750, "A Discourse Concerning Unlimited Submission and Non-Resistance to the Higher Powers," was such a sensation when first preached, and has always been such a landmark for historians (see Akers 1964). Its celebration of the execution of Charles I by Parliament and its Puritan allies, which had taken place 100 years earlier, offered a potent blend of liberal religion, commonwealth politics, and fervent rhetoric; it advanced beyond what had been heard during King George's War and pointed toward what would soon become standard colonial rhetoric.

The renewal of hostilities against France in 1754 offered other colonists the opportunity to advance the political conjunctions that Mayhew had stressed (see Hatch 1977). During this new imperial crisis, the Real Whig vocabulary spread everywhere. For example, in 1755 the Presbyterian Samuel Davies of Virginia preached the first of several stirring war sermons that dressed orthodox theology in the garments of Whig liberty. The ostensible purpose of the sermon was to exploit the calamities of war as an appeal for repentance and the New Birth, but Davies' analysis of the war was thoroughly republican: "our religion, our liberty, our property, our lives, and everything sacred to us are in danger," especially of being "enslaved" by "an arbitrary, absolute monarch" enforcing conformity to "the superstition and idolatries of the church of Rome" (Davies 1828, vol. 3, p. 173).

By the end of active fighting against the French in 1760, an unusually strong bond had emerged in the American colonies between republican political ideology and traditional religious convictions. The crisis over the Stamp Act that followed immediately—and then the spiraling process of alienation from Britain—deepened, expanded, and sharpened American Christian republicanism. Specific events tightened the link between Christian and Real Whig reasoning (see Lambert 2003).

Thus, colonists in the 1760s resisted efforts by Anglicans to place a bishop in the colonies as a threat to both civil and religious liberty. They looked upon the Quebec Act of 1774, which legalized establishment status for the French Catholics of that colony, as proof of Britain's opposition to true religion and promotion of civil tyranny. It was not, however, conflict with Britain over specifically religious matters that encouraged colonial Protestants to accept Real Whig republicanism; rather, it was the mingling of what had been previously antagonistic concepts that took place in the traumas of war with France that occurred well before overt hostility flamed against the mother country.

On the eve of warfare with Great Britain, the merger of Protestant convictions about providence, covenant, and virtue with secular convictions about liberty, rights, and virtue, which had once been only occasional and adventitious, was now ubiquitous and systemic. The result for patriot leaders was the availability of a vocabulary that could make the political struggle into a clash of deep moral principle. For the churches, the conflict with Britain took on apocalyptic significance. For later American history, it was of greatest significance that this mixture of political and religious viewpoints was fixed in place at the dawn of national existence.

RELIGION AND POLITICS IN WAR, CONFEDERATION, AND BEYOND

During and after the War for Independence, American patriots accepted what was, for the time, a singular combination of Protestant Christian beliefs and secular political convictions. For supporters of the struggle against Britain, traditional Protestant and traditional republican vocabularies became almost interchangeable (see Bloch 1985, pp. 53–74; Noll 2006, pp. 53–60). The two perspectives merged in describing human nature as potentially noble but also as needing constant restraint to avoid the natural drift toward corruption. They used similar language to describe the relation between individual morality and public well-being—specifically, that the personal exercise of virtue provided the necessary foundation for a free and well-balanced society. In turn, liberty—civil *and* religious—was a prerequisite for the cultivation of virtue. Tyranny not only revealed the degeneracy of rulers, but made it impossible for virtue to be cultivated. Without virtue, there could be no true liberty; without liberty, no health in society.

In addition, republicans and the heirs of the Puritans saw the progress of liberty as an ongoing drama of cosmic significance. Patriotic Real Whigs pored over the past to chart the cyclical fortune of freedom and its decay. Evangelicals enjoyed a long history of resisting tyranny, and traced this resistance to its origin in the Reformation, and behind the Reformation to the words of Jesus and Paul. Together, Whigs and awakened Protestants came to see the triumph of liberty in

British North America as a climactic scene in the story of humanity. When republicanism became Christian republicanism, views of history were altered in two ways. Historical cycles now found an end point in the millennium, a theme that surged in prominence at the start of the French and Indian wars and the Revolutionary War (Bloch 1985). For republicans, the blind sovereignty of *Fortuna* was given a purpose as religious leaders, especially in New England, recalled the sovereign will that had created the covenant with those who first fled into the American wilderness for the sake of liberty. In the immediate context of war, the exchange of religious and political concepts gave the argument against Parliament the emotive force of revival.

When Tom Paine published *Common Sense* in 1776, he probably already had come to the conclusion, as he put it later, that most of the Old Testament, with "a few phrases excepted . . . deserves either our abhorrence or our contempt" (Paine 1794, p. 218). However, this opinion did not prevent him from citing the Hebrew scriptures at great length in his influential attack on monarchy, or from using a religiously charged vocabulary to subvert accepted British notions of hereditary power (Paine 1776, pp. 19–27). In the same year, 1776, the theological liberal Samuel West of Dartmouth, Massachusetts, and the theological conservative Samuel Sherwood of Weston, Connecticut, both used the imagery of the beast from Revelation 13 to describe British oppression (Sherwood 1776; West 1776). Similarly, during the war itself several patriots invoked the Curse of Meroz from Judges 5:23 against those who refused to fight for colonial liberty (Heimert 1966, pp. 332–334, 500–509).

Benjamin Rush (1745–1813), a leading Philadelphia physician, a signer of the Declaration of Independence, and a tireless reformer, illustrated the tight connections between religious and political thinking. Rush's prewar experience included intimate contact with revivalistic New Side Presbyterianism, resistance to the Stamp Act, medical training in Europe, and personal acquaintance with radical political leaders like Tom Paine and John Wilkes (see D'Elia 1974). In the crucible of Revolutionary America, Rush's political and religious faiths became one, and they would remain so after the war was over. As he wrote to an English correspondent in 1783: the "language" of American independence "has for many years appeared to me to be the same as that of the heavenly host that announced the birth of the Saviour of mankind. It proclaims 'glory to God in the highest—on earth peace—good will to man'" (as quoted in D'Elia 1974, p. 52).

The main political payoff from the creation of a distinctly American Christian republicanism was that religion played a major role in how the major founding fathers pictured a well-functioning social order (see especially West 1996). Although they differed among themselves on many questions of religion as well as politics, agreement on this point took in John Jay and John Witherspoon, who were evangelicals in something like the modern sense of the term; James Wilson and Alexander Hamilton, whose attachment to Christian orthodoxy fluctuated; George Washington and James Madison, who shared devotion to the republic and an extreme reticence about disclosing their personal religious beliefs; and Benjamin Franklin, John Adams, and Thomas Jefferson, who although Unitarian, or even

Deist, nonetheless thought religion had a vital role to play in the new nation. All of these major founders wanted the new United States to promote religious liberty and none wanted the national government to dictate religious beliefs or practices. They were thoroughly committed to the radical innovation of separating church and state. Yet, the founders also agreed among themselves that the free exercise of religion was essential in a republic of the sort they wanted to create.

John Witherspoon, the era's most politically active cleric, exemplified the founders' convictions from his post as president of the College of New Jersey at Princeton and in his service to the Continental Congress (see Morrison 2005). Thus, Witherspoon's moral philosophy represented a conservative Presbyterian appropriation of Francis Hutcheson's version of "the moral sense" along with a scientific approach to morals, and so paralleled similar convictions that Madison and Hamilton deployed in the *Federalist Papers*. Witherspoon's orientation toward pragmatic results instead of doctrine or metaphysics also spoke for the founding generation as a whole. Where he stood out was by offering support for independence with citations from John Calvin's famous authorization for "lesser magistrates" to take arms under duress to change regimes. After the conflict was over, Witherspoon's efforts at transforming the Presbyterian church into a truly national body inculcated the same commitments to religious freedom and cohesive national action in his church that he had worked to promote in the nation.

The surprising degree to which less orthodox founders agreed with frankly Christian leaders like Witherspoon rested on two shared assumptions: first, that the moral goods promoted by the Protestant churches largely coincided with the moral goods promoted by a republican government, and second, that these churches had a role to play in making the moral calculus of republicanism actually work. During and after the war, this moral calculus occupied an unusually prominent place in public life. It held that religion could and should contribute to the morality that was necessary for the virtuous citizens without which a republic could not survive. The practical challenge for the churches was to figure out a way to promote morality in a public sphere from which the old forms of establishment had been excluded by the new nation's commitment to religious freedom.

While the churches worked on that task, the founders continued to look to religion as a key support for their republican experiment. The classic expression was George Washington's Farewell Address of 1796. As a primer in classical republicanism, this speech warned about the dangerous public effects of passion, praised the Constitution as "sacredly maintained," and cautioned against standing armies and political factions. As an expression of Christian republicanism, it underscored the promotion of religion as central to Washington's purpose: "Can it be, that Providence has not connected the permanent felicity of a Nation with its virtue?" For maintaining that virtue, Washington evoked religion: "Of all the dispositions and habits which lead to political prosperity, Religion and morality are indispensable supports.... A volume could not trace all their connections with private and public felicity.... And let us with caution indulge the supposition, that morality can be maintained without religion.... 'Tis substantially true, that virtue or morality is a necessary spring of popular government" (Washington 1796).

The unprecedented torrent of memorial sermons after the death of Washington in late 1799—a torrent united by the common conviction that Washington's republican dignity had been an antitype fulfilling biblical typology for a godly ruler—testified to the ongoing strength of the convergence between religious and political thinking (see Smylie 1976).

As steadily as the founders stressed the need for religion to support republican government, a noticeable change in political thinking did take place during the last third of the 18th century. For the major founders, civic humanist themes of liberty as the fruit of virtue, tyranny as the product of vice, and social well-being as incompatible with arbitrary power were at first more prominent than the Lockean themes of natural rights, social contract, and civic individualism, even though the former by no means excluded the latter. The way in which Lockean themes enriched the republican–Christian mixture was well illustrated by a proclamation issued by the Continental Congress on November 1, 1777, as it fixed a day of public thanks for the recent victory at Saratoga. Samuel Adams, who composed the resolution, began with a Puritan–like reminder that it was "the indispensable duty of all men to adore the superintending providence of Almighty God; to acknowledge with gratitude their obligation to him for benefits received, and to implore such farther blessings as they stand in need of" (on the Puritan echo, see Morgan [1967]). However, Adams went on in republican and Lockean tones to say that similar adoration was due to God for his providential aid "in the prosecution of a just and necessary war, for the defense and establishment of our unalienable rights and liberties." Congress was calling the people to prayer on December 18 so that they might "consecrate themselves to the service of their divine benefactor; and … join the penitent confession of their manifold sins, whereby they had forfeited every favour, and their humble and earnest supplication that it may please God, through the merits of Jesus Christ, mercifully to forgive and blot them out of remembrance." Congress also asked the people to pray for material prosperity, but ended by stressing the need to cultivate "the principles of true liberty, virtue and piety, under his nurturing hand, and to prosper the means of religion for the promotion and enlargement of that kingdom which consisteth 'in righteousness, peace and joy in the Holy Ghost'" (*Journals* [1777] 1907; pp. 854–855; see Davis [2000] for context). Whatever the degree of religious sincerity among the Congressmen who passed this resolution, they were successfully blending the ideological elements that long defined American political discourse.

In the decades after the war, these ingredients remained constant, but the proportions within the mix underwent a shift. After the first years of the war, ideology moved to accentuate commercial expansion, economic and political rights, and the fulfillment of the individual self. In a word, classical republican views gradually yielded more place to Lockean principles and the practices of democratic individualism. When and how rapidly that shift took place does remain a historically contested question. A few historians date the transition as early as the

1760s (e.g., Kramnick 1990, p. 171), a few during the Revolutionary War itself (McCoy 1980, pp. 66–75), others in the years immediately after that conflict (e.g., Wood 1992), and still more during the early years of the 19th century (e.g., Wiebe 1984; Watts 1987). John Murrin (1987, p. 226) summarized the historiographical debate expertly: Virtually all students "have insisted . . . that there was a transition, a before and after. We do not believe that America was born modern [i.e., liberal]. . . . We probably do agree that the shift to modernity was virtually complete by the 1820s, but no doubt we can still quarrel about how it happened, among whom, and why." This shift was one of emphasis. Lockean accounts of natural rights were present all along; the classical republican account of disinterested public virtue never passed away.

Once it is understood that America's increasing liberalism did not necessarily obliterate a broad commitment to republican values—in other words, that a simple antithesis between republicanism and liberalism is a modern construct rather than a historical reality—much else becomes clear about the early national period. Americans of almost all political convictions did embrace stronger notions of individual rights, and most of them also wanted to see the powers of government limited to at least some degree. However, these commitments did not represent a repudiation of the republican heritage of the Revolutionary era. In an analysis of why concern for corruption was so great in the early United States, Murrin (1994, p. 138) concedes that "we surely ought to see republicanism as the recessive and liberalism as the dominant configuration by 1815." Yet he also insists that "we cannot even begin to make sense of the content of public life unless we see the two as a continuing dichotomy. . . . Without continuing acceptance of republican values, corruption would not have become a serious issue, much less an obsession, in an environment that was rapidly becoming more participatory and democratic" (Murrin 1994, pp. 138–139). The result was a national environment in which strong convictions about virtue, corruption, and freedom (as the absence of tyranny) long coexisted alongside strong notions of rights, contract, and freedom (as the liberty of individuals). Abraham Lincoln and Jefferson Davis would both draw on these parallel streams, and they survived together well into the 20th century, with special force during episodes of hot or cold war.

For the later history of North America, it was especially significant that the patriots' Christian republicanism overwhelmed political principles defined by moderate Christian loyalism that had been widespread in the colonies until 1776. Moderate Loyalist views of social well-being drew heavily on doctrines of creation (whereby God established rulers in their places) and of nature (where the harmonious working of the created order was thought to mirror God's providential control of the cosmos). Moderate Christian Loyalists often also adopted various forms of Whig political thought. Yet the conceptual bond between moderate Christian Loyalist and Real Whig principles was never as strong as the bond between revivalistic Protestantism and republican thought that prevailed in the new United States. The reason may have been that, as a religion stressing creation and nature, Christian loyalism could not resonate in a situation thought to be imperiled by tyranny as powerfully as revivalistic evangelicalism with its emphasis on redemption and dramatic rescue from sin. The American road not taken would, however, define the political history of Canada, where 40,000 to 50,000 United Empire Loyalists found a home after leaving the new United States. By 1815, in both the Maritime Provinces and Upper Canada (later Ontario), a Protestantism similar in its formal doctrines to what was held by Americans was establishing an ideology in which Christianity was valued because of support it gave for *rejecting* revolution. Egerton Ryerson, an evangelical who was the key early figure in both Upper Canadian Methodism and early Ontario public education, and many later commentators have thus regarded the contrasting ideologies of the United States and British North America (later Canada) as arising from the contrasting ways in which Protestants in the colonies responded to the challenge of revolutionary republicanism (see Ryerson 1880; Lipset 1990).

The widespread American acceptance of the Protestant–republican–Lockean politics that triumphed in the War for Independence has made it difficult for Americans to evaluate the Revolution morally. Issues at stake include questions about the just character of the war itself and also about the American founders' toleration for slavery. That Christian patriots perceived the conflict with Britain as a just war is clear. However, modern historians like Gordon Wood have described a reality for American colonists that did not reach the extremity of conditions justifying conflict in traditional just war doctrine. In his words, the colonists "were freer, had less inequality, were more prosperous and less burdened with cumbersome feudal restraints than any other part of mankind in the eighteenth century, and more important they knew it" (Wood 1983, p. 16). Yet the confidence bestowed by political and religious certainty has short-circuited later efforts to ask, for example, whether the course of diplomacy in the 1770s had been allowed to run its course (the criterion of last resort) or whether the wrongs suffered by colonists at the hands of Parliament were gross enough to require armed insurrection (the criterion of comparative justice).

Equally troubling, patriotic Christian republicans failed to see discrepancies between their complaints against Parliament's "tyranny" and the actual enslavement of African Americans. Prominent British voices like John Wesley's (1775) were joined by a few American pastors, like the white Samuel Hopkins (1776) and the black Lemuel Haynes (1776, pp. 17–30), who used both Christian and republican arguments to attack chattel bondage. But for the most part, patriots were too self-righteous in their own ideological understanding of slavery to heed the enslavement of African Americans.

Times of war are not ideal for creative ethical or theological reflection. During and after the American Revolution, the bond between a certain type of Protestantism and a certain type of republicanism was assumed more than defended. Partly for that reason it long continued as an instinctive reality in later American history.

RELIGION AND THE CONSTITUTION

A long tradition has regarded the American Constitution as so unique in the annals of humanity as to make it, in effect, a divine document. Alexander MacWhorter (1793, pp. 11–12), a respected New Jersey Presbyterian, expressed what was already a common view when he said in 1793: "Perhaps it is not in the reach of beings, of no more extended intelligence than man, to work up any thing nearer absolute perfection, consistent with, and creative of freedom, order and happiness, than the cardinal principles of our glorious Civil Constitution." One of Great Britain's most famous political leaders, speaking more than a century later, testified to the same effect. The Constitution, said William Gladstone, was "the most wonderful work ever struck off at a given time by the brain and purpose of man" (as cited in Wood 1973, p. v).

Others have not been so sure. A British contemporary of Gladstone, Walter Bagehot thought the Constitution so divided principles of sovereignty as to invite chaos or the manipulation of government by backstage operators. To him, the secret of the United States' political success was not the Constitution, but the American people: "[I]f they had not a genius for politics; if they had not a moderation in action singularly curious where superficial speech is so violent; if they had not a regard for law, such as no great people have yet evinced ... —the multiplicity of authorities in the American Constitution would long ago have brought it to a bad end" (Bagehot 1896, p. 296). Even more dubious were abolitionists who scorned the Constitution for how it supported slavery—by stipulating that slaves be counted as three fifths of a person for determining representation in Congress; by prohibiting even the possibility of terminating the slave trade before 1808; and, in the provision that galled the most, by mandating in Article IV that all states were required to return any "Person held to Service or Labour in one State, under the Laws thereof," if such a slave escaped to a free state. For these objections, William Lloyd Garrison held that the Constitution was nothing less than an "agreement with Hell" (Finkelman 1987, p. 188).

Close attention to the era in which the Constitution was written opens a door for understanding why it said what it said (and did not say) about religion. It also offers the beginning point for adjudicating later disputes over constitutional interpretation of religious controversies.

The Articles of Confederation, which were to govern the newly independent United States, went into effect in 1781. Very soon thereafter, influential figures in all parts of the new nation began to ask whether this instrument of government could protect the liberties won in the War for Independence. Under the Articles, the country possessed a weak, rotating executive. Each state, despite large discrepancies in population, had an equal vote in all deliberations. The Confederation Congress had no authority to raise money by its own initiative, but was required to request funds from the states. And the Articles could be amended only by the unanimous consent of all 13 states.

Compounding economic and political problems were moral concerns that troubled James Madison and several others who took the lead in calling for a new instrument of government. Madison was especially upset at the way in which government under the Articles seemed to be violating republican principles. With like-minded observers, he was appalled at the factionalism dividing states into a debtor class advocating "easy money" and a creditor class demanding a stable currency. They were particularly dismayed at the short-lived, but troubling debtors' "rebellion" led by Daniel Shays in western Massachusetts. Because, as Gordon Wood (2006, p. 605) has observed, "most of the new state constitutions created in 1776–7 were meant . . . to be republican copies of what the English constitution should have been," the new state constitutions had vested vast powers in large, popularly elected legislatures. But Madison and others observed that, instead of electing morally responsible men of substance to conduct the affairs of the states, voters were turning to men of little consequence—even to rabble-rousers and demagogues. Even worse, the legislatures conducted by such common individuals often acted with extraordinary disregard for checks and balances on power. In one particularly disturbing example, the New Hampshire legislature repeatedly vacated or suspended the judgments of judges, arbitrarily examined appeals and initiated cases in law, and in general arrogated to itself many traditionally executive and judicial functions.

The question Madison, Alexander Hamilton, John Adams, and other veterans of the Revolutionary struggle asked themselves was a grave one. Had the war to preserve republicanism against Britain succeeded only to witness the decline of republicanism in an independent America? The call in 1787 for a convention to consider a remedy for such defects seemed to offer a last chance for bringing together "popular government" and "individual freedom."

When it emerged, the new Constitution mostly fulfilled the expectations of the nationalists. To antifederalists who opposed the new document, too much power was being vested in the central government. But to federalist supporters, the genius of the Constitution lay in its balance of powers that prevented any one segment of the national government from becoming too powerful, even as it enabled the national government to check the arbitrary exercise of government in the states. So on the national level, the legislature, the president, and the courts were created in such a way so that each exercised some kind of restraint on the other two. At the same time, the people at large were provided a significant voice in protecting their own liberties, directly through the election of representatives to the House of Representatives and indirectly in the choice of state legislatures who, in turn, selected U.S. senators and the electors for president. At several points in the Constitution, as well as in the Tenth Amendment of the Bill of Rights, the Constitution was balanced by retaining a considerable measure of state power. This Bill of Rights, or the first 10 amendments to the Constitution, which were passed immediately after the formation of the new government, also contained many other provisions guaranteeing the liberties of individual citizens.

The 85 *Federalist Papers*—an influential series authored by Madison, Hamilton, and John Jay—made the central argument that the Constitution offered the best means for republican ideals to work in a nation with the size and political diversity of the United States. The most famous of these essays was Madison's "Tenth Federalist," which made the case that republicanism required a large and diverse country. Europe's experiments at republican government had failed largely because they had been attempted in tiny places where the popular will could be manipulated by local potentates. In America, it was different. Madison admitted that both the democratic provisions of the Constitution and the powerful national offices it provided could be abused. Yet because the United States was so large, because it included so many diverse interests (economically, religiously, politically), the republican balance of powers had a better chance to work here than anywhere else.

In contrast with the conflicts of the Revolution (and also with the constitutional crises leading to the Civil War), overt religion played a relatively scant role in deliberations leading to the Constitution. To be sure, within the context of ever-expanding practices of religious freedom, the Continental and Confederation congresses made many accommodations from 1774 to 1789 (see Davis 2000). For example, these bodies called for public days of thanksgiving and prayer, they authorized prayers to open its daily sessions and retained chaplains to offer them, they attended sermons (including Roman Catholic sermons) and church funerals in a body, they sponsored chaplains in the military, they used much more language about God in official documents than would appear in the Constitution, they incorporated religious symbols into the nation's Great Seal, and they provided federal lands in the Northwest Ordinance of 1787 for education to promote "Religion, morality, and knowledge" (Davis 2000, p. 169). Yet, as would be true for writing the Constitution, most of these actions were pragmatic efforts to achieve immediate results rather than consistently reasoned efforts at establishing carefully defined principles. The most common congressional action was consistently to refer religious questions to the states.

In the tidal wave of published commentary generated during debates on whether to ratify the Constitution, quotations from scripture abounded. The Bible, in fact, was quoted much more often than any other authority (see Lutz 1984). However, most of this quotation was ceremonial and rhetorical; only rarely did religious concerns enter into the deliberations at Philadelphia or the give-and-take marking the struggle for ratification (see Bailyn 1993).

Practicalities, not principles, dictated that religion be excluded from constitutional debate. If there was to be any kind of functioning national government, it was imperative that the different ways the states were supporting religion and the various (and contradictory) religious tests they prescribed for office holding be removed from discussion. As Americans debated whether to ratify the new Constitution, five of the nation's 14 states (Vermont had joined the original 13) provided some tax support for ministers, and those five plus seven others continued religious tests for public office. Only Virginia and Rhode Island practiced the kind of separation of church and state that has since become the American norm—where government provides no money for churches and poses no religious conditions for participation in public life (see Curry 1986). In John F. Wilson's (2007, p. 84) perceptive summary: "At root, while the founding fathers were not antireligious individually or collectively, their overriding and commonly held objective of achieving an adequate federal government would only be frustrated if the issue of religion's relationship to regime were allowed to introduce a dimension of continuing divisiveness into their work" (see also Marty 2006, pp. 510–511; Hutson 2008, pp. 139–144).

Throughout the Constitution-writing process and then during debates on its merits, however, several religious matters remained important. As expressed in George Washington's Farewell Address, the founders presupposed that government under the Constitution would prosper only so long as a morality backed by religion remained strong among the people at large (Hutson 2003). The Massachusetts Constitution of 1780 stated the same message in words that were picked up by other states as well: "the happiness of a people, and the good order and preservation of civil government, essentially depend on piety, religion, and morality" (Hutson 2008, p. 109). This same document explained why it was necessary for states to promote education by using the same logic: "wisdom and knowledge, as well as virtue, diffused generally among the body of the people [is] necessary for the preservation of their rights and liberties" (*The Founders' Constitution* 1987, vol. 1, p. 637). This motive also lay behind the many informal services that the early state and federal governments rendered to religion. These included promoting national slogans like "In God We Trust," invoking God on state mottos and seals, calling for days of thanksgiving and prayer, supporting missionaries to Native Americans, and exempting church property from taxes (see Hutson 2008, p. 167).

The founders also sought a wide scope for the free practice of religion. Although influential spokesmen like Patrick Henry of Virginia and most of the political leaders of New England thought it should be possible to continue some governmental support of churches and other religious activities, none of them wanted the burdensome constraints that had characterized almost all European state–church establishments for the preceding thousand years. In their view, state-supported bishops, ecclesiastical courts, and religious tests for public office all subverted the right to life, liberty, property, and the pursuit of happiness.

In addition, the American colonies enjoyed strong traditions that opposed religious establishments for ideological rather than political reasons. Roger Williams was expelled from Massachusetts in the 1630s and forced to settle in Rhode Island because he argued that churches were corrupted by power when they allied themselves with the state. His viewpoint had been resurrected by Baptists in the Revolutionary era, when for the first time Williams' principles began to exert a wide influence. Also strong were similar opinions propelled more by the 18th-century Enlightenment than by Protestant Dissent. So Benjamin Franklin, from his secular vantage point, expressed the opinion that "when a religion is good, I conceive it will support itself; and when it cannot support itself . . . so that its Professors are oblig'd to call for the help of the Civil Power, it is a sign, I apprehend, of its being a bad one" (Kurland and Lerner 1987, vol. 4, p. 634).

Thomas Jefferson's statute for religious freedom, which was adopted by Virginia in 1786, pioneered what would be the American path. It began with a ringing declaration: "Whereas Almighty God hath created the mind free; that all attempts to influence it by temporal punishments or burthens, or by civil incapacitations, tend only to beget habits of hypocrisy and meanness, and are a departure from the plan of the Holy author of our religion" (Kurland and Lerner 1987, vol. 5, p. 84). During debate on this law an amendment was proposed to make it read "a departure from the plan of Jesus Christ, the holy author of our religion" (Kurland and Lerner 1987, vol. 5, p. 85). Virginia's Deists and other advocates of the Enlightenment opposed the amendment, but so also did several members who, in the words of James Madison, "were particularly distinguished by their reputed piety and Christian zeal." The argument of these Protestant Dissenters against the amendment was, in Madison's summary, "that the better proof of reverence for that holy name would be not to profane it by making it a topic of legislative discussion, and particularly by making his religion the means of abridging the natural and equal rights of all men, in defiance of his own declaration that his Kingdom was not of this world" (Kurland and Lerner 1987, vol. 5, p. 103).

An additional factor moving the founders to divide institutions of church and state was the growing awareness that America might eventually become home to settlers who were not Christians. Petitions of Philadelphia Jews in the 1780s were a straw in the wind. The new Pennsylvania Constitution affirmed specifically the liberty to worship freely, but it also required office holders in the state government to swear their belief that "the Scriptures of the old and new Testament [were] given by divine inspiration." A plaintive petition of the Philadelphia Synagogue to the government of Pennsylvania in 1783 asked if this provision was in keeping with the republican liberties secured in the Revolution. The petitioners asked "leave to represent, that in the religious books of the Jews, which are or may be in every man's hands, there are no such doctrines or principles established as are inconsistent with the safety and happiness of the people of Pennsylvania, and the conduct and behaviour of the Jews in this and the neighbouring States, has always tallied with the great design of the Revolution" (Kurland and Lerner 1987, vol. 4, p. 635). At the Federal Convention in Philadelphia four years later, the delegates received a similar petition from an individual Jew, Jonas Phillips, making the same points (Kurland and Lerner 1987, vol. 4, pp. 638–639). Whatever the precise influence of such petitions, and whatever the founders felt it was appropriate for the states to require of state officials, they ensured that Jews, Catholics, and others who did not hold to the Protestant faiths then dominant in America would be able to serve in the national government. In the words of Article VI, clause 3: "no religious Test shall ever be required as a Qualification to any Office or public Trust under the United States."

The reticence of the Constitution concerning public philosophy, including religion, complicates questions about its modern application. Sixteen simple words in The First Amendment of 1791 have been the focal point of endless discussion: "Congress shall make no law respecting an establishment of religion, or prohibiting the free exercise thereof."

Almost from the beginning, it was recognized that the precise meaning of these principles could pose a difficulty. James Madison, who promoted a strict separation between the institutions of government and those of the state, confessed as an old man in 1832, "I must admit . . . that it may not be easy, in every possible case, to trace the line of separation between the rights of religion and the Civil authority with such distinctness as to avoid collisions and doubts on unessential points" (Kurland and Lerner 1987, vol. 5, p. 107). Joseph Story, a Supreme Court justice and the author of an influential commentary on the Constitution, felt that religion and politics could cooperate much more closely than Madison held. Yet when he expressed that viewpoint in 1833, he perceived the same potential for confusion that Madison saw: A "real difficulty" lay in the path of "ascertaining the limits, to which the government may rightfully go in fostering and encouraging religion" (Kurland and Lerner 1987, vol. 5, p. 108).

Questions about constitutional intent are also complicated by the great number of its "authors." To whom did the original document belong? To Madison and others who drafted it? To the delegates at Philadelphia who approved it? To the voters who elected representatives to the state ratifying conventions? To those representatives as they gave the approval, often by slim margins, in their states? To the first Congress, which added the Bill of Rights in response to requests from several state ratifying conventions? Or even to that most amorphous entity mentioned in the very first words of the Constitution, "We the people of the United States?"

Despite these difficulties, it simply is not the case that the Constitution, or its First Amendment, may mean whatever anyone wants them to mean. The "free exercise" clause meant that citizens of the United States were to have their own choice in religious belief and practice. One after another of the new state constitutions had spelled out this principle, as did New Hampshire's Constitution of 1784: "Every individual has a natural and unalienable right to worship God according to the dictates of his own conscience, and reason; and no subject shall be hurt, molested, or restrained in his person, liberty or estate for worshipping God, in the manner and season most agreeable to the dictates of his conscience, or for his religious profession, sentiments or persuasion." The states clearly held that the right of "free exercise" was absolute, provided only that people, as New Hampshire put it, do "not disturb the public peace, or disturb others, in their religious worship" (Kurland and Lerner 1987, vol. 5, p. 81).

The founders also maintained equally clear opposition to "an establishment of religion," at least in general terms. When the first Congress debated the Bill of Rights in August 1789, a representative wondered if the proposed wording of the First Amendment might ever be twisted "to abolish religion altogether." James Madison, who was lukewarm to the idea of a Bill of Rights because he felt that the liberties it specified were already possessed by the people, nonetheless spoke up immediately. As he saw it, the provision in the First Amendment meant "that Congress should not establish a religion, and enforce the legal observation of it by law, nor compel men to worship God in any manner contrary to their conscience"

(Kurland and Lerner vol. 5, p. 93). The United States, in other words, would never authorize public support for one denomination in the way that the British Parliament supported the Church of England. No citizens of the United States would ever be forced to attend or pay taxes for a national church.

At the center, the First Amendment was clear enough. But what of the states? And what of complexities that developed over time? How did the founders themselves interpret the words of the First Amendment? And what weight should those interpretations continue to have?

The views of Thomas Jefferson are well known, but also controversial. Jefferson was not present at the Constitutional Convention, but he was influential in Virginia's ratification process and through his constitutionally significant decisions as chief executive from 1801 to 1809. Jefferson wrote his famous words about "a wall of separation between Church and State" to the Danbury, Connecticut Baptist Association in 1802. These words articulated a separatistic principle that Jefferson had stated many times before, but they were uttered by a president who willingly attended services of Christian worship that convened in the U.S. capitol and who wrote to the Connecticut Baptists to strengthen his party's political standing in New England as much as he did to lay down timeless principles of government (see Hutson et al. 1999; Dreisbach 2002).

Other founders, moreover, did not see eye to eye with Jefferson. Along with Chief Justice John Marshall, Joseph Story was the most important interpreter of the Constitution in the years before the Civil War. Story was named to the Supreme Court in 1812 and served for more than 30 years, while at the same time he rejuvenated the Harvard Law School and published his famous commentaries. Story articulated greater room for accommodating religion and government than did Jefferson: "The promulgation of the great doctrines of religion," Story wrote in his 1833 commentary on the First Amendment, can "never be a matter of indifference to any well ordered community." Especially, "a republic" needed "the Christian religion, as the great basis, on which it must rest for its support and permanence." The First Amendment therefore allowed "Christianity . . . to receive encouragement from the state, so far as was not incompatible with the private rights of conscience, and the freedom of public worship" (Kurland and Lerner 1987, vol. 5, pp. 108–110).

James Madison had yet another view, closer to Jefferson's than Story's, yet with a difference. Madison believed that church and state should be separated to the point of prohibiting public payments for chaplains in the military and Congress, and of vetoing acts of Congress that incorporated churches in the District of Columbia. Although he "recommended" days of public prayer while president, Madison felt he had no authority to authorize or mandate them. In these particulars he stood quite close to Jefferson. At the same time, Madison also felt that it was quite appropriate for chaplains and other religious professionals to work in public areas and play a role in public events, *if* they were supported by *voluntary* contributions.

Jefferson, Story, and Madison all believed in separating the institutions of the state from denominational institutions. They all believed that no citizen should be forced to act against conscience in supporting religious beliefs or practices. Yet beyond this, the three were different. Jefferson went further to conceive a firm division between religion and politics. Story felt that government should promote religion, just as long as it did not support any particular denomination or religious institution. Madison, while siding generally with Jefferson, also held that voluntarily supported religious activities should be allowed in the public arena. None of the founders interpreted the First Amendment as prohibiting religious-based arguments for public policies. None seemed to worry about incidental benefits coming to religious institutions from legislation passed for the good of the citizenry as a whole. Yet none of the framers thought that it would be an easy matter to support religion generally without giving unfair advantage to one group of citizens. Even Justice Story wanted the public arena left as wide open as possible. To him it was important that "the Catholic and the Protestant, the Calvinist and the Arminian, the Jew and the Infidel," be able to "sit down at the common table of the national councils, without any inquisition into their faith, or mode of worship" (Kurland and Lerner 1987, vol. 5, p. 110).

If religion was a relatively subdued factor in the writing and passage of the Constitution, and if the role of religion in American constitutional life was ambiguous from the beginning, it leads naturally to the historical question: Why was this the case? One answer may lie in the religious situation of the 1780s, when the Constitution took shape, for this period witnessed something quite different from what came before and what came after. Looking more broadly at religious history, recognizing that the era of Constitution-making overlapped with only a small portion of that history helps to provide a clearer picture of the whole period's complex religious–political interactions.

POLITICS AND EARLY AMERICAN RELIGION

The history of religion in the new republic strongly influenced the way in which Revolutionary era achievements were appropriated in the new United States. With practices of establishment fading from the 1770s, Americans were venturing into uncharted waters. The result for both religion in itself and religion in connection to public life was confusion, and this confusion was felt most strongly during the years between the end of the War of Independence and the implementation of the Constitution. However, from the 1790s onward, a new kind of distinctly American religious practice took held, and with a vengeance. Rather than the leaders of colonial religious life—Congregationalists, Anglicans/Episcopalians, Presbyterians —upstart Methodists and Baptists were now paving the way (see Hatch 1989; Noll 2002, pp. 161–208).

Methodists, unlike many of their Protestant peers, did not stress the millennial future of the new American republic, and they expelled dissidents like James

O'Kelly, who tried to merge Methodist religion and revolutionary politics (see Andrews 2000). Within the main body of Methodists, many shades of opinion did exist on political questions, as did some latitude for political participation. However, a surprising number of the early Methodists shared the sentiments of John Mann, who wrote to a fellow-itinerant in 1795 that republicanism "eats [religion] out of many hearts" (Andrews 2000, p. 7). The Methodists' most important early leader, Francis Asbury (1745–1816), was also the one who defined the general Methodist stance toward politics, which was unusually cautionary. Asbury and his Methodist colleagues preached a message singularly well adapted to the conflicts, dislocations, and widely shared longings for personal and communal identity that characterized the early republic. Yet it was also a message that at first transcended this-worldly political preoccupations. The Methodists' greatest impact on public life came indirectly, as they demonstrated how a thoroughly voluntaristic approach to religion could succeed in the new United States.

The form of religion that flourished so luxuriantly during the first years of the 19th century was certainly republican—the whole range of Protestants along with the tiny Catholic minority had internalized the fear of unchecked authority and the commitment to private virtue that drove the ideology of the first political founding. However, it was also "Christian republicanism"—the virtue that both energetic itinerants and settled pastors promoted was not classical manliness but humility in Christ. The religion that came to prevail was more antiformal than formal. It did not trust in ascribed authority or inherited bureaucracies, but rather trusted in achieved authority and ad hoc networking. It was populist or democratic; it championed the ability of any white man to assume leadership in any religious assembly. It was oriented to the Bible alone—it spoke of the scriptures as a supreme authority that trumped or even revoked all other religious authorities.

Above all, this religious style followed the voluntary path marked out by the Methodists. Voluntarism was a mind-set keyed to innovative leadership, proactive public advocacy, and entrepreneurial goal setting. Voluntarism was also the means through which private religion could mobilize on behalf of social and political causes. As self-created vehicles for preaching the Christian message, distributing Christian literature, encouraging Christian civilization, and networking philanthropic activity, the voluntary societies came into their own after about 1810. The best funded and most dynamic societies—like the American Board of Commissioners for Foreign Missions (1810), the American Bible Society (1816), or the American Education Society (1816)—were rivaled only by the Methodist church in their shaping effects on national culture.

Along with the revivalism promoted by Methodists, Baptists, other newly formed movements, and (eventually) Congregationalists, Presbyterians, and some Episcopalians, voluntary agencies transformed the shape of American religion. A period of tumultuous and contentious innovation first reversed the downward slide of Protestantism and then began, as an almost inevitable process, to shape all of American society in a voluntaristic mold. Most remarkably, evangelicals even conquered the South, where an honor-driven culture of manly self-assertion had presented a far less propitious field for labor than regions to the North, where Puritanism had flourished.

The antebellum period's dynamic voluntary evangelicalism established an enduring template for the nation. Later religious movements would move well beyond the boundaries of evangelical Protestant belief and practice. However, religions that have flourished in the United States have done so by adopting, to at least some degree, many of the free-form, populist, and voluntaristic traits that evangelicals pioneered during the early national period.

The success of this kind of religion has posed a problem for interpreting the meaning of religion and politics in the Revolutionary age. The paradigmatic importance of the Revolutionary and Constitutional era is beyond question. However, it is also true that a great deal of contingent history succeeded the first founding, and that this history has led to political–religious realities very different from what existed during the last decades of the 18th century.

For the religious–political principles hammered out during the Revolutionary era, the main business was to protect the new nation from the excesses, abuses, corruptions, and intrinsic failures of European Christendom. But for the realities soon to exist in this new nation, the main business has been to establish guidelines appropriate for voluntary religious association rather than the weight of religious establishments. As they were formulated, the religious–political principles of the Revolutionary era looked backward to guard against abuses from a European past; by contrast, the religious–political realities of the new nation defined issues, problems, and situations created by new circumstances for both religion and politics. The effort to appropriate the founding history has, therefore, created a challenge, especially in recent decades, to grasp both what the founders accomplished and how changes since their era affect contemporary application of their legacy.

OPEN-ENDED QUESTIONS

Appropriation of the history of religion and the founding has constituted a special challenge in recent decades because of the difficulty in bringing together both what the founders accomplished and how changes since their era affect contemporary application of their legacy. The most obvious area of ongoing contention concerns interpretation of the First Amendment's guarantees concerning no establishment of religion and the free exercise of religion. Such controversy has become increasingly ardent since the 1940s, when the protections of rights guaranteed by the Fourteenth Amendment of 1868 were extended to the states. Resulting debate has stimulated the publication of outstanding general texts (e.g., Witte 2005), bibliographies (e.g., Wilson 1986–1987), and documentary collections (e.g., Wilson and Drakeman 2003), as well as high-quality arguments over how the founding texts should be applied to contemporary issues. The latter range widely, but can be divided roughly between those that see the Constitution as a flexible document with a relaxed boundary between religion and public life (that is, an accomodationist position [e.g., McConnell 1985; Hamburger 2002; Hutson 2003]) and those who view it as posing a sharp divide between anything religious and everything governmental—that is, a separationist position (e.g., Levy 1986; Kramnick and Moore 2005; Waldman 2008). The framers' decision to keep detailed consideration of religion out of their deliberations in the late 1780s has, with the passage of time, ensured the centrality of religion in contemporary constitutional debate.

Yet if controversies over the First Amendment dominate contemporary scholarship on religion in the founding era, other subjects also deserve more attention than they have recently received. These include heightened efforts to harvest the fruit of the increasingly nuanced scholarship on the founding era's political thought. What that sophisticated work makes possible are studies focused on which American religious groups used which strands of the era's multivalent political thought for which purposes in which specific regions (for a fresh example of such research, see Calvert [2008]). Because of the extensive scholarship that now exists on all aspects of the Revolutionary period and early republic, it would also be possible, as intimated earlier, to reopen normative questions such as whether the War for Independence was a just war or whether the Canadian Loyalists succeeded better than the Americans they left behind in creating a just society.

Another normative question with immense contemporary relevance is the question of how important the maintenance of African American slavery was for the creation of American independence. This question has been the subject of classic works of scholarship (e.g., Morgan 1975; Davis 1999). It has recently been carried into the years of the early republic (Einhorn 2006; Mason 2006) and out into the broader Atlantic world (Schama 2005); but for a nation so fixated on its heritage of liberty, the subject should remain a perennial topic of historical inquiry. As an extension of that particular concern, the broader issue of how religious contributions to independence, the formation of the Constitution, and the development of civic life under the Constitution may have contributed to religious–political entanglements during the era of the Civil War has been the subject of increasing scholarly attention (e.g., Miller, Stout, and Wilson 1998; Hochgeschwender 2006; Stout 2006). However, as "big picture" history pushes back against the recent tide of microhistorical scholarship, that question should offer an unusually important theme for scholars to research and a wide reading public to ponder.

The United States did not have a religious founding as such. Yet because all aspects of the founding were surrounded, encouraged, interpreted, contested, or resisted by religion, study of political–religious connections, which has produced such good results in the recent past, may actually be poised to do even better in the years to come.

REFERENCES

Akers, Charles W. 1964. *Called unto Liberty: A Life of Jonathan Mayhew, 1720–1766.* Cambridge, Mass.: Harvard University Press.

Andrews, Dee. 2000. *The Methodists and Revolutionary America.* Princeton, N.J.: Princeton University Press.

Appleby, Joyce. 1992. *Liberalism and Republicanism in the Historical Imagination.* Cambridge, Mass.: Harvard University Press.

Bagehot, Walter. 1896. *The English Constitution.* London: K. Paul, Trench, and Trübner.

Bailyn, Bernard. 1967. *The Ideological Origins of the American Revolution.* Cambridge, Mass.: Harvard University Press.

Bailyn, Bernard. 1993. *The Debate on the Constitution: Federalist and Antifederalist,* 2 vols. New York: Library of America.

Bloch, Ruth H. 1985. *Visionary Republic: Millennial Themes in American Thought, 1756–1800.* New York: Cambridge University Press.

Bonomi, Patricia U. 2003. *Under the Cope of Heaven: Religion, Society, and Politics in Colonial America.* 2nd ed. New York: Oxford University Press.

Burke, Edmund. 1960. "Speech on Conciliation with America." In *The Debate on the American Revolution, 1761–1783.* 2nd ed., ed. Max Beloff, 205–228. London: A. & C. Black.

Calvert, Jane E. 2008. *Quaker Constitutionalism and the Origins of American Civil Disobedience.* New York: Cambridge University Press.

Chauncy, Charles. 1745. *Marvellous Things Done by the Right Hand and Holy Arm of God in Getting Him the Victory.* Boston, Mass.: M. Cooper.

Clark, J. C. D. 1994. *The Language of Liberty, 1660–1832: Political Discourse and Social Dynamics in the Anglo-American World.* New York: Cambridge University Press.

Clark, J. C. D. 2000. *English Society, 1660–1832: Religion, Ideology, and Politics During the Ancient Regime.* 2nd ed. New York: Cambridge University Press.

Curry, Thomas J. 1986. *The First Freedoms: Church and State in America to the Passage of the First Amendment.* New York: Oxford University Press.

Davies, Samuel. 1828. "God the Sovereign of all Kingdoms" (March 5, 1755). In *Sermons on Important Subjects.* 3 Vols., 4th American ed. New York: J. & J. Harper.

Davis, David Brion. 1999. *The Problem of Slavery in the Age of Revolution, 1770–1823.* New ed. New York: Oxford University Press.

Davis, Derek H. 2000. *Religion and the Continental Congress, 1774–1789: Contributions to Original Intent.* New York: Oxford University Press.

D'Elia, Donald J. 1974. *Benjamin Rush: Philosopher of the American Revolution* (Transactions, vol. 64, part 5). Philadelphia, Pa.: American Philosophical Society.

Dreisbach, Daniel L. 2002. *Thomas Jefferson and the Wall of Separation between Church and State.* New York: New York University Press.

Einhorn, Robin L. 2006. *American Taxation, American Slavery.* Chicago, Ill.: University of Chicago Press.

Elliott, Emory. 1979. "The Puritan Roots of American Whig Rhetoric." In *Puritan Influences in American Literature,* ed. Emory Elliott, 107–127. Urbana, Ill.: University of Illinois Press.

Engeman, Thomas S., and Michael P. Zuckert, eds. 2004. *Protestantism and the American Founding.* Notre Dame, Ind.: University of Notre Dame Press.

Finkelman, Paul. 1987. "Slavery and the Constitutional Convention: Making a Covenant with Death." In *Beyond Confederation: Origins of the Constitution and American*

National Identity, eds. Richard Beeman, Stephen Botein, and Edward Carter III, 188–225. Chapel Hill, N.C.: University of North Carolina Press.

Gaustad, Edwin. 1976. *Historical Atlas of American Religious History*. Rev. ed. New York: Harper & Row.

Grasso, Christopher. 1999. *A Speaking Aristocracy: Transforming Public Discourse in Eighteenth-Century Connecticut*. Chapel Hill, N.C.: University of North Carolina Press.

Hamburger, Philip. 2002. *Separation of Church and State*. Cambridge, Mass.: Harvard University Press.

Hartz, Louis. 1955. *The Liberal Tradition in America*. New York: Harcourt, Brace.

Hatch, Nathan O. 1977. *The Sacred Cause of Liberty: Republican Thought and the Millennium in Revolutionary New England*. New Haven, Conn.: Yale University Press.

Hatch, Nathan O. 1989. *The Democratization of American Christianity*. New Haven, Conn.: Yale University Press.

Haynes, Lemuel. [1776] 1990. "Liberty Further Extended." In *Black Preacher to White America: The Collected Writings of Lemuel Haynes, 1774–1833*, ed. Richard Newman, 17–30. Brooklyn, N.Y.: Carlson.

Heimert, Alan. 1966. *Religion and the American Mind, from the Great Awakening to the Revolution*. Cambridge, Mass.: Harvard University Press.

Hochgeschwender, Michael. 2006. *Wahrheit, Einheit, Ordnung: Die Sklavenfrage und der amerikanische Katholizismus, 1835–1870*. Paderborn: Schöningh.

Hopkins, Samuel. 1776. *A Dialogue, Concerning the Slavery of the Africans*. Norwich, Conn.: J. P. Spooner.

Hutson, James H. 2003. "'A Future State of Rewards and Punishment': The Founders' Formula for the Social and Political Utility of Religion." In *Forgotten Features of the Founding: The Recovery of Religious Themes in the Early American Republic*, ed. James H. Hutson, 1–44. Lanham, Md.: Lexington.

Hutson, James H. 2008. *Church and State in America: The First Two Centuries*. New York: Cambridge University Press.

Hutson, James H., et al. 1999. "Thomas Jefferson's Letter to the Danbury Baptists: A Controversy Rejoined." *William and Mary Quarterly* 56: 775–824.

Journals of the Continental Congress, 1774–1789, vol. 9 (Oct. 3–Dec. 31, 1777). 1907. Washington, D.C.: Government Printing Office.

Kidd, Thomas S. 2007. *The Great Awakening: The Roots of Evangelical Christianity in Colonial America*. New Haven, Conn.: Yale University Press.

Kramnick, Isaac. 1990. *Republicanism and Bourgeois Radicalism: Political Ideology in Late Eighteenth-Century England and America*. Ithaca, N.Y.: Cornell University Press.

Kramnick, Isaac, and R. Laurence Moore. 2005. *The Godless Constitution: A Moral Defense of the Secular State*. 2nd ed. New York: W. W. Norton.

Kurland, Philip B., and Ralph Lerner, eds. 1987. *The Founder's Constitution*. 5 Vols. Chicago, Ill.: University of Chicago Press.

Lambert, Frank. 2003. *The Founding Fathers and the Place of Religion in America*. Princeton, N.J.: Princeton University Press.

Levy, Leonard W. 1986. *The Establishment Clause: Religion and the First Amendment*. New York: Macmillan.

Lipset, Seymour Martin. 1990. *Continental Divide: The Values and Institutions of the United States and Canada*. New York: Routledge.

Lutz, Donald. 1984. "The Relative Influence of European Writers on Late Eighteenth-Century American Political Thought." *American Political Science Review* 78: 189–197.

MacIntyre, Alasdair. 1984. *After Virtue: A Study in Moral Theology.* 2nd ed. Notre Dame, Ind.: University of Notre Dame Press.

MacWhorter, Alexander. 1793. *A Festival Discourse, Occasioned by the Celebration of the Seventeenth Anniversary [sic] of American Independence.* Newark, N.J.: John Woods.

Marini, Stephen A. n.d. "The Government of God in Revolutionary America, 1764–1792." Unpublished ms.

Marty, Martin E. 2006. "The American Revolution and Religion, 1765–1815." In *The Cambridge History of Christianity: Enlightenment, Reawakening and Revolution, 1660–1815,* ed. Stewart J. Brown and Timothy Tackett, 497–516. Cambridge: Cambridge University Press.

Mason, Matthew. 2006. *Slavery and Politics in the Early American Republic.* Chapel Hill, N.C.: University of North Carolina Press.

McConnell, Michael W. 1985. "Accommodation of Religion." *Supreme Court Review* 1985: 1–59.

McCoy, Drew R. 1980. *The Elusive Republic: Political Economy in Jeffersonian America.* Chapel Hill, N.C.: University of North Carolina Press.

Miller, Randall M., Harry S. Stout, and Charles Reagan Wilson, eds. 1998. *Religion and the American Civil War.* New York: Oxford University Press.

Morgan, Edmund S. 1967. "The Puritan Ethic and the American Revolution." *William and Mary Quarterly* 24: 3–43.

Morgan, Edmund S. 1975. *American Slavery, American Freedom: The Ordeal of Colonial Virginia.* New York: Norton.

Morrison, Jeffrey H. 2005. *John Witherspoon and the Founding of the American Republic.* Notre Dame, Ind.: University of Notre Dame Press.

Murrin, John M. 1987. "Self-Interest Conquers Patriotism: Republicans, Liberals, and Indians Reshape the Nation." In *The American Revolution: Its Character and Limits,* ed. Jack P. Greene, 224–229. New York: New York University Press.

Murrin, John M. 1994. "Escaping Perfidious Albion: Federalism, Fear of Aristocracy, and the Democratization of Corruption in Postrevolutionary America." In *Virtue, Corruption, and Self-Interest: Political Values in the Eighteenth Century,* ed., 103–147. Richard K. Matthews. Bethlehem, Pa.: Lehigh University Press.

Murrin, John M. 2007. "Religion and Politics in America from the First Settlements to the Civil War." In *Religion and American Politics: From the Colonial Period to the Present,* 2nd ed., ed. Mark A. Noll and Luke E. Harlow. New York: Oxford University Press.

Noll, Mark A. 2002. *America's God: From Jonathan Edwards to Abraham Lincoln.* New York: Oxford University Press.

Noll, Mark A. 2003. *The Rise of Evangelicalism: The Age of Edwards, Whitefield and the Wesleys.* Downers Grove, Ill.: InterVarsity Press.

Noll, Mark A. 2006. *Christians in the American Revolution.* 2nd ed. Vancouver: Regent College Publishing.

Paine, Tom. [1776] 1960. *Common Sense and the Crisis.* Garden City, N.Y.: Doubleday.

Paine, Tom. [1794] 1989. *The Age of Reason.* In *Political Writings,* ed. Bruce Kuklick, 265–318. New York: Cambridge University Press.

Pocock, J. G. A. 1975. *The Machiavellian Moment: Florentine Political Thought and the Atlantic Republican Tradition.* Princeton, N.J.: Princeton University Press.

Rahe, Paul A. 1992. *Republics Ancient and Modern: Classical Republicanism and the American Revolution.* Chapel Hill, N.C.: University of North Carolina Press.

Ryerson, Egerton. 1880. *The Loyalists of America and Their Times: From 1620 to 1816.* 2 Vols. Toronto: W. Briggs.

Schama, Simon. 2005. *Rough Crossings: Britain, the Slaves and the American Revolution.* London: BBC Books.

Sewall, Joseph. 1745. *The Lamb Slain.* Boston, Mass.: D. Henchman.

Sherwood, Samuel. 1776. *The Church's Flight into the Wilderness: An Address on the Times.* New York: S. Loudon.

Smylie, James H. 1976. "The President as Republican Prophet and King: Clerical Reflections on the Death of Washington." *Journal of Church and State* 18: 233–252.

Stout, Harry S. 2006. *Upon the Altar of the Nation: A Moral History of the Civil War.* New York: Viking.

Tennent, Gilbert. 1745. *The Necessity of Praising God for Mercies Receiv'd: A Sermon Occasion'd, By the Success of the Late Expedition.* Philadelphia, Pa.: William Bradford.

Waldman, Stephen. 2008. *Founding Faith: The Birth of Religious Freedom in America.* New York: Random House.

Walter, Nathaniel. 1745. *The Character of a True Patriot.* Boston, Mass.: D. Henchman.

Washington, George. [1796] 1997. "Farewell Address." In *Writings*, ed. John Rhodehamel, 962–977. New York: Library of America.

Watts, Steven. 1987. *The Republic Reborn: War and the Making of Liberal America, 1790–1820.* Baltimore, Md.: Johns Hopkins University Press.

Wesley, John. [1775] 1991. "A Calm Address to Our American Colonies." In *Political Sermons of the American Founding Era, 1730–1805*, ed. Ellis Sandoz. Indianapolis, Ind.: Liberty Press.

West, John G., Jr. 1996. *The Politics of Revelation and Reason: Religion and Civic Life in the New Nation.* Lawrence, Kans.: University Press of Kansas.

West, Samuel. 1776. *A Sermon Preached before the Honorable Council.* Boston, Mass.: John Gill.

Wiebe, Robert H. 1984. *The Opening of American Society: From the Adoption of the Constitution to the Eve of Disunion.* New York: Knopf.

Wilson, John F., ed. 1986–1987. *Church and State in America: A Bibliographical Guide.* 2 Vols. New York: Greenwood.

Wilson, John F. 2007. "Religion, Government, and Power in the New American Nation." In *Religion and American Politics: From the Colonial Period to the Present*, 2nd ed., Mark A. Noll and Luke E. Harlow, 79–92. New York: Oxford University Press.

Wilson, John F., and Donald L. Drakeman, eds. 2003. *Church and State in American History: Key Documents, Decisions, and Commentary from the Past Three Centuries.* 3rd ed. Boulder, Colo.: Westview Press.

Witte, John, Jr. 2005. *Religion and the American Constitutional Experiment.* 2nd ed. Boulder, Colo.: Westview Press.

Wood, Gordon S. 1969. *The Creation of the American Republic, 1776–1787.* Chapel Hill, N.C.: University of North Carolina Press.

Wood, Gordon S., ed. 1973. *The Confederation and the Constitution: The Critical Issues.* Boston, Mass.: Little, Brown.

Wood, Gordon S. 1983. "This Land Is Our Land," *New York Review of Books*, February 3, pp. 16–21.

Wood, Gordon S. 1992. *The Radicalism of the American Revolution.* New York: Knopf.

Wood, Gordon S. 2006. "The American Revolution." In *The Cambridge History of Eighteenth-Century Political Thought*, ed. Mark Goldie and Robert Wokler. Cambridge: Cambridge University Press.

CHAPTER 3

....

RELIGION AND AMERICAN VOTING BEHAVIOR, 1830s TO 1930s

....

ROBERT P. SWIERENGA

FOR years, historians largely rejected out of hand the premise that religion had influenced American politics since the birth of the republic. Only during World War II did social scientists begin to take religious variables into account in their analyses of American voting behavior. Paul Lazarsfeld, Samuel Lubell, and Seymour Martin Lipset led the way in the 1950s, and historians Lee Benson and Samuel Hays completed the reorientation in the 1960s by their writings and by tutoring a host of graduate students (Lubell 1956; Benson 1957; Hays 1959; Benson 1961; Johnson 1962; Lipset 1964; Silbey, Bogue, and Flanigan 1978; Bogue 1978; Hays 1980; McCormick 1986).

By the 1970s, the new approach in American political history had a name—the ethnocultural or ethnoreligious interpretation[1]—and a bevy of adherents, or "schools," who made it the reigning orthodoxy, replacing the populist–progressive paradigm that "economics explains the mostest," as Charles Beard famously stated (Swierenga 1971; McSeveney 1973; Stout 1975). In the 1980s and 1990s, a resurgent neoprogressive, or "new left," historiography, led by cultural Marxists, challenged the ethnoreligious interpretation (McCormick 1986), but the edifice, which stands on solid research at the grassroots, remains largely intact (Noll 1990; Leege and Kellstedt 1993; Gjerde 1997; Fogel 2001; Noll and Harlow 2007). Religious belief, Kathleen Conzen noted in 2004, "has been and remains a vital force in public as well as private life." For this reason, Conzen (2004, pp. 69, 114) concluded, scholars must confront, rather than bracket, the nexus between religious belief and politics.

This chapter summarizes the accumulated evidence in support of the thesis that religion was a salient factor in 19th-century voting behavior—and even to the advent of the New Deal. How and why religion was at the center is extremely complex, as are the related issues of documentation and measurement. Essentially, the United States is an immigrant nation, populated by peoples with different languages, religions, cultures, social values, and work experiences. This resulted in a nation with a relatively high degree of cultural pluralism, ethnic diversity, and conflicting norms and values. Not surprisingly, religion has been a salient factor in American politics at least since the Jacksonian era of the 1820s. Hence, a religious interpretation of voting behavior enhances our understanding of American political culture from the eras of Andrew Jackson to Franklin D. Roosevelt.

THE REDISCOVERY OF RELIGION

The revolution in American political history began when Lazarsfeld and his associates at the Bureau of Applied Social Research at Columbia University systematically surveyed voters during the 1940 presidential election campaign in Erie County, Ohio. To their surprise, they found that voters were most influenced by their churches, or, in sociological jargon, their "social reference groups." Protestants and Catholics clearly differed in voting and party identification, even when "controlling" for socioeconomic factors (Lipset 1964; Silbey, Bogue, and Flanigan 1978). In one giant step, Lazarsfeld brought into political analysis the religious variable that the first generation of professional historians and political scientists had jettisoned. The prevailing wisdom was basically summarized in James Bryce's terse assertion in 1894: "Religion comes very little into the American party" (Jensen 1970, p. 325). Sectional economic rivalries, class conflicts, and melting pot doctrines were the reigning orthodoxies following the influential historians Frederick Jackson Turner and Charles Beard. Why the rising professoriate was blind to expressions of religious values in politics is complex. Put simply, they were highly secularized and believed religion should be privatized, with a wall separating church and state. The doctrine of the melting pot, then dominant, also held that ethnic and religious differences were narrowing in society and politics.

So strong was this thinking during the 20th century that the first political pollsters of the modern era never considered religious questions when gathering data on voting behavior. Indeed, when Lazarsfeld told George Gallup, the first professional pollster and himself a Protestant churchgoer, of his startling finding, Gallup expressed disbelief (Lipset 1964, p. 71). Even as late as 1959, during the Kennedy–Nixon presidential race, Elmo Roper, another leading pollster, challenged the "myth of the Catholic vote" and denied any connection between religion and voting (Roper 1959, p. 22). However, the pollsters' skepticism gave way when Lipset, the prestigious director of the Institute of International Studies at the University of California, Berkeley, further documented the place of religion in American culture and politics. Yet, Lipset still deferred to the neo-Marxist explanation then in decline. Religion did not "explain everything," he allowed; class position was equally determinative (Lipset 1964, pp. 120–21).

The next challenge to the progressive paradigm carried the day. In 1961, Lee Benson, a young historian who had studied 19th-century voting patterns at Lazarsfeld's bureau in the mid 1950s, published one of the most significant books in American political history, *The Concept of Jacksonian Democracy: New York as a Test Case*. Benson began his research as a convinced economic determinist, but his analysis of group voting behavior led him to develop a sociological–psychological model based on ethnoreligious conflict. His key conclusion is the now classic statement: "At least since the 1820s, when manhood suffrage became widespread, ethnic and religious differences have tended to be *relatively* the most important source of political differences in the United States" (1961, p. 165). Benson made no attempt to "prove" his proposition other than to demonstrate its validity in the 1844 presidential election in New York State. Intuitively, he felt that this theory conformed to common sense: "Since the United States is highly heterogeneous, and has high social mobility," he reasoned, "I assume that men tend to . . . be more influenced by their ethnic and religious group membership than by their membership in economic classes or groups" (Benson 1961, p. 165).

Within a decade, a host of historians completed additional research on 19th-century elections that generally confirmed the religious dimension. Their research, which used quantitative and social science methods and theories, demonstrated that religion and ethnicity were basic to American voting patterns (Kleppner 1970; Formisano 1971; Jensen 1971; Kleppner 1979; Formisano 1983, 1993).[2] This conclusion should not have been surprising. Keen foreign observers of the time, such as Alexis de Tocqueville, had noted the high religiosity of American society, especially after the Second Great Awakening filled empty churches with new converts. As Richard Jensen (1971, p. 62) stated: "The most revolutionary change in nineteenth century America was the conversion of the nation from a largely dechristianized land in 1789 to a stronghold of Protestantism by mid-century. The revivals did it." By 1890, church affiliation was more than 70 percent in the Midwest, with the new revivalist sects and churches claiming more than half. The revivals sparked confrontation in every denomination. Again quoting Jensen (1971, pp. 63–64): "Until the mid-1890s the conflict between pietists and liturgicals was not only the noisiest product of American religion, it was also the force which channeled religious enthusiasm and religious conflicts into the political arena." This was all the more true because the militant evangelicals sought to link Christian reform and republicanism into an unofficial Protestant establishment that virtually equated the Kingdom of God with the nation (Marsden 1970).

From Religion to Politics: Values and Culture

The mechanism for translating religion into political preferences is complicated and much disputed. Lazarsfeld, Lipset, Lubell, Benson, and Hays all stressed the socialization process (Benson 1961; Hays 1964; Lipset 1964; Hays 1980). Individuals learned attitudes and values early in life from family, church, and community, which then shaped their perception of the larger world and gave them ethical values to live by. Citizens, if you will, absorbed voting habits with their mother's milk, and clerics and other community opinion makers then reinforced these subconscious dispositions. One political party was "right"; the other was "wrong." Parties were bound to conflict in a society flooded by wave after wave of immigrants or ethnoreligious groups, each with its own social character, historical experience, and theological beliefs. Each had its friends and enemies, or, in Robert K. Merton's words, its positive and negative reference groups.[3] Irish Catholics, for example, reacted against New England Protestants, who tended to be Whigs, by joining the Democratic Party. Then, new British immigrants voted Whig because Irish Catholics voted Democratic, and so on.

The ethnoreligious thesis, on one level, shifted the focus from national to local issues and from elites to the behavior of voters at the grassroots. At a deeper level, it substituted religious culture for class conflict and sectionalism as a significant independent variable in voting choices. As Hays (1964, p. 54) explained simply: "Party differences in voting patterns were cultural, not economic" in that "[e]thnocultural issues were far more important to voters than were tariffs, trusts, and railroads. They touched lives directly and moved people deeply" (Hays 1967, p. 300). Instead of battles in Washington and statehouses over economic benefits and favors, ethnoreligionists stressed fights over prohibition of alcohol, abolition of slavery, Sunday closing laws, parochial school funding, foreign language and Bible usage in public schools, anti-Catholic nativism and alien suffrage, sexual conformity and capital punishment, and a host of lesser crusades. These moral issues, rather than pocketbook interests, impelled 19th-century voters and precipitated the major political conflicts of the day. Rather than be assimilated, ethnoreligious groups clung to their customs, beliefs, and identities for generations, and as they clashed over public policy at the polls, their values and attitudes were hardened, reshaped, or mellowed, depending on changing historical circumstances. As Lipset (1964, p. 71) noted, this made "religious variation a matter of political significance in America."

Political socialization of individuals and structural conflict among social groups may explain how voters absorbed their values and prejudices, and had them reinforced as groups fought to defend or advance their interests in the political arena. However, this does not explain why particular ethnoreligious groups voted as they did. In other words, why were Irish Catholics Democrats and New England Congregationalists Whig and Republican?

Ethnoreligionists have offered at least three distinct, but often intertwined, theories to explain how religious group impulses became political ones. Benson

(1957, 1961) emphasized reference group theory, especially negative reactions. Although valid in limited historical settings, such as Boston in the 1840s, when Irish Catholic immigrants overran the Anglo-Protestant center, reference group theory is rather limited and simplistic, especially the notion that group members merely "absorb" political ideas and "react" to other groups. Hays (1959, pp. 66, 87) added a refinement—that of group hegemonic goals, which he called the "social analysis of politics." Ethnoreligious groups use political means to try to extend the domain of their cultural practices or, conversely, to protect themselves from legal or legislative attacks. For example, as Irish and German Catholic immigrants seemed to inundate the United States, native-born Protestants turned to nativist laws to keep Sabbath desecration and saloons in check. Again, this social approach begs the question of the sources of differing lifestyles. If groups clashed because of historic antagonisms and conflicting cultural traditions, it was because their religious roots differed.[4]

This led to the third theory, that "theology rather than language, customs, or heritage, was the foundation of cultural and political subgroups in America" (Jensen 1971, p. 82). "Political choices were thus derived from beliefs about God, human nature, the family, and government. Citizens were not robots, but reflective beings whose value system had been 'sanctified' by their family, friends, and congregations" (Kleppner 1970, p. 37; Jensen 1971; Kleppner 1979; Formisano 1983). Different ways of living and voting derive from different ways of believing. Moral decisionmaking rests on religious values, theological distinctions, or, more broadly, worldviews (Carwardine, 1993).[5]

Paul Kleppner (1979, pp. 183–185) cogently explained the nature of belief. Religion "involves a rationale for existence, a view of the world, a perspective for the organization of experience; it is a cognitive framework consisting of a matrix within which the human actor perceives his environment." Although it is not the only perspective, it "penetrates all partial and fragmentary social worlds in which men participate; it organizes and defines how they perceive and relate to society in general." Religiosity, Kleppner continues, comprises five core dimensions: belief, knowledge, practice, experience, and consequences. Various denominations emphasize different dimensions and the way in which they may be linked together, and out of this emerge behavioral differences.

It must be admitted that any attempt to explain voting behavior on the basis of Christian theology, liturgy, or lifestyle is a sticky wicket. Voters do not *always* act consistently with their ultimate beliefs. They may be cross-pressured by competing and conflicting religious "oughts." Finney evangelicals, for example, worked to free slaves but not women. Voters may delude themselves and vote their pocketbook, while claiming to follow ulterior motives. Churches and historical issues and pressures also changed over time, and generalizations are thus necessarily limited in time and place. Scholars have also struggled with theological typologies that can adequately categorize the many denominations according to their various belief systems.

The Liturgical–Pietist Continuum

Kleppner (1970, 1979) and Jensen (1971) offered the first sophisticated religious theory of American voting in the 19th century. Based on a wide reading in the sociology of religion and the history of individual denominations and groups, they developed the ritualist–pietist, or liturgical–pietist continuum, which locates ethnoreligious groups and denominations along a single dimension based on the central tendency of their theological orientation.[6] On the one side were ecclesiastic, ritualistic, and liturgically oriented groups; on the other were the sectlike evangelicals or pietists who stressed a living, biblical faith, and the imminent return and rule of the Messiah. The liturgical churches (e.g., Roman Catholic, Episcopal, and various Lutheran synods) were credally based, sacerdotal, hierarchical, nonmillennial, and particularistic. These ecclesiasticals were ever vigilant against state encroachment on their churches, parochial schools, and the moral lives of their members. God's kingdom was otherworldly, and human programs of conversion or social reform could not usher in the millennium. God would restore this inscrutable, fallen world in His own good time and in His own mighty power.

The pietists (e.g., Baptists, Methodists, Disciples, Congregationalists, Quakers) were New Testament–oriented, antiritualist, congregational in governance, active in parachurch organizations, and committed to individual conversion and societal reform to usher in the millennial reign of Christ. Pietists did not compartmentalize religion and civil government. "Right belief" and "right behavior" are two sides of the same spiritual coin. The liturgicals excommunicated heretics; the pietists expelled or shunned sinners.

These theological differences directly affected politics in the Jacksonian era, because the Yankee pietists launched a crusade to Christianize America, and the liturgicals resisted what they viewed as an enforced Anglo-conformity.[7] The pietists staged a two-pronged public program. First, they created the "benevolent empire" during the 1810s to spread the gospel and teach the Bible. Then, during the 1820s, they established reform societies to eradicate slavery, saloons, Sabbath desecration, and other social ills. Finally, during the 1830s, they entered the political mainstream by joining the new Whig Party against Jacksonian Democrats. By the 1840s, in fear of the growing Catholic immigrant menace, the Whigs added nativist legislation to their agenda, especially extending the naturalization period from 5 to 14 years. As the reformed-minded Yankees threatened to gain control of the federal and state governments through the Whig Party and, after 1854, the Republican Party, the liturgicals, who were mainly immigrants, fought back through the Democratic Party (Holt 1999).

Why the liturgicals joined the democracy and the more pietistic Christians gravitated toward the Whig and Republican parties requires a brief explanation of party ideologies and programs. With Thomas Jefferson as its patron saint and Andrew Jackson as its titular head, the Democratic Party from its inception in the 1820s espoused egalitarian, libertarian, and secularist goals (Kelley 1979; Ashworth 1983). The Democrats were social levelers who believed in a limited, populist government and a society rooted in self-interest and individual autonomy. They sought a secular state that did not try to legislate social behavior and was free of church control. An editorial in an Ohio Democratic newspaper condemned all reform movements that were motivated by "ascetic law, force, terror, or violence" (Georgetown *Democratic Standard*, September 12, 1843; cited in Fox 1979, p. 257). A Michigan editor declared: "We regard a man's religious belief as concerning only himself and his Maker" (Ann Arbor *Argus*, February 1, 1843; cited in Formisano 1971, p. 110). Government must thus restrain all economic power brokers and promote a laissez-faire society. Democratic theorists like George Bancroft believed that "the voice of the people is the voice of God" (Bancroft 1855). The highest good was universal manhood suffrage, majoritarian rule, a nonexploitative society, and a government that granted no undue favors. The Democrats easily attracted immigrants from the beginning and always stood for cultural and ethnic diversity (Kelley 1979; Ashworth 1983).

The Whig, or "Yankee" Party, was more elitist, paternalistic, cosmopolitan, entrepreneurial, and legalistic (Howe 1979; Holt 1999). It viewed government positively, trusted the governors more than the governed, and believed in absolute law based on eternal verities. The goal of the northern Whigs was to enlist all Christians and their clerical leaders who sought collectively to promote moral behavior and social harmony.[8] The Whigs, said Robert Kelley (1979, p. 160), were "the party of decency and respectability, the guardians of piety, sober living, proper manners, thrift, steady habits, and book learning." The Whig agenda of building a "righteous empire" received a boost initially from the Second Great Awakening. Indeed, without the spiritual revivals, the Whig leaders could not have built a viable mass party. Later, during the 1840s, the backlash against mass immigration and the perceived Irish menace further strengthened the Anglo-Whig party. When Bishop John Hughes of New York City objected to the reading of the King James Bible in the public schools as an attempt to proselytize Catholic children, and tried to obtain public funding for Catholic schools, Protestant leaders became alarmed and turned to the Whig Party to enact nativist laws to weaken or contain the Catholic threat (Ahlstrom 1972). To Yankees, the Irish were English "blacks," social pariahs who were infesting Protestant America (Kelley 1979, p. 172). In the end, the revivalist disposition convulsed the political parties, especially the Whigs, and caused the breakup of the second party system and the emergence of a new system led by a nascent coalition, the Republican Party (Kleppner 1981).

Given the opposing ethnoreligious groups, it is not surprising that historians find many links between religion and politics. Liturgicals demanded maximum personal freedom and state neutrality regarding personal behavior. They tended to find a congenial home in the Democratic Party. Pietists, on the other hand, felt an obligation to "reach out and purge the world of sin," and they found in the Whigs a vehicle to accomplish this (Jensen 1971, pp. 67–68). Kleppner's (1979, p. 74) generalization is the standard summary of the ethnoreligious thesis: "The more ritualistic the religious orientation of the group, the more likely it was to support the Democracy; conversely, the more pietist the group's outlook the more intensely

Republican its partisan affiliation." In short, "the primary cleavage line of party oppositions pitted evangelical pietistics against ritualistic religious groups" (Kleppner 1979, p. 363).

Was this political and social conflict between religious groups rooted in simple ethnic and religious prejudices and differing lifestyles? Or did theological beliefs underlie the behavioral distinctions? Some scholars (Benson 1957, 1961, and Ronald Formisano 1971, 1983 for example) stressed the clash of cultures, the historic reference group hatreds and prejudices, the group defenses, and hegemonic goals. Although there is no dearth of historical evidence for such patterns of brokenness, it does not mean that human behavior is usually (or always) unthinking, reactive, and culturally determined. As noted earlier, to explain that German Catholics supported the Democrats because that party opposed prohibition, and Quakers voted Whig because that party favored prohibition is not to explain the behavior at all. To claim that Irish Catholics voted Democratic because they hated Yankee Whigs does not explain the source of the prejudice. The reason that people voted this way ultimately lies deeper than symbols or culture; it is rooted in religious worldviews (Kleppner 1979).[9] People act politically, economically, and socially in keeping with their ultimate beliefs. Their values, mores, and actions, whether in the polling booth, on the job, or at home, are an outgrowth of the god (or gods) they hold at the center of their being.

In a nation of immigrants, where members of ethnoreligious groups often lived out their daily lives together in churches, schools, societies and clubs, work and play, and in marriage and family life, group norms were readily passed from parents to children, along with a strong sense of identity and a commitment to their political and social goals. Such groups were understandably ready to promote or defend their beliefs when public policy issues arose that touched their lives directly. Religious issues, more than social class, status, or sectional interests, were at the crux. As Kleppner (1979, p. 371) asserts: "Attachments to ethnoreligious groups were *relatively* more important as determinants of nineteenth-century social group cohesiveness and party oppositions than were economic attributes or social status." Notice the word *relatively*.

Ethnoculturalists do not claim that their findings *exclusively* explain mass voting patterns, only that differing religious beliefs *best* explain that behavior. They also recognize that in the South, the race issue was paramount (Kleppner 1979).[10] Ethnoculturalists also acknowledge that cross-pressures and particular historical contexts may change patterns or create unique situations (Kleppner 1979). The Pella (Iowa) Dutch pietists continued to vote Democratic after the Civil War when other Dutch Reformed colonies in the Midwest switched en masse to the Republican Party. The nativist attacks on the Pella community in the 1850s had been too strong and bitter to forget (Swierenga 1965; Kleppner 1979).

Ethnoreligious sensitivities were powerful motivators, but they could also be instruments of manipulation in the hands of skillful politicos, as Jon Gjerde (1997, p. 311) noted in his ethnocultural analysis of the "minds" of the rural Midwest. Political parties learned to manage ethnic subgroups and submerge them into larger coalitions of voters. Over time, this meant that the particular perspectives of ethnoreligious groups became "muted" and homogenized into "clusters of voters defined by attributes of social class, region of birth, and race" (p. 311). Ethnoreligious groups lived on two-way streets. They brought their perspectives on issues into the public square, but party leaders conflated particular concerns and accentuated collective points of reference to win elections. The "structure of political debate informed, truncated, and transformed many of these convictions" (p. 311). In the end, therefore, the "acids of modernity . . . inexorably corroded the institutional structures on which ethnic communities were based" (p. 317). Political parties were Trojan horses that might destroy ethnoreligious groups.

MEASUREMENT PROBLEMS

Having explained the religious roots of voting behavior, I now turn to the pithy question Lee Benson first posed in 1957 (p. 122): "Who voted for whom, when?" How ethnoreligious group members voted is a factual question that requires an empirical answer. (Kleppner, 1979). Although the question is straightforward, finding the answers has been very difficult. Two basic measurement problems keep cropping up. The first is to determine the religious affiliation of party members and voters, and the second is to measure the extent to which religious values acted in conjunction with socioeconomic and other factors to determine voting behavior.

Identifying the religion of voters is by far the more difficult problem. Federal census publications did not report the number of church members or communicants until the 1890 census. Beginning in 1850, however, the census enumerated church seating capacity per community. Because "sittings" were not directly proportionate with membership, particularly in the Catholic church, some scholars estimated pre-1890 membership by assuming that the 1890 ratio of members to sittings was a reasonable approximation of the earlier ratio (Jensen 1971, pp. 85–87; Kleppner 1979, pp. 204–205).[11] Some scholars simply used sittings, or an even cruder measure, the number of church buildings. It is also recognized that church attendance consistently exceeded membership, but nominal and occasional members likely shared the values and worldviews of full members (Lipset 1964, pp. 101–102).

In some areas, local sources such as county biographical directories occasionally state the religious affiliation of family heads (Jensen 1970; Peterson 1970; Jensen 1971). However, locals had to pay to be listed in these "mug books," so they do not include all potential voters. Poll books of active voters survive in some counties and, when these are collated with church membership records, it is possible to determine precisely the religion of voters (Formisano 1971; Rozett, 1976; Hammarberg 1977; Bourke and DeBats 1980, 1995; Winkle 1983). Such individual-level data are ideal, but rare. One scholar estimated Catholic strength in minor civil divisions by linking fathers and godfathers in baptism records with federal census records, multiplying by the ratio of births per adult member (15:1 in 1860), and thereby estimating the Catholic population (Kremm 1974, 1977).

Another common method of measuring religion was to note the state or country of birth in the manuscript censuses (recorded from 1850 onward) as a proxy for ethnoreligious identity, and then to find "homogeneous" counties (or, preferably, townships and wards) that were predominantly German Lutheran, Dutch Reformed, Swedish Lutheran, New England Yankee, and so on. The voting behavior in these homogeneous townships is then taken to represent the entire group in a state or region (Benson 1963; Hays 1964).[12] Critics charged that such ethnoreligious communities are atypical, because group pressures would be unduly strong there. Would a German Lutheran living in a largely German village in Wisconsin vote differently than a fellow church member who was living among Irish Catholics in Chicago?

The alternative to finding homogeneous communities is to estimate the relative proportion of ethnoreligious groups per county for an entire state or section of the country, either in whole or by sampling. The ideal, which no one has yet attempted, is to draw a random township and ward sample of the northeastern United States; compile township-level aggregate data on religion, ethnicity, occupation, wealth, and other pertinent variables during the period 1850 to 1900; and then, using multiple regression analysis, determine the relative relationships between religion and voting, taking into account the effects of all the other variables (Kousser 1976). Until such a large project is undertaken, scholars must rely on the numerous state and local case studies of the past 40 years, which cover the period from 1830 to 1900 in the northeastern and midwestern states (Wyman 1968; Holt 1969; Luebke 1969; McSeveney 1972; Fox 1973, 1977; Hammond 1979; Baum 1984; Giennap 1987).

Ethnoreligious Groups

Although regional variations existed, the findings generally agree in the political alignment of the major ethnoreligious groups. They can best be grouped in four categories: strongly Democrat (>75 percent), moderately Democratic (50 percent to 75 percent), moderately Whig or Republican (50 percent to 75 percent), and strongly Whig or Republican (>75 percent). As shown in table 3.1, strongly Democratic groups were all Catholics (Irish, German, French, French Canadian, Belgian, Bohemian, and so on), and Southern Baptists and Southern Methodists. Moderately Democratic groups were Old (i.e., colonial) German Lutheran, Old German and Old Dutch Reformed, Old British Episcopalians, New England Universalists, and Southern Presbyterians and Disciples of Christ. (Groups designated "Old" immigrated before the American Revolution; "New" arrived afterward.) Moderately Whig and Republican in their voting were the German pietist sects (Brethren,

Table 3.1 Political Orientation of Major Ethnoreligious Groups, 1830–1890

Strongly Whig/ Republican, 75%–100%	Moderately Whig/ Republican, 50%–75%	Strongly Democratic, 75%–100%	Moderately Democratic, 50%–75%
Quaker	Christian Church- Disciples Missionary Baptist	Irish Catholic	Old British Episcopal
Scotch-Irish Presbyterian	Regular Baptist	German Catholic	Southern Presbyterian
Free Will Baptist	Universalist (Midwestern)	French Catholic	Universalist (New England)
Congregationalist	Old School Presbyterian	Bohemian Catholic	Southern Disciples of Christ
New School Presbyterian	New German Lutheran	French Canadian	Old German Lutheran
Unitarian	Danish Lutheran	French Southern Baptist	Old German Reformed
Northern Methodist	German Pietist Groups	Southern Methodist	Old Dutch Reformed
Irish Methodist	Amish		
Cornish Methodist	Brethren		
Welsh Methodist	Mennonite		
Swedish Lutheran	Moravian		
Norwegian Lutheran	Dutch Christian Reformed		
Haugean Norwegian			
English Episcopal			
Canadian English Episcopal			
New Dutch Reformed			
French Huguenot			
Black Protestant			

Source: Kleppner (1970, 1979), Jensen (1971), and Formisano (1971).

Mennonites, Moravians, Amish), New German and Danish Lutheran, New Dutch Christian Reformed, Old School Presbyterians, Regular and Missionary Baptists, Midwestern Universalists, and the Christian Church. Strongly Whig and Republican were Northern Methodists (including Irish and Cornish Methodists), Free Will Baptists, Congregationalists, New School Presbyterians, Unitarians, Quakers,

French Huguenots, Swedish and Norwegian Lutherans, Haugean Norwegians, New Dutch Reformed, Canadian English and New England Episcopalians, and blacks.

Ethnoreligious specialists deserve credit for discovering these voting patterns, some of which are extremely subtle. For example, among Michigan's Dutch Calvinist immigrants of the mid-19th century, the majority affiliated with the largely Americanized Old Dutch Reformed Church in the East, but a minority opposed the union, seceded, and formed an independent immigrant church—the Christian Reformed Church. One of the major doctrinal issues in the split was the conviction of the seceders that the Old Dutch espoused a revivalist, free-will theology and used evangelical hymns and other "tainted" aspects of Yankee pietism (Swierenga and Bruins 1997; Fabend 2000). In their politics, Kleppner (1979, pp. 166–169) found that the Old Dutch Reformed after the Civil War consistently voted Republican more strongly than the Christian Reformed (66 percent vs. 59 percent). Thus, even among a homogeneous immigrant group like the Dutch Calvinists, the inroads of revivalism strengthened commitments to the Yankee political party.

Religion and Politics

Revivalism was the "engine" of political agitation not only for Dutch Calvinists but for all ethnoreligious groups (Formisano 1971, p. 104). Evangelist Charles G. Finney began preaching in the mid 1820s throughout New England and its colonies in western New York. By 1830, religious enthusiasm had reached a fever pitch in Yankeedom, and mass conversions swept town after town. Church membership doubled and tripled, and Protestant churches reclaimed large portions of the populace. Finney challenged his followers to pursue "entire sanctification," or perfectionism, and to become Christian social activists. The converts first entered politics in the anti-Masonic movement in New York in 1826 to 1827. By the mid 1830s, the evangelicals entered national politics in opposition to slavery, alcohol, and other social ills that they believed the Jackson administration condoned. Converts such as Theodore Dwight Weld became leaders in the antislavery movement, and in the next decades revivalist regions of the country developed strong antislavery societies and voted Liberty, Whig, and later Republican (Hammond 1979, Howe, 1990, 1991). Ultimately, the allegiance of pietists to the Whig Party led to its demise, because pietists put ethical goals, such as abolition of slavery, above party loyalty. The idea of a party system built on patronage and discipline was much stronger in Democratic than in Whig ranks. Evangelicals had a disproportionate share of antiparty men. In their estimation, Popery, Masonry, and Party were all threats to freedom of conscience and Christian principles (Formisano 1971, Howe 1979).

The disintegration of the Whig Party during the early 1850s, followed by the brief appearance of the Know-Nothings and then of the new Republican Party, and the fissure of the Democratic Party in 1860, were the main components of the political realignment of that decade. The second electoral system gave way to the third system (Smidt 2001). But, "Yankee-cultural imperialism" now expressed through the Republican Party continued as the dynamic force, carrying out God's will against racists and other sinners in the Democratic Party. Broadly speaking, during the third electoral era, pietist religious groups (both native born and immigrant) led the Republican Party against antipietist Democrats (Kleppner 1979).

The 1860 presidential election signaled the future direction of the social bases of partisanship. Catholic voter groups of all ethnic backgrounds and across all status levels voted more solidly Democratic than ever before. Meanwhile some former Democrats moved toward the Republicans—notably, Yankee Methodists and Baptists, and pietistic Norwegians, Dutch Reformed, and Germans. The increasingly Catholic character of the democracy, as well as that party's presumed responsibility for the Civil War, drove these Protestants away.

Cleveland, a city founded by New England Yankees, lay astride the immigrant route from the Port of New York to points west, and by 1860 the majority of the population was foreign born, mainly German and Irish Catholics. The Catholic influx led to a nativist backlash, as in Boston. The Protestant majority believed Catholics were un-American for rejecting the "public religion" of the republic. Moreover, the Catholic church was an "undemocratic engine of oppression." As the editor of the Cleveland *Express* declared on January 30, 1855, "Roman Catholics, whose consciences are enslaved, . . . regard the King of Rome—the Pope—as the depository of all authority" (as cited in Kremm 1977, p. 82). Religious tensions were also stirred by Catholic opposition to public school tax levies, by their "European" use of the Sabbath for recreation, and by their consistent bloc voting for the Democrats. Irish Catholics, charged the editors of the Cleveland *Leader*, "were sots and bums who crawled out of their 'rotten nests of filth' on election days to cast 'ignorant' ballots for the candidates of the 'slavocracy.' These 'cattle' lured to the polls by huge quantities of whisky, worshipped the three deities of the Ruffian Party—the Pope, a whisky barrel, and a nigger driver" (as cited in Kremm 1977, p. 85).

This level of invective suggests that the Cleveland electorate divided along Catholic versus non-Catholic lines, rather than over slavery extension. Voting analysis of the 1860 election proves this. The percentage of Catholic voters per ward and the Douglas vote were almost perfectly correlated. Similarly, the percentage of non-Catholic voters and the Lincoln vote were almost perfectly correlated. Even when removing the effects of ethnicity, occupation, and wealth, religion explains more than 80 percent of the variation across wards in the Republican and Democratic percentages. Religion, Kremm (1977, pp. 80–81) concluded, was the "real issue," the "overriding factor determining party preference in 1860." Catholics voted for the Democratic candidate, Stephen Douglas; non-Catholics, irrespective of other socioeconomic factors, voted for Lincoln (Kremm 1977, p. 76).

The rise of the Republican Party in Pittsburgh in the 1850s is similar to the Cleveland story. As Michael Holt (1969) discovered, the Republican coalition rose on a wave of anti-Catholic sentiment among native-born Protestants, which flared over Sabbatarian laws and parochial schools. The growing Irish and German Catholic population increasingly voted the Democratic ticket. Holt's statistical correlations at the ward level between voting patterns and ethnoreligious and economic character- istics revealed that "economic issues made no discernible contribution to Republican strength. . . . Instead, social, ethnic, and religious considerations often determined who voted for whom between 1848 and 1861. Divisions between native-born Amer- icans and immigrants and between Protestants and Catholics, rather than differences of opinion about the tariff or the morality of slavery, distinguished Whigs and Republicans from Democrats" (Holt 1969, pp. 7, 9).

The temperance issue and other social concerns, except abolition of slavery, lessened during the Civil War years, but during the early 1870s legal moves against alcohol and saloons resurfaced. The Republicans, who were generally supportive, lost voting support over temperance agitation. The Yankee Party also had a negative fallout from the economic depression set off by the financial panic of 1873 (Kleppner 1979). The Democrats, meanwhile, benefited from the Catholic fertility "bomb" that exploded in the 1870s. The relative strength of the ritualists thus grew at the expense of the pietists. In 1860, pietists outnumbered ritualists nationwide by 21 points (50 percent to 29 percent); but by 1890, pietists led by only five points (40 percent to 35 percent). The population increase among pietist groups averaged 2.4 percent per year, compared with 5.3 percent among liturgicals and 6.2 percent among Catholics (Kleppner 1979, table 6.3).

Out of political desperation, as well as concern for the moral decline in American society, the Republican pietists in the 1870s and 1880s revived the "politics of righteousness"—Sabbatarian and temperance laws, anti-Catholic pro- paganda, defense of Protestant public schools, and English-only language instruc- tion. Despite these efforts, the Democrats, bolstered by the "solid South," surged after 1876, winning three of four presidential elections by close margins. In effect, the northern supporting groups held steady in both camps for several decades until the major realignment of the 1890s, when William Jennings Bryan molded the old democracy into a new "party of reform," and William McKinley redirected the Republicans into a middle-of-the-road position that fought against silver coinage rather than alcoholic beverages (Kleppner 1970).

Rapid industrialization and the economic crises of the 1870s and 1890s opened the door for third-party movements, such as the Greenback–Labor, Socialist, and Populist parties, which pushed only pocketbook issues—the eight-hour day, rail- road rate regulation, paper money and "free" silver coinage, trust busting, and the like. Even in the face of severe hard times, however, recent multivariate statistical analyses of individual-level poll book data found that the two major parties held their traditional ethnocultural voting blocs, for whom noneconomic issues re- mained salient. The socialist fringe parties attracted those who had no ethnic or religious group identification, because they were susceptible to the rhetoric of class conflict (DeBats 2004; DeCanio 2007; DeCanio and Smidt 2007).[13]

McKinley's triumph over populism in 1896 and 1900 crushed radical politics for a generation, until the Great Depression, and ethnocultural voting patterns continued under the third electoral system until the New Deal coalition in 1932.

The prewar years, 1900 to 1915, witnessed the final immigrant push of southern and eastern European Catholic and Orthodox Christians, and Russian and Polish Jews. These newcomers raised ethnoreligious tensions to a fever pitch during World War I and the postwar years. Thus, although the Ku Klux Klan emerged in the South during Reconstruction as an organization with a focus on restricting the freedom of blacks, it became more rooted in the North during the 1920s as an effort to limit the opportunities of Catholic and Jewish immigrants (Jackson 1967). Voting along religious lines continued to be the norm, especially when the first Roman Catholic candidate, Al Smith, ran on the Democratic ticket.

This is confirmed in studies of the cities of New Haven, Chicago, St. Louis, Cincinnati, and the states of Massachusetts and Wisconsin, to name a few. In New Haven (Wolfinger 1965), where poor Italian Catholic immigrants comprised one third of the population by 1910, they split their vote evenly between the two parties for 30 years, which allowed Republicans to carry the city for 30 years. Then, during the Great Depression, the Italians increasingly turned Republican, becoming even more so during World War II. In 1939, William C. Celetano, a self-made mortician and son of a fruit peddler, won the Republican nomination for mayor and became New Haven's first Italian to win major political office. He held the office for 14 years, until 1953. Despite economic assimilation, ethnicity dictated voting behavior, and once initial patterns were set, partisan affiliation persisted for decades. New Haven's Italian Republican loyalties were a product of local politics, but ethnic loyalties were equally important. In Newark, where Italians comprised 40 percent to 45 percent of the electorate after the war, compatriots running on either the Republican or Democratic ticket could count on their support (Pomper 1966).

Chicago's major ethnic groups—Czechoslovakian, Polish, Lithuanian, Yugoslavian, Italian, German, and Swedish—voted Republican until the late 1920s and early 1930s (Allswang 1970). Then, Anton Cermak, the local Czech Democratic leader, upstaged his Republican rival, William Hale Thompson, and captured the loyalty of the New Immigrant voters. Cermak rode the coattails of Alfred E. Smith in the 1928 presidential campaign. The pair were a catalyst in the radical shift among Chicago's ethnics that firmly fixed a Democratic voting tradition. In Massachusetts, Al Smith, the "Happy Warrior," also capitalized on urban ethnic rivalries to capture the rock-ribbed Republican state of Massachusetts from Herbert Hoover (Huthmacher 1959). Smith swung the southern and eastern European Catholic immigrants in interior cities as well, including St. Louis, where a "persistent Democratic inclination" among the new immigrants continued "unto the fourth generation and later" (Greer 1961, p. 624).

In the upper Midwest, ethnic voting patterns set in the 1890s also continued for 50 years and more. Swedish Lutherans in Rockford, Illinois, faithfully voted Republican since the Civil War era, with the exception of the 1930s, when the Depression threatened their livelihood and brought a temporary switch to Democrats (Homer 1964). The Dutch Reformed in Chicago could not be swayed from their Republican proclivities, even while suffering economically along with the

Swedes, although a minority of intellectuals and small businessmen did defect in 1932 and 1936 (Swierenga 2002). German and Scandinavian groups in Wisconsin who had supported populism and Robert LaFollette progressivism at the turn of the century backed Senator Joseph McCarthy in the 1950s, as did Polish and Czech Catholics (Rogan 1967). Cincinnati's German Catholics, Democrats ever since the 1840s, turned Republican in the 1930s when F. D. Roosevelt adopted an anti-German foreign policy (Allen 1964).

American religious life changed markedly between 1880 and 1930. Organized Protestantism lost its political dominance, and narrowly defined ethnoreligious groups gave way to "mainline" Protestants, who coalesced in the Federal Council of Churches (1908), against the rising Catholic and Jewish immigrants. Political conflict, however, continued over values issues—the "social gospel" against poverty and vice, prohibition and prostitution, new immigrants who refused to "assimilate," Henry Ford's promise of a "car in every garage," Hollywood's sexual revolution on "silent screen," and the revolt against Victorian mores by novelists and flappers. Then came the sudden economic shift from the "prosperity decade" to the "dismal decade." With the economy in tatters, pocketbook issues took precedence over sociocultural differences, and hyphenated politics gave way to class conflict. The New Deal majority swept under its banner Catholics, blacks, Jews, white evangelical southerners, and unionized workers. The Republican Party continued to rest on northern Protestant votes, as it had done since the 1860s. Calvin Coolidge and Herbert Hoover were Protestant heroes; and Franklin Roosevelt was their demigod. In terms of behavioral attachments, blacks and Jews changed allegiances, but most ethnocultural groups continued to vote as they had since the Civil War.

Contributions and Critique

There are many positive results of the ethnoreligious interpretation of American voting behavior. Most important is the realization that religious beliefs significantly affected mass voting behavior. Religious groups and political parties had a symbiotic relationship. Churches influenced political agenda by determining that slavery or alcohol or some other moral problem required legislative action (VanderMeer 1981). Parties, in turn, built constituencies from various religious groups with worldviews that jibed with the party's programs and goals. The relationship between religion and politics was so close during the 19th century that Kleppner rightly calls the parties "political churches" and their ideologies "political confessionalism" (Kleppner 1979, p. 196).

The ethnoreligionists made their case convincingly, even to the point of "boredom and hostility," in the words of Sean Wilentz (1982, p. 47). By 1970, religion had become the new orthodoxy in voting studies. As critic James Wright admitted, the behavioralists had "done their work well. It is virtually impossible to avoid their frame of reference" (Wright 1973, p. 40). Since the mid 1970s, political historians have had to *disprove* the salience of religion and culture as major explanations of voting patterns. Cultural Marxists were even factoring religious forces into their economic models (compare with Johnson [1978]).

A second impact of ethnoreligious research was to shift attention from the national level to the local level, from political elites to voters at the grassroots. This radically different perspective, working "from the bottom up," brought great excitement to the new political history during the 1960s and 1970s, and sparked many new studies (Bogue 1983).

After the publication of Kleppner's *Third Electoral System* in 1979 and For-misano's *Transformation of Political Culture* in 1983, one scholar, Jean Baker (1983, p. 11), concluded that "the limits have been reached"; ethnoreligious political analysis "as originally conceived, was at a dead end." However, new scholarship continued during the 1980s that blended the political ideology of republicanism and the rising forces of capitalism with the social analysis of politics (McCormick 1974). Moreover, the best new work incorporated more sophisticated social statis-tical techniques (multivariate correlation and regression analysis, partialing, path analysis) to explain the relationship between voting choices and occupation, wealth, status, religion, and ethnicity. These studies proved again that the politics of "'Amens' and 'Hallelujahs'" determined voting more than class and social status (Kleppner 1979, pp. 326–328, 361–363).

Critics have leveled against the ethnoreligionists many charges, only a few of which are valid. Unsubstantiated charges are that they are monocausalists who exaggerated the religious variable to the point of "religious determinism," that they have a "fixation" with vague "symbolic" aspects of politics while ignoring concrete issues, that they are ahistorical in treating religion independently of time and place, that they ignored the unchurched or nominally churched half of the population, that their statistical methods were weak and misguided, and that their case study approach was not representative of the nation at large (Wright 1973; Foner 1974; Kousser 1976; Latner and Levine 1976; Bogue, Clubb, and Flanigan 1977; Ham-marberg 1977; Lichtman and Langbein 1978; Pessen 1979; Bogue 1983; Shade n.d.). The cultural Marxists have also reiterated their a priori assumptions about the centrality of economic forces (Kleppner 1979; Baum 1984; McCormick 1986; Egnal 2001).

There are two valid criticisms. One relates to the religious model and the other to research design. Most problematic is the pietist–liturgical continuum, which predicted how doctrinal beliefs were translated into voting patterns. It is an inadequate instrument not because religious beliefs were "seldom dominant" in voting decisions, as one critic charged (cited in Kleppner, 1979, 186), but because ultimate values and beliefs, which are always dominant in human decision making, are too complex for a one-dimensional "either-or" scale. To counter this criticism, Kleppner (1979, pp. 187–188) developed a more complex model that treated the pietistic and ritualistic perspectives as "more-or-less" characteristic of the various denominations, rather than divide them into two mutually exclusive types. He also drew distinctions among pietists between northern "evangelicals" and. southern "salvationists," and among Lutheran and Catholic ritualists, centering on the extent to which these groups compartmentalized the sacred from the secular. The sharper the division, the less the moral legislation.

However, this more sophisticated model still failed to incorporate necessary distinctions among northern pietists in mainline denominations such as Congregationalists, in perfectionist denominations such as Wesleyan Methodists, in primitivist denominations such as the Churches of Christ, and in separatist groups such as the Amish (VanderMeer 1981). Issues of theology, polity, and praxis separated these groups, and we still need a model that incorporates these complexities and yet is sufficiently simple to be useful in research (the jargon word is *operational*). Kleppner's newer model (Kleppner 1979) points in the right direction—that is, the relationship between the church and the world. Niebuhr (1951) identified five historic views: Christ *against* culture, Christ in *agreement* with culture, Christ *above* culture, Christ in *tension* with culture, and Christ *transforming* culture. Niebuhr's (1951) categories need revision, however, especially since the current religious Right has made a shambles of the oppositional model that stressed separation from culture. Yet the key issue remains: How do persons of faith relate to the political world? Specialists in American religious history, such as Marsden (1990), could make a major contribution to political history by developing a usable theological topology.

The other challenge is for political historians with good statistical skills to undertake the massive study Morgan Kousser called for 30 years ago (Kousser 1976). This is to validate the ethnoreligious interpretation by drawing random samples of rural townships and city wards, collect relevant socioeconomic facts for several decennial censuses during the 19th century for these sample areas, and then undertake multivariate statistical analyses to uncover the key determinants in voting patterns. Such a study might well yield a more generalized model of American voting behavior. It might even convince skeptics that religious institutions and values counted heavily in American politics and American history in general.

For now, the best data we have are scattered precinct polling lists and county historical directories. Recently, DeCanio and Smidt (2007) used regression analysis to tease information about 19th-century voting behavior from the data bases of the InterUniversity Consortium for Political and Social Research. Melvyn Hammarberg (1974, 1977) compiled data in the 1970s from *The People's Guide* directory for Indiana and the *Past and Present* directories for Illinois. These files, by county, list individuals by name, party identity, ethnicity, occupation, value of property, religious affiliation, and distance of residence from town. Their conclusions are familiar—that the political allegiances of 19th-century voters "were rooted in ethnocultural appeals and values that were isolated from economic conditions" (DeCanio and Smidt 2007, p. 23).

It is notable that in recent years political scientists, not historians, are publishing individual-level statistical analyses of historical voting patterns. And their findings suggest that "culture and the economy both mattered" (Lynch 1999, 2002a, b; DeCanio and Smidt 2007; DeCanio 2007). Political historians have shifted their attention to complex public policy issues and societal groups. Historians have turned to race, class, and gender studies; they prefer to mine nonquantitative sources, such as memoirs, stories, imagery, and symbols. Few historians today master social statistics and quantitative techniques, which are the tools needed to study voting behavior of past populations. The values issues of ethnocultural voting behavior also find little resonance with a generation steeped in postmodernism. The "new history" of the progressive period and its quantitative offspring in the 1960s rested on the now-outmoded search for "truth." Kamphoefner (1991, 1999, 2004), Kawaguchi (1994), Gjerde (1997), Baum (1998), Steckel (1998), Lorenz-Meyer (2000), and Conzen (2004) are among the few historians who continued to explore ethnoreligious factors in 19th-century politics, but none use statistical methods.

Whether and why churches were primary value-generating institutions during the past two centuries are no longer interesting questions. Religion may have been the "stuff of political choice" (Silbey et al. 1978, p. 23) for earlier generations of scholars, but no longer. During the 20th century, American intellectuals jettisoned belief for ideology. Theological perspectives of particular denominations, they assume, could not possibly explain past voting behavior. Politics has replaced theology, and denominations are giving way to megachurch and parachurch organizations. Yet, the ethnoreligious scholars of the 1960s to the 1980s deserve accolades for providing coherent explanations of American voting behavior from Andrew Jackson to Franklin D. Roosevelt. Until proved otherwise by new research, the legacy of their work stands.

NOTES

1. Fuchs (1956, p. 13) coined the term *ethnoreligious* because of its "inclusive quality"; it incorporated ethnic groups such as the Irish, religious groups such as Jews and Quakers, and even racial groups such as blacks.

2. Although omitted in this chapter, Jews also had bloc voting for Jeffersonian Republicans and Jacksonian Democrats during the early republic, and after the 1840s they switched and became solid Republican until the New Deal (Heitzmann 1975).

3. Derived from Merton's observation that "men frequently orient themselves to groups *other than their own* in shaping their behavior and evaluations" (Merton 1957, p. 288).

4. McCormick (1974) perceptively explains that the ethnocultural scholars somewhat carelessly intermixed these three theories.

5. Kleppner (1979) followed Milton Rokeach, J. Milton Yinger, Rodney Stark, Charles Glock, Peter Berger, and other psychologists and sociologists of religion. Although acknowledging religious values, some scholars believe that political parties took shape independently and then they either attracted or repelled religious groups, depending on their platforms and programs. This is only a variant on the interest group interpretation (Ashworth 1983). Churches preceded parties in America, and it is logical to assume that religious preference preceded partisan preference (Swierenga 1990).

6. Baird (1844, p. 220) divided all denominations into "evangelical" and "unevangelical." Scholars have struggled with other terms to identify the same distinction: Benson (1961),

Puritan/non-Puritan; Formisano (1971), evangelical/antievangelical; Formisano (1983), center/
periphery; VanderMeer (1981), church/sect; Peterson (1970), traditionalist/pietist; and
Kantowitz (1980), insider/outsider and dogmatist/pietist. Benson and Formisano are more
reluctant than the other scholars to associate liturgical and pietist values with theology, rather
than to offer sociological explanations (McCormick 1986).

7. Alternatively, some have argued that the Jacksonians were rationalistic, as
republican nation builders enlisted Protestant imagery and symbols to legitimate and
unify the "new experiment in self-government" and create a "public religion," to use
Benjamin Franklin's phrasing. Mead (1963) argues that during the second half of
the 19th century, Protestantism was amalgamated with "Americanism" to form an
all-encompassing "civil religion," the "Religion of the Republic" (compare with Marsden
[1970] and Marty [1984]).

8. The Reverend Ezra Stiles Ely, pastor of Philadelphia's Third Presbyterian Church,
was one such cleric who called for a Christian citizens movement, a loosely organized
"Christian party in politics," to influence Christians to vote for avowed Christian candidates
(cited in Bodo [1954]; compare with Benson [1961]).

9. McCormick (1986, p. 367) allows that religious beliefs explain the political
behavior of pietists but not liturgicals, who simply acted in self-defense. Their
worldview, says McCormick, had "no political significance until they were assaulted by
pietists." However, it is illogical to hold that pietist theology was intrinsically political
and liturgical theology was intrinsically apolitical. Liturgicals were on the defensive in
the antebellum era because the Great Awakening impelled revivalists toward social
activism. During the progressive era, however, pietist fundamentalists made the "great
reversal" and withdrew from political life, whereas the liturgicals launched the social
gospel movement (Moberg 1972).

10. Kelley (1979, p. 164) speaks of a "marginal preponderance."

11. Baum (1980, p. 120) argues that systematic underenumeration in counting "seats,"
especially for Catholic churches, which served several groups of parishioners, would "make
no difference" in statistical analyses. The censuses of "Social Statistics" from 1850 list each
church by denomination in every town and give the number of "accommodations" or
"seats" in each building. The percentage of each denomination's seats of the total seats
indicates the "religious preferences" of each township.

12. Benson (1963) and Hays (1964) pioneered this technique, which Kousser (1976,
pp. 5–6) castigate as "gestalt correlation," and "proving correlation by intimidation."
McCormick (1974) is also critical.

13. Poll books, in the tradition of British viva voce elections, record voters by name and
the candidates and parties for whom they announced support. Scholars have uncovered poll
books in various counties in Illinois, Indiana, Kentucky, and Virginia, among others.

REFERENCES

Ahlstrom, Sydney E. 1972. *A Religious History of the American People.* New Haven, Conn.:
    Yale University Press.
Allen, Howard W. 1964. "Isolationism and German-Americans." *Journal of the Illinois State
    Historical Society* 57: 143–149.

Allswang, John M. 1970. *A House for All Peoples: Ethnic Politics in Chicago, 1890–1936.* Lexington, Ky.: University of Kentucky Press.

Ashworth, John. 1983. *'Agrarians' and 'Aristocrats': Party Political Ideology in the United States, 1837–1846.* London: Royal Historical Society.

Baird, Robert. 1844. *Religion in America.* New York: Harper & Row.

Baker, Jean H. 1983. *Affairs of Party: The Political Culture of Northern Democrats in the Mid-Nineteenth Century.* Ithaca, N.Y.: Cornell University Press.

Bancroft, George. 1855. "The Office of the People in Art, Government and Religion." *Literary and Historical Miscellanies* (New York). In *Social Theories of Jacksonian Democracy: Representative Writings of the Period, 1825–1850,* ed. Joseph L. Blun, 263–273. Indianapolis, Ind.: Bobbs-Merrill.

Bancroft, George. 1855. "The Office of the People in Art, Government and Religion." *Literary and Historical Miscellanies* (New York). Pp. 263–273 in Joseph L. Blau, ed. 1954. *Social Theories of Jacksonian Democracy: Representative Writings of the Period, 1825–1850.* Indianapolis, Ind.: Bobbs-Merrill.

Baum, Dale. 1980. "The 'Irish Vote' and Party Politics in Massachusetts, 1860–1876." *Civil War History* 26 (2): 117–141.

Baum, Dale. 1984. *The Civil War Party System: The Case of Massachusetts, 1848–1876.* Chapel Hill, N.C.: University of North Carolina Press.

Baum, Dale. 1998. *The Shattering of Texas Unionism: Politics in the Lone Star State during the Civil War Era.* Baton Rouge, La.: Louisiana State University Press.

Benson, Lee. 1957. "Research Problems in American Political Historiography." In *Common Frontiers of the Social Sciences,* ed. Mira Komarovsky, 113–183. Glencoe, Ill.: Free Press.

Benson, Lee. 1961. *The Concept of Jacksonian Democracy: New York as a Test Case.* Princeton, N.J.: Princeton University Press.

Benson, Lee. 1963. *The Concept of Jacksonian Democracy: New York as a Test Case.* Princeton, N.J.: Princeton University Press. [Paperback edition.]

Bodo, John R. 1954. *The Protestant Clergy and Public Issues, 1812–1848.* Princeton, N.J.: Princeton University Press.

Bogue, Allan G. 1978. "The New Political History of the 1970s." In *Clio and the Bitch Goddess: Quantification in American Political History,* ed. Allan G. Bogue, 113–135. Beverly Hills, Calif.: Sage.

Bogue, Allan G. 1983. *Clio and the Bitch Goddess: Quantification in American Political History.* Bevery Hills., Calif.: Sage.

Bogue, Allan G., Jerome M. Clubb, and William H. Flanigan. 1977. "The New Political History." *American Behavioral Scientist* 21: 201–220.

Bourke, Paul F., and Donald A. DeBats. 1980. "Individuals and Aggregates: A Note on Historical Data and Assumptions." *Social Science History* 4: 229–250.

Bourke, Paul F., and Donald A. DeBats. 1995. *Washington County [Ohio]: Politics and Community in Antebellum America.* Baltimore, Md.: Johns Hopkins University Press.

Carwardine, Richard. 1993. *Evangelicals and Politics in Antebellum America.* New Haven, Conn.: Yale University Press.

Conzen, Kathleen Neils. 2004. "Immigrant Religion and the Public Sphere: The German Catholic Milieu in America." In *German-American Immigration and Ethnicity in Comparative Perspective,* ed. Wolfgang Helbich and Walter D. Kamphoefner, 69–114. Madison, Wisc.: University of Wisconsin Madison.

DeBats, Donald. 2004. "German and Irish Political Engagement: The Politics of Cultural Diversity in an Industrial Age." In *German-American Immigration and Ethnicity in*

Comparative Perspective, ed. Wolgang Helbich and Walter D. Kamphoefner, 171–217. Madison, Wisc.: University of Wisconsin Madison.

DeCanio, Samuel, 2007. "Religion and 19th Century Voting Behavior: A New Look at Some Old Data." *Journal of Politics* 69: 339–350.

DeCanio, Samuel, and Corwin Donald Smidt. 2007. "Prelude to Populism: Mass Electoral Supporters for the Grange and Greenback Parties." Presented at the annual meeting of the Midwest Political Science Convention, Chicago, April.

Egnal, Marc. 2001. "The Beards Were Right: Parties in the North, 1840–1860." *Civil War History* 47 (1): 30–56.

Fabend, Firth Haring. 2000. *Zion on the Hudson: Dutch New York and New Jersey in the Age of Revivals*. New Brunswick, N.J.: Rutgers University Press.

Fogel, Robert. 2001. *The Fourth Great Awakening and the Future of Egalitarianism*. Chicago, Ill.: University of Chicago Press.

Foner, Eric. 1974. "The Causes of the American Civil War: Recent Interpretations and New Directions." *Civil War History* 20: 197–214.

Formisano, Ronald P. 1971. *The Birth of Mass Political Parties: Michigan, 1827–1861*. Princeton, N.J.: Princeton University Press.

Formisano, Ronald P. 1983. *The Transformation of Political Culture: Massachusetts Parties, 1790s–1840s*. New York: Oxford University Press.

Formisano, Ronald P. 1993. "The New Political History and the Election of 1840." *Journal of Interdisciplinary History* 23: 661–682.

Fox, Stephen C. 1973. "The Group Bases of Ohio Political Behavior, 1803–1848." Ph.D. diss., University of Cincinnati.

Fox, Stephen C. 1977. "Politicians, Issues, and Voter Preference in Jacksonian Ohio: A Critique of an Interpretation," *Ohio History* 86: 155–170.

Fox, Stephen C. 1979. "The Bank Wars, The Idea of 'Party,' and the Division of the Electorate in Jacksonian Ohio." *Ohio History* 88 (3): 253–276.

Fuchs, Lawrence 1956. *The Political Behavior of American Jews*. Glencoe, Ill.: Free Press.

Giennap, William E. 1987. *The Origins of the Republican Party, 1852–1856*. New York: Oxford University Press.

Gjerde, Jon. 1997. *The Minds of the West: Ethnocultural Evolution in the Rural Middle West, 1830–1917*. Chapel Hill, N.C.: University of North Carolina.

Greer, Scott. 1961. "Catholic Voters and the Democratic Party." *Public Opinion Quarterly* 25: 611–625.

Hammarberg, Melvyn. 1974. "Indiana Farmers and the Group Basis of the Last Nineteenth-Century Political Parties." *Journal of American History* 61: 91–115.

Hammarberg, Melvyn. 1977. *The Indiana Voter: The Historical Dynamics of Party Allegiance During the 1870s*. Chicago, Ill.: University of Chicago Press.

Hammond, John L. 1979. *The Politics of Benevolence: Revival Religion and American Voting Behavior*. Norwood, N.J.: Abbey.

Hays, Samuel P. 1959. "History as Human Behavior," in Hays 1980. *American Political History as Social Analysis*, pp. 51–65. Knoxville, Tenn.: University of Tennessee Press.

Hays, Samuel P. 1967. "Political Parties and the Community–Society Continuum," in Hays. 1980. *American Political History as Social Analysis*, pp. 87–132. Knoxville, Tenn.: University of Tennessee Press.

Hays, Samuel P. 1980. *American Political History as Social Analysis*. Knoxville, Tenn.: University of Tennessee Press.

Heitzmann, William Ray. 1975. *American Jewish Voting Behavior: A History and Analysis*. San Francisco, Calif.: R & E Research Associates.

Holt, Michael F. 1969. *Forging a Majority: The Formation of the Republican Party in Pittsburgh 1848–1860*. New Haven, Conn.: Yale University Press.

Holt, Michael F. 1999. *The Rise and Fall of the American Whig Party*. New York: Oxford University Press.

Homer, Dorothy T. 1964. "The Rockford Swedish Community." *Journal of the Illinois State Historical Society* 57: 149–155.

Howe, Daniel Walker. 1979. *The Political Culture of the American Whigs*. Chicago, Ill.: University of Chicago Press.

Howe, Daniel Walker. 1990. "Religion and Politics in the Antebellum North." In *Religion & American Politics from the Colonial Period to the 1980s*, ed. Mark Noll, 121–145. New York: Oxford University Press.

Howe, Daniel Walker. 1991. "The Evangelical Movement and Political Culture in the North during the Second Party System." *Journal of American History* 77: 1216–1239.

Huthmacher, J. Joseph. 1959. *Massachusetts: People and Politics, 1919–1933*. Cambridge, Mass.: Harvard University Press.

Jackson, Kenneth. 1967. *The Ku Klux Klan in the City, 1915–1930*. New York: Oxford University Press.

Jensen, Richard. 1970. "The Religious and Occupational Roots of Party Identification: Illinois and Indiana in the 1870s." *Civil War History* 16 (4): 325–343.

Jensen, Richard. 1971. *The Winning of the Midwest: Social and Political Conflict: 1888–96*. Chicago, Ill.: University of Chicago Press.

Johnson, Benton. 1962. "Ascetic Protestantism and Political Preference." *Political Science Quarterly* 26: 35–46.

Johnson, Paul E. 1978. *A Shopkeeper's Millennium: Society and Revivals in Rochester, New York, 1815–1837*. New York: Hill and Wang.

Kamphoefner, Walter D. 1991. "German-Americans and Civil War Politics: A Reconsideration of the Ethnocultural Thesis." *Civil War History* 37: 226–240.

Kamphoefner, Walter D. 1999. "New Perspectives on Texas Germans and the Confederacy." *Southwestern Historical Quarterly* 102: 441–455.

Kamphoefner, Walter D. 2004. "German and Irish Big City Mayors: Comparative Perspectives on Ethnic Politics." In *German-American Immigration and Ethnicity in Comparative Perspective*, ed. Wolfgang Helbig and Walter D. Kamphoefner, 221–242. Madison, Wisc.: University of Wisconsin Madison.

Kantowitz, Edward R. 1980. "Politics." In *Harvard Encyclopedia of American Ethnic Groups*, ed. Stephan Thernstrom, Ann Orlov, and Oscar Handlin, 803–804. Cambridge, Mass.: Harvard University Press.

Kawaguchi, Lesley Ann. 1994. "Diverging Affiliations and Ethnic Perspectives: Philadelphia Germans and Antebellum Politics." *Journal of American Ethnic History* 13: 3.

Kelley, Robert. 1979. *The Cultural Pattern in American Politics: The First Century*. New York: Knopf.

Kleppner, Paul. 1970. *The Cross of Culture: A Social Analysis of Midwestern Politics, 1850–1900*. New York: Free Press.

Kleppner, Paul. 1979. *The Third Electoral System, 1853–1892: Parties, Voters, and Political Cultures*. Chapel Hill, N.C.: University of North Carolina Press.

Kleppner, Paul. 1981. "Partisanship and Ethnocultural Conflict: The Third Electoral System, 1853–1892." In *The Evolution of American Electoral Systems*, ed. Paul Kleppner, Walter Dean Burnham, Ronald P. Formisano, Samuel P. Hays, Richard Jensen, and William G. Shade, 113–146. Westport, Conn.: Greenwood Press.

Kousser, J. Morgan. 1976. "The 'New Political History': A Methodological Critique." *Reviews in American History* 4: 1–14.

Kremm, Thomas A. 1974. "The Rise of the Republican Party in Cleveland, 1848–1860." Ph.D. diss., Kent State University.

Kremm, Thomas A. 1977. "Cleveland and the First Lincoln Election: The Ethnic Response to Nativism." *Journal of Interdisciplinary History* 8: 69–86.

Latner, Richard B., and Peter Levine. 1976. "Perspectives on Antebellum Pietistic Politics." *Reviews in American History* 4: 15–24.

Leege, David, and Lyman A. Kellstedt, eds. 1993. *Rediscovering the Religious Factor in American Politics.* Armonk, N.Y.: M. E. Sharpe.

Lichtman Allan J., and Laura. I. Langbein. 1978. "Ecological Regression Versus Homogeneous Units: A Specification Analysis." *Social Science History* 2: 172–193.

Lipset, Seymour Martin. 1964. "Religion and Politics in the American Past and Present." In *Religion and Social Conflict,* ed. Robert Lee and Martin E. Marty, 69–126. New York: Oxford University Press.

Lorenz-Meyer, Martin. 2000. "United in Difference: The German Community in Nativist Baltimore." *Yearbook of German-American Studies* 35: 1–26.

Lubell, Samuel. 1956. *The Future of American Politics.* Garden City, N.Y.: Doubleday Anchor.

Luebke, Frederick C. 1969. *Immigrants and Politics: The Germans of Nebraska, 1880–1900.* Lincoln, Neb.: University of Nebraska Press.

Lynch, Patrick. 1999. "Presidential Elections and the Economy, 1872 to 1896: The Times They are A' Changing, or the Song Remains the Same?" *Political Research Quarterly* 52 (4): 825–844.

Lynch, Patrick. 2002a. "Midterm Elections and Economic Fluctuations: The Response of Voters over Time." *Legislative Studies Quarterly* 27 (2): 265–294.

Lynch, Patrick. 2002b. "U.S. Presidential Elections in the Nineteenth Century: Why Culture and the Economy Both Mattered." *Polity* 35 (1): 29–50.

Marsden, George M. 1970. *The Evangelical Mind and the New School Experience.* New Haven, Conn.: Yale University Press.

Marsden, George M. 1990. "Afterword: Religion, Politics, and the Search for an American Consensus." In *Religion & American Politics from the Colonial Period to the 1980s,* ed. Mark Noll, 380–390. New York: Oxford University Press.

Marty, Martin E. 1984. *Pilgrims in Their Own Land: Five Hundred Years of Religion in America.* New York: Viking Penguin.

McCormick, Richard L. 1974. "Ethnocultural Interpretations of Nineteenth Century American Voting Behavior," 29–63. Reprinted in McCormick. 1986. *The Party Period and Public Policy: American Politics from the Age of Jackson to the Progressive Era.* New York: Oxford University Press.

McCormick, Richard L. 1974. "Ethnocultural Interpretations of Nineteenth Century American Voting Behavior," 29–63. Reprinted in McCormick. 1986. *The Party Period and Public Policy: American Politics from the Age of Jackson to the Progressive Era.* New York: Oxford University Press.

McCormick, Richard L. 1986. *The Party Period and Public Policy: American Politics from the Age of Jackson to the Progressive Era.* New York: Oxford University Press.

McSeveney, Samuel T. 1972. *The Politics of Depression: Political Behavior in the Northeast, 1893–1896.* New York: Oxford University Press.

McSeveney, Samuel T. 1973. "Ethnic Groups, Ethnic Conflicts, and Recent Quantitative Research in American Political History." *International Migration Review* 7: 59–79.

Mead, Sidney E. 1963. *The Lively Experiment: The Shaping of Christianity in America.* New York: Harper & Row.

Merton, Robert K. 1957. *Social Theory and Social Structure.* Glencoe, Ill.: Free Press.

Moberg, David O. 1972. *The Great Reversal: Evangelicalism Versus Social Concern.* Philadelphia, Pa.: Lippincott.

Niebuhr, H. Richard. 1951. *Christ and Culture.* New York: Harper.

Noll, Mark A. ed. 1990. *Religion & American Politics from the Colonial Period to the 1980s.* New York: Oxford University Press.

Noll, Mark A., and Luke E. Harlow. eds. 2007. *Religion & American Politics from the Colonial Period to the Present.* 2nd ed. New York: Oxford University Press.

Pessen, Edward. 1979. "Review of Robert Kelley, *The Cultural Pattern in American Politics: The First Century*" *Civil War History* 25: 279–281.

Peterson, Roger D. 1970. "The Reaction to a Heterogeneous Society: A Behavioral and Quantitative Analysis of Northern Voting Behavior, 1845–1870, Pennsylvania a Test Case." Ph.D. diss., University of Pittsburgh.

Pomper, Gerald. 1966. "Ethnic and Group Voting in Nonpartisan Municipal Elections." *Public Opinion Quarterly* 30: 79–97.

Rogan, Michael P. 1967. *The Intellectuals and McCarthy: The Radical Specter.* Cambridge, Mass.: Harvard University Press.

Roper, Elmo. 31 Oct. 1959. "The Myth of the Catholic Vote." *Saturday Review of Literature,* p. 22.

Rozett, John M. 1976. "Racism and Republican Emergence in Illinois, 1848–1860: A Re-Evaluation of Republican Negrophobia." *Civil War History* 22: 101–115.

Shade, William G. n.d. "Banner Units and Counties: An Empirical Comparison of Two Approaches." Unpublished ms.

Silbey, Joel B., Allan G. Bogue, and William H. Flanigan, eds. 1978. *The History of American Electoral Behavior.* Princeton, N.J.: Princeton University Press.

Smidt, Corwin. 2001. "Religious Groups and the Political Order: An Historical Perspective." Unpublished ms.

Steckel, Richard H. 1998. Migration and Political Conflict: Precincts in the Midwest on the Eve of the Civil War." *Journal of Interdisciplinary History* 28: 583–605.

Stout, Harry S. 1975. "Ethnicity: The Vital Center of Religion in American Political History." *Ethnicity*: 204–224.

Swierenga, Robert P. 1965. "The Ethnic Voter and the First Lincoln Election." *Civil War History* 11: 27–43.

Swierenga, Robert P. 1971. "Ethnocultural Political Analysis: A New Approach to American Ethnic Studies." *Journal of American Studies* 5: 59–79.

Swierenga, Robert P. 1990. "Ethnoreligious Political Behavior in the Mid-Nineteenth Century." In *Religion & American Politics from the Colonial Period to the 1980s,* ed. Mark A. Noll, 146–171. New York: Oxford University Press.

Swierenga, Robert P. 2002. *Dutch Chicago: A History of the Hollanders in the Windy City.* Grand Rapids, Mich.: Wm B. Eerdmans.

Swierenga, Robert P., and Elton J. Bruins. 1997. *Family Quarrels in the Dutch Reformed Churches of the Nineteenth Century.* Grand Rapids, Mich.: Wm B. Eerdmans.

VanderMeer, Philip R. 1981. "Religion, Society, and Politics: A Classification of American Religious Groups." *Social Science History* 5: 3–24.

Wilentz, Sean. 1982. "On Class and Politics in Jacksonian America." *Reviews in American History* 10 (December): 47–48.

Winkle, Kenneth J. 1983. "A Social Analysis of Voter Turnout in Ohio, 1850–1860." *Journal of Interdisciplinary History* 13: 411–435.

Wolfinger, Raymond E. 1965. "The Development and Persistence of Ethnic Voting." *American Political Science Review* 59: 896–908.

Wright, James E. 1973. "The Ethnocultural Model of Voting: A Behavioral and Historical Critique." In *Emerging Theoretical Models in Social and Political History*, ed. Allan G. Bogue, pp. 35–56. Beverly Hills, Calif.: Sage.

Wyman, Roger E. 1968. "Wisconsin Ethnic Groups and the Election of 1890." *Wisconsin Magazine of History* 51: 269–293.1.

....

CHAPTER 4

RELIGION AND AMERICAN POLITICAL THOUGHT

....

MICHAEL LIENESCH

To study American political thought is to be struck, as Tocqueville was on his arrival in the new United States, by the pervasiveness of religion. From 17th-century sermons to contemporary democratic discourse, American writers have used sacred and transcendent terms to describe and give meaning to their politics, persistently portraying themselves as a chosen people with a millennial mission. Yet it has been only during the past several decades, beginning in the last quarter of the 20th century and continuing today, that significant numbers of scholars have seriously taken up the study of religion's role in American political thought. To carry out this change, they have had to look beyond several powerful paradigms—the philosophical liberalism of John Rawls, the Lockean interpretation of American history made popular by Louis Hartz, and the secularization theory of 20th-century sociologists from Max Weber to Daniel Bell—which combined to present a picture of American politics as uniformly liberal, individualistic, and secular. In breaking—or better, stretching—the bonds of these paradigms, this new generation of scholars has rediscovered religion's presence in the public realm. It has also produced a remarkable stream of scholarship, so much that Eldon Eisenach (2004, p. 44) has described the study of religion in American political thought today as "not only flourishing, it threatens to overwhelm us."

In reviewing this work, this chapter concentrates on three general approaches to the study of political thought: *political philosophy, history of political theory*, and (for want of a more precise term) *contemporary social and political thought*. In each section it describes the changing conceptions of religion's role, discussing how secular understandings have been challenged by religious ones, and showing how the political meaning and purpose of religion has continued to be contested. Since only a limited number of sources can be discussed, those chosen are selected for their importance in defining the direction of the field or in representing various schools or viewpoints. Although treatments of this topic are thoroughly interdisciplinary, including a sizable amount of popular writing, attention is given here to those works that come closest to the academic area of American political thought. In addition to providing an overview of several decades of existing literature, this chapter evaluates the current status of scholarship in the field, while also suggesting some directions for future study.

POLITICAL PHILOSOPHY

Any account of the role of the role of religion in recent American political philosophy must begin with the influence of Rawlsian liberalism. In his *A Theory of Justice*, the late Harvard philosopher John Rawls (1971) articulated a version of liberalism that presumed the primacy of rights and the requirement of public reason. Identifying liberalism as a response to the wars of religion, Rawls consistently claimed that one of its chief contributions was its commitment to toleration, which not only established a society of civility and respect but also provided the personal freedom for individuals to pursue their own life plans. To achieve this toleration, public policies had to be premised on public reason, or what he called in his *Political Liberalism* (Rawls 1993; see also Rawls 1997) an "overlapping consensus" of reasonable views about the meaning of justice. Yet as Rawls implied, and others (Larmore 1990; Nagel 1991; Audi 2000) made explicit, public reason in a pluralistic society cannot include those religious doctrines that presuppose comprehensive conceptions of the good life (see Owen 2001; Woodiwiss 2001b). It follows, according to liberal theorists like Bruce Ackerman (1980), Ronald Dworkin (1985), and Stephen Macedo (1990, 1995), that religion should exist primarily not in the public but in the private realm, where it can be protected while also being prevented from limiting the rights of others. To ensure that religion remains in its proper place, legal and political boundaries must be established and policed: church should be separated from state, religious considerations should be clearly distinguished from political ones, and public authorities should be strictly neutral in matters of religion, neither favoring one religious view over another nor religion generally over nonreligion. Those believers who accept the requirements of public reason, who are able and willing to speak a common civic language, are welcome in the public sphere. Those who do not must remain in the private one. "They must pay a price," writes Macedo (1995, p. 496) in his *Liberal Virtues*, "for living in a free pluralistic society."

Responding to Rawls was a growing chorus of critics. Among the earliest and most formidable of these was a diverse group of thinkers who shared common concerns about the individualistic and rationalistic presuppositions of liberalism, along with similar commitments to recovering the role of community in public life. In his *After Virtue*, Alasdair MacIntyre (1981) launched an unsparing critique of modern liberal theory, arguing that its egoistic and skeptical assumptions had led, by the end of the 19th century, to a collapse of the Western moral order. Turning to Aristotle as an antidote to both Kantian and utilitarian liberalism, MacIntyre (1981) proceeded to make the philosophical case for a society based less on personal rights and more on public moral goods, in which those goods are defined by the practices of a community of virtuous persons. Although his early work said little about the religious content of this ethical community, and at times could be scathingly critical of theological systems, including Christian ones, by the time of his *Whose Justice? Which Rationality?*, MacIntyre (1988) had adopted teleological assumptions about the importance of moral ends from Aquinas, and since then has developed an extensive neo-Thomist synthesis that describes how Christian communities, existing at the margins of modern democratic societies, can provide a moral counterpoint to modern liberalism. At about the same time, arguing on Hegelian and Heideggerian assumptions, Charles Taylor (1989) introduced a similar critique of Rawls's liberalism in his *Sources of the Self*, in which he proposed that agency and identity were the products not of personal choice, but of communal practice, being constructed dialogically in social and communal relationships with others. A committed Catholic, Taylor's conception of the self allowed a prominent place for religion, which he saw not only as an antidote to the atomizing effects of modernity, but also as a site for creating moral meaning in the modern world. Throughout the 1980s, communitarian thinkers such as Michael Sandel (1982), Michael Walzer (1983), and Mary Ann Glendon (1991) made similar arguments, criticizing the Rawlsian conception of the "unencumbered" self and insisting that any complete conception of personhood requires an understanding of the roles that people play in a common democratic experience that allows for family, friendship, and faith. Applying these assumptions to contemporary legal debates, which they described as dominated by what Glendon (1991) called "rights talk," these thinkers argued that far from a matter of personal choice, faith was for most believers less a choice than a duty, and less a matter of personal rights than public responsibility. In removing religion from the public realm, they concluded, Rawlsian liberalism had undercut liberal society itself, "impoverishing political discourse," as Sandel (1996, p. 23) put it, "and eroding the moral and civic resources necessary to self-government."

Also responding to Rawls, and in part inspired by his communitarian critics, was a second group of scholars who worked within the liberal tradition while also attempting to open it to a broader and more diverse set of moral values. Among these "civic liberals" (see Spragens 1999), William Galston took the lead in arguing that Rawls' abstract assumptions about autonomy had led previous liberal thinkers to the unrealistic premise that societies can remain neutral in evaluating competing conceptions of what is good and valuable. In his *Liberal Purposes* (Galston 1991), he proposed an alternative view, insisting that modern liberal states ought to be committed to a distinctive conception of the good life, one that allowed for the greatest possible diversity in pursuit of public purposes. To achieve this value pluralism, Galston insisted that the public realm must be open to the largest possible variety of moral views, allowing maximum space for citizens to discuss and resolve their differences, including those that touch on fundamental values. Above all, as he made clear in his *Liberal Pluralism* (Galston 2002; see also Galston 2005), liberalism must be committed to religious toleration, accommodating even those who embrace illiberal values, such as groups like the Old Order Amish. At about the same time, a cohort of liberal pluralist scholars was beginning to look more closely at the problems posed to democratic societies by such religious groups. Among these, Michael J. Perry (1991, 1997), Kent Greenawalt (1995), and others (Thiemann 1996; Eberle 2002; Weithman 2002) were particularly active in attempting to map the place of religion in the public sphere, seeking to set rules that were ecumenical without being sectarian. In theory, all agreed that believers should be welcomed into the conversation of democracy, at least as long as they agreed to articulate their religious views while also embracing basic democratic values. In practice, however, the authors often found it difficult to distinguish acceptable from unacceptable religious viewpoints, let alone religious practices, and some have shifted their views substantially, embracing a more inclusive role for religion in politics (Perry 2003) or returning to a more restrictive one (Hamilton 2005). Political theorist Jeff Spinner-Halev (2000) has addressed the problems posed by the appearance of exclusive religious groups in the public square, suggesting principles for their accommodation and legal standards that would allow them latitude to practice their religious views while also protecting the rights of others. And in a provocative work, Lucas Swaine (2006) has gone so far as to argue that to be true to their own principles of toleration, liberal societies must allow considerable latitude even to antiliberal theocrats, protecting freedom of conscience by providing them with what he calls "quasi-sovereignty."

In addition to the liberal critics, a diverse collection of democratic thinkers have suggested alternatives to Rawlsian theory. Among these, contemporary pragmatists have had some of the greatest influence on American philosophy, with writers like Jeffrey Stout, Cornel West, and Richard Rorty attempting to open the public realm to more democratic voices, including religious ones. Writing in his *Ethics After Babel* (Stout 2001) and *Democracy and Tradition* (Stout 2004), Stout turned to Emerson, Whitman, and Dewey to criticize both Rawls' rights-based liberalism and Jürgen Habermas' conception of ideal speech, arguing that by opening public discussion to the most inclusive range of moral issues and the widest variety of religious and other views, democratic societies enable a more ethically and politically virtuous civic life. Cornel West, writing in a series of studies including his *Race Matters* (West 1993; see also West 1989, 1996a), made a similar case, contending that it is precisely when American democracy has allowed a diversity of voices, including especially those inspired by their religious faith, that moral achievements such as those of the civil rights movement have become possible. Indeed, in his *Achieving Our Country*, Richard Rorty (1998), who at one time expressed confidence that religion would one day wither away, made the case for what he called a "religion of democracy," a new public faith in the democratic community that combined belief, hope, and human solidarity. Joining such pragmatists in the desire to open the public sphere to religious views are antifoundationalist and poststructuralist writers. Among these, Stanley Fish (1999) has argued that liberal claims of tolerance and religious freedom, being based on norms of reasoned deliberation, are in fact designed to exclude religious believers who put more stock in faith than reason. Chantal Mouffe (2000, 2006) has insisted that for liberal democracies to be true to their principles, citizens with religious views must be allowed to contest not only ethical and political precepts, but also constitutional ones that structure and legitimate democratic debate, as part of the ongoing agonistic struggle of democratic politics. Finally, in his *Why I Am Not a Secularist*, William Connolly (1999) has envisioned a politics in which citizens move beyond tolerance to active engagement in a multipluralistic process of exchange that finds ethical inspiration in a variety of sources, including Christian and other theistic ones (see also White 2000; Bennett 2006; Brown 2006; Connolly 2006).

Not surprisingly, among the critics of contemporary liberal theory some of the most active in considering the role of religion have been those who work from within religious traditions, primarily Christian ones. Here the voices are many and the traditions vast and varied, ranging from Anabaptist to Calvinist to Thomistic to contemporary evangelical. At the forefront are the theologians, among them John Milbank, Nicholas Wolterstorff, and Stanley Hauerwas, who draw on different faith perspectives to level a combined critique against modern liberalism and its devotion to secular reason. Arguing from within an Anglo-Catholic tradition, John Milbank (1991) has proposed a radically orthodox metanarrative, an Augustinian account of the world in which classical conceptions of rationality are replaced by a Christian epistemology of communal harmony and spiritual peace. The Reformed theologian Nicholas Wolterstorff (1997; see also Alston 1991; Plantinga 1993), mixing Calvinism with commonsense philosophy, also criticizes liberal reliance on secular reason, contending that Christian commitment should serve as a starting place for practical rationality, and that liberal states should recognize that people should not be expected to live their lives in separate religious and nonreligious realms. The prolific and outspoken Stanley Hauerwas (1981; see also Hauerwas 1995, 2000) offers still another view, drawing on Anabaptist roots (see Yoder 1984) to label secular liberalism a philosophy that has corrupted not only modern culture and the modern state, but also the contemporary church, and calling on Christians to create alternative "communities of character." Joining the theologians have been political theorists like J. Budziszewski (1986), Glenn Tinder (1989), and Clarke

Cochran (1990), who draw respectively on Aquinas, Niebuhr, and Catholic social teaching to critique secular liberalism and offer alternative accounts of the role of religion in politics. Following in their footsteps, a new cohort of Christian political theorists has carried on the critique. Applying Anabaptist teachings, Thomas Heilke (2001) asks Christians to assume a critical stance toward the power politics of the modern state while also creating communities that can witness justice and peace to the world. Timothy Sherratt (2001) brings neo-Calvinist notions of "sphere sovereignty" to bear in advocating a constitutionally limited but morally purposeful modern state that can share authority with societal institutions and act as an agent of public justice. Ashley Woodiwiss (2001a) combines insights from Milbank and Hauerwas with those from agonistic democrats like Mouffe to argue that Christian communities must assume a "subaltern status" in modern society, playing an engaged but restrained role in which they attempt to bring virtues of humility, hospitality, and openness into public life while still claiming no sovereignty over it. Most recently, Kristen Deede Johnson (2007) has combined Milbank's Augustinianism with Connolly's conception of a radically responsive democracy to make the case that Christians should contribute to a public conversation that celebrates difference while leaving open the possibility that citizens can learn from one another, transforming both themselves and their society in the process.

As the criticism of Rawlsian liberalism continues, and as alternatives to it proliferate, thinkers today are describing a more pluralistic public realm in which religion has become an active participant. Yet as the boundaries between church and state become less distinct, the problems of defining religion's role in public life have become more difficult, creating continuing controversies over the meaning of First Amendment provisions concerning religious establishment and free exercise. Thus, while some thinkers (Laycock 1990; McConnell 1992; Monsma 1993; Greenawalt 2000; McConnell 2000a) have attempted to establish broad constitutional conditions or principles for defining religious freedom, others have preferred to proceed issue by issue and even case by case. In the area of public education, for example, erstwhile Rawlsian liberal Stephen Macedo (2000) has come to accept that in some situations school vouchers may be desirable even if they allow students to attend religious schools, but he continues to insist that public schools retain control of their curriculum, arguing that religious freedom does not extend to the desire of parents to exempt their children from legitimate educational requirements for religious reasons (see also Gutmann 1987). Turning to employment law, Nancy Rosenblum (2000) has examined how courts have conceptualized the role of religion in the workplace, criticizing recent decisions as being too accommodating to religious associations while also arguing that both too much and too little autonomy for such groups can subvert the moral basis of pluralism. Others have considered other issues, such as the presence of faith-based groups in programs such as Charitable Choice, with advocates (Monsma 1996; McConnell 2000b) and critics (Sullivan 1992; Gill 2004) agreeing on general principles, but sharply disagreeing on the legal status of particular activities and groups. Still others have investigated religious involvement in a growing number of domestic issues, ranging from health care (Cochran 2001) and welfare reform (Hecht 2001; Coleman 2003) to land use and the rights of prisoners (Hamilton 2005).

Moreover, students of democratic pluralism have increasingly come to see the issues posed by the political presence of religion in international context. For liberals, certain human rights must always reach beyond national boundaries. Thinkers from other traditions, including Christian ones, often argue that conscience must in many cases be considered superior to state sovereignty. Among liberal democrats, Susan Moller Okin (1999) was particularly outspoken in pointing out that religious groups often present rationales for controlling the lives of their members, especially their female members, and that those who value rights at home should value them abroad as well. Such views have provoked a wide range of responses (see, for example, Nussbaum 1999; Parekh 1999; Sunstein 1999), suggesting the difficulty of reconciling the rights of individuals with the cultural claims of religious groups in nonliberal societies. In the same way, arguing from a Christian natural law perspective, Daniel Philpott (2001) has made a strong case for international humanitarian intervention, calling for an expanded response to a diverse collection of moral crises in countries across the world. As borders between states become more porous, religious issues take on increasing international importance, with religious groups becoming more involved in what were once considered the internal affairs of other nations. As Martha Nussbaum (1997, 2000, 2006) has demonstrated, the challenges posed by these changes are daunting, creating an ever-lengthening line of hard cases involving religious dress, expression, and practice. Today, writes David Hollenbach (2003, p. 231), "the role of religion in forming cultural values has become central in reflection on the ethical dimensions of global politics."

All told, in today's complex and interconnected world, Rawlsian attempts to confine religion to a private realm of personal rights seem increasingly unrealistic. At home and abroad, we face seemingly intractable moral issues—from abortion and same-sex marriage to climate change, the transnational transmission of diseases like AIDS, and the proliferation of the weapons of war—that cannot be solved without some shared vision of the common good. Today, political philosophers seem to be in agreement that religious communities must play some part in creating this vision, not only because of the moral insights they can contribute, but also for the political dangers they pose if excluded. As to exactly how and where these communities are to express their convictions, and how far they may go in enacting them before violating the rights of others, there remains considerably less agreement. Thus, for the future, students of political philosophy must be expected to continue to reach beyond Rawls, proceeding in a more problem-driven manner—principle by principle, issue by issue, case by case—in seeking the proper place for religion in an expanded conception of human rights. In this effort, writes Michael J. Perry (2007, p. 141), "the necessary work is just beginning."

HISTORY OF POLITICAL THEORY

As John Rawls provides a starting point for any discussion of late-20th-century American political philosophy, Louis Hartz plays a similar part for the history of political theory. In his *The Liberal Tradition in America*, Hartz (1955), a Harvard government professor, argued that political thought in the United States was the product of a pervasive liberalism, a way of thinking that arose from the absence of a feudal society, and that led inexorably to a logic of personal liberty. This Lockean (Hartz wrote "Lockian") liberalism predisposed Americans to practice a politics of individual self-interest, eschewing the social divisions that created the conflicts that had characterized European society. Although Hartz (1955) concentrated mostly on the absence of class in the United States, his analysis downplayed the presence of other divisions as well, including race and religion. Thus, in addition to seeing the American South as an exception to his overall outline, he said almost nothing about American Puritanism, beginning his book with the American Revolution. Indeed, *The Liberal Tradition in America* (Hartz 1955) contains almost no discussion of religion whatsoever, with the exception of references to how little it mattered in American politics. As Hartz (1955, p. 41) put it in a passage on Revolutionary New England, "instead of being forced to pull the Christian heaven down to earth," American liberals "were glad to let it remain where it was." Moreover, as James Kloppenberg (2003) has argued, this disregard for religion extended even beyond the book, because Hartz's interpretation was influential enough to convince an entire generation of students that American political theory, such as it was, could be reduced to a continuing rationalization of secular market capitalism. And it is true that for the next several decades, with few exceptions (see McWilliams 1973; Eisenach 1979; Kelly 1984), scholars remained blithely unconcerned when it came to the influence of religion on American political thought. As Wilson Carey McWilliams and Marc K. Landy (1984, p. 210) observed in an 1984 review of the field, real knowledge of the role of religion remained at the time "depressingly slight."

By the mid 1980s, however, some were beginning to rediscover religion. Prodded by intellectual historians like Perry Miller (1939, 1953), Alan Heimert (1966), and Sacvan Bercovitch (1975, 1978), and by political ones like Bernard Bailyn (1967) and Gordon Wood (1969), a growing group of scholars had concluded that Hartz's single-minded focus on Lockean liberalism had led him to overlook other traditions of thought, including religious and republican ones. Among the first to make this case was McWilliams (1973, 1984), who described the development of a biblically based republicanism that not only served as a counterpoint to Enlightenment rationalism, but also became the basis for continuing democratic and populist revolts. Joining him was John Patrick Diggins (1984), who accepted Hartzian arguments about the hegemony of liberal theory, but argued that a second strain, the product of Calvinist convictions about the certainty of sin and the possibility of salvation, had struggled unsuccessfully against it, creating what he called the "lost soul" of American politics. Meanwhile, a small phalanx (Lutz 1980, 1984; Lienesch 1988; Sandoz 1990; Miller 1991; Shain 1994; Elazar 1998) was at work on the founding, documenting how Americans of the Revolutionary and Constitutional eras relied not only on Locke, but also on covenant theology, sacred conceptions of history, and millennialist visions of the future to shape their thinking. In his *The Lincoln Persuasion*, J. David Greenstone (1993) followed some of the same themes into the 19th century, claiming that Abraham Lincoln's great political genius was his ability to reconcile interest-based liberalism with a powerful moral perfectionism, the product of a New England Protestant tradition that ran from early Calvinists through John Adams to northern abolitionist radicals. Eldon Eisenach (1994) showed how American Progressivism before World War I was rooted not in abstract conceptions of rights, but in an evangelical spirit of nationalistic social reform. More recently, James E. Block (2002) directed a full frontal assault against Hartzian interpretations, contending in *A Nation of Agents* that American political thought was, at its heart, based on a conception of self—primarily the product of evangelicalism— that stressed agency rather than autonomy, so that even while celebrating individual freedom, Americans can better be understood as craving the connectedness of communal and religious life. In *Hellfire Nation*, James A. Morone (2003) went one better, suggesting that neither liberal nor communitarian theories can capture the Puritan moralistic impulse that lies at the heart of American identity and that is manifested in the worst and best of American politics, running the gamut from 17th-century witch hunters and 1950s anticommunists to social gospel reformers and civil rights activists. And in several studies reflecting on the fears of decline expressed most provocatively in the wake of terrorism and war, Andrew Murphy (2005, 2009; see also Murphy and Miller 2006) has investigated the enduring influence of the American jeremiad, the sermon style that calls for repentance and return to a collective redemptive mission, tracing it from colonial preachers to contemporary critics and politicians. All told, for many scholars today, the history of American political thought is seen as moving, not from contract to contract, but from revival to revival. After almost four centuries of moralistic reform, as Morone (2003, p. 497) concludes, Americans "remain Puritans all."

In recovering America's religious roots, no period has provoked more scholarship than the Constitutional founding. Controversial then as now, the issue of religion's role in the new nation divided the nation's founders, inspiring some of the period's most profound political theory while also raising legal and political questions about establishment and free exercise that continue to be troubling in our own time. In *The Godless Constitution*, Isaac Kramnick and R. Laurence Moore (1996) helped initiate the most recent round of scholarly debate, arguing forcefully that although the founders subscribed to a variety of Christian views, they devised a document that included neither Christianity nor God, and that left religious convictions to be matters of personal conscience. Kramnick and Moore (1996) described the fears of many Americans of the time who thought that the absence of religious tests would open the new national government to control by Quakers,

Catholics, or Jews. They also showed how those like Madison and Jefferson, together with their allies in Baptist and other minority denominations, reached back into American experience and English law to argue that the best means to counter control by any religious group was to create a strong wall of separation between church and state. Although they cited neither Rawls nor Hartz, Kramnick and Moore (1996) captured many of the basic claims of both, locating the origins of American liberalism in the removal of religion to the private realm and the creation of a neutral, secular state. Admittedly polemical, their broadside provoked considerable criticism, some of it based on significant new scholarship. Thus, in *The Politics of Revelation and Reason*, John G. West, Jr. (1996b) accepted the argument that the founders solved the problem of the dual allegiance to God and government by separating church and state, but went on to show that they also believed that church and state would agree on the shared moral standards—the product of reason and revelation—that became the basis of political action in the new republic. Picking up on the theme, Daniel Dreisbach (2002) contended in his *Thomas Jefferson and the Wall of Separation between Church and State* that claims about Jefferson's famous wall must be understood in the context of the Danbury letter in which the metaphor was first used, and even more in the context of the federal constitutional structure, which removed religion from the new national government to allow the individual states freedom to decide for themselves how to define the relation between church and state. Extending this interpretation in his *Separation of Church and State*, Philip Hamburger (2002) insisted that Jefferson's concept of separation was extreme at the time, that most of the founders intended to prevent only a national church, and that the true source of separation came much later, when 19th-century Protestants adopted the doctrine to counter the growing ecclesiastical power of the Roman Catholic church. This revisionist view has been countered by others (McConnell 2000a; Murphy 2001; Lambert 2003; Feldman 2005; Beneke 2006) who document deeper roots of religious diversity in 17th- and 18th-century America, while also stressing the role of dissenter groups in securing liberty of conscience and toleration for their religious views. Debates over specifics notwithstanding, however, most scholars have come to accept the general finding that the founders brought religious thinking to bear in framing constitutional doctrines concerning religious freedom. As John Witte (2005, p. 5) puts it, "We cannot pretend that the First Amendment is a purely secular trope, or just another category of liberty and autonomy, and expect citizens to believe in it."

Then there is Tocqueville. Among analysts of American democracy, Alexis de Tocqueville may have been the most emphatic in declaring the essential role of religion, and the most elusive in describing it. Thus, although insisting that religion was, in his famous phrase, the "first" of America's political institutions, he went on in his *Democracy in America* (2003) to celebrate the separation of church and state, and to claim that churches (like other civic associations) served to nurture the customs and mores that were the source of democratic stability. Following in Hartz's footsteps, mid-20th-century scholars described Tocqueville as relegating religion to the private realm, suggesting that he saw it as a kind of sociological strategy in which sacred myths were put to work controlling the excesses of democratic individualism and equality. In recent years, however, analysts have come to see more complex conceptions of the relationship between religion and politics in his thinking, and to disagree among themselves about them. In a series of studies, Sanford Kessler (1977, 1992, 1994) presented one line of interpretation, contending that Tocqueville viewed American Christianity, with its roots in Puritan conceptions of covenant and conscience, as the true source of democratic politics, encouraging the development of liberty and equality while fending off self-interested individualism and mass mediocrity. Speaking for a second school, Joshua Mitchell (1995) described Tocqueville as less interested in civil than in revealed religion, which he saw as an antidote to the restlessness of America's "Augustinian self," moderating the extreme swings of introverted individualism and extroverted egalitarianism that personified the democratic character. The debate has been protracted, with those on one side (Allen 2005; Villa 2006; see also earlier essays by Zuckert 1981; Galston 1987; Koritansky 1990) contending that Tocqueville saw religion primarily as a contributor to the democratic social order, and those on the other (Mansfield and Winthrop 2006; Mélonio 2006; see also Hinckley 1990; Hancock 1991) insisting that he considered it to be the salvation of the democratic soul. In his *Tocqueville between Two Worlds*, Sheldon Wolin (2002) reads *Democracy in America* as containing both versions, with religion being described differently in the book's two volumes—in one as a source of solace; in the other, of social control. And in his *Christianity and American Democracy*, Hugh Heclo (2007, p. 213) argues that Tocqueville saw Christianity's contribution to democracy as both public and private, teaching Americans "how to sustain ordered liberty in democratic politics as well as how to uphold the spiritual nobility of human beings against the threats of a materialistic, mass democracy."

In accepting Tocquevillian assumptions, historians of political thought have been forced to revise radically the existing narratives of the American democratic experience. In Hartz's version of the story, 18th-century demands for rights had given way to 19th-century cravings for profit and property that were strong enough to sweep aside all other possibilities of politics. Thus, Diggins (1984) argued that even at the time of the founding, Christian and classical forms of virtue had already disappeared, and although those such as Lincoln and Herman Melville struggled against the tide in attempting to revive them, the Christian ideals they represented had by the late 19th century "died out" (Diggins 1984, p. 341). Yet as West (1996b; see also Noll 2002) demonstrated in his study of the early republic, American evangelicals exerted considerable political power throughout the postfounding period, being active in a host of movements ranging from efforts to end the Sunday mails to the campaign to prevent Cherokee removal. By the middle of the 19th century, despite the much-heralded innovation of religious freedom in the new nation, an evangelical moral establishment had introduced issues of temperance, sexual purity, and the suppression of vice into American law and politics, in what Morone (2003; see also Foster 2002) has called the "Victorian quest for virtue." In his *Civic Ideals* (Smith 1997; see also Smith 1993), Rogers Smith took the story from there, describing how Protestant elites were deeply implicated in attempts to institutionalize the "ascriptive Americanism" that was seen in Gilded Age opposition to Catholicism, Mormonism, and atheistic socialism, along with nativist and racist initiatives to ensure Anglo-Saxon racial supremacy. By the end of the century, as described by Eldon Eisenach (1994) in his *The Lost Promise of Progressivism*, Progressive academics and intellectuals, drawing on social gospel teachings, were offering a reformist alternative to the existing evangelical moral establishment, capturing state institutions and expanding civil society in an effort to bring social Christianity to bear in creating a new democratic nationalism. Others (Williams and Alexander 1994; Creech 2006) have shown how Populist reformers of the same time drew on religious rhetoric to establish legitimacy for their movement and imbue it with a sacred sense of urgency. Indeed, in a review of American historical scholarship, Eisenach (2004, p. 46) has concluded that in place of the Hartzian model a new consensus has been built, and that today there is almost universal agreement that throughout the 19th century, religious belief was, in his words, "inseparable from politics."

The same can be said about the more recent American past. According to Hartz's historiography, the American aversion to socialism had doomed any serious alternative to a piecemeal and pragmatic interest-based liberalism, be that alternative radical, conservative, or otherwise. However, inspired by the movement politics of the 20th century, historians of political theory have been rediscovering a politics that is not only less liberal, but also more distinctly religious. Led by Neal Riemer (1984) and Michael Walzer (1985), who introduced the idea of prophetic politics to contemporary historians of political thought, and by Garry Wills (1990) who applied it broadly across American politics, scholars have been documenting the persistence of the biblical practice of prophecy in a score of modern movements. In tracing the tradition of prophetic protest, many have turned to African American Protestantism, describing the prophetic voices within the black church that influenced abolitionism (Rogers 1996), antilynching and union organizing campaigns (West 1996a), and the civil rights movement (Howard-Pitney 1990; Marsh 2005; see also Shulman 2008). Others have concentrated on the Catholic church, where prophetic themes have been present in Christian feminism (Daly 1973; Reuther 1996), liberation theology (Pottenger 1996), and social teachings on economic justice and peace (Formicola 1996). Some (Auerbach 1996) have written on Judaism, finding strong links between the prophetic tradition and the commitment to intergenerational justice that many Jews bring to issues of social welfare and human rights. In his *Prophetic Politics*, David S. Gutterman (2005; see also Gutterman 2006) found prophetic themes across a broad spectrum of religious leaders and movements, from Billy Sunday to Martin Luther King, Jr., and from the conservative men's group Promise Keepers to the progressive antipoverty organization Call to Renewal. Working at about the same time, other scholars have concentrated on conservative thinking, tracing the influence of religious themes in the writings of those in the New Christian Right (Lienesch 1993; Apostolidis 2000; Harding 2000), the Christian Identity movement (Barkun 1996), Christian

Reconstructionism (Pottenger 2007), and contemporary creationism (Lienesch 2007). Still others, like Robert Booth Fowler (1995; see also Bowersox 2006) have looked at liberal Protestantism, analyzing ideas of creation care and stewardship that have fueled the growing interest in environmental issues within mainstream churches. And in a recent work, Allen Hertzke (2004) has documented the concerns of activists from many faiths who have converged in the campaign for global human rights.

Today it is almost impossible to imagine a serious study of American political thought that does not pay some attention to the role of religion. It is also impossible to imagine one in which the treatment of religion is not controversial. The Hartzian liberal tradition may be a relic of the past, its blindness to religion's place in politics no longer even a possibility, but liberal interpretations have by no means been banished from American political thought. Thus, most scholars have followed those like Michael Zuckert (1996; see also Kloppenberg 1998) in continuing to consider Lockean natural rights philosophy a central contributor to the liberal republicanism of the founders, while at the same time seeing it as only one of several components of a theoretical synthesis that included Protestant Christianity, classical republicanism, and the common law tradition. The debates about the respective roles of these strains has been heated and prolonged (see, for example, Engeman and Zuckert 2004). Moreover, they have turned increasingly away from well-worn treatments of Jefferson and Madison to examinations of other founding figures, including Washington (Muñoz 2004), Adams (Witte 2004), Witherspoon (Morrison 2004), Franklin (Lubert 2004), James Wilson (Hall 2004), George Mason (Dreisbach 2004), the Carrolls of Maryland (Stoner 2004), and others, including Antifederalist thinkers (see Cornell 1999). In the same way, the ever-enigmatic Tocqueville continues to inspire controversy about the character of democratic faith, with commentators (see Deneen 2005; Mitchell, 2006) seeing him less as celebrating religion's role as an antidote to the excesses of democratic politics and more as warning about the extremes of democratic religion, particularly the type practiced by certain fundamentalists. In addition to Lincoln, who inspires interest in every era (see Wills 1992; Morel 2000; White 2002; Holland 2007), scholars have given growing attention to democratic theorists like Emerson, Whitman, and Dewey, examining their respective conceptions of what Patrick Deneen (2005) has called "democratic faith." Among those who study American thought in the 20th century, growing numbers (see Warren 1997; Martin 2003; Nurser 2005; Skillen 2005) have been recovering religion's role in foreign policy, resurrecting the forgotten influence of religious thinkers from John Foster Dulles to Reinhold Niebuhr in shaping America's role in the Cold War and contributing to international agreements like the Universal Declaration of Human Rights. Finally, as today's world becomes ever smaller, scholars (see Johnston and Sampson 1994; Carlson and Owens 2003; Fox and Sandler 2004) are giving growing attention to the international implications of American religious politics, and the trend seems certain to continue. As Hertzke (2004, p. 6) puts it, "to grasp something of the global future, we must understand American religion."

Today, Hartz's classic account of contracts and individuals continues to be challenged by a competing historical narrative of covenants and congregations. To look ahead is to predict that scholars will soon be portraying a past in which these separate stories come together into one. That is to say, having rediscovered the role of religion in public life, historians of political thought can now go on describe in detail how religion and politics have been interconnected—indeed, inextricably intertwined—throughout America's past. The topics still to be treated are countless, calling for a reexamination of much of the nation's political experience from earliest times to today. After all, to borrow the metaphor of Hugh Heclo (2007, p. 35), America's very DNA is the product of religion and politics coming together in tension, "a kind of double-stranded helix," as he has described it, "spiraling through time."

CONTEMPORARY SOCIAL AND POLITICAL THOUGHT

Among mid-20th-century American social and political thinkers, the assumption of secularization was every bit as pervasive as Rawls' liberalism and Hartz's Lockean reading of history. The product of a sophisticated sociological theory with roots in Marx, Weber, and Durkheim, the concept held that the emergence of Enlightenment reason had challenged the sacred status of religion, reconstructing the social order along more secular lines and relegating religion to a matter of personal choice rather than public obligation. In *The Sacred Canopy*, sociologist Peter Berger (1966) elaborated on the process, explaining how the relentless rationality of the modern world had shattered its "sacred canopy," the religious beliefs and rituals that had provided legitimacy to the older social order, differentiating church from state while also exposing individuals to a diversity of religious views. Those views in turn had come to be secularized themselves, their sacred status being stripped of deeper moral meaning. Applied to America, the theory explained what writers like Will Herberg (1955) had described in his *Protestant–Catholic–Jew* as an all-encompassing shallowness in which the contents of religious life had been emptied out, replaced by a bland sense that religion was really a form of sociability. By the 1970s, with studies showing declining attendance at churches and the decreasing importance of religion to individuals, students of American religion seemed convinced that while traditional religion remained a force in society, it was slowly and surely dying out. Social critics across the spectrum, from neoconservatives like Daniel Bell (1978) to democratic socialists like Michael Harrington (1983), described what they saw as the exhaustion of modernism, a spiritual poverty that left people hungering for more meaningful lives. Religion continued to serve as a source of support in the private lives of people, but it had surrendered any semblance of providing the public with a more transcendent sense of purpose. Among the critics, few held out much hope for the revival of religion's political role. Concluded Harrington (1983, p. 218) in his *The Politics at God's Funeral*, "the political and social God of the Western tradition is dying."

Beginning in the mid 1980s, however, scholars began to look beyond such laments, criticizing the secularization thesis while also developing more elaborate explanations for the apparent inability of religion to exert greater influence on secular society. Responding to the sudden surge of political activism seen in the New Christian Right, analysts were forced to reevaluate the theories that had so confidently predicted not only declining membership in religious organizations, but also their steady retreat from the public realm. In his *The Naked Public Square*, Richard John Neuhaus (1984), a Lutheran minister who would soon become a Catholic priest, delivered a stinging rebuke to conventional opinion, arguing that American society, far from secular, was more religious than ever, and that the reason people of faith had failed to exercise more influence on politics was because advocates of a secular state had pushed them out of the public square, leaving behind a politics that lacked any fundamental moral grounding. At about the same time, Robert Bellah, Richard Madsen, William Sullivan, Ann Swidler, and Steven Tipton (1985), writing in their best-selling *Habits of the Heart*, were rediscovering religious roots beneath the surface of American secular society. To all appearances, the authors admitted, Americans seemed to be individualistic utilitarians, self-consumed practitioners of privatized forms of religion like that captured in the famous "Sheilaism" of one pseudonymous respondent who described her personal faith as "my own little voice." Yet in carrying out extensive interviews with middle-class respondents, the authors were surprised to discover a deeper set of alternative ethical traditions, including biblical and republican ones, that contributed to the mores and practices—what Tocqueville (2003, p. 336) called the "habits of the heart"—by which Americans actually lived their lives. Writing in his *Unconventional Partners*, Robert Booth Fowler (1989) found a similar religious presence, arguing that although much of America's secular culture was indeed individualistic, leading at the extreme to personal and political isolation, religion offered an active alternative to it, a refuge from relativism that ironically played a critical role in supporting liberal society. Although their arguments were at points decidedly different, betraying contrasting traditionalist, communitarian, and liberal perspectives, Neuhaus (1984), Bellah et al. (1985), and Fowler (1989) were in agreement that, far from being strangled by secularization, religion was not only alive and well, but also increasingly important in American public life. Indeed, as social theorist José Casanova (1994) would argue, what was really new about religion in the 1980s was that it had become "deprivatized," meaning that religious people were now no longer willing to accept the marginal role that theories of secularization had reserved for them. To put it simply, observed Casanova (1994, p. 3), religion in the 1980s "went public."

Yet many scholars were troubled by religion's new public role. In particular, the rise of the New Christian Right, mobilizing millions of previously apolitical religious conservatives, was seen by many as encouraging a politics that was both dangerously moralistic and deeply polarizing. The sociologist of religion Robert Wuthnow (1988) had seen it coming, arguing in *The Restructuring of American Religion* that traditional denominational divisions had become largely meaningless, having been supplanted by belief-based fault lines that cut across churches, sharply separating religious conservatives from religious progressives. In his landmark book *Culture Wars*, James Davison Hunter (1991) developed the insight, describing how American elites had become divided into competing camps based on mutually antagonistic moral visions. In one camp were the culturally orthodox, those committed to a literal and transcendent conception of authority, who included fundamentalist and conservative evangelical Protestants, along with traditionalist Catholics, Orthodox Jews, and a few secular allies. In the other were cultural progressives, consisting primarily of liberal Protestants, Catholics, and Jews, all of whom saw moral authority as more rational and subjective, together with secular activists from organizations like the American Civil Liberties Union and the National Organization of Women. Tracing the historical roots of these camps, describing their competing moral visions, and examining cases in several areas of conflict, he concluded that although the American experiment was not on the brink of collapse, this continuing culture war had strained the social fabric and posed a serious threat to democratic political practice. Hunter's (1991) book itself provoked considerable conflict, with many embracing his military metaphor to describe contemporary politics, whereas others expressed skepticism. Examining the evidence, scholars led by Green, Guth, Smidt, and Kellstedt (1996) found evidence of a deepening religious divide, especially among elites and political activists, but less support for the view that American politics had become thoroughly polarized. Others, including Wuthnow (1989), argued that bipolar categories of orthodox and progressive were too simple, overlooking a good deal of diversity within them. Among the most active critics was Alan Wolfe (1998), who contended in his *One Nation, After All* that although some elites may have encouraged cultural conflict, most Americans—including even many religious conservatives—were "instinctive moderates," tolerant people who believed that morality was mainly a private matter. A few analysts went so far as to deny the existence of a culture war altogether, declaring the theory a "myth" (Williams 1997; see also Fiorina 2005). In looking back over the period, however, most observers came to the conclusion that the reappearance of religion in the political realm had indeed introduced considerable moral conflict, at least on a number of issues, and especially among elites, and that it had encouraged polarization within American politics. As Wolfe (1998, p. 276) himself admitted, "on moral matters, there is no unanimity in America."

In the wake of the culture wars, a growing cadre of thinkers struggled to find less polarizing ways to bring religion to bear on politics. Seeking neither to return to secularism nor to populate the no-longer-naked public square with moral partisans, these writers attempted to define a democratic discourse that would encourage moral convictions while also providing ways for citizens to work out their deepest moral differences. In his popular *The Culture of Disbelief*, Yale constitutional law professor Stephen L. Carter (1993) set the tone for them, making the case for a democratic politics that embraced the broadest expression of faith while also maintaining the essential separation between church and state. Writing as a liberal Episcopalian and reminding readers of the long tradition of religious reform that had culminated in the civil rights movement, Carter insisted that religion was an essential ingredient of American democracy. At the same time, chiding mainstream Protestants for their unwillingness to believe that America could be a force for good in the world, he attempted to lay the basis for a new political religion, one that maintained a center of civility while also allowing for a diversity of democratic views. Writing at about the same time, a broad cross-section of thinkers joined the call for a less polarizing role for religion in politics, stressing the need for civil discourse (Elshtain 2000, 2001), self-restraint (Perry 2000), and a new civic consensus or "common ground" (Haynes 2001). Tapping themes of community and social obligation in Christian (Segars 2000; Tinder 2000), Jewish (Dorff 2000; Elazar 2000), and Islamic thought (al-Hibri 2001), these thinkers made the case that people of faith must play a meliorating role in public life, connecting rather than dividing citizens from one another. In fact, in his widely read *Bowling Alone*, Robert Putnam (2000; see also Verba, Schlozman, and Brady 1995) contended that faith communities were essential to the success of modern democratic states, serving as the single most important repository of "social capital" (see also Coleman 1997; Smidt 2003). Other writers (Hollenbach 1997; Thiemann 2000; Coles 2005) contended that religious groups could contribute to the development of democracy not only by contributing to civil society, but also by participating directly in the political realm, with churches serving as sites for civic education and community building. Eldon Eisenach (2000b; see also Eisenach 2000a) took the argument from there, calling on believers to become part of what he termed the "next religious establishment," a loose and voluntary alliance of moral authorities (including secular intellectuals) committed to creating a new national ethic of civility and toleration that could be the basis for democratic pluralism in a "post-Protestant America."

In attempting to define a more public role for religion, some thinkers turned to the concept of civil religion. Introduced by sociologist Robert Bellah (1967), the concept captures a form of public religiosity, existing alongside but independent of established religion, that gives transcendent meaning to the national experience. Found in public texts and celebrated in political rituals, this civic faith consists primarily of a common set of biblical tropes—chosen people, promised land, city on a hill—that allow Americans to affirm a divine mission and appeal for God's blessing. Although enormously influential, the concept soon came to be criticized (Wilson 1979), and eventually even Bellah (1992) himself stopped using it, fearing that it had become synonymous with the idolatrous worship of the state. Never-theless, it has continued to find advocates as well as detractors, and to provoke heated controversy. Thus, Wilfred McClay (2004) has contended that civil religion can be misused, but it can also contain an element of transcendental accountability that serves to check rather than enable nationalistic excesses. By contrast, those like Rogers Smith (2008; see also Riswold 2004), criticizing President George W. Bush's use of religious rhetoric in the wake of the 9/11 terrorist attacks, has argued that by providing sacred legitimation for otherwise partisan policies, it can close off criticism and define dissent not only as unpatriotic, but also as unrighteous or evil. Other scholars (Wuthnow 1988; Lincoln 2003) have described different versions of civil religion, contrasting conservative preservationist strains with liberal prophetic ones, and describing how the two can sometimes become entangled. In any case, as Wuthnow (2005) has reported, strong strains of civil religion can be detected in the American public, with more than half of all respondents telling researchers that America's strength comes from its faith in God. And, as Melissa Wilcox (2006, p. 44) has observed, one of the lessons of the 9/11 aftermath was that the rhetoric of civil religion can be enormously powerful, carrying the potential "to unmake and re-make a society."

Today the search to find the proper place for faith in our politics continues, made more challenging by the growing diversity of American religion. With immigration bringing believers from every part of the world, and with reform and schism ceaselessly creating new forms of faith, religious life is being transformed, creating problems and opportunities for democratic politics. For those like Samuel P. Huntington (2004), writing in his *Who Are We? Challenges to American National Identity*, this ever-expanding pluralism poses serious questions about whether an increasingly diverse society can merge conflicting cultures, languages, and religious worldviews into a common conception of national purpose. Warning ominously of fragmentation, Huntington (2004) advances the case for a single "Anglo-Protestant culture," arguing unapologetically that Christianity has been the basis of an American creed that combines commitment to hard work and individual self-improvement with the sense of moral responsibility required for republican self-government. In response, critics have taken him to task, citing historical inaccuracies and chastising him for overlooking the contributions of other ethnic and religious groups. For these writers, the sacred canopy has been replaced by what Christian Smith (1998, p. 106) has called "sacred umbrellas," a multitude of faith-sustaining religious worlds that believers construct for themselves. Moreover, as Barbara McGraw (2003, 2005) and others have argued, although the diversity of American religion can be confusing and sometimes threatening, it can also create a more active and participatory public life. Thus, a growing group of scholars has considered the contributions to the public forum from those of many faiths, including not only Protestants, Catholics, and Jews, but also Mormons (Pottenger 2005), Muslims (Kahn 2005), Hindus (Rambachan 2005), Buddhists (Gross 2005), and Confucianists (Selover 2005). Others have investigated the role of those who are active in minor religions (Eck 2001), or who participate in spiritual movements such as ecofeminism (Sturgeon 1997) or spiritual ecology (Woolpert 2005). Still others (see Kao and Copulsky 2007) focus on the small but steadily increasing number who claim no particular religious views whatsoever. In addition, scholars have begun to investigate the interaction that is taking place as this growing collection of groups comes into contact with one another and with the state, analyzing how citizens from a variety of faith perspectives deal with issues ranging from abortion (Formicola 2005) and same-sex marriage (Josephson and Burack 2006) to public policies like Charitable Choice (Carlson-Thies 2003; Hawkins 2006), the death penalty (Owens, Carlson, and Elshtain 2004), and local conflicts over community health care, homelessness, and zoning (Button 2006, Djupe and Olson 2007). As Diana Eck (2001) has argued, the ability to define a politics that can deal with this ever-expanding religious pluralism is among the most important challenges Americans face today. She concludes:

> Whether the vibrant new religious diversity that is now part and parcel of the United States will, in the years ahead, bring us together or pull us apart depends greatly on whether we are able to imagine our national community anew. And the fate of a vibrant pluralism in the U.S. will have an important impact on the fate of religious pluralism worldwide. (Eck 2001, p. 385)

In short, the secularization theory of the mid 20th century has failed to predict what has become the unimaginably contested and pluralistic religious politics of the 21st century. The theory's failure is not to deny the reality of secularization. We live, says Charles Taylor (2007), in "a secular age," by which he means one in which the sacred has not been banished by the secular, but rather has been challenged, confronted, and constantly changed by it. Thus today, and even more for the future, students of social and political thought must be turning their attention to how secularity, far from expelling the sacred, has become closely and often inseparably bound up with it. For as we look ahead to the coming century, we can be confident of one thing: that religion will continue to be a powerful force in our politics. Writes Taylor (2007, p. 535), "we are just at the beginning of a new age of religious searching, whose outcome no one can foresee."

CONCLUSION

During the course of the past several decades, students of American political thought have rediscovered religion. Challenging powerful paradigms—the liberalism of John Rawls, the Lockean historical interpretation of Louis Hartz, and the secularization theory developed by modern sociologists from Max Weber to Daniel Bell—they have reached beyond popular preconceptions of American politics as uniformly liberal, individualistic, and secular. Inspired by the sudden appearance of millions of religious activists in the 1980s, and by the continuing presence of religious voices ever since, they have redefined the study of American political thought, providing a more secure place for religion in political philosophy, the history of theory, and contemporary social and political thought.

The classic paradigms have not completely disappeared. Indeed, in recent years a few authors have tried to revive them, reasserting the essential rightness of Rawls (Dombrowski 2001), Hartz (Abbott 2005), and the secularization theorists (Bruce 1996; Norris and Inglehart 2004; Martin 2005). Yet in recognizing religion, American political thought has been changed in significant ways, and the changes promise to continue. Thus, for political philosophers today, the boundaries between faith and reason, public and private, church and state are less clear and more contested, challenged by an increasingly diverse collection of religious groups. Historians of political theory, no longer content with single explanations, now construct multifaceted narratives, opening the telling of America's story to multiple traditions, including religious ones. Social and political thinkers struggle to define a public discourse that allows for expressions of faith from an ever-growing variety of voices. The inclusion of religion has had methodological implications as well, for with the stretching of paradigms, abstract theories have been supplemented by analyses of actual issues; sweeping descriptions of American ideology have given way to more specific studies of the ideas of individuals and groups; and conceptions of a common culture have been replaced by a richer sense of the variety of worldviews. Meanwhile, as scholars come to terms with religion's reach, their research must, of necessity, become more interdisciplinary in character as well as more international in focus.

Much remains to be done. For the foreseeable future, it seems improbable that new paradigms will appear, fully formed, to replace the older and increasingly outdated ones. More predictable is a period of dialogue and experimentation in which scholars continue to bring religion to bear on the study of American political thought. Among political philosophers, the increasing presence of religious pluralism has already led to more serious engagement between liberal, Christian, and antifoundational theorists (see Johnson 2007), suggesting philosophical possibilities that point beyond both tolerance and agonistic indifference. For students of the history of American political theory, recent scholarship citing the centrality of religion to Lockean liberalism (Waldron 2002; see also Gilchrist 2006) demonstrates that assumptions about multiple traditions must be extended to include multiple overlapping ones, in which religion is no longer considered an independent component of American thought, but a contributor to almost every aspect of it. To those who study contemporary social and political thought, the work of Christian Smith (2003) and his collaborators suggests that secularization should be seen not as an abstract historical theory, but as a particularistic political process that can best be examined by applying contemporary concepts of resource mobilization, issue framing, and political opportunity structures. Indeed, in studying the increasingly intricate interplay of religion and politics, the best future scholarship can be expected to move beyond conventional categories altogether, combining philosophical, historical, and empirical methods in more problem-driven, case-specific, and comparative ways.

Whatever our views, the primary lesson we have learned during the past quarter century is that religion is an essential ingredient of American political thought. Critics like Richard Dawkins (2006), Daniel Dennett (2006), and Sam Harris (2004, 2006) may decry its inherent irrationality, seeking to banish it from the public realm. Older paradigms notwithstanding, however, we have come to see that religion has been a permanent presence in our political thinking. For the future, our research agendas must be focused not on whether it plays a role, but how, when, where, and with what consequences. Students of religion in American political thought have more than enough to keep us occupied for some time to come.

ACKNOWLEDGMENTS

For the their advice and suggestions, I acknowledge and thank Clarke Cochran, Eldon Eisenach, Andrew Murphy, Jeff Spinner-Halev, and Ashley Woodiwiss.

REFERENCES

Abbott, Phillip 2005. "Still Louis Hartz after All These Years: A Defense of the Liberal Society Thesis." *Perspectives on Politics* 3: 93–109.

Ackerman, Bruce. 1980. *Social Justice in the Liberal State*. New Haven, Conn.: Yale University Press.

al-Hibri, Azizah Y. 2001. "Standing at the Precipice: Faith in the Age of Science and Technology." In *Religion in American Public Life: Living with Our Deepest Differences*, ed. Azizah Y. al-Hibri, Jean Bethke Elshtain, and Charles C. Haynes, 62–95. New York: W. W. Norton.

Allen, Barbara. 2005. *Tocqueville, Covenant, and the Democratic Revolution*. Lanham, Md.: Rowman & Littlefield.

Alston, William P. 1991. *Perceiving God: The Epistemology of Religious Experience*. Ithaca, N.Y.: Cornell University Press.

Apostolidis, Paul. 2000. *Stations of the Cross: Adorno and Christian Right Radio*. Durham, N.C.: Duke University Press.

Audi, Robert. 2000. *Religious Commitment and Secular Reason*. New York: Cambridge University Press.

Auerbach, Bruce E. 1996. "Intergenerational Justice and the Prophetic Tradition." In *Let Justice Roll: Prophetic Challenges in Religion, Politics, and Society*, ed. Neal Riemer, 169–186. Lanham, Md.: Rowman & Littlefield.

Bailyn, Bernard. 1967. *The Ideological Origins of the American Revolution*. Cambridge, Mass.: Belknap Press of Harvard University Press.

Barkun, Michael. 1996. *Religion and the Racist Right: The Origins of the Christian Identity Movement*. Chapel Hill, N.C.: University of North Carolina Press.

Bell, Daniel. 1978. *The Cultural Contradictions of Capitalism*. New York: Basic Books.

Bellah, Robert N. 1967. "Civil Religion in America." *Journal of the American Academy of Arts and Sciences* 96: 1–21.

Bellah, Robert N. 1992. *The Broken Covenant: American Civil Religion in Time of Trial.* 2nd ed. Chicago, Ill.: University of Chicago Press.

Bellah, Robert N., Richard Madsen, William M. Sullivan, Ann Swidler, and Steven M. Tipton. 1985. *Habits of the Heart: Individualism and Commitment in American Life.* Berkeley, Calif.: University of California Press.

Beneke, Chris. 2006. *Beyond Toleration: The Religious Origins of American Pluralism.* New York: Oxford University Press.

Bennett, Jane. 2006. "The Agency of Assemblages and the North American Blackout." In *Political Theologies: Public Religions in a Post-Secular World,* ed. Hent de Vries and Lawrence E. Sullivan, 602–616. New York: Fordham University Press.

Bercovitch, Sacvan. 1975. *The Puritan Origins of the American Self.* New Haven, Conn.: Yale University Press.

Bercovitch, Sacvan. 1978. *The American Jeremiad.* Madison, Wisc.: University of Wisconsin Press.

Berger, Peter L. 1966. *The Sacred Canopy: Elements of a Sociological Theory of Religion.* Garden City, N.Y.: Doubleday.

Block, James E. 2002. *A Nation of Agents: The American Path to a Modern Self and Society.* Cambridge, Mass.: Harvard University Press.

Bowersox, Joe. 2006. "Greening the Divine: Religion, the Environment, and Politics in Twenty-first Century North America." In *Religion, Politics, and American Identity: New Directions, New Controversies,* ed. David S. Gutterman and Andrew R. Murphy, 199–219. Lanham, Md.: Rowman & Littlefield.

Brown, Wendy. 2006. "Subjects of Tolerance: Why We Are Civilized and They Are the Barbarians." In *Political Theologies: Public Religions in a Post-Secular World,* ed. Hent de Vries and Lawrence E. Sullivan, 298–317. New York: Fordham University Press.

Bruce, Steve. 1996. *Religion in the Modern World: From Cathedrals to Cults.* New York: Oxford University Press.

Budziszewski, J. 1986. *The Resurrection of Nature: Political Theory and the Human Character.* Ithaca, N.Y.: Cornell University Press.

Button, Mark. 2006. "Religion on Main Street: Toward a New Politics of the Sacred and Secular." In *Religion, Politics, and American Identity: New Directions, New Controversies,* ed. David S. Gutterman and Andrew R. Murphy, 129–149. Lanham, Md.: Rowman & Littlefield.

Carlson, John D., and Erik Owens, eds. 2003. *The Sacred and the Sovereign: Religion and International Politics.* Washington, D.C.: Georgetown University Press.

Carlson-Thies, Stanley W. 2003. "Charitable Choice: Bringing Religion Back into American Welfare." In *Religion Returns to the Public Square: Faith and Policy in America,* ed. Hugh Heclo and Wilfred M. McClay, 269–297. Washington, D.C.: Woodrow Wilson Center Press.

Carter, Stephen L. 1993. *The Culture of Disbelief: How Law and Politics Trivialize Religious Devotion.* New York: Basic Books.

Casanova, José. 1994. *Public Religions in the Modern World.* Chicago, Ill.: University of Chicago Press.

Cochran, Clarke E. 1990. *Religion in Private and Public Life.* New York: Routledge.

Cochran, Clarke E. 2001. "Taking Ecclesiology Seriously: Catholicism, Religious Institutions, and Health Care Policy." In *The Re-enchantment of Political Science:*

Christian Scholars Engage Their Discipline, ed. Thomas W. Heilke and Ashley Woodiwiss, 169–192. Lanham, Md.: Lexington Books.

Coleman, John A. 1997. "Deprivatizing Religion and Revitalizing Citizenship." In *Religion and Contemporary Liberalism*, ed. Paul J. Weithman, 162–181. Notre Dame, Ind.: University of Notre Dame Press.

Coleman, John A. 2003. "American Catholicism, Catholic Charities USA, and Welfare Reform." In *Religion Returns to the Public Square: Faith and Policy in America*, ed. Hugh Heclo and Wilfred M. McClay, 229–267. Washington, D.C.: Woodrow Wilson Center Press.

Coles, Romand. 2005. *Beyond Gated Communities: Reflections for the Possibility of Democracy*. Minneapolis, Minn.: University of Minnesota Press.

Connolly, William. 1999. *Why I Am Not a Secularist*. Minneapolis, Minn.: University of Minnesota Press.

Connolly, William. 2006. "Pluralism and Faith." In *Political Theologies: Public Religions in a Post-Secular World*, ed. Hent de Vries and Lawrence E. Sullivan, 278–297. New York: Fordham University Press.

Cornell, Saul. 1999. *Anti-Federalism and the Dissenting Tradition in America, 1788–1828.* Chapel Hill, N.C.: University of North Carolina Press.

Creech, Joe. 2006. *Religion and the Populist Revolution*. Urbana, Ill.: University of Illinois Press.

Daly, Mary. 1973. *Beyond God the Father: Toward a Philosophy of Women's Liberation.* Boston, Mass.: Beacon Press.

Dawkins, Richard. 2006. *The God Delusion*. Boston, Mass.: Houghton Mifflin.

Deneen, Patrick J. 2005. *Democratic Faith*. Princeton, N.J.: Princeton University Press.

Dennett, Daniel C. 2006. *Breaking the Spell: Religion as a Natural Phenomenon*. New York: Viking Press.

De Tocqueville, Alexis. 2003. *Democracy in America and Two Essays on America*, trans. Gerald E. Bevan, ed. Isaac Kramnick. London: Penguin Books.

Diggins, John Patrick. 1984. *The Lost Soul of American Politics: Virtue, Self-Interest, and the Foundation of Liberalism*. New York: Basic Books.

Djupe, Paul A., and Laura R. Olson, eds. 2007. *Religious Interests in Community Conflict: Beyond the Culture Wars*. Waco, Texas: Baylor University Press.

Dombrowski, Daniel A. 2001. *Rawls and Religion: The Case for Political Liberalism*. Albany, N.Y.: State University of New York Press.

Dorff, Elliot N. 2000. "The King's Torah: The Role of Judaism in Shaping Jews' Input in National Policy." In *A Nation under God? Essays on the Future of Religion in American Public Life*, ed. R. Bruce Douglass and Joshua Mitchell, 203–221. Lanham, Md.: Rowman & Littlefield.

Dreisbach, Daniel L. 2002. *Thomas Jefferson and the Wall of Separation between Church and State*. New York: New York University Press.

Dreisbach, Daniel L. 2004. "George Mason's Pursuit of Religious Liberty in Revolutionary Virginia." In *The Founders on God and Government*, ed. Daniel L. Dreisbach, Mark D. Hall, and Jeffry H. Morrison, 207–249. Lanham, Md.: Rowman & Littlefield.

Dworkin, Ronald. 1985. *A Matter of Principle*. Cambridge, Mass.: Harvard University Press.

Eberle, Christopher J. 2002. *Religious Conviction in Liberal Politics*. Cambridge, UK: Cambridge University Press.

Eck, Diana. 2001. *A New Religious America: How a "Christian Country" Has Now Become the World's Most Religiously Diverse Nation*. New York: HarperCollins.

Eisenach, Eldon J. 1979. "The American Revolution Made and Remembered." *American Studies* 20: 71–91.

Eisenach, Eldon J. 1994. *The Lost Promise of Progressivism.* Lawrence, Kans.: University Press of Kansas.

Eisenach, Eldon J. 2000a. "Post-Protestant America? Some Hegelian Reflections on the History and Theology of Religious Establishment." In *A Nation under God? Essays on the Future of Religion in American Public Life,* ed. R. Bruce Douglass and Joshua Mitchell, 135–161. Lanham, Md.: Rowman & Littlefield.

Eisenach, Eldon J. 2000b. *The Next Religious Establishment: National Identity and Political Theology in Post-Protestant America.* Lanham, Md.: Rowman & Littlefield.

Eisenach, Eldon J. 2004. "Emerging Patterns in America's Political and Religious Self-Understanding." *Studies in American Political Development* 18: 44–59.

Elazar, Daniel J. 1998. *Covenant and Constitutionalism: The Great Frontier and the Matrix of Federal Democracy.* New Brunswick, N.J.: Transaction Books.

Elazar, Daniel J. 2000. "Recovenanting the American Polity." In *A Nation under God? Essays on the Future of Religion in American Public Life,* ed. R. Bruce Douglass and Joshua Mitchell, 65–90. Lanham, Md.: Rowman & Littlefield.

Elshtain, Jean Bethke. 2000. "How Should We Talk?" In *A Nation under God? Essays on the Future of Religion in American Public Life,* ed. R. Bruce Douglass and Joshua Mitchell, 163–176. Lanham, Md.: Rowman & Littlefield.

Elshtain, Jean Bethke. 2001. "Faith of Our Fathers and Mothers: Religious Belief and American Democracy." In *Religion in American Public Life: Living with Our Deepest Differences,* ed. Azizah Y. al-Hibri, Jean Bethke Elshtain, and Charles C. Haynes, 39–61. New York: W. W. Norton.

Engeman, Thomas S., and Michael P. Zuckert, eds. 2004. *Protestantism and the American Founding.* Notre Dame, Ind.: University of Notre Dame Press.

Feldman, Noah. 2005. *Divided by God: America's Church–State Problem—and What We Should Do about It.* New York: Farrar, Straus and Giroux.

Fiorina, Morris P. 2005. *Culture War? The Myth of a Polarized America.* New York: Pearson Longman.

Fish, Stanley. 1999. *The Trouble with Principle.* Cambridge, Mass.: Harvard University Press.

Formicola, Jo Renee. 1996. "The American Catholic Bishops and Prophetic Politics." In *Let Justice Roll: Prophetic Challenges in Religion, Politics, and Society,* ed. Neal Riemer, 115–132. Lanham, Md.: Rowman & Littlefield.

Formicola, Jo Renee. 2005. "Catholicism and Pluralism: A Continuing Dilemma for the Twenty-first Century." In *Taking Religious Pluralism Seriously: Spiritual Politics on America's Sacred Ground,* ed. Barbara A. McGraw and Jo Renee Formicola, 61–86. Waco, Texas: Baylor University Press.

Foster, Gaines. 2002. *Moral Reconstruction: Christian Lobbyists and the Federal Legislation of Morality, 1865–1920.* Chapel Hill, N.C.: University of North Carolina Press.

Fowler, Robert Booth. 1989. *Unconventional Partners: Religion and Liberal Culture in the United States.* Grand Rapids, Mich.: William B. Eerdmans Publishing.

Fowler, Robert Booth. 1995. *The Greening of Protestant Thought.* Chapel Hill, N.C.: University of North Carolina Press.

Fox, Jonathan, and Shmuel Sandler. 2004. *Bringing Religion into International Relations.* New York: Palgrave Macmillan.

Galston, William. 1987. "Tocqueville on Liberalism and Religion." *Social Research* 54: 499–518.

Galston, William. 1991. *Liberal Purposes: Goods, Virtues, and Diversity in the Liberal State.* New York: Cambridge University Press.

Galston, William. 2002. *Liberal Pluralism: The Implications of Value Pluralism for Political Theory and Practice.* New York: Cambridge University Press.

Galston, William. 2005. *Public Matters: Essays on Politics, Policy and Religion.* Lanham, Md.: Rowman & Littlefield.

Gilchrist, Brent. 2006. *Cultus Americanus: Varieties of the Liberal Tradition in American Political Culture, 1600–1865.* Lanham, Md.: Lexington Books.

Gill, Emily R. 2004. "Religious Organizations, Charitable Choice, and the Limits of Freedom of Conscience." *Perspectives on Politics* 2: 741–755.

Glendon, Mary Ann. 1991. *Rights Talk: The Impoverishment of Political Discourse.* New York: Free Press.

Green, John C., James L. Guth, Corwin E. Smidt, and Lyman A. Kellstedt. 1996. *Religion and the Culture Wars: Dispatches from the Front.* Lanham, Md.: Rowman & Littlefield.

Greenawalt, Kent. 1995. *Private Consciences and Public Reasons.* Oxford, UK: Oxford University Press.

Greenawalt, Kent. 2000. "Five Questions about Religion Judges Are Afraid to Ask." In *Obligations of Citizenship and Demands of Faith: Religious Accommodation in Pluralist Democracies,* ed. Nancy L. Rosenblum, 196–244. Princeton, N.J.: Princeton University Press.

Greenstone, J. David. 1993. *The Lincoln Persuasion: Remaking American Liberalism.* Princeton, N.J.: Princeton University Press.

Gross, Rita M. 2005. "Buddhist Contributions to the Civic and Conscientious Public Forums." In *Taking Religious Pluralism Seriously: Spiritual Politics on America's Sacred Ground,* ed. Barbara A. McGraw and Jo Renee Formicola, 215–234. Waco, Texas: Baylor University Press.

Gutmann, Amy. 1987. *Democratic Education.* Princeton, N.J.: Princeton University Press.

Gutterman, David S. 2005. *Prophetic Politics: Christian Social Movements and American Democracy.* Ithaca, N.Y.: Cornell University Press.

Gutterman, David S. 2006. "Stories of Sinfulness: Narrative Identity in America." In *Religion, Politics, and American Identity: New Directions, New Controversies,* ed. David S. Gutterman and Andrew R. Murphy, 73–84. Lanham, Md.: Rowman & Littlefield Publishers.

Hall, Mark D. 2004. "James Wilson: Presbyterian, Anglican, Thomist, or Deist?" In *The Founders on God and Government,* ed. Daniel L. Dreisbach, Mark D. Hall, and Jeffry H. Morrison, 181–205. Lanham, Md.: Rowman & Littlefield.

Hamburger, Philip. 2002. *Separation of Church and State.* Cambridge, Mass.: Harvard University Press.

Hamilton, Marci A. 2005. *God vs. the Gavel: Religion and the Rule of Law.* New York: Cambridge University Press.

Hancock, Ralph. 1991. "The Uses and Hazards of Christianity in Tocqueville's Attempt to Save Democratic Souls." In *Interpreting Tocqueville's Democracy in America,* ed. Ken Masugi, 348–393. Lanham, Md.: Rowman & Littlefield.

Harding, Susan F. 2000. *The Book of Jerry Falwell: Fundamentalist Language and Politics.* Princeton, N.J.: Princeton University Press.

Harrington, Michael. 1983. *The Politics at God's Funeral: The Spiritual Crisis of Western Civilization.* New York: Holt, Rinehart and Winston.

Harris, Sam. 2004. *The End of Faith: Religion, Terror, and the Future of Reason.* New York: W. W. Norton.

Harris, Sam. 2006. *Letter to a Christian Nation.* New York: Alfred A. Knopf.

Hartz, Louis. 1955. *The Liberal Tradition in America: An Interpretation of American Political Thought since the Revolution.* New York: Harcourt, Brace & World.

Hauerwas, Stanley. 1981. *A Community of Character.* Notre Dame, Ind.: University of Notre Dame Press.

Hauerwas, Stanley. 1995. *In Good Company: The Church as Polis.* Notre Dame, Ind.: University of Notre Dame Press.

Hauerwas, Stanley. 2000. *A Better Hope: Resources for a Church Confronting Capitalism, Democracy, and Postmodernity.* Grand Rapids, Mich.: Brazos Press.

Hawkins, Larycia A. 2006. "Religion, Race, and Rhetoric: The Black Church, Religious Interest Groups, and Charitable Choice." In *Religion, Politics, and American Identity: New Directions, New Controversies,* ed. David S. Gutterman and Andrew R. Murphy, 221–245. Lanham, Md.: Rowman & Littlefield.

Haynes, Charles C. 2001. "From Battleground to Common Ground: Religion in the Public Square of 21st Century America." In *Religion in American Public Life: Living with Our Deepest Differences,* ed. Azizah Y. al-Hibri, Jean Bethke Elshtain, and Charles C. Haynes, 96–136. New York: W. W. Norton.

Hecht, Stacey Hunter. 2001. "The State of the States: A Perspective on Federalism and Biblically Just Social Policy." In *The Re-enchantment of Political Science: Christian Scholars Engage Their Discipline,* ed. Thomas W. Heilke and Ashley Woodiwiss, 193–224. Lanham, Md.: Lexington Books.

Heclo, Hugh. 2007. *Christianity and American Democracy.* Cambridge, Mass.: Harvard University Press.

Heilke, Thomas. 2001. "At the Table: Toward an Anabaptist Political Science." In *The Re-enchantment of Political Science: Christian Scholars Engage Their Discipline,* ed. Thomas W. Heilke and Ashley Woodiwiss, 35–62. Lanham, Md.: Lexington Books.

Heimert, Alan. 1966. *Religion and the American Mind: From the Great Awakening to the Revolution.* Cambridge, Mass.: Harvard University Press.

Herberg, Will. 1955. *Protestant–Catholic–Jew: An Essay in Religious Sociology.* New York: Doubleday.

Hertzke, Allen D. 2004. *Freeing God's Children: The Unlikely Alliance for Global Human Rights.* Lanham, Md.: Rowman & Littlefield.

Hinckley, Cynthia J. 1990. "Tocqueville on Religious Truth and Political Necessity." *Polity* 23: 39–52.

Holland, Matthew S. 2007. *Bonds of Affection: Civic Charity and the Making of America—Winthrop, Jefferson, and Lincoln.* Washington, D.C.: Georgetown University Press.

Hollenbach, David. 1997. "Politically Active Churches: Some Empirical Prolegomena to a Normative Approach." In *Religion and Contemporary Liberalism,* ed. Paul J. Weithman, 162–181. Notre Dame, Ind.: University of Notre Dame Press.

Hollenbach, David. 2003. *The Global Face of Public Faith: Politics, Human Rights, and Christian Ethics.* Washington, D.C.: Georgetown University Press.

Howard-Pitney, David. 1990. *The Afro-American Jeremiad: Appeals for Justice in America.* Philadelphia, Pa.: Temple University Press.

Hunter, James Davison. 1991. *Culture Wars: The Struggle to Define America.* New York: Basic Books.

Huntington, Samuel P. 2004. *Who Are We? The Challenges to America's National Identity.* New York: Simon and Schuster.

Johnson, Kristen Deede. 2007. *Theology, Political Theory, and Pluralism: Beyond Tolerance and Difference.* Cambridge, UK: Cambridge University Press.

Johnston, Douglas, and Cynthia Sampson, eds. 1994. *Religion, the Missing Dimension of Statecraft.* New York: Oxford University Press.

Josephson, Jyl J., and Cynthia Burack. 2006. "Inside, Out, and In-Between: Sexual Minorities, the Christian Right, and the Evangelical Lutheran Church in America." In *Religion, Politics, and American Identity: New Directions, New Controversies*, ed. David S. Gutterman and Andrew R. Murphy, 247–265. Lanham, Md.: Rowman & Littlefield Publishers.

Kahn, M. A. Muqtedar. 2005. "American Muslims and the Rediscovery of America's Sacred Ground." In *Taking Religious Pluralism Seriously: Spiritual Politics on America's Sacred Ground*, ed. Barbara A. McGraw and Jo Renee Formicola, 127–148. Waco, Texas: Baylor University Press.

Kao, Grace Y., and Jerome E. Copulsky. 2007. "The Pledge of Allegiance and the Meanings and Limits of Civil Religion." *Journal of the American Academy of Religion* 75: 121–149.

Kelly, George Armstrong. 1984. *Politics and Religious Consciousness in America*. New Brunswick, N.J.: Transaction Books.

Kessler, Sanford. 1977. "Tocqueville on Civil Religion and Liberal Democracy." *Journal of Politics* 39: 119–146.

Kessler, Sanford. 1992. "Tocqueville's Puritans: Christianity and the American Founding." *Journal of Politics* 54: 776–792.

Kessler, Sanford. 1994. *Tocqueville's Civil Religion: American Christianity and the Prospects for Freedom*. Albany, N.Y.: State University of New York Press.

Kloppenberg, James T. 1998. *The Virtues of Liberalism*. New York: Oxford University Press.

Kloppenberg, James T. 2003. "From Hartz to Tocqueville: Shifting the Focus from Liberalism to Democracy in America." In *The Democratic Experiment: New Directions in American Political History*, ed. Meg Jacobs, William J. Novak, and Julian E. Zelizer, 350–380. Princeton, N.J.: Princeton University Press.

Koritansky, John C. 1990. "Civil Religion in Tocqueville's *Democracy in America*." *Interpretation* 17: 389–400.

Kramnick, Isaac, and R. Laurence Moore. 1996. *The Godless Constitution: A Moral Defense of the Secular State*. New York: W. W. Norton.

Lambert, Frank. 2003. *The Founding Fathers and the Place of Religion in America*. Princeton, N.J.: Princeton University Press.

Larmore, Charles. 1990. "Political Liberalism." *Political Theory* 18: 339–360.

Laycock, Douglas. 1990. "Formal, Substantive, and Disaggregated Neutrality toward Religion." *DePaul Law Review* 39: 993–1018.

Lienesch, Michael. 1988. *New Order of the Ages: Time, the Constitution, and the Making of Modern American Political Thought*. Princeton, N.J.: Princeton University Press.

Lienesch, Michael. 1993. *Redeeming America: Politics and Piety in the New Christian Right*. Chapel Hill, N.C.: University of North Carolina Press.

Lienesch, Michael. 2007. *In the Beginning: Fundamentalism, the Scopes Trial, and the Making of the Antievolution Movement*. Chapel Hill, N.C.: University of North Carolina Press.

Lincoln, Bruce. 2003. *Holy Terrors: Thinking about Religion after September 11*. Chicago, Ill.: University of Chicago Press.

Lubert, Howard L. 2004. "Benjamin Franklin and the Role of Religion in Governing Democracy." In *The Founders on God and Government*, ed. Daniel L. Dreisbach, Mark D. Hall, and Jeffry H. Morrison, 147–180. Lanham, Md.: Rowman & Littlefield.

Lutz, Donald S. 1980. *Popular Consent and Popular Control: Whig Theory in the Early State Constitutions*. Baton Rouge, La.: Louisiana State University Press.

Lutz, Donald S. 1984. "The Relative Influence of European Writers on Late Eighteenth-Century American Political Thought." *American Political Science Review* 78: 189–197.

Macedo, Stephen. 1990. "Liberal Civic Education and Religious Fundamentalism: The Case of *God v. John Rawls?*" *Ethics* 105: 468–496.

Macedo, Stephen. 1995. *Liberal Virtues: Citizenship, Virtue, and Community in Liberal Constitutionalism.* Oxford, UK: Clarendon Press.

Macedo, Stephen. 2000. *Diversity and Distrust: Civic Education in a Multicultural Democracy.* Cambridge, Mass.: Harvard University Press.

MacIntyre, Alasdair. 1981. *After Virtue: A Study in Moral Theory.* Notre Dame, Ind.: University of Notre Dame Press.

MacIntyre, Alasdair. 1988. *Whose Justice? Which Rationality?* Notre Dame, Ind.: University of Notre Dame Press.

Mansfield, Harvey C., Jr., and Delba Winthrop. 2006. "Tocqueville's New Political Science." In *The Cambridge Companion to Tocqueville,* ed. Cheryl B. Welch, 81–107. New York: Cambridge University Press.

Marsh, Charles. 2005. *The Beloved Community: How Faith Shapes Social Justice, from the Civil Rights Movement to Today.* New York: Basic Books.

Martin, David. 2005. *On Secularization: Towards a Revised General Theory.* Aldershot, UK: Ashgate.

Martin, William. 2003. "With God on Their Side: Religion and U.S. Foreign Policy." In *Religion Returns to the Public Square: Faith and Policy in America,* ed. Hugh Heclo and Wilfred M. McClay, 327–359. Washington, D.C.: Woodrow Wilson Center Press.

McClay, Wilfred M. 2004. "The Soul of a Nation." *The Public Interest* 155: 4–19.

McConnell, Michael W. 1992. "Religious Freedom at a Crossroads." *University of Chicago Law Review* 50: 115–194.

McConnell, Michael W. 2000a. "Believers as Equal Citizens." In *Obligations of Citizenship and Demands of Faith: Religious Accommodation in Pluralist Democracies,* ed. Nancy L. Rosenblum, 90–110. Princeton, N.J.: Princeton University Press.

McConnell, Michael W. 2000b. "The Problem of Singling Out Religion." *DePaul Law Review* 50: 1–47.

McGraw, Barbara A. 2003. *Rediscovering America's Sacred Ground: Public Religion and Pursuit of the Good in a Pluralistic America.* Albany, N.Y.: State University of New York Press.

McGraw, Barbara A. 2005. "Introduction to America's Sacred Ground." In *Taking Religious Pluralism Seriously: Spiritual Politics on America's Sacred Ground,* ed. Barbara A. McGraw and Jo Renee Formicola, 1–25. Waco, Texas: Baylor University Press.

McWilliams, Wilson Carey. 1973. *The Idea of Fraternity in America.* Berkeley, Calif.: University of California Press.

McWilliams, Wilson Carey. 1984. "The Bible and the American Political Tradition." In *Religion and Politics,* ed. Myron J. Aronoff, 11–46. New Brunswick, N.J.: Transaction Books.

McWilliams, Wilson Carey, and Marc K. Landy. 1984. "On Political Education, Eloquence and Memory." *PS: Political Science and Politics* 17: 203–210.

Mélonio, Françoise. 2006. "Tocqueville and the French." In *The Cambridge Companion to Tocqueville,* ed. Cheryl B. Welch, 337–358. New York: Cambridge University Press.

Milbank, John. 1991. *Theology and Social Theory: Beyond Secular Reason.* Oxford, UK: Blackwell.

Miller, Joshua. 1991. *The Rise and Fall of Democracy in Early America, 1630–1789.* University Park, Pa.: Pennsylvania State University Press.

Miller, Perry. 1939. *The New England Mind: The Seventeenth Century.* New York: Macmillan.

Miller, Perry. 1953. *The New England Mind: From Colony to Province.* Boston, Mass.: Beacon Press.

Mitchell, Joshua. 1995. *The Fragility of Freedom: Tocqueville on Religion, Democracy, and the American Future.* Chicago, Ill.: University of Chicago Press.

Mitchell, Joshua. 2006. "Tocqueville on Democratic Religious Experience." In *The Cambridge Companion to Tocqueville,* ed. Cheryl B. Welch, 276–302. New York: Cambridge University Press.

Monsma, Stephen V. 1993. *Positive Neutrality: Letting Religious Freedom Ring.* Westport, Conn.: Greenwood Press.

Monsma, Stephen V. 1996. *When Sacred and Secular Mix: Religious Nonprofit Organizations and Public Money.* Lanham, Md.: Rowman & Littlefield.

Morel, Lucas E. 2000. *Lincoln's Sacred Effort: Defining Religion's Role in American Self-Government.* Lanham, Md.: Rowman & Littlefield.

Morone, James. A. 2003. *Hellfire Nation: The Politics of Sin in American History.* New Haven, Conn.: Yale University Press.

Morrison, Jeffry H. 2004. "John Witherspoon's Revolutionary Religion." In *The Founders on God and Government,* ed. Daniel L. Dreisbach, Mark D. Hall, and Jeffry H. Morrison, 117–146. Lanham, Md.: Rowman & Littlefield.

Mouffe, Chantal. 2000. *The Democratic Paradox.* London: Verso.

Mouffe, Chantal. 2006. "Religion, Liberal Democracy, and Citizenship." In *Political Theologies: Public Religion in a Post-Secular World,* ed. Hent de Vries and Lawrence E. Sullivan, 318–326. New York: Fordham University Press.

Muñoz, Vincent Philip. 2004. "Religion and the Common Good: George Washington on Church and State." In *The Founders on God and Government,* ed. Daniel L. Dreisbach, Mark D. Hall, and Jeffry H. Morrison, 1–22. Lanham, Md.: Rowman & Littlefield.

Murphy, Andrew R. 2001. *Conscience and Community: Revisiting Toleration and Religious Dissent in Early Modern England and America.* University Park, Pa.: Penn State Press.

Murphy, Andrew R. 2005. "One Nation under God, September 11, and the Chosen Nation: Moral Decline and Divine Punishment in American Public Discourse." *Political Theology* 6: 9–30.

Murphy, Andrew R., and Jennifer Miller. 2006. "The Enduring Power of the American Jeremiad." In *Religion, Politics, and American Identity: New Directions, New Controversies,* ed. David S. Gutterman and Andrew R. Murphy, 49–72. Lanham, Md.: Rowman & Littlefield.

Murphy, Andrew R. 2009. *Prodigal Nation: Moral Decline and Divine Punishment from New England to 9/11.* Oxford, UK: Oxford University Press.

Nagel, Thomas. 1991. *Equality and Partiality.* Oxford, UK: Oxford University Press.

Neuhaus, Richard John. 1984. *The Naked Public Square: Religion and Democracy in America.* Grand Rapids, Mich.: William B. Eerdmans Publishing.

Noll, Mark A. 2002. *America's God: From Jonathan Edwards to Abraham Lincoln.* New York: Oxford University Press.

Norris, Pippa, and Ronald Inglehart. 2004. *Sacred and Secular: Religion and Politics Worldwide.* Cambridge, UK: Cambridge University Press.

Nurser, John S. 2005. *For All Peoples and All Nations: The Ecumenical Church and Human Rights.* Washington, D.C.: Georgetown University Press.

Nussbaum, Martha C. 1997. "Religion and Women's Human Rights." In *Religion and Contemporary Liberalism,* ed. Paul J. Weithman, 93–137. Notre Dame, Ind.: University of Notre Dame Press.

Nussbaum, Martha C. 1999. "A Plea for Difficulty." In *Is Multiculturalism Bad for Women?*, ed. Joshua Cohen, Matthew Howard, and Martha C. Nussbaum, 105–114. Princeton, N.J.: Princeton University Press.

Nussbaum, Martha C. 2000. *Women and Human Development: The Capabilities Approach.* Cambridge, UK: Cambridge University Press.

Nussbaum, Martha C. 2006. *Frontiers of Justice: Disability, Nationality, Species Membership.* Cambridge, Mass.: Harvard University Press.

Okin, Susan Moller. 1999. "Is Multiculturalism Bad for Women?" In *Is Multiculturalism Bad for Women?*, ed. Joshua Cohen, Matthew Howard, and Martha C. Nussbaum, 9–24. Princeton, N.J.: Princeton University Press.

Owen, J. Judd. 2001. *Religion and the Demise of Liberal Rationalism: The Foundational Crisis of the Separation of Church and State.* Chicago, Ill.: University of Chicago Press.

Owens, Erik C., John D. Carlson, and Eric P. Elshtain. 2004. *Religion and the Death Penalty: A Call for Reckoning.* Grand Rapids, Mich.: William B. Eerdmans Publishing.

Parekh, Bhikhu. 1999. "A Varied Moral World." In *Is Multiculturalism Bad for Women?*, ed. Joshua Cohen, Matthew Howard, and Martha C. Nussbaum, 69–75. Princeton, N.J.: Princeton University Press.

Perry, Michael J. 1991. *Love and Power: The Role of Religion and Morality in American Politics.* New York: Oxford University Press.

Perry, Michael J. 1997. *Religion in Politics: Constitutional and Moral Perspectives.* Oxford, UK: Oxford University Press.

Perry, Michael J. 2000. "Christians and Political Self-Restraint: The Controversy over Same-Sex Marriage." In *A Nation under God? Essays on the Future of Religion in American Public Life,* ed. R. Bruce Douglass and Joshua Mitchell, 177–202. Lanham, Md.: Rowman & Littlefield.

Perry, Michael J. 2003. *Under God? Religious Faith and Liberal Democracy.* Cambridge, UK: Cambridge University Press.

Perry, Michael J. 2007. *Toward a Theory of Human Rights: Religion, Law, Courts.* Cambridge, UK: Cambridge University Press.

Philpott, Daniel. 2001. "The Christian Case for Humanitarian Intervention." In *The Re-enchantment of Political Science: Christian Scholars Engage Their Discipline,* ed. Thomas W. Heilke and Ashley Woodiwiss, 225–255. Lanham, Md: Lexington Books.

Plantinga, Alvin. 1993. *Warrant and Proper Function.* New York: Oxford University Press.

Pottenger, John R. 1996. "Liberation Theology, Prophetic Politics, and Radical Social Critique: *Quo Vadis?*" In *Let Justice Roll: Prophetic Challenges in Religion, Politics, and Society,* ed. Neal Riemer, 133–154. Lanham, Md.: Rowman & Littlefield.

Pottenger, John R. 2005. "The Mormon Religion, Cultural Challenges, and the Good Society." In *Taking Religious Pluralism Seriously: Spiritual Politics on America's Sacred Ground,* ed. Barbara A. McGraw and Jo Renee Formicola, 103–126. Waco, Texas: Baylor University Press.

Pottenger, John R. 2007. *Reaping the Whirlwind: Liberal Democracy and the Religious Axis.* Washington, D.C.: Georgetown University Press.

Putnam, Robert. 2000. *Bowling Alone: The Collapse and Revival of American Community.* New York: Simon and Schuster.

Rambachan, Anantanand. 2005. "The Hindu Tree on America's Sacred Ground." In *Taking Religious Pluralism Seriously: Spiritual Politics on America's Sacred Ground,* ed. Barbara A. McGraw and Jo Renee Formicola, 173–190. Waco, Texas: Baylor University Press.

Rawls, John. 1971. *A Theory of Justice.* Cambridge, Mass.: Harvard University Press.

Rawls, John. 1993. *Political Liberalism.* New York: Columbia University Press.

Rawls, John. 1997. "The Idea of Public Reason Revisited." *University of Chicago Law Review* 64: 765–807.

Reuther, Rosemary Radford. 1996. "Prophetic Tradition and the Liberation of Women: A Story of Promise and Betrayal." In *Let Justice Roll: Prophetic Challenges in Religion, Politics, and Society,* ed. Neal Riemer, 59–69. Lanham, Md.: Rowman & Littlefield.

Riemer, Neal. 1984. *The Future of the Democratic Revolution: Toward a More Prophetic Politics.* New York: Praeger.

Riswold, Caryn D. 2004. "A Religious Response Veiled in a Presidential Address: A Theological Study of Bush's Speech on 20 September 2001." *Political Theology* 5: 39–46.

Rogers, William B. 1996. "Frederick Douglass, William Lloyd Garrison, and the Prophetic Tradition in Nineteenth-Century America." In *Let Justice Roll: Prophetic Challenges in Religion, Politics, and Society,* ed. Neal Riemer, 71–88. Lanham, Md.: Rowman & Littlefield.

Rorty, Richard. 1998. *Achieving Our Country: Leftist Thought in Twentieth-Century America.* Cambridge, Mass.: Harvard University Press.

Rosenblum, Nancy L. 2000. "*Amos*: Religious Autonomy and the Moral Uses of Pluralism." In *Obligations of Citizenship and Demands of Faith: Religious Accommodation in Pluralist Democracies,* ed. Nancy L. Rosenblum, 165–195. Princeton, N.J.: Princeton University Press.

Sandel, Michael. 1982. *Liberalism and the Limits of Justice.* Cambridge, UK: Cambridge University Press.

Sandel, Michael. 1996. *Democracy's Discontent: America in Search of a Public Philosophy.* Cambridge, Mass.: Harvard University Press.

Sandoz, Ellis. 1990. *A Government of Laws: Political Theory, Religion, and the American Founding.* Baton Rouge, La.: Louisiana State University Press.

Segars, Mary C. 2000. "Where Are We Now? 'The Catholic Moment' in American Politics." In *A Nation under God? Essays on the Future of Religion in American Public Life,* ed. R. Bruce Douglass and Joshua Mitchell, 111–133. Lanham, Md.: Rowman & Littlefield.

Selover, Thomas. 2005. "Confucianism on America's Sacred Ground." In *Taking Religious Pluralism Seriously: Spiritual Politics on America's Sacred Ground,* ed. Barbara A. McGraw and Jo Renee Formicola, 45–60. Waco, Texas: Baylor University Press.

Shain, Barry Alan. 1994. *The Myth of American Individualism: The Protestant Origins of American Political Thought.* Princeton, N.J.: Princeton University Press.

Sherratt, Timothy. 2001. "Rehabilitating the State in America: Abraham Kuyper's Overlooked Contribution." In *The Re-enchantment of Political Science: Christian Scholars Engage Their Discipline,* ed. Thomas W. Heilke and Ashley Woodiwiss, 121–148. Lanham, Md.: Lexington Books.

Shulman, George M. 2008. *American Prophecy: Race and Redemption in American Political Culture.* Minneapolis, Minn.: University of Minnesota Press.

Skillen, James W. 2005. *With or against the World? America's Role among the Nations.* Lanham, Md.: Rowman & Littlefield.

Smidt, Corwin, ed. 2003. *Religion as Social Capital: Producing the Common Good.* Waco, Texas: Baylor University Press.

Smith, Christian. 1998. *American Evangelicalism: Embattled and Thriving.* Chicago, Ill.: University of Chicago Press.

Smith, Christian, ed. 2003. *The Secular Revolution: Power, Interests, and Conflict in the Secularization of American Public Life.* Berkeley, Calif.: University of California Press.

Smith, Rogers M. 1993. "Beyond Tocqueville, Myrdal, and Hartz: The Multiple Traditions in America." *American Political Science Review* 87: 549–566.

Smith, Rogers M. 1997. *Civic Ideals.* New Haven, Conn.: Yale University Press.

Smith, Rogers M. 2008. "Religious Rhetoric and the Ethics of Public Discourse." *Political Theory* 36: 272–300.

Spragens, Thomas A., Jr. 1999. *Civic Liberalism: Reflections on Our Democratic Idealism.* Lanham, Md.: Rowman & Littlefield Publishers.

Spinner-Halev, Jeff. 2000. *Surviving Diversity: Religion and Democratic Citizenship.* Baltimore, Md.: Johns Hopkins University Press.

Stoner, James R. 2004. "Catholic Politics and Religious Liberty in America: The Carrolls of Maryland." In *The Founders on God and Government,* ed. Daniel L. Dreisbach, Mark D. Hall, and Jeffry H. Morrison, 251–271. Lanham, Md.: Rowman & Littlefield.

Stout, Jeffrey. 2001. *Ethics after Babel: The Languages of Morals and Their Discontents.* Princeton, N.J.: Princeton University Press.

Stout, Jeffrey. 2004. *Democracy and Tradition.* Princeton, N.J.: Princeton University Press.

Sturgeon, Noel. 1997. *Ecofeminist Natures: Race, Gender, Feminist Theory, and Political Action.* New York: Routledge.

Sullivan, Kathleen M. 1992. "Religion and Liberal Democracy." *University of Chicago Law Review* 59: 195–223.

Sunstein, Cass R. 1999. "Should Sex Equality Law Apply to Religious Institutions?" In *Is Multiculturalism Bad for Women?,* ed. Joshua Cohen, Matthew Howard, and Martha C. Nussbaum, 85–94. Princeton, N.J.: Princeton University Press.

Swaine, Lucas. 2006. *The Liberal Conscience: Politics and Principle in a World of Religious Pluralism.* New York: Columbia University Press.

Taylor, Charles. 1989. *Sources of the Self: The Making of Modern Identity.* Cambridge, Mass.: Harvard University Press.

Taylor, Charles. 2007. *A Secular Age.* Cambridge, Mass.: Harvard University Press.

Thiemann, Ronald F. 1996. *Religion in Public Life.* Washington, D.C.: Georgetown University Press.

Thiemann, Ronald F. 2000. "Public Religion: Bane or Blessing for Democracy?" In *Obligations of Citizenship and Demands of Faith: Religious Accommodation in Pluralist Democracies,* ed. Nancy L. Rosenblum, 73–89. Princeton, N.J.: Princeton University Press.

Tinder, Glenn E. 1989. *The Political Meaning of Christianity: An Interpretation.* Baton Rouge, La.: Louisiana State University Press.

Tinder, Glenn E. 2000. "Faith, Doubt, and Public Dialogue." In *A Nation under God? Essays on the Future of Religion in American Public Life,* ed. R. Bruce Douglass and Joshua Mitchell, 223–241. Lanham, Md.: Rowman & Littlefield.

Verba, Sidney, Kay Lehman Schlozman, and Henry E. Brady. 1995. *Voice and Equality: Civic Voluntarism in American Politics.* Cambridge, Mass.: Harvard University Press.

Villa, Dana. 2006. "Tocqueville and Civil Society." In *The Cambridge Companion to Tocqueville,* ed. Cheryl B. Welch, 216–244. New York: Cambridge University Press.

Waldron, Jeremy. 2002. *God, Locke, and Equality: Christian Foundations of John Locke's Political Thought.* New York: Cambridge University Press.

Walzer, Michael. 1983. *Spheres of Justice: A Defense of Pluralism and Equality.* New York: Basic Books.

Walzer, Michael. 1985. *Exodus and Revolution.* New York: Basic Books.

Warren, Heather. 1997. *Theologians of a New World Order: Reinhold Niebuhr and the Christian Realists, 1920–1948.* New York: Oxford University Press.

Weithman, Paul J. 2002. *Religion and the Obligations of Citizenship.* Cambridge, UK: Cambridge University Press.

West, Cornel. 1989. *The American Evasion of Philosophy: A Genealogy of Pragmatism.* Madison, Wisc.: University of Wisconsin Press.

West, Cornel. 1993. *Race Matters.* Boston, Mass.: Beacon Press.

West, Cornel. 1996a. "The Prophetic Tradition in Afro-America." In *Let Justice Roll: Prophetic Challenges in Religion, Politics, and Society,* ed. Neal Riemer, 89–100. Lanham, Md.: Rowman & Littlefield.

West, John G., Jr. 1996b. *The Politics of Revelation and Reason: Religion and Civic Life in the New Nation.* Lawrence, Kans.: University Press of Kansas.

White, Ronald C., Jr. 2002. *Lincoln's Greatest Speech: The Second Inaugural.* New York: Simon and Schuster.

White, Stephen K. 2000. *Sustaining Affirmation: The Strengths of Weak Ontology in Political Theory.* Princeton, N.J.: Princeton University Press.

Wilcox, Melissa M. 2006. "Discourse Bless America." In *Religion, Politics, and American Identity: New Directions, New Controversies,* ed. David S. Gutterman and Andrew R. Murphy, 25–47. Lanham, Md.: Rowman & Littlefield.

Williams, Rhys H., ed. 1997. *Cultural Wars in American Politics: Critical Reviews of a Popular Myth.* New York: Aldine de Gruyter.

Williams, Rhys H., and Susan M. Alexander. 1994. "Religious Rhetoric in American Populism: Civil Religion as Movement Ideology." *Journal for the Scientific Study of Religion* 33: 1–15.

Wills, Garry. 1990. *Under God: Religion and American Politics.* New York: Simon and Schuster.

Wills, Garry. 1992. *Lincoln at Gettysburg: The Words That Remade America.* New York: Simon and Schuster.

Wilson, John F. 1979. *Public Religion in American Culture.* Philadelphia, Pa.: Temple University Press.

Witte, John, Jr. 2004. "One Public Religion, Many Private Religions: John Adams and the 1780 Massachusetts Constitution." In *The Founders on God and Government,* ed. Daniel L. Dreisbach, Mark D. Hall, and Jeffry H. Morrison, 23–52. Lanham, Md.: Rowman & Littlefield.

Witte, John, Jr. 2005. *Religion and the American Constitutional Experiment: Essential Rights and Liberties.* 2nd ed. Boulder, Colo.: Westview Press.

Wolfe, Alan. 1998. *One Nation, After All: What Middle-Class Americans Really Think about God, Country, Family, Racism, Welfare, Immigration, Homosexuality, Work, The Right, The Left, and Each Other.* New York: Viking.

Wolin, Sheldon S. 2001. *Tocqueville between Two Worlds: The Making of a Political and Theoretical Life.* Princeton, N.J.: Princeton University Press.

Wolterstorff, Nicholas. 1997. "Why We Should Reject What Liberalism Tells Us about Speaking and Acting in Public for Religious Reasons." In *Religion and Contemporary Liberalism,* ed. Paul J. Weithman, 162–181. Notre Dame, Ind.: University of Notre Dame Press.

Wood, Gordon S. 1969. *The Creation of the American Republic, 1776–1787.* Chapel Hill, N.C.: University of North Carolina Press.

Woodiwiss, Ashley. 2001a. "Deliberation or Agony? Toward a Post-Liberal Christian Democratic Theory." In *The Re-enchantment of Political Science: Christian Scholars Engage Their Discipline,* ed. Thomas W. Heilke and Ashley Woodiwiss, 149–166. Lanham, Md.: Lexington Books.

Woodiwiss, Ashley. 2001b. "Rawls, Religion, and Liberalism." In *The Re-enchantment of Political Science: Christian Scholars Engage Their Discipline*, ed. Thomas W. Heilke and Ashley Woodiwiss, 65–83. Lanham, Md.: Lexington Books.

Woolpert, Stephen. 2005. "Greening America's Sacred Ground: Eco-spirituality and Environmental Politics." In *Taking Religious Pluralism Seriously: Spiritual Politics on America's Sacred Ground*, ed. Barbara A. McGraw and Jo Renee Formicola, 87–102. Waco, Texas: Baylor University Press.

Wuthnow, Robert. 1988. *The Restructuring of American Religion*. Princeton, N.J.: Princeton University Press.

Wuthnow, Robert. 1989. *The Struggle for America's Soul: Evangelicals, Liberals, and Secularism*. Grand Rapids, Mich.: William B. Eerdmans Publishing.

Wuthnow, Robert. 2005. *America and the Challenges of Religious Diversity*. Princeton, N.J.: Princeton University Press.

Yoder, John Howard. 1984. *The Priestly Kingdom: Social Ethics as Gospel*. Notre Dame, Ind.: University of Notre Dame Press.

Zuckert, Catherine. 1981. "Not by Preaching: Tocqueville on the Role of Religion in American Democracy." *The Review of Politics* 43: 259–280.

Zuckert, Michael. 1996. *The Natural Rights Republic: Studies in the Foundation of the American Political Tradition*. Notre Dame, Ind.: University of Notre Dame Press.

....

CHAPTER 5

CULTURE, RELIGION, AND AMERICAN POLITICAL LIFE

....

KENNETH D. WALD
AND DAVID C. LEEGE

Of all the terms commonly used when scholars discuss religion and American politics, none is so confusing nor as essential as *culture*. Virtually everybody who writes about the topic portrays religion as intimately tied to and expressive of culture, but each study offers a unique explanation of what is meant by the term. The student who delves into this literature encounters a bewildering array of views about what culture actually denotes. The problem is not unique to the analysis of religion in American political life. The meaning and significance of culture are strongly contested in all the social sciences regardless of the specific object of inquiry.

This chapter explores the role of religion in American culture and, ultimately, in political life. Reflecting the absence of any single authoritative understanding of culture, we utilize the concept in two different ways. We start with culture in its most traditional sense to encapsulate the content and meaning of core American values. In this holistic conceptualization, religion is an important element in the system of beliefs and values widely shared by the people of the United States. In the discipline of political science, culture has often been narrowed to refer only to core beliefs and values relevant to governance and public life. Accordingly, we focus our attention on the religious elements of American *political culture* or what is some-times called *American civil religion*.

Another section of the chapter explores culture and religion through an alternative framework. Recent work on culture has tended to see it not as a "thing" or "entity" attached to a plot of land or a group of people, as in the holistic understanding, but rather as a socially constructed process or form of relationship. The emphasis of this perspective is on culture as a distinct sphere of human activity in which society transmits meaning through specialized institutions that enable individuals to locate themselves in the social order. Most accounts of culture written from this viewpoint emphasize diversity rather than unity, asserting that multiple subcultures abound and brush up against each other in the social and political sphere. Consistent with this emerging perspective, this chapter thus considers culture as a source of identities and norms for behavior, and explores how such subcultures are mobilized on behalf of political ends. We conclude with thoughts on future research directions in the study of culture, religion, and politics.

Culture as a Concept

Before exploring how culture and religion intersect to influence American political life, we must first try to clarify culture as a concept. Reviewing how "culture" has been conceptualized and used by social scientists, William Sewell (1999) usefully distinguishes between two basic approaches. As Gupta and Ferguson (1992) explain, the older approach tends to associate culture with collectivities defined typically by either geography (e.g., French culture, the American South) or race and ethnicity (typified by, say, Arab culture). In this view, culture consists of the ultimate values that knit together people with some kind of common ancestral tie, real or imagined. Each such collectivity develops a distinct package of "knowledge, beliefs, and values" that demarcates the group from others (Kuper 1999, p. 16). Culture thus represents "a concrete and bounded world of beliefs and practices" that belongs to a group (Sewell 1999, p. 39). In some treatments of culture from this perspective, culture is portrayed as so deeply rooted, so fixed, such a quintessential trait of persons from a group, that it almost seems like a "natural" trait. (Viewing cultural traits as primordial qualities, likening them to biological or genetic factors, is known as *essentialism*.) It is that sense of the term—culture as a collective property—that we use, for the most part, in the sections devoted to religion as an element of American culture and as a source of its political culture. We label this traditional approach *holistic*, because it posits a common culture that suffuses a collectivity.

For at least two reasons, social scientists grew increasingly dissatisfied with this approach during the 1970s. First, culture seemed to be so vague and diffuse a concept that it could seemingly be stretched to describe almost anything that was not otherwise accounted for in theories of political behavior. Scholars almost reflexively attributed the residual variance in any analysis to the influence of "culture," reducing the concept to little more than a label. Aside from that shortcoming, other scholars wondered how something that seemed so durable and fundamental could explain political change. If culture was deeply rooted and durable, how could it be utilized to account for the dynamic nature of political development? Hence, political scientists began to explore alternative ways to think about the phenomenon of culture (Spiro 1987; Eckstein 1988; Wedeen 2002).

Rather than start with something entirely new, they drew on the idea of culture as a process, "a theoretically defined category or aspect of social life that must be abstracted out from the complex reality of human existence" (Sewell 1999, p. 39). Culture in this new key has to be distinguished from other causal agents such as "political and economic forces, social institutions, and biological processes" (Kuper 1999, p. xi). Culture so defined is distinctive in several aspects that have been elaborated by the advocates of the "cultural turn" in the 1980s and 1990s. For one thing, culture is *learned*. People are not born *with* a culture but *into* a culture that has to be created by humans and passed on from one generation to the next through the process of socialization. (This was not a new observation, but something given greater significance than it had enjoyed in the holistic approach.) As a distinct sphere of human learning, culture is about the infusion of *meaning*:

> Culture comprises the symbols and meanings that give coherence to a society; basically it constitutes those forms of expression that link individuals together by serving as a means of understanding how each group or individual relates to another. In this sense, culture or tradition is reproduced through a number of means (such as language) and acts like ballast, providing a sense of collectivity that holds individuals together. (Yengoyan 1986, p. 372)

Accordingly, scholars must pay attention to the "practices of meaning-making" (Wedeen 2002, p. 714) by the sphere of society that specializes in *transmission* of culture. This comprises institutions "devoted specifically to the production, circulation and use of meanings"—institutions that include education, art, literature, media, and, most important for our purposes, religion (Sewell 1999, p. 41). Furthermore, culture is typically expressed in terms of *myths* and *symbols*. Cultural ideas are most effectively communicated and understood not on the cognitive plane, but through affective symbols and images that evoke powerful emotional reactions—the American flag, the Twin Towers of 9/11, Willie Horton, the welfare mother, educated elites (eggheads, pointy-headed intellectuals, effete snobs, social planners), and so on. Culture is also expressed through *practice*. To take but one example, American private citizens who patrol the shared Mexican border and build fences to separate the United States from its southern neighbor call themselves "Minutemen," claiming common ancestry with the patriots who battled British colonial authorities at the time of the American Revolution. Theirs is a form of cultural labor intended to harness a powerful symbol on behalf of an exclusive definition of citizenship and law. Finally, culture is increasingly understood as *dynamic* rather than static, a redefinition that seriously subverts the holistic view of culture as largely fixed. Ann Swidler (1986) famously characterized culture as a "tool kit" of resources that can be drawn upon to cope with changing circumstances. Cultures grow, adapt, and adjust, providing individuals with no single road map, but instead with a plethora of templates to understand and respond to social change.

Even with these diverse approaches to culture, it seems obvious why religion and culture would intersect in scholarly accounts of religious influence on American politics. The holistic concept of culture as a package of ultimate values—"the whole body of practices, beliefs, institutions, customs, habits, myths and so on" that characterize a people (Sewell 1999, p. 40)—makes it virtually impossible to discuss American culture without referring to religion. If religion is central to culture, then it seems almost inevitable that religion contributes to American life and to core understandings about the purpose of governance. In this sense, religion is thought to be an integrative force that promotes consensus about political ends. The alternative approach to culture reminds us that religion can also be a force for difference and disintegration when it helps to form distinctive subcultures. Religions develop and promote meaning about such basic questions as the purpose of life and standards of behavior, meanings that may not be universally shared by all members of society. Virtually all cultures identify and demonize an "Other"—a group of people who are not "us"—and draw distinctions between themselves and outsiders as a means of boundary maintenance. Moreover, people often derive their notions of what political ideas logically "go with" religious values through education in religious institutions. In this sense, religion as culture may provide the basis for political disagreement and conflict. We need to consider both possibilities—that religion has the capacity to promote political cohesion and political difference.

RELIGION IN AMERICAN CULTURE

From the colonial period through the present day, European visitors to the United States have commented on the powerful current of religiousness that appears to affect all aspects of American life. The most celebrated foreign observer of American society, Alexis de Tocqueville, could not escape the pervasiveness of religion in the early American republic and described it as the first of American institutions (Bryant 2005). Tocqueville was not alone in this perception. Observers from abroad frequently echoed his assessment of the primacy of religion, one going so far as to label the United States "a nation with the soul of a church" (Chesterton 1922). Not all of these perceptive visitors respected the religious leavening of American culture, but few denied its palpable presence.

Whether we examine belief, belonging, or behavior, the religious motif of American culture remains quite striking today. Surveys of American opinion document that religious belief is widespread: Nearly all Americans profess a belief in God, anticipate an afterlife, and report that religion is important in their lives. Beyond these affirmations, which even Tocqueville suggested might have more to do with habit than conviction, religious zeal is also evident when Americans are asked by pollsters to assess various groups in society. Since the 1930s, the Gallup organization has asked Americans if they would vote for well-qualified presidential candidates from various minority groups defined by race, religion, gender, and other traits. In 2007, more Americans said they would refuse to vote for an atheist than for a candidate from any other group—including a homosexual (Jones 2007). In fact, an atheist was the *only* candidate in the survey who would draw electoral support from less than a majority of voters simply because of his or her religious (in this case, nonreligious) identity. According to a national survey by Edgell, Gerteis, and Hartmann (2006, p. 218), atheists topped the list of social groups whom Americans believe do *not* share their vision of society, leadings gays by almost two to one, and "recent immigrants" by three to one. In terms of social boundaries, more Americans would disapprove if their child wanted to marry an atheist (47.6 percent) than a Muslim (33.5 percent). As Edgell et al. (2006) conclude, part of what it means to be a "good American" to most citizens is some kind of religious faith, a perspective that seems to have changed rather little during the past half century (Herberg 1955).

For most Americans, religious belief is expressed through affiliation with religious organizations. Despite a tendency to venerate spirituality above "organized religion" (Wuthnow 1998), most Americans do in fact maintain some kind of connection with formal religious traditions. At the most abstract level, typically 80 percent to 90 percent of respondents to opinion surveys are willing to identify themselves with a specific local church, denomination, or religious tradition (Kosmin and Keysar 2006, p. 24). Although there are legitimate doubts about how accurately we can measure these kinds of things, somewhere between one half (Kosmin and Keysar 2006, p. 51) and two thirds (Winseman 2005) of adult Americans belong to churches, mosques, synagogues, and other religious institutions. That membership percentage far exceeds the equivalent figure from what some people imagine as the Golden Age of American religion during the late 18th century, when it is reckoned that less than one fifth of the population was similarly affiliated (Finke and Stark 1992). Church membership also dwarfs the level of affiliation with any other voluntary social institution in the United States, and is much higher in the United States than other countries (Curtis, Grabb, and Baer 1992).

What of the so-called "unchurched," the large percentage of Americans who do not belong to churches or otherwise affiliate religiously? One describes these people as "secular" with great reservation, because many if not most who fall in this category are not lacking religious belief nor are they hostile to religion at all. In fact, as Reimer (1995, p. 452) documented, strong majorities of Americans who rarely, if ever, attend church and foreswear religious labels nonetheless share beliefs in the existence of God, sin, the soul, life after death, and the efficacy of prayer. Although lack of religious attachment indicates anticlericalism in most societies, Americans who are religiously unfettered in organizational terms are not always different in their religious beliefs and behavior from the church affiliated. They may simply pursue their spiritual life through noninstitutional paths (Fuller 2001).

Saying one believes in God and or even writing a check to a religious organization are relatively passive activities, so one might legitimately wonder if we find the same high level of engagement when we turn to the realm of behavior.[1] Most Americans say that religion is important in their lives and figures prominently in their decision making.[2] Americans do not just join religious institutions; they participate in them. Roughly 4 in 10 Americans tell pollsters they have attended religious services each week, and the number would increase if we added persons who did not attend but watched or listened to religious broadcasts from home.

Apart from formal worship, Americans join congregational groups that serve a remarkably wide array of interests, participate on the boards and committees of religious institutions, and devote considerable time to volunteer work on behalf of religious concerns. Drawing on the tangible resources provided by congregants, religious institutions are by far the most favored source of and target for philanthropy (Brown, Harris, and Rooney 2004). Collectively, religious institutions spend more on social welfare activities, broadly defined, than any source other than the government. Religious institutions send abroad more representatives—disaster relief workers, missionaries, teachers, doctors, and other personnel—than the U.S. State Department (Nichols 1988, p. 21; McDonough 1994). In fact, the U.S. government is a primary source of funds for religiously connected nongovernmental organizations (NGOs) because of their reputation for efficient and effective social service delivery (Degeneffe 2003, p. 381). This trend was established long before the adoption of Charitable Choice and other efforts to increase the flow of federal funds to what have been called faith-based social service agencies.

Should these data be taken at face value to indicate that religion suffuses American life and culture? Among the many voices that argue otherwise, we can discern four broad critiques of American religiosity. Many foreign visitors who were impressed by the breadth of religious sentiment in the United States were equally strongly put off by its apparent lack of depth. (In Nebraska they have a saying that preachers, politicians, and the Platte River have two things in common—they are all a mile wide and a foot deep.) As surveys have repeatedly shown, Americans know remarkably little about religious doctrine, and often understand it in simplistic terms (Prothero 2007).[3] Moreover, they change denominational loyalties, if not religious traditions, quite frequently. All of these traits raise a question about the authenticity of such apparently shallow religiousness. Second, contemporary critics have argued that Americans do not practice what they preach or, rather, do not tell the truth about how often they hear preaching. According to careful observations of congregational worship, actual attendance at church services is well below the levels reported in surveys (Hadaway and Marler 2005).[4] The tendency to inflate attendance appears strongest among white evangelical Protestants and Catholics, two groups that report attendance rates well above the general population. The discovery that churches that place a premium upon attendance also generate the highest levels of inaccurate recall suggests that overreporting is a function of group cultural norms. In another assault on the image of the United States as a society with a deeply religious culture, various studies of "popular religiosity" show how Americans often believe doctrines and practice rituals that are inconsistent with the official views of their religious communities. Throughout history, for example, Americans have simultaneously participated in orthodox religious rites and dabbled in magic (Butler 1990). Nancy Reagan, the former first lady, was not the first avowed Christian who consulted an astrologer before making major decisions, even though such behavior is deemed heterodox within Christianity. Finally, some observers wonder how Americans can simultaneously pursue God and Mammon. Noting the strong emphasis on material values characteristic of American attitudes and behavior (McClosky and Zaller 1984), there is some doubt that people so focused on the here and now are truly influenced by deeper views about the ultimate purpose of life.

Although these criticisms certainly raise questions about the meaning of religiousness to many Americans, they do not necessarily cast fundamental doubt on the centrality of religion in American culture. It could just as easily be argued that many of the practices simply constitute a particularly American way of being religious. Consider the claim that Americans know very little about religion and act in heterodox ways. If one defines religiousness as familiarity with the details of religious doctrine, then the unfamiliarity of many Americans with their denominational creed surely undercuts the image of a nation with the soul of a church. However, observers going back to Tocqueville have noted that American religious intensity was not expressed via deep learning about denominational creeds, but rather focused on visions of common morality. Perhaps, as Johnson (2006) speculates, this lack of attentiveness to denominational niceties reflects a tradition in which preachers were "called" to the pulpit rather than trained for it in formal seminaries. In any case, Americans embrace what is sometimes called "religion in general," rather than making sharp distinctions between different denominations or sects. Changing from one local church or denomination to the next does not seem so significant in this environment.

By the same token, the ability of some Americans to believe in both traditionalist religious doctrine and alternate forms of folk spirituality seems quite common across the world. Elements of pagan worship styles—statuary, prayer to ancestors (saints) other than God—quickly took their place in Christianity. Many of the great Christian worship centers were built on the holy sites of other religions. Voodoo and animism accompany Christianity in many West African and Caribbean locales. Field goal kickers and free-throwers commonly make the sign of the cross before performing their decidedly nonreligious behavior—probably evidence of superstition. By distinguishing between "official" and "popular" religiosity in theoretical terms, the field of religious studies has demonstrated convincingly that belief in a church-prescribed creed is seldom the sole marker of strong religious identity. Even in the most doctrinaire churches, individuals often develop their own "practical" or "everyday" theologies that reflect personal experience and immediate concerns without in any way diminishing the importance of the church to them (Moon 2004).

The argument that Americans overstate their religious behavior—specifically, their rate of church attendance—is harder to dismiss but, from a cultural perspective, it seems more important that church attendance is deemed worthy enough to exaggerate. Survey research on truth-telling in surveys suggests that respondents are prone to exaggerate behavior that is valued highly, such as making charitable contributions and voting on election day (Cahalan 1968). That attendance at worship is similarly inflated attests obliquely to the continuing status of religious behavior as a highly valued activity.

Finally, the strong emphasis on both materialism and spirituality in American culture may seem strange, but is hardly evidence that religion is trivial. Max Weber (1958) noted the "elective affinity" between Protestantism and capitalist development in his famous "Protestant ethic" thesis. He contended that the Protestant Reformation put a premium on habits and behavior that could translate into entrepreneurial zeal and economic success, explaining the strong connection he observed in Europe between nations' Protestant affiliation and economic prosperity. In a religious tradition in which a person's status in the eyes of God could not be known for certain, material prosperity was often interpreted as evidence of God's grace. This "prosperity gospel" has become a powerful force in contemporary African American Protestantism and white Pentecostalism, and also in church growth dogma and televangelist preaching across traditions. Although this perspective can legitimately be considered "instrumental," using religion for purposes other than pure faith and moral uplift, it does not mean that religiousness is inauthentic.[5]

Having established the importance of religion in American culture, we now confront the puzzle of its persistence. The continuing strength of religious attachment in the United States, a key component of so-called "American exceptionalism" first noted by Tocqueville, has drawn attention from both scholars and foreign observers (Tiryakian 1982). As we just noted, some people "explain" the persistence of religion by casting doubt upon its seriousness or meaningfulness. However, those who take seriously the high level of religiousness in the United States still have to explain how it coexists with two other traits typically associated with low levels of religious commitment: modernity and a secular system of government. As a rule, the populations of economically developed nations with high rates of urbanization and education exhibit less attachment to traditional religious values (Wald and Calhoun-Brown 2006, pp. 8–9). The persistence of strong religious loyalties in a society that has long defined "modernity" runs counter to this pattern. The strength of religious sentiment and institutions in the United States also confounds observers who assume that a secular state must perforce be hostile to religion. The government of the United States is secular in at least two ways: the state does not endorse or subsidize religion (although at times it provides it with benefits such as property tax exemptions), and citizenship is not contingent on membership in any religious community. At the time of the founding, this feature was revolutionary because it contradicted the almost universal belief that strong religion required state patronage.

Scholars have offered multiple explanations for the persistence of traditional religion in what appears to be such an inhospitable environment. We will group them into (1) theories that highlight the "need" for religion as a consequence of American social and economic development, and (2) explanations that emphasize religious diversity as a spur to high levels of religiousness. The former are functional because they treat religion as a factor that remedies defects in American life whereas the latter are structural, identifying rules and institutions that enhance religious vitality.

An immigrant nation like no other, America drew people from many lands and its population continues to grow via immigration. For many immigrant groups, particularly in the first and second generations, the church and the party machine, often overlapping, functioned as institutions that addressed both immediate needs and the desire for fellowship. The church and precinct organizations were perhaps the only institutions where the poor immigrant could expect to be treated with dignity and respect. Detailed studies of contemporary immigrant churches and congregations demonstrate that they still meet the multiple social, economic, and cultural needs that would otherwise be unfilled in the lives of members (Min 1992; Nanlai 2005). Religion serves similar purposes for other Americans, Robert Booth Fowler (1989) has argued, because it supplies consolation otherwise lacking in American society. Although liberalism has been an important and constructive element in American life, he argues, its emphasis on the autonomy of the individual often leaves people without either a meaningful sense of community or clear standards for behavior. Religion thrives, Fowler (1989) asserts, because it addresses these important needs in a liberal society. It provides people with both a set of standards for living a morally upright life and a group of fellow believers with whom one can share fellowship. This approach can be understood as a more general version of the ethnic diversity argument.

The second functional explanation—economic and psychological insecurity—accepts the general argument about the negative relationship between religiousness and economic development, but accommodates the American experience to it. According to Norris and Inglehart (2004), traditional religion appeals most powerfully to people who experience existential stress and insecurity in their lives. As a consequence of the development of the welfare state and social safety net programs, people in more developed societies generally experience reduced risks to their lives and health, and have less need for religious consolation. However, Norris and Inglehart (2004) note that such conditions are not universal and that highly developed societies may nonetheless have substantial pockets of poverty. Moreover, despite a high level of societal affluence, Americans face considerable economic insecurity because the traditional Protestant emphasis on personal responsibility has retarded the growth of the welfare state. This forces many Americans to "face risks of unemployment, the dangers of sudden ill health without adequate private medical insurance, vulnerability to becoming a victim of crime, and the problems of paying for long-term care of the elderly" (Norris and Inglehart 2004, p. 108). Such a precarious state of affairs may reinforce belief in the supernatural as a means to ward off insecurity. Thus, the United States may fit the general model more closely than is realized.

The structural explanations deal explicitly with religious diversity. As a consequence of its immigrant population, the United States quickly became one of the most religiously heterogeneous societies in the world. The diversity was further strengthened by the development of new religious traditions by religious entrepreneurs (Marty 1984) and by new immigrants who carried with them religious traditions that were not well established in the United States (Eck 2001). This diverse religious environment, it has been argued, has created a virtual "religious marketplace," a "divine supermarket" (Ruthven 1989), that offered consumers a startling array of choices. This diversity forced the state to forego religious regulation. In most countries, where it was taken for granted that the nation had a particular religious identity and that the government was obligated to support it in various ways, the state typically granted one religion what amounted to monopoly status. State churches were—often still are (Fox 2007)—provided financial support in the form of tax support for church buildings, the education of church leadership, funding of clerical salaries, and so forth. Such provisions are often accompanied by limitations on competing religions, restrictions that further privilege the dominant religious tradition at the expense of alternative belief systems.

Drawing from economic theory, scholars liken such favored churches to "lazy monopolies" that are protected from competition by their own resources and regulations that hamper alternative traditions: Lacking incentives to appeal to a captured market, they simply refuse to innovate or to worry much about customer service (Stark and Finke 2000). Accordingly, religious enthusiasm withers. Before the Revolution, the American colonies typically followed this pattern by giving various benefits and legal privileges to certain religious groups (Borden 1984). The religious regulation that was common during the colonial period could not survive in the face of the robust growth of and enthusiasm for disfavored religions whose members demanded a state that would be neutral in matters of religion. By the early 1800s, the benefits of state patronage had been withdrawn in all the 13 states at the behest of religious groups who had grown dramatically and who resented state favoritism for their competitors (Lambert 2003; Gill 2008). Stripped of all privileges (with nonestablishment guaranteed), religions were placed on equal footing and forced to vie for adherents. The consequence, it is argued, is a religious sector in which institutions compete for market share by offering appeals that will capture the loyalties of citizens and in which some traditions prosper by identifying unfilled "niches." Some of the very qualities that seem to make American religion "thin"—the low level of doctrinal awareness or knowledge—may be a consequence of the pressure to simplify the product to compete successfully in an unregulated environment.

Having examined the centrality of religion to American culture, we now turn to the more explicitly political dimension. The next section of the chapter explores how the pervasiveness of religion in American culture affects the operation of the political system. The emphasis on religious diversity in this section of the chapter has raised an interesting and perplexing question about how a nation whose citizens follow so many different religious traditions manages, nonetheless, to hold together. Can a diverse religious heritage contribute to an integrated political tradition or does it necessarily undermine civic unity? For many scholars, the answer depends on the phenomenon of *civil religion*.

RELIGION AND CIVIC INTEGRATION

According to British historian Paul Johnson (2006, p. 18), "No one who studies the key constitutional documents in American history can doubt for a moment the central and organic part played by religion in the origins and development of American republican government" (see Witte [1990] for details). The strength of religion in American culture has translated into political ideas. During the colonial period, when the Bible was by far the most common book in the United States, and public discussion was couched in religious language, certain religious ideas exerted a powerful impact on the nature of governance (Lutz 1984). The biblical covenant became a model for the voluntary associations formed by early settlers (Lutz 1994). The founders justified democracy and a republican form of government on the basis of the Christian notion of original sin (Wright 1949). If no person was above temptation, as they believed, government could not be entrusted to a single person (a monarch or elected official) and would best operate if authority was divided among multiple centers of institutional power, each jealous to defend its own prerogatives. Thus, the concept of separation of powers was justified by reference to widely shared religious doctrines, and religious thinking provided one set of influences that affected the design of the state. But in time, as secular justifications gained more influence, the role of religion became politically significant primarily by how it helped define and maintain America's national identity as a democratic nation.

Although it is easy to take for granted how religion contributes to American unity and the persistence of democracy, a glance around the globe dispels any idea that such a connection is automatic. The U.S. invasion of Iraq and the removal of Saddam Hussein created a power vacuum that was filled, in part, by religious communities. The consequence was something that looked a great deal like a civil war based on competing sects of Islam (with an ethnic Kurdish component on the side). If Iraq seems familiar, it is because so many states have similarly experienced civil war in which religion defined the contestants. The breakup of the former Yugoslavian state produced a bloody internal conflict in which Orthodox Serbs fought Muslims and Catholic Croats. Lebanon has periodically been fractured by Christian–Muslim hostility, whereas the contest in Northern Ireland has pitted Protestants against Catholics. Algeria and Turkey have struggled with yet another variant of religious competition—near civil war between Muslims who call for state adoption of Islamic identity and secularists who want no such mingling of mosque and state. Postcolonial India, a land mass containing an enormous range of ethnic groups, tribes, and religions, was fractured into two nations—one primarily Hindu (India) and one Islamic (Pakistan), and a region (Kashmir) that remains a festering conflict. East and West Pakistan, separated geographically, soon became distinct nations—Pakistan and Bangladesh (which involved many Christians). All three resulting nations are frequently unsettled by communal warfare. These examples suggest that religious differences are incendiary forces that can easily overwhelm a political system because they involve deep matters of faith that simply cannot be compromised (Rose and Urwin 1969). That insight has become the basis for an influential school of thought that anticipates a post-Cold War era of civilizational conflict, with religion as the cultural basis of contestation (Huntington 1996).

So why has the United States escaped the same fate? At times and in certain places, religion has certainly stimulated or justified political violence in American life. Anti-Catholic riots were a common occurrence during the 19th century. Unconventional religions like Mormonism encountered state-sponsored violence during their formative period, and some people believe that same dynamic was responsible for the federal government's 1993 onslaught against the Branch Davidian compound in Waco, Texas (Tabor and Gallagher 1995). Although the Civil War was not fundamentally about religion, it took on added ferocity because northerners and southerners alike believed fervently that God was on their side (Woodworth 2001). The Ku Klux Klan, born in the Reconstruction South as a mechanism of white resistance to black freedom, and reborn in the 1960s in response to the civil rights movement, actually reached its peak of national power in the 1920s, when it appealed most strongly to those fundamentalist Protestants who feared the insidious effects of Catholic and Jewish immigrants on the American character (Jackson 1967). The nativism of the Klan has found an echo in the so-called patriot movement that has promoted and inspired various acts of violence since the 1960s (Aho 1991). The liberalization of abortion laws in 1972 has also stimulated isolated assaults against abortion providers and property (Blanchard and Prewitt 1993).

Despite these outbreaks, the United States stands out by the ease with which the political system has accommodated religious differences. The influential British weekly *The Economist* recently rendered such a verdict with its backhanded compliment that America "has mastered the politics of religion at home, but not abroad" ("Lesson from America" 2007, p. 21). Scholars from Tocqueville onward recognized that much of the activity that sustained a viable democracy would come from civil society, including religion. For Tocqueville, religious institutions would nurture respect for others and provide transcendent standards of justice by which to measure the effects of legislation. He contrasted the kinds of Puritan and low-church Protestantism dominant in the young United States with the Catholicism dominant in France. He liked the fact that rank in the community— knowing who to trust in economic bargains and to whom to entrust political authority—paralleled the hurdles of membership in religious congregations. It instilled active behavior rather than the passivity of receiving sacraments for the remission of sin, while expecting priests to be hired holy men. Given the separation of powers, multiple levels of government, the minimization of the state, and the penchant of organizations in the civil society to solve collective problems, he did not spend much time worrying about the threat of religious fanaticism to the viability of the American democratic experiment.

To explain American exceptionalism further, contemporary scholars have deployed what might be considered both negative and positive explanations. That is, some theories argue that the United States lacks qualities that have made religion such a lethal political force elsewhere, whereas others argue that religion has been a cohesive force in and of itself.

Students of religiously based political conflict have suggested at least two reasons why the American experience has differed from the global model. One explanation distinguishes between plural societies—states in which conflict is essentially limited to two competing groups—and pluralistic states with high levels of fractionalization (Rabushka and Shepsle 1972). In places with just two major players, politics is likely to be a zero-sum game, such that a victory by one side produces defeat for the other. The side with fewer resources—population, wealth, power—is likely to lose every election and thus has little or no incentive to partici- pate in conventional politics. Options such as secession or terrorist action make more sense as a minority strategy in such environments. However, when the population is extremely fragmented, as in the United States, when there are many different religious communities and politically relevant differences such as race and region that further fracture the population, no single group is likely to win consis- tently. Diversity encourages a politics of coalition formation and logrolling: Groups cohere on the basis of common interests but divide and re-form new groupings as interests change. Political participation offers a chance to small groups.

Nevertheless, despite the presence of religious pluralism within the American context, some scholars believe that religion actually serves to integrate Americans. The 19th-century social theorist Emile Durkheim argued that religion should be understood as a means by which societies develop common myths to sustain national unity (Pals 2006, chap. 3). The nation is treated not as a mere collection of people who live together, but as a force sanctioned by the divine and serving a larger purpose than mere security or collective self-interest. By sanctifying the state, this so-called "civil religion" constitutes "a projection by a civic order of its experiences and values onto the cosmic order for the sake of social solidarity. It is, so to speak, society worshiping the image of itself, from the bottom up" (Stackhouse 2004, p. 291).[6] Despite its religious diversity, it is argued, the United States has developed its civil religion by selecting common elements of various creeds to unite people around a shared identity. This is not a collection of sectarian doctrines that compete in any way with religious traditions, but rather a culture of its own that transcends differences that otherwise divide Americans into compet- ing religious communities.

Discerning the content of a concept as vague as *civil religion* is challenging. In a broad sense, as Robert Bellah (1966) argued in his classic statement about the phenomenon, civil religion is the common belief that the United States stands for something more noble than self-interest. In the eyes of its citizenry, the nation embodies humankind's aspirations for freedom and peace. Leroy Rouner (1999, p. 4) distilled the essence of the civil religious creed from the Declaration of Independence and the Constitution. In his view, it comprised the values of sacrifice, loyalty, brotherhood, sisterhood, and freedom. These are the values repeatedly invoked and venerated in American political discourse, especially in moments of national crisis such as the aftermath of the 9/11 attacks. Like religions in general, civil religion has holidays (Memorial Day, the Fourth of July), monuments like the Constitution and Lincoln Memorial (Meyer 2001), temples and priests (the Supreme Court), solemn rites (inauguration, citizenship ceremonies), sacred relics in the form of the flag (Welch 2002), and a corpus of popular music (Meizel 2006). With such a civil religious background, patriotism is as much love of the American Idea as of America the country. To become American is to assent to this idea. Hence becoming an American does not require the sacrifice of any religious beliefs or conversion to other gods. America does not have civic religion—a common dogma enforced by the power of the state—but a civil religion that sustains the political order through voluntary absorption and personal commitment (Rouner 1999, p. 5).

How do we know this rather poetic construct is real or that it matters to the maintenance of national identity and political cohesion? To avoid a circular argument—the survival of the United States "proves" that it has a common religiously based political culture—there needs to be some evidence that assesses the civil religion hypothesis. Scholars have searched for that evidence in American political culture by using such disparate research tools as participant observation, survey research, and ethnographic studies. Several scholars have parsed the content of American political rhetoric in search of civil religious themes. Presidential inaugural addresses and similar political addresses have been especially fertile territory for such analysis because the occasion seems ripe for recitations of core American values (Toolin 1983; Linder 1996; Hansen 2006). A number of community surveys have reported widespread public agreement with such themes as American destiny, the sacredness of freedom, the religious status of the Constitution, and the like (Wimberly 1976; Christenson and Wimberly 1978; Wimberly 1979). Smidt (1980, 1982) found similar sentiments widespread among American school children. Participant observation techniques used by Gamoran (1990) also found some evidence that civil religion is an important motif in schools, socializing institutions that play an important role in providing meaning for young people. When they content analyzed the publications of a major fraternal organization, Jolicoeur and Knowles (1978) discovered persistent repetition of major civil religion themes (but see Thomas and Flippen 1972).

Although civil religion appears to exist as an integrative factor, it has also been cited as a destructive influence on American political life. Some critics believe that civil religion is nothing more than "a form of patriotic self-celebration"

(Stackhouse 2004, p. 275), mere religious nationalism that leads to excessive pride, an aversion to self-criticism, and a degree of nationalist assertion that disfigures American foreign policy. How can one criticize "God's country" without criticizing God? Scholars associated with the influential "realist" school of international relations contend that moral considerations undermine the rational pursuit of national self-interest and call on the United States to forego such pursuits, molding foreign policy around power rather than rectitude (Donnelly 2000).

Defenders of civil religion believe that it has a built-in self-correcting mechanism. At its best, Bellah (1966) argued, civil religion is a blend of two impulses. The priestly dimension of civil religion does indeed amount to a kind of blessing of the country, emphasizing that it is a force for good. But alongside the tendency to endow the nation with transcendent qualities, civil religion also contains a prophetic element. The idea of a nation "under God" means both that the nation enjoys divine sanction *and* that it is responsible to divine authority in the exercise of power. Each dimension should balance the other.

The two components may fuse in the idea that the United States will continue to enjoy the blessings of Providence only so long as it acts consistently with biblical morality. Critics of both the Left and Right have found reasons to chastise the nation for straying from the main path. Both Abraham Lincoln and Martin Luther King argued that the United States had abandoned Divine will, first by tolerating slavery and then by accepting the oppression of blacks after Emancipation. During the Vietnam era, war critics argued that U.S. behavior violated accepted codes of morality. With the rise of Christian conservatism a decade later, the same logic undergirded critiques of American social policy. By tolerating such moral outrages as abortion, homosexuality, drug use, and sexual experimentation, some movement leaders argued, America had forfeited God's protection. As an extreme but no means atypical expression of that view, two prominent Protestant televangelists explicitly interpreted the 9/11 attacks as God's punishment for American licentiousness. Recently, a sectarian group in Kansas has disrupted the funerals of American soldiers killed in Iraq by arguing that the soldiers were punished for America's willingness to tolerate homosexuality.

Even though Bellah (1966) identified both priestly and prophetic components as necessary for a constructive civil religion, it may be that essentially two different civil religions have developed (Wuthnow 1988). The priestly civil religion tends to venerate the United States and assumes that it is on the side of the angels. Such a perspective, described by Bellah (1966, p. 16) as "an American Legion–type of ideology that blends God, country, and flag" is relatively intolerant of any self-criticism. With that kind of perspective, some defenders of the American mission in Iraq publicly cloaked the mission in religious terms, effectively rendering disagreement with the war as tantamount to support for terrorism (Boyer 2005). On the popular side, a substantial part of religious America argued that George W. Bush, a man of God, was chosen by God to lead this Christian nation in a time of trials against fundamentalist Islam. The alternative prophetic tradition constantly holds the nation up to high standards of morality and finds that it invariably falls short—whether its intervention is meant to stop genocide in Bosnia by defending Muslims or to take sides in the Muslim civil war that has overtaken Iraq. Taken to extremes, as it has been from time to time, this approach may simply paralyze action by arguing that American intervention always involves self-interest and material gain rather than a higher purpose, and the nation should thus refrain from any military engagements outside its borders. Neither perspective is particularly useful alone because of what it refuses to see or consider.

The debate over civil religion reminds us that deep-seated cultural values may divide as easily as they unite. In the next section, we turn to cultural differences as source of political conflict and competition. This section will draw heavily on the newer stream of cultural studies outlined earlier in the chapter.

CULTURAL DIFFERENCES IN AMERICAN POLITICS

The cultural turn in social science (Bonnell and Hunt 1999) called attention to the multiplicity of cultural conflicts and forms that persist in most societies. This research emphasizes the divisive capacity of group differences in society, politics, and economics. This reality is most apparent when we shift focus from political culture as a holistic phenomenon to ongoing cultural conflicts that arise over specific issues, policies, and campaigns.

Long before social scientists rediscovered the divisive aspects of culture, historians had already noted its potency in American political life. Beginning with the work of Lee Benson and Samuel Hays in the 1950s (see Swierenga, chapter 3, this volume), historians began to challenge conventional wisdom about the dominance of economic interests in American political development. A new school of "ethno-cultural" political analysis called attention to ethnic and religious communities as key forces in party competition (McCormick 1974). Most important, this stream of research joined social and political history by demonstrating that many political issues were at base conflicts over ultimate values rooted in cultural understandings. For example, northern workers opposed slavery not simply on economic grounds but because it offended their ideas about the nobility of free labor and encouraged immoral behavior by slaveholders (Holt 1969; Oestreicher 1988). Battles over free trade were similarly rendered into broader symbolic contests over competing ways of life that touched on deeply held communal values. The Cold War was not solely a competition between different styles of economic policy, but rather, in the eyes of some protagonists, a larger struggle between Godliness and atheism (Canipe 2003). This work usefully broadened the discussion of culture beyond a single-minded focus on overtly religious issues.

Unlike history, however, political science was slow to appreciate the political significance of cultural differences rooted in religious understanding. At the time American political science developed as a discipline in the late 19th century, religion was often thought to be a relic of the past, a form of tribalism to be overcome, not a positive force contributing to democratic development, as it had been at Tocqueville's time. In part this reflected the heavy Hegelian and post-Hegelian influence on the American academy. In part it reflected the liberation from old binding sources through the higher education of the sons of families wealthy enough to send them to college. Even the social science professoriate, drawn disproportionately from children of mainline Protestant clergy (Ross 1991; Fox 1993), saw science as the solution to social ills, and religion as a limiting force that created a false consciousness. It is no surprise then that neither the most influential work in comparative politics with "culture" in its title, Almond and Verba's (1965) *The Civic Culture*, nor its successors, paid much attention to religious institutions and religious values as positive or negative forces for democracy.[7]

The awareness of religion as a basis of cultural politics first seeped into political science through the subfield of public policy. Focusing more intently on a class of disputes over what became known as "morality politics," political scientists have investigated the roots of this apparently unique and quintessentially American style of political conflict (Meier 1994; Clark and Hoffman-Martinot 1998; Sharp 1999; Morone 2003; Tatalovich and Daynes 2005). These studies have drawn on the seminal work of Daniel Elazar (1984), who argued that differences in the style and content of public policy among the American states often reflected settlement patterns that went far back in time. Ethnic groups carried with them divergent moral cultures as they migrated across North America, each bringing a distinctive ethos to the area where its members concentrated. This insight fueled a surge of studies demonstrating a powerful linkage between social composition (typically operationalized by ethnic and religious profiles) and public policy adoption (summarized in Meier 1994). In time, scholars developed a general model of morality politics that differentiated it from other forms of conflict (see Koopman, chapter 20, this volume). Such conflict was largely unrelated to tangible economic interests, focused more heavily on symbolic debates over ultimate moral values, and typically engaged a wider array of actors than other kinds of political issues (Mooney 2001). A particularly compelling theory of political parties uses morality politics, narrowly defined, to show how party goals and composition changed during the latter half of the 20th century (Layman 2001).

A sociologist, James Davison Hunter (1991), provided a general framework for this literature through his work on "culture wars." Although the phrase was borrowed from 19th-century German politics (and mistranslated *Kulturkampf*, as *Kampf* became "wars" instead of "enduring struggles"), the concept itself was an extended version of "New Class" theory popularized by some sociologists in the 1970s (Bruce-Biggs 1979; Kellner and Berger 1992). New Class theorists argued that modernity had given rise to a new set of social actors whose principal task was symbol manipulation. These new professionals—university professors, social workers, journalists, public school teachers, and the like—were said to constitute a distinctive stratum that was not tied to traditional institutions. With an essentially oppositional perspective on American life, it was claimed, they set out to undermine traditionalist institutions and values. They were able to mount an effective attack on older verities by virtue of their concentration in key sectors of cultural socialization—education, the mass media, government, and so on. New Class theory, which relied on a large number of assertions that were belied by careful academic investigation (Brint 1994), became part of Hunter's culture war model.

In Hunter's (1991) version of culture war theory, there are two broad camps—defined by their differing notions of moral authority—contesting for public supremacy in the United States. One bloc, committed to traditional values anchored in belief in a transcendent God, defends moral values in public life. It competes with a "progressive" alliance, essentially the New Class, some of which want nothing of religion or moral suasion in public life and others of which see morality as compelling yet situational. This battle between the two camps is joined over questions about sexuality, the flag, drug use, and other symbols of public morality. To some degree, this underlying conflict is really an ongoing debate about the 1960s (Himmelfarb 1999). In the eyes of traditionalists (or, as Hunter [1991] labeled them, the "orthodox"), the '60s spawned a variety of social movements that undercut traditional values and introduced damaging alternative lifestyles to Americans. Those who feel to the contrary, a group labeled "progressives," contend that the '60s represented cultural revitalization, embrace the new trends, and continue to question received cultural norms long after the decade has passed. However, not all who initially embraced the spirit of the 1960s remained in that camp. Observers have suggested that so many of the '60s generation later "found" churches and religious values because drugs, music, and sex failed to answer ultimate questions about meaning and behavior (Tipton 1982). One reason Hunter's (1991) *Culture Wars* was found compelling by many is that he developed a typology of cultural differences in the origin and binding nature of authority for an anomic society.

The language of culture war was soon picked up by political elites as a rallying cry and was reflected in journalism through simplistic red state–blue state terminology. Whatever the label, the perspective assumes a massive increase in polarization at both the elite and mass levels, fueled by cultural differences, that has generated a new and somewhat toxic politics of conviction.

On the whole, Hunter's work (1991), like New Class theory, has not fared well in empirical research. On the one hand, one cannot deny the seeming growth in irreligion among many people in the younger age cohorts as a product of advanced education.[8] The emergence of this sector offers an appealing target for politicians who want to inflame cultural tensions. By the same token, there has been a growth in polarization among the mass electorate (Green, Guth, Smidt, and Kellstedt 1996; Abramowitz and Saunders 2005; Campbell 2005; Nivola and Brady 2006). Yet, whether using in-depth interviews in local communities or sample surveys of the entire population, scholars have raised strong doubts that the American public (as opposed to elites) is deeply polarized, that such differences reflect cultural fault lines that threaten the stability of the country, or that such differences drive political conflict beyond a narrow range of issues (compare with Olson and Carroll

1992; Carroll 1995; Davis and Robinson 1996; Evans 1997; Williams 1998; Wolfe 1998; Miller and Hoffmann 1999; Fiorina 2005; Bartels 2006; Layman and Green 2006). As Nicholas J. Demerath (2001, p. 166), trenchantly observed after a global tour of states like Rwanda, Lebanon, and Northern Ireland that were torn apart by ethnoreligious differences, "applying the phrase 'culture war' to the United States makes a mockery of nations elsewhere that fulfill the criteria all too well." This is not to deny that American politics reflects cultural *differences*, which are not the same thing as culture war, nor to challenge evidence that religious communities have group affinities in the voting booth. Rather, culture war theory is simply too broad and theoretically underdeveloped to capture the complexity of cultural tensions in the American polity.

One important alternative to culture war theory, represented by the scholarship of Ronald Inglehart (1990, 1997), called readers' attention to materialist and post-materialist values in advanced industrial societies. In Inglehart's view, cultural values largely reflect the social conditions in which people are raised. Those who come of age in periods of war and economic deprivation will prize political order and affluence above all such social values, preferring political movements that give priority to those ends. On the other hand, people raised in times when political order and affluence can be taken for granted—the post-World War II cohorts in most western democracies— look to politics for what Abraham Maslow called "self-actualization." They care passionately about quality-of-life issues and freedom of expression, and judge politi-cal movements accordingly. This divide creates a tension between traditionalism—in which religion may well be a constitutive element—and progressivism, which might incorporate secularist viewpoints. Inglehart (1990, 1997) argues that this latent con-flict underlies political conflict in many societies.

For all their insights, neither of these approaches to culture explains how culture is drawn into the political realm. This defect of culture war theory has prompted scholars to pay more attention to the process by which cultural tensions are translated into social and political debates, drawing on the "culture as process" approach that was identified early in the chapter. Unlike Hunter (1991) and others who seem to think that religion is the basis of culture and somehow becomes automatically ingrained in partisan conflict, this alternative scholarship has at-tempted to break down the steps involved in politicizing cultural differences. Aaron Wildavsky's (1987) seminal article set the stage by reminding political scientists that there are several viable cultural traditions in American life that provide answers to the existential questions that all people face: questions of identity, behavior, and boundaries. At any time, advocates of these various perspectives may be engaged in political efforts to enshrine their own cultural values as public policy.

The great virtue of Wildavsky's (1987) work was to emphasize the role of social construction in cultural debates. Such conflicts are not natural or inevitable, but must be treated as variable. Most social practices are not intrinsically offensive to alternative cultures, but have to be framed in certain ways so that they resonate politically. In like manner, Swidler (1986) spoke of culture as a tool kit from among many optional answers about a moral order. Alternate choices could be used by elites or groups to justify statuses in the social order. In the hands of political elites, choices can be quite fluid. In 1980, Ronald Reagan ran for the Republican presidential nomination as a pro-life candidate, although as governor of California he had signed a very permissive abortion bill into law. George H. W. Bush, Reagan's successor, was pro-choice in 1980, but by 1988 he had converted into the pro-life candidate. Senator Al Gore of Tennessee was pro-life in those days but became pro-choice by the time he ran for president in 2000. Former Massachusetts governor Mitt Romney has undergone similar "learning" experiences as he changed his policy positions in a way that conforms more closely to those of his party's electoral bases in the 2008 presidential campaign. Fluid selection among the tool kit of values is probably more common among ambitious political elites than among the general public (Beck and Parker 1985). Conversion of politicians' positions to conform to the cultural values of strategic sectors of the electoral base is implicated in both Layman's (2001) and Gill's (2008) treatment of party transformation and politicians' interests.

The work of cultural education takes place in a variety of social institutions— schools, churches, voluntary associations, and so forth. Whatever the locale, individuals must learn to think of themselves as members of a community or subculture, develop grievances linked to their personal identity, locate the source of their unhappiness, and develop an overarching cognitive framework—a schema— that tells them how best to respond to the grievance. This can certainly happen in religious environments. Kristi Andersen (1988) recounted interviews with Ohio women active in the movement against the proposed Equal Rights Amendment (ERA) to the U.S. Constitution. These activists did not oppose the ERA until they understood it as a fundamental challenge to their worldview. That is, they first needed to perceive this legal provision as part of a larger onslaught on the proper moral order governing the social roles of men and women. The ERA became linked in their minds to such unsettling social trends as liberalized abortion law, tolerance and celebration of homosexuality, easy divorce, and the embrace of moral relativism in public education. Rather than a simple measure that empowered women, they came to view the ERA as an important pillar of cultural degradation and a revolt against God's law. This transformation occurred under the tutelage of clergymen and conservative political activists who helped the women link their concern about several moral trends to the underlying "threat" posed by the amendment. Catholic women, who were more likely to be employed outside the home than other women and who would have had a stronger interest in equal pay for equal work, were recruited to both the antiabortion movement (Luker 1984) and the anti-ERA movement by means of a similar process (Mansbridge 1986; Leege, Wald, Krueger, and Mueller 2002).

The centrality of public education as a venue of cultural transmission accounts for the sometimes ferocious political conflicts that arise in this domain. If one understands public education not as a place merely for the inculcation of tangible skills that enhance one's economic prospects, but as an environment in which cultural values are propagated, the stakes over control become much easier to appreciate (Peshkin 1987; Rose 1987). That is why, for example, traditionalist groups are vigilant in monitoring what they see as cultural pollution in public school curricula. Numerous conflicts have broken out over the adoption of texts that emphasize such progressive ideas as autonomy, skepticism, gender equality, and relativism—values seen to be in conflict with such religiously sanctioned ideas as self-discipline, self-control, gender complementarity, and immutable truths grounded in revealed religion. The exclusion of state-sponsored religious exercises from public schools at the behest of the U.S. Supreme Court, a trend that progressives celebrate as a victory for free inquiry, strikes some traditionalists instead as a policy that excludes their cultural perspectives from the public realm. The emergence of antidiscrimination policies that cover sexual orientation, gay-friendly curricula, and gay-themed student organizations similarly is taken as evidence that control over socialization has been captured by advocates of immorality. For various reasons, including both the content and quality of education provided, some parents choose to remove their children from what they denounce as "government schools" in favor of home schooling or religious schools, where their personal or group values will be propagated and reinforced. All these tensions can be understood as conflicts over controlling the authoritative transmission of meaning to young people.

In the political realm, this framing is often done effectively on a mass scale by extralegal (meaning unofficial) social movements, a term that denotes organizations and constituents who mobilize to achieve broad social goals. Such movements are not created out of whole cloth, but usually capitalize upon the links of communication, social interaction, and cultural values of preexisting institutions. This process of identity creation, grievance generation, and interpretive framework has been on display in the movement to restrict illegal immigration by people from Mexico (Preston 2007). In mid 2007, the Republican president urged Congress to enact a comprehensive bill that would, among other provisions, permit immigrants who had crossed the border illegally to apply for citizenship after demonstrating a period of good behavior and paying a fine. This produced a firestorm of cultural rage. Grassroots activists who opposed legislation granting what they called "amnesty" to illegal immigrants repeatedly described themselves as ordinary, hardworking Americans who followed the law and played by the rules. Ranged against them, "the Others" were identified as a subculture of "undeserving immigrants who do not speak English and would soon become a burden on public services that Americans need in a time of economic uncertainty." Although economic resources were part of the argument, the conflict was not simply or primarily about tangible resources (Citrin, Green, Muste, and Wong 1997). Rather, the rhetoric of immigration opponents was suffused with the kind of normative language typically found in cultural conflicts. Despite an emphasis on "taking care of our own people first," many of the activists who fought the bill had limited encounters with illegal immigrants and could not identify any personal harm they had suffered on that account. Rather than focus on self-interest, they objected in cultural terms, in terms of right and wrong, to the proposal that would, in their eyes, degrade the value of American citizenship and thus undermine the moral order of Americanism.

They publicized their views through websites and talk radio programs, and recruited like-minded friends and neighbors from organizational networks, public demonstrations, gun shows, and other venues (see "Minutemen" 2007). Judging by the failure of the legislation that enjoyed support from Democratic leaders, some Republicans in the Senate, and President Bush, this movement achieved its short-term political aim.

For any of this to happen requires the intervention of political activists and elites (Layman 2001). Indeed, the most important and original argument of Hunter's critics is that the autonomy of the political sphere facilitates or impedes political mobilization based on cultural grievances. In one ambitious effort, Leege et al. (2002) developed a systematic model of cultural conflict that puts political entrepreneurs at the center of the electoral process. In their view, ambitious politicians constantly monitor the landscape for social conflicts with the potential to produce political gain. Although the short-term goal may be to raise a faction to majority status within the party, cultural conflict is most useful as a means of gaining control of government institutions. This objective is driven by the simple rules of the electoral process. Parties can win elections by either mobilizing all their supporters (if they happen to enjoy latent majority support) or, in the case of minority parties, by persuading members of the majority coalition to abstain from voting or by encouraging sizable numbers of them to cross party lines. In practice, it is easier to utilize cultural appeals to persuade people not to vote for their customary party than to cross over to the other side.

Thus, parties often direct their campaigns to members of a majority coalition who seem rife for disaffection and thus for demobilization. This outcome is encouraged by a particular style of issue framing. Voters react powerfully to emotional symbols, perhaps more so than to rational appeals to self-interest (Marcus, Neuman, and MacKuen 2000; Neuman, Marcus, Crigler, and MacKuen 2007). The key to cementing and undermining voter blocs is to manipulate symbols that evoke powerful feelings. The candidate that the opposing party's voters would normally support must be portrayed as out of sympathy with the core cultural values of that party. This was accomplished with great effectiveness by the GOP's usage of the Willie Horton advertisement in the 1988 presidential election. Threatened by low poll numbers for its candidate, the Republican campaign sought to portray the Democratic nominee, Michael Dukakis, as a threat to social order and thus not worthy of the support of normally Democratic voters who were worried about personal security. To convey the notion that the Democratic nominee was soft on crime, George H. W. Bush's campaign promoted an ad that linked Dukakis to Horton, a convicted felon who committed a rape while on furlough from a state prison. Horton, described by Bush's campaign manager as "a big black rapist" (Blumenthal 1990, p. 265), was a perfect distillation of white fears about dangerous black males who were coddled by liberal politicians (Mendelberg 1997). Cultural norms about race and crime were fused, tied to the Democratic candidate (who had continued a program introduced in federal prisons under President Reagan's watch) and used with great effectiveness to depress participation by erstwhile Democrats on election day. Even *within* a party, the same process is used to undercut support for a rival within an undecided bloc—witness Governor Mike Huckabee's central description of himself not as a governor, but as a "Christian leader" to draw contrast with front-runner Governor Mitt Romney's Mormonism during the 2008 Iowa caucus campaign (Luo 2007).

As a minority party (in terms of baseline support by the electorate), the GOP has been more inclined to embrace this style. During the 2006 midterm election, however, some Democrats took a page from their opponents' playbook by capitalizing on one of the scandals that had broken out among GOP congressional representatives. Congressman Mark Foley, a Florida Republican, was publicly revealed to have sent suggestive emails to young male pages in the House of Representatives. Reports indicated that the House GOP leadership had been warned by staff members of Foley's behavior but did nothing to stop him. This scandal tapped into various moral orders—such as beliefs about rectitude and corruption in public office, and fears about homosexual predators, and had been sharpened by recent revelations of pedophile priests—that were ripe for exploitation. Armed with this information, Democrats accused their Republican opponents of guilt by association with Foley and with those in the House Republican leadership who had looked the other way. The ads run by Democrats in many districts featured Foley prominently and attempted to link GOP candidates to him. Tying the GOP to immorality (homosexual advances against underage legislative pages) and political corruption (a coverup) was a classic cultural strategy.

Advances in the tools used in modern campaigns make it possible to micro-target specific groups and subcultures with powerful cultural appeals. For example, Monson and Oliphant (2007) and Campbell and Monson (2007) examined the mass mailings the Republican National Committee made to 24 target groups in 2004. Some, from the party's base, were to be enraged, and thus mobilized, by the appeal. Others, from the opposition's base, were to be demobilized with graphic information about what their party had become. In several battleground electoral college states, Campbell and Monson (2007) demonstrated that antigay materials provided by the Republican National Convention seemed to have tipped the balance to President Bush. Direct mailings, narrow-cast television, talk radio, videos, and DVDs permit candidates to aim at smaller, confined populations with incendiary messages rather than muting the appeal to be acceptable to general audiences.

Many studies have shown that voters, far from being atomistic consumers, make decisions based on processing of information within social groups and networks (Wald, Owen, and Hill 1988; Huckfeldt, Plutzer, and Sprague 1993; Djupe and Gilbert 2006). Because voters are embedded in social groups, no matter how informal, it is easier for candidates to demonize the "other" (a form of *social categorization*) and to enhance the solidary power of one's own *reference group*. That is because *meaning* inheres in those groups with which we interact frequently (*social cohesion*) or identify with closely (*social identification*). Many such groups and networks are religious in composition, as we noted earlier. This would enhance boundary-maintaining appeals to religiously rooted moral values. However, many groups are also not about religion, and often relate to interests—economic or status-maintaining. Individuals hold overlapping memberships and identifications that may mute cultural appeals. Choice becomes a calculus based on priorities in any given election and on issue framing. Often, then, the campaigner will try to frame cultural material to appeal to a sense of *relative deprivation*: The "other" practices immoral values or is undeserving of the recognition or rewards that the opposing party affords. But again, the process of heightening cultural appeals is a strategic choice that political elites make, not some inexorable outcome that depends on rank-and-file group properties. With their ears to the ground, elites seek advantage—within the boundaries of America's general sense of tolerance.[9]

This approach improves on culture war theory in significant ways. First, it calls attention to the mechanism by which social tension becomes politically relevant—namely, the activities of partisans and political activists. Second, it emphasizes the potency of emotion-inducing symbols in the conflict over cultural norms by using the behavioral theory of affective intelligence (Marcus et al. 2000; Neuman et al. 2007). Third, it explains why such campaigning is rational from the perspective of candidates and activists, particularly those associated with the minority party. Even more fundamentally, however, the alternative approach in Leege et al. (2002) overcomes the tendency of culture war advocates to limit culture to the realm of religion and religiously based issues such as prayer in school, abortion, homosexuality, gender roles, and such. Drawing on recent cultural theorists (summarized in Wuthnow 1987), Leege et al. (2002) argue that there are multiple moral orders that cover a wide range of issues—international policy, domestic economics, race relations, and immigration. When debating such issues, people raise questions about fairness, justice, the source of authority, and the right way to order society. Such questions tap into moral concerns every bit as much as the issues commonly deemed "religious." Certainly, religious groups may offer certain perspectives on these questions, but voters do not seem to react based solely or principally on religious affiliation. This approach thus suggests that cultural analysis needs to move beyond its preoccupation with religion and recognize that virtually any issue has the capacity to be approached from a cultural perspective (Mockabee 2007). The ongoing debate over immigration is a case in point.

CULTURAL IMPACT ON RELIGION IN POLITICS: RESEARCH OPPORTUNITIES

This chapter has explored the cultural dimensions of religion in American public life. We began by noting the conceptual confusion and disagreement that characterize "culture" in the social sciences. Out of a morass of conflicting and overlapping definitions, we extracted two broad approaches to culture. The first or holistic approach treats culture as a property of social collectivities and spatial units, and tends to emphasize culture as a common property that infuses a community and promotes political integration. Many scholars regard American culture as heavily weighted with religious sensibilities and therefore as an important source of American political norms and institutions. The most important manifestation of this tendency is the prevalence of a *civil religion* that provides powerful symbols, ideas, and themes that stress the transcendent nature of American nationhood. There is a second approach to culture, however, that emphasizes its capacity to undermine unity and to promote conflict. In this perspective, culture needs to be understood principally as an inherently conflictual realm of society devoted to promoting meaning. One important, albeit deeply flawed, manifestation of this approach, culture war theory, illustrates how differences over the source of social authority may become grist for competing political movements. A theory of cultural conflict offers a more nuanced understanding of the dynamics of moral debate in public life. Culture provides individuals with a sense of identity, standards of behavior, and an identification of outsiders. Conflicting views about these matters can be made politically relevant when elites sense political advantage in making them salient. The effect is likely to be disintegrative in the sense that it encourages polarization.

It is commonplace to note the growing multicultural nature of American life, a product of increased exposure to world currents transmitted by globalization and transnationalism. This growing social complexity appears to offer fodder for cultural conflict in politics as evident in recent disputes over immigration, language issues, diaspora engagement in foreign policy, representation, and other areas. More so than at anytime during the 1920s, Americans seem to debate "who we are" as a people (Huntingon 2004) and how we should order our lives. As a consequence of these fissures, issue entrepreneurs who troll the political seas in search of potentially divisive issues with the capacity to confer political advantage face a decidedly bullish market.

As the foregoing discussion suggests, we see the most productive research opportunities on religion and politics in the cultural studies approach that has developed during the past 20 years. Although the holistic approach to culture has offered some important insights, its essentially static nature seems ill-equipped to explain a dynamic political system in which religious appeals wax and wane. That is why, for instance, empirical research on topics such as "civic culture" and "civil religion" has largely reached a conceptual dead end. The newer approach to culture offers more promise because it recognizes the fluidity of a socially constructed domain of culture. Such a perspective warrants that scholars pay closer attention to at least three phenomena.

First, it is important to broaden the understanding of "culture" beyond overtly religious issues to appreciate how cultural conflict inheres in debates over a wide range of issues that do not appear on the surface to be religious in nature. Scholars of religion and politics often work with a preset domain of "cultural" issues—for example, abortion, gay marriage, educational values, evolution, family preservation and promiscuous sex, and so on. How can this be reconciled with evidence that most of the partisan mobility during the post-New Deal period, including the shift of many Protestant evangelicals toward the Republican Party, was the result of attitudes toward African Americans and the role of the federal government in furthering equality of opportunity (Leege et al. 2002, chap. 9; Valentino and Sears 2005)? There is no paradox here if we remember that race has been a "carrier" for debates over cultural values associated with competing moral orders—as in the case of affirmative action. Some opponents of compensatory programs—whether minority preference in college admissions or "set-asides" for minority contractors on public projects—argue their case against such programs in a way that draws on such hallmarks of cultural thinking as group categorization, relative deprivation, and reference groups. On the assumption that black Americans no longer face discrimination because of civil rights laws, these critics contend that any failure by blacks to achieve full inclusion in the American dream owes principally to deficiencies in their own culture. Specifically, because black Americans "do not conform to traditional American values, particularly the work ethic, as well as obedience to authority (as in schools, the workplace or law enforcement) and impulse control (concerning such issues as alcohol, drugs, sexuality, and prudent use of money)," they suffer bad economic outcomes (Sears, Henry, and Kosterman 1999 p. 77). Hence, claims for government preference to offset the effects of these outcomes are perceived as illegitimate demands for "special" benefits rather than legitimate policies to compensate individuals for the harm done to them. Government affirmative action programs, it follows, amount to a capitulation to those who are undeserving of such assistance. None of this makes sense unless we remember that culture encompasses ideas that legitimate policies as right or wrong based on a moral calculus.

Moving into the third millennium of the Common Era, many journalists and scholars have missed the cultural value priorities that frame vote preferences among religious conservatives. For many Americans, the events of 9/11 raised concerns about war, national security, and terrorism to the top of the public agenda, pushing social issues farther down the queue. However, religious conservatives did not abandon their traditional political priorities, but rather accommodated the newest threats to their worldview. They did so by applying to this phenomenon the same kind of cultural frame once used against global communism (Durham 2004). Terrorism looms so large for some in this sector of the electorate because it is *Islamic* terrorism, and this has become for them another part of the *kampf* between Christian culture and Islamic culture. From this perspective, Muslims are the infidel devils, not merely a political adversary. Accordingly, some religious conservatives may have given support for President Bush's war in Iraq because they believed God had placed him in the White House at this time of tribulation to stop such adversaries in their tracks. Similarly, even after what they acknowledge as failed military policies, many have argued against withdrawal from Iraq as giving renewed vigor to the terrorist forces (Lawton 2006).

A theory of cultural politics should never start with a limited and predefined domain of issues. Rather, it spreads the net widely to find what religious values are behind what appear to be straightforward nonreligious issues. And it uses multi-variate tools to estimate which dimensions are dominant and by what paths they are linked to the outcome. We have used race and national defense/patriotism to illustrate the matter, but we could do just as well with economic issues. The debate over "welfare reform" is inexplicable without recognizing the underlying power of religious views about the "deserving" and "undeserving" poor.

Second, religiously based political behavior should be understood to encompass both positive acts and forms of withdrawal. Much attention is given to mobilization because it is thought easy to measure from survey data (past record of participation) or, better, precinct books that map turnout over time. Hence, many studies trace change in the partisan orientation of religious groups from one election to the next. However, potential voters face two choices in an election—which candidate to support (the datum normally reported) and the prior decision of whether to vote at all. It is every bit as easy to measure demobilization—purposive nonvoting—and its antecedents. Leege et al. (2002) regressed vote or failure to vote on a variety of issue and group factors, along with demographic variables that helped interpret turnout in past participation studies (compare with Verba et al. 1995). Coefficients for groups targeted by campaigners were compared—both cross-group comparisons and through-time comparisons—to assess the unsettling (dissonant) effects of campaign themes and candidate personae. For example, when Democrats decided to push civil rights measures, white southern Democratic turnout declined well beyond what demographic factors predicted. Eventually this dissonant information led white southern Democrats to seek consistency in the Republican Party. We know from the statements and behaviors of campaign managers that suppressing turnout among vulnerable target groups in the rival party's coalition is an important strategy in modern campaigning (see Wirthlin 1981; Monson and Oliphant 2007). Clearly, religion and politics specialists would do well to build failure to vote into their models.

Third, and finally, it is absolutely critical to study the role of government and political elites as forces that facilitate cultural expression in American politics. Early sociological studies and empirical research by various political scientists (Wilson and Banfield 1964) displayed how WASP (white Anglo-Saxon Protestant) culture among mainline Protestants reinforced a strong commitment to the Republican Party. By contrast, a very different cultural orientation to politics undergirded the worldviews of Catholic and Irish Protestant immigrants, manifested in a strongly Democratic partisan identification. Both these tendencies have subsequently frayed under the influence of cultural change. In *The Inheritance: How Three Catholic Families Moved from Roosevelt to Reagan and Beyond*, journalist Samuel Freedman (1996) examines successive generations of two Irish Catholic families in New York City and upstate New York and a Polish Catholic family in Baltimore. Freedman (1996) shows how the norms of a tight cultural community sustained loyalty to Democratic candidates, but when the national parties changed policy objectives and the cultural backgrounds of leaders, later generations shifted to Reagan's Republicanism. For their part, WASP Republicans have often reacted uneasily to the growing religious enthusiasm and cultural Puritanism expressed by the GOP as it has become decidedly more southern and evangelical. Such pillars of northeastern Republicanism as John Danforth and Christine Todd Whitman have warned about the "capture" of their party by forces that now appear hostile to the cultural values that once dominated the GOP. This should not be confused with secularism, as Hunter's model tends to do, but with a different way of linking religious values to political causes.

These ideas merely suggest some productive possibilities for social analysis of religion and politics that is informed by newer approaches to cultural studies. Such work will help to resurrect culture as more than a residual category to be used when analysts cannot otherwise account for patterns of mass political behavior. In time, a cultural theory of politics may join the economic and sociological models that still dominate the study of American political behavior, putting religion back into the equation, but broadening its meaning considerably.

NOTES

1. This section draws on Wald and Calhoun-Brown (2006, chap. 1).

2. For a useful summary of data on this point from one of the most respected academic surveys, see the section on religion and religious practices at "Social and Religious Characteristics of the Electorate," American National Election Studies, http://www.electionstudies.org/nesguide/gd-index.htm#1.

3. This tendency was documented memorably by an episode in the satirical fake news television program, the *Colbert Report*. While interviewing a Georgia congressional representative who had repeatedly sponsored legislation mandating the display of the Ten Commandments, the genial host asked his guest to name the commandments. The congressman came up with only three. This priceless interview is available at http://ww.crooksandliars.com/index.php?s=COLBERT+%22TEN+COMMANDMENTS%22.

4. Some scholars believe that inflated attendance reports may be the consequence of oversampling people who are members of churches.

5. In a classic study, Allport and Ross (1967) distinguished between "intrinsic" and "extrinsic" religious motivation, suggesting that the latter tendency to embrace religion for its social advantages represented a less authentic form of commitment. But as Lenski (1963) demonstrated, religions also serve a communal purpose that is equally as meaningful as other forms of commitment. Cohen, Hall, Koenig, and Meador (2005) have forcefully argued that devaluing such communal attachment amounts to adopting an exclusively Protestant model of religiosity that devalues the communal dimension of faiths such as Roman Catholicism and Judaism.

6. Left-Hegelian philosopher Ludwig Feuerbach, in exploring the notion of alienation and false consciousness, had argued that, at the level of the individual, the Divine is nothing more than the best human traits and aspirations projected onto a transcendent Other. His anthropomorphic interpretation of Christianity addressed individuals, whereas Durkheim addressed broader institutions of the whole society.

7. It is interesting to note that Verba's highly influential later work (Verba, Schlozman, and Brady 1995) treats religion as a major factor in explanations of political participation.

8. However, there is some evidence to suggest otherwise. See the discussion on religious socialization found in chapter 6 of this volume.

9. A perceptive discussion of reality framing during both the 2000 Florida vote count and post-9/11 America is provided in Jamieson and Waldman (2003).

REFERENCES

Abramowitz, Alan, and Kyle Saunders. 2005. "Why Can't We All Just Get Along? The Reality of a Polarized America." *The Forum* 3. http://www.bepress.com/cgi/viewcontent.cgi?article=1076&context=forum (accessed December 31, 2007).

Aho, James A. 1991. *The Politics of Righteousness: Idaho Christian Patriotism.* Seattle, Wash.: University of Washington Press.

Allport, Gordon W., and James M. Ross. 1967. "Personal Religious Orientation and Prejudice." *Journal of Personality and Social Psychology* 5: 432–443.

Almond, Gabriel, and Sidney Verba. 1965. *The Civic Culture.* Boston, Mass.: Little Brown.

Andersen, Kristi. 1988. "Sources of Pro-Family Belief." *Political Psychology* 9: 229–243.

Bartels, Larry M. 2006. "Review: What's the Matter with *What's the Matter with Kansas?*" *Quarterly Journal of Political Science* 1: 201–226.

Beck, Paul Allen, and Suzanne Parker. 1985. "Consistency in Policy Thinking." *Political Behavior* 7: 37–56.

Bellah, Robert N. 1966. "Civil Religion in America." *Daedalus* 134: 40–55.

Blanchard, Dallas A., and Terry J. Prewitt. 1993. *Religious Violence and Abortion: The Gideon Project.* Gainesville, Fla.: University Press of Florida.

Blumenthal, Sidney. 1990. *Pledging Allegiance: The Last Campaign of the Cold War.* New York: HarperCollins.

Bonnell, Victoria E., and Lynn Hunt, eds. 1999. *Beyond the Cultural Turn: New Directions in the Study of Society and Culture.* Berkeley, Calif.: University of California Press.

Borden, Morton. 1984. *Jews, Turks and Infidels.* Chapel Hill, N.C.: University of North Carolina Press.

Boyer, Paul. 2005. "Biblical Prophecy and Foreign Policy." In *Quoting God: How Media Shape Ideas about Religion and Culture*, ed. Claire Badarraco, 67–78. Waco, Texas: Baylor University Press.

Brint, Steven. 1994. *In an Age of Experts: The Changing Role of Professionals in Politics and Public Life.* Princeton, N.J.: Princeton University Press.

Brown, Melissa S., Joseph Claude Harris, and Patrick M. Rooney. 2004. "Reconciling Estimates of Religious Giving." Indianapolis, Ind.: Center on Philanthropy, Indiana University.

Bruce-Briggs, B., ed. 1979. *The New Class?* New Brunswick, N.J.: Transaction.

Bryant, Clell. 2005. "Tocqueville's America." *Smithsonian Magazine*, July: 104–107.

Butler, Jon. 1990. *Awash in a Sea of Faith: Christianizing the American People.* Cambridge, Mass.: Harvard University Press.

Cahalan, Don. 1968. "Correlates of Respondent Accuracy in the Denver Validity Survey." *Public Opinion Quarterly* 32: 607–621.

Campbell, David E., and J. Quin Monson. 2007. "The Case of Bush's Reelection: Did Gay Marriage Do It?" In *A Matter of Faith: Religion in the 2004 Presidential Election*, ed. David E. Campbell, 120–141. Washington, D.C.: Brookings Institution Press.

Campbell, James E. 2005. "Why Bush Won the Presidential Election of 2004: Incumbency, Ideology, Terrorism, and Turnout." *Political Science Quarterly* 120: 219–241.

Canipe, Lee. 2003. "Under God and Anti-Communist: How the Pledge of Allegiance Got Religion in Cold War America." *Journal of Church & State* 45: 305–323.

Carroll, Jackson W. 1995. "Culture Wars? Insights from Ethnographies of Two Protestant Seminaries." *Sociology of Religion* 56: 1–19.

Chesterton, G. K. 1922. *What I Saw in America*. London: Hodder & Stoughton.

Christenson, James, and Ronald C. Wimberly. 1978. "Who Is Civil Religious?" *Sociological Analysis* 39: 77–83.

Citrin, Jack, Donald P. Green, Christopher Muste, and Cara Wong. 1997. "Public Opinion toward Immigration Reform: The Role of Economic Motivations." *Journal of Politics* 59: 858–881.

Clark, Terry Nichols, and Vincent Hoffman-Martinot, eds. 1998. *The New Political Culture*. Boulder, Colo.: Westview Press.

Cohen, Adam B., Daniel E. Hall, Harold G. Koenig, and Keith G. Meador. 2005. "Social Versus Individual Motivation: Implications for Normative Definitions of Religious Orientation." *Personality and Social Psychology Review* 9: 48–61.

Curtis, James E., Edward G. Grabb, and Douglas E. Baer. 1992. "Voluntary Association Membership in Fifteen Countries." *American Sociological Review* 57: 139–152.

Davis, Nancy J., and Robert V. Robinson. 1996. "Are the Rumors of War Exaggerated? Religious Orthodoxy and Moral Progressivism in America." *American Journal of Sociology* 102: 756–787.

Degeneffe, Charles Edmund. 2003. "What Is Catholic about Catholic Charities?" *Social Work* 48: 374–383.

Demerath, Nicholas J. 2001. *Crossing the Gods: World Religions and Worldly Politics*. New Brunswick, N.J.: Rutgers University Press.

Djupe, Paul A., and Christopher P. Gilbert. 2006. "The Resourceful Believer: Generating Civic Skills in Church." *Journal of Politics* 68: 116–127.

Donnelly, Jack. 2000. *Realism and International Relations*. New York: Cambridge University Press.

Durham, Martin. 2004. "Evangelical Protestantism and Foreign Policy in the United States after September 11." *Patterns of Prejudice* 38: 145–158.

Eck, Diana L. 2001. *A New Religious America: How a "Christian Country" Has Now Become the World's Most Religiously Diverse Nation*. San Francisco, Calif.: Harper.

Eckstein, Harry. 1988. "A Culturalist Theory of Political Change." *American Political Science Review* 82: 789–804.

Edgell, Penny, Joseph Gerteis, and Douglas Hartmann. 2006. "Atheists as 'Other': Moral Boundaries and Cultural Membership in American Society." *American Sociological Review* 71: 211–234.

Elazar, Daniel J. 1984. *American Federalism: A View from the States*. 3rd ed. New York: Harper and Row.

Evans, John. H. 1997. "Worldviews or Social Groups as the Source of Moral Value Attitudes: Implications for the Culture Wars Thesis." *Sociological Forum* 12: 371–404.

Finke, Roger and Rodney Stark. 1992. *The Churching of America, 1776–1990: Winners and Losers in Our Religious Economy*. New Brunswick, New Jersey: Rutgers University Press.

Fiorina, Morris P. 2005. *Culture War? The Myth of a Polarized America*. New York: Pearson Longman.

Fowler, Robert Booth. 1989. *Unconventional Partners: Religion and Liberal Culture in the United States.* Grand Rapids, Mich.: William B. Eerdman's.

Fox, Jonathan. 2007. "Do Democracies Have Separation of Religion and State?" *Canadian Review of Political Science* 40: 1–24.

Fox, Richard Wightman. 1993. "The Culture of Liberal Protestant Progressivism, 1875–1925." *Journal of Interdisciplinary History* 23: 639–660.

Freedman, Samuel G. 1996. *The Inheritance: How Three Families and America Moved from Roosevelt to Reagan and Beyond.* New York: Simon and Schuster.

Fuller, Robert C. 2001. *Spiritual, But Not Religious: Understanding Unchurched America.* New York: Oxford University Press.

Gamoran, Adam. 1990. "Civil Religion in American Schools." *Sociological Analysis* 51: 235–256.

Gill, Anthony. 2008. *Political Origins of Religious Liberty.* New York: Cambridge University Press.

Green, John C., James L. Guth, Corwin E. Smidt, and Lyman A. Kellstedt. 1996. *Religion and the Culture Wars: Dispatches from the Front.* Lanham, Md.: Rowman & Littlefield.

Gupta, Akhil, and James Ferguson. 1992. "Beyond 'Culture': Space, Identity, and the Politics of Difference." *Cultural Anthropology* 7: 6–23.

Hadaway, C. Kirk, and Penny Long Marler. 2005. "How Many Americans Attend Worship Each Week? An Alternative Approach to Measurement." *Journal for the Scientific Study of Religion* 44: 307–322.

Hansen, Andrew C. 2006. "The Religious Text in Daniel Webster's First Bunker Hill Address." *Southern Communication Journal* 71: 383–400.

Herberg, Will. 1955. *Protestant–Catholic–Jew.* Garden City, N.Y.: Doubleday.

Himmelfarb, Gertrude. 1999. *One Nation, Two Cultures.* New York: Alfred A. Knopf.

Holt, Michael F. 1969. *Forging a Majority: The Republican Party in Pittsburgh, 1848–1860.* New Haven, Conn.: Yale University Press.

Huckfeldt, Robert, Eric Plutzer, and John C. Sprague. 1993. "Alternative Contexts of Political Behavior: Churches, Neighborhoods, and Individuals." *Journal of Politics* 55: 365–381.

Hunter, James Davison. 1991. *Culture Wars: The Struggle to Define America.* New York: Basic Books.

Huntington, Samuel P. 1996. *The Clash of Civilizations and the Remaking of World Order.* New York: Simon and Schuster.

Huntington, Samuel P. 2004. *Who Are We?* New York: Simon and Schuster.

Inglehart, Ronald. 1990. *Culture Shift in Advanced Industrial Society.* Princeton, N.J.: Princeton University Press.

Inglehart, Ronald. 1997. *Modernization and Postmodernization: Cultural, Economic, and Political Change in 43 Societies.* Princeton, N.J.: Princeton University Press.

Jackson, Kenneth T. 1967. *The Ku Klux Klan in the City, 1915–1930.* New York: Oxford University Press.

Jamieson, Kathleen Hall, and Paul Waldman. 2003. *The Press Effect: Politicians, Journalists, and the Stories That Shape the Political World.* New York: Oxford University Press.

Johnson, Paul. 2006. "The Almost-Chosen People." *First Things* 17–22.

Joliceur, Pamela M., and Louis K. Knowles. 1978. "Fraternal Organizations and Civil Religion: Scottish Rite Freemasonry." *Review of Religious Research* 20: 3–22.

Jones, Jeffrey M. 2007. *Some Americans Reluctant to Vote for Mormon, 72-Year-Old Presidential Candidates.* Washington, D.C.: Gallup News Reports.

Kellner, Hansfried, and Berger, Peter L. 1992. "Life-Style Engineering: Some Theoretical Reflections." In *Hidden Technocrats: The New Class and Capitalism*, ed. Hansfried Kellner, 1–22. New Brunswick, N.J.: Transaction.

Kosmin, Barry A., and Ariela Keysar. 2006. *Religion in a Free Market*. Ithaca, N.Y.: Paramount Market Publishing.

Kuper, Adam. 1999. *Culture: The Anthropologists' Account*. Cambridge, Mass.: Harvard University Press.

Lambert, Frank. 2003. *The Founding Fathers and the Place of Religion in America*. Princeton, N.J.: Princeton University Press.

Lawton, Kim. 2006 (March 24). "Interview: Richard Land." *Religion & Ethnics Newsweekly*. http://www.pbs.org/wnet/religionandethics/week930/interview.html (accessed December 31, 2007).

Layman, Geoffrey C. 2001. *The Great Divide: Religious and Cultural Conflict in American Party Politics*. New York: Columbia University Press.

Layman, Geoffrey C., and John C. Green. 2006. "Wars and Rumours of Wars: The Contexts of Cultural Conflict in American Political Behaviour." *British Journal of Political Science* 36: 61–89.

Leege, David C., Kenneth D. Wald, Brian S. Krueger, and Paul D. Mueller. 2002. *Politics of Cultural Differences: Social Change and Voter Mobilization Strategies in the Post-New Deal Period*. Princeton, N.J.: Princeton University Press.

Lenski, Gerhard. 1963. *The Religious Factor*. Garden City, N.Y.: Doubleday-Anchor.

"Lesson from America." 2007. *Economist* November 3: 21–22.

Linder, Robert D. 1996. "Universal Pastor: President Bill Clinton's Civil Religion." *Journal of Church and State* 38: 733–750.

Luker, Kristin. 1984. *Abortion and the Politics of Motherhood*. Berkeley, Calif.: University of California Press.

Luo, Michael. 2007 (November 27). "Huckabee Lays out His Claim as an 'Authentic Conservative.'" *New York Times*. http://www.nytimes.com (accessed January 5, 2008).

Lutz, Donald S. 1984. "The Relative Influence of European Writers upon Late 18th-Century American Political Thought." *American Political Science Review* 78: 189–197.

Lutz, Donald S. 1994. "The Evolution of Covenant Form and Content as the Basis for Early American Political Culture." In *Covenant in the Nineteenth Century*, ed. Daniel J. Elazar, 31–48. Lanham, Md.: Rowman and Littlefield.

Mansbridge, Jane J. 1986. *Why We Lost the ERA*. Chicago, Ill.: University of Chicago Press.

Marcus, George E., W. Russell Neuman, and MacKuen Michael. 2000. *Affective Intelligence and Political Judgment*. Chicago, Ill.: University of Chicago Press.

Marty, Martin E. 1984. *Pilgrims in Their Own Land*. Boston, Mass.: Little, Brown.

McCloskey, Herbert, and John Zaller. 1984. *The American Ethos*. Cambridge, Mass.: Harvard University Press.

McCormick, Richard L. 1974. "Ethno-Cultural Interpretations of Nineteenth Century American Voting Behavior." *Political Science Quarterly* 89: 351–377.

McDonough, Peter. 1994. "On Hierarchies of Conflict and the Possibility of Civil Discourse: Variations on a Theme by John Courtney Murray." *Journal of Church and State* 36: 115–142.

Meier, Kenneth J. 1994. *The Politics of Sin: Drugs, Alcohol, and Public Policy*. Armonk, N.Y.: M. E. Sharpe.

Meizel, Katherine. 2006. "A Singing Citizenry: Popular Music and Civil Religion in America." *Journal for the Scientific Study of Religion* 45: 497–503.

Mendelberg, Tali. 1997. "Executing Hortons: Racial Crime in the 1988 Presidential Campaign." *Public Opinion Quarterly* 61: 134–157.

Meyer, Jeffrey F. 2001. *Myths in Stone: Religious Dimensions of Washington, D.C.* Berkeley, Calif.: University of California Press.

Miller, Alan S., and John P. Hoffmann. 1999. "The Growing Divisiveness: Culture Wars or a War of Words?" *Social Forces* 78: 721–746.

Min, Pyong Gap. 1992. "The Structure and Social Functions of Korean Immigrant Churches in the United States." *International Migration Review* 26: 1370–1394.

"Minutemen Making Inroads in Iowa." 2007 (September 7). *Cedar Rapids Gazette.* http://www.gazetteonline.com/apps/pbcs.dll/article?Date=20070908&Category=NEWS&ArtNo=70908046&Template=printart (accessed December 31, 2007).

Mockabee, Stephen. 2007. "A Question of Authority: Religion and Cultural Conflict in the 2004 Election." *Political Behavior* 29: 221–248.

Monson, J. Quin, and J. Baxter Oliphant. 2007. "Microtargeting and the Instrumental Mobilization of Religious Conservatives." In *A Matter of Faith: Religion in the 2004 Presidential Election,* ed. David E. Campbell, 95–119. Washington, D.C.: Brookings Institution Press.

Moon, Dawne. 2004. *God, Sex, and Politics: Homosexuality and Everyday Theologies.* Chicago, Ill.: University of Chicago Press.

Mooney, Christopher Z., ed. 2001. *The Public Clash of Private Values: The Politics of Morality Policy.* Chatham, N.Y.: Chatham House.

Morone, James A. 2003. *Hellfire Nation: The Politics of Sin in American History.* New Haven, Conn.: Yale University Press.

Nanlai, Cao. 2005. "The Church as a Surrogate Family for Working Class Immigrant Chinese Youth: An Ethnography of Segmented Assimilation." *Sociology of Religion* 66: 183–200.

Neuman, W. Russell, George E. Marcus, Ann N. Crigler, and Michael MacKuen, eds. 2007. *The Affect Effect: Dynamics of Emotion in Political Thinking and Behavior.* Chicago, Ill.: University of Chicago Press.

Nichols, J. Bruce. 1988. *The Uneasy Alliance: Religion, Refugee Work, and U.S. Foreign Policy.* New York: Oxford University Press.

Nivola, Pietro S., and David W. Brady, eds. 2006. *Red and Blue Nation: Characteristics and Causes of America's Polarized Politics.* Washington, D.C.: Brookings Institution Press.

Norris, Pippa, and Ronald Inglehart. 2004. *Sacred and Secular: Religion and Politics Worldwide.* New York: Cambridge University Press.

Oestreicher, Richard. 1988. "Urban Working-Class Political Behavior and Theories of American Electoral Politics, 1870–1940." *Journal of American History* 74: 1257–1286.

Olson, Daniel V. A., and Jackson W. Carroll. 1992. "Religiously Based Politics: Religious Elites and the Public." *Social Forces* 70: 765–786.

Pals, Daniel. 2006. *Eight Theories of Religion.* New York: Oxford University Press.

Peshkin, Alan. 1987. *God's Choice: The Total World of a Fundamentalist Christian School.* Chicago, Ill.: University of Chicago Press.

Preston, Julia. 2007. "Grass Roots Roared and Immigration Plan Collapsed." *New York Times* June 10. http://www.nytimes.com/2007/06/10/washington/10oppose.html

Prothero, Stephen. 2007. *Religious Literacy: What Every American Needs to Know—And Doesn't.* New York: Harper Collins.

Rabushka, Alvin, and Kenneth Shepsle. 1972. *Politics in Plural Societies: A Theory of Democratic Instability.* Columbus, Ohio: Charles E. Merrill.

Reimer, Samuel H. 1995. "A Look at Cultural Effects on Religiosity: A Comparison between the United States and Canada." *Journal for the Scientific Study of Religion* 34: 445–457.

Rose, Richard, and Derek Urwin. 1969. "Social Cohesion, Political Parties, and Strains in Regimes." *Comparative Political Studies* 2: 7–67.

Rose, Susan D. 1987. *Keeping Them Out of the Hands of Satan: Evangelical Schooling in America.* New York: Routledge.

Ross, Dorothy. 1991. *The Origins of American Social Science.* New York: Cambridge University Press.

Rouner, Leroy. 1999. "Civil Religion, Cultural Diversity, and American Civilization." *The Key Reporter* 64: 1–6.

Ruthven, Malise. 1989. *The Divine Supermarket: Shopping for God in America.* New York: William Morrow.

Sears, David O., P. J. Henry, and Rick Kosterman. 1999. "Egalitarian Values and Contemporary Racial Politics." In *Racialized Politics: The Debate about Racism in America*, ed. David O. Sears, Jim Sidanius, and Lawrence Bobo, 75–117. Chicago, Ill.: University of Chicago Press.

Sewell, William H. 1999. "The Concept(s) of Culture." In *Beyond the Cultural Turn: New Directions in the Study of Society and Culture*, ed. Victoria E. Bonnell and Lynn Hunt, 35–61. Berkeley, Calif.: University of California Press.

Sharp, Elaine B. ed. 1999. *Culture Wars in Local Politics.* Lawrence, Kans.: University Press of Kansas.

Smidt, Corwin. 1980. "Civil Religious Orientation among Elementary School Children." *Sociological Analysis* 41: 25–40.

Smidt, Corwin. 1982. "Civil Religious Orientations and Children's Perception of Political Authority." *Political Behavior* 4: 147–162.

Spiro, Melford. 1987. *Culture and Human Nature.* Chicago, Ill.: University of Chicago Press.

Stackhouse, Max L. 2004. "Civil Religion, Political Theology and Public Theology: What's the Difference?" *Political Theology* 5: 275–293.

Stark, Rodney, and Roger Finke. 2000. *Acts of Faith: Explaining the Human Side of Religion.* Berkeley, Calif.: University of California Press.

Swidler, Ann. 1986. "Culture in Action: Symbols and Strategies." *American Sociological Review* 51: 273–286.

Tabor, James D., and Eugene V. Gallagher. 1995. *Why Waco? Cults and the Battle for Religious Freedom in America.* Berkeley, Calif.: University of California Press.

Tatalovich, Raymond, and Bryon W. Daynes, eds. 2005. *Moral Controversies in American Politics.* Armonk, N.Y.: M. E. Sharpe.

Thomas, Michael C., and Charles C. Flippen. 1972. "American Civil Religion: An Empirical Study." *Social Forces* 51: 218–225.

Tipton, Steven M. 1982. *Getting Saved from the Sixties: Moral Meaning in Conversion and Cultural Change.* Berkeley, Calif.: University of California Press.

Tiryakian, Edward A. 1982. "Puritan America in the Modern World: Mission Impossible." *Sociological Analysis* 43: 351–368.

Toolin, Cynthia. 1983. "American Civil Religion from 1789–1981: A Content Analysis of Presidential Inaugural Addresses." *Review of Religious Research* 25: 39–48.

Valentino, Nicholas A., and David O. Sears. 2005. "Old Times There Are Not Forgotten: Race and Partisan Realignment in the Contemporary South." *American Journal of Political Science* 49: 672–688.

Verba, Sidney, Kay Lehman Schlozman, and Henry E. Brady. 1995. *Voice and Equality*. Cambridge, Mass.: Harvard University Press.

Wald, Kenneth D., and Allison Calhoun-Brown. 2006. *Religion and Politics in the United States*. 5th ed. Lanham, Md.: Rowman & Littlefield.

Wald, Kenneth D., Dennis E. Owen, and Samuel S. Hill, Jr. 1988. "Churches as Political Communities." *American Political Science Review* 82: 531–548.

Weber, Max. 1958. *The Protestant Ethic and the Spirit of Capitalism*. New York: Charles Scribner's.

Wedeen, Lisa. 2002. "Conceptualizing Culture: Possibilities for Political Science." *American Political Science Review* 96: 713–728.

Welch, Michael. 2002. *Flag Burning: Moral Panic and the Criminalization of Protest*. New York: Aldine de Gruyter.

Wildavsky, Aaron. 1987. "Choosing Preferences by Constructing Institutions: A Cultural Theory of Preference Formation." *American Political Science Review* 81: 3–21.

Williams, Rhys H., ed. 1998. *Cultural Wars in American Politics: Critical Reviews of a Popular Myth*. New York: Aldine de Gruyter.

Wilson, James Q., and Edward C. Banfield. 1964. "Public-Regardingness as a Value Premise in Voting Behavior." *American Political Science Review* 58: 876–887.

Wimberly, Ronald. 1976. "Testing the Civil Religion Hypothesis." *Sociological Analysis* 37: 341–352.

Wimberly, Ronald C. 1979. "Continuity in the Measurement of Civil Religion." *Sociological Analysis* 40: 59–62.

Winseman, Albert L. 2005. "How Many Americans are 'Unchurched'?" *Gallup Poll Tuesday Briefing* October 11, 1–4.

Wirthlin, Richard B. 1981. "The Republican Strategy and Its Electoral Consequences." In *Party Coalitions in the 1980s*, ed. Seymour Martin Lipset, 235–266. San Francisco, Calif.: Institute for Contemporary Studies.

Witte, John, Jr. 1990. "How to Govern a City on a Hill: The Early Puritan Contribution to American Constitutionalism." *Emory Law Journal* 39: 41–64.

Wolfe, Alan. 1998. *One Nation, After All*. New York: Viking.

Woodworth, Steven E. 2001. *While God Is Marching On: The Religious World of Civil War Soldiers*. Lawrence, Kans.: University Press of Kansas.

Wright, Benjamin F. 1949. "The Federalist on the Nature of Political Man." *Ethics* 59: 1–31.

Wuthnow, Robert. 1987. *Meaning and Moral Order: Explorations in Cultural Analysis*. Berkeley, Calif.: University of California Press.

Wuthnow, Robert. 1988. *The Restructuring of American Religion*. Princeton, N.J.: Princeton University Press.

Wuthnow, Robert. 1998. *After Heaven: Spirituality in America Since the 1950s*. Berkeley, Calif.: University of California Press.

Yengoyan, Aram A. 1986. "Theory in Anthropology: On the Demise of the Concept of Culture." *Comparative Studies in Society and History* 28: 368–374.

CHAPTER 6

RELIGION AND POLITICAL SOCIALIZATION

SHANNA PEARSON-MERKOWITZ
AND JAMES G. GIMPEL

POLITICAL socialization is the process by which citizens learn about political leaders, governmental institutions, and political processes, and acquire their political beliefs and practices. Socialization is *developmental* in nature. As individuals mature from youth to adulthood, and even during the latter, they continue to learn new political information. This ongoing process of learning serves to shape values, political commitments, and political skills, which in turn determine which policies, candidates, and political parties are favored. Put another way, the socialization process provides the conceptual tools needed to render judgment on political matters. The academic study of political socialization attempts to answer questions such as: Why do some citizens participate whereas others do not? Why do some have crystallized, well-defined political views whereas others have ambivalent or apathetic perspectives? In short, how do individuals develop attitudes toward politics and government in the way that they do?

The research on political socialization in the American context has been based on an implicit normative foundation—namely, that positive socialization experiences communicate values conducive to the maintenance of democratic political institutions (Dennis 1968). Scholars assume that it is better to develop attitudes that favor political participation than to develop cynical, nonparticipatory ones; to create attitudes supportive of governmental institutions and processes than foster more negative ones; and to acquire knowledge about the political system and how it works rather than remain ignorant of its operation. Successful political socialization involves the formation of "informed" opinions on issues (Sears and Valentino 1997) as well as respect for the outcomes of the political process, especially when the latter are not in one's personal interest. Thus, overall, practices that further the goals of participation, knowledge, opinion holding, and support for the democratic process are deemed superior to practices that undermine these goals.

Our nation has become better educated during the past half century, with its population possessing more years of formal schooling with each successive decade. Yet, the higher educational attainment of today's young adults raises the quandary of why political participation rates have fallen during the past several decades (at least until its upsurge beginning in 2004), and why young people exhibit less political awareness and knowledge today than their parents and grandparents did at the same age (Nie, Junn, and Stehlik-Barry 1996; Zukin 2000). In terms of normative expectations, it appears that many Americans have been "poorly socialized."

The central argument of this chapter is that the process by which citizens acquire political knowledge, political attitudes, and expectations concerning political activity is poorly understood. This is the case despite a half century of political socialization research. In the first section of the chapter, we summarize the history of political socialization as a field of study and describe the role different agents have played in the socialization process. We also discuss religious socialization and religion as an influence on both youth and adult political socialization. In the second section, we review literature that specifically addresses how churches serve as socializing and mobilizing venues for otherwise politically quiescent religious groups. And, in the final section, we discuss possible avenues for future research.

THE HISTORY OF SOCIALIZATION RESEARCH

Childhood Political Socialization

By 1970, the subfield of political socialization was a "growth stock" within political science (Greenstein 1970). Between 1961 and 1968, the term *political socialization* went from being an occasional passing reference within the discipline to a major subfield of specialization that garnered as many section members as some of the more established areas of research in the discipline (Greenstein 1970, p. 969). What attracted many scholars to the field was its effort to discern how the protest generation of the 1960s acquired their political attitudes, which seemed to conflict with those of their more conservative parents. As a result, leading investigators initiated studies on the causes and consequences of political learning and how it affected political activity and opinion later in life.

Much of early research was based on two major assumptions about the process of political socialization—namely, the primacy principle and the structuring principle (Searing, Schwartz, and Lind 1973). The primacy principle holds that what is learned early is retained the longest. And just what kinds of things are learned early? Generally, it is not specific attitudes about public policy or detailed information about institutional processes; children lack the cognitive capacity to acquire such things. Rather, conceptions of morality, broad orientations toward authority (e.g., toward authority figures, the law), and various identities (e.g., national identity, sexual identity, religious identity, partisan identity) are the phenomena learned at an early age.

The structuring principle holds that what is learned early is not only retained, but molds later learning as well—structuring the acquisition of later attitudes and behavior. Early orientations and identities serve as "filters" in terms of who and what is to be believed or trusted as well as who and what might be accordingly dismissed as untrustworthy. For example, a partisan identity acquired early in life serves as a filter in assessing candidates and issue positions as maturation takes place.

However, two alternative models of the effects of childhood socialization have subsequently emerged within the literature on political socialization: the persistence model and the impressionable years model (Sears and Levy 2003, p. 78). The persistence model posits that residues of preadult learning persist throughout one's lifetime, perhaps becoming less susceptible to change over time. Thus, it is consistent with the contentions associated with the primary and structuring principles, but less strongly stated. On the other hand, the impressionable years model holds that one's political attitudes are particularly susceptible to influence during the years of late adolescence and early adulthood, and that such attitudes tend to persist thereafter. These two models are normally contrasted with the view that adults are more responsive to the events of their "times" (see our later discussion for a further description of these alternative models related to adult socialization).

Several major agents of socialization are typically identified as playing primary roles in learning about the political world during childhood: parents, schools, peers, and the mass media. In early socialization research, parents attracted the lion's share of the academic inquiry on how children acquire political interest and knowledge, as both the primacy and the structuring principles drew attention to parents (Beck 1977, p. 122). Not only can parents largely determine what messages are communicated to the child early in life, but they are able to select or screen many of the other socializing agents that might affect their children. Thus, parents can work to ensure the messages communicated at home (whether about morality, orientations toward authority, or identity) are reinforced elsewhere (e.g., by selecting those churches or schools that convey similar messages). Likewise, parents can seek to prevent exposure to other socializing agents that communicate messages contrary to parental wishes (e.g., certain media programs). Not surprisingly, therefore, in his seminal review of the early socialization research, Hyman (1959, p. 51) concluded: "Foremost among agencies of socialization into politics is the family."

Nevertheless, as political socialization research unfolded, the findings did not consistently reveal the primacy of parents in the process. In the initial waves of their monumental multiwave panel study of parent–child pairings, Jennings and Niemi (1968) found that parents were not as central to the political development of children as scholars had generally assumed—at least for the particular generation of youth they were studying. For example, they found a surprisingly low correspondence between the parents' level of political interest and that of the child. And later studies revealed that, although parents appeared to transmit their party identification to their children, little else appeared to be passed on (Sears 1975; Jennings and Niemi 1981).

More recent research, however, has revealed that the relationship of political values between parent and child is generally strong among highly politicized parents, but not among those who are apolitical or only occasionally political (Beck and Jennings 1991; Jennings, Stoker, and Bowers 1999). Thus, the relatively weak associations previously found between child and parental attitudes may have been an artifact of a particular generation in which parent–child ties were strained by politically dealigning forces, rather than a generalization holding across all generations (Beck and Jennings 1991, p. 759).

Among the early researchers on political socialization, Hess and Torney (1967) argued that schools were critical to political socialization—in part because children spent so much time there. Research on schools has focused on the effects of formal instruction and routines (e.g., civic courses), the effects of teachers, and the effects of extracurricular activities. With regard to the first, most early studies showed that the civics education curriculum did not contribute greatly to increased students' political awareness or participation among students, but simply reinforced community norms (e.g., Litt 1963; Langton and Jennings 1968). The classic study by Jennings and Niemi (1968; see also Langton and Jennings 1968) found that the civics curriculum increased the likelihood of participation among disadvantaged minority students, but that variation in school curricula had only a minimal effect on socialization. However, more recent studies suggest that students do gain political knowledge from the civics curriculum, although what they learn politically varies across student subgroups and is not limited to the civics curriculum (Galston 2001). For example, Conover and Searing (2000) examine the role of high schools in fostering civic understanding and behavior, and find that different elements of the school experience affect the civic consciousness and practice of young people. Niemi and Junn (1998) find that the recency and extent of civic coursework, along with the variety of courses studied, and the frequency of discussion of contemporary events in the classroom had significant effects on the acquisition of civic knowledge. Likewise, increased political knowledge varies by topic, with more knowledge shown in matters that have greater personal relevance, such as criminal and civil rights, than in those of less direct relevance (Niemi and Junn 1998, p. 36). And what is learned politically is also shaped by the level of political heterogeneity evident within such learning environments (e.g., Gimpel, Lay, and Schuknecht 2003; Campbell 2006).

The strongest case for substantial teacher influence was made by Hess and Torney (1967, p. 110) who argued: "The public school appears to be the most important and effective instrument of political socialization in the United States." However, their study suffered from several important methodological problems (see, for example, Beck 1977, p. 129).[1] And, when more methodologically sound studies were conducted, the results showed that teacher–student agreement was even lower than that of parents and students on all political orientations examined (Jennings, Ehman, and Niemi 1994). The effect of the school has been noted in other ways. Children who are involved in extracurricular activities are more likely to be involved in political activity later in life (Beck and Jennings 1982; McNeal 1995).

The findings from early studies on the influence of peers on the development of political attitudes were relatively unclear and, at times, contradictory (e.g., Campbell 1980; Tedin 1980; Rosenberg 1985). Langton (1967) contended that peer groups could inculcate and reinforce positive values, because heterogeneous class environments could "resocialize" lower status youngsters toward the "superior" civic values of upper income groups. Although later investigations did find that certain attributes may be more amenable to peer influence than others, political attitudes were usually not of sufficient importance to a respondent's peers to be subject to group pressures toward conformity (Campbell 1980). Although students often knew their parents' political attitudes, they were less likely to know those of their peers (Tedin 1980, p. 148). And, according to reference group theory, on which investigations of peer influence were largely based (Festinger, Schacter, and Bach 1950), a group's influence only extends to particular domains of relevance.

With regard to the mass media as socializing agents, a number of studies have examined their influence on adolescents (Chaffee, Ward, and Tipton 1970; Conway, Stevens, and Smith 1975; Conway, Wyckoff, Feldbaum, and Ahern 1981; Garramone 1983; Garramone and Atkin 1986). During the 1950s and '60s, scholars largely ignored the role of the mass media as a socializing agent, but during the 1970s and '80s they saw a larger role for the news media—in fact, one scholar went so far as to term television "the new parent" (Hollander 1971). Given that the news media are a primary source of political information for adults (Zaller 1992), it is hardly surprising to learn that news consumption rises steadily as children age, and that children who are exposed to informational programming on television are more knowledgeable about politics and current events than those who are not (Chafee, Ward, and Tipton 1970; Garramone and Atkin 1986). However, although media may play a major role in cognitive learning about politics, there is little evidence beyond self-reporting that they have a substantial direct influence in shaping political opinions and attitudes (Chaffee, Ward, and Tipton 1970). Evidence suggesting that media messages have "unmediated and substantive effects" are limited (Leighley 2004, p. 169). Nevertheless, others have argued that media both molds and reinforces political position taking and participation (Ansolabehere and Iyengar 1995; Patterson 2002; Kellstedt 2003; Zukin, Keeter, Andolina, Jenkins, and Delli Carpini 2006). In addition, television exposure may alter the basis on which political evaluations are made; those who are more reliant on television than newspapers tend to base their evaluations on more affective reactions than on cognitive information, suggesting that media influence the very basis of political judgment itself (Leighley 2004, p. 170).

The rise of the information economy, the rapid evolution of computer technology, and the explosion of the Internet are new and important socializing agents. In 1965, there were only two or three television channels from which to choose, and the six-o'clock news was the only program available for all who chose to watch television at that time. By the early 1990s, it was common to have scores of channels from which to choose, making it easier for people to avoid news programs altogether (Zukin 2000). For many, network television has been replaced by cable channels and the personal computer, with its explosion of options on the Internet. Not only do presidential candidates have their own websites, they also "advertise" on sites like Facebook, a widely used site for teenagers.

Finally, unique historical events make a great deal of difference to the development of political values, offering "occasions for socialization" (Beck and Jennings 1991; Sears and Valentino 1997; Valentino and Sears 1998). Accordingly, each generation is conditioned by its own unique historical circumstances, resulting in political socialization that is generationally contingent. This is the case for several reasons. First, consider some of the major events that have happened between the mid 1970s and the first decade of the 21st century that might have shaped political learning: Watergate and the Nixon resignation; the Carter presidency, which was plagued by domestic economic and foreign policy crises; the Reagan–Bush era with its massive defense spending, strong economic growth, an ideological repudiation of much of the 40 previous years of domestic policy making, and the Iran–Contra scandal; the dramatic collapse of the Soviet Union and the fall of the Berlin wall, Tiananmen Square, and the emergence of the United States as the world's sole superpower; the first Gulf War; the Los Angeles riots of 1992; the moral scandal of the Clinton–Lewinsky affair; the shocking Columbine High School shootings; the events of 9/11; and, the current war in Iraq.

Second, not only are events and circumstances likely to vary by generation, but the meaning and significance of socialization agents can change over time as well. For example, family life has undergone dramatic change, particularly with the increase in single-parent households. Having two parents in the household increases the likelihood that children will hear adult conversations, some of which may be about politics, therefore enhancing their exposure to political information (Niemi and Junn 1998, p. 57).

All of this suggests that research on adolescents should be ongoing and that earlier work should be revisited regularly, because political learning may vary from one generation to the next as a result of changing events and circumstances. Nevertheless, because the field was not altogether successful in explaining gaping differences across generations, interest in childhood political socialization studies declined significantly by the mid 1980s.[2] Timeless general laws did not emerge (except that political socialization is time bound or subject to period effects). Instead, generational and subpopulation differences were discovered. Studies revealed so many inconsistent findings that researchers may have grown discouraged and abandoned the study.[3] Consequently, already by the early 1980s, some were willing to offer the study of political socialization its last rites (e.g., Cook 1985), and research in the subfield during the 1980s and '90s became primarily the province of a few prominent specialists (Jennings and Niemi 1981; Niemi and Junn 1998).

Unfortunately, those who turned away from its study did not realize that generational and subpopulation differences in socialization are among the main reasons why the process of political socialization is worth studying and continually in need of revisiting. Some research in the field was done more indirectly, largely under different guises such as political psychology or studies of contextual effects on political behavior, but only a few scholars openly admitted they were engaging in political socialization research—even if they were.

Childhood Religious Socialization

During the halcyon days of political socialization research, little attention was given to the study of the religious beliefs, affiliation, and behavior of youth (for exceptions, see Wuthnow 1976; Nelson and Provin 1980; Cornwall 1988). However, in recent years, research on religion among teens has simply exploded (for reviews of this research, see Regnerus, Smith, and Fritsch 2003; Smith 2003; Bartkowski 2007).[4] This research has revealed several basic and relatively consistent findings, some of which stand in contrast to prevailing assumptions about the religious character of young people today that posit an "increasing secularization of youth" (Gallup and Lindsay 1999, p. 160).

The overwhelming proportion of youth today (85 percent) claim a denominational affiliation (e.g., Smith and Faris 2002; Smith and Denton 2005). Most such affiliations are linked to conventional forms of religious organization, with a little more than half claiming to be Protestant, and another one quarter affiliating with the Roman Catholic Church. Nor are teens generally alienated from or hostile toward organized religion (Smith 2003). Thus, any claims that contemporary youth are "spiritual seekers," largely devoid of ties to organized forms of religion, appear to be incorrect (Smith and Denton 2005). In addition, there is evidence that youth who are religiously active do better on a variety of outcome variables related to academic achievement in school and noninvolvement in risky behaviors (e.g., drug and alcohol use, sexual promiscuity) than those who are not religiously engaged (Smith and Denton 2005, pp. 221–223).

Moreover, most teens take their religion quite seriously. Data gathered through the Monitoring the Future study[5] revealed that, in 1996, approximately three in five high school seniors reported that religion was important in their lives, and nearly one in three claimed it was "very important"' (Smith and Faris 2002). On the other hand, less than one in six (15 percent) in the 1996 study stated that religion was "not important" to them (Smith and Faris 2002). Data subsequently gathered in 2002 through 2003 through the National Study of Youth and Religion (NSYR), revealed similar patterns—with more than half of the NSYR youth reporting that their faith was "extremely important" in shaping their daily lives, whereas less than 1 in 10 indicated that their faith was "not at all important" (Smith and Denton 2005).

American young people today not only report religious affiliations and relatively high levels of religious salience, but there is also evidence of at least modest levels of religious belief.[6] More than four out of five profess belief in God, and three in five report belief in angels and in divine miracles (Smith and Denton 2005, chap. 2). Finally, there is evidence that young people are also relatively active religiously. In the 1996 wave of the Monitoring the Future study, nearly one in three high school students indicated that they attended religious services once per week or more often (Smith and Faris 2002), a somewhat lower level than that claimed among adults. However, such religious activity and salience varied by religious tradition, as those affiliated with more theologically orthodox traditions tended to attend religious services more frequently (Smith, Denton, Faris, and Regnerus 2002) and rate their faith as being more important to them (Smith 2003).

Religiously active youth are more likely to express moral compassion and commitment to justice than are nonreligious youth. In contrast to the latter, religiously active youth are more likely to volunteer, be civically engaged, and render service to their communities (Smith and Denton 2005, pp. 226–232; Marcelo, Lopez, and Kirby 2007). Our own research from a large survey sample of youth indicated that what mattered most for racial and ethnic tolerance was the regularity of religious observance (Gimpel, Lay, and Schuknecht 2003). Regardless of religious tradition or denomination, those who attended church services every week were more tolerant than those who never attended or attended only occasionally. Even as early as adolescence, a significant division emerges between the religiously committed and the less committed—less so between mainline and evangelical Protestants, between Protestants and Catholics, or between Christians and non-Christian traditions.

When examined over time, weekly attendance at worship services among high school seniors dropped from around 40 percent (1976–1981) to 31 percent in 1991, although it has remained fairly stable throughout the 1990s (Regnerus and Uecker 2006, p. 218). However, reported attendance at religious services declines as one compares eighth graders with sophomores and sophomores with seniors (Smith et al. 2002, p. 605). On the other hand, little, if any, change has occurred between 1976 and 1996 in the general affect expressed by youth toward organized religion (Smith 2003). And, overall, seniors in high school "consistently agree with their parents' religious views, render a generally positive evaluation of religious institutions, express a desire for religious institutions to be influential in society, and have given or would give financially to religious organization provided they have the monetary means to do so" (Bartkowski 2007, p. 503). In fact, in a unique 60-year-long study of close to 200 Protestant and Catholic men and women born in the 1920s,[7] the data show that the "variation in levels of adolescent religious involvement in the 1930s and 1940s closely parallels studies of religiousness among adolescents today" (Dillon and Wink 2007, p. 46).

Such religious continuity is also evident in a cross-time replication study of college students enrolled in nine different evangelical colleges. Students enrolled in 1996 expressed the same level of religious beliefs and moral values, and they exhibited the same religious practices as students attending these same colleges in 1982 (Penning and Smidt 2002). What changed over time among these evangelical college students was not their religious characteristics, but their political characteristics. They became more Republican in political party identifications and more conservative in terms of ideological orientations (Penning and Smidt 2002). Thus, although political socialization may be largely generationally specific, with important changes transpiring over time, religious socialization may be less subject to such generational divergence.[8]

Still, though there have been studies on political socialization and other studies on religious socialization, little work has been done to relate the two. Within traditional studies of political socialization, there have been only vague allusions to the role religion may play as a primary instrument of political information transmission among the young (Jennings and Niemi 1981, pp. 182–184). As a result, questions such as how religious participation as an adolescent may affect their political participation and beliefs as they emerge into adulthood, when ties to a church may wane or lapse, remain unanswered. Moreover, aside from schools, churches are among the few places where youth interact with adults outside their family—in other words, other citizens who may expose them to information and ideas that may be absent, or poorly communicated, in their home (Smith and Denton 2005, p. 69). How important, then, is participation in religious congregations during one's youth in the shaping of political attitudes and behavior of such adolescents when they reach adulthood? An answer to the question calls for longitudinal or cohort analysis.

RELIGION AND ADULT POLITICAL SOCIALIZATION

Emphases on adult political socialization are generally based on one of two different models (Sears and Levy 2003, p. 79). The first is the lifelong openness model. Here, individuals remain open throughout their lifetime to political influence and learning. The second is the life cycle model. This particular approach holds that people are typically attracted to certain kinds of attitudes at particular stages in their life cycle (e.g., liberalism in youth and conservatism in old age).

At least since *The American Voter* (Campbell, Converse, Miller, and Stokes 1960), political scientists have argued that the American public is largely uninformed and unsophisticated politically. Not only do many Americans lack a basic understanding of American government, they frequently fail to form clear and consistent opinions about political subjects. This situation continues to be true long after the seminal studies on the subject were published.

By the early 1990s, "political knowledge" and "political awareness" became central concepts for study, as scholars began to examine how those with greater awareness thought and behaved compared with those who were less aware and less informed (Delli Carpini and Keeter 1991; Zaller 1992; Delli Carpini and Keeter 1996; Converse 2000). As political scientists have learned more about the causes and consequences of possessing varying levels of information, researchers have again turned to examine how different agents of socialization contribute to what individuals learn about politics and how likely they are to become politically engaged later in life. This time around, however, researchers are expanding the scope of data collection and hypothesis testing beyond family and school-related variables, incorporating measures of discussion within social networks, neighborhood contexts, as well as religious institutions, into a more complete understanding of the roots of political engagement (Verba, Schlozman, Brady, and Nie 1993; Verba, Schlozman, and Brady 1995; Gimpel, Lay, and Schuknecht 2003; Campbell 2006). In this more recent body of research, the school, community, and neighborhood contexts are considered essential elements of explanation, as they structure (1) exposure to the political beliefs and activities of others, (2) regulate the flow of political information, and (3) shape the character of interpersonal interaction (Huckfeldt and Sprague 1995; Anderson 1996; Alesina and La Ferrara 2000; Beck, Dalton, Greene, and Huckfeldt 2002; Gimpel, Lay, and Schuknecht 2003; Campbell 2006).

Major religious traditions express a striking degree of conformity of opinion among their congregants when it comes to political matters and political party preference, even after controlling for confounding factors such as race and socioeconomic status. For example, 68 percent of Jews identified themselves as Democrats in 2004, whereas only about one quarter of evangelical Protestants did so (Green 2007, p. 88). A similar degree of homogeneity appears when examining ideological orientations and issue positions (Barker and Carman 2000; Mayer 2004; Green 2007, p. 86; Wald and Calhoun-Brown 2007), with differences between adherents and nonadherents greatly exacerbated on moral and cultural issues such as women's rights, gay marriage, and abortion (Wuthnow 1988; Hunter 1991; Davis and Robinson 1996; DiMaggio, Evans, and Bryson 1996; Layman 2001; Weisberg 2005).[9] In addition, strongly held religious beliefs and high levels of religious practice are associated with highly constrained political attitudes suggesting the importance of religious institutions as socializing agents.

Scholars have begun to examine the role of religion in the process of opinion formation and political participation, particularly among adults, because there is a growing recognition that adults continue to learn about politics and can be socialized and resocialized throughout the various stages of the life cycle and in a variety of institutions. For example, in recent years, religious beliefs have been cited as an important foundation for economic values (Barker and Carman 2000; Wald and Calhoun-Brown 2007; Wilson, chapter 7, this volume), foreign policy attitudes (Mayer 2004; Guth, Green, Kellstedt, and Smidt 2005; Guth, chapter 9, this volume), and, most notably, views about "social" issues such as abortion, women's rights, prayer in school, homosexual unions, and sex education (Wuthnow 1988; Hunter 1991; Davis and Robinson 1996; Dimaggio, Evans, and Bryson 1996; Layman 2001; Wilcox and Norrander 2002; Weisberg 2005; Jelen, chapter 8, this volume). In these matters, greater attention has been given to churches, religious media, religious interest groups, and clergy as agents of political socialization.

Churches as Agents of Political Socialization

If religious beliefs and practices have important political consequences, the primary socializing agent for these beliefs and practices is the local church. In the following section, we examine the role of the local church in this regard.

Sources of Theological Perspectives and Moral Judgments

Religious congregations are among the most important, active, and far-reaching institutions in America (Putnam 2000, p. 66). They are the source of theological and moral perspectives that guide judgments about public policy. Moral commitments undergird a wide variety of public policy goals (Tetlock 2000, p. 247). These values, usually religiously informed, are expressed at the ballot box, ultimately directing political decision making on governmental matters such as the redistribution of wealth, equality, tolerance for deviance and the limits on individual freedom, the severity of criminal punishment, policies relating to family structure, gender roles, and the value of human life. Political differences that touch on competing understandings of right and wrong have come to constitute passionate divisions in contemporary politics.

With this in mind, the acquisition of specific values and value hierarchies has been described as the starting point for political socialization research (Feldman 2003). The question remains, however, as to what *specific* beliefs should be "the starting point." Theological perspectives on God, life after death, the Bible, the historicity of Jesus Christ, and the origins of life are all possibilities. All are linked to a traditionalist–modernist divide (see chapter 1, this volume) that could serve as the appropriate starting point for socialization research within congregations.

In addition, belief systems vary in terms of the appropriate role for both the church and the individual in society. For example, many churches focus on a moral reform agenda (see Harris 1994; Guth, Green, Smidt, Kellstedt, and Poloma 1997; Smidt, Crawford, Deckman, Gray, Hofrenning, Olson, Steiner, and Weston 2003; Smidt 2004), whereas others emphasize a social justice agenda. A variety of studies have analyzed the nature, frequency, and ability of clergy to speak their minds to their members and the public (Hadden 1969; Quinley 1974; Guth et al. 1997; Olson 2000; Crawford and Olson 2001; Jelen 2001; Smidt 2004; Smith 2005).[10] Clergy may make political speeches from the pulpit to encourage their members to participate, and participate in a specific manner (Djupe and Gilbert 2002). However, the extent to which clergy address matters of public affairs varies based on differences in resources and opportunities (Guth et al. 1997; Olson 2000; Crawford and Olson

2001), and differences in terms of theology and ideology (Stark, Foster, Glock, and Quinley 1970, 1971), although differences between evangelical and mainline Protestant clergy in addressing matters of public affairs have narrowed over time (Smidt 2004, chap. 23).

Thus, those who voluntarily assemble for worship services and who observe and listen carefully are likely to receive certain messages about what things they should pay attention to, care about, and act upon—and often these cues are not ignored (Wald, Owen, and Hill 1988, 1990; Olson and Crawford 2001). This is especially true when clergy address certain issues frequently and when they address issues that are salient to their congregations and to society (Djupe and Gilbert 2001).

Finally, clergy are generally perceived to be spiritual and moral leaders—people who are more likely than most of their congregants to be aware of, and concerned with, the moral dimensions of the problems found in the world around them. As a result, on some issues, congregation members may give more credence to a pastoral perspective than they would to an issue position heard or read in some news medium (Buddenbaum 2001). Thus, pastors may not only play a vital role in setting the political agenda of their congregants by the issues they choose to emphasize, but they may also serve to shape their congregants' views on such issues.

These explicit injunctions, as well as the more indirect cues given, can be particularly effective when clergy provide legitimate warrants for their positions (e.g., citing biblical support or historic confessional statements of the church that may be accepted as authoritative), and when those positions do not completely alienate congregation members from the dominant culture (Jelen 2001). Under such circumstances, these messages and cues are not usually ignored (Wald, Owen, and Hill 1988, 1990; Penning and Smidt 2000; Fetzer 2001; Olson and Crawford 2001). Still, in many cases, pastors may be "preaching to the converted." However, even under such circumstances, clergy can still influence their congregations by intensifying their attachments and reinforcing their preferences, which can in turn lead to activism (Jelen 2001). Much more research is needed on how different types of churches serve as sources of theological and social theological perspectives and moral judgments. Understanding the learning process will help us grasp why these beliefs have such robust relationships with political variables (Layman 2001).

Transmitter of Group Norms

Although religion as a font of values may provide a simple explanation for the widespread agreement among congregants on some political issues, it is less obvious why such clear policy congruence holds with regard to issues that are less easily understood in religious terms. Religious congregations and associations are important in that they are usually bound by strong affective ties and frequent patterns of social interaction. These qualities make them well suited to influence the transmission of group norms both to offspring and to new congregants, and they highlight the important difference between socialization that is assumed to generate from a "force of psychological consonance stemming directly from theology" (White 1968, p. 25) and that which stems from social interaction.

As noted earlier, one of the most important ways in which political dispositions are affected by religion is through the local context that churches provide for the interaction of like-minded individuals. In addition, congregations serve as "political communities" (Wald, Owen, and Hill 1988), reinforcing accepted ideas and practices and providing pressures for individuals who are ambivalent or undecided. Even if ministerial leadership does not espouse clearcut political positions from the pulpit, churches can still serve as strong socializing agents, providing members with information and skills relevant to political engagement and participation (Wald, Owen, and Hill 1988; Verba, Schlozman, and Brady 1995).

Religious houses of worship do this by providing opportunities for members to communicate political messages and to influence each other. The regular meeting of those who are relatively of one accord morally and religiously promotes further social interaction and communication. Moreover, departure from community norms can bring punishment. Congregations can discipline, shun, or "disfellowship" members who stray too far, although this power is more sharply constrained in contemporary times compared with earlier centuries. Particularly in "strict churches" (i.e., those that accentuate rule keeping and require members to devote substantial time to the church outside of Sunday services), members are less likely to have as extensive a social network outside of the church or to challenge the conventional political values held by members of the congregation (Finke and Stark 1992). As Laurence Iannacone (1994) notes, strict churches make nonchurch activity highly costly; but, in so doing, such institutions not only screen out weakly committed members, they also stimulate higher levels of involvement among those who remain.

Building Civic Skills

As politically socializing institutions, churches can directly promote engaged citizenship by providing regular attendees with opportunities to build the skills necessary to participate actively in politics (Verba, Scholzman, and Brady 1995). By participating in church activities beyond attendance at services, members learn skills that make them more likely to participate in politics because they perceive less cost in doing so, (in fact, it is less costly) and because they are prepared to apply organizational skills they have learned in church. Thus, developing members' skill sets is largely a by-product of church participation. Religious traditions vary as to how likely they are to provide training opportunities for the skills essential for political participation, with hierarchically organized churches less likely to do so, whereas congregationally based churches are more likely to do so (Verba, Schlozman, and Brady 1995; but see Jones-Correa and Leal 2001).

Certainly not all churches encourage their members to participate in political and civic activity. Many churches in the United States do not take an active role in the political process, and their leadership resists endorsing parties or candidates. "Activist" or "political churches," on the other hand, see it as their mission to take an aggressive role in making the governmental system more just and enabling their congregants to participate. In these churches, congregants are in fact *expected* to participate and work actively to make the world a better place (Wald 2003, p. 155).

Politicized churches are also very important because political topics are discussed during worship services and worshipers receive clear political instructions and admonishments directly from their clergy (Calhoun-Brown 1996; Djupe and Gilbert 2002).

Political scientists, as a rule, agree that the many citizens remain ignorant of basic aspects of government and politics, and are unsure about how their values align with their political preferences (Campbell et al. 1960; Converse 1964; Zaller 1992). Likewise, legions of Americans are unable to respond accurately to questions about how the parties or candidates are positioned on salient political topics. Recent research has found that it is only individuals who are aware of party polarization on issues that are able to make well-reasoned decisions about which party they should belong to given their beliefs (Layman and Carsey 2002; Carsey and Layman 2006). Positions clearly enunciated from the pulpit, or in a Sunday school class, can assist those parishioners with limited information and interest in politics in making the connection between their moral values and current political debates. In addition, because clergy specifically encourage their members to vote, and some may publicly support particular candidates (although primarily off the pulpit), activist churches do motivate congregants to act on the information they receive (Guth et al. 1997; Djupe and Gilbert 2002). As noted earlier, Verba et al. (1995) found differences in the promotion of civic skills among different types of church structures. This finding is promising, but limited in terms of its application to the wide variety of churches in the United States, opening up numerous research opportunities for comparison of local churches, denominations, and religious traditions.

Loci for Direct Mobilization

Finally, churches serve as sites in which those who attend regularly may be mobilized directly to become politically engaged. Churches help to politicize and mobilize voters. Churches may sponsor voter registration drives, and pastors may encourage participation in campaigns (e.g., Harris 1999; Wielhouwer 2000; Olson, chapter 13, this volume; Wielhouwer, chapter 14, this volume).

Church attendance facilitates political contacting, because regular worshipers are more prone to engage in informal political discussions with friends, more likely to pick up a voter guide left in the church, or may even find themselves on some mailing list of an organization promoting a moral or social issue agenda (Guth, Kellstedt, Smidt, and Green 1998, p. 180). The most common form of religious political contact is clergy encouraging their parishioners to register and vote, with about one half of black Protestants and evangelical Protestants reporting such urging in the 2004 election campaign (Guth, Kellstedt, Green, and Smidt 2006, p. 162). The second most common form is the informal political discussion that takes place at church, also varying by religious tradition as well as by time—with evangelical Protestants the most likely to report such discussions and with the percentage doing so increasing monotonically over the 1996, 2000, and 2004 presidential election cycles (Guth et al. 2006, p. 164).

Although press accounts have often highlighted the use of voter guides to provide cues to parishioners regarding how to vote, less than 10 percent in 2004 reported the presence of such guides at their houses of worship (Guth et al. 2006, p. 165). This represents a fairly significant decline from that reported in 1996, when some 27 percent of churchgoers reported receiving some kind of information at church about candidates or parties (Kohut, Green, Keeter, and Toth 2000). Based on data from the American National Election Studies, Wilcox and Sigelman (2001) have also shown that the presence of such guides varies by religious tradition and that their presence has declined over time. Thus, during the past three presidential elections, it appears that political talk at church has increased, that voter guides are less common, and that the already small numbers of clergy endorsements remain relatively rare.

However, the role that churches play in political mobilization needs to be placed within a broader perspective. Given the relative weakness of party organizations in general and given the difficulty to locate and activate sympathetic voters, regular church attenders provide an inviting opportunity to contact voters who share relatively similar values and perspectives. The ability to reach such a substantial number of voters because they attend church on a regular basis is no small matter. Religious interest groups, in particular, may seek to target members of different churches based on attitude similarities among such church members. As a result, religious interest groups have become significant competitors (and sometime adjuncts) to party committees, candidate organizations, and traditional interest groups (Guth, Kellstedt, Green, and Smidt 2002, p. 171). Nevertheless, members of religious houses of worship are more likely to be mobilized through conversations with their fellow congregational members. These "informal religious social networks" increase the likelihood of participation (McKenzie 2004) as well as shape political beliefs among its members (Wald, Owen, and Hill 1988).

In sum, churches have a significant role to play in the socialization process. They are the primary teachers of theological perspectives and moral attitudes, they transmit group norms, they build civic skills, and they provide a location for political mobilization. How churches do this and how successful they are in this regard are important avenues for future research.

African American Churches as Socializing Agents

Black churches have played an important role historically within the African American community. As a location for the political socialization of African Americans, the black church has been ideal—a safe place where communication about all sorts of topics could take place, including political communication. Political candidates, particularly Democrats, have recognized this as they regularly make appearances in black churches during the course of election campaigns. In addition, as a source of political mobilization, the church has been particularly important for African Americans, who as a group have less access to other institutions that socialize and recruit congregants for political action (Tate 1993; Harris

1994; Verba, Schlozman, and Brady 1995; Alex-Assensoh and Assensoh 2001; Barnes 2005). Pastors in the black church have regularly enlisted their congregations to participate in political protests and demonstrations. Preachers have been the negotiators of accommodation with white society, agents of social change, and, at times, the "objects of messianic expectations of deliverance" (McTighe 2000, p. 595).

Until recently, the careers of most prominent African American political leaders originated in the church, as ordained ministers. From Martin Luther King, Jr., to Jesse Jackson, Jr., to Al Sharpton, black political leaders have relied on the homogeneous community that the church provides as a power base and mobilizing force. Compared with other institutions, the church is arguably the fundamental unit of political mobilization within the African American community.

To be sure, the largely Protestant denominations and independent congregations present in African American communities are a different mix from those in neighborhoods with largely white residents. These denominations differ by name, doctrine, and style of worship, primarily because of the historical and cultural traditions of the communities that African American churches serve. Despite this, African Americans are consistently more liberal ideologically and aligned more fully with the Democratic Party in their economic views than are whites who belong to churches in the same denomination (Wald and Calhoun-Brown 2007). This difference is attributed to the distinctive socioeconomic interests of African Americans as a group and to the fact that many of the major black congregations were founded in a direct response to racism (Lincoln and Mamiya 1990), with many of these congregations later serving as platforms for the civil rights movement.

Still, there are some important religious and political differences between different kinds of African American churches. For example, clergy from the African Methodist Episcopal (AME) church are much more likely than pastors from the Church of God in Christ (COGIC) to approve the formation of action groups in their congregations to accomplish some social or political goal, to participate in a protest march, or to commit some act of civil disobedience. Similar differences were found between AME and COGIC clergy in terms of public policy positions and voting in presidential elections, with the COGIC pastors more conservative (see McDaniel 2004a, b). Documenting differences in the socialization of congregants in a variety of African American churches is a fruitful avenue for future research.

DIRECTIONS FOR FUTURE RESEARCH

In this final section, we will explore several ideas for future research related to religion and political socialization. Rather than pointing to some very specific research questions, our discussion will focus on several broad topics that merit further scholarly analysis.

Religious and Political Socialization

First, there has been very little effort to relate religious and political socialization within childhood and early adolescence. Rather, one strand of research has basically focused on childhood and adolescent political socialization, whereas another strand has examined childhood and adolescent religious socialization. However, the extent to which the two facets reinforce each other or remain separated is not well understood. For example, when children and adolescents are socialized to accept religious authority, does such acceptance have a "spillover effect" and lead to the acceptance of political authority? Early political socialization research emphasized the president and the policeman as the points of contact where children became aware of a larger political world (e.g., Easton and Dennis 1969). Interestingly, much of the early images that children had of the president (e.g., he was benevolent and omnipotent) are attributes frequently associated with God within the Abrahamic faith traditions. Consequently, is socialization toward authority within the religious sphere linked to socialization in the political arena?

Likewise, we know that many religious faiths emphasize a separation between religious and political authority, so that remaining true to one's religious faith may entail the rejection of the legitimacy of authorities, or even structures of government. How do children and adolescents come to separate their religious and their political identity?

We also lack panel studies of children and adolescents that track children and adolescents into adulthood to ascertain whether the particular relationships evident between religion and political orientations and behavior during earlier years in life continue to be evident later in life.[11] Do the linkages between religious and political variables become stronger, weaker, or remain largely the same over time? And, if changes occur, what factors are associated with modifying such relationships?

Recent Immigrants and Civic Participation

New religions and greater religious diversity have arisen in the wake of the quickened pace of emigration to the United States since the late 1960s (Eck 2001). The presence of new immigrants provides an opportunity to study the socialization and outcomes among preadult immigrants, but also to analyze the resocialization of older adults (Jennings 2007, p. 39). Recent immigrants are generally more religious here in the United States than they were in their native countries, possibly because religion facilitates the preservation of cultural identities (Smith 1978; Williams 1988).

Immigrants to the United States confront many disadvantages and obstacles to participation in the political process. They often come from countries with non-participatory political traditions, many of which are extremely oppressive and authoritarian. In addition, immigrants arrive without social networks to provide the information necessary to facilitate political learning and engagement. Others confront language barriers that place critical bits of political information out of their reach. In this regard, houses of worship frequently serve as "schools for living, where immigrants and others address many of the issues of living in a strange new land and acquire tools and resources, moral and spiritual as well as social and economic, for making their way in society" (Foley and Hoge 2007, p. 22).

As yet, we know very little about the processes by which those affiliated with various nonwestern immigrant religions are incorporated socially and politically within American life. We continue to know very little about the power of non-western religious tenets on the politics of these religious minorities, particularly in terms of succeeding generations. For example, Islam does not recognize a separation of church and state, and so there is the whole issue of how first-, second-, and third-generation Muslim immigrants to this country come to view the principle of separation of church and state within the context of American politics.

Reversing the Causal Direction

The socialization experience that churches offer their members is never a clean and neat product of religious doctrine alone. Theological systems are intricate, and typically some tenets are ignored whereas others are given great emphasis; in fact, much of the impact of doctrine may be mediated by the characteristics of a particular community that churches serve. A congregation serving a mixed-race urban population may choose to emphasize social justice and Jesus' merciful ministry to the poor and oppressed, whereas a congregation within the same denomination serving a white suburban population may emphasize scriptural teachings against abortion, homosexuality, divorce, and sexual promiscuity.

The differences in message framing and moral emphasis *within traditions* pose a challenge to the dominant thrust of social scientific research on religion, which has favored running the arrow of causality from religious doctrine to political beliefs, explaining the latter in terms of the former. Churches and church leaders depend upon local populations for their financial well-being. In settings of high mobility, many churches are in a fluid market for adherents, and must therefore present themselves in a favorable light, as local conditions may dictate. If they do not cater to the values and dispositions of local populations, they risk stagnation, or going under entirely.[12] Attending to the needs of the people in the pews may lead different congregations within the same denominational tradition to express rather different perspectives on political matters because the values of their worshipers may be dictating the content of preaching from the pulpit. If so, political differences between two congregations, just a few miles apart, will not disappear simply because the two churches share confessional tenets. Although it is unlikely that individuals pick congregations solely on the basis of their political orientations, it is conceivable that, within the same denomination or larger faith tradition, individuals may choose a particular congregation based first on consideration of their general theological or confessional perspectives, and then, within that context, select a congregation that is more congruent with their own political orientation.

Where such phenomena occur, religion's influence as a socialization force may give way to local partisan and cultural influences, ceding its power as a force for individual and collective transformation. Examining this possibility will call for imaginative research designs that use a variety of techniques—lengthy periods of observation, content analysis of sermons and other types of teaching, in-depth interviews with clergy, and surveys of congregations.

Of course, these broad arenas for research on religion and political socialization do not exhaust the possibilities for such investigation. There is clearly a need for continued research that examines the links between religion—in its various facets of expression—and political learning. Given that socialization is a process, this effort will likely test the skills that scholars in the various disciplines have to offer.

NOTES

1. Beck (1977, p. 128) notes that several methodological difficulties have hampered researchers in demonstrating the influence of schools in the political socialization process: (1) the fact that they are institutions, and not individuals, diminishes the appropriateness of measures of agreement frequently used to indicate parental influence; and (2) virtually all young adults are exposed to schools, "thus rendering the reliable statistical technique of comparing control and experimental groups inoperative."

2. However, Jennings (2007, p. 29) argues that "[i]t would be a mistake ... to say that an interest in political socialization disappeared for any great length of time." He does note that relatively few studies were published that focused on preadults between the mid 1970s and the early 1990s. By the 1990s, however, scholarly analysis of political socialization had clearly increased, although such attention "has focused on adolescents, young adults, and beyond" (Jennings 2007, p. 30).

3. Increased difficulty in gaining access to public schools may also have been a contributing factor to the decline in socialization research.

4. This section draws heavily on a review of religious socialization by John Bartkowski (2007).

5. Monitoring the Future is an ongoing study of the attitudes, values, and behaviors of American secondary school students. Each year approximately 50,000 students in the 8th, 10th, and 12th grades are surveyed. See http://www.monitorthefuture.org for more information.

6. On the other hand, these more positive assessments of the religious lives of American teens are also coupled with other, less positive, findings. In particular, smost teens find it difficult to explain what they believe and what the implications of their beliefs are for their lives (Smith and Denton 2005, p. 262).

7. The study of Dillon and Wink (2007) draws on a 60-year-long study of nearly 200 mostly Protestant and Catholic men and women who were born in the 1920s but who were interviewed during their adolescence and then again each decade between the 1950s and the late 1990s.

8. However, Smith (2004) using National Opinion Research Center (NORC) GSS data compared those age 18 to 24 in 1997 with those of similar age in 1973 and those of similar age in 1985. Youth in the 1990s were more likely than their counterparts in the 1970s and 1980s to view the world with mistrust and cynicism. They were also more disconnected from society on a number of fronts: They were less likely to read a newspaper, attend church, vote for president, or identify with a political party than previously. In addition, they were less likely to believe people are trustworthy, helpful, or fair, and they were less likely to believe that humans are naturally good or that the world reflects God's goodness.

9. For example, almost 70 percent of Jewish respondents surveyed in 2004 said they supported legal recognition of gay marriages, but less than 10 percent of evangelical Protestants did so (Green 2007, p. 80). The stands of members of different religious groups on the legal right to an abortion reveal a similar divide: Less than 10 percent of evangelical Protestants supported abortion on demand, whereas more than 50 percent of Jews did so (Green 2007, p. 80).

10. The next four paragraphs draw heavily from the literature review provided by Smidt and Schaap (forthcoming).

11. Jennings (2007, p. 38) notes that there are "two intriguing questions" about the influence of parents on socialization: (1) "how enduring is parental influence," and (2) "are there differences in parental impact across generations?"

12. The success of megachurches in recent decades may be the result of effective attentiveness to market forces.

REFERENCES

Alesina, Alberto, and Eliana La Ferrara. 2000. "Participation in Heterogeneous Communities." *Quarterly Journal of Economics* 115 (3): 847–904.

Alex-Assensoh, Yvette, and A. B. Assensoh. 2001. "Inner-City Contexts, Church Attendance, and African-American Political Participation." *The Journal of Politics* 63 (3): 886–901.

Anderson, Christopher J. 1996. "Political Action and Social Integration." *American Politics Quarterly* 24 (1): 105–125.

Ansolabehere, Stephen D., and Shanto Iyengar. 1995. *Going Negative: How Political Advertisements Shrink and Polarize the Electorate*. New York: Free Press.

Barker, David C., and Christopher Jan Carman. 2000. "The Spirit of Capitalism? Religious Doctrine, Values, and Economic Attitude Constructs." *Political Behavior* 22 (1): 1–27.

Barnes, Sandra L. 2005. "Black Church Culture and Community Action." *Social Forces* 84 (2): 967–994.

Bartkowski, John. 2007. "Religious Socialization among American Youth, How Faith Shapes Parents, Children, and Adolescents." In *Handbook of the Sociology of Religion*, ed. James A. Beckford and N. Jay Demerath III, 495–509. Thousand Oaks, Calif.: Sage Publications.

Beck, Paul Allen. 1977. "The Role of Agents in Political Socialization." In *Handbook of Political Socialization: Theory and Research*, ed. Stanley A. Renshon, 115–141. New York: The Free Press.

Beck, Paul Allen, Russell J. Dalton, Steven Greene, and R. Robert Huckfeldt. 2002. "The Social Calculus of Voting: Interpersonal, Media and Organizational Influences on Presidential Choices." *American Political Science Review* 96 (1): 57–74.

Beck, Paul Allen, and M. Kent Jennings. 1982. "Pathways to Participation." *American Political Science Review* 76 (1): 94–108.

Beck, Paul Allen, and Edward T. Jennings. 1991. "Family Traditions, Political Periods, and the Development of Partisan Orientations." *Journal of Politics* 53 (4): 742–763.

Buddenbaum, Judith. 2001. "The Media, Religion, and Public Opinion: Toward a Unified Theory of Influence." In *Religion and Popular Culture: Studies on the Interactions of Worldviews*, ed. Daniel Stout and Judith Buddenbaum, 19–37. Ames, Iowa: Iowa State University Press.

Calhoun-Brown, Allison. 1996. "African American Churches and Political Mobilization: The Psychological Impact of Organizational Resources." *Journal of Politics* 58 (4): 935–953.

Campbell, Angus, Phillip E. Converse, Warren E. Miller, and Donald E. Stokes. 1960. *The American Voter*. Chicago, Ill.: University of Chicago.

Campbell, Bruce A. 1980. "A Theoretical Approach to Peer Influence in Adolescent Socialization." *American Journal of Political Science* 24 (2): 324–344.

Campbell, David E. 2006. *Why We Vote*. Princeton, N.J.: Princeton University Press.

Carsey, Thomas M., and Geoffrey C. Layman. 2006. "Changing Sides or Changing Minds? Party Identification and Policy Preference." *American Journal of Political Science* 50 (2): 464–477.

Chaffee, Steven H., L. Scott Ward, and Leonard P. Tipton. 1970. "Mass Communication and Political Socialization." *Journalism Quarterly* 47 (4): 647–659.

Conover, Pamela Johnston, and Donald D. Searing. 2000. "A Political Socialization Perspective." In *Rediscovering the Democratic Purposes of Education*, ed. Lorraine M. McDonnell, P. Michael Timpane and Roger Benjamin, 91–125. Lawrence, Kans.: Kansas University Press.

Converse, Phillip E. 1964. "The Nature of Belief Systems in Mass Publics." In *Ideology and Discontent*, ed. David Apter. 206–61. New York: Free Press.

Converse, Phillip E. 2000. "Assessing the Capacity of Mass Electorates." *Annual Review of Political Science* 3 (1): 331–353.

Conway, M. Margaret, A. Jay Stevens, and Robert G. Smith. 1975. "The Relation between Media Use and Children's Civic Awareness." *Journalism Quarterly* 52: 531–538.

Conway, M. Margaret, Mikel L. Wyckoff, Eleanor Feldbaum, and David Ahern. 1981. "The News Media in Children's Political Socialization." *The Public Opinion Quarterly* 45 (2): 164–178.

Cook, Timothy E. 1985. "The Bear Market in Political Socialization and the Costs of Misunderstood Psychological Theories." *American Political Science Review* 79 (4): 1079–1093.

Cornwall, Marie. 1988. "The Influence of Three Agents of Socialization." In *The Religion and Family Connection*. Vol. 16, ed. Darwin Thomas, 207–231. Provo, Utah: Brigham Young University Press.

Crawford, Sue E. S, and Laura R. Olson, eds. 2001. *Christian Clergy in American Politics*. Baltimore, Md.: Johns Hopkins University Press.

Davis, Nancy J., and Robert V. Robinson. 1996. "Are the Rumors of War Exaggerated? Religious Orthodoxy and Moral Progressivism in America." *The American Journal of Sociology* 102 (3): 756–787.

Delli Carpini, Michael X., and Scott Keeter. 1991. "Stability and Change in the U.S. Public's Knowledge of Politics." *The Public Opinion Quarterly* 55 (4): 583–612.

Delli Carpini, Michael X., and Scott Keeter. 1996. *What Americans Know about Politics and Why It Matters.* New Haven, Conn.: Yale University Press.

Dennis, Jack. 1968. "Major Problems of Political Socialization Research." *Midwest Journal of Political Science* 12 (1): 85–114.

Dillon, Michele, and Paul Wink. 2007. *In the Course of a Lifetime: Tracing Religious Belief, Practice, and Change.* Berkeley, Calif.: University of California Press.

Dimaggio, Paul, John Evans, and Bethany Bryson. 1996. "Have Americans' Social Attitudes Become More Polarized?" *Social Science Quarterly* 84 (1): 71–90.

Djupe, Paul A., and Christopher P. Gilbert. 2001. "Congregational Resources for Clergy Political Action." Presented at the annual meeting of the Midwest Political Science Association, Chicago, Illinois, April 19–22.

Djupe, Paul A., and Christopher P. Gilbert. 2002. "The Political Voice of Clergy." *The Journal of Politics* 64 (2): 596–609.

Easton, David, and Jack Dennis. 1969. *Children in the Political System: Origins of Political Legitimacy.* New York: McGraw-Hill.

Eck, Diana. 2001. *A New Religious America: How a 'Christian Country' Has Now Become the World's Most Religiously Diverse Nation.* San Francisco, Calif.: HarperSanFrancisco.

Feldman, Stanley. 2003. "Values, Ideology, and the Structure of Political Attitudes." In *Oxford Handbook of Political Psychology,* ed. David O. Sears, Leonie Huddy, and Robert Jervis, 477–508. New York: Oxford University Press.

Festinger, Leon, Stanley Schacter, and Kurt Bach. 1950. *Social Pressures in Informal Groups.* New York: Harper.

Fetzer, Joel. 2001. "Shaping Pacifism: The Role of the Local Anabaptist Pastor." In *Christian Clergy in American Politics,* ed. Sue Crawford and Laura Olson, 177–187. Baltimore, Md.: Johns Hopkins University Press.

Finke, Roger, and Rodney Stark. 1992. *The Churching of America, 1776–1990: Winners and Losers in Our Religious Economy.* New Brunswick, N.J.: Rutgers University Press.

Foley, Michael W., and Dean R. Hoge. 2007. *Religion and the New Immigrants: How Faith Communities Form Our Newest Citizens.* Oxford: Oxford University Press.

Gallup, George, and Michel Lindsay. 1999. *Surveying the Religious Landscape: Trends in U.S. Beliefs.* Harrisburg, Pa.: Morehouse.

Galston, William A. 2001. "Political Knowledge, Political Engagement, and Civic Education." *Annual Review of Political Science* 4 (1): 217–234.

Garramone, Gina M. 1983. "Television News and Political Socialization." In *Communication Yearbook 7,* ed. Robert N. Bostrom. Beverly Hills, Calif.: Sage.

Garramone, Gina M., and Charles Atkin. 1986. "Mass Communication and Political Socialization: Specifying the Effects." *Public Opinion Quarterly* 50 (1): 76–86.

Gimpel, James G., J. Celeste Lay, and Jason E. Schuknecht. 2003. *Cultivating Democracy.* Washington, D.C.: Brookings Institute Press.

Green, John C. 2007. *The Faith Factor: How Religion Influences American Elections.* Westport, Conn.: Praeger.

Greenstein, Fred I. 1970. "A Note on the Ambiguity of 'Political Socialization': Definitions, Criticisms, and Strategies of Inquiry." *The Journal of Politics* 32 (4): 969–978.

Guth, James L., John C. Green, Lyman A. Kellstedt, and Corwin E. Smidt. 2005. "Faith and Foreign Policy: A View from the Pews." *Faith & International Affairs* 3: 3–10.

Guth, James L., John C. Green, Corwin E. Smidt, Lyman A. Kellstedt, and Margaret M. Poloma. 1997. *The Bully Pulpit: The Politics of Protestant Clergy.* Lawrence, Kans.: University of Kansas Press.

Guth, James, Lyman Kellstedt, John Green, and Corwin Smidt. 2002. "A Distant Thunder? Religious Mobilization in the 2000 Election." In *Interest Group Politics.* 6th ed., ed. Allan Cigler and Burdett Loomis, 161–184. Washington, D.C.: CQ Press.

Guth, James, Lyman Kellstedt, John Green, and Corwin Smidt. 2006. "Getting the Spirit? Religious and Partisan Mobilization in the 2004 Elections." In *Interest Group Politics.* 7th ed., ed. Allan Cigler and Burdett Loomis, 157–181. Washington, D.C.: CQ Press.

Guth, James, Lyman Kellstedt, Corwin Smidt, and John Green. 1998. "Thunder on the Right? Religious Interest Group Mobilization in the 1996 Election." In *Interest Group Politics.* 5th ed., ed. Allan Cigler and Burdett Loomis, 169–192. Washington, D.C.: CQ Press.

Hadden, Jeffrey K. 1969. *The Gathering Storm in the Churches.* Garden City, N.Y.: Doubleday.

Harris, Fredrick C. 1994. "Something Within: Religion as a Mobilizer of African-American Activism." *Journal of Politics* 56 (1): 42–68.

Harris, Fredrick C. 1999. *Something Within: Religion in African-American Political Activism.* New York: Oxford University Press.

Hess, Robert, and Judith Torney. 1967. *The Development of Political Attitudes in Children.* Garden City: Doubleday.

Hollander, Neil. 1971. "Adolescents and the War: The Sources of Socialization." *Journalism Quarterly* 48: 472–479.

Huckfeldt, R. Robert, and John Sprague. 1995. *Citizens, Politics, and Social Communication.* Cambridge: Cambridge University Press.

Hunter, James Davison. 1991. *Culture Wars.* New York: Basic Books.

Hyman, Herbert. 1959. *Political Socialization.* Glencoe, Ill.: The Free Press.

Iannacone, Laurence. 1994. "Why Strict Churches Are Strong." *American Journal of Sociology* 99 (5): 1180–1211.

Jelen, Ted G. 2001. "Notes for a Theory of Clergy as Political Leaders." In *Christian Clergy in American Politics,* ed. Sue Crawford and Laura Olson, 15–29. Baltimore, Md.: Johns Hopkins University Press.

Jennings, M.Kent., and Richard Niemi. 1981. *Generations and Politics.* Princeton, N.J.: Princeton University Press.

Jennings, M. Kent, Lee H. Ehman, and Richard Niemi. 1994. "Social Studies Teachers and Their Pupils." In *The Political Character of Adolescence,* ed. Edward Jennings and Richard Niemi, 207–228. Princeton, N.J.: Princeton University Press.

Jennings, M. Kent., Laura Stoker, and Jake Bowers. 1999. "Politics across Generations: Family Transmission Re-examined." Presented at the annual meeting of the American Political Science Association, Atlanta, Georgia, September 2–5.

Jennings, M. Kent. 2007. "Political Socialization." In *The Oxford Handbook on Political Behavior,* ed. Russell Dalton and Hans-Dieter Klingemann, 29–44. New York: Oxford University Press.

Jennings, M. Kent, and Richard Niemi. 1968. "The Transmission of Political Values from Parent to Child." *American Political Science Review* 62 (1): 169–184.

Jones-Correa, Michael A., and David L. Leal. 2001. "Political Participation: Does Religion Matter?" *Political Research Quarterly* 54 (4): 751–770.

Kellstedt, Paul M. 2003. *The Mass Media and the Dynamics of American Racial Attitudes.* Cambridge: Cambridge University Press.

Kohut, Andrew, John C. Green, Scott Keeter, and Robert C. Toth. 2000. *The Diminishing Divide: Religion's Changing Role in American Politics.* Washington, D.C.: Brookings.

Langton, Kenneth P. 1967. "Peer Group and School and the Political Socialization Process." *American Political Science Review* 61 (3): 751–758.

Langton, Kenneth P., and M. Kent Jennings. 1968. "Political Sophistication and the High School Civics Curriculum in the United States." *American Political Science Review* 62 (3): 852–867.

Layman, Geoffrey C. 2001. *The Great Divide*. New York: Columbia University Press.

Layman, Geoffrey C., and Thomas M. Carsey. 2002. "Party Polarization and Conflict Extension in the American Electorate." *American Journal of Political Science* 46 (4): 786–802.

Leighley, Jan. 2004. *Mass Media and Politics: A Social Science Perspective*. Boston, Mass.: Houghton Mifflin.

Lincoln, C. Erik, and Lawrence H. Mamiya. 1990. *The Black Church in the African American Experience*. Durham, N.C.: Duke University Press.

Litt, Edgar. 1963. "Civic Education, Community Norms, and Political Indoctrination." *American Sociological Review* 28 (1): 69–75.

Marcelo, Karlo B., Mark Hugo Lopez, and Emily Hoban Kirby. 2007. "Fact Sheet: Civic Engagement among Young Men and Women." College Park, Md.: CIRCLE: The Center for Information & Research on Civic Learning & Engagement. Also available online at http://www.civicyouth.org/PopUps/FactSheets/FS07_Gender_CE.pdf (accessed December 2, 2007).

Mayer, Jeremy D. 2004. "Christian Fundamentalists and Public Opinion toward the Middle East: Israel's New Best Friends?" *Social Science Quarterly* 85 (3): 695–712.

McDaniel, Eric. 2004a. "African Methodist Episcopal Church." In *Pulpit and Politics: Clergy in American Politics at the Advent of the Millennium*, ed. Corwin E. Smidt, 247–258. Waco, Texas: Baylor University Press.

McDaniel, Eric. 2004b. "Church of God in Christ." In *Pulpit and Politics: Clergy in American Politics at the Advent of the Millennium*, ed. Corwin E. Smidt, 259–271. Waco, Texas: Baylor University Press.

McKenzie, Brian D. 2004. "Religious Social Networks, Indirect Mobilization, and African-American Political Participation." *Political Research Quarterly* 57 (4): 621–632.

McNeal, Ralph B. 1995. "Extracurricular Activities and High School Dropouts." *Sociology of Education* 68 (1): 62–81.

McTighe, Michael J. 2000. "Jesse Jackson and the Dilemmas of a Prophet in Politics." *Journal of Church and State* 32 (3): 585–608.

Nelson, Hart, and Raymond Provin. 1980 "Toward Disestablishment: New Patterns of Social Class, Denomination, and Religiosity among Youth." *Review of Religious Research* 22: 137–154.

Nie, Norman, Jane Junn, and Kenneth Stehlik-Barry. 1996. *Education and Democratic Citizenship in America*. Chicago, Ill.: Chicago University Press.

Niemi, Richard, and Jane Junn. 1998. *Civic Education: What Makes Students Learn?* New Haven, Conn.: Yale University Press.

Olson, Laura R. 2000. *Filled with Spirit and Power: Protestant Clergy in American Politics*. Albany, N.Y.: State University of New York Press.

Olson, Laura R., and Sue E. S. Crawford. 2001. "Clergy in Politics: Political Choices and Consequences." In *Christian Clergy in American Politics*, ed. Sue Crawford and Laura Olson, 3–14. Baltimore, Md.: Johns Hopkins University Press.

Patterson, Thomas E. 2002. *The Vanishing Voter*. New York: Alfred A. Knopf.

Penning, James M., and Corwin E. Smidt. 2000. "The Political Activities of Reformed Clergy in the United States and Scotland." *Journal for the Scientific Study of Religion* 39: 204–219.

Penning, James M., and Corwin E. Smidt. 2002. *Evangelicalism: The Next Generation.* Grand Rapids, Mich.: Baker Academic.

Putnam, Robert D. 2000. *Bowling Alone: The Collapse and Revival of American Community.* New York: Simon and Schuster.

Quinley, Harold E. 1974. *The Prophetic Clergy: Social Activism among Protestant Ministers.* New York: Wiley.

Regnerus, Mark, Christian Smith, and Melissa Fritsch. 2003. *Religion in the Lives of American Adolescents: A Review of the Literature: Research report of the National Study of Youth and Religion, no. 3.* Chapel Hill N.C.: The National Study of Youth and Religion. Also available online at http://www.youthandreligion.org.

Regnerus, Mark, and Jeremy Uecker. 2006. "Finding Faith, Losing Faith: The Prevalence and Context of Religious Transformations among Adolescents." *Review of Religious Research* 47: 217–237.

Rosenberg, Shawn. 1985. "Sociology, Psychology, and the Study of Political Behavior: The Case of Research on Political Socialization." *The Journal of Politics* 47: 415–452.

Searing, D. D., Joel J. Schwartz, and Alden E. Lind. 1973. "The Structuring Principle: Political Socialization and Belief Systems." *American Political Science Review* 67: 415–542.

Sears, David O. 1975. "Political Socialization." In *Handbook of Political Science: Volume II*, ed. Fred I. Greenstein and Nelson Polsby, 93–153. Reading, Mass: Addison-Wesley.

Sears, David O., and Sheri Levy. 2003. "Childhood and Adult Political Development." In *Oxford Handbook of Political Psychology*, ed. David O. Sears, Leonie Huddy, and Robert Jervis, 60–109. New York: Oxford University Press.

Sears, David O., and Nicholas A Valentino. 1997. "Politics Matters: Political Events as Catalysts for Preadult Socialization." *American Political Science Review* 91 (1): 45–65.

Smidt, Corwin E., ed. 2004. *Pulpit and Politics.* Waco, Texas: Baylor University Press.

Smidt, Corwin E., Sue Crawford, Melissa Deckman, Donald Gray, Dan Hofrenning, Laura Olson, Sherrie Steiner, and Beau Weston. 2003. "The Political Attitudes and Activities of Mainline Protestant Clergy in the Election of 2000: A Study of Six Denominations." *Journal for the Scientific Study of Religion* 42: 515–532.

Smidt, Corwin E., and Brain Schaap. In press. "Public Worship and Public Engagement: Pastoral Cues within the Context of Worship Services." *Review of Religious Research.*

Smith, Christian. 2003. "Theorizing Religious Effects among American Adolescents." *Journal for the Scientific Study of Religion* 42: 17–30.

Smith, Christian, and Melinda L. Denton. 2005. *Soul Searching: The Religious and Spiritual Lives of American Teenagers.* Oxford: Oxford University Press.

Smith, Christian, Melinda L. Denton, Robert Faris, and Mark Regnerus. 2002. "Mapping American Adolescent Religious Participation." *Journal for the Scientific Study of Religion* 41: 597–612.

Smith, Christian, and Robert Faris. 2002. *Religion and American Adolescent Delinquency, Risk Behaviors and Constructive Social Activities.*" Research report of the National Study of Youth and Religion, *no. 1.* Chapel Hill, N.C.: The National Study of Youth and Religion. Also available online at http://www.youthandreligion.org.

Smith, Gregory. 2005. "The Influence of Priests on the Political Attitudes of Roman Catholics." *Journal for the Scientific Study of Religion* 44: 291–306.

Smith, Timothy. 1978. "Religion and Ethnicity in America." *American Historical Review* 83: 1155–1185.

Smith, Tom. 2004. "Generation Gaps in Attitudes and Values from the 1970s to the 1990s." In *On the Frontier of Adulthood: Theory, Research and Public Policy*, ed. Richard Settersten, Jr., Frank Furstenberg, Jr., and Ruben Rumbaut, 177–221. Chicago, Ill.: University of Chicago Press.

Stark, Rodney, Bruce D. Foster, Charles Y. Glock, and Harold E. Quinley. 1970. "Sounds of Silence." *Psychology Today* April: 38–41, 60–61.

Stark, Rodney, Bruce D. Foster, Charles Y. Glock, and Harold E. Quinley. 1971. *Wayward Shepherds: Prejudice and the Protestant Clergy*. New York: Harper & Row.

Tate, Katherine. 1993. *From Protest to Politics: The New Black Voters in American Elections*. Cambridge, Mass.: Harvard University Press.

Tedin, Kent L. 1980. "Assessing Peer and Parent Influence on Adolescent Political Attitudes." *American Journal of Political Science* 24 (1): 136–154.

Tetlock, Philip E. 2000. "Coping with Trade-offs: Psychological Constraints and Political Implications." In *Elements of Reason*, ed. Arthur Lupia, Mathew McCubbins, and Samuel Popkin. 239–263 Cambridge: Cambridge University Press.

Valentino, Nicholas A., and David O. Sears. 1998. "Event-Driven Political Communication and the Preadult Socialization of Partisanship." *Political Behavior* 20 (2): 129–154.

Verba, Sidney, Kay Lehman Schlozman, and Henry E. Brady. 1995. *Voice and Equality*. Cambridge, Mass.: Harvard University Press.

Verba, Sidney, Kay Lehman Schlozman, Henry Brady, and Norman H. Nie. 1993. "Race, Ethnicity and Political Resources: Participation in the United States." *British Journal of Political Science* 23 (4): 453–497.

Wald, Kenneth D. 2003. *Religion and Politics in the United States*. 4th ed. Lanham, Md.: Rowan & Littlefield.

Wald, Kenneth D., and Allison Calhoun-Brown. 2007. *Religion and Politics in the United States*. 5th ed. Lanham, Md.: Rowan & Littlefield.

Wald, Kenneth D., Dennis E. Owen, and Samuel S. Hill, Jr. 1988. "Churches as Political Communities." *The American Political Science Review* 82 (2): 531–548.

Wald, Kenneth D., Dennis E. Owen, and Samuel S. Hill, Jr. 1990. "Political Cohesion in Churches." *Journal of Politics* 52: 197–215.

Weisberg, Herbert F. 2005. "The Structure and Effects of Moral Predispositions in Contemporary American Politics." *The Journal of Politics* 67 (3): 646–668.

White, Richard H. 1968. "Toward a Theory of Religious Influence." *The Pacific Sociological Review* 11 (1): 23–28.

Wielhouwer, Peter. 2000. "Releasing the Fetters: Parties and the Mobilization of African-Americans." *American Journal of Political Science* 38: 211–229.

Wilcox, Clyde, and Barbara Norrander. 2002. "Of Moods and Morals: The Dynamics of Opinion on Abortion and Gay Rights." In *Understanding Public Opinion*, ed. Barbara Norrander and Clyde Wilcox, 121–148. Washington, D.C.: CQ Press.

Wilcox, Clyde, and Lee Sigelman. 2001. "Political Mobilization in the Pews." *Social Science Quarterly* 82: 524–535.

Williams, Raymond Brady. 1988. *Religions of Immigrants from India and Pakistan: New Threads in the American Tapestry*. New York: Cambridge University Press.

Wuthnow, Robert. 1976. "Recent Patterns of Secularization." *American Sociological Review* 41: 850–867.

Wuthnow, Robert. 1988. *The Restructuring of American Religion*. Princeton, N.J.: Princeton University Press.

Zaller, John. 1992. *The Nature and Origins of Mass Opinion*. Cambridge: Cambridge University Press.

Zukin, Cliff. 2000. "Across the Generational Divide: Political Engagement, Civic Engagement and Social Attitudes." Presented at the annual meeting of the American Association for Public Opinion Research, Portland, Oregon, May.

Zukin, Cliff, Scott Keeter, Molly Andolina, Krista Jenkins, and Michael X. Delli Carpini. 2006. *A New Engagement? Political Participation, Civic Life, and the Changing American Citizen.* New York: Oxford University Press.

CHAPTER 7

RELIGION AND AMERICAN PUBLIC OPINION: ECONOMIC ISSUES

J. MATTHEW WILSON

MANY of the most fundamental and enduring political issues in any society center on the generation and distribution of wealth. Whether framed as the very pragmatic question of "who gets what, when, how" (Lasswell 1936) or as more abstract debates about "what's fair" (Hochschild 1981), competing visions of distributive justice frequently undergird individuals' political worldviews and structure the basic identities of political parties. In addition, there is perhaps no command more universally normative in the world's great religious traditions than the imperative of charity toward the poor. Thus, it would seem natural to assume a powerful nexus between religious belief and economic policy attitudes. Surely, if one wishes to explain issue preferences so clearly rooted in fundamental conceptions of justice, equality, and community, religious traditions and perspectives are a natural place to look for influences on individuals' worldviews.

Or so one would think. However, an analysis of empirical, social–scientific work on attitudes toward the economy and the welfare state reveals a stunning absence of religious variables. Most of the classic works on American economic policy attitudes (Lane 1962; Hochschild 1981; Feldman and Zaller 1992) ignore religion almost entirely, despite focusing heavily on concepts like individualism, humanitarianism, and communitarianism that have clear religious overtones.[1] In an important recent work on the subject, Feldman and Steenbergen (2001) identify "humanitarian" orientations as the prime motivator of social welfare liberalism, an obvious opening to discuss the impact of religion on economic attitudes, but merely note in passing that humanitarianism is positively correlated with church attendance. Clearly, work in political science on the public's economic policy preferences has remained largely insensitive to potential religious influences.

At the same time, work by scholars of religion and politics has also tended not to focus on economic issues. Since the 1980s, when political scientists began to identify religion as an important variable in modern American politics, most of the attention has been on social or "moral" issues like abortion, homosexuality, and school prayer, or on religion's role in driving partisan realignments. This concentration is understandable to a degree; most religiously based political activism during the past several decades *has* centered on issues of human life and sexual morality, and it is not economic concerns that have driven millions of evangelical Protestants and traditional Catholics toward the Republican Party over the last 30 years. Nonetheless, this focus on noneconomic issues has meant that political scientists understand the relationship between faith and social welfare attitudes far less well than the links between faith and positions on abortion or gay rights.

That said, a close and careful analysis of extant work in religion in politics does reveal a variety of interesting findings and controversies surrounding the interaction of Americans' religious faith and their economic policy attitudes. Certain broad patterns seem fairly well established: Jews and black Protestants are very liberal on a wide range of economic/social justice questions, including welfare spending, national health insurance, and tax policy, whereas Catholics and mainline Protestants are generally centrist, and evangelical Protestants tend to be rather conservative (Smidt 2001; Wald and Calhoun-Brown 2007). These broad-brush impressions are fairly robust across time and across issues, as data from the American National Election Studies (ANES) make clear. Table 7.1 reports the mean positions of respondents from each of America's five largest faith traditions (evangelical Protestants[2], mainline Protestants, black Protestants, Catholics, and Jews) on three key and recurring measures of economic liberalism: whether government should spend more or less on social services, whether government should guarantee every American a job, and whether there should be a national health care system in the United States (see notes below table 7.1 for specific question wordings). In all years, on every issue examined, black Protestants are by far the most liberal group in the sample, followed by Jews, then Catholics in the center, to the left of the two white Protestant groups. In recent decades, mainline Protestants are consistently to the left of evangelicals, as conventional wisdom would suggest (although this relationship is not apparent in 1968). Thus, taken as a whole, these five religious groups have for some time exhibited rather predictable patterns of response to economic questions.

However, as the remainder of this chapter will make clear, considerable nuance and qualification is needed when speaking about the relationship between religious faith and economic attitudes for any of these groups. Various strands of rather disparate work—gleaned from political science, history, and sociology, and using

Table 7.1 Mean Positions on Economic/Social Welfare Issues by Religious Tradition, Selected Years (high values = liberal positions)

	Evangelical Protestants	Mainline Protestants	Black Protestants	Catholics	Jews
2004					
Services/spending[1]	0.50	0.54	0.75	0.58	0.61
Job guarantee[2]	0.36	0.44	0.66	0.43	0.55
Health care[3]	0.45	0.52	0.61	0.54	0.58
1992					
Services/spending	0.43	0.46	.070	0.50	0.57
Job guarantee	0.37	0.38	0.64	0.43	0.45
Health care	0.51	0.55	0.67	0.60	0.60
1980					
Services/spending	0.50	0.52	0.77	0.59	0.73
Job guarantee	0.33	0.37	0.68	0.39	0.47
1968					
Job guarantee	0.33	0.30	0.84	0.44	0.61
Health care	0.61	0.51	1.00	0.64	0.95
1956					
Job guarantee	0.59	0.59	0.91	0.67	0.83
Health care	0.55	0.55	0.90	0.69	0.79

Cell entries reflect mean values for members of each religious tradition who attend religious services at least "often" (for 1956–1968) or "once or twice a month" (for 1980–2004). All entries have been rescaled to run from 0 to 1. Source: American National Election Studies.

1. Wording of services/spending questions is as follows:

    1992–2004: "Some people think the government should provide fewer services even in areas such as health and education in order to reduce spending.... Other people feel it is important for the government to provide many more services even if it means an increase in spending.... Where would you place yourself on this scale, or haven't you thought much about this?" (Response values from 0 to 6 points.)

    1980: "Some people think the government should provide fewer services even in areas such as health and education in order to reduce spending. Other people feel it is important for the government to continue the services it now provides even if it means no reduction in spending. Where would you place yourself on this scale, or haven't you thought much about this?" (Response values from 0 to 6 points.)

2. Wording of job guarantee questions is as follows:

    1968–2004: "Some people feel the government in Washington should see to it that every person has a job and a good standard of living.... Others think the government should just let each person get ahead on their own.... Where would you place yourself on this scale, or haven't you thought much about this?" (Response values from 0 to 6 points 1980 to –2004; from 0 to 2 points in 1968.)

    1956: "The government in Washington ought to see to it that everybody who wants to work can find a job." (Agree or disagree; response values from 0 to 4 points.)

3. Wording of health care questions is as follows:

    1992, 2004: "Some people feel there should be a government insurance plan which would cover all medical and hospital expenses for everyone.... Others feel that all medical expenses should be paid by individuals, and through private insurance plans like Blue Cross or other company paid plans.... Where would you place yourself on this scale, or haven't you thought much about this?" (Response values from 0 to 6 points.)

    1968: "Some say the government in Washington ought to help people get doctors and hospital care at low cost; others say the government should not get into this. Have you been interested enough in this to favor one side over the other? What is your position?" (Response values from 0 to 2 points.)

    1956: "The government ought to help people get doctors and hospital care at low cost." (Agree or disagree; response values from 0 to 4 points.)

wide-ranging methodologies—when pulled together offer important insights and tantalizing hints about religion and economic opinions within America's varied faith traditions. The remainder of this chapter focuses on the patterns that these works have uncovered and on the (considerable) research frontiers that remain.

AMERICAN PROTESTANTISM AND THE ECONOMY: A HISTORICAL PERSPECTIVE

The relative paucity of contemporary work on the relationship between religion and economic attitudes is particularly surprising given America's history of religiously based social justice activism. As Noonan (1998) notes, most major American sociopolitical movements have been fueled by religious conviction, and many (including abolition, prohibition, workers' rights, and civil rights) have taken on the form of "crusades." None more clearly fit this pattern than the social gospel movement of the late 19th and early 20th centuries, which focused on curbing the excesses of industrial capitalism, improving conditions for workers, creating at least a minimal social safety net for families, and ameliorating structural inequities in American political and economic life. Although these same objectives were shared by many secular and even socialist activists, it is clear that the movement for social reform and a more humane state often took on an explicitly religious cast, fueled by what Niebuhr (1951) terms "conversionist" Christianity. As one Tennessee woman said in a 1911 address to the National Council of Mothers, a reform organization committed to social gospel principles: "If our public mind is maternal, loving, and generous, wanting to save and develop all, our government will express this senti-ment.... Every step we make toward establishing government along these lines means an advance toward the Kingdom of Peace" (Skocpol 2000, p. 36).

In this articulation, the relationship between social reform and Christian millennial theology could hardly be clearer; moreover, these sorts of explicit, public linkages between Christian theology and economic uplift of the poor were com-mon during this era (Trattner 1999; Bartkowski and Regis 2003). Indeed, for the near century between emancipation and the onset of the civil rights movement, economic initiatives stemming from a social gospel mentality constituted the primary form of religious activism in American public life (Noll 1990; Bane, Coffin, and Thiemann 2000).

It is important to note that, at least at the outset, social gospel activism spanned all religious traditions[3] within American Protestantism (Russell 1976; Handy 1990).[4] There was no greater receptivity to the economic reform agenda in the mainline churches than in their evangelical counterparts (a distinction that, in any event, was less clear then than it is today). In fact, any apparent differences ran in the *opposite* direction, with evangelicals often undertaking the most aggressive social gospel activism and spearheading the earliest reform efforts (Magnuson 1977). Beginning in the 1920s, however, this consensus started to fragment. Many evangelicals grew concerned that the economic agenda of their mainline counterparts had become detached from its Christian moorings, abandoning a theology of personal responsibility and redemption for one of collectivism (or, frankly, for no theology at all [see Marsden 2006]). Some even suggested that the political objectives of many social gospel proponents smacked of Godless socialism (Handy 1952). Thus, by the middle of the 20th century, the stage was set for the conventional wisdom that has emerged in recent years—that American evangelicals espouse laissez-faire as a matter of faith, whereas mainline Protestants, particularly that subset that has come to be known as the "Christian Left," carry the torch of religiously motivated economic progressivism.

CONTEMPORARY EVANGELICAL AND MAINLINE ATTITUDES TOWARD ECONOMIC POLICY

As is so often the case, the truth is much more contested and complicated than the previous neat summation would indicate. Certainly, the dominant view among modern scholars is that evangelicalism is associated with a greater propensity to endorse capitalism and to be suspicious of the welfare state (Stark and Glock 1968; Hollinger 1983; Green, Guth, Smidt, and Kellstedt 1996; Wilcox 1996). George Marsden (1973, p. 18) characteristically argues that American evangelicalism is marked by an embrace of "free enterprise economics, success-oriented competitive individualism, opposition to expansion of the federal government, [and] extreme fear of socialism." This perspective was originally articulated, quite famously, by Max Weber (1930), who argued that the individualist, Calvinist theology of conservative Protestantism, which had been very influential in the United States, was directly linked to a capitalist economic outlook. The evangelical conviction that "poverty and damnation were individual matters, and only the individual could overcome them" (Trattner 1999, p. 55) was assumed to be at the root of conservative economic policy positions. In their consideration of the poor and disadvantaged, evangelicals tend to prefer "relational" approaches (Smith 1998), emphasizing the charitable efforts of congregations and of individual Christians over broad, impersonal (and thoroughly secular) government programs.

This view has received considerable empirical support. Johnstone (1988) and Hargrove (1989) both find evidence that evangelicals celebrate individualism and the entrepreneurial ideal, with Johnstone (1988, p. 129) noting their "corresponding disapproval of social action and public welfare programs." Work by Jelen, Smidt, and Wilcox (1993) demonstrates that "born-again" identification is associated with lower support for government antipoverty programs, while

Wilcox, Jelen, and Leege (1993) show that "evangelical," "fundamentalist," and "charismatic" self-identifications all reduce support for liberal economic policies. Guth, Kellstedt, Smidt, and Green (2006), in an analysis of the 2004 presidential election, note that evangelicals (particularly "traditionalist" ones—the bulk of the evangelical sample) are more supportive of large tax cuts than are other groups, and are less likely to emphasize economic issues in their voting calculus. The most in-depth, empirical demonstration of the link between evangelical Protestantism and economically conservative positions, however, is provided by Barker and Carman (2000). Using data from the ANES and building sophisticated structural equations models, they demonstrate that "doctrinarian" Christianity (which they identify with evangelicalism and operationalize with a self-reported born-again measure) strongly shapes attitudes toward economic policy. Its influence is both direct and indirect (through the intervening media of ideology, broad cultural attitudes, and party identification), and survives controls for region, income, education, age, gender, ethnicity, and racial attitudes. Taken in tandem with previous impressionistic accounts and less comprehensive empirical treatments that reach the same conclusions, the Barker and Carman (2000) work provides evidence for a link between evangelical Protestant religious belief and economic conservatism in the mass public.

This view at the mass level is reinforced by work on the attitudes of evangelical opinion leaders, most particularly clergy. Classic treatments of Protestant ministers' political attitudes have found sharp distinctions between evangelical and mainline clergy that go back decades, with evangelical leaders (or those with "orthodox theology") focused on a relatively narrow range of "moral" and "decency" issues, and avoiding economic advocacy (Hadden 1969; Quinley 1974). More recent work by Jelen (1993) confirms this pattern, with evangelical ministers tending to see morality and public order, not economic redistribution, as their central political objectives. Major studies of clerical lobbying in Washington reveal that evangelical ministers tend to draw a sharp distinction between moral issues, which they regard as within the legitimate political purview of the church, and economic concerns, which they view as outside their sphere of responsibility (Hertzke 1988; Hofrenning 1995). All of these patterns are confirmed, elaborated, and reinforced in the landmark study by Guth, Green, Smidt, Kellstedt, and Poloma (1997) of clergy political attitudes and activism. Drawing on nationwide surveys of and interviews with Protestant clergy in eight different denominations, they find that identification of economic issues as central national problems is negatively associated with doctrinal orthodoxy; ministers in the evangelical Southern Baptist and Assemblies of God denominations are much less likely to raise economic and social equity concerns than mainline Presbyterian or Disciples of Christ pastors. Indeed, Guth et al. (1997, p. 84) go so far as to say that "most evangelicals ignore the social justice agenda, whether on civil rights, the environment, military spending, employment, or women's issues." Clearly, the economic conservatism and acceptance of laissez-faire that many scholars have noted in the mass public finds strong reinforcement at the elite, clerical level.

There is, however, a countervailing view in the literature—a minority perspective to be sure, but a nontrivial one. A small group of scholars, beginning in the late 1980s, has maintained that certain elements of evangelical belief actually contribute to more *liberal* positions on the economy and on antipoverty efforts (Tamney, Burton, and Johnson 1989; Hart 1992; Iannaccone 1993; Wuthnow 1994; Clydesdale 1999). At the very least, if the poor are perceived as "deserving" (Will and Cochrane 1995), or if their own class interests are implicated (Pyle 1993), evangelicals are potentially stronger supporters of economic redistribution than their mainline counterparts.[5] Although this view certainly runs counter to conventional wisdom in the field, it has some plausibility given the strong emphasis on justice for the poor in the Old Testament prophetic tradition and in the gospels, the aforementioned history of evangelical activism in American social justice movements, and the relatively modest socioeconomic circumstances of many evangelicals (Davis and Robinson 1996; Corbett and Corbett 1999).[6] Indeed, Jim Wallis (2005) has famously argued that evangelical Christianity should lead naturally to a focus on social equity and economic reform. Wuthnow's (1994) empirical evidence, drawn from both a national survey and in-depth interviews, documents a propensity among conservative Protestants to take their obligation to the poor quite seriously; they are "substantially more likely to have thought about it," he notes, "than either moderates or liberals" (Wuthnow 1994, p. 196). Finally, Regnerus, Smith, and Sikkink (1999) strongly dispute the notion that there is any pervasive hostility or indifference toward the poor among conservative Protestants, arguing that these individuals are actually significantly more generous in their charitable giving than people of other religious persuasions—a claim reinforced by more recent work (Brooks 2006; Smidt, den Dulk, Penning, Monsma, and Koopman 2008).

What, then, might account for these disparate findings? One possibility is that scholars are not all considering exactly the same group of believers. Some of the work focuses on "evangelicals," whereas other pieces examine "conservative Protestants," "fundamentalists," "born-again Christians," "traditionalists," or "doctrinarians." Although there is considerable overlap between these various concepts, they are not interchangeable, and each taps a slightly different element of religious believing, belonging, or behaving.[7] Another possibility is suggested by Wilson (1999), who argues that evangelical Protestants are both suspicious of "big government" *and* inclined to try to remedy economic inequities individually or through their local churches. "Paradoxically," he argues, "evangelicals seem simultaneously more anxious to help disadvantaged people and more hostile toward government programs that seek to do exactly that" (Wilson 1999, p. 434). Thus, evangelicals respond negatively to questions about spending on "welfare" or "food stamps," but positively to the somewhat more nebulous idea that government ought to spend more to help the poor, the unemployed, and the homeless. The possibility of such ambivalence is also acknowledged by Barker and Carman (2000, p. 10), who concede that "doctrinarians might believe fervently in the Christian responsibility to care for the poor and to wage war against social oppression and inequality, while objecting strongly to the stipulation that the secular humanistic government should be the strategists of such a war." In a similar vein, Regnerus, Smith, and Sikkink (1999, p. 483) caution against "confusing generosity *per se* with support for the political project of the welfare state." If this ambivalence does in fact exist, then the apparent relationship between evangelicalism and support for social welfare policies will be highly sensitive to both the specific character of the policy in question and to the perceived character of its beneficiaries, a pattern that is in fact discerned by Will and Cochrane (1995) and by Wilson (1999). In any event, the exact nature of the relationship between evangelical Protestantism and conservative economic policy attitudes, along with the question of whether any such relationship is rooted in doctrine, denominational socialization, and/or nonreligious influences, remains an important area for future research.

If one must exercise some caution in generalizing about the economic policy attitudes of evangelical Protestants, it is even more difficult to speak with any precision about the preferences of their mainline counterparts. They are perhaps the most politically and ideologically eclectic religious tradition in the United States, as mainline churches display sizable segments of both very conservative and very liberal members. That said, many of the same sources referenced earlier that find evangelicals to be conservative on economic questions (e.g., Johnstone 1988; Hargrove 1989; Leege and Kellstedt 1993; Green et al. 1996; Smidt 2001, 2007; Wald and Calhoun-Brown 2007) also find mainline Protestants receptive to the programs of the welfare state, at least by comparison. Members of mainline churches tend to focus on structural, societal causes for poverty instead of personal character deficiencies or moral failings, and are more likely to view social action rather than simply private charity as the appropriate remedy (Thuesen 2002). One should not push these conclusions too far, however. The predominant ideological perspective in mainline congregations is moderate rather than liberal (Roof and McKinney 1987; Smidt 2007), and they still typically give a small majority of their votes to Republican candidates. Given that mainline Protestants tend to be relatively affluent, this is not particularly surprising. Indeed, in response to survey questions, they evince a level of contentment with the status quo in American society surpassing that expressed by any other major religious tradition (Olson 2007; Smidt 2007), and a corresponding distaste for political activism of either a liberal *or* a conservative variety. Thus, one should hardly expect to find the mainline Protestant tradition, taken as a whole, a locus for any radical redistributionist politics or significant social justice activism.

There are, however, segments within the broader mainline tradition that are much more clearly and aggressively liberal on economic questions. One of these is the currently small but historically important movement that one might term the *Christian Left*. This group finds its center in the mainline Protestant tradition, especially (although by no means exclusively[8]) in traditionally liberal denominations such as the United Church of Christ and in "Peace Protestant" groups like Quakers, Mennonites, and Brethren (Olson 2007). Although most do not reject capitalism per se, they tend to unite around an economic agenda including universal health insurance, an increase in the minimum wage, aid for the unemployed, and strong support for organized labor (Craig 1992; Wuthnow and Evans 2002). These individuals *do* tend to identify as liberals, to vote heavily for Democratic candidates (Kellstedt et al. 2007; Olson 2007), and to engage in social justice activism, especially at the community level (Hart 2001; Warren 2001; Wood 2002; Djupe and Olson 2007). The political power of their economic liberalism, however, is hampered by two important factors. First, the denominations that constitute the core of this Christian Left are either stagnant or declining in membership (Roof and McKinney 1987; Finke and Stark 1992; Kosmin and Keyser 2006). Second, members of these traditions tend to be strong church–state separationists, and thus suspicious of too much religiously based political activism (Kellstedt et al. 2007; Olson 2007). For these reasons, the Christian Left movement, although important, is insufficient to push mainline Protestant opinion as a whole solidly into the camp of economic liberalism.

Another locus of economic liberalism within the mainline tradition is found among the clergy. Although the economic policy views of mainline congregations are quite varied and generally moderate, ministers in many mainline denominations lean much more decisively to the Left. This pattern is reflected both in Guth et al.'s (1997) major nationwide survey of Protestant clergy and in numerous case study and anecdotal accounts of clerical activism (e.g., Crawford and Olson 2001; Wuthnow and Evans 2002; Djupe and Olson 2007). Mainline clergy are considerably more open to the idea of direct political action by religious leaders than their evangelical counterparts, and their activism tends to be focused on issues of social and economic justice. Mainline clergy generally reject what they see as the overly narrow definition of moral concerns embraced by evangelicals. Guth et al. (1997, p. 88) quote a typical mainline pastor as saying that he and his colleagues "find it hard to make a clear distinction between moral and political." As another pastor argues, "the Lordship of Christ makes all political issues moral issues" (Parham 1996, p. 3). For these ministers, economic inequality is a fundamental moral concern, and a legitimate focus for explicitly Christian political action.

The practical political impact of the mainline clergy's economic liberalism is, however, sharply constrained by the reality that they have largely failed to persuade their congregations of their views on this score. The disconnect between liberals in the pulpits and moderates in the pews has been noted for decades within the mainline churches (Hadden 1969; Quinley 1974), and has been confirmed in more recent empirical studies. For example, Guth et al. (1997), using data collected after the 1988 presidential election, found *majorities* of pastors within the Methodist, Presbyterian, and Disciples of Christ traditions reporting that they were "much more liberal" than their congregations, a truly striking pattern of discontinuity. "The situation described . . . a generation ago," they argue, "still obtains: liberal mainline clergy confront laity with a distinctly more conservative coloration than their own" (Guth et al. 1997, p. 112).

However, the ideological divide between mainline clergy and their parishioners had narrowed considerably by the turn of the millennium. This can be seen in table 7.2, which analyzes clergy from three evangelical and four mainline Protestant

Table 7.2 Clergy Perceptions of Congruity with Parishioners' Views over Time (measured as a percentage)

| | 1989 | | | 2001 | | | 2001 | | |
| | Most Issues | | | Social Issues | | | Economic Issues | | |
	More Conservative	About Same	More Liberal	More Conservative	About Same	More Liberal	More Conservative	About Same	More Liberal
Evangelical Protestants	25	47	28	26	63	11	24	64	12
Assemblies of God	39	45	16	19	75	3	16	77	7
Christian Reformed	8	40	52	25	55	20	28	53	19
Southern Baptists	17	57	15	34	58	8	28	63	9
Mainline Protestants	6	20	75	32	42	26	32	45	23
Disciples of Christ									
Presbyterian Church USA	3	10	87	30	47	23	33	47	20
Reformed Church	8	38	54	27	48	25	28	51	21
United Methodist	14	14	72	33	42	25	32	45	23

Sources: 1989 data from Guth et al. 1997 p. 111; 2001 data drawn from the Cooperative Clergy Study; see Smidt (2004).

denominations who were randomly surveyed in 1989 and again in 2001. In the earlier survey, clergy were asked how their political views related to the political views of members of their congregation. Nearly half (47 percent) of evangelical Protestant clergy reported in 1989 that their political views were about the same as their congregants, with about as many reporting their political views were more conservative (25 percent) as more liberal (28 percent) than their parishioners. In contrast, only one fifth of mainline Protestant clergy reported their political views to be similar to their parishioners, with more than 12 times as many reporting their views to be more liberal (74 percent) than to be more conservative (6 percent) than their parishioners.

In 2001, clergy of these same denominations were once again asked to compare their views on social and economic issues with most members of their congrega-tions. Reported differences in the views of clergy and their parishioners had narrowed considerably during the 12 years. The percentage of evangelical and mainline Protestant clergy who reported that their views were similar to their congregants had increased considerably, more than doubling among mainline Protestant clergy. Mainline Protestant clergy were still, overall, more likely than evangelical Protestant clergy to report that they held more liberal views than their congregants. Even more striking, however, is the fact that the percentage of mainline Protestant clergy in 2001 who reported their views to be more conserva-tive than their parishioners actually exceeded the percentage who reported their views to be more liberal than their parishioners—regardless of whether one examines economic or social issues. Thus, although many mainline clergy still perceive themselves to be more socially and economically liberal than their par-ishioners, the clergy–laity gap within mainline Protestantism today is not nearly as great as it was 20 years ago.

American Catholicism and Economic Liberalism: Effect or Artifact?

The relationship between religious belief and economic policy attitudes among American Catholics is similarly complex and contested. Certainly, if one looks to the teaching and action of the church hierarchy, both in the United States and globally, there is considerable reason to expect a link between Catholicism and welfare state liberalism. Since Pope Leo XIII's landmark encyclical *Rerum Novarum* in 1891, the Vatican has taken a consistent stance in favor of regulated capitalism with significant humanitarian safeguards, rejecting both socialism and laissez-faire in favor of moderate social democracy. This approach, with its concomitant emphasis on communitarianism at the expense of individualism, is broadly char-acteristic of Catholic social thought, according to both Weber (1930) and

Durkheim (1951). In America, Cross (1967) documents a concerted push for work-ers' rights and various social insurance measures led by Catholic clergy and intellectuals beginning as early as 1900. Looking internationally, Lipset and Rokkan (1967) establish Catholic predispositions toward collectivism and the welfare state, rooted in the Church's social doctrine, as an important line of partisan cleavage in European politics.

During the past 25 years, these general principles of Catholic social teaching have been reaffirmed and reemphasized by church leaders in both Rome and the United States. In the mid 1980s, the U.S. Conference of Catholic Bishops' statement *Economic Justice for All* (1986) received considerable notoriety, and was seen as a rebuke of the Reagan administration's "trickle-down" economic policies. In it, the bishops affirm universal human rights to life, food, clothing, shelter, rest, medical care, education, and employment, and call on the state to enact policies to secure these rights. In addition, the bishops' statement asserts that "as followers of Christ, we are challenged to make a fundamental 'option for the poor'—to speak for the voiceless, to defend the defenseless, to assess lifestyles, policies, and social institu-tions in terms of their impact on the poor" (p. 3). This message was reinforced globally with the issuance in 2005 of the *Compendium of the Social Doctrine of the Church* by the Pontifical Council for Justice and Peace, reaffirming (among many other things) the church's doctrines of solidarity and the preferential option for the poor.

Given this long-established body of teaching by church authorities, it is not surprising that many scholars have asserted a link between Catholicism and economic liberalism in American public opinion. Tracy (1981) and Greeley (1990) argue for the existence of a distinctively Catholic "analogical" or "sacramental" imagination that stands in contrast to the individualistic orientation of Protestant-ism, and is thus more amenable to state action to alleviate poverty and social disadvantage.

Empirical studies of public opinion and voting behavior have lent support to this notion as well. As far back as the 1940s, political scientists were documenting the central role of Catholics in the New Deal coalition, arguing that they were tightly bound to the Democratic Party by their preference for welfare state liberal-ism (Lazarsfeld, Berelson, and Gaudet 1948). Work in more recent decades has also identified a tendency among American Catholics to support liberal economic policies (Hanna 1979; Gallup and Castelli 1987; Greeley 1989; Wagner 1998), even as their partisan unity has fragmented. According to Froehle and Gautier (2000, p. 32), "even among Catholics who identify with and vote for the Republican Party, there is a tendency to be more liberal on issues involving help for the needy and respect for the rights of others than is the case among their fellow political partisans from other religious traditions." Clearly, the predominant view has been and continues to be that Catholicism in America is associated with greater receptivity to expansions of the welfare state. Gallup and Castelli (1987, p. 76) confidently and characteristically assert the point: "American Catholics remain and will continue to remain supporters of an idea rooted in both their faith and their experience: the belief that government must play a strong role in guaranteeing a healthy economic climate and meeting the needs of its people."

Despite this consensus, however, some skeptical voices have begun to emerge in recent years. Although the fact that Catholics have historically been both loyal Democrats and strong supporters of the American welfare state is beyond doubt, there is reason to question what role (if any) theology and religious belief per se played in these alignments. For most of American history, Catholics were a socially disadvantaged population, comprised largely of immigrants and the children of immigrants (Hennesey 1981); support for economically liberal policies would come naturally to such a group, regardless of religious convictions. Indeed, Byrnes (1991) suggests that the American bishops' economic policy activism during the first half of the 20th century was driven as much by the material interests of their flock as by their broader theological convictions. In the 1960s, however, American Catholics' material and educational circumstances began to converge with those of American Protestants, and the socioeconomic basis of Catholic liberalism began to erode (Kenski and Lockwood 1991). This reality, combined with effective Republican appeals to Catholic voters on racial, cultural, and national security issues (Leege, Wald, Krueger, and Mueller 2002), gradually undermined Catholic support for both the Democratic Party and liberal welfare state policies (Prendergast 1999). Indeed, by 2004, strong majorities of observant white Catholics, especially young ones, were both voting Republican and endorsing (implicitly or explicitly) conservative economic policies (Mockabee 2007; Wilson 2007).

How, then, does one reconcile these trends with the strong evidence of continued Catholic clerical liberalism on economic questions, and the assertions of earlier scholars that Catholicism was associated with economic liberalism in the mass public? To begin with, one should not assume that clerical guidance on these issues is effectively transmitted to or absorbed by ordinary American Catholics. As Greeley (1990, p. 146) concedes, "less than a fifth of Catholic laity have even heard of the National Conference's much touted pastoral letters on nuclear weapons and poverty." Moreover, most of the conventional wisdom about Catholic support for welfare-state liberalism was based on impressionistic evidence and bivariate correlations, a dubious proposition when there are obvious potential confounding factors like socioeconomic status and historical, ethnocultural attachments to the Democratic Party.

Although much work remains to be done, emerging scholarship based on sophisticated, multivariate analysis is beginning to debunk the link between Catholic religious belief and economically liberal policy attitudes, at least among the laity. If the link between Catholicism and support for the welfare state is indeed based on *religion* (as opposed to a spurious artifact of other variables that happen to be correlated with Catholicism), then more committed/observant/orthodox Catholics ought to be more liberal on social welfare questions, *ceteris paribus,* than their more nominally Catholic counterparts. In a very meticulous analysis using a range of demographic and partisan controls, Leege and Mueller (2004) examine the independent and interactive effects of Mass attendance, importance of religion in daily life, and feelings of closeness to other Catholics on a range of policy attitudes, including national health insurance, a government role in guaranteeing equal opportunity, assistance for blacks, and opinions about various disadvantaged social groups. They find no evidence of any religiosity effect on these issues; their array of religious commitment variables is "never a powerful predictor of . . . measures of social justice or of warmth toward people not like oneself or of lower status than oneself" (Leege and Mueller 2004, p. 233). Wilson (2004), in another multivariate examination, goes even further, arguing that observant Catholics have *never* been more liberal than their nominal counterparts on economic questions, at least in the era that public opinion data permit a reliable comparison. As far back as the 1960s, regular Mass attenders were significantly and consistently more conservative on the issues of national health insurance and a governmental full employment guarantee than infrequent attenders,[9] despite the clear inclination of Catholic clergy to the contrary.

If these more recent accounts are correct about the lack of a link between American Catholic religious belief and welfare liberalism (or even the existence of an inverse relationship), then the real research frontier is to answer why. After all, church teachings seem influential for the political attitudes of observant Catholics in a variety of areas (Leege and Mueller 2004; Wilson 2004), moving them in a conservative direction on some (e.g., abortion and homosexuality) and a liberal direction on others (e.g., the death penalty). Why are economic issues the seeming exception? It could be because these church teachings receive less attention in the media. It might be because it is harder to translate these moral principles into specific, binding political directives. Alternatively, the answer may lie with the efforts (or lack thereof) of political parties to mobilize Catholic voters on these issues. Whatever the answer may be, it has heretofore been the subject only of speculation in the social science literature, and awaits more thorough and systematic analysis.

ECONOMIC POLICY ATTITUDES AMONG MINORITY RELIGIOUS TRADITIONS

If the link between faith and economic policy preferences in America's major white religious traditions is ambiguous and contested, it is much clearer among African American Christians. General surveys of religion and political attitudes consistently find black Protestants to be the most economically leftist religious group in America, generally supporting sharply higher taxes on the affluent and significant increases in spending on welfare-state programs (Leege and Kellstedt 1993; Wilson 1999; Smidt 2001; Wald and Calhoun-Brown 2007). Moreover, African Americans are the only group in the electorate for whom increased religious commitment is associated with more liberal issue positions (at least on econom-ic questions) and greater likelihood of voting Democratic (Guth, Kellstedt, Green, and Smidt 2001; McDaniel 2007)—preferences that generally endure even as they become more affluent (Dawson 1994).

Clearly, this economic liberalism is motivated in large part by African Amer-icans' own material circumstances and sense of community solidarity. At the same time, however, it also powerfully reinforced by important elements of black theology. Some early sociological accounts emphasized the passivity and other-worldliness of the African American church and argued that it inhibited the black struggle for social justice (Frazier 1963; Orum 1966), but most more recent treat-ments argue that black churches have served as important vehicles for organizing black political activism and articulating demands for economic justice, at least since the civil rights era (Morris 1984; Lincoln and Mamiya 1990; Harris 1999). This activism has been fueled to a significant degree by the emergence during the late 1960s and early 1970s of black liberation theology, which explicitly links redistribu-tive (and often radical) economic policies with Christianity. A full summary of the tenets of black liberation theology is beyond the scope of this chapter,[10] but it is important to note that it emphasizes Jesus' own humble life circumstances and his solidarity with the poor and disadvantaged. According to the movement's founders (Cleage 1968; Cone 1969; Roberts 1971), support for the poor, not only through personal charity, but also through direct social and political action, is at the heart of the Christian calling. In a characteristic formulation, the Reverend Joseph Johnson (1993, p. 206) calls on Christians (especially *black* Christians) to envision "Jesus walking the dark streets of the ghettos of the North and the sharecropper's farm in the Deep South, without a job, busted, and emasculated," and to remember that "Jesus was born in a barn, wrapped in a blanket used for sick cattle, and placed in a stall." The political imperative to support redistributive economic policies could not be clearer, and indeed is often made explicit by black theologians.

Thus, there is general agreement in the literature that black Protestant liberal-ism on economic questions is almost universal, and that it is rooted to some degree in the theology and practice of African American Christianity. At the same time, however, recent scholars have hastened to point out that one should be cautious about reifying the "progressive black church," because individual congregations vary considerably in their level of politicization and in the radicalism of their economic vision, if not in their general preference for Democratic candidates and liberal economic policies (Calhoun-Brown 1996; Harris-Lacewell 2007). Pinn (2002) argues that scholars have a tendency to exaggerate the importance of black liberation theology (largely the product of academic theologians), and that its radically redistributive economic vision has had a limited impact on the attitudes of most ordinary African Americans.

Indeed, it may be that the "prosperity gospel" is having a greater impact today in the African American community than is black liberation theology, thereby pushing blacks away from redistributive economic perspectives. Nowhere is this truer than in the growing number of African American megachurches. These churches, on the rise since the 1990s, tend to deemphasize organized political activism and demands for radical economic restructuring (Smith and Tucker-Worgs 2000; Hutchinson 2001). Instead, many preach a "prosperity gospel" that stresses individual prudence, faith, and righteousness, rather than collective political action, as the cure for African American economic woes (Harris-Lacewell 2007). This theology, Harris-Lacewell (2007) argues, has tangible political consequences, both dampening activist politics and creating potential openings for Republican candidates. As the megachurch and prosperity gospel movements become increasingly important parts of the black religious experience, scholars will do well to monitor whether these trends attenuate the traditionally strong link between African American religion and economic liberalism.

Considerably less work has been done on the relationship between religious faith and economic policy attitudes among Latinos, but the little that exists suggests several notable patterns. First, Latinos of all religious backgrounds share generally liberal positions on economic and social welfare questions, and generally conservative positions on moral and cultural issues (DeSipio and de la Garza 2002; DeSipio 2007).[11] Second, Latino churches have historically not been nearly as active as African American churches in fostering political activism on behalf of social and economic justice, although this has begun to change during the past several decades, particularly at the local level (Rogers 1990; Warren 2001; Espinosa, Elizondo, and Miranda 2005). Finally, some of the most interesting work on Latino religion and politics is beginning to examine differences between Protestant and Catholic Latinos. Protestants have traditionally been a very small segment of America's Latinos, and they will remain a minority for the foreseeable future; nonetheless, their numbers have been growing significantly, to the point that, according to some scholars, they now comprise about a fifth of the Latino population in the United States, most of them evangelicals (Hunt 2000; DeSipio 2007). In fact, the recent massive Pew Forum survey (Pew Forum on Religion & Public Life 2008) places the Protestant share of Latinos at 26 percent in 2007.

Although their policy positions, as just mentioned, are generally similar to those of Catholic Latinos, Protestant Latinos tend to place more emphasis on moral issues and less emphasis on economic ones in their voting decisions, creating opportunities for Republican candidates (Suro, Fry, and Passel 2005). Moreover, controlling for standard sociodemographic factors, research has generally found that Protestant Latinos participate politically at lower rates than their Catholic counterparts (Jones-Correa and Leal 2001; Lee, Pachon, and Barreto 2002; DeSipio 2007), although Latino Protestant participation seems to have surged in 2004, perhaps in response to mobilization by the Bush campaign (Green, Kellstedt, Smidt, and Guth 2007). In sum, Latino Protestants are somewhat less likely to engage in political activity than Latino Catholics, and when they do, they tend not to focus on economic issues. Any religiously based economic activism in the Latino community will thus almost certainly have to be centered primarily in Catholic churches; whether and how these churches foster that activism will be an important area of research in the years to come.

Finally, a brief word is in order about the link between religious belief and economic policy attitudes among adherents of America's non-Christian faiths. Because these groups have always been a tiny sliver of the American religious pie (although many are now growing rather rapidly), work on faith and politics in these traditions has been scarce; more specifically, work on the religiously based economic attitudes of these groups is practically nonexistent. Nonetheless, a few studies suggest some interesting patterns. America's longest-established non-Christian tradition is Judaism, and American Jews have long been noted for their liberalism on issues across the board, including—despite their own relative afflu-ence—economic questions (Himmelfarb 1985; Greenberg and Wald 2001; Djupe 2007). As Milton Himmelfarb (1985, p. 40) famously quipped, Jews "earn like Episcopalians and vote like Puerto Ricans." Fuchs (1956) argues for a distinctively religious source for this Jewish economic liberalism, rooting it in *tzedakeh*, or concern for the poor and dispossessed. Others, however, question the religious basis for these attitudes, arguing that they are just as strong among secular Jews as they are among observant ones (Cohen and Liebman 1997; Greenberg and Wald 2001). A similar pattern has been noted in the nascent literature on the political attitudes of American Muslims, where Djupe and Green (2007) find adherents of Islam in this country to be very strong supporters of universal health care and more generous aid to the poor, despite their own generally high socioeconomic status. These findings are confirmed by the largest study of Muslim public opinion ever conducted in the United States, *Muslim Americans: Middle Class and Mostly Mainstream* (Pew Research Center 2007, p. 44), which shows that most Muslims believe that the federal government should do more to help the needy, with Muslim opinion being much more liberal on these issues than the public at large. Again, however, it is not clear what role (if any) religion per se plays in motivating these attitudes. Clearly, these studies only scratch the surface of the relationship between religious belief and economic attitudes in America's non-Christian communities of faith. As Muslims, Hindus, Buddhists, and other non-Christian traditions become more significant parts of the nation's social and political fabric, this literature is sure to grow.

AN AGENDA FOR RESEARCH

As the preceding discussion makes clear, significant research frontiers remain in the study of religion and American economic policy attitudes. Although there are many interesting and important questions to be explored within each of the religious traditions discussed here, some basic, overarching themes also emerge. These will likely form the core of research in this area in the coming years.

One major recurring question centers on the influence of religious elites on public opinion. Why do clergy and theologians in some of America's largest religious traditions find it so difficult to lead on questions of economic justice? It is not for lack of conviction. As the works cited earlier demonstrate, clergy in the Catholic and mainline Protestant traditions (and more sporadically in the evangelical tradition) are deeply committed to redistributive economic policies, and express those commitments both from the pulpit and in public statements. Moreover, political elites certainly seem influenced by religion in their approach to economic questions, as religious variables are significant predictors of economic policy attitudes among party convention delegates (Layman 2001) and members of Congress (Guth 2007). Yet the public opinion data consistently show that religious leaders who seek to shape the economic views of the mass public meet with little success; their guidance on economic issues does not have nearly the same impact, even with religiously committed members of the flock, as their guidance on other moral questions. Even among black Protestants, the call to radical economic restructuring inherent in black liberation theology, so influential among theologians and intellectuals, has not resonated with many ordinary churchgoers, as evidenced by the proliferation of the "prosperity gospel." One major task for scholars is to explain this disconnect.

In religious groups where there *is* an apparent embrace of liberal economic policies (Jews, Muslims, black Protestants, Latino Catholics, the white Christian Left), the challenge for scholars is to identify what, if any, specifically *religious* factors contribute to these attitudes. For African Americans and Latinos, it is difficult to separate the effects of theologies of liberation from those of simple self-interest (or group interest) among disadvantaged populations. Is religion in these cases a real motivator for social and political action, or is it merely a part of supporting and rationalizing political behaviors that materialist politics would be inducing anyway? Among Jews and white Christian liberals, there is clearly something more than material self-interest going on (because these groups tend to be quite affluent), but the religious basis for their social justice activism can still be quite difficult to discern. Very often, their issue agendas look just like those of the secular Left, not only in their range of objectives, but also in their articulation. When observant members of these religious traditions are indistinguishable in their preferences from nonreligious people of the same ethnicity and ideology, it casts doubt on the importance of theology in motivating their economic policy preferences. And yet, a wealth of case studies and anecdotal evidence suggests that many members of these traditions *do* feel a powerful moral force undergirding their economic liberalism. It remains for scholars, then, to trace and demonstrate more fully and compellingly the relationship between religious faith and economic liberalism in those groups for which one may exist.

Both of these issues feed into one larger question: Will we in American politics see a resurgence of large, meaningful, religiously based campaigns for economic justice and equality? Historically, the current situation, in which large-scale religious activism is focused almost solely on issues of personal morality, is an anomaly. The history of religiously motivated political movements in the United States, as discussed previously, includes a substantial focus on economic concerns. If such a movement were to reassert itself, from whence would it come? On what specific issues might it find broad-based support, and on which ones would it likely be confined to a fringe movement of the religious Left? What sorts of moral appeals for social justice have greater or lesser resonance across religious traditions? How might such a movement interact with the existing political parties? Might it be co-opted, channeled, or diffused by one or the other? These questions, informed by the modest but growing body of work on religion and economic attitudes in the American public, are of great significance for both political science and American politics more broadly.

NOTES

1. Jennifer Hochschild's (1981) book *What's Fair?*, the most comprehensive extant treatment of American perspectives on economic justice, is typical in this regard. Despite running more than 300 pages and discussing extensively different ideological and value dispositions related to economic philosophy, the book is virtually silent on the possible religious origins of these orientations. Indeed, it does not even contain index entries for *religion* or *Christianity*.

2. In this analysis, evangelical and mainline Protestants are differentiated according to their views of the Bible; those Protestants who report that the Bible is "literally true" are classified as evangelicals, whereas those with lower views of scripture are classified as mainline. This is an admittedly imprecise measure, but it is the most consistent rubric available across the wide span of time covered here, and parallels that used in at least one other important analysis (Clydesdale 1999). For more recent years, where the Bible item is available alongside detailed denominational measures, categorization based on either produces similar results. In the 1956 study, it is impossible to distinguish between evangelical and mainline Protestants (as neither a Bible item nor detailed denominational data are available); thus, that year's figures reported for both groups in table 7.1 reflect the overall white Protestant means.

3. For an excellent explanation of the concept of *religious tradition,* as well as a discussion of the general differences between the evangelical and mainline Protestant traditions, see Smidt (2007).

4. Although many Catholics, Jews, and others were certainly sympathetic to the policy aims of the social gospel movement, there were relatively fewer of them in American society than there are today, and they were more politically marginalized. Social gospel activism is generally regarded as a Protestant phenomenon, because both the theology underlying the movement and the ground-level impetus for social change were clearly rooted in American Protestantism.

5. Clydesdale (1999) also finds an interesting conditional relationship between "biblical conservatism" and support for redistributive economic policies. In his analysis, highly educated biblical conservatives are strongly opposed to governmental antipoverty efforts, largely because of their tendency to accept individual rather than structural explanations for poverty, whereas less educated biblical conservatives are strongly supportive of those same efforts. These findings, which run clearly counter to the normal relationship between education/sophistication and structural attributions (see Gomez and Wilson 2006), bear further testing and examination by scholars.

6. Although evangelicals do, on average, have lower levels of education and income than mainline Protestants, the gap has closed during the past several decades (Smidt 2007), and is often overstated in the popular press (Bolce and De Maio 2007).

7. For some discussion of these different ways of conceptualizing religious groups, see Leege and Kellstedt (1993). In political science, the classification of individuals into religious traditions based largely on denomination, outlined by Green et al. (1996), has become the generally accepted "industry standard," but this does not mean that it is universally observed. Moreover, work in history, sociology, and religious studies tends to use different categorization schemes entirely, as does work in all disciplines prior to the 1990s. To what extent is an analysis of the beliefs or behavior of "evangelicals" comparable with one of "fundamentalists" or "traditionalist Protestants?" This is one of the endemic questions in all areas of religion and politics research.

8. As Kellstedt, Smidt, Green, and Guth (2007) demonstrate, the religious Left in America, although it is disproportionately strong in mainline Protestantism, extends beyond that tradition to encompass significant numbers of Catholics, Jews, and black Protestants, and even a few evangelicals.

9. These results survive an array of demographic controls, including gender, race, region, age, education, income, and union membership.

10. For more comprehensive summaries of the tenets and development of black liberation theology, see Hopkins (1999) and Harris-Lacewell (2007).

11. The major exception to this generalization, as to many about Latino politics, is Cuban Americans, who are more conservative and Republican across the board than other Latinos (DeSipio 1996).

REFERENCES

Bane, Mary Jo, Brent Coffin, and Ronald Thiemann, eds. 2000. *Who Will Provide?: The Changing Role of Religion in American Social Welfare.* Boulder, Colo.: Westview Press.

Barker, David C., and Christopher Jan Carman. 2000. "The Spirit of Capitalism?: Religious Doctrine, Values, and Economic Attitude Constructs." *Political Behavior* 22: 1–27.

Bartkowski, John P., and Helen A. Regis. 2003. *Charitable Choices: Religion, Race, and Poverty in the Post-Welfare Era.* New York: New York University Press.

Bolce, Louis, and Gerald De Maio. 2007. "Secularists, Anti-Fundamentalists, and the New Religious Divide in the American Electorate." In *From Pews to Polling Places: Faith and Politics in the American Religious Mosaic,* ed. J. Matthew Wilson, 251–276. Washington, D.C.: Georgetown University Press.

Brooks, Arthur C. 2006. *Who Really Cares: The Surprising Truth about Compassionate Conservatism.* New York: Basic Books.

Byrnes, Timothy A. 1991. *Catholic Bishops in American Politics.* Princeton, N.J.: Princeton University Press.

Calhoun-Brown, Allison. 1996. "African American Churches and Political Mobilization: The Psychological Impact of Organizational Resources." *The Journal of Politics* 58: 935–953.

Cleage, Albert B., Jr. 1968. *The Black Messiah: The Religious Roots of Black Power*. New York: Sheed and Ward.

Clydesdale, Timothy T. 1999. "Toward Understanding the Role of Bible Beliefs and Higher Education in American Attitudes toward Eradicating Poverty, 1964–1996." *Journal for the Scientific Study of Religion* 38: 103–118.

Cohen, Steven M., and Charles S. Liebman. 1997. "American Jewish Liberalism: Unraveling the Strands." *Public Opinion Quarterly* 61: 405–430.

Cone, James H. 1969. *Black Theology and Black Power*. New York: Seabury.

Corbett, Michael, and Julia Mitchell Corbett. 1999. *Politics and Religion in the United States*. New York: Garland.

Craig, Robert H. 1992. *Religion and Radical Politics: An Alternative Christian Tradition in the United States*. Philadelphia, Pa.: Temple University Press.

Crawford, Sue E. S., and Laura R. Olson, eds. 2001. *Christian Clergy in American Politics*. Baltimore, Md.: Johns Hopkins University Press.

Cross, Robert D. 1967. *The Emergence of Liberal Catholicism in America*. Cambridge, Mass.: Harvard University Press.

Davis, Nancy J., and Robert V. Robinson. 1996. "Are the Rumors of War Exaggerated?: Religious Orthodoxy and Moral Progressivism in America." *American Journal of Sociology* 102: 756–787.

Dawson, Michael C. 1994. *Behind the Mule: Race and Class in African American Politics*. Princeton, N.J.: Princeton University Press.

DeSipio, Louis. 1996. *Counting on the Latino Vote: Latinos as a New Electorate*. Charlottesville, Va.: University of Virginia Press.

DeSipio, Louis. 2007. "Power in the Pews?: Religious Diversity and Latino Political Attitudes and Behaviors." In *From Pews to Polling Places: Faith and Politics in the American Religious Mosaic*, ed. J. Matthew Wilson, 161–184. Washington, D.C.: Georgetown University Press.

DeSipio, Louis, and Rodolfo O. de la Garza. 2002. "Forever Seen as New: Latino Participation in American Elections." In *Latinos: Remaking America*, ed. Marcelo Suárez-Orozco and Mariela M. Páez, 398–409. Berkeley, Calif.: University of California Press.

Djupe, Paul A. 2007. "The Evolution of Jewish Pluralism: Public Opinion and Political Preferences of American Jews." In *From Pews to Polling Places: Faith and Politics in the American Religious Mosaic*, ed. J. Matthew Wilson, 185–212. Washington, D.C.: Georgetown University Press.

Djupe, Paul A., and John C. Green. 2007. "The Politics of American Muslims." In *From Pews to Polling Places: Faith and Politics in the American Religious Mosaic*, ed. J. Matthew Wilson, 213–250. Washington, D.C.: Georgetown University Press.

Djupe, Paul A., and Laura R. Olson. 2007. *Religious Interests in Community Conflict: Beyond the Culture Wars*. Waco, Texas: Baylor University Press.

Durkheim, Emile. 1951. *Suicide: A Study in Sociology*. Trans. John A. Spaulding and George Simpson. Glencoe, Ill.: Free Press.

Espinosa, Gaston, Virgilio Elizondo, and Jesse Miranda, eds. 2005. *Latino Religions and Civic Activism in the United States*. New York: Oxford University Press.

Feldman, Stanley, and Marco R. Steenbergen. 2001. "The Humanitarian Foundation of Public Support for Social Welfare." *American Journal of Political Science* 45: 658–677.

Feldman, Stanley, and John Zaller. 1992. "The Political Culture of Ambivalence Ideological Responses to the Welfare State." *American Journal of Political Science* 36: 268–307.

Finke, Roger, and Rodney Stark. 1992. *The Churching of America, 1776–1990: Winners and Losers in Our Religious Economy*. New Brunswick, N.J.: Rutgers University Press.

Frazier, E. Franklin. 1963. *The Negro Church in America*. New York: Schocken.

Froehle, Bryan T., and Mary L. Gautier. 2000. *Catholicism USA: A Portrait of the Catholic Church in the United States*. Maryknoll, N.Y.: Orbis.

Fuchs, Lawrence. 1956. "American Jews and the Presidential Vote." *American Political Science Review* 49: 385–401.

Gallup, George, Jr., and Jim Castelli. 1987. *The American Catholic People: Their Beliefs, Practices, and Values*. Garden City, N.Y.: Doubleday.

Gomez, Brad T., and J. Matthew Wilson. 2006. "Rethinking Symbolic Racism: Evidence of Attribution Bias." *The Journal of Politics* 68: 611–625.

Greeley, Andrew M. 1989. *Religious Change in America*. Cambridge, Mass.: Harvard University Press.

Greeley, Andrew M. 1990. *The Catholic Myth: The Behavior and Beliefs of American Catholics*. New York: Collier.

Green, John C., James L. Guth, Corwin E. Smidt, and Lyman A. Kellstedt. 1996. *Religion and the Culture Wars: Dispatches from the Front*. Lanham, Md.: Rowman & Littlefield.

Green, John C., Lyman A. Kellstedt, Corwin E. Smidt, and James L. Guth. 2007. "How the Faithful Voted: Religious Communities and the Presidential Vote." In *A Matter of Faith: Religion and Politics in the 2004 Presidential Election*, ed. David E. Campbell, 15–36. Washington, D.C.: Brookings Institution Press.

Greenberg, Anna, and Kenneth D. Wald. 2001. "Still Liberal after All These Years?: The Contemporary Political Behavior of American Jews." In *Jews in American Politics*, ed. L. Sandy Maisel and Ira Forman, 167–199. Lanham, Md.: Rowman & Littlefield.

Guth, James L. 2007. "Religion and Roll Calls: Religious Influences on the U.S. House of Representatives, 1997–2002." Presented at the annual meeting of the American Political Science Association, Chicago, Illinois (September 1).

Guth, James L., John C. Green, Corwin E. Smidt, Lyman A. Kellstedt, and Margaret M. Poloma. 1997. *The Bully Pulpit: The Politics of Protestant Clergy*. Lawrence, Kans.: University Press of Kansas.

Guth, James L., Lyman A. Kellstedt, John C. Green, and Corwin E. Smidt. 2001. "America Fifty/Fifty." *First Things* October: 19–26.

Guth, James L., Lyman A. Kellstedt, Corwin E. Smidt, and John C. Green. 2006. "Religious Influences in the 2004 Presidential Election." *Presidential Studies Quarterly* 36: 223–242.

Hadden, Jeffrey K. 1969. *The Gathering Storm in the Churches*. Garden City, N.Y.: Doubleday.

Handy, Robert T. 1952. "Christianity and Socialism in America, 1900–1920." *Church History* 21: 39–54.

Handy, Robert T. 1990. "Protestant Theological Tensions and Political Styles in the Progressive Period." In *Religion and American Politics: From the Colonial Period to the 1980s*, ed. Mark A. Noll, 281–301. New York: Oxford University Press.

Hanna, Mary T. 1979. *Catholics and American Politics*. Cambridge, Mass.: Harvard University Press.

Hargrove, Barbara. 1989. *The Sociology of Religion: Classic and Contemporary Approaches*. Arlington Heights, Ill.: Harlan Davidson.

Harris, Fredrick C. 1999. *Something Within: Religion in African-American Political Activism*. New York: Oxford University Press.

Harris-Lacewell, Melissa. 2007. "Liberation to Mutual Fund: Political Consequences of Differing Conceptions of Christ in the African American Church." In *From Pews to Polling Places: Faith and Politics in the American Religious Mosaic*, ed. J. Matthew Wilson, 131–160. Washington, D.C.: Georgetown University Press.

Hart, Stephen. 1992. *What Does the Lord Require? How American Christians Think about Economic Justice*. New York: Oxford University Press.

Hart, Stephen. 2001. *Cultural Dilemmas of Progressive Politics: Styles of Engagement among Grassroots Activists*. Chicago, Ill.: University of Chicago Press.

Hennesey, James S. J. 1981. *American Catholics: A History of the Roman Catholic Community in the United States*. New York: Oxford University Press.

Hertzke, Allen D. 1988. *Representing God in Washington: The Role of Religious Lobbies in the American Polity*. Knoxville, Tenn.: University of Tennessee Press.

Himmelfarb, Milton. 1985. "Another Look at the Jewish Vote." *Commentary* December: 39–44.

Hochschild, Jennifer L. 1981. *What's Fair?: American Beliefs about Distributive Justice*. Cambridge, Mass.: Harvard University Press.

Hofrenning, Daniel J. B. 1995. *In Washington But Not of It*. Philadelphia, Pa.: Temple University Press.

Hollinger, Dennis. 1983. *Individualism and Social Ethics: An Evangelical Syncretism*. Lanham, Md.: University Press of America.

Hopkins, Dwight N. 1999. *Introducing Black Theology of Liberation*. Maryknoll, N.Y.: Orbis.

Hunt, Larry L. 2000. "Religion and Secular Status among Hispanics in the United States: Catholicism and the Varieties of Hispanic Protestantism." *Social Science Quarterly* 81: 344–362.

Hutchinson, Earl Ofari. 2001. "New Worries about Mega-Black Churches." *Black World Today* February 2: 1–5.

Iannaccone, Laurence R. 1993. "Heirs to the Protestant Ethic?: The Economics of American Fundamentalists." In *Fundamentalisms and the State*, ed. Martin E. Marty and R. Scott Appleby, 342–366. Chicago, Ill.: University of Chicago Press.

Jelen, Ted G. 1993. *The Political World of the Clergy*. Westport, Conn.: Praeger.

Jelen, Ted G., Corwin E. Smidt, and Clyde Wilcox. 1993. "The Political Effects of the Born-Again Phenomenon." In *Rediscovering the Religious Factor in American Politics*, ed. David C. Leege and Lyman A. Kellstedt, 199–215. Armonk, N.Y.: M. E. Sharpe.

Johnson, Joseph A. 1993. "Jesus, the Liberator." In *Black Theology: A Documentary History*, ed. James H. Cone and Gayraud S. Willmore, 203–216. Maryknoll, N.Y.: Orbis.

Johnstone, Ronald L. 1988. *Religion in Society: A Sociology of Religion*. Englewood Cliffs, N.J.: Prentice-Hall.

Jones-Correa, Michael, and David Leal. 2001. "Political Participation: Does Religion Matter?" *Political Research Quarterly* 54: 751–770.

Kellstedt, Lyman A., Corwin E. Smidt, John C. Green, and James L. Guth. 2007. "A Gentle Stream or a 'River Glorious?': The Religious Left in the 2004 Election." In *A Matter of Faith: Religion in the 2004 Presidential Election*, ed. David E. Campbell, 232–256. Washington, D.C.: Brookings Institution Press.

Kenski, Henry C., and William Lockwood. 1991. "Catholic Voting Behavior in 1988: A Critical Swing Vote." In *The Bible and the Ballot Box: Religion and Politics in the 1988 Election*, ed. James L. Guth and John C. Green, 173–187. Boulder, Colo.: Westview Press.

Kosmin, Barry A., and Arila Keyser. 2006. *Religion in a Free Market*. Ithaca, N.Y.: Paramount Market Publishing.

Lane, Robert E. 1962. *Political Ideology: Why the American Common Man Believes What He Does.* Glencoe, Ill.: Free Press.

Lasswell, Harold D. 1936. *Politics: Who Gets What, When, How.* New York: McGraw-Hill.

Layman, Geoffrey C. 2001. *The Great Divide: Religious and Cultural Conflict in American Party Politics.* New York: Columbia University Press.

Lazarsfeld, Paul F., Bernard Berelson, and Hazel Gaudet. 1948. *The People's Choice: How the Voter Makes up His Mind in a Presidential Campaign.* New York: Columbia University Press.

Lee, Jongho, Harry P. Pachon, and Matt Baretto. 2002. "Guiding the Flock: Church as a Vehicle of Latino Participation." Presented at the annual meeting of the American Political Science Association, Boston, Massachusetts (August 31).

Leege, David C., and Lyman A. Kellstedt, eds. 1993. *Rediscovering the Religious Factor in American Politics.* Armonk, N.Y.: M. E. Sharpe.

Leege, David C., and Paul D. Mueller. 2004. "How Catholic Is the Catholic Vote?" In *American Catholics and Civic Engagement: A Distinctive Voice,* ed. Margaret O'Brien Steinfels, 213–250. Lanham, Md.: Rowman & Littlefield.

Leege, David C., Kenneth D. Wald, Brian S. Krueger, and Paul D. Mueller. 2002. *The Politics of Cultural Differences: Social Change and Voter Mobilization Strategies in the Post-New Deal Period.* Princeton, N.J.: Princeton University Press.

Lincoln, C. Eric, and Lawrence H. Mamiya. 1990. *The Black Church in the African American Experience.* Durham, NC: Duke University Press.

Lipset, Seymour Martin, and Stein Rokkan. 1967. "Cleavage Structures, Party Systems, and Voter Alignments: An Introduction." In *Party Systems and Voter Alignments: Crossnational Perspectives,* ed. Seymour Martin Lipset and Stein Rokkam, 1–64. New York: Free Press.

Magnuson, Norris. 1977. *Salvation in the Slums: Evangelical Social Work, 1865–1920.* Metuchen, N.J.: Scarecrow.

Marsden, George M. 1973. "The Gospel of Wealth, the Social Gospel, and the Salvation of Souls in Nineteenth-Century America." *Fides et Historia* 5: 10–21.

Marsden, George M. 2006. *Fundamentalism and American Culture.* 2nd ed. New York: Oxford University Press.

McDaniel, Eric L. 2007. "The Black Church: Maintaining Old Coalitions." In *A Matter of Faith: Religion in the 2004 Presidential Election,* ed. David E. Campbell, 215–231. Washington, D.C.: Brookings Institution Press.

Mockabee, Stephen T. 2007. "The Political Behavior of American Catholics: Change and Continuity." In *From Pews to Polling Places: Faith and Politics in the American Religious Mosaic,* ed. J. Matthew Wilson, 81–104. Washington, D.C.: Georgetown University Press.

Morris, Aldon D. 1984. *The Origins of the Civil Rights Movement: Black Communities Organizing for Change.* New York: Free Press.

Niebuhr, H. Richard. 1951. *Christ and Culture.* New York: Harper.

Noll, Mark A. 1990. *Religion and American Politics: From the Colonial Period to the 1980s.* New York: Oxford University Press.

Noonan, John T. 1998. *The Lustre of Our Country: The American Experience of Religious Freedom.* Berkeley, Calif.: University of California Press.

Olson, Laura R. 2007. "Whither the Religious Left?: Religio-Political Progressivism in Twenty-First Century America." In *From Pews to Polling Places: Faith and Politics in the American Religious Mosaic,* ed. J. Matthew Wilson, 53–79. Washington, D.C.: Georgetown University Press.

Orum, Anthony. 1966. "A Reappraisal of the Social and Political Participation of Negroes." *American Journal of Sociology* 72: 32–46.

Parham, Robert. 1996. "Honest Speech in Church." *Ethics Report* 4: 1–3.

Pew Forum on Religion & Public Life. 2008. *U.S. Religious Landscape Survey.* Washington, D.C.: Pew Forum on Religion & Public Life.

Pew Research Center. 2007. *Muslim Americans: Middle Class and Mostly Mainstream.* Washington, D.C.: Pew Forum on Religion & Public Life.

Pinn, Anthony B. 2002. *The Black Church in the Post-Civil Rights Era.* Maryknoll, N.Y.: Orbis.

Pontifical Council for Justice and Peace. 2005. *Compendium of the Social Doctrine of the Church.* Vatican City: Libreria Editrice Vaticana.

Pope Leo XIII. 1891. *Rerum Novarum.* Vatican City: Libreria Editrice Vaticana.

Prendergast, William B. 1999. *The Catholic Voter in American Politics: The Passing of the Democratic Monolith.* Washington, D.C.: Georgetown University Press.

Pyle, Ralph E. 1993. "Faith and Commitment to the Poor: Theological Orientation and Support for Government Assistance Measures." *Sociology of Religion* 54: 385–401.

Quinley, Harold E. 1974. *The Prophetic Clergy: Social Activism among Protestant Ministers.* New York: Wiley.

Regnerus, Mark D., Christian Smith, and David Sikkink. 1999. "Who Gives to the Poor?: The Influence of Religious Tradition and Political Location on the Personal Generosity of Americans toward the Poor." *Journal for the Scientific Study of Religion* 37: 481–493.

Roberts, J. Deotis. 1971. *Liberation and Reconciliation.* Philadelphia, Pa.: Westminster Press.

Rogers, Mary Beth. 1990. *Cold Anger: A Story of Faith and Power Politics.* Denton, TX: University of North Texas Press.

Roof, Wade Clark, and William McKinney. 1987. *American Mainline Religion: Its Changing Shape and Future.* New Brunswick, N.J.: Rutgers University Press.

Russell, C. Allyn. 1976. *Voices of American Fundamentalism.* Philadelphia, Pa.: Westminster.

Skocpol, Theda. 2000. "Religion, Civil Society, and Social Provision in the U.S." In *Who Will Provide?: The Changing Role of Religion in American Social Welfare,* ed. Mary Jo Bane, Brent Coffin, and Ronald Thiemann, 21–50. Boulder, Colo.: Westview Press.

Smidt, Corwin E. 2001. "Religion and American Public Opinion." In *In God We Trust?: Religion and American Public Life,* ed. Corwin E. Smidt, 96–117. Grand Rapids, Mich.: Baker Academic.

Smidt, Corwin E., ed. 2004. *Pulpit and Politics: Clergy in American Politics at the Advent of the Millennium.* Waco, Texas: Baylor University Press.

Smidt, Corwin E. 2007. "Evangelical and Mainline Protestants at the Turn of the Millennium: Taking Stock and Looking Forward." In *From Pews to Polling Places: Faith and Politics in the American Religious Mosaic,* ed. J. Matthew Wilson, 29–51. Washington, D.C.: Georgetown University Press.

Smidt, Corwin E., Kevin R. den Dulk, James M. Penning, Stephen V. Monsma, and Douglas L. Koopman. 2008. *Pews, Prayers, and Participation: Religion and Civic Responsibility in America.* Washington, D.C.: Georgetown University Press.

Smith, Christian. 1998. *American Evangelicalism: Embattled and Thriving.* Chicago, Ill.: University of Chicago Press.

Smith, R. Drew, and Tamelyn Tucker-Worgs. 2000. "Megachurches: African-American Churches in Social and Political Context." In *The State of Black America 2000,* ed. Lee Daniels, 180–200. New York: National Urban League.

Stark, Rodney, and Charles Y. Glock. 1968. *American Piety.* Berkeley, Calif.: University of California Press.

Suro, Roberto, Richard Fry, and Jeffrey Passel. 2005. *Hispanics and the 2004 Election: Population, Electorate, and Voters.* Washington, D.C.: Pew Hispanic Center.

Tamney, Joseph B., Ronald Burton, and Stephen D. Johnson. 1989. "Fundamentalism and Economic Restructuring." In *Religion and Political Behavior in the United States,* ed. Ted G. Jelen, 67–82. New York: Praeger.

Thuesen, Peter. 2002. "The Logic of Mainline Churchliness: Historical Background since the Reformation." In *The Quiet Hand of God: Faith-Based Activism and the Public Role of Mainline Protestantism,* ed. Robert Wuthnow and John Evans, 27–53. Berkeley, Calif.: University of California Press.

Tracy, David. 1981. *The Analogical Imagination: Christian Theology and the Culture of Pluralism.* New York: Crossroads.

Trattner, Walter I. 1999. *From Poor Law to Welfare State: A History of Social Welfare in America.* New York: Free Press.

United States Conference of Catholic Bishops. 1986. *Economic Justice for All: Catholic Social Teaching and the U.S. Economy.* Washington, D.C.: United States Conference of Catholic Bishops.

Wagner, Steven. 1998. "The Catholic Voter Project." *Crisis* November: 2–8.

Wald, Kenneth D., and Allison Calhoun-Brown. 2007. *Religion and Politics in the United States.* 5th ed. Lanham, Md.: Rowman & Littlefield.

Wallis, Jim. 2005. *God's Politics: Why the Right Gets It Wrong and the Left Doesn't Get It.* San Francisco, Calif.: HarperCollins.

Warren, Mark R. 2001. *Dry Bones Rattling: Community Building to Revitalize American Democracy.* Princeton, N.J.: Princeton University Press.

Weber, Max. 1930. *The Protestant Ethic and the Spirit of Capitalism.* Trans. Talcott Parsons. New York: Scribner.

Wilcox, Clyde. 1996. *Onward Christian Soldiers?: The Religious Right in American Politics.* Boulder, Colo.: Westview Press.

Wilcox, Clyde, Ted G. Jelen, and David C. Leege. 1993. "Religious Group Identifications: Toward a Cognitive Theory of Religious Mobilization." In *Rediscovering the Religious Factor in American Politics,* ed. David C. Leege and Lyman A. Kellstedt, 72–99. Armonk, N.Y.: M. E. Sharpe.

Will, Jeffry A., and John K. Cochran. 1995. "God Helps Those Who Help Themselves?: The Effects of Religious Affiliations, Religiosity, and Deservedness on Generosity toward the Poor." *Sociology of Religion* 56: 327–338.

Wilson, J. Matthew. 1999. " 'Blessed Are the Poor': American Protestantism and Attitudes toward Poverty and Welfare." *Southeastern Political Review* 27: 421–437.

Wilson, J. Matthew. 2004. "American Catholic Attitudes on Poverty and Welfare: Distinctiveness or Convergence?" Presented at the annual meeting of the Midwest Political Science Association, Chicago, Illinois (April 15).

Wilson, J. Matthew. 2007. "The Changing Catholic Voter: Comparing Responses to John Kennedy in 1960 and John Kerry in 2004." In *A Matter of Faith: Religion in the 2004 Presidential Election,* ed. David E. Campbell, 163–179. Washington, D.C.: Brookings Institution Press.

Wood, Richard L. 2002. *Faith in Action: Religion, Race, and Democratic Organizing in America.* Chicago, Ill.: University of Chicago Press.

Wuthnow, Robert. 1994. *God and Mammon in America.* New York: Free Press.

Wuthnow, Robert, and John H. Evans, eds. 2002. *The Quiet Hand of God: Faith-Based Activism and the Public Role of Mainline Protestantism.* Berkeley, Calif.: University of California Press.

CHAPTER 8

....

RELIGION AND AMERICAN PUBLIC OPINION: SOCIAL ISSUES

....

TED G. JELEN

Since the 1960s, the salience of noneconomic domestic, or the so-called social, issues has risen dramatically (Scammon and Wattenberg 1971). Their importance was readily apparent in the 1972 election, when opponents characterized Democrat George McGovern as the candidate of "Acid, Amnesty, and Abortion." And, subsequently, the political importance of these issues has only increased during the final two decades of the 20th century and into the first decade of the 21st.

In fact, analysts such as James Davison Hunter (1991, 1994) have gone so far as to suggest that "lifestyle issues" superseded economic divisions as the principal axis of political conflict in the United States, labeling the divide a "culture war." Although the culture wars thesis is controversial (Davis and Robinson 1996; Williams 1998; Miller and Hoffman 1999; Fiorina 2005), at the very least it can be said that the increased attention paid to social issues has had important conse-quences for American politics.

Changes in the religious landscape have been critical in elevating social issues to the forefront of American politics. Prior to the 1970s, religious differences were mainly between Protestants and Catholics. These differences had political conse-quences, particularly outside the South, with Protestants aligned with the Republi-can Party, whereas Catholics and their Jewish allies identified with the Democrats. Increasingly, after 1970, conflict has taken place *within* religious groups, with battles over gay rights, abortion, and women's roles. Inevitably, these differences also had political consequences. Strategic elites in both parties found it advantageous to raise such issues, ensuring their prominence on the public agenda (Jelen 2000; Layman 2001; Jelen and Wilcox 2003; McTague and Layman, chapter 12, this volume). As Layman (2001) has argued, politicians and political parties saw new opportunities in these religious differences. Democrats aligned themselves with religious modernists in taking pro-choice positions on abortion and liberal stances on gay rights. In contrast, Republicans took the other side on both issues, joining religious traditionalists. The result was a "social issue evolution" (Adams 1997), similar to the racial issue evolution described by Carmines and Stimson (1980).

One result of these changes was the realignment of white evangelical Protestants into the Republican Party; such "values voters" now constitute an essential component of the GOP coalition. Meanwhile, mainline Protestants, the former bulwark of the Republican Party, moved to the center based, in part, on social issues, as did Roman Catholics, the old champions of the Democrats. The GOP's social issue stance had special appeal to "traditionalist" religionists, particularly in the South, and helped transform that region from a Democratic Party bastion to a Republican stronghold by the end of the 20th century. Moreover, the increased visibility of issues such as abortion, gay rights, and school prayer occasioned the rise of the Christian Right during the late 1970s (Wilcox, Goldberg, and Jelen 2000). Thus, the emergence of social issues has occasioned mobilization and counter-mobilization among both religious liberals and conservatives.[1]

Some issues considered here (e.g., abortion and gay rights) concern sexual morality. In part, these issues arose as the result of changing attitudes toward gender roles, as well as important changes in the technology surrounding procreation. The mobilization of women into the paid labor force during World War II (symbolized by "Rosie the Riveter") may have occasioned a demand for control over fertility. This demand was met by the introduction of oral contraception, widely available by the mid 1960s (Halberstam 1997). Such changes provided the backdrop for changing attitudes toward the meaning of sexuality. Sexual activity—within or outside of marriage—was no longer simply tied to procreation, but was seen as a means of personal and emotional fulfillment. Arguably, once sexuality and reproduction were uncoupled, the "unnaturalness" of homosexuality became more controversial. Thus, changes in social relations between men and women, as well as advances in medical technology, may have provided both the impetus for "the sexual revolution" and the traditionalist reaction.

Other social issues considered in this chapter deal with educational policy and have a longer pedigree than gay rights and abortion. For example, organized prayer in public schools has been controversial since the latter part of the 19th century (Delfattore 2004), whereas the teaching of evolution has been an issue since the Scopes "Monkey Trial" of 1925 (see Wills, 1990). Contemporary political controversies over these issues are largely rooted in modern cases decided by the U.S. Supreme Court.

Several other social issues are not considered in this chapter because of space constraints and the lack of sustained attention by public opinion scholars. These include Charitable Choice and school vouchers (the limited opinion data show that the public does not have firm views on these issues) as well as public displays of religious symbols, such as nativity scenes, the Christian cross on public buildings, or monuments commemorating the Ten Commandments. In sum, the focus of the chapter is on attitudes toward sexual morality and educational policy and their linkages to religion.

OVERVIEW

Do the diverse questions subsumed under the rubric of "social issues" fit together or form some type of unidimensional scale? In an early piece, I suggested that even committed religious conservatives do not organize their attitudes in this manner (Jelen 1990), but some later research has found a unidimensional pattern, or at least substantial attitude constraint (Wilcox 1993). Carmines and Layman (1997) also found a unidimensional structure in American National Election Studies (ANES) questions concerning social issues from 1972 to 1992. Even more recent scholarship (Kohut, Green, Keeter, and Toth 2000; Kellstedt, Smidt, Green, and Guth 2007; Layman and Hussey 2007) finds similar patterns. An analysis that I performed of social issue items in the 2004 General Social Survey (GSS) reveals that the average correlation among attitudes toward abortion, school prayer, same-sex marriage, the morality of homosexuality, and evolution is approximately .35 (with the correlation between attitudes toward school prayer and abortion at .19).[2] These are relatively high given the typically low correlations among issue positions in the mass public (see the classic argument of Converse [1964, 1970]).

Moreover, clergy and political activists usually exhibit a strong pattern of social issue attitude constraint. By the 1980s, many clergy embraced a "moral reform" agenda, encompassing numerous social issues (Guth, Green, Smidt, Kellstedt, and Poloma 1997, p. 101) and a similar pattern was found in 2001 (Smidt 2004, p. 316). This is important evidence given the key role of pastors in instructing their congregants on moral concerns. Similarly, Layman (2001) and Carmines and Woods (2002) find strong evidence of an underlying social issue dimension among party activists, a pattern that extends to political elites. Adams (1997) and Guth (2007) show that members of Congress vote in consistent fashion on social issues, suggesting that there is strong underlying attitude constraint to these issues among members. In sum, responses to the social issues appear similar at the level of the mass public, activists, and governmental elites. No wonder these issues are so divisive.

Nevertheless, it is difficult to generalize about the specific religious variables that are most strongly related to attitudes toward different social issues. In part, this is the result of the wide variety of religious variables used from study to study. For example, some analysts (Woodrum and Hoban 1992) have suggested that biblical literalism is a stronger predictor of attitudes toward the creation/evolution controversy than for school prayer, where more general measures of religiosity such as church attendance are central. Such a finding makes intuitive sense, because a major component of the creation/evolution issue involves the authority of the Bible. However, a more recent study (Haider-Markel and Joslyn 2008) does not include a measure of biblical literalism, but shows that a "born-again" experience is related to most aspects of the issue. A promising avenue for future research involves determining which aspects of religion (affiliation, beliefs, practices) have the strongest relationships with attitudes toward social issues.

Moreover, there may be substantial variation in public attitudes *within* a particular issue domain. For example, the correlates of approval for a "moment of silence" in public schools are quite distinct from those associated with approval of public prayer at high school sporting events (Jelen 2005a). Similarly, many respondents who do not hold a "high" view of scripture approve of the teaching of creationism as an alternative to evolution.

Why should this be so? It may result from the way that issues are framed. American political culture is characterized by widely held values such as individualism and egalitarianism (Jelen 2005b). Arguably, the master narrative in American political discourse involves autonomous individuals making uncoerced or unrestricted decisions for themselves. The importance of "rights talk" (Glendon 1991) poses a problem for those who seek to limit or proscribe legal abortion, or to prohibit same-sex marriage. Moral traditionalists who seek to restrict such choices must provide compelling counterframes to the dominant individualist culture. To the extent that religious or political leaders can characterize traditionalist positions on social issues as accessing the values of individual freedom or equality, they will be advantaged in public debate. Thus, if school prayer is successfully framed as an application of religious liberty (rather than government establishment of religion), or if "equal time" measures for creation science can be described as allowing all sides in a debate to be heard, conservative positions might attract more support.

"Pelvic Politics"

Two issues I deal with in this study are related to attitudes toward sexual morality, which Leege and Kellstedt (1993) have termed "pelvic politics." The controversy over gay rights is a relatively recent addition to the public agenda, whereas abortion has been center stage in American politics for more than a generation. Both issues have incited emotional (and, in the case of abortion, occasionally violent) controversies in U.S. politics during the late 20th and early 21st centuries.

Gay Rights

Throughout the past decade, the legal rights of homosexuals have been among the most visible and most divisive issues in American politics. Some analysts have even suggested that the issue of same-sex marriage was a decisive factor in George W. Bush's winning campaign for the presidency in 2004, particularly in the so-called "battleground" states (compare with Guth, Kellstedt, Smidt, and Green 2006; Campbell and Monson 2007; Keeter 2007).

The issue of gay rights has evolved during the past generation. Some observers date the contemporary gay rights movement from the Stonewall incident in 1968, in which patrons of a gay bar in New York fought back against police officers attempting to close the establishment. Like most issues discussed in this chapter, the movement for the rights of gays and lesbians was fueled by court decisions. These would include *Bowers v. Hardwick* (478 US 186 [1986]), in which the U.S. Supreme Court upheld a Georgia antisodomy statute; *Romer v. Evans* (517 US 620 [1996]), in which an amendment to the Colorado state constitution which prohibited all state and local laws designed to protect homosexuals was overturned; *Lawrence v. Texas* (530 US 558 [2003]), which reversed *Bowers* on privacy grounds; and *Goodridge v. Department of Public Health* (798 N.E. 2d 941 [Mass. 2003]), in which the Massachusetts Supreme Court ruled that laws proscribing same-sex marriage violated guarantees of equal protection under the constitution of the Commonwealth of Massachusetts.

Because gay rights might be considered an "easy issue" (Carmines and Stimson 1980), it is not surprising that the matter is quite salient in the arena of public opinion. In recent years, a growing and sophisticated literature has enhanced our understanding of the dynamics of public attitudes on this issue.

Perhaps the most important finding is the increasing public acceptance of homosexuality, and the rise of public support for protecting the rights of gays. It is important that the distinction between these two points be maintained. Although public approval of the morality of homosexuality is increasing, most Americans do not approve of sexual relations between members of the same sex.[3] At the same time, support for protecting the civil liberties of gays and lesbians, and for laws providing equal treatment for such citizens, is also increasing, even among Americans who regard homosexuality as immoral (see Loftus 2001; Wilcox and Norrander 2002). In general, virtually all studies point to increasing public acceptance and tolerance of homosexuality (Yang 1997; Bowman and O'Keefe 2004). Yet such attitudes are by no means universal, and there remains substantial opposition to gay rights.[4]

What accounts for liberalizing attitudes toward homosexuality and gay rights? Wilcox and Norrander (2002) show that much of the observed change can be attributed to generational replacement, with more tolerant and accepting younger cohorts gradually replacing less tolerant elders (see also Brewer 2003a, b). In turn, these developments are occasioned by changing aspects in political and popular culture. In recent decades, media treatment of gays has become more sympathetic, and prominent celebrities have "come out," revealing their sexual orientations. Perhaps not coincidentally, an increasing number of Americans report being acquainted with someone who is gay or lesbian (Wilcox and Wolpert 2000). Arguably, homosexuality might seem less threatening when this characteristic is embodied by a neighbor, coworker, or acquaintance. Moreover, increasing numbers of citizens have come to believe that homosexuality is a genetic trait, or, at the very least, is involuntary (Copeland and Hamer 1994; Wilcox and Norrander 2002; Wilcox, Brewer, Shames, and Lake 2007).

Finally, as the issue of gay rights continues to be debated, it has increasingly been subsumed under the rubric of American core values such as moral traditionalism, egalitarianism, and individualism (Brewer 2003a, b; Craig, Martinez, Kane, and Gainous 2005; Martinez, Craig, Kane, and Gainous 2005). In particular, the "equal protection" and "individual rights" frames have been applied to questions involving the rights of gays and lesbians. For example, Wilcox et al. (2007) have shown that equality values are significantly related to support for antidiscrimination laws, as well as to support for the right of homosexuals to adopt children. However, such values are not related to support for gays in the military, or for same-sex marriage.

These findings raise the question of the dimensionality of attitudes toward the rights of gays and lesbians. Martinez et al. (2005) have suggested that a distinction exists between attitudes toward gays and "family and children's issues" (adoption, marriage, teaching in schools, joining the Boy Scouts) and "adult" activities (support for antidiscrimination laws, equality in obtaining health benefits, and so forth). Wilcox et al. (2007) have shown that attitudes toward adoption by gays, gays in the military, same-sex marriage, and laws prohibiting discrimination against gays and lesbians are analytically and empirically distinct, and have different sources. Clearly, attitudes toward gay rights issues are not driven by a simple "culture wars" model. Different aspects of the gay rights issue may involve different core values, or, at a minimum, different weights for competing values. The organization of attitudes toward gay rights and the different sources of such attitudes are promising areas for research.

Virtually all the research on attitudes toward gay rights underscores the importance of religion as a source of opposition to gay rights. However, the precise aspects of religious belief, affiliation, and practice that affect such attitudes remain unclear. There appears to be general agreement that church attendance and religious salience, as well as attitudes toward scripture and membership in an evangelical denomination are significant predictors of attitudes toward gays and lesbians, and toward the rights of homosexuals.[5] One study found that being a frequent church-attending Roman Catholic is not a significant predictor of attitudes toward antidiscrimination laws (Wilcox and Norrander 2002). Clearly, given the size of the Catholic electorate, and the potential electoral importance of issues of gay rights, understanding Catholic attitudes on these issues is of some importance.

In recent years, some empirical research has dealt explicitly with attitudes toward same-sex marriage. Support for same-sex marriage has been increasing

(Wilcox et al. 2007), although such unions remain quite unpopular. Although it has been suggested that civil unions constitute a middle ground between legally recognized marriages between couples of the same sex and their prohibition (Brewer and Wilcox 2005), the correlates of support for civil unions are similar, but distinct, from those for same-sex marriage (Olson, Cadge, and Harrison 2006). It is possible that public attitudes toward same-sex marriage are conditioned by beliefs that marriage is both a religious and legal institution, and the apparent violation of religious prerogatives contributes to the unpopularity of same-sex unions. Future research might well focus on whether the issue of same-sex marriage is *sui generis*, or whether support for such unions represents the most extreme point on something resembling a Guttman scale.[6]

Clearly, disparate findings such as these can be attributed to the precise framing of the dependent variable, different samples, or divergent model specifications. Indeed, it is a common practice to include control variables such as affect toward gays, moral traditionalism, or political ideology in multivariate models of attitudes toward gay rights. As noted earlier, religious beliefs and affiliations affect these general values, and both traditional (or orthodox) beliefs and frequent church attendance may exert indirect, as well as direct, influence on attitudes toward homosexuality and the rights of gays and lesbians. Thus, complex multivariate models that measure only the direct effects of religious variables may, in fact, underestimate the role of religion in fostering opposition to gay rights or same-sex marriage. Future research might well focus on core values, or attitudes toward gays and lesbians, as intervening variables between religion and political attitudes toward gay rights.

Abortion

One of the most thoroughly studied areas in the social sciences involves public opinion and abortion (for an overview, see Jelen and Wilcox [2003]). Even before the Supreme Court's landmark decision in *Roe v. Wade* (410 US 113 [1973]), abortion was becoming a controversial issue (Luker 1984; Faux 1988; Cook, Jelen, and Wilcox 1992). The GSS makes it clear that there has been some movement toward a pro-life position over time, but that it has been relatively small in magnitude.[7] However, the greatest change has been among strong partisans. The GSS data reveal that "strong" Democrats were actually more pro-life than "strong" Republicans in the 1970s. The Republicans caught up in the 1980s, surpassed the Democrats in pro-life attitudes during the 1990s, and accelerated the trend during the first years of the 21st century.[8] These findings are not surprising given the heated partisan battles regarding abortion in recent elections, and the strong efforts by the two Bush presidential campaigns to mobilize supporters around this issue (Layman 2001).

Given the relationship of the abortion issue to ultimate concerns of human life, and to questions of sexual morality, it is not surprising that much opposition to legal abortion has had a religious basis. In the first years after *Roe*, opposition was presumed to be primarily a Catholic concern (Luker 1984; Faux 1988; Welch, Leege, and Cavendish 1995). The centralized authority of the Roman Catholic hierarchy, as well as the church's explicit opposition to abortion (and, indeed, to contraception) rendered Catholic politics the focus of "pro-life" activity. As the issue developed, however, the religious basis of opposition changed, as evangelical Protestants became more "pro-life" (Cook et al. 1992; Hoffman and Miller 1997).

Sullins (1999) has shown that American Protestants of all types have become more opposed to legal abortion in the years since *Roe*,[9] whereas Roman Catholics have become more accepting of "pro-choice" policies.[10] Sullins (1999) attributed these changes to different patterns of church attendance, as many Protestants (especially those from the evangelical tradition) began to attend religious services more frequently, whereas Mass attendance among Catholics declined.[11] If the relationship between religious and abortion attitudes remains somewhat unclear, other research (Cook et al. 1992; Emerson 1996) has shown that increased religiosity is related to conservative attitudes on abortion, regardless of denomination. As Evans (2002a) has shown, and as examination of GSS and ANES time series data confirms, *intra*denominational polarization over the abortion issue has increased over time, again in response to differences in attendance at religious services. Thus, it is unclear whether church attendance is the key or whether frequent church attenders supplement the religious socialization encountered in church with other religious communications, such as religious television (see Jelen and Wilcox 1993; Newman and Smith 2007).

Some research also suggests that abortion attitudes are contingent on the larger social contexts in which political learning occurs. For example, although individual Roman Catholics are more likely than the median voter to adopt "pro-life" attitudes, the presence of large numbers of Catholics in a given state appears to occasion countermobilization among non-Catholics (Cook, Jelen, and Wilcox 1993). In other words, non-Catholics living in heavily Catholic Massachusetts are more likely to hold permissive attitudes on legal abortion than their coreligionists in Mississippi or Utah. However, O'Connor and Berkman (1995) have shown that there is no corresponding countermobilization with respect to evangelical Protestants, and that the effects of evangelicalism seem simply additive. Why would Catholicism appear to exert a contextual effect on abortion attitudes among people outside the faith, whereas evangelicalism does not? Perhaps the strong organizational presence of the church in heavily Catholic states makes its pro-life stance more visible, and more salient, to Protestants, Jews, and the unchurched (Segers and Byrnes 1995).

Among the more perplexing findings is the relative stability of abortion attitudes at the aggregate level prior to the year 2000 (Sharp 1999; Wilcox and Norrander 2002; Jelen and Wilcox 2005). Indeed, since 2000, aggregate attitudes toward abortion have moved slightly in a more conservative (pro-life) direction.[12] What makes this result surprising is that the American population has been changing in ways that would suggest a liberalization of abortion attitudes.

Attributes generally associated with pro-choice attitudes, such as higher education and female participation in the paid labor force, have been increasing, as has acceptance of sexual activity outside marriage. In addition, equal rights for women are much more popular today than in the 1970s.[13] Why, then, have abortion attitudes remained relatively stable (in contrast to attitudes toward gay rights)? One possibility is that the "rights" frame (in which autonomous individuals exercise independent choices) does not unambiguously support a pro-choice position. Indeed, activists on both sides of the abortion issue use the language of rights: A "right to choose" is contrasted with a fetal "right to life." Indeed, Wilcox and Norrander (2002) have shown that most Americans value both the potential life of the fetus and the autonomy of the pregnant woman. Moreover, Saletan (2003) has suggested that pro-life activists have turned the "right to choose" on its head by suggesting that families, not isolated individuals, should make choices among reproductive alternatives. Thus, the framing of the abortion controversy as conflict between competing rights has characterized the issue since *Roe*, and may account for the apparent stability of the aggregate distribution of abortion attitudes. An alternative explanation is a political one and involves three interrelated aspects: the movement of the South (the most religious region of the country) in a Republican direction, the lessoning of the traditional Democratic edge in partisan identification (at least through 2004), and the aggressive efforts by the Bush presidential campaigns in 2000 and 2004 to highlight abortion in their efforts to mobilize support. Nevertheless, the puzzle of this relative stability is by no means settled, and it continues to pose an important topic for future research.

Arguably, pro-life leaders have made some headway in public opinion by approaching the abortion issue indirectly. Rather than simply attacking *Roe*, they have emphasized other aspects of the controversy. For example, abortion opponents worked to pass the "Hyde amendment" during the late 1970s, prohibiting the federal funding of abortions, and public opinion supports that position.[14] Parental consent for minors seeking abortions has been another issue of contention.[15] The controversy over intact dilation and extraction (partial-birth abortion), a late-term procedure, has seen pro-life groups pressuring state governments as well as the U.S. Congress to ban the procedure. The congressional ban has been upheld by the U.S. Supreme Court (*Gonzales v. Carhart*, 2007).[16] Thus, by focusing public attention on these aspects of the abortion issue, pro-life elites may have provided the rhetorical, intellectual, and political resources to counteract presumed pro-choice demographic shifts. Again, there is little empirical evidence to relate changes in the framing of the abortion question to shifts in public opinion, and although the statics and dynamics of abortion attitudes have received a great deal of attention, there is still much to be learned about causal mechanisms.

Of course, not all changes in issue frames cut in a pro-life direction. During recent years, a controversy has been growing over the question of embryonic cell research for therapeutic medical purposes. Obviously, controversies over "stem cell research" or "human cloning" involve a core issue in the abortion debate: the ontological status of human embryo or fetus. Like abortion, embryonic cell research involves fundamental questions—literally, "matters of life and death."

Again, there is little empirical work on the relationship between abortion attitudes and those concerning newer medical technologies. Saad (2002) has shown that opposition to human and animal cloning is relatively widespread, and is based in large part on church attendance and self-identification as "pro-life" or "pro-choice." However, Evans (2002b) has suggested that attitudes toward embryonic cell research are highly sensitive to variations in issue framing. Norrander and Norrander (2007) have shown that support for stem cell research is strongly related both to religious tradition and church attendance, but that this issue had little effect on vote choice in the 2004 presidential election (see also Guth et al. 2006).[17] In sum, it seems clear that the issue of embryonic cell research is in flux, and researchers have an excellent opportunity to monitor changes in public attitudes toward this question and to determine whether the way the issue is framed matters.

Finally, a few studies have suggested that abortion issue framing has become less explicitly religious and more likely to invoke secular or scientific rationales for opposition to abortion (Grindstaff 1994; Dillon 1996). In a religiously pluralistic society such as the United States, manifestly religious warrants such as scripture or natural law theology may not be publicly accessible to large numbers of Americans (see especially Greenawalt 1988). Thus, there has been a tendency for pro-life advocates to make more explicit use of science in opposing legal abortion (Jelen 1992). To what extent do ordinary citizens find secular or religious arguments against abortion more compelling? This is a promising topic for future research, and indeed is an area in which experimental designs hold out a great deal of potential.

Pelvic Politics: The Partisan Connection

During recent decades, the relationships between attitudes toward issues of sexual morality, such as gay rights and abortion, and ideological and party identification have become substantially stronger (Layman 2001). In addition, there is substantial evidence that these issues affect vote decisions at a variety of electoral levels (Cook, Jelen, and Wilcox 1994a, b; Abramowitz 1995; Guth et al. 2006), fueled by self-identified liberals and political independents (Haeberle 1999; Lewis and Rogers 1999; Sherrill and Yang 2000; but see Lindaman and Haider-Markel 2002). In sum, party polarization seems to have occurred with respect to both of the issues considered here.

Yet the question remains: Is it religion at the mass level or governmental and party elites driving the changes? As several analysts (Adams 1997; Carsey and Layman 1999) have pointed out, the direction of causality is not entirely clear. Political parties in the United States have long been regarded as agents of political socialization, and it is at least plausible to argue that, in some instances, party has supplanted religion as a source of attitudes on abortion and gay rights. It follows that scholars should explore the interaction between partisan and religious socialization on these issues. Do people who identify as Republicans on other grounds (such as economic or racial attitudes, or as the result of parental socialization) come to adopt the stances of their party on these issues?[18] If political parties constitute an independent source of political socialization on these issues, it would be useful to understand the manner in which partisanship and religious belief or affiliation interact. Although the problems of estimating the relative magnitude of causal arrows running in opposite directions are formidable indeed, the potential payoff in increasing our understanding of the sources of attitudes toward abortion and gay rights would be enormous.

The Politics of Education

Despite the apparent clarity of Jesus' admonition to "Render unto Caesar that which is Caesar's, and render unto God that which is God's," (Matthew 22:21), the historical course of politics in the United States has shown that there is substantial overlap between the realms of the secular and the sacred. This is perhaps most apparent in the education of the young, which has been a traditional priority of religious communities and which became an important governmental responsibility during the 20th century.

In this section I consider the empirical research that exists concerning two issues involving religion and public education: school prayer (which includes other expressions of religious values in public schools) and the controversies surrounding the teaching of evolution. With respect to both issues, political disagreement has largely been driven by the efforts of educational leaders such as school boards (and, perhaps by extension, popular majorities) to provide for the expression or protection of religious values in the setting of public schools, and by court decisions that have largely limited such expressions in governmental institutions like public schools. In contrast to gay rights and abortion, these matters have not become political issues at the national level, although they have sparked controversies at the local level (Deckman 2004; Djupe and Olson 2007).[19]

School Prayer

The issue of religious expressions in public schools, such as organized school prayer, has been a controversial one for much of American history (Delfattore 2004). Questions about the propriety of explicit or implicit religious messages in public schools have been raised periodically, although the practice was quite common for many years in all parts of the country.

As with the other issues discussed in this chapter, public controversy over religious expression in public schools was exacerbated by decisions of the U.S. Supreme Court. Prior to *Everson v. Board of Education* (1947), such conflicts were dealt with in state courts. Almost immediately after *Everson*, the court struck down an Illinois law providing for released time for religious education on school premises (*McCullom v. Board of Education* 1948). This decision produced a firestorm of protest, leading the court to declare that released time was constitutional if the instruction took place off school property (*Zorach v. Clauson* 1952)—a result that has never been challenged. The most famous of the religious expression cases was *Engel v. Vitale* (1962), which banned mandatory prayers, composed by government, in public schools. The *Engel* decision was followed in short order by *Abingdon School District v. Schempp* (1963), which struck down Bible reading for devotional purposes in public schools.[20] More recent court decisions have prohibited posting of the Ten Commandments in public schools (*Stone v. Graham* 1980), "moments of silence" for prayer or meditation (*Wallace v. Jaffree* 1985),[21] public prayer by clergy at high school graduations (*Lee v. Weisman*, 1992), and public prayer at high school sporting events (*Santa Fe Independent School District v. Doe* 2000). In each case, the court ruled (with occasionally bitter dissents) that such practices constituted violations of the Establishment Clause of the First Amendment.

An impressive body of research has shown that prayer in public schools, as well as other affirmations of religious values, has been consistently popular within the mass public (Elifson and Hadaway 1985; Green and Guth 1989). These attitudes are quite stable in the aggregate, although support for organized Bible reading has declined slightly during recent years (Servin-Gonzalez and Torres-Reyna 1999). Large majorities have consistently favored organized prayer and other religious expressions in public schools (typically on the order of 70 percent to 80 percent).[22] Court decisions banning religious symbols and expression in public schools are extremely unpopular, even among those expressing no religious preference (Jelen and Wilcox 1995).

Furthermore, despite the fact that Roman Catholics have historically opposed prayer in public schools (Delfattore 2004), there are few significant differences among members of different Christian denominations (Elifson and Hadaway 1985; Jelen and Wilcox 1995), although some research suggests polarization of attitudes toward these issues in recent years (Miller and Hoffman 1999). In general, religiosity (operationalized either as attendance at religious services or as the subjective importance of religion) is positively associated with support for school prayer (Woodrum and Hoban 1992), although it remains the case that school prayer is fairly popular even among those who are not particularly religious. Among religious traditions, Jews oppose school prayer, whereas differences between Protestants and Catholics are minimal.

The popularity of school prayer and other expressions of religious values in public schools is perplexing. The percentage of Americans who favor school prayer far exceeds the proportion of Americans who are members of evangelical denominations, who regard the Bible as literally true, or who regularly attend religious services. Why should this be so? One possibility is that many Americans regard school prayer as a matter of religious free exercise, rather than religious establishment. Indeed, religious and political elites who support religious expression in public schools have emphasized the "voluntary" nature of such activities and have suggested that those who oppose such expression are opposed to religious freedom (Jelen 2000). It is, of course, an empirical question regarding whether mass publics have internalized the "free exercise" framing of the issue, which has not, to my knowledge, been addressed by scholars of public opinion.

It has been shown that support for school prayer is less widespread among political activists than among members of the mass public (Green and Guth 1989), and the same lower levels of support are observed among academic, business, media, and government leaders (Jelen and Wilcox 1995). This pattern of elite–mass differences may result from the fact that many members of the mass public have limited exposure to genuine religious diversity, and may not see how difficult it is to produce genuinely neutral or nondiscriminatory public expressions of religious values. Wilcox, Goldberg, and Jelen (2002) have shown that, in general, support for separationist positions on issues involving religious establishment is related to the religious diversity of the community in which a survey respondent lives. Newport (2003) has shown that, in a Gallup survey, 77 percent of respondents disapproved of a court decision mandating removal of a display of the Ten Commandments from a courthouse in Montgomery, Alabama, whereas, in the same survey, only 10 percent approved of the public display of exclusively Christian symbols in government buildings (and 58 percent approved of displaying the symbols of "other religions" along with Christianity).[23]

Some qualitative findings bear on this question. I conducted focus groups on church–state relations in 1993, soliciting opinions on school prayer. Initially, virtually all participants endorsed organized prayer, seeing nothing objectionable about starting the school day with a nondenominational prayer. When asked about the difficulty of composing such a prayer, most did not see this as a problem, but when asked about the possibility that atheists, Muslims, or Hindus might be offended, the reaction began to change. Although few worried about atheists, the problem of offending Muslims or Hindus became more apparent (both had a small, but visible, presence in the local community). Concern rose when participants confronted the task of composing a prayer neutral between monotheism (Christianity, Islam) and polytheism (Hinduism). When I suggested that a different student lead the prayer each day from her/his tradition, the idea was very unpopular. As one respondent put it, "I don't want my child praying to Buddha." Most (but not all) participants eventually abandoned support for school prayer in face of the complexities of dealing with pronounced religious diversity (Jelen and Wilcox 1995; Jelen 2005a).

Such a study suggests that exposure to religious diversity is not part of the daily experiences of most Americans, and that, absent such exposure, many citizens fail to discern potential problems in fashioning genuinely neutral religious expressions in public settings. Even many who favor church–state separation in the abstract also favor prayer in public schools, public displays of the Ten Commandments, and prayers at graduation ceremonies. This is possible because many citizens do not perceive a problem of religious establishment on matters that are largely regarded as consensual, particularly in religiously homogeneous communities.

Thus, research on attitudes toward school prayer contains some obvious findings, but at least one anomaly. Support for school prayer (and related issues) appears to be related to religiosity and religious salience, a highly intuitive result. It stands to reason that support for public expressions of religion would be most frequent among people for whom religion is important. However, support for school prayer is also very high among members of the mass public for whom religion is not particularly salient, and who display low levels of religiosity. Whether this is the result of the effectiveness of a counterframe (public religious expression as an element of religious free exercise) or as the result of a lack of contextual information is worth future investigation.

There has also been little work on the dimensionality of attitudes toward types of religious expression in public schools. For the most part, systematic attention has focused on school prayer, with only sporadic attention to moments of silence; prayer at organized sporting events or graduation; organized religious activities before, during, or after school; or the display of religious symbols. However, it is not clear whether attitudes toward such issues represent a single dimension or whether respondents make distinctions among them. For example, I have shown elsewhere (Jelen 2005a) that biblical literalism is a significant predictor of support for organized prayer at sporting events at public high schools, but is not significantly related to support for "moments of silence." Similarly, Catholics are as supportive of moments of silence as are evangelicals, but are more than twice as likely to oppose public prayer at sporting events (Jelen and Wilcox 1995). The reasons for these findings are not clear. Do respondents hold a lower standard of church–state separation at "voluntary" events such as football games than activities in the normal school day? Are people skeptical about a genuinely neutral public prayer, but persuaded that a "moment of silence" conveys no specific religious message? Because these issues are likely to remain on the public agenda, research into the organization of public attitudes on such questions merits attention.

Evolution and Creationism

At least since the Scopes "Monkey Trial" of 1925, the teaching of evolution has been a recurring dispute in American politics. Many believe that the idea that humans evolved from different or "lower" forms of life presents a challenge to the account of creation in Genesis, and, perhaps by extension, to religious belief more generally (see Wills 1990).

Two Supreme Court cases illustrate the recurring nature of this issue. In the 1960s, Arkansas passed a law prohibiting the teaching of evolution in public schools, which was struck down by the court in *Epperson v. Arkansas* (1968). Two decades later, a Louisiana statute mandating the teaching of creationism along with evolution in public schools was also invalidated by the court (*Edwards v. Aguillard* 1987). The Court held that both laws violated the Establishment Clause of the First Amendment (Jelen 2000).

More recently, an active movement has promoted the teaching of "intelligent design" as a nontheistic alternative to evolution. Essentially, the "theory" of intelligent design assumes that human beings are irreducibly complex, and that the development of such complex forms through "random" processes such as genetic mutation and natural selection is extremely improbable. Such complex organisms, it is argued, result from the conscious efforts of an intelligent, intentional designer.[24] Such a designer might be the God of the Judeo-Christian tradition, or something akin to Aristotle's "unmoved mover." Although the Supreme Court has not ruled on requiring the teaching of intelligent design in the science curricula of public schools, a federal district judge has held that this requirement violates the Establishment Clause (*Kitzmiller v. Dover Area School District* 2005).

The evolution/creation controversy thus has a long history, and has occasioned a great deal of legal, journalistic, and polemical attention. Indeed, in debates before the 2008 presidential election, several Republican candidates expressed strong reservations about the theory of evolution. Despite these expressions, evolution has not been a matter of partisan contention at the national level. And, for our purposes, there has been little empirical research on public attitudes toward this issue (Bishop 2007).

In a series of surveys conducted by Gallup since 1982, respondents have been asked to choose among a creationist alternative, theistic evolution (evolution depicted as a process guided by God), and evolution in which God played no role. Despite variations in question wordings over time, a plurality of Americans has endorsed special creation over the other alternatives. Furthermore, this percentage has not changed substantially in the 25 years that Gallup has posed variations of this question (Bishop 2007).

The strongest predictors of belief in creationism have been education, biblical literalism, religiosity, and evangelical self-identification (Woodrum and Hoban 1992; Mazur 2004, Bishop 2007). It is, of course, not surprising that religious variables, especially biblical literalism, are important correlates of belief in special creation. However, it is interesting that skepticism about evolution persists even among highly educated Americans, as well as among those who do not hold high views of scripture. Bishop (2007) suggests that the manner in which Gallup poses questions regarding beliefs about creationism and evolution might tap more general beliefs in God. Because such beliefs are widespread among Americans and have not varied systematically over time (Wald and Calhoun-Brown 2007), question phrasing may thus account for the results.

There has also been very little research on the effects of alternative frames of the creation/evolution debate. One possible frame is to characterize evolution as "only a theory," implicitly distinguished from "fact." Newport (2006) has shown that there is widespread support for the proposition that evolution is only one of several different theories about the origins of life, and one that has not been decisively confirmed by evidence. It is possible that proponents of special creation have successfully framed the issue around the vagueness of the word *theory* to suggest that the scientific basis of evolution is open to question.

The question of framing is perhaps especially compelling as it applies to the teaching of evolution or creationism in public schools. In many jurisdictions, school boards have proposed or enacted "equal time" provisions, in which creationism is to be taught alongside evolution as an alternative, with students encouraged to "make up their own minds." Although some research has posed questions on the teaching of evolution in this manner (Wilcox 1993; Jelen and Wilcox 1995, Keeter 2005; Masci 2007), there has been little, if any, methodological experimentation with alternative frames. It seems likely that many respondents would respond to cues of "fairness" or "equality" in proposals to provide "balanced" treatment between evolution and creationism. Haider-Markel and Joslyn (2008) have shown that church attendance is related to most aspects of the evolution controversy, but that it is not significantly related to approval of teaching evolution *and* creationism. Possibly, this latter finding can be attributed to the value of "fairness" among nonreligious respondents.[25]

Thus, the question of issue frames is a promising avenue for future research on attitudes toward creationism, evolution, and the teaching of the origins of life in public schools. At least two research strategies seem promising. Experimentation in questionnaire design could determine whether posing explicitly political, rather than scientific or religious, values has a discernable effect on attitudes toward these issues. Alternatively, qualitative techniques could be used, allowing respondents to offer their own rationales for taking the positions they hold. Such open-ended surveys (with necessarily small samples) could provide the basis for more sophisticated hypotheses, and further research using sample surveys.

CONCLUSION

As this chapter has shown, empirical research on attitudes toward social issues has been productive: We have learned much about how attitudes on personal morality or attitudes toward the role of religion in public education are affected by religious affiliation, beliefs, and practices. Nevertheless, there is a great deal more to learn, and I conclude by posing three general directions for research.

First, attitudes on three of the four general issues considered here have been relatively stable over time. Only on gay rights do we observe substantial change during recent years. For those who take secularization or modernization theory seriously (see especially Casanova 1994), the gay rights issue might be a template to which other issues under discussion might be compared. Demographic changes and period effects have occasioned a liberalization of attitudes toward homosexuality and toward the rights of homosexuals. Increases in education, media coverage, and generational replacement have changed the public landscape rather drastically.

Why has liberalization not occurred on the other issues as well? Why has support for legal abortion actually declined slightly, despite increased levels of education, female participation in the paid labor force, and public acceptance of sex outside of marriage? These demographic and cultural changes have likely been offset by pro-life period effects, occasioned by religious and secular leaders who seek to limit or eliminate access to legal abortion. To what extent does religion play a role in stemming changes in the mass public that might be expected to produce attitudinal changes in a "pro-choice" direction? Or, have political parties supplanted religion as a source of socialization on this issue?

The stability of attitudes toward school prayer and evolution raises similar questions. Is support for school prayer, displaying the Ten Commandments, or prayer at school sporting events a reaction to dissatisfaction with public education generally? Does such support represent an attempt to utilize the public schools to counteract the possibly secularizing effects of the popular culture? Why should evolution continue to evoke such intense opposition in a society in which science (and particularly medical science) has achieved such a high level of legitimacy? Why have increased levels of education not resulted in declining beliefs in creationism, or in declining support for inclusion of creationism in public school curricula?

For all these questions, we need to know much more about the subjective basis for such attitudes. Specifically, how does religion affect such attitudes, and, in the case of educational issues, why does support for school prayer or the inclusion of creationism in educational institutions remain so high even among relatively irreligious people?

The aggregate stability of attitudes toward abortion, school prayer, and creationism leads naturally to the second general direction for future research: the question of issue frames, or of the relationship of attitudes toward social issues to core values of the American political culture. Religious values such as biblical literalism, or religiously motivated values such as moral traditionalism, must compete with more secular regime values such as individualism and egalitarianism. Indeed, the recent changes in attitudes toward gay rights might be attributable to the pervasive framing of the issue in terms of individual freedom or equal protection, and the apparent inability of social traditionalists to produce plausible counterframes.

Thus, the relative stability of attitudes toward abortion may be attributed at least in part to the availability of the "rights" frame to both sides: A "right to life" is typically depicted as opposing a "right to choose." Because a dominant core value (individual rights) is available to both sides, the application of "rights talk" to abortion may result in a rhetorical "draw," in which neither protagonist has an advantage. Similarly, advocates of "creationism," "creation science," or "intelligent design" may be advantaged by general public agreement on values such as individual freedom and equality. Although empirical research is rather limited, the assertion of the value of "equal time" for creationism and evolution, in which students are allowed to "think for themselves" and "make up their own minds" might allow even some irreligious people to support such activities. Conceivably, but perhaps less plausibly, framing school prayer as a matter of religious freedom may account for its popularity among respondents whose religious commitments make such support seem unlikely. Additional qualitative research, as well as survey research involving experimental designs, might well be fruitful to help resolve some of these questions.

Finally, the question of attitude organization within each issue domain has not been addressed systematically. To what extent are attitudes toward same-sex marriage related to those on gays in the military, or toward disability benefits for same-sex couples? Do mass publics distinguish between school prayer, religious displays in public schools, and "moments of silence?" If so, on what basis? Is support for "equal treatment" of creationism or intelligent design based on religious beliefs about the nature of human origins or upon attitudes toward "fairness" or "equal treatment?" To answer such questions, we need surveys with extensive batteries of items from these issue domains. Single survey items about school prayer or beliefs about the origins of humanity will not provide subjectively adequate accounts of attitude organization or structure. Happily, recent empirical research into religion and politics has supplemented the use of national sample surveys, such as the ANES and GSS, in favor of smaller scale efforts in which individual researchers have more control over questionnaire content. As research into the religious basis of public attitudes on social issues continues, smaller scale surveys, as well as qualitative research designs, are likely to play a central role in enhancing our understanding.

NOTES

1. Some analysts have suggested that the emergence of conservative political activity is a periodic feature of American politics (Jelen 1991; Wilcox 1992).

2. Unfortunately, the 2004 GSS used a split-half method, in which not all respondents were asked all questions. In one version of the 2004 GSS questionnaire, respondents were asked about legal abortion, school prayer, and the morality of homosexuality. In another version, respondents were asked two questions about evolution and another about same-sex marriage. This division of questions across different surveys makes conventional dimensional analysis (such as factor analysis) impractical.

3. The GSS have asked the following question throughout its time series: "What about sexual relations between two adults of the same sex—do you think it is always wrong, almost always wrong, wrong only sometime, or not wrong at all?" In the 1970s, 46 percent of Americans responded "always" or "mostly" wrong; this declined to 38 percent after 1990. Evangelical Protestant percentages for the two time periods were 55 and 50 percent

respectively. Jews and seculars were the least likely to consider such relations to be wrong, with the percents declining over time. See Wilcox and Norrander (2002) for data from the 1970s until 2000.

4. The ANES first asked the following question in 1988 and has repeated it in surveys taken since then: "Do you favor or oppose laws to protect homosexuals against job discrimination?" In 1988, just more than half the national sample favored the idea. By 2004, that percentage had increased to almost three quarters. Evangelicals opposed the proposition at higher rates than any of the other large religious traditions, whereas Jews and seculars were the most favorable. See Wilcox and Norrander (2002) for data from 1988 to 2000.

5. The 2004 ANES provides support for this conclusion. Just more than four fifths of the national sample (and almost two thirds of evangelicals) supported gays serving in the military; three quarters of the national sample (and half of evangelicals) favored job discrimination laws protecting homosexuals, and nearly half (but only a quarter of evangelicals) favored adoption by gays. Clearly, multivariate analysis is needed to sort out the causal relationships among the religious variables, other sources of attitudes toward gays, and the attitudes themselves.

6. It is also possible that some respondents who are strongly committed to the rights of same-sex couples may reject civil unions as an inadequate substitute (following the logic of the *Goodridge* decision). Guth et al. (2006) show that just more than one half of their 2004 national sample favored traditional marriage. In data not shown, just less than one fifth of the population favored civil unions, whereas just more than one quarter supported same-sex marriage. Predictably, religious affiliations, beliefs, and practices were central to attitudes, with those exhibiting evangelical affiliation, "traditionalist" beliefs, and high levels of religious practice strongly in support of traditional marriage.

7. The pro-life trend varies from 2 percentage points on the item concerned with abortion when the woman's health is endangered to 10 points when abortion is the result of family poverty.

8. This trend exists on all the GSS measures and is strongest on the items that are the most contentious and weakest on those for which most Americans agree that an abortion should be legal—mother's health at risk, pregnancy resulting from rape, and when there are serious birth defects in the baby. The partisan differences are accentuated when the focus is on whites only.

9. This conclusion needs some qualification. For the years that Sullins (1999) examined in the GSS time series, the movement among Protestants toward a pro-life stance was concentrated among evangelicals. The attitudes of mainline Protestants were stable until 1998, when a pro-life trend can be detected on three of the GSS items: a legal abortion should be possible in (1) cases of family poverty, (2) when a married woman does not want any more children, and (3) when the woman is single and does not wish to marry the father.

10. In the GSS time series, Roman Catholics held remarkably stable attitudes toward abortion from the 1970s until the beginning of the 21st century, when a shift in the pro-life direction can be noted.

11. We find a somewhat different pattern in the GSS church attendance data. The time series shows a gradual decline in attendance since 1972, with the pattern accentuated among Catholics and to a somewhat less extent among mainline Protestants. Evangelical and black Protestant attendance remains stable.

12. The GSS shows a somewhat more significant drop in pro-choice sentiment from 2002 to 2004, whereas the ANES also shows a decline from 2000 to 2004, albeit smaller than

the GSS. The explanation for this is unclear, although partisan differences between Democrats and Republicans were greater in 2004 than previously.

13. In the ANES data, support for equal rights for women increased from 69 percent in the 1970s to 82 percent in 2004. The issue did not divide the parties during the early period and did so only modestly in 2004, when Democrats were slightly more favorable to women's rights. Evangelical Protestants were somewhat less favorable to the rights of women in both time periods, although 75 percent took an equal rights position in 2004.

14. ANES data in 2004 reveal that only 38 percent of the national sample favored federal funding of abortion.

15. ANES data in 2000 indicated that 80 percent of the public favored parental consent provisions. There was a 16-point gap between strong Republicans and strong Democrats on the issue. Unfortunately, the question was not repeated in 2004.

16. Public opinion data on this procedure is of recent vintage; ANES data from 2000 found fully three quarters of respondents favored a ban on partial-birth abortions. Partisan differences on the issue were modest in 2000, but quite large in 2004, when 80 percent of strong Republicans favored a ban on the procedure compared with only 47 percent of strong Democrats. By 2004, the overall percentage of the public who favored such a ban declined to a little more than three fifths (63 percent).

17. The latter study finds that attitudes toward banning stem cell research vary by religious "traditionalism." In other words, strong "traditionalist" beliefs and high levels of religious practice are associated with favoring a ban on stem cell research among those affiliated with churches in evangelical, mainline, and Catholic religious traditions, whereas "modernists" in these traditions favor continuing such research. Only 30 percent of the sample as a whole favored banning stem cell research.

18. This process certainly seems to occur among GOP presidential candidates, as observers of George W. Bush, Mitt Romney, and Rudi Guliani can attest.

19. School vouchers have received some attention in recent surveys. Both the ANES 2000 and 2004 surveys included a question on school vouchers. The results vary dramatically from 2000 to 2004, with 55 percent favoring vouchers in 2000, but only 32 percent in 2004. Strong Republicans were more favorable to vouchers in both years. In 2002, the Supreme Court upheld an Ohio statute that provided for vouchers (*Zelman v. Simmons-Harris* 536 US 639 [2002]). The *Zelman* decision and the publicity surrounding it may have been a factor in the decline in support for vouchers. There is, however, one other "education" issue that is not covered in the sections that follows—namely, whether school vouchers should be provided to parents to send their children from "failing" public schools to private or religious schools. The issue has not become a major partisan issue, and public opinion data on this subject are rare and difficult to interpret.

20. The decision banned state-mandated Bible reading and prayer, but it did argue that the teaching of religion should be part of the school curriculum. Such instruction could include the role of religion in history, the study of comparative religions, and even the study of the Bible as literature.

21. The Alabama moment-of-silence law was declared unconstitutional, in part, because in both the hearings and floor debate on the bill, legislators made it clear that this was an effort to reinstitute school prayer.

22. The ANES asked whether school prayer should be allowed in 1964, 1966, 1968, and again in 1980 and 1984. The GSS has also included a school prayer item in its time series. The GSS question asks respondents whether they approve or disapprove of the Supreme Court decision that "ruled that no state or local government may require the reading of the

Lord's Prayer or Bible verses in public schools." Responses were remarkably stable over time, with just more than 60 percent of those with an opinion disapproving of the court decision.

23. The apparent contradiction becomes understandable when it is made clear that most respondents do not regard the Ten Commandments as a Christian (or Judeo-Christian) symbol. In the Gallup survey in question, 73 percent of respondents disagreed with the statement that the Ten Commandments "gave special consideration to Jews and Christians," whereas only 25 percent agreed (Jelen, 2005a).

24. The literature on intelligent design is voluminous. For an overview of competing perspectives, see Pennock (2001).

25. In this study, born-again status and Roman Catholicism are significantly related to support for "equal time" provisions.

REFERENCES

Abramowitz, Alan. 1995. "It's Abortion, Stupid: Policy Voting in the 1992 Presidential Election." *Journal of Politics* 57: 176–186.

Adams, Greg D. 1997. "Abortion: Evidence of an Issue Evolution." *American Journal of Political Science* 41: 718–737.

Bishop, George F. 2007. "Evolution, Religion, and the 'Culture War' in American Politics." Presented at the annual meeting of the American Political Science Association, Chicago, Illinois, September.

Bowman, Karlyn, and Bryan O'Keefe. 2004. *Attitudes about Homosexuality and Gay Marriage.* Washington, D.C.: American Enterprise Institute Studies in Public Opinion.

Brewer, Paul R. 2003a. "The Shifting Foundations of Public Opinion about Gay Rights." *Journal of Politics* 65: 1208–1220.

Brewer, Paul R. 2003b. "Values, Political Knowledge, and Public Opinion about Gay Rights: A Framing-Based Account." *Public Opinion Quarterly* 67: 173–201.

Brewer, Paul R., and Clyde Wilcox. 2005. "Trends: Same-Sex Marriage and Civil Unions." *Public Opinion Quarterly* 69: 599–616.

Campbell, David E., and J. Quin Monson. 2007. "The Case of Bush's Reelection: Did Gay Marriage Do It?" In *A Matter of Faith: Religion in the 2004 Presidential Election,* ed. David E. Campbell, 120–141. Washington, D.C.: The Brookings Institution.

Carmines, Edward G., and Geoffrey C. Layman. 1997. "Issue Evolution in Postwar American Politics: Old Certainties and Fresh Tensions." In *Present Discontents,* ed. Byron E. Shafer, 89–134. Chatham, N.J.: Chatham House Publishers.

Carmines, Edward G., and James A. Stimson. 1980. "The Two Faces of Issue Voting." *American Political Science Review* 74: 78–91.

Carmines, Edward G., and James Woods. 2002. "The Role of Party Activists in the Evolution of the Abortion Issue." *Political Behavior* 24: 361–377.

Carsey, Thomas M., and Geoffrey C. Layman. 1999. "Changing Parties or Changing Attitudes: Uncovering the Partisan Change Process." Presented at the annual meeting of the Midwest Political Science Association, Chicago, Illinois, April.

Casanova, Jose. 1994. *Public Religions in the Modern World.* Chicago, Ill.: University of Chicago Press.

Converse, Philip E. 1964. "The Nature of Belief Systems in Mass Publics." In *Ideology and Discontent,* ed. David Apter, 106–161. New York: Free Press.

Converse, Philip E. 1970. "Attitudes and Non-Attitudes: Continuation of a Dialogue." In *The Quantitative Analysis of Social Problems,* ed. Edward R. Tufte, 168–179. Reading, Mass.: Addison-Wesley.

Cook, Elizabeth Adell, Ted G. Jelen, and Clyde Wilcox. 1992. *Between Two Absolutes: Public Opinion and the Politics of Abortion.* Boulder, Colo.: Westview Press.

Cook, Elizabeth Adell, Ted G. Jelen, and Clyde Wilcox. 1993. "Catholicism and Abortion Attitudes in the American States: A Contextual Analysis." *Journal for the Scientific Study of Religion* 32: 375–383.

Cook, Elizabeth Adell, Ted G. Jelen, and Clyde Wilcox. 1994a. "Issue Voting in Gubernatorial Politics: Abortion and Post-*Webster* Politics." *Journal of Politics* 36: 187–199.

Cook, Elizabeth Adell, Ted G. Jelen, and Clyde Wilcox. 1994b. "Issue Voting in U.S. Senate Elections: The Abortion Issue in 1990." *Congress and the Presidency* 21: 99–112.

Copeland, Dean, and Peter Hamer. 1994. *The Science of Desire: The Search for the Gay Gene and the Biology of Behavior.* New York: Simon and Schuster.

Craig, Stephen C., Michael D. Martinez, James G. Kane, and Jason Gainous. 2005. "Core Values, Value Conflict, and Citizens' Ambivalence about Gay Rights." *Political Research Quarterly* 58: 5–17.

Davis, Nancy, and Robert Robinson. 1996. "Are Rumors of War Exaggerated? Religious Orthodoxy and Moral Progressivism in America." *American Journal of Sociology* 102: 756–776.

Deckman, Melissa M. 2004. *School Board Battles: The Christian Right in Local Politics.* Washington, D.C.: Georgetown University Press.

Delfattore, Joan. 2004. *The Fourth R: Conflict over Religion in America's Public Schools.* New Haven, Conn.: Yale University Press.

Dillon, Michele. 1996. "Cultural Differences in the Abortion Discourse of the Catholic Church: Evidence from Four Countries." *Sociology of Religion* 57: 25–39.

Djupe, Paul A., and Laura R. Olson. 2007. *Religious Interests in Community Conflict: Beyond the Culture Wars.* Waco, Texas: Baylor University Press.

Elifson, Kirk W., and C. Kirk Hadaway. 1985. "Prayer in Public Schools: When Church and State Collide." *Public Opinion Quarterly* 49: 317–326.

Emerson, Michael O. 1996. "Through Tinted Glasses: Religion, Worldviews, and Abortion Attitudes." *Journal for the Scientific Study of Religion* 35: 41–55.

Evans, John H. 2002a. "Polarization in Abortion Attitudes in U.S. Religious Traditions, 1972–1998." *Sociological Forum* 17: 397–422.

Evans, John H. 2002b. "Religion and Human Cloning: An Exploratory Analysis of First Available Opinion Data." *Journal for the Scientific Study of Religion* 41: 749–760.

Faux, Marian. 1988. *Roe v. Wade.* New York: MacMillan.

Fiorina, Morris P. 2005. *Culture War? The Myth of a Polarized America.* New York: Pearson Longman.

Glendon, Mary Ann. 1991. *Rights Talk.* New York: Free Press.

Green, John C., and James L. Guth. 1989. "The Missing Link: Political Activists and Support for School Prayer." *Public Opinion Quarterly* 52: 41–57.

Greenawalt, Kent. 1988. *Religious Convictions and Political Choice.* New York: Oxford University Press.

Grindstaff, Laura. 1994. "Abortion and the Popular Press: Mapping Media Discourse from *Roe* to *Webster*." In *Abortion Politics in the United States and Canada: Studies in Public Opinion*, ed. Ted G. Jelen and Mathe A. Chandler, 57–88. Westport, Conn.: Praeger.

Guth, James L. 2007. "Religion and Roll Calls: Religious Influences on the U.S. House of Representatives, 1997–2002." Presented at the annual meeting of the American Political Science Association, Chicago, Illinois, September.

Guth, James L., John C. Green, Corwin E. Smidt, Lyman A. Kellstedt, and Margaret M. Poloma. 1997. *The Bully Pulpit: The Politics of Protestant Clergy.* Lawrence, Kans.: The University Press of Kansas.

Guth, James L., Lyman A. Kellstedt, Corwin E. Smidt, and John C. Green. 2006. "Religious Influences in the 2004 Presidential Election." *Presidential Studies Quarterly* 36: 223–242.

Haeberle, Steven H. 1999. "Gay and Lesbian Rights: Emerging Trends in Public Opinion and Voting Behavior." In *Gays and Lesbians in the Democratic Process: Public Policy, Public Opinion, and Political Representation*, ed. Ellen D. B. Riggle and Barry L. Tetlock, 146–169. New York: Columbia University Press.

Haider-Markell, Donald P., and Mark R. Joslyn. 2008. "Pulpits Versus Ivory Towers: Socializing Agents and Evolution Attitudes." *Social Science Quarterly* 89: 665–683.

Halberstam, David. 1997. *The Fifties.* New York: Fawcett.

Hoffman, John P., and Alan S. Miller. 1997. "Social and Political Attitudes among Religious Groups: Convergence and Divergence over Time." *Journal for the Scientific Study of Religion* 36: 52–70.

Hunter, James Davison. 1991. *Culture Wars: The Struggle to Define America.* New York: Basic Books.

Hunter James Davison. 1994. *Before the Shooting Begins: Searching for Democracy in America's Culture War.* New York: Free Press.

Jelen, Ted G. 1990. "Religious Belief and Attitude Constraint." *Journal for the Scientific Study of Religion* 29: 118–125.

Jelen, Ted G. 1991. *The Political Mobilization of Religious Beliefs.* Westport, Conn.: Praeger.

Jelen, Ted G. 1992. "The Clergy and Abortion." *Review of Religious Research* 34: 132–151.

Jelen, Ted G. 2000. *To Serve God and Mammon: Church–State Relations in American Politics.* Boulder, Colo.: Westview Press.

Jelen, Ted G. 2005a. "Ambivalence and Attitudes toward Church–State Relations." In *Ambivalence, Politics, and Public Policy*, ed. Stephen C. Craig, and Michael D. Martinez, 127–144. New York: Palgrave/MacMillan.

Jelen, Ted G. 2005b. "Political Esperanto: Rhetorical Resources and Limitations of the Christian Right in the United States." *Sociology of Religion* 66: 303–321.

Jelen, Ted G., and Clyde Wilcox. 1993. "Preaching to the Converted: The Causes and Consequences of Viewing Religious Television." In *Rediscovering the Religious Factor in American Politics*, ed. David C. Leege and Lyman A. Kellstedt, 255–269. Armonk, N.Y.: M. E. Sharpe.

Jelen, Ted G., and Clyde Wilcox. 1995. *Public Attitudes toward Church and State.* Armonk. N.Y.: M. E. Sharpe.

Jelen, Ted G., and Clyde Wilcox. 2003. "Causes and Consequences of Public Attitudes toward Abortion: A Review and Research Agenda." *Political Research Quarterly* 56: 489–500.

Jelen, Ted G., and Clyde Wilcox. 2005. "Continuity and Change in Attitudes toward Abortion: Poland and the United States." *Politics and Gender* 1: 297–315.

Keeter, Scott. 2005. "Reading Polls on Evolution and Creationism." *Pew Research Center Pollwatch*, September 28. Washington, D.C.: Pew Research Center.

Keeter, Scott. 2007. "Evangelicals and Moral Values." In *A Matter of Faith: Religion in the 2004 Presidential Election*, ed. David E. Campbell, 80–92. Washington, D.C.: The Brookings Institution.

Kellstedt, Lyman A., Corwin E. Smidt, John C. Green, and James L. Guth. 2007. "A Gentle Stream or a 'River Glorious?' The Religious Left in the 2004 Election." In *A Matter of Faith: Religion in the 2004 Presidential Election*, ed. David E. Campbell, 232–256. Washington, D.C.: The Brookings Institution.

Kohut, Andrew, John C. Green, Scott Keeter, and Robert Toth. 2000. *The Diminishing Divide: Religion's Changing Role in American Politics*. Washington, D.C.: The Brookings Institution.

Layman, Geoffrey C. 2001. *The Great Divide: Religion and Cultural Conflict in American Party Politics*. New York: Columbia University Press.

Layman, Geoffrey C., and Laura S. Hussey. 2007. "George W. Bush and the Evangelicals: Religious Commitment and Partisan Change among Evangelical Protestants, 1960–2004. In *A Matter of Faith: Religion in the 2004 Presidential Election*, ed. David E. Campbell, 180–198. Washington, D.C.: The Brookings Institution.

Leege, David C., and Lyman A. Kellstedt. 1993. "Religious Worldviews and Political Philosophies: Capturing Theory in the Grand Manner through Empirical Data." In *Rediscovering the Religious Factor in American Politics*, ed. David C. Leege and Lyman A. Kellstedt, 216–231. Armonk, N.Y.: M. E. Sharpe.

Lewis, Gregory B., and Marc A. Rogers. 1999. "Does the Public Support Equal Employment Rights for Gays and Lesbians?" In *Gays and Lesbians in the Democratic Process: Public Policy, Public Opinion, and Political Representation*, ed. Ellen D. B. Riggle and Barry L. Tetlock, 118–145. New York: Columbia University Press.

Lindaman, Kara, and Donald B. Haider-Markel. 2002. "Issue Evolution, Political Parties, and the Culture Wars." *Political Research Quarterly* 55: 91–110.

Loftus, Jeni. 2001. "America's Liberalization in Attitudes toward Homosexuality, 1973 to 1998." *American Sociological Review* 66: 762–782.

Luker, Kristin. 1984. *Abortion and the Politics of Motherhood*. Berkeley, Calif.: University of California Press.

Martinez, Michael D., Stephen C. Craig, James G. Kane, and Jason Gainous. 2005. "Ambivalence and Value Conflict: A Test of Two Issues." In *Ambivalence, Politics, and Public Policy*, ed. Stephen C. Craig and Michael D. Martinez, 63–82. New York: Palgrave/MacMillan.

Masci, David. 2007. "How the Public Resolves Conflicts between Faith and Science." Washington, D.C.: Pew Research Center. Also available online at http://pewresearch. org/pubs/578/how-the-public-resolves-conflicts-between-faith-and-science.

Mazur, Allan. 2004. "Believers and Disbelievers in Evolution." *Politics and the Life Sciences* 23: 55–61.

Miller, Alan S., and John P. Hoffman. 1999. "The Growing Divisiveness: Culture Wars or a War of Words?" *Social Forces* 78: 721–745.

Newman, Brian, and Mark Caleb Smith. 2007. "Fanning the Flames: Religious Media Consumption and American Politics." *American Politics Research* 35: 846–877.

Newport, Frank. 2003. "Americans Approve of Public Displays of Religious Symbols." *Gallup Poll News Services* October 3. http://www.gallup.com.

Newport, Frank 2006. "Almost Half of Americans Believe Humans Did Not Evolve." *Gallup News Service* June 5. www.galluppoll.com.

Norrander, Barbara, and Jan Norrander 2007. "Stem Cell Research." In *A Matter of Faith: Religion in the 2004 Presidential Election*, ed. David E. Campbell, 142–159. Washington, D.C.: The Brookings Institution.

O'Connor, Robert E., and Michael B. Berkman. 1995. "Religious Determinants of State Abortion Policy." *Social Science Quarterly* 76: 447–459.

Olson, Laura R., Wendy Cadge, and James T. Harrison. 2006. "Religion and Public Opinion about Same-Sex Marriage." *Social Science Quarterly* 87: 340–360.

Pennock, Robert T., ed. 2001. *Intelligent Design and Its Critics: Philosophical, Theological, and Scientific Perspectives.* Cambridge, Mass.: MIT Press.

Saad, Lydia. 2002. "'Cloning' Humans Is a Turnoff to Most Americans." *Gallup News Service.* http://www.gallup.com/poll/releases/pr020516.asp.

Saletan, William. 2003. *Bearing Right: How Conservatives Won the Abortion War.* Berkeley, Calif.: University of California Press.

Scammon, Richard M., and Ben J. Watternberg. 1971. *The Real Majority.* New York: Coward, Mcann, and Geoghegan.

Segers, Mary C., and Timothy A. Byrnes, eds. 1995. *Abortion Politics in States.* Armonk, N.Y.: M.E. Sharpe.

Servin-Gonzalez, Mariana, and Oscar Torres-Reyna. 1999. "Trends: Religion and Politics." *Public Opinion Quarterly* 63: 592–621.

Sharp, Elaine B. 1999. *The Sometime Connection: Public Opinion and Social Policy.* Albany, N.Y.: SUNY Press.

Sherrill, Kenneth, and Alan Yang. 2000. "From Outlaws to In-Laws." *Public Perspective* 11: 20–23.

Smidt, Corwin E. 2004. *Pulpit and Politics: Clergy in American Politics at the Advent of the Millennium.* Waco, Texas: Baylor University Press.

Sullins, Paul D. 1999. "Catholic/Protestant Trends on Abortion: Convergence and Polarity." *Journal for the Scientific Study of Religion* 38: 354–369.

Wald, Kenneth D., and Allison Calhoun-Brown. 2007. *Religion and Politics in the United States.* 5th ed. Lanham, Md.: Rowman & Littlefield.

Welch, Michael R., David C. Leege, and James C. Cavendish. 1995. "Attitudes toward Abortion among U.S. Catholics: Another Case of Symbolic Politics?" *Social Science Quarterly* 76: 142–157.

Wilcox, Clyde. 1992. *God's Warriors: The Christian Right in the 20th Century.* Baltimore, Md.: Johns Hopkins University Press.

Wilcox, Clyde. 1993. "The Dimensionality of Public Attitudes toward Church-State Establishment Issues." *Journal for the Scientific Study of Religion* 32: 169–176.

Wilcox, Clyde, Paul R. Brewer, Shauna Shames, and Celinda Lake. 2007. "If I Bend This Far, I Will Break? Public Opinion and Same-Sex Marriage." In *The Politics of Same-Sex Marriage*, ed. Craig A. Rimmerman and Clyde Wilcox, 215–242. Chicago, Ill.: University of Chicago Press.

Wilcox, Clyde, Rachel Goldberg, and Ted G. Jelen. 2000. "Full Pews, Musical Pulpits: The Christian Right at the Turn of the Millennium." *The Public Perspective* 11: 36–39.

Wilcox, Clyde, Rachel Goldberg, and Ted G. Jelen. 2002. "Public Attitudes on Church and State: Coexistence or Conflict." In *Piety, Politics, and Pluralism: Religion, the Courts, and the 2000 Election*, ed. Mary C. Segers, 221–233. Lanham, Md.: Rowman & Littlefield.

Wilcox, Clyde, and Barbara Norrander. 2002. "Of Moods and Morals: The Dynamics of Opinion on Abortion and Gay Rights." In *Understanding Public Opinion*, ed. Barbara Norrander and Clyde Wilcox, 121–148. Washington, D.C.: CQ Press.

Wilcox, Clyde, and Robin Wolpert. 2000. "Gay Rights in the Public Sphere: Public Opinion on Gay and Lesbian Equality." In *The Politics of Gay Rights*, ed. Craig A. Rimmerman, Kenneth D. Wald, and Clyde Wilcox, 409–432. Chicago, Ill.: University of Chicago Press.

Williams, Rhys, ed. 1998. *Culture Wars in American Politics: Critical Reviews of a Popular Myth*. New York: Aldine de Gruter.

Wills, Garry. 1990. *Under God: Religion and American Politics*. New York: Simon and Schuster.

Woodrum, Eric, and Thomas Hoban. 1992. "Support for Prayer in School and Creationism." *Sociological Analysis* 53: 309–321.

Yang, Alan S. 1997. "Attitudes toward Homosexuality." *Public Opinion Quarterly* 61: 477–507.

CHAPTER 9

....

RELIGION AND AMERICAN PUBLIC OPINION: FOREIGN POLICY ISSUES

....

JAMES L. GUTH

ALTHOUGH the study of religion's role in American political life has made enormous strides during the past two decades, the progress has been uneven. As other chapters in this volume reveal, scholars have put religious factors on the agenda in the fields of voting behavior, party politics, and, to a lesser extent, public opinion. In recent years, there has also been a growing initiative to bring religion into international relations (see, for example, Johnston and Sampson 1994; Fox and Sandler 2004; Farr 2008). Indeed, several academic research centers are now devoted to that task. Few political scientists, however, have considered the way that religion influences the foreign policy attitudes of the American public, despite J. Bryan Hehir's reminder that "religious convictions and concerns" have permeated U.S. foreign policy since World War II (Hehir 2001, p. 36).

This neglect of religion by political scientists has recently been highlighted by an enormous outpouring from journalists (Mead 2004, 2006; Phillips 2006; Clark 2007), historians (Boyer 2005; Guyatt 2007; Oren 2007), diplomats (Carter 2005; Urquhart 2005; Albright 2006), religion scholars (Northcott 2004; Marsh 2007; Urban 2007), sociologists (Martin 1999; Derber and Magrass 2008), philosophers (Singer 2004), and even literature and communications analysts (Domke 2004; Collins 2007). These authors have made strong claims both for the influence of religion on public attitudes on foreign policy and about its impact on political leaders. Such assertions are even more common overseas, both among intellectual elites and in the mass public. Indeed, no one reading European journals of opinion, from *The Economist* to *Le Monde*, would doubt that European intellectuals believe that American foreign policy reflects religious influences, or that this notion has widespread appeal among ordinary citizens as well (Braml 2004; Kohut and Stokes 2006).

This emerging literature makes wide-ranging claims and draws from a capacious storeroom of religious labels. A major theme alleges a pernicious influence of evangelicals on American foreign policy transmitted through President George W. Bush, invariably regarded as a paradigm of that religious community's worldview. In this account, presidential policies have been shaped by key characteristics of an evangelical mind-set: militarism, dogmatic unilateralism, dualistic moralism, nationalistic assertiveness, antiscientific attitude, and apocalyptic attachment to Israel (Marsden 2008). This perspective is labeled variously as *fundamentalist, premillennialist, dispensationalist, biblical literalist,* or *messianic.* And for most observers, these disturbing views are descended from those infusing earlier themes in American history, such as Manifest Destiny or Special Providence (McCartney 2004; Judis 2005). Only a few observers find other, more redeeming, traits in the foreign policy concerns of evangelicals (Kristof 2002; Guth, Green, Kellstedt, and Smidt 2005; Mead 2006; den Dulk 2007). In any event, literally thousands of articles in elite and popular journals of opinion—in the United States and abroad—have repeated and elaborated upon these arguments (see Guth [2006] and Kohut and Stokes [2006] for typical examples).

These claims are based on a simplistic view of American religion. Few such accounts consider the 75 percent of the American public that does not affiliate with evangelical churches, creating an analytical dualism that arrays evangelicals against "secular" opinion (presumably everyone else).[1] Also ignored is the fact that Catholic and mainline Protestant churches, as well as American Jewish leaders, have long sought to influence both public attitudes and the decisions of policy makers, perhaps more doggedly and over a longer period than evangelical bodies. Nor does it consider the possibility that the growing unaffiliated or secularist public (Hout and Fischer 2002) may have truly distinctive foreign policy preferences as well. Thus, the emerging literature, both polemical and scholarly, often overstates the distinctiveness of one religious group, ignores the potential influence of others, and treats American religion in an invariably simplistic manner.

The task of understanding religion's role in shaping public opinion on foreign policy faces other obstacles. Although many observers exaggerate the impact of religion, other analysts counter such misunderstandings by denying its influence altogether. To take one example, Kohut and Stokes' (2006, p. 94) extensive and much-cited review of international and American opinion stresses that "with the exception of policy toward Israel, religion has little bearing on how they think about international affairs." Despite the belief of many Europeans and Americans to the contrary, Kohut and Stokes (2006, p. 94) find "little evidence that faith drives support for the unilateralist U.S. foreign policy that has fueled anti-Americanism in recent years."

As we shall see, there is substantial evidence that Kohut and Stokes are mistaken. If political scientists are going to discover the threads of religious influence in attitudes toward American foreign policy, they must be willing to do the hard work of understanding American religion first. In this chapter, we focus on the ways that religious factors may influence public opinion on foreign policy issues. First, we review recent political science perspectives on the shape of public opinion on foreign policy that have emphasized the coherence of competing public orientations toward American policy in the world. We then consider the extant work on religion and public opinion, discovering much incidental evidence that religion has had—and continues to have—considerable impact on those orientations, both during the Cold War and its aftermath. The evidence is even stronger that religion has influenced critical religious and political elites: clergy, religious activists, party activists, and even legislators. This review concludes with an illustration of the advantage that a fuller accounting of religious factors can provide for analysts of public support for the "Bush doctrine." This doctrine is the central focus of much of the critical literature cited earlier and a useful test case for the influence of religious factors on public opinion (McCormick 2004; Jervis 2005, pp. 79–101).

RELIGION AND FOREIGN POLICY ATTITUDES IN THE MASS PUBLIC

One of the most fascinating tasks confronting analysts of American foreign policy is to characterize public opinion on international issues. After World War II, the conventional wisdom was based on the "Almond-Lippmann consensus" (Holsti 2004, pp. 25–40), which holds that most Americans were uninterested in—and ill-informed about—international events, and that their orientation toward countries and issues lacked both coherence and stability. Given this lack of opinion constraint, public opinion exerted little, if any, impact on the policy process.

There is evidence that the American public's interest in foreign affairs has not grown significantly in recent years, although some analysts would qualify that observation (Aldrich, Sullivan, and Borgida 1989). Nevertheless, prominent scholars have argued that public attitudes are in fact shaped by structured beliefs that are fairly stable over time, especially in the aggregate. In studies of the mass public (Peffley and Hurwitz 1993; Holsti 2004), elites (Chittick and Billingsley 1989; Holsti and Rosenau 1990), and both masses and elites (Wittkopf 1990; Page 2006), scholars have uncovered overarching attitude structures that allow citizens to be "cognitive misers." For example, Wittkopf's (1990) review of quadrennial surveys by the Chicago Council on Foreign Relations (CCFR), found that Americans organize their attitudes around two dimensions: *militant internationalism* and *cooperative internationalism*. Taking a slightly different approach, Peffley and Hurwitz (1993) argued that the mass public derives specific opinions from two "postures": *militarism* and *containment*. More recently, Benjamin Page (2006) has contended that Americans have *purposive belief systems* that, in aggregate, contribute to coherent sets of collective preferences on foreign policy issues. Although it is not possible to reconcile these various approaches entirely, it is clear that the dimensions involved include orientations toward the degree of American involvement in the world, willingness to use military force, and, finally, preference for unilateral or multilateral action on the part of the United States (see Barker et al. 2008).

Although scholars have made some progress in identifying such generalized orientations, there has been little sustained work on uncovering their cognitive and demographic antecedents. Ideology, partisanship, education, gender, and other variables have been considered, but as Chittick, Billingsley, and Travis (1995, p. 323) noted a decade ago, "the truth is that we have hardly begun to identify such sources." And religion is not often seen as a possibility at all. In an otherwise thorough review, Ole Holsti (2004, pp. 163–239) does not even consider religion as a "background attribute" that might shape attitudes. In a similar vein, Page (2006, p. 233ff) argues (at least initially) that demographic characteristics such as religion contribute little to explaining policy preferences, at least in comparison with attitudes, beliefs, and ideas largely independent of such traits.

Is there evidence that religion influences attitudes on specific policies or, more important, on the basic orientations that structure public opinion? A review of relevant literature since World War II reveals severe limitations in our ability to answer this query. The problems discussed in chapter 1 are especially evident in the foreign policy opinion literature. First of all, religious variables are seldom present in most opinion surveys, such as the important studies conducted by the CCFR. Thus, we must often depend on analyzing occasional foreign policy items in other surveys that also contain at least one, and occasionally more, religious items. Although this lack of data has recently been alleviated in part by the advent of extensive polling on foreign policy issues by other organizations, especially the Pew Research Center for the People and the Press, in most cases the number of religious variables available has been minimal, usually confined to crude measures of affiliation. Only rarely are detailed affiliation, doctrinal belief, and religious practice items present in the same survey with extensive batteries of foreign policy questions. Finally, there is seldom much explicit theorizing behind the choice of religious items or much understanding of how those variables might influence public attitudes on foreign policy (for a conspicuous exception, see Barker et al. 2008).

Religion and Foreign Policy Attitudes: The Cold War Era and Beyond

The neglect of religion in foreign policy opinion studies is rather surprising in one respect, given Alfred O. Hero's (1973) pioneering (and massive) treatment, based on public opinion polls from the late 1930s up through the early years of the Vietnam

War. An early leader in the study of public attitudes about foreign affairs, Hero had to work with broad religious affiliation measures, usually categories such as "Protestant, Catholic, or Jewish." He was careful to control for race when possible, and even for ethnicity among Catholics, but he lamented the paucity of belief and behavior items in the polls (Hero 1973, pp. 8–12). Nevertheless, his sophisticated understanding of American religion made even crude measures into useful instruments, revealing significant differences on important issues that often survived available controls.

Although the posture of religious groups varied with the specific international issues confronting the United States after 1936, Hero (1973) found some distinct patterns. Throughout the period, Jews were much more internationalist in orientation, followed by Protestants, whereas Catholics tended toward isolationism, as did black Protestants. Such tendencies shifted somewhat after World War II, as Catholics and black Protestants moved toward more internationalist attitudes, supporting American involvement abroad, and simultaneously providing stronger backing for multilateral institutions, such as the United Nations (UN) and international aid agencies. And although Catholics were more militarist and anti-Communist during the early Cold War (*militant internationalist*), by the late 1960s they were becoming less supportive of U.S. military ventures and more accommodating of détente with the Soviet Union and other Communist states (*cooperative internationalist*).

Unlike later analysts less conversant with American religion, Hero was curious about the factors influencing religious differences in foreign policy opinion. At times, he thought religious differences reflected sociodemographic variation among believers: The isolationism of black Protestants before the 1960s, for example, might be a reflection of their modest levels of education and income. Similar attitudes among evangelical Protestants might be the result of the same background factors, whereas the internationalism of Episcopalians reflected their higher socioeconomic status. At other times, Hero (1973) saw the postures of specific traditions shaped by interest in the welfare of coreligionists abroad: American Jews' concern for Jews in prewar Europe and, later, for Israel, fed their internationalism, as did Catholics' worries about their eastern European brethren under Soviet domination after World War II.

Hero (1973) also speculated that religious belief might influence attitudes in specific traditions: For example, white Protestants' disdain for foreign aid might reflect the "Protestant work ethic," whereas greater Catholic support for international programs might arise from Catholic social teachings. Of course, the absence of belief items in surveys made these observations purely speculative. Still, Hero (1973) was inclined to think that, by the 1960s, religious beliefs were becoming more important in shaping Americans' foreign policy attitudes, a view supported by a good bit of circumstantial evidence.

A more testable hypothesis was that distinctive attitudes of specific traditions might stem from leadership cues, reflecting the considerable effort by mainline Protestant and Catholic denominational leaders to influence parishioners' ideas about foreign policy, usually in a cooperative internationalist direction. However, Hero (1973) was most puzzled by his finding that, despite leadership pronounce-ments, there seemed to be little or no difference between regular churchgoers and the less observant. This sparse evidence suggested that religious involvement was not an independent source of foreign policy attitudes, nor did it reenforce the implications of theological beliefs, or buttress the impact of leadership cues among those in the pews (Hero 1973, p. 173).

Thus, Hero (1973) considered several possibilities for religious influence over public attitudes, but simply lacked the raw material for constructing a full under-standing of that influence. No subsequent study focused on religion with his comprehensive sweep, but later analysts did introduce a multidimensional ap-proach to religion—at least if their scattered findings are aggregated. Although the only study to use several religious variables simultaneously with a significant number of discrete foreign policy issues was Jelen's (1994) review of the 1990–1991 ANES special panel study, we can combine his findings with a collection of other results to discover some intriguing patterns.

First, there is solid evidence that evangelical affiliation, orthodox doctrine, and high religious commitment fostered anti-Communist attitudes and support for higher defense spending—the makings of the dimensions of *militarism* or *militant internationalism* discovered by foreign policy opinion analysts (Wittkopf 1990, pp. 43–44; Guth and Green 1993; Hurwitz, Peffley, and Seligson 1993; Jelen 1994; Greeley and Hout 2006; Barker et al. 2008). These effects, however, varied by religious tradition and era. High religious commitment among Catholics encour-aged anti-Communist militancy after World War II, but then reversed effects during the 1970s and 1980s, perhaps with the Vietnam War (Gartner, Seguara, and Wilkening 1997), or, alternatively, with the bishops' letter on nuclear war (Wald 1992; Jelen 1994). Jews continued to hold distinctive internationalist atti-tudes, were more critical of the Vietnam War than other citizens (Gartner, Seguara, and Wilkening 1997), but were more supportive of Israel (Greenberg and Wald 2001). Evangelicals, and especially theological dispensationalists, increasingly sup-ported a strong alliance with Israel—one of the few amply demonstrated effects of religious affiliation and doctrine on foreign policy attitudes (Guth, Fraser, Green, Kellstedt, and Smidt 1996; Mayer 2004; Guth, Kellstedt, Smidt, and Green 2006; Mearsheimer and Walt 2007; Barker et al. 2008; Baumgartner, Francia, and Morris 2008).

Like Hero (1973), few studies have found that mainline Protestant affiliation produced distinctive foreign policy attitudes, despite the clear preferences of many denominational leaders and local clergy for cooperative internationalist policies. Sometimes this conclusion reflects the analytical use of mainline Protestants as a part of the omitted reference group in multivariate analysis (e.g., Jelen 1994; Page 2006), but more often it seems to have resulted from centrist stances of this large and diverse religious tradition. In the same vein, "nonaffiliated" or "secular" citizens were usually ignored, as were other religious minorities, perhaps because of their small numbers. Some cross-national evidence hinted, however, that secular citizens may have been especially supportive of foreign aid and other cooperative internationalist ventures (Nelson 1988; Greeley and Hout 2006, p. 84). The growing number of secular citizens and of a variety of religious minorities certainly argues for their inclusion in any comprehensive analysis of contemporary attitudes (compare with Hout and Fischer 2002).

We suspect, then, that a full accounting of religious variables might not only help explain specific policy attitudes, but perhaps even attitudes toward the general orientations discussed by many scholars (Peffley and Hurwitz 1993). Of course, with the end of the Cold War, some scholars have detected the collapse of overarching frameworks for public understanding of foreign policy. Perhaps this reduces the relevance of religious factors (e.g., with the demise of "Godless communism"), but there are reasons to expect that religion might be even *more* strongly related to contemporary foreign policy views. First, the great elite and public debate over America's role in the post-Cold War world still seems to elicit "purposive belief systems," focusing on isolationism, multilateral cooperation, or unilateral interventionism (Page 2006). If, for example, Americans divide over whether the United States should engage in preemptive military actions, religious factors may influence those views through their impact on militarism, just as they did during the Cold War. In this vein, for example, Gary Jacobson (2005) found that "religious conservatives" more often accepted President Bush's justifications for the Iraq war than did other citizens, corroborating earlier findings from a variety of polls (Guth 2004b). Even more fundamentally, Barker et al. (2008) have argued that "messianic militarism" may contribute to a general propensity to support militant policies abroad, based on core values of "traditionalistic Christian religion."

Second, "Godless" communism may well have been replaced as a competing value system by militant Islam. Samuel Huntington (1996) has famously interpreted contemporary international politics as a "clash of civilizations" rooted in conflicting religious worldviews. Even if this claim is overstated, religious values may still have a powerful effect on attitudes, as believers are influenced by their own traditions' characteristic approach to religious competitors. Some Americans, for example, might see Muslims as religious enemies (Cimino 2005; Smidt 2005). Other scholars have concluded that the conflict over globalization is dividing religious traditions, whether over international trade and its distributive effects or over the impact of massive immigration on domestic communities, raising the possibilities for cultural conflict (Daniels 2005).

Third, American religious leaders are playing an increasingly vocal role in addressing foreign policy. As noted earlier, mainline Protestant councils and clergy have continued a long tradition of "prophetic witness" on international issues, usually in a cooperative internationalist or even pacifist vein (Kurtz and Fulton 2002; Tipton 2007), but they have now been joined by evangelical Protestants, who are widely believed to have a more "militaristic" perspective on foreign policy (Marsh 2007; Barker et al. 2008). Similarly, both the Vatican and the American Catholic bishops have expressed views on a vast range of questions, from UN population control policies to the recent war in Iraq (opposing both).

Although Hero (1973) concluded that the pronouncements of denominational leaders and church council officials were not heard very far away from headquarters in the 1950s and '60s, by the 1970s local clergy were in fact increasingly divided on foreign policy issues along theological lines. The earliest studies of Protestant clergy attitudes by Hadden (1969) and Quinley (1974) found clear divisions over defense spending, the Vietnam War, support for the UN, and action on world poverty. Theologically liberal "new breed" clergy were clearly on the cooperative internationalist side, whereas theological conservatives were less active politically, but favored militant internationalist policies. Such divisions deepened by the early 1990s, as increasingly active theological conservatives favored higher defense spending, demanded support for Israel over the Palestinians, expressed skepticism about strategic arms limitation treaties, and gave backing to the *contras* in Central America, with theological liberals arrayed on the other side (Guth, Green, Smidt, Kellstedt, and Paloma 1997; Tipton 2007). Needless to say, the policy stances of religious elites still differ substantially by tradition (and especially by theology), but if parishioners hear and heed such messages, they may exhibit distinctive attitudes (Guth 2007b).

A final trend pointing to the heightened relevance of religion is the assimilation of foreign policy issues into the structures that shape domestic politics. Not only are domestic economic and social issues increasingly intertwined with international ones, but the very ideational constructs that inform domestic political choices— ideology and partisanship—now have more influence over foreign policy attitudes (Holsti 2004; Page 2006, pp. 238–239). From the late 1980s to the present, both partisanship and ideology have played a greater role in shaping citizen responses to international questions (Brewer, Gross, Aday, and Willnat 2004; Jacobson 2005). This tendency may well reflect diverging stances of Republican and Democratic elites on international issues, as residues of the Cold War elite consensus disappear and as domestic divisions extend into international issues (compare with Powlick and Katz 1998; Layman and Carsey 2002; Green and Jackson 2007).

All this integration has occurred as partisanship and ideology have been infused by religious and cultural factors. This raises the possibility that the religious effect may often be indirect, transmitted through partisanship and ideology, often obscuring the total impact of religious affiliation, commitment, and beliefs. Although there is only fragmentary evidence available on this point, religious factors certainly seem to have structured the foreign policy attitudes of political activists and elites in much the same way that they have divided clergy. A massive study of large financial contributors to party political action committees (PACs) and finance committees during the late 1980s showed that religious commitment was strongly related to a scale tapping "hardliner/accommodationist" attitudes (Green, Guth, and Fraser 1991), whereas a secondary analysis of the same data showed that activists who felt close to the Christian Right strongly supported militant internationalism, whereas those close to the mainline National Council of Churches favored cooperative internationalism (Aguilar, Fordham, and Lynch 1997; compare with Barker et al. 2008). In the same vein, analysis of U.S. House voting from 1997 to 2002 showed that doctrinal traditionalism among members was negatively correlated with foreign policy liberalism (cooperative internationalism), but that affiliation with minority religious traditions (black Protestant, Hispanic Catholic, Jewish, or secular) had a positive influence. In addition, congressional district religious membership, especially of evangelicals, had an additional independent impact, reducing support for cooperative international policies. Both findings survived controls for partisanship and other important predictors (Guth 2007a). Narrower studies of U.S. Senate and U.S House voting and bill sponsorship on issues related to Israel similarly demonstrated the importance of the members' religious affiliation, with Jews and evangelical Protestants most supportive, but with less evidence of additional impact from constituency religious composition (Oldmixon, Rosenson, and Wald 2005; Rosenson, Oldmixon, and Wald 2009).

Thus, as party and ideology become more relevant to foreign policy attitudes, and as religious and political elites increasingly reveal religious differences on foreign policy questions, citizens may in fact exhibit distinct religious profiles on these issues, just as they do on domestic ideological and partisan alignments (Layman 2001; Guth 2004a; Barker et al. 2008). Of course, the causal direction may still be at issue: Do religious perspectives influence partisanship and ideology, and thereby have an indirect effect on foreign policy attitudes? Or are the foreign policy views of religious groups shaped by cues from political leaders, and "absorbed" in conformity with religious citizens' ideological and partisan commitments? In either case, religion plays an important role in shaping attitudes and deserves attention.

At this point we consider the one major recent scholarly work incorporating religion in a rigorous analysis of foreign policy attitudes. Page's *The Foreign Policy Disconnect* (2006) uses the 2002 and 2004 CCFR mass public and elite studies to investigate the sources of public opinion and its impact on policy elites. Fortunately, recent CCFR mass public surveys incorporate basic religious affiliation questions (Protestant, Catholic, Jewish, Muslim, Other, No Religion), and differentiate "evangelical" and "mainline" Protestants with a religious identity question ("fundamentalist, evangelical, charismatic, or Pentecostal" vs. "moderate to liberal"). Although this approach has many of the conceptual and measurement deficiencies discussed in chapter 1, such drawbacks are partially offset by the size of the national sample and the range of policy questions asked (although split-half survey design often vitiates these advantages in specific analyses, both by limiting the number of cases for analysis and precluding much scale building).

Page (2006) argues that demographic factors explain little variation in important attitudes, at least in comparison with *basic attitudes*, such as preferences for international involvement, partisanship, and ideology, but he includes dummies for four religious traditions—evangelicals, Catholics, Jews, and Muslims—in analyzing specific policy attitudes. And a careful perusal of text, notes, and tables soon leaves the reader with the impression that religious affiliation may be more important than the author initially suggests. This is especially true of evangelicals, who stand out on many issues: in favor of defense spending, skeptical of the UN and other multilateral projects, supportive of Israel and against a Palestinian state, opposed to the Kyoto Protocol on global warming, in favor of military action against terrorism, negative toward remaining Communist regimes and "Axis of Evil" nations, and favoring expanded homeland security programs and intelligence gathering abroad.

All this evidence points to evangelicals as a key source of public support for militant internationalism or, perhaps, unilateralist internationalism—a bit like the popular literature suggests (and in conformity with the careful analysis of Barker et al. [2008]). Other religious groups are less frequently distinctive: Catholics were more positive about defense spending and homeland security, more likely to oppose diplomatic relations with Cuba and Iran, but also more supportive of at least some multilateral institutions and of a comprehensive nuclear test ban treaty. They also put higher priorities on stopping illegal drugs from entering the country, spreading democracy to the rest of the world, and protecting American workers from the effects of globalization. And, despite their small numbers in the sample, even Jews and Muslims were distinctive on some issues and especially on orientations toward specific nations, such as Israel and predominantly Muslim countries.

In the analysis by Page (2006) the influence of religious affiliations often disappears when *basic attitudes* and *foreign policy goals* are incorporated in the equation, suggesting that they work indirectly through those variables. Thus, it is impossible to determine the total effect of religious affiliation on a specific policy item. And because mainline Protestants, other religions, and the unaffiliated constitute the omitted reference group across the analyses, there is no way to assess the influence of these affiliations. In addition, because the CCFR surveys included no measures of religious belief or practice, Page (2006, p. 268) could not test their impact, although he assumed that religious involvement would increase the affiliation effects.

Although he speculated little about the religious differences he found, he belatedly recognized their significance: "We were surprised by the potent effect upon quite a few foreign policy opinions of certain religious affiliations, especially evangelical Protestantism," concluding that the "current centrality of evangelical Protestants in Republican Party politics has important implications for the making of U.S. foreign policy when that party is in power" (Page 2006, p. 234). Thus, although Page's assessment of the contribution of religion shifts almost visibly from the beginning to the end of the book, his data and analytical approach made it impossible to say much about critical issues: the sources of evangelical attitudes, the influence of other religious traditions or secular citizens, or the effects of religious belief and behavior. Nevertheless, this pathbreaking work not only confirms the importance of religion in shaping public opinion on foreign policy, but also tends to confirm the contentions raised by the new literature cited at the beginning of this chapter. We now turn a test of these arguments.

Religion and Foreign Policy Attitudes: A Full Accounting and an Example

To illustrate the advantages of a fuller accounting of religious variables in explaining public attitudes on foreign policy, we use an example directly relevant to the central contentions of the recent literature on religion and foreign policy: public support for the Bush doctrine. This much-controverted strategic posture emphasizes the necessity of preemptive U.S. military action to ward off potential dangers to its security and its willingness to take action unilaterally without international backing, asserts special responsibilities of the United States for world order, and supports Israel as a linchpin of Middle East policy (McCormick 2004; Jervis 2005). Indeed, many of the complaints cited earlier are directed at the religious contribution to these foreign policy stances.

To test for religious support for the Bush doctrine, we use the 2004 NSRP, conducted by the University of Akron and cosponsored by the Pew Forum on Religion and Public Life. This survey is unique in possessing both a comprehensive battery of religious measures and several foreign policy items. In table 9.1, the dependent variable (support for the Bush doctrine) is a factor score based on five such items (see the appendix for information on variable construction).[2] Table 9.1 reports results from several alternative models of religious influence. As demographic controls, we use standard variables identified by many scholars as influencing foreign policy attitudes: political knowledge, education level, income, gender, and age (Holsti 2004; Page 2006).

First, we evaluate the utility of the type of religious measures available in major polls on foreign policy attitudes, such as the CCFR surveys used by Page (model 1) and by many Pew Research Center reports (model 2) by replicating those variables in virtually identical form in the NSRP data. Next, we introduce fuller models based on the expansive religious batteries of the 2004 NSRP: one using a more detailed affiliation measure (model 3); one that adds religious belief, behavior, and movement measures (model 4); and one that incorporates Page's *basic attitudes* to determine whether religion has a direct impact on foreign policy attitudes, or whether such influence is channeled primarily through other, more proximate variables (model 5).

Although our interest is in the religious roots of support for the Bush doctrine, we note that demographics do have some impact on public attitudes. On balance, higher income predicts greater support, whereas extended education, political knowledge, age, and female gender work in the other direction. Model 1, using the CCFR/Page religious classification and the four religious dummies he tests, shows evangelicals quite supportive of the Bush doctrine, followed at a distance by Catholics and Jews. Muslims, on the other hand, are less positive than the omitted reference group of all other religious and nonreligious citizens. These results are quite compatible with the findings by Page (2006) in *The Foreign Policy Disconnect* on issues for which evangelicals have distinctive policy preferences. Together with other demographic variables, the religious dummies explain

Table 9.1 Support for Bush Doctrine by Religious Variables, National Survey of Religion and Politics, 2004 (standardized Ordinary Least Square regression coefficients)

	Model 1: Demographics and Tradition (evangelical by ID)	Model 2: Demographics and Tradition (evangelical born again)	Model 3: Demographics and Tradition Based on Detailed Affiliation	Model 4: Demographics and Tradition, Beliefs, and Behavior	Model 5: Demographics and Tradition, Beliefs, Behavior, and "Dispositions"
Demographic controls					
Political knowledge	−.05*	−.05*	−.05*	−.03	−.08‡
Education	−.07†	−.06†	−.06†	−.01	−.03
Income	.11‡	.12‡	.13‡	.10‡	.04*
Female	−.06‡	−.07‡	−.08‡	−.08‡	−.04†
Age	−.07†	−.08†	−.08‡	−.03	−.04*
Religious tradition					
Evangelical	.23‡	.27‡	.22‡	.07†	.01
Latter-day Saints	—	—	.08‡	.05†	.01
Mainline Protestant	—	.07‡	.01	.02	−.02
White Catholic	.05*	.08‡	.03	.03	−.01
Jewish	.06‡	.07‡	.06†	.10‡	.08‡
Muslim	−.06†	—	.01	−.03	−.03
Black Protestant	—	−.01	−.05*	−.10‡	−.02
Other non-Christians	—	—	−.07†	−.03	−.02
Secular	—	—	−.10‡	−.02	−.01
Agnostics/atheists	—	—	−.14‡	−.03	−.05*
All others	—	—	—	—	—

Beliefs and behavior					
Civil religion				.28‡	.15‡
Traditionalism				.16‡	.08‡
Moral absolutism				.16‡	.12‡
Religious involvement				−.10‡	−.10‡
Traditional movement				.08‡	.05†
Political predispositions					
"Active part"					.23‡
Strong GOP					.25‡
Strong conservative					.09‡
Strong liberal					−.07‡
Strong Democrat					−.08‡
R^2 value	.079	.086	.125	.27	.438

*P 0.05, †P 0.01, ‡P 0.001. N = 2731.

almost 8 percent of the variance, also comparable with Page's results (2006) on the sorts of policy preferences embodied in our Bush doctrine score.

Model 2 reproduces the classification strategy often used by the Pew Research Center and other polling organizations, based on broad religious traditions, with white Protestants differentiated by born-again status. The main analytical difference from Page's strategy is that we have incorporated mainline and black Protestants in the regression, removing them from the omitted reference group. As in model 1, the analysis reveals that evangelicals are significantly more positive toward the Bush doctrine than other groups, but it also shows mainline Protestants joining white Catholics and Jews in providing more modest backing. Black Protestants do not differ significantly from the omitted reference group of all other religious and nonreligious respondents. Model 2 not only tells us more about the influence of specific groups than model 1, but it also does slightly better in prediction, explaining almost 9 percent of the variance.

What if we use a more detailed accounting of religious affiliation? Model 3 is based on religious affiliation variables from the 2004 NSRP. Although the choice of smaller traditions to analyze is somewhat arbitrary, we included several that we expect should differ significantly from the national mean. The results exhibit the advantages of a more accurate and detailed measure of religious affiliation. First, although we discover once again that evangelicals buttress support for the Bush doctrine (now with aid from Mormons), we are also able to pinpoint sources of opposition. In this analysis, black Protestants tend to oppose the doctrine, as do members of non-Christian faiths (other than Judaism and Islam), secular respondents (those with no religious affiliation or salience), and explicit agnostics and atheists. Mainline Protestants and white Catholics—and, interestingly, Muslims—on the other hand, do not differ from the omitted centrist reference group made up of Hispanic Protestants and Catholics, all other Christian groups (such as Eastern Orthodox), and religious but unaffiliated citizens. As a result of the more accurate affiliation measures (and choice of omitted reference groups closer to the center of opinion), model 3 produces a 50 percent improvement in variance explained by the demographic and religious affiliation variables alone. Substantively, it also portrays a modest "culture war" developing over foreign policy, anchored by evangelicals at one end, with seculars and various religious minorities at the other (Hunter 1991; Fiorina 2005; Barker et al. 2008).

Can we do better with additional religious measures? In theoretical terms, the vast literature cited earlier seems to require measures of religious belief and behavior. Although some authors are content to blame evangelicals (however defined) for the undesirable trends they see in American opinion (Derber and Magrass 2007), others emphasize theological conservatism, Protestant premillennialism or dispensationalism (Judis 2005; Guyatt 2007), American civil religion or "sacralization ideology" (McCartney 2004; Froese and Mencken 2009), religious dualism or moralism (Domke 2004), or, simply, American religiosity (Kohut and Stokes 2006). Obviously, if researchers are to justify the time and space for more religious items to test such assertions, they must produce substantial improvements in explanation.

Although we do not have space to test all the variant hypotheses offered by such accounts, we can illustrate the payoff from more sophisticated religious measures. In model 4 we introduce several religious scores discussed in chapter 1: theological traditionalism, religious activity or behavior (*religious involvement* in table 9.1), and traditionalist religious movement identification. In addition, given arguments about the nature of public support for the Bush administration that stress moralistic dualism and belief in civil religion, we have included measures of both. As table 9.1 shows, the addition of religious belief, behavior, and movement measures more than doubles the variation explained in model 3, and triples that explained by models 1 and 2—a dramatic improvement.

Not surprisingly, belief and behavior measures reduce the effects—often to insignificance—of religious affiliation (compare with Jelen 1994). Although evangelicals, Mormons, and Jews are still slightly more likely to support the Bush Doctrine, and black Protestants are more likely to oppose it, the resistance of other religious groups is accounted for by their scores on belief and behavior measures. Indeed, adherence to civil religion, theological traditionalism, moral absolutism, and identification with traditionalist religious movements produce potent support for the Bush doctrine. Although high religious involvement is also associated with support for the doctrine at the bivariate level, the sign reverses when the other religious measures are in the equation. In the absence of conservative religious beliefs, then, religious involvement actually works *against* support for the doctrine (compare with Green [2007] and Barker et al. [2008] for similar findings and provocative speculations on this reversal). All these findings suggest considerable empirical warrant for the recent jeremiads by Bush doctrine critics—and caution about accepting Kohut and Stokes' (2006) dismissal of religion as an influence over Americans' attitudes on foreign policy. Just because Americans *say* that their foreign policy views are not consciously influenced by religion does not thereby demonstrate the absence of religious influences.

We should emphasize that the extensive religious data in the 2004 NSRP permits many other kinds of analysis as well. For example, does dispensationalist theology bolster support for the Bush doctrine, as suggested by many scholars (e.g., Northcott 2004; Weber 2004; Boyer 2005)? Including a variable tapping dispensationalism in model 4 shows that this theology, although strongly correlated with support for the Bush doctrine at the bivariate level, does not add explanatory power to the religious factors already in the equation (data not shown). Does theological traditionalism have a greater impact on some traditions than others? A test with interaction terms for theology within the major Christian traditions shows that traditionalism's effect does not vary significantly by tradition. Does belief in religious pluralism—the idea that all religious traditions offer a way to salvation—enhance opposition to the doctrine? Not beyond that produced by the other religious variables. Nor does a citizen's use of religious information sources or hearing pastoral pronouncements on related issues make any difference. The sole exception is with regard to the Mideast, where evangelicals are more supportive of Israel if a congregational leader addresses that region (compare with Barker et al. 2008). Does involvement with religious Right and religious Left groups influence attitudes? Not beyond that predicted by the variables already in the equation. These latter findings tend to confirm Alfred Hero's (1973) conjecture that direct influence of religious leaders and groups on foreign policy attitudes is minimal, and that the more likely impact is indirect through inculcation of explicitly *theological* understandings, with consequent implications for public attitudes.

Do religious factors influence public attitudes directly? Or, as Page (2006) asserts, is their influence primarily indirect, through partisanship, ideology, and more general predispositions toward American involvement in the world? The final test for religious variables is to include them in a full model with the *basic attitudes* emphasized by Page (2006), Holsti (2004), and other scholars as the contemporary foundation of foreign policy attitudes. In model 5 we add Page's *active part internationalism* to control for citizens' general propensity to favor American global involvement (Page 2006, pp. 70–72). In addition, we incorporate two ideological and two partisan measures, with moderates and true independents as the reference points (scored zero). This procedure captures any asymmetrical effects, say, of strong liberalism or strong conservatism.

The results in model 5 are impressive. First, as Page (2006) might predict, *active part internationalism* produces stronger backing for the Bush doctrine, as do Republican identification and, to a lesser extent, conservatism. Liberalism and Democratic partisanship naturally work in the other direction, although not with as much force. Second, although religious variables contribute powerfully to partisan and ideological identification (see chapter 1), and thus to support for or opposition to the doctrine, their influence is by no means entirely indirect. *All* the belief and behavior measures retain substantial and significant coefficients, although these are reduced somewhat by the introduction of the political predispositions, which they influence. The religious affiliation coefficients, on the other hand, almost disappear, with only the dummy variables for Jews and agnostics/atheists retaining significance. All in all, model 5 performs impressively, explaining almost 44 percent of the variance.

By comparison, if political predispositions are added to models 1 and 2, the variance explained is significantly less—38 percent in each case. And some of the affiliation dummies remain significant whereas partisanship and ideology become more important, because they capture a part of the "lost" religious influence (data not shown). On the whole, then, the analysis shows that we gain a better understanding of the religious influence over foreign policy attitudes by a more complete specification of religious variables. Clearly, it is religious and quasi-religious *beliefs* that are the most important factor, not affiliation per se, which is at best a weak proxy for those beliefs. And these religious factors have a considerable impact, working both through other political predispositions and, in at least the case of the Bush doctrine, directly as well.

CONCLUSIONS

We have argued that there are significant advantages to the inclusion of religious measures in surveys of foreign policy attitudes. Not only is there evidence that religious factors have influenced public opinion on foreign policy for many decades, but there is also reasonable suspicion that religious differences shape contemporary American opinion on a wide range of policy questions. As our test case involving the Bush doctrine shows, sensitive religious measures can help us understand the sources of partisan and ideological divisions over foreign policy in the mass public, and certainly among religious and political elites.

Of course, not all scholars and pollsters will want to use the full batteries of religious items used in the quadrennial NSRP. At a minimum, though, they would be well advised to include detailed denominational screens, one or two religious practice items (especially attendance at religious services), and, if possible, questions on theological traditionalism, moralism, and civil religion (see chapter 1).[3] Such questions will permit them to address the question of how religious variables influence foreign policy attitudes, and how these influences interact with other important demographic and ideational variables.

In this task, the most promising line of inquiry is also the most difficult. As we have seen, not only have many of the authors addressing religion and foreign policy stressed various theological factors in their explanations, but, empirically, belief factors have the strongest influence on foreign policy attitudes. Yet these are the most costly and difficult data to acquire. As a result, despite the outpouring of books and articles connecting theological perspectives (ranging from dispensationalism to liberation theology) with elite and public attitudes, there are few empirical studies that test these relationships, and most are based on local or purposive samples (e.g., Williams, Bliss, and McCallum 2006). Even the best studies often incorporate very limited religious belief measures, designed to tap only religious conservatism (e.g., Barker et al. 2008). The growing diversity of American religion makes it even more difficult to design survey instruments that can assess the varying theological perspectives of myriad religious groups. However, the importance of this intellectual project requires that pollsters and scholars develop a new appreciation for the power of religious influences, and new techniques for measuring and assessing those influences.

APPENDIX ON VARIABLES FOR TABLE

Bush doctrine is a factor score derived from a principal components analysis of five items tapping support for the Iraq war, willingness for the United States to take preemptive military action, support for Israel in the Middle East, preference for unilateral action by the United States over multilateral action in international affairs, and the belief that the United States has a special role to play in world politics (*theta reliability* = .70). Additional items that might be incorporated include the respondent's evaluation of President Bush's foreign policy and preference for putting the task of spreading democracy as a high priority for American foreign policy. Inclusion of these items improves the reliability of the score even further and, when the score is analyzed, produces very similar results to those in table 9.1. We have omitted the evaluation item from the score because it might run the risk of conflating partisan with policy considerations in the analysis. We thank Benjamin Page for this suggestion. (In this vein we think the inclusion of a "trust Bush" variable (highly correlated with evangelical affiliation) as a predictor of Bush doctrine scores explains some of the puzzling conclusions about religious influences in the otherwise interesting article by Froese and Mencken [2009]). We also decided to omit the spreading democracy item on the dual grounds that it was a "goal" rather than a policy question, and was measured with a substantially different metric than the other items.

Active part taps Page's (2006) "active part internationalism" by asking respondents how strongly they agreed or disagreed with the statement: "The U.S. should mind its own business and let other nations get along as best they can on their own." Although this NSRP question differs slightly from the CCFR item, the marginal distributions for agreement and disagreement are almost identical in the two 2004 surveys.

Theological traditionalism is the factor score described in chapter 1 of this volume, utilizing five belief questions appropriate to the religious traditions of the vast majority of Americans. *Religious involvement* is the religious activity or behavior measure also described in chapter 1, based on five common religious practices. We should note that a single measure of attendance at religious services is only slightly less powerful than the full factor score.

Moralism is a single Likert-scale item asking how strongly the respondent agreed or disagreed with the statement: "There are clear and absolute standards for right and wrong."

Civil religion is a factor score derived from a principal components analysis of nine items tapping the respondent's preferences for religion in public life. These include the perceived importance of religious faith to the respondent's own choices, regardless of whether the president has a strong religious faith, the appropriateness of the involvement of religious groups and institutions in the political process, and similar queries (*theta reliability* =.87).

Traditionalist movement is the alternative religious movement measure described in chapter 1, based on two questions asking respondents whether they usually identified with those attempting to preserve or to modernize their own faith tradition.

NOTES

1. Even one of the few political science works to consider the influence of religion on foreign policy attitudes, the otherwise insightful article by Barker, Hurwitz, and Nelson (2008), focuses exclusively on "evangelicals," without any consideration of how religious factors might influence other religious and secular communities.

2. We have used the Bush doctrine score here for purposes of illustration, but analysis of the five individual items reveals very similar patterns of religious influence, although the variables predicting support for Israel are somewhat distinctive.

3. The work of Barker et al. (2008) suggests that items tapping dogmatism, nationalism, and authoritarianism might be useful additions, although these may well overlap with our measures of moralism and civil religion.

REFERENCES

Aguilar, Edwin E., Benjamin O. Fordham, and G. Patrick Lynch. 1997. "The Foreign Policy Beliefs of Political Campaign Contributors." *International Studies Quarterly* 41: 355–366.

Albright, Madeleine K. 2006. *The Mighty and the Almighty.* New York: HarperCollins.

Aldrich, John H., John L. Sullivan, and Eugene Borgida. 1989. "Foreign Affairs and Issue Voting: Do Presidential Candidates 'Waltz Before a Blind Audience'" *American Political Science Review* 83: 123–141.

Barker, David C., Jon Hurwitz, and Traci L. Nelson. 2008. "Of Crusades and Culture Wars: 'Messianic' Militarism and Political Conflict in the United States." *Journal of Politics* 70 (2): 307–322.

Baumgartner, Jody C., Peter L. Francia, and Jonathan S. Morris. 2008. "A Clash of Civilizations? The Influence of Religion on Public Opinion of U.S. Foreign Policy in the Middle East." *Political Research Quarterly* 61: 171–179.

Boyer, Paul S. 2005. "Biblical Policy and Foreign Policy." In *Quoting God*, ed. Claire H. Badaracco, 107–122. Waco, Texas: Baylor University Press.

Braml, Josef. 2004. "The Religious Right in the United States: The Base of the Bush Administration?" SWP research paper. Berlin: German Institute for International and Security Affairs.

Brewer, Paul R., Kimberly Gross, Sean Aday, and Lars Willnat. 2004. "International Trust and Public Opinion about World Affairs." *American Journal of Political Science* 48: 93–109.

Carter, Jimmy. 2005. *Our Endangered Values: America's Moral Crisis.* New York: Simon and Schuster.

Chittick, William O., and Keith R. Billingsley. 1989. "The Structure of Elite Foreign Policy Beliefs." *The Western Political Quarterly* 42: 201–224.

Chittick, William O., Keith R. Billingsley, and Rick Travis. 1995. "A Three-Dimensional Model of American Foreign Policy Beliefs." *International Studies Quarterly* 39: 313–333.

Cimino, Richard. 2005. "No God in Common: American Evangelical Discourse on Islam after 9/11." *Review of Religious Research* 47: 162–174.

Clark, Victoria. 2007. *Allies for Armageddon: The Rise of Christian Zionism.* New Haven, Conn.: Yale University Press.

Collins, Christopher. 2007. *Homeland Mythology: Biblical Narratives in American Culture.* University Park, Pa.: Pennsylvania State University Press.

Daniels, Joseph P. 2005. "Religious Affiliation and Individual International–Policy Preferences in the United States." *International Interactions* 31: 273–301.

den Dulk, Kevin R. 2007. "Evangelical 'Internationalists' and U.S. Foreign Policy During the Bush Administration." In *Religion and the Bush Presidency,* ed. Mark J. Rozell and Gleaves Whitney, 213–234. New York: Palgrave Macmillan.

Derber, Charles, and Yale R. Magrass. 2008. *Morality Wars: How Empires, the Born-Again, and the Politically Correct Do Evil in the Name of Good.* Boulder Colo.: Paradigm Publishers.

Domke, David. 2004. *God Willing? Political Fundamentalism in the White House, the 'War on Terror' and the Echoing Press.* London: Pluto Press.

Farr, Thomas F. 2008. "Diplomacy in an Age of Faith." *Foreign Affairs* 87 (2): 110–124.

Fiorina, Morris, with Samuel J. Abrams and Jeremy C. Pope. 2005. *Culture War? The Myth of a Polarized America.* New York: Pearson Longman.

Fox, Jonathan, and Shmuel Sandler. 2004. *Bringing Religion into International Relations.* New York: Palgrave Macmillan.

Froese, Paul, and F. Carson Mencken. 2009. "A U.S. Holy War? The Effects of Religion on Iraq War Policy Attitudes." *Social Science Quarterly* 90: 103–116.

Gartner, Scott Sigmund, Gary M. Segura, and Michael Wilkening. 1997. "All Politics Are Local: Local Losses and Individual Attitudes toward the Vietnam War." *The Journal of Conflict Resolution* 41: 669–694.

Greeley, Andrew, and Michael Hout. 2006. *The Truth about Conservative Christians.* Chicago, Ill.: University of Chicago Press.

Green, John C. 2007. "Religion and Torture: A View from the Polls." *Faith & International Affairs* 5: 23–28.

Green, John C., James L. Guth, and Cleveland R. Fraser. 1991. "Apostles and Apostates? Religion and Politics among Party Activists." In *The Bible and the Ballot Box: Religion and Politics in the 1988 Election,* ed. James L. Guth and John C. Green, 113–136. Boulder, Colo.: Westview Press.

Green, John C., and John S. Jackson. 2007. "Faithful Divides: Party Elites and Religion in 2004." In *A Matter of Faith: Religion in the 2004 Presidential Election,* ed. David E. Campbell, 37–62. Washington, D.C.: Brookings Institution Press.

Greenberg, Anna, and Kenneth D. Wald. 2001. "Still Liberal after All These Years?" In *Jews in American Politics,* ed. L. Sandy Maisel and Ira N. Forman, 161–193. Lanham, Md.: Rowman & Littlefield.

Guth, James L. 2004a. "George W. Bush and Religious Politics." In *High Risk and Big Ambition: The Presidency of George W. Bush,* ed. Steven E. Schier, 117–141. Pittsburgh, Pa.: University of Pittsburgh Press.

Guth, James L. 2004b. "The Bush Administration, American Religious Politics and Middle East Policy: The Evidence from National Surveys." Presented at the annual meeting of the America Political Science Association, Chicago, Illinois, September 2–5.

Guth, James L. 2006. "Religion and Foreign Policy Attitudes: The Case of the Bush Doctrine." Presented at the annual meeting of the Midwest Political Science Association, Chicago, Illinois, April 20–22.

Guth, James L. 2007a. "Religion and Roll Calls: Religious Influences on the U.S. House of Representatives, 1997–2002." Presented at the annual meeting of the American Political Science Association, Chicago, Illinois, August 20–September 2.

Guth, James L. 2007b. "Religious Leadership and Support for Israel: A Study of Clergy in Nineteen Denominations." Presented at the annual meeting of the Southern Political Science Association, New Orleans, Louisiana, January 3–7.

Guth, James L., Cleveland R. Fraser, John C. Green, Lyman A. Kellstedt, and Corwin E. Smidt. 1996. "Religion and Foreign Policy Attitudes: The Case of Christian Zionism." In *Religion and the Culture Wars: Dispatches from the Front*, ed. John C. Green, James L. Guth, Corwin E. Smidt, and Lyman A. Kellstedt, 330–360. Lanham, Md.: Rowman & Littlefield.

Guth, James L., and John C. Green. 1993. "Salience: The Core Concept?" In *Rediscovering the Religious Factor in American Politics*, ed. David C. Leege and Lyman A. Kellstedt, 157–174. Armonk, N.Y.: M. E. Sharpe.

Guth, James L., John C. Green, Lyman A. Kellstedt, and Corwin E. Smidt. 2005. "Faith and Foreign Policy: A View from the Pews." *The Review of Faith and International Affairs* 3: 3–9.

Guth, James L., John C. Green, Corwin E. Smidt, Lyman A. Kellstedt, and Margaret M. Poloma. 1997. *The Bully Pulpit: The Politics of Protestant Clergy*. Lawrence, Kans.: University Press of Kansas.

Guth, James L., Lyman A. Kellstedt, Corwin E. Smidt, and John C. Green. 2006. "Religious Influences in the 2004 Presidential Election." *Presidential Studies Quarterly* 36: 223–242.

Guyatt, Nicholas. 2007. *Have a Nice Doomsday*. New York: Harper Perennial.

Hadden, Jeffrey. 1969. *The Gathering Storm in the Churches*. New York: Doubleday.

Hehir, J. Bryan. 2001. "Religious Freedom and U.S. Foreign Policy." In *The Influence of Faith: Religious Groups and U.S. Foreign Policy*, ed. Elliott Abrams, 33–52. Lanham Md.: Rowman & Littlefield.

Hero, Alfred O. 1973. *American Religious Groups View Foreign Policy: Trends in Rank-and-File Opinion, 1937–1969*. Durham, N.C.: Duke University Press.

Holsti, Ole R. 2004. *Public Opinion and American Foreign Policy*. Ann Arbor, Mich.: University of Michigan Press.

Holsti, Ole R., and James N. Rosenau. 1990. "The Structure of Foreign Policy Attitudes: American Leaders, 1976–1984." *Journal of Politics* 52: 94–125.

Hout, Michael, and Claude S. Fischer. 2002. "Why Americans Have No Religious Preference: Politics and Generations." *American Sociological Review* 67: 165–190.

Hunter, James D. 1991. *Culture Wars*. New York: Basic Books.

Huntington, Samuel P. 1996. *The Clash of Civilizations and the Remaking of World Order*. New York: Simon and Schuster.

Hurwitz, Jon, Mark Peffley, and Michael A. Seligson. 1993. "Foreign Policy Belief Systems in Comparative Perspective: The United States and Costa Rica." *International Studies Quarterly* 37: 245–270.

Jacobson, Gary C. 2005. "The Public, the President, and the War in Iraq." Presented at the annual meeting of the Midwest Political Science Association, Chicago, Illinois, April 7–10.

Jervis, Robert. 2005. *American Foreign Policy in a New Era*. New York: Routledge.

Jelen, Ted G. 1994. "Religion and Foreign Policy Attitudes: Exploring the Effects of Denomination and Doctrine." *American Politics Quarterly* 22: 382–400.

Johnston, Douglas, and Cynthia Sampson, eds. 1994. *Religion, the Missing Dimensions of Statecraft*. New York: Oxford University Press.

Judis, John. 2005. "The Chosen Nation: The Influence of Religion on U.S. Foreign Policy." Policy Brief 37. Washington, D.C.: Carnegie Endowment for International Peace.

Kohut, Andrew, and Bruce Stokes. 2006. *America against the World*. New York: Henry Holt.

Kristof, Nicholas. 2002. "Following God Abroad." *New York Times* May 21, A21.

Kurtz, Lester, and Kelly Goran Fulton. 2002. "Love Your Enemies? Protestants and United States Foreign Policy." In *The Quiet Hand of God: Faith-Based Activism and the Public Role of Mainline Protestantism*, ed. Robert Wuthnow and John H. Evans, 364–380. Berkeley, Calif.: University of California Press.

Layman, Geoffrey. 2001. *The Great Divide: Religious and Cultural Conflict in American Party Politics*. New York: Columbia University Press.

Layman, Geoffrey, and Thomas M. Carsey. 2002. "Party Polarization and 'Conflict Extension' in the American Electorate." *American Journal of Political Science* 46: 786–802.

Marsden, Lee. 2008. *For God's Sake: The Christian Right and US Foreign Policy*. London: Zed Books.

Marsh, Charles. 2007. *Wayward Christian Soldiers*. Oxford: Oxford University Press.

Martin, William. 1999. "The Christian Right and American Foreign Policy." *Foreign Policy* 114: 66–80.

Mayer, Jeremy. 2004. "Christian Fundamentalists and Public Opinion toward the Middle East." *Social Science Quarterly* 85: 694–712.

McCartney, Paul. 2004. "American Nationalism and U.S. Foreign Policy from September 11 to the Iraq War." *Political Science Quarterly* 119 (3): 399–423.

McCormick, James M. 2004. "The Foreign Policy of the George W. Bush Administration." In *High Risk and Big Ambition*, ed. Steven E. Schier, 189–223. Pittsburgh, Pa.: University of Pittsburgh Press.

Mead, Walter Russell. 2004. *Power, Terror, Peace, and War*. New York: Alfred A. Knopf.

Mead, Walter Russell. 2006. "Religion and U.S. Foreign Policy." *Foreign Affairs* 85: 24–43.

Mearsheimer, John J., and Stephen M. Walt. 2007. *The Israel Lobby and U.S. Foreign Policy*. New York: Farrar, Straus and Giroux.

Nelson, Lynn D. 1988. "Religion and Foreign Aid Provision: A Comparative Analysis of Advanced Market Nations." *Sociological Analysis* 49: 49–63.

Northcott, Michael. 2004. *An Angel Directs the Storm: Apocalyptic Religion and American Empire*. London: I. B. Taurus.

Oldmixon, Elizabeth, Beth Rosenson, and Kenneth Wald. 2005. "Conflict over Israel: The Role of Religion, Race, Party and Ideology in the U.S. House of Representatives, 1997–2002." *Terrorism and Political Violence* 17: 407–426.

Oren, Michael B. 2007. *Power, Faith, and Fantasy: America in the Middle East, 1776 to the Present*. New York: W. W. Norton.

Page, Benjamin I., with Marshall M. Bouton. 2006. *The Foreign Policy Disconnect: What Americans Want from Our Leaders But Don't Get*. Chicago, Ill.: University of Chicago Press.

Peffley, Mark, and John Hurwitz. 1993. "Models of Attitude Constraint in Foreign Affairs." *Political Behavior* 15: 61–90.

Phillips, Kevin. 2006. *American Theocracy: The Peril and Politics of Radical Religion, Oil and Borrowed Money in the 21st Century*. New York: Viking.

Powlick, Philip J., and Anthony Z. Katz. 1998. "Defining the American Public Opinion/ Foreign Policy Nexus." *Mershon International Studies Review* 42: 29–61.

Quinley, Harold. 1974. *The Prophetic Clergy: Social Activism among Protestant Ministers.* New York: Wiley.

Rosenson, Beth, Elizabeth Oldmixon, and Kenneth Wald. 2009. "U.S. Senators' Support for Israel Examined through Sponsorship/Co-sponsorship, 1993–2002: The Influence of Elite and Constituency Factors." *Foreign Policy Analysis* 5: 73–91.

Singer, Peter. 2004. *The President of Good and Evil: The Ethics of George W. Bush.* New York: E. P. Dutton.

Smidt, Corwin. 2005. "Religion and American Attitudes towards Islam and an Invasion of Iraq." *Sociology of Religion* 66: 243–261.

Tipton, Steven M. 2007. *Public Pulpits: Methodists and Mainline Churches in the Moral Argument of Public Life.* Chicago, Ill. University of Chicago Press.

Urban, Hugh B. 2007. *The Secrets of the Kingdom; Religion and Concealment in the Bush Administration.* Lanham Md.: Rowman & Littlefield.

Urquhart, Brian. 2005. "Extreme Makeover." *New York Review of Books* February 24, 4–5.

Wald, Kenneth. 1992. "Religious Elites and Public Opinion: The Impact of the Bishops' Peace Pastoral." *Review of Politics* 54: 112–143.

Weber, Timothy P. 2004. *On the Road to Armageddon: How Evangelicals Became Israel's Best Friend.* Grand Rapids, Mich.: Baker Books.

Williams, Robert L., Stacy L. Bliss, and R. Steve McCallum. 2006. "Christian Conservatism and Militarism among Teacher Education Students." *Review of Religious Research* 48 (1): 17–32.

Wittkopf, Eugene R. 1990. *Faces of Internationalism: Public Opinion and Foreign Policy.* Durham, N.C.: Duke University Press.

CHAPTER 10

....

RELIGION AND
SOCIAL
MOVEMENTS

CLYDE WILCOX AND
GREGORY FORTELNY

RELIGION has been a resource for most social movements that have transformed American politics and society. Consider, for example, the adoption in 1848 of a declaration of women's rights in Seneca Falls, New York, that protested (among other things) the exclusion of women from leadership positions in churches; or the "Underground Railroad" that in defiance of the law hid runaway slaves in the homes of Methodists, Baptists, Quakers, and Catholics; or even the Women's Christian Temperance Union's efforts to pass a prohibition amendment during the late 1800s and early 1900s. Fast-forward to the late 20th century, and one could note that during the early 1960s, African Americans met in countless churches in the South to hear sermons condemning segregation, and then later marched into the face of likely violence armed with the assurance of religious faith, or the more than 500 American congregations that joined together in the 1980s to shelter illegal immigrants from El Salvador and Guatemala, despite federal prosecutions.[1]

During the past several decades, however, the most substantial religiously based social movement has been the Christian Right. During the late 1970s, a network of groups, including the Moral Majority, Religious Roundtable, and Christian Voice, sought to mobilize conservative white evangelicals around a broad issue agenda and an explicitly partisan electoral program. And, after Reagan's victory in the 1980 presidential election, they attracted substantial media attention and significant scholarly interest as well. During the late 1980s and early 1990s, new organizations formed, including the Christian Coalition.

As attention to the Christian Right has grown, scholars have pondered the absence of a similarly visible and influential religious Left. There has been some research on the religious Left, largely seeking to ascertain whether a movement parallel to the Christian Right may emerge. In this chapter, we first consider why social movements are important in American politics, and how religion can aid their mobilization. We then review research on the Christian Right and the religious Left, and conclude by noting questions for future research.

Social Movements and American Politics

Social movements have profoundly affected American society and politics. They have, for example, altered the way we think and talk about race, gender, and sexual diversity; they have also influenced public policy, sponsoring both broad legal changes (e.g., outlawing gender discrimination) and narrower ones (e.g., requiring companies to include contraception in worker health plans).

Yet social movements do not speak with one voice. They are decentralized, somewhat disorganized, and spontaneous. They frequently involve a multiplicity of leaders, organizations, grievances, and ideologies. Social movement entrepreneurs compete and cooperate to define the movement and its constituency. The existence of multiple and competing social movement voices enables grassroots activists to define social movements, at least in part, by choosing to support one set of leaders and organizations rather than another. Social movement organizations may seek to attract one or more types of potential movement supporters, with some aiming for more radical elements and others seeking to attract moderates.

Social movement organizations and activists form uneasy relationships with political parties. Social movements value parties as a mechanism to elect policy makers who can enact laws embodying movement goals, whereas parties seek to win elections and thus desire the support of social movements. However, parties do not necessarily seek to transform society, and, as a result, party activists may resist pressure to adopt social movement agendas, fearing that it might cost them victory. In turn, movements may withhold support from candidates who do not endorse their agenda (Schwartz 2006; Witko 2009).

America's weak and permeable political parties allow social movements to shape party platforms and to play a major role in selecting nominees (Baer and Bositis 1988, Rozell and Wilcox 1996; Green, Rozell, and Wilcox 2001). Some party rules enhance the influence of social movements in the nomination process (Green, Guth, and Wilcox 1998), and low turnout in American primary and general elections further bolsters social movement influence. Politicians depend on movement organizations to mobilize voters, providing activists with leverage over policy makers.

Different theories explain why social movements form and are successful. Early social science theories focused on the grievances of disadvantaged groups. These grievances may involve objections to discrimination, which have served to mobilize blacks, women, and gays and lesbians, denied important societal benefits during the 20th century (McAdam 1999; Klein 1984). Other scholars have argued that grievances may result simply from perceived threats to social status. For example, Gusfield (1963) claimed that the rise of the temperance movement was partially the result of a perception by evangelical, small-town Protestants that their values were declining in society; similar arguments have been applied to the mobilization of the Christian Right in the 1980s (Wald, Owen, and Hill 1989; Green, Guth, and Wilcox 1998).

Yet, as Wald, Silverman, and Fridy (2005) note, countless groups have grievances but do not organize into social movements. Social movement success, rather, depends on many factors, including the presence of critical issues, the mobilization of resources, and the ability of entrepreneurs to construct common identities and collective action frames (Mueller 1992; Tarrow 1994). Entrepreneurs are needed to build organizations to convince potential movement members that they share a common identity that can be transformed into group consciousness— a politicized identity that entails support for collective action (Miller, Gurin, Gurin, and Malanchuk 1981).

Religion has provided key material and ideological resources for social movements throughout American history (Mitchell 2007; Wilcox 2007; Wilcox forthcoming). Religious institutions can provide important organizational space, as they did for African Americans in the South, where blacks could meet in churches with limited white interference. Religious institutions can also provide communication networks through individual churches, denominations, and larger religious coalitions, as well as even broader audiences through their broadcasts and publications. And, finally, religious institutions can supply key leaders (e.g., in the civil rights movement, African American pastors often had educational and organizational skills that were critical to mobilization).

The concrete resources that religious institutions provide help subsidize collective action costs, and they are used within a context and culture that tends to maximize their importance. Churches, synagogues, and mosques are more than buildings; they are communities that meet regularly—in some cases once a week or more. And pastors are more than simply educated leaders with good rhetorical skills; they enjoy a certain level of support and trust from their congregants.

Religion also contributes to social movements in less tangible, but no less important, ways. Religious ideas and theology can mobilize movements. Tinder (1989) argues that there are three elements of Christian faith[2] that can lead to support for radical social transformation. First, Christianity offers a transcendent critique of the established order. As a result, grievances may be viewed as violations of God's will and not simply reflections of personal discontent.[3] Second, religious faith demands that followers act on their beliefs, making efforts to overcome collective action costs a moral obligation. This does more than increase the likelihood that potential members will join a movement; it makes members more likely to endure hardships. Finally, religion may help social movements by providing faith that can sustain action against great odds. Accordingly, the "blessed assurance" of God's protection helped civil rights activists stare down rows of policemen, and provided the dream that allowed them to endure after terrible treatment (Harris 1999).

THE CHRISTIAN RIGHT

Of all of the religiously based movements in American history, few have inspired more controversy than the Christian Right. The Christian Right has aroused considerable animosity among journalists and political activists (Boston 2000; Kaplan 2004; Hedges 2006), who have often seen it as a monolithic and powerful movement generating antidemocratic passions among uncompromising citizens. Certainly, various pronouncements by early movement leaders were intolerant and extreme.[4] Soon after the 1980 election, journalists began to write with some surprise and no small degree of misunderstanding about the sudden appearance of so many organizations—and their apparent success in helping elect Reagan. Scholars took a bit longer to respond, but soon a cottage industry of Christian Right scholarship developed.[5]

This profusion of scholarly attention has not always resulted in clarity. Extant studies display myriad theoretical, conceptual, and empirical approaches. These studies also reach different conclusions about the nature of the movement, its political activities, and its impact on American politics. In the following sections, we will discuss these different scholarly interpretations of the nature of the Christian Right, how it mobilized, its activities, and finally its impact on American politics and public life.

The Nature of the Christian Right

First, there is disagreement about whether the Christian Right is a social movement, a religious movement, or simply the partisan mobilization of a targeted voting bloc. A majority of scholars have described the Christian Right as a genuine social movement seeking to mobilize conservative Christians, and primarily white evangelicals, into political action (Zwier 1982; Liebman 1983; Wilcox 1992a; Bates 1993; Rozell and Wilcox 1996; Green et al. 2001; Wald et al. 2005).

Baer and Bositis (1988) have argued, to the contrary, that the Christian Right is really a religious movement, but this contention faces some strong objections. They observe, first of all, that not all evangelicals support the Christian Right, but this is also true with regard to workers and the labor movement or with women and the feminist movement. Second, Baer and Bositis (1988) argue that some movement leaders (e.g., Jerry Falwell) were unpopular among evangelicals, but other social movement leaders have also been unpopular among their target constituencies. Third, they note that the televangelists leading the movement are not disadvantaged economically, but then again neither are the leaders of many other movements, and not all movements are focused on economic grievances. And, finally, Baer and Bositis (1988) claim that the Christian Right had no mass membership organizations, and although this may have been true for a time, it certainly was not true by the 1990s.[6]

Other analysts have viewed the Christian Right largely as the partisan mobilization of specific religious groups (e.g., Martin 1996). Instead of spontaneous and decentralized uprisings, the movement can be seen as a carefully planned effort by Republican strategists to build a winning coalition. From this perspective, the Christian Right movement of the 1980s was planned by, and received substantial support from, Republican activists (Martin 1996). And its second-wave organizations (e.g., the Christian Coalition) were also formed by Republican activists, staffed by Republican professionals, and funded initially by GOP donors (Wilcox forthcoming). Thus, the movement may represent little more than Republican efforts to use wedge issues to divide and demobilize the Democratic base, and to create and energize a new party base (Leege 1992; Layman 1997; Leege, Wald, Krueger, and Mueller 2002).

Whether we view the Christian Right as a social movement or as a political mobilization depends in part on why and how these organizations were formed, how they were funded, and who joined them and why. Here the evidence is mixed, as perhaps were the motives of those who founded and those who later joined the organizations. Certainly there were spontaneous social movement protests prior to the appearance of Christian Right groups during the late 1970s (Wald and Calhoun-Brown 2007), and scattered spontaneous protests and organizing afterward (Bates 1993; Rozell and Wilcox 1996). Thus, the Christian Right cannot be viewed *only* as a partisan mobilization.

However, partisan activists did notice these spontaneous uprisings, and channeled major resources into the movement in efforts to meet their electoral goals (Wilcox forthcoming), particularly mobilizing voters behind Republican candidates. When movement organizations became less effective in doing this in 2000, the Republican Party began to centralize voter mobilization within the party. Thus, the Republican Party did for George W. Bush in 2004 what the Christian Coalition did for his father in 1992.

There are two other issues in the conceptualization of the Christian Right. First, how do we view the historical mobilizations of similar constituencies? Were these earlier manifestations a reflection of the same, or distinctively different, movements? During the 1920s, fundamentalists mobilized against the teaching of evolution in public schools (Lienesch 2006; Marsden 2006). Still, one of the movement's spokespersons, William Jennings Bryan, held very leftist views on the economy and might instead be considered a figure of the religious Left (Kazin 2006). And, in the 1950s, a much smaller Christian Right mobilization formed around anticommunism, with continued opposition to teaching evolution (Wolfinger, Wolfinger, Prewitt, and Rosenhack 1964; Ribuffo 1983; Wilcox 1987a).

Because of these differences, the Christian Right of the 1970s and '80s was often called the *New Christian Right* in early scholarship (Liebman and Wuthnow 1983), and the most recent incarnation of the Christian Right really constitutes more of a series of related, but distinct, mobilizations than a single, highly coordinated movement. During the late 1970s, fundamentalist (and to a lesser extent Pentecostal) Christians mobilized into a series of organizations such as the Moral Majority, Christian Voice, and Religious Roundtable (Guth 1983a; Liebman 1983; Moen 1989). There was considerable, but far from perfect, overlap with the pro-life movement, which also appealed to moderate and even liberal Catholics.

In 1988, the presidential campaign of Pat Robertson brought many Pentecostals to activist politics (Smidt and Penning 1991; Wilcox 1992b; Hertzke 1993; Green 1996; Oldfield 1996), but many fundamentalist leaders such as Falwell did not endorse Robertson. From the ashes of Robertson's failed campaign sprung the Christian Coalition, and during the 1990s a new wave of organizations such as Focus on the Family and Family Research Council became prominent, and older groups such as the Concerned Women for America became more active. The Christian Coalition was a very different organization, and attracted very different activists, than the Moral Majority (Bendyna and Wilcox 1997; Wilcox, DeBell, and Sigelman 1999). Thus, as some scholars (e.g., Bruce 1988) were pronouncing the Christian Right movement dead, a new wave of mobilization was already underway.

Second, although the Christian Right is often conceived as a single movement, it might be better viewed as a coalition of related movements—a pro-life movement, a homeschooling movement, an antigay rights movement, and a movement supporting traditional gender roles. Although there is considerable overlap among these movements, many activists care principally about one set, rather than a full spectrum, of issues. This is especially true at the state level, where the Christian Right varies considerably depending on state-specific issues, key organizers and politicians, and its own religious composition (Bruce 1995; Gilbert and Peterson 1995; Lunch 1995; Rozell and Wilcox 1996; Guth and Smith 1997), as the religious composition of Christian Right activists varies considerably across states (Bendyna 2000; Bendyna, Green, Rozell, and Wilcox 2001).

Mapping Movement Boundaries

Of course, any conceptualization of a movement involves some understanding of its boundaries—not just what organizations and issues are included, but those excluded. Defining the limits of the Christian Right is complicated, because movement leaders and organizations do not use *Christian Right*, preferring generic terms such as *Christian conservative* or *pro-family movement*. Scholars use the term to distinguish the movement from more centrist conservative Christians, many of whom do not support the movement, and from many religious and secular liberal groups who also consider themselves "pro-family." It is also important to distinguish between the social movement and those it seeks to mobilize. Just as the feminist movement is different from its target constituency of all women, so, too, the Christian Right differs from the white evangelical population it seeks to enlist. Studies have consistently showed that only a minority of white evangelicals support Christian Right groups (Wilcox 1989).[7]

Among scholars, there are differences in classifying various social movement organizations. There is consensus that the Christian Right would at least include organizations at the national, state, and local levels that seek to mobilize conservative Christians into political action. Thus the Moral Majority, Christian Voice, Christian Coalition, Focus on the Family, Concerned Women for America, and Citizens for Excellence in Education are all included without reservation. Some scholars include pro-life groups, arguing that they are the heart of the movement (Shields 2007), whereas others exclude such groups because they include some moderate and even liberal Americans (Wilcox and Gomez 1990). Likewise, there are disagreements about inclusion of antifeminist organizations like Eagle Forum, and a few scholars have added more extreme groups such as Christian Identity (Aho 1990; Barkun 1994), which most Christian Right leaders would repudiate.

Operational Definitions of the Christian Right

Empirical research on the Christian Right has used various operational definitions of the movement. Frequently, this variation reflects the limits of available data; in other cases, it results from different conceptualizations of the movement or different theoretical interests (e.g., between mass support and elite participation). To draw conclusions from these studies, it is important to understand their different foci. Many scholars have sought to measure and explain mass *support* for the Christian Right. Those using the American National Elections Studies (ANES) have used ratings of Christian Right groups on "feeling thermometers," and some have used such measures in their own surveys (Buell and Sigelman 1985; Wilcox 1987b, c; Jelen 1992; Robinson 2006). Other studies have asked respondents to rate various Christian Right groups favorably or unfavorably (Tamney and Johnson 1988). Similarly, studies have used data from exit polls that ask whether voters support the religious Right (Rozell 2002).[8] Other studies have focused on those who give positive ratings to candidates associated with the movement (Wilcox 1990, 1992b). The various measures are not strictly comparable, but give a reasonably consistent estimate that between 11 percent and 16 percent of white Americans support (as opposed to belong to) the movement.

A second approach to measuring support for the Christian Right has been to identify those who back the movement's policy preferences (Simpson 1984). This approach is used less often, both because it is difficult to determine what constitutes support for the platform (Sigelman and Presser 1988), and because support for an agenda and support for the movement itself are conceptually distinct. Yet, many movements draw support from citizens who do not support their entire agenda.[9]

Others have studied movement activists, specifically those who have contributed to candidates and movement organizations, who say they are members, and who in some cases play leadership roles. These studies have focused on contributors to Christian Right candidates such as Pat Robertson (Green and Guth 1988; Wilcox 1992a), on donors to Christian Right organizations such as the Concerned Women for America (Guth and Green 1991; Green, Guth, Kellstedt, and Smidt 1994; Robinson 2008), and on members and activists in Christian Right organizations such as the Moral Majority or the Christian Coalition (Wilcox 1986; Green, Guth, and Hill 1993; Wilcox, Jelen, and Linzey 1995; Berkowitz and Green 1997). Such studies are limited by the availability of membership and donor lists, but they typically focus on donors because groups and candidates frequently must disclose their contributions to the Federal Election Commission.[10]

Understanding Christian Right Mobilization

Studies that seek to understand the mobilization of the Christian Right have taken two tracks. Some have sought to analyze movement activists; others have sought to understand the process of mobilization. During the 1950s, and to a lesser extent during the 1980s and '90s, scholars focused attention on who joined Christian Right groups, and why. This earlier literature assumed that rational, well-adjusted people would never support the movement. Such studies sought explanations rooted in personality disorders, alienation, and the displacement of anxiety related to social status (Jelen 1991). In contrast, more recent studies have largely sought to understand the Christian Right within broader social movement theories (Wald, Owen, and Hill 1989; Wilcox 1992a; Wald et al. 2005).

During the 1950s, the Christian Anti-Communism Crusade and other groups perceived a worldwide Communist conspiracy of staggering proportions, and scholars wrote of the paranoid style of the movement and the authoritarian and dogmatic personalities of its supporters. Studies published during the 1960s concluded that Christian Right activists (and members of similar groups) were more authoritarian, dogmatic, and intolerant than other Americans (Elms 1969; Rohter 1969). Other scholars suggested that the authoritarian style of the Christian Right arose from socialization processes—and not personality disorders (Hofstadter 1965).

However, only a few scattered works since the 1980s have considered personality theories as bases for Christian Right support (Johnson and Tamney 1984). Although surveys of the Indiana Moral Majority membership showed high levels of authoritarianism and dogmatism, no comparisons were ever made with other activists or other Indiana citizens (Wilcox et al. 1995). One study did test for the existence of personality traits among supporters and nonsupporters of the

Christian Right movement, finding supporters higher in "authority mindedness," but this was defined as a cognitive style and not a personality trait (Owen, Wald, and Hill 1991).

Other studies have linked support for the Christian Right to alienation (Conover and Gray 1983), although most find activists to be located in dense social networks and not the isolated individuals that mass society theories posit. Some research has argued that support for the movement derives from anxiety over social status (Rohter 1969), although most studies discount this (e.g., Wolfinger et al. 1964; Smidt 1988b). Wald et al. (1989) argue that it is not individual anxiety over economic or social status that matters, but rather collective dissatisfaction with social respect given to traditionalist groups and institutions.

Most studies in the 1980s and since have portrayed Christian Right supporters as rational—or at least as rational as other activists. Support for the movement is seen as stemming from religious and political sources, and is highest among white evangelicals with conservative positions on sociomoral issues. Supporters are distinctive in their evangelical religious doctrine, high public religiosity, and conservative moral stances. Activists have even higher levels of doctrinal orthodoxy and religiosity, and are more conservative on social, economic, and foreign policy issues than supporters. They are generally well educated and affluent, although less so than other activists. They are frequently active in political, partisan, and social groups, and they often display considerable intolerance toward those with opposing viewpoints—at least when compared with other activists (Green and Guth 1988; Guth and Green 1991; Wilcox 1992a).

A second strand of research has generally applied various social movement theories to explain how the Christian Right mobilized. Most accounts point to a mix of grievances that spurred mobilization during the late 1970s, including liberalized abortion laws, changes in women's roles, foreign policy, increased regulation of religious schools, and potential regulation of televangelism (Moen 1989; Smith forthcoming). Some Christian Right activists are narrowly focused on single issues, such as abortion or Christian schools, but others are concerned with a range of issues. Evangelical communities appear to have been especially challenged by social changes during the 1960s, which may have crystallized into concern over certain symbolic issues (e.g., abortion and gay and lesbian rights),[11] but also reflected a wider social critique (Fried 1988; Wilcox 2007c).[12]

Many activists portray their activity as a defensive action to protect their lifestyle (Lorentzen 1980; Bates 1993). Education issues are central because they fear a decline in their ability to raise their children to share their values. Movement leaders try to frame issues along defensive themes (e.g., opposition to same-sex marriage is cast as a defense of traditional marriage) in part because they believe that society undermines their moral authority, ridicules them, and is openly hostile to their way of life. Thus, for many, specific policy issues are part of a more generic assault on evangelical lifestyles and beliefs.[13]

Social movements need to build group consciousness, stressing to potential members the importance of collective action that transcends intragroup divisions.

The Christian Right confronted a serious theological obstacle to its original mobilization, as doctrinal differences between fundamentalists, Pentecostals, and neo-evangelicals made building a coherent movement difficult (Smidt 1988a, 1989; Wilcox 1992a; Jelen 1993a). Consequently, leaders sought to build a more comprehensive identity, such as "evangelical," or Ralph Reed's more inclusive "people of faith." Surveys show that the movement eventually smoothed over some divisions among Protestants, and that by the 1990s many evangelicals had even warmed toward Catholics (Wilcox, Rozell, and Gunn 1996; Bendyna, Green, Rozell, and Wilcox 2000).

The Activities of the Christian Right

Although the activities of Christian Right groups have been described in some detail, there has been little empirical work that carefully documents those activities, and practically no effort has been made to put them into a broader theoretical focus. Most research has concentrated on electoral activity. The organizations formed during the 1970s and, especially, the 1980s were heavily involved in electoral work—particularly, voter mobilization. Some groups, such as the Christian Coalition, made electoral mobilization their central focus. Electoral activities extended beyond the boundaries of the organizations themselves in that they sought to register and mobilize like-minded voters who might never contribute to, let alone join, Christian Right groups. These efforts have been greatest during presidential elections, but have been substantial in statewide contests as well (Gilbert and Peterson 1995; Lunch 1995).

Yet it is difficult to do more than describe the actions of Christian Right organizations, for the boundaries between these activities and those by parties and candidates are difficult to draw. For example, Christian Coalition voter guide distribution was financed in part by partisan activists, some of whom were also members of the movement. Candidates who court the Christian Right and ask its leaders to mobilize supporters on the candidates' behalf are often not themselves part of the movement—and, in some cases, may not even be supporters. Moreover, movement electoral activities frequently involve disseminating materials to non-members. For this reason, most theoretical work has sought to incorporate Christian Right electoral activities into broader theories of cultural politics (Wald and Leege, chapter 5, this volume) or voting behavior (Layman and McTague, chapter 12, this volume).

Several Christian Right organizations have undertaken significant electoral mobilization. Although there are many anecdotal reports of Moral Majority voter registration drives during the 1980 and 1984 elections, it is difficult to estimate their extent.[14] The Christian Coalition voter guides from the 1990s have been described in detail, but as yet there have been no statistical analysis of their impact, although such studies are possible.[15] There have been examinations, however, of the aggregate effects of voter contacting by conservative religious groups, which suggest that a significant number of evangelicals and others were reached (Wilcox 1991; Guth, Kellstedt, Green, and Smidt 2007).[16]

Christian Right efforts in state elections have been described in detail (Rozell and Wilcox 1995; Green, Rozell, and Wilcox 2003, 2006). In some cases the movement has sought to gain access to, and control of, state and local party organizations, whereas in others it functions more as one competing party faction (Green, Guth, and Wilcox 1998; Green et al. 2001). As discussed later, the interaction between party and movement has, over time, served to change both.

The Christian Right has also recruited and trained candidates for office, from school boards through state legislatures and governors to Congress. Generally, movement candidates have fared poorly in high-stake elections, but have had a bit more success in state legislatures and school boards (Deckman 2004).[17] Christian Right groups have lobbied Congress (Moen 1989; Green and Bigelow 2005), state legislatures (Cleary and Hertzke 2006), and local governments. Most accounts are primarily descriptive, although one study systematically compared Christian Right advocacy strategies with those of other child advocacy groups (Gormly and Cymrot 2006).

Finally, movement organizations have also gone to court (Bates 1993; Brown 2004; Hacker 2005). In recent years, Christian Right law firms have switched their legal arguments from efforts favoring public accommodation of religion to free exercise rights. Such firms have been especially active in threatening action against schools that appear to deny free exercise rights to evangelicals, and in defending churches and other religious groups active in politics.

The Impact of the Christian Right

Social movements have the ability to transform social and political life profoundly.[18] It is always difficult to assess the impact of a social movement, because we cannot observe a world where it did not exist. Without the Christian Right there would still be morally conservative evangelical voters, and candidates would still appeal for their votes. Moreover, even without the Christian Right, Republicans might have targeted white evangelical voters with different cultural messages.[19] The latest incarnation of the Christian Right has been active in American public life for nearly 30 years, and here we consider four types of effects that the movement might have (1) on the political mobilization of evangelical Christians, (2) on public support for the movement's agenda, (3) on public policy, and (4) on political discourse and the civic virtues of movement members.

There has been little systematic study of the impact of Christian Right mobilization efforts on voter turnout among evangelicals and other conservative Christians. Of course, when mobilization efforts by both Christian Right organizations and political candidates/parties target and reach the same individuals, it is difficult to isolate the effects of Christian Right mobilization. Turnout among evangelicals increased in 1980 when the Moral Majority first organized registration drives, but this may well have been because both Reagan and Carter claimed to be born-again Christians, and both campaigns targeted evangelicals (Wilcox 1991). Similarly, evangelical partisanship has changed dramatically during the past two decades, but this is part of a broader movement of southern conservatives into the GOP— one spurred by the campaign strategies of candidates as well as the Christian Right. It seems clear that the Christian Right did bring some previously apolitical people into politics, and that it helped to move some evangelicals from Democratic to Republican partisanship, but it is difficult to sort out the magnitude of this effect. Moreover, there is some evidence that Christian Right efforts sparked a counter-mobilization of religious moderates and secular citizens (Wilcox 1992a), although other studies do not confirm this (Campbell 2006).

More broadly, how successful has the Christian Right been in persuading the culture of its moral claims? After 30 years of mobilization, the Christian Right has not seemingly influenced the culture in the same way that the civil rights, feminist, or even the gay and lesbian rights movements have. Public opinion on abortion has remained relatively constant over time, although opinion is more consistent with partisanship today (Layman and Carsey 2002). The public has become more liberal on gender roles, and far more liberal on gay and lesbian rights. Indeed, there are few issues today where the mass public is closer to the Christian Right's position than it was when the Moral Majority was formed in 1979. Even the strong reaction to same-sex marriage in 2004 is actually a demonstration of how quickly that debate has shifted, because when the Moral Majority was founded, gay marriage was not even remotely on the political agenda.

Many Christian Right activists have taken positions in GOP state and county organizations. As a result, the GOP itself may have been transformed as Christian Right activists have become party leaders. The Christian Right may also have helped to change the evangelical community by focusing on issues that resonated among evangelicals, moving them toward greater politicization and identification with the GOP.

The movement's success in enacting policy is relatively unimpressive. After 30 years of activism, there are many more state regulations on abortion, but few seem to have had any real impact on abortion rates.[20] States have more policies that allow women to join the labor force, even when they have small children. Likewise, there are far more protections for same-sex couples than in the past. Still, despite such liberal advances, Christian Right activists argue that the movement has succeeded in blocking even more rapid liberal policy change.

The Christian Right has enjoyed the greatest success when its appeals have echoed traditional social movement themes of fair treatment and equality. The movement has managed to reverse laws and policies that it saw either as limiting religious freedom or creating an unequal field between religious and secular organizations. It also has had some success in winning federal funds for favored programs, in part because funding is still viewed as a nonzero sum process. Thus, the national government has provided funding for abstinence-based sex education programs in the United States and abroad, although the requirement that anti-AIDS funds must include some portion of funding devoted to abstinence was reversed by Congress in 2007.

The Christian Right may also have influenced the broader political debate in America, the extent of cultural polarization, and the civility of the dialogue. The rise of the Christian Right coincides with the advent of the American "culture war": focused cultural conflict over highly symbolic issues. As the Christian Right joined ranks with the Republican Party, Democratic candidates sought to paint the GOP as a party of religious extremists. This led more secular citizens to align with the Democrats, and more religious ones, especially those with orthodox religious views, to move into the GOP (Layman 2001).

To exploit these cultural cleavages, groups and party activists on both sides used inflammatory communications that sought to increase fear and decrease tolerance of the other side. The mail of Christian Right organizations warned that liberals wanted to take away Christian Bibles and that gay rights activists secretly sought to promote pedophiles of the "New World Order," whereas the mail of opponents warned that Christian Right leaders wanted to establish a theocracy on par with Iran. Such efforts may prove useful in fundraising, but they pose important barriers to democratic discourse (M.E. Warren 1999, 2001). Many surveys show that Christian Right activists are low on various democratic virtues, including compromise and tolerance (Guth and Green 1991; Green, Guth, Kellstedt, and Smidt 1994; Wilcox et al. 1995). Christian Right direct mail may not be distinctive in its reliance on messages that stoke fear and distrust, but it reaches activists whose theology may be especially focused on the dangers of their opponents and whose certitude of their own beliefs is unusually strong.

Still, the Christian Right has helped to ease some barriers of religious particularism. From the early 20th century through the early 1980s, Pentecostals and fundamentalists exchanged heated accusations on the public stage, but today evangelicals of all theological stripes are more accommodating. Fundamentalists were also quite hostile to Catholics during the same period (Kellstedt 1988), but the movement has sparked a dialogue between evangelicals and Catholics that has led to interesting exchanges on both sides (Robinson 2008).

THE RELIGIOUS LEFT

The organized and active presence of the Christian Right during the past 20 years has moved political activists and scholars to ask: Why is there so little evidence of a viable religious Left?[21] The existence of a "God gap" in which the most religious voters support Republican candidates has led many to assume that religion can only be mobilized on behalf of conservative causes. This is ironic inasmuch as Christian political activity in the United States had long been the province of the

Left, whereas theological conservatives were politically quiescent, largely concerned with saving souls.

In sharp contrast to the wealth of studies on the Christian Right, there is a paucity of studies on the religious Left.[22] Indeed, many scholars question whether such a movement exists or could even be created (Marty 1999; Alpert 2000). The general consensus about the religious Left is that "to the extent that it exists at all, [it is] a loosely knit coalition of religious people who approach politics from a liberal/progressive vantage point" (Olson 2007c, p. 54).

The Nature of the Religious Left

As is the case with *Christian Right*, the label *religious Left* is not often used by organizations and activists in contemporary American politics. Some scholars have also eschewed the label, favoring jaw benders such as *religiopolitical progressives*. Many scholars have referred to the religious Left as a nascent or latent movement—that is, an unformed, but potential, movement.

Olson (2006) argues that mainline Protestants have sustained a rich *culture* emphasizing social gospel principles, thereby giving congregants a cultural identity on which to draw for private and social behavior. Through their churches and movement organizations, a Protestant Left can mobilize necessary *resources*, such as leaders, communication networks, finances, and physical space, although the religious Left still lacks the dense network of parachurch organizations available to the Christian Right. Yet, it is important to distinguish between doctrinal orthodoxy and political progressivism. Even doctrinally orthodox Christians can find strong support for progressive economic policies in scripture (Roelofs 1988), and doctrinally liberal Christians may take conservative positions on issues such as same-sex marriage.

No analyst has described the religious Left as primarily a religious movement; indeed, low levels of religious observance among potential members may limit its mobilization. However, once again religious doctrine is important to understanding the movement and even defining it, for any successful religious Left would transcend the boundaries of Christianity. American Jews have long been a mainstay in progressive politics (Sigelman 1991; Wald and Calhoun-Brown 2007). In smaller numbers, Buddhists and some other religious minorities have joined in progressive traditions, making the religious Left a more eclectic coalition than the Christian Right.

Opposing social movements need not be mirror opposites. Thus, it is possible for the Christian Right to center its mobilization around the doctrinally orthodox, whereas as a more eclectic religious coalition the religious Left may be united on political principles.[23] In fact, the religious Left may be very different in nature from the Christian Right, focusing more on policies and social change rather than elections—much as other social movements have done historically. In addition, several works have focused on the religious Left's efforts to influence local policies and conditions.

Still, it is also possible to conceive of the religious Left as an effort by Democratic Party activists to build a credible movement to counter the Christian Right. Democratic donors and activists helped to launch the Interfaith Alliance, and Democratic strategists have worked to try to build a social movement counterweight to the Christian Right in politics. This has been especially true after George Bush's reelection in 2004, which many progressives interpreted as demonstrating the power of religious mobilization.

And as with the Christian Right, there are questions of how to consider waves of social movement mobilization in the past. Even more than the Christian Right, early religious Left movements can be conceived as separate mobilizations of related movements. During the 1920s, first-wave feminism and temperance shared some of the same religious constituencies and activists. However, it was during the 1960s that the religious Left most resembled a broader coalition that might balance the Christian Right. Many of the same activists were involved in the civil rights and antiwar movements, as well as being mobilized on issues such as hunger and poverty. The movement was sufficiently visible and influential to draw strong denunciations from religious conservatives. Today, the religious Left might be thought of as a set of organizations and activists who engage in a variety of issues, sometimes intertwined, sometimes separate (Alpert 2000).

Mapping Movement Boundaries

Drawing the boundaries of a religious Left is as difficult conceptually as determining those for the Christian Right. First, it is perhaps important to distinguish genuine religious progressive politics from more secular politics, as many progressive activists are secular. Kellstedt, Smidt, Green, and Guth (2007) argue that progressive activists with minimal religious affiliation lie outside any potential religious Left; they do, however, allow for theological flexibility because nontraditional spirituality might serve as a genuinely religious Left. It is also important to distinguish the religious Left from any religious constituencies that it might target. African American Protestants typically vote for Democratic candidates, support gender equality, and identify as moderately liberal, but many take conservative positions on sociomoral issues such as abortion and same-sex marriage (Thomas and Wilcox 1992; Shaw and McDaniel 2007). Mainline Protestant denominations have substantial resources and are a logical core for any religious Left, but these denominations are frequently divided on these same issues (Wuthnow and Evans 2002; Djupe and Gilbert 2003).

The divisions in these faith traditions are echoed in others as well. Catholic doctrine does not fit neatly into Left/Right categories. Consider, for example, Cardinal Joseph Bernardin's famous "seamless garment" of life. Bernardin argued that a Catholic's "moral, political, and economic responsibilities do not stop at the moment of birth," and a consistently Christian viewpoint should include "specific political and economic positions on tax policy, employment generation, welfare policy, nutrition and feeding programs" (Kelly 1999, p 104).[24]

There are some religious groups that support abortion rights (e.g., the Religious Coalition for Reproductive Choice) and others that support gay and lesbian rights. However, it might be more useful to think of a religious Left that is not the mirror opposite of the Christian Right, but instead is orthogonal to it. Although the Christian Right has focused on "sex sins" and personal morality, the religious Left concentrates on social justice, equality, and peace (Hall 1997). Under this conception, groups could oppose same-sex marriage and abortion, but still be considered part of the religious Left if they focused on income redistribution, health care for the poor, living wages, environmental issues, and so forth.

Some organizations (e.g., the Interfaith Alliance and Call to Renewal) fit conceptions of a religious Left as a counterweight to the Christian Right in electoral mobilization. However, these organizations are smaller and less successful than the Christian Right. The Sojourners have sought to mobilize liberal evangelicals into both elections and policy making. Other types of organizations that might be part of the religious Left are more focused on policy than elections.[25]

Operational Definitions of the Religious Left

Because there are far fewer studies of the religious Left than the Christian Right, there have been far fewer efforts to define the movement operationally. The ANES have included only one feeling thermometer question in 1972 that referred to "ministers who lead protest marches." Several surveys measure feelings toward "civil rights leaders," many of whom were religious, but such items tap racial attitudes more than religious ones. A few studies compare Christian Right and religious Left activists who participated in movement organizations (Guth, Green, Kellstedt, and Smidt 1995; Hall 1997), but surveys of activists are limited by availability of membership lists. Unlike the case of the Christian Right, there have been no major religious Left presidential candidates and few religious Left Political Action Committees, and thus donor lists are difficult to obtain (Robinson 2008).[26]

Although theological progressivism and political progressivism are distinct concepts, some scholars have used both theology and support for liberal policies to define the movement. In a number of studies, Olson (2006, 2007a, b), has identified the religious Left as a "loosely knit" collection of individuals with "intertwining themes of liberalism—theological and political" (Olson 2007c, p. 82). Kellstedt et al. (2007) combine theology, religious behavior, and political views to identify a core and periphery of the religious Left. They combine measures of political liberalism (based on ideological self-classification) and religious liberalism (based on measures of religious beliefs and behavior), describing the religious Left core constituency as politically liberal and theologically modernist. Three additional groups are peripheral constituents—specifically, the politically liberal and theologically centrist, the politically liberal and theologically traditionalist, and the politically moderate and theologically modernist—but each differs in many respects from core constituents (Kellstedt et al. 2007).

Understanding Religious Left Mobilization (or Lack Thereof)

As was the case with the Christian Right, a number of studies have described supporters of the movement. Because the religious Left is currently smaller than the Christian Right, many studies have also assessed potential support—a strategy that has proved useful in the study of other social movements (Cook 1989). Kellstedt et al. (2007) note that various potential constituencies of the religious Left are demographically distinctive, with significant variations in race, gender, education, and geography. Olson (2007a) finds that religious liberals are better educated, more likely to be female, and less likely to be married than fundamentalists and evangelicals.

There is a core of issues that appeals to religious Left citizens, and some entrepreneurs who have sought to mobilize them (e.g., Jim Wallis). However, mobilization efforts are less visible at the national level, and there have been few studies of individuals involved in community-level mobilization. Thus, we know little about the ability of the nascent movement to build a common identity or even a common set of grievances.

Surveys show that religious Left activists want the church to concentrate more on social justice and less on personal morality. Many members of religious Left organizations identify as political moderates, and although there is consensus among members on government programs to aid the poor and protect the environment, narrower majorities favor gender equality, condom distribution in public schools, and gay and lesbian rights. A majority of religious Left activists favor restrictions on legal abortion and on pornography (Hall 1997), a finding consistent with our earlier argument that the key issues of concern for the religious Left and Christian Right may differ.

The Activities of the Religious Left

There have been a few scattered studies of the religious Left in electoral politics (Kellstedt et al. 2007). Religious Left groups have passed out voter guides and have sought to publicize candidate positions on key issues. During the 2004 presidential election, Sojourners advertised "God is not a Republican . . . or a Democrat." Although there have been few careful estimates of the extent of this activity, it is obviously far less than the mobilization of the Christian Right. In one recent study, Guth et al. (2007) reported that fully 83 percent of evangelical traditionalists had received at least one electoral contact during the 2004 election, compared with only 38 percent of modernist mainline Protestants.

During the 1960s, many clergy and concerned laity took part in large protest marches, especially as part of the civil rights and antiwar movements (Friedland

1998). Hadden (1970) estimated that 2600 clergy and seminarians demonstrated against the Vietnam War in the Clergy Mobilization March on Washington in 1967. He noted that some studies found that clergy in California were twice as likely to oppose as to support the war, and that among the former, many had signed antiwar petitions, marched, joined a peace organization, contacted a public official, or even participated in acts of civil disobedience.

Case studies of lobbying by religious Left groups suggest they may have political skills that amplify their voice (Cleary and Hertzke 2006). Mainline Protestants, a core constituency of the religious Left, retain considerable political resources despite their diminishing numbers (Wuthnow and Evans 2002; Francia 2003; Smidt 2007). This leads religious Left groups not only to protest, but to consider lobbying strategies that utilize personal connections of movement activists.

The Impact of the Religious Left

Religious progressives have participated in some of the most sweeping social movements of the past century.[27] During the 1960s, religious resources helped the civil rights movement succeed against long odds. The religious Left was an element in the antiwar movement as well, although perhaps less centrally so. However, both the civil rights and the antiwar movements divided churches, and they may have accelerated the decline of mainline Protestantism. Whole case studies suggest that perhaps the most important activity of the religious Left is in community politics. These case studies have yet to cumulate enough data to build valid theoretical generalizations, but they do suggest interesting avenues for future inquiry. These studies have suggested that the religious Left is especially successful in forging broad coalitions and creating bridging social capital (M.R.Warren 2001; Wood 2002).

RIGHT, LEFT, AND CENTER: UNDERSTANDING THE DYNAMICS OF RELIGIOUS MOBILIZATION

During the 1960s, liberal churches were actively involved in mobilizing their resources on behalf of progressive causes such as civil rights, poverty, and the war in Vietnam. Conservative pastors decried the intertwining of religion and politics, frequently denouncing pastors who led protest marches from the pulpit. Twenty years later, however, conservative churches were actively involved in mobilizing congregants on abortion, homosexuality, pornography, and other moral issues, but this mobilization focused more on ballots than on marches. And, in this case, liberal clergy often complained about turning pews into precincts.

As scholars have sought evidence of a nascent or latent religious Left, they have implicitly asked why the Christian Right has been the most visible religiously based movement since the 1980s and why the religious Left has been quiescent. Conversely, why was the religious Left so active during the 1960s, but the Christian Right was not? Many accounts of the current Christian Right and nascent religious Left focus on characteristics of the movement's supporters. One important difference is that Christian Right activists have far higher levels of public religiosity than those of the religious Left. Kellstedt et al. (2007) report that only 26 percent of the core members of the religious Left attend church weekly, compared with 93 percent of core members of the Christian Right. Fully 13 percent of core religious Left respondents were unaffiliated with a church, and the rest were scattered across traditions. Meanwhile, none of the core Christian Right respondents were unaffiliated, and more than half were members of evangelical Protestant churches. Moreover, the Christian Right core is relatively unified on theological issues,[28] whereas the core of the religious Left is more divided.[29]

These religious differences suggest that Christian Right supporters may be simply easier to mobilize. They are found in a narrower range of churches, and they are more likely to attend every week. They share a common theology, which permits easier rhetorical mobilization. Yet, Kellstedt et al. (2007, p. 240) do find one peripheral religious Left group which they call *traditionalist liberals*, who attend church regularly and hold orthodox religious beliefs, but who also hold liberal political views.

Second, some have argued that the Christian Right is simply more unified on key issues than the religious Left. Kellstedt et al. (2007, p. 248) emphasize the diversity of opinion among the peripheral and core religious Left groups; they conclude that "in 2004 the hot-button social issues divided the secular from the religious left and also created fissures among religious left groups." Yet the core of the Christian Right is divided on economic issues and some foreign policy issues. Moreover, surveys of Christian Right activists show considerable differences on precise positions on abortion and gay rights. One survey of Concerned Women for America revealed that many members would allow abortions under certain circumstances (Wilcox and Larson 2006). What contributes to the Christian Right appearing unified on social issues is that such issues are now debated in directional terms—in other words, whether we should have more conservative policies on abortion, not when it should be permitted.

Taken together, though, these explanations would suggest that the Christian Right should always be better mobilized than the religious Left, but this was certainly not true during the 1960s. So how can we explain the change over time? In part, this may reflect the changing sizes of religious communities. The mainline Protestant denominations at the core of the religious Left are in decline, whereas white evangelical churches are remaining stable and thereby growing as a proportion of all American Protestants (Smidt 2007). And divisions within mainline Protestant churches on social issues may make mainline pastors less likely to risk dividing their congregations by talk about politics, because their resource base is insecure.[30] White mainline pastors are also less likely to claim divine guidance for their political stands or to link them to scripture (Jelen 1993b). On many issues, they face congregations that are not eager to hear religion and politics linked, and they can speak with less authority about why members should mobilize. Although all this may well work against the religious Left, it is also possible that the visible Christian Right rhetoric of linking religion to conservative politics may have pushed religious liberals toward a more secular stance (Hout and Fisher 2002; Marwell and Demerath 2003).

Perhaps more important, the issue cycle has made it more difficult to mobilize religious liberals, but perhaps easier to mobilize conservatives. Between the 1960s and 1990s, progressive issues shifted from being "easy" issues to more complex ones, difficult to use in mass mobilization. Segregation was an easy target during the 1960s, but it is more difficult to mobilize white Christians on behalf of affirmative action plans. The Iraq war is unpopular, but the draft made the Vietnam War highly relevant for congregations in a way that the volunteer army does not. Poverty and hunger remain, but the new decentralized approach to these issues moves the fight from national politics to less visible struggles in state legislatures and city councils. As these issues become more complex, the debate has shifted to issues regarding sexual morality, which divide the religious Left and provide some unity to the Christian Right. If *Roe v. Wade* is overturned, however, positional cues on abortion would not be possible, and the abortion issue may become harder for the Right.

What is perhaps most interesting about the past 20 years is how myriad religious groups in America have lined up into two coalitions on the Left and Right. Many political issues are not obviously liberal or conservative, and many religious constituencies (e.g., Catholics and African American Protestants) hold positions that do not fit neatly into either ideological group. However, political party activists have spent significant sums trying to attract religious citizens, and seeking to build distrust between the two camps.

Today, however, there appear to be more voices from the religious center, reasserting the importance of prophetic critiques of political parties and the state. Moreover, the Christian Right appears to be in disarray, and a new generation of evangelical leaders appears eager to work with moderates, and even with liberals, when issue agendas overlap. Thus, it is possible that a growing moderation will serve to transform the debate.

QUESTIONS FOR FUTURE RESEARCH

There are many possible questions for fruitful research about the Christian Right and religious Left. Here we point to a few related questions that might prove productive for future scholars. First, there is fruitful conceptual work still to be done. One possibility is to consider how the Christian Right has influenced the Republican Party and in turn has been influenced by it. Clearly, the Christian Right has changed the Republican Party and provided resources for certain types of candidates, but it is almost certain that Republican resources helped to mold the contours of the movement in a more accommodating, and more partisan, direction. If partisans helped to shape the movement, then it is worth considering whether the movement has influenced the way religion is experienced in churches that have supported it. Although political scientists have focused most of their attention on how religion influences politics, politics in turn influences religion. During the 1980s, for example, many Ohio churches were deeply divided by Christian Right mobilization, and during the past few years several prominent activist pastors have stepped back from political involvement.

When considering the religious Left, it is worth pondering why we expect a movement that would be the mirror opposite of the Christian Right. The Christian Right during the 1980s differed from many earlier social movements in its focus on electoral politics and a broad issue agenda. Could not the religious Left have a more limited agenda, or focus more on local mobilization? Moreover, instead of focusing on potential supporters of a movement to counter the Christian Right, it might be more profitable to theorize about the circumstances under which a religious Left might emerge. However unlikely such a movement may seem, it was equally implausible during the 1960s to imagine the Christian Right some 20 years later. So what political, social, and religious conditions would be needed to foster a broader religious Left? And if partisan politics becomes less polarized, or if younger evangelicals seek more moderate policies, could Christian Right mobilization decline?

Some older questions about the rise of the Christian Right still await definitive answers. Although there have been scores of studies about who supports the Christian Right, there is still no definitive test to reject past theories that the movement attracts those with dogmatic or authoritarian personalities, or those who are nonrational in their political support. Likewise, there may be substantial numbers of "true believers" within the religious Left. A definitive test would require a comparison of those who choose to join such organizations with those in a similar religious and social environment who choose not to join. Moreover, the impact of the Christian Right on elections has not been estimated with much precision. Copies of Christian Coalition voter guides are archived at various locations, and information about the number distributed in various states (and sometimes in congressional districts) is available, making more precise work possible. Similar kinds of studies have been completed on labor mobilization (Jacobson 1999).

There are a number of newer questions to be answered as well. Although there is a great deal of descriptive information on the Christian Right electoral activity at the state level, there is far less research on the policy impact that the Christian Right has had there. Here researchers would need to take into account state political institutions, political parties, and the ecology of supporting and opposing interest groups.

Another important research question is the extent to which the Christian Right has expanded the civic capacities of members. The Christian Coalition did make some effort to train their members in the norms of compromise and civility (Rozell and Wilcox 1995). And, recently some scholars (e.g., Shields 2007) have argued that the Christian Right generally produced tolerant activists. Yet, other studies show that Christian Right activists have low levels of tolerance and are more likely to fear and dislike their political opponents than those outside its ranks.

In a related vein, is it possible that the training of activists led to increased tolerance, whereas direct mail solicitations for money to less active members pushed them in the opposite direction? Yet, there is little empirical evidence to assess the democratic effects of the movement on its members and target constituency. It is, of course, important to consider the baseline: Christian Right activists come from a population that is less tolerant and less oriented to compromise than other Americans. So how, then, does movement involvement change them? To sort this out, longitudinal data on members and nonmembers are needed. Without longitudinal data, studies might focus on long-time versus new members, and also on those who attend meetings at least occasionally compared with those who only receive direct mail and contribute money to the organizations. Such results have important implications for democratic theory, because the impact of groups on individual capacities and on collective processes remains controversial (Rosenblum 1998; M.E. Warren 2001).

Similar questions about the possible mobilization of a religious Left might bear even greater fruit, because recently considerable resources have been invested by political actors trying to jump-start the movement. One could gather data before such a movement gathers shape, and then with panel data track who joins movement groups, and why. It is even possible that some disaffected religious liberals might be drawn back to organized religious activity if churches began to articulate clearer messages on issues that liberals care about. In addition, studies of the religious Left need to move beyond the interesting and careful case studies of community mobilization into more systematic comparison of communities and cases. This would enable us to develop theories better about when and where mobilization occurs, and whether it is effective.

Finally, future research on the religious center might be especially useful, as Catholics emerge as swing voters and new moderate voices are amplified among white evangelicals. Although the recent polarization of American politics may have led many to expect religious groups to polarize as well, there are in fact many Christians and other religious citizens who do not neatly fit into the Left or Right. Such voters merit our attention.

NOTES

1. Nevertheless, although religion was a source of movement mobilization, it was also in each case a source of opposition to the movement. For example, white churches in the South defended slavery and segregation, conservative churches opposed suffrage and feminism, and Catholics opposed the temperance movement.

2. Similar claims could likely be made for Judaism, Islam, and other religions.

3. For example, abolitionists argued that slavery was contrary to the laws of God; suffragettes argued that allowing women to vote would help marshal religious purity of women into politics; and civil rights activists could argue that God made all people in His image, so that racism was an evil doctrine that violated God's will.

4. For example, in one fundraising letter, Pat Robertson, then head of the Christian Coalition, warned that the feminist movement was a "socialist, anti-family political movement that encourages women to leave their husbands, kill their children, practice witchcraft, destroy capitalism and become lesbians."

5. A JSTOR search in October 2007 revealed nearly 75 articles with the phrases *Christian Right* or *religious Right*, or the names of major movement organizations in the title, and nearly 2000 articles with the mention of these terms in the text. The Christian Right has been the subject of more than 65 doctoral dissertations during this period, and scores of scholarly books.

6. Although the argument that the Christian Right is simply a religious movement is unconvincing, it does remind us of the important theological elements of the Christian Right. Earlier waves of Christian Right mobilization followed major theological ferment (Wilcox 1992a), and drew resources from parachurch organizations such as the World Christian Fundamentals Association in the 1920s and the American Council of Christian Churches in the 1950s (Furniss 1963). During the late 1970s, the movement was initially mobilized among fundamentalist denominations, then later among Pentecostals and other evangelical groups facing challenges of religious particularism (Guth 1983b; Jelen 1991; Green 1996). Similarly, many journalists and a few scholars confuse the Christian Right with the religious ministries or business enterprises of Christian Right leaders. Because Pat Robertson and the late Jerry Falwell both had television shows, and James Dobson has a widely distributed radio program, some have included their media broadcasts as part of the Christian Right (Kintz and Lesage 1998; Apostolidi 2000). However, Falwell's television program was essentially a broadcast of his sermons at the Liberty Baptist Church, and Dobson's radio program is more frequently focused on advice to parents than on politics. Christian schools and universities may well educate children in values consistent with the Christian Right position, but Liberty Baptist University (founded by Jerry Falwell) is distinct from the movement itself (Robinson and Wilcox 2005).

7. Thus, the Southern Baptist Convention has many members who support the Christian Right, but the Southern Baptist Convention is itself a religious denomination and not part of the Christian Right. Moreover, the National Association of Evangelicals sometimes supports Christian Right positions, such as opposition to abortion and same-sex marriage, but it also takes positions against global warming and the use of torture in interrogations of prisoners, which are not part of the Christian Right agenda.

8. The wording in the exit polls has differed over time, making comparisons difficult.

9. However, the approach is useful in some circumstances. For example, one might conceive of Republican activists who support the Christian Right agenda as part of the movement, even if they currently belong to no social movement organizations (Wilcox 1992a).

10. Finally, some have studied the writings of movement leaders (Lienesch 1993), and the political actions of their elites and organizations (Wilcox 1988; Moen 1989; Deckman 2004). In these instances, the movement is defined from the top down, rather than the bottom up.

11. To suggest that these issues may serve as symbolic issues is not to deny that there are important moral or substantive concerns related to such issues.

12. Thus, debates about abortion may entail a broader concern with the breakdown of families, and discussion of Christian schools may come to encapsulate worries about lawlessness and social disintegration.

13. Social movement accounts have also focused on the entrepreneurs who assembled Christian Right groups, and the various resources they are able to bring to bear (Guth 1983a; Liebman 1983; Brown, Powell, and Wilcox 1995; Martin 1996). Less attention has been paid to the "changing of the guard" in the Christian Right, with the gradual replacement of televangelists with political actors (Lindsay 2007). Some of these new entrepreneurs, however, appear to be outside the boundaries of the Christian Right.

14. It is clear that the Moral Majority and, to a lesser extent, other Christian Right groups were active in some states such as North Carolina and Virginia (Rozell and Wilcox 1996).

15. This is possible because voter guides are archived at various locations, and the Christian Coalition partially disclosed the number of guides that they claimed to have distributed to the Federal Election Commission. For an example of how this type of analysis might work, see Jacobson (1999).

16. In the 2004 election, some studies focused on contacting voters in relationship to the same-sex marriage issue in the 2004 election (Monson and Oliphant 2007), but this was done more by the Republican National Committee than by Christian Right groups.

17. Most writing on this type of activity has documented case studies.

18. The civil rights movement not only ended legal barriers for African Americans to use public facilities, live wherever they wanted, and attend public schools and universities, it also transformed the way we think and talk about race in the United States. Similarly, the feminist movement not only ended legal barriers for women's advancement in education and business, it also changed attitudes on women's roles and the acceptability of various types of conduct, language, and humor.

19. Indeed, clearly a complex blend of religious, cultural, nationalist, and race appeals have been used by Republican candidates to target the same voting bloc.

20. The reported decline in the number of abortions during the past decade may be a function of other factors, such as a decline in the number of doctors who are willing to perform abortions.

21. The designation *religious Left* is used rather than *Christian Left* because its supporters are drawn from a much greater diversity of religious groups, many of whom are outside the Christian faith.

22. A JSTOR search shows only two articles with *Christian Left* or *religious Left* in the title, and only 100 that mention the terms even in passing in the body of the study.

23. However, some scholars have argued that progressive theological views are an essential element to identifying any existing or potential religious Left, as discussed later.

24. This pro-life, but otherwise progressive, package is similar to that of liberal evangelicals such as the Sojourners, and the now defunct JustLife PAC (Bendyna 1994). Although some on the Left might insist that pro-choice policies are a prerequisite for any label such as *Left* or *progressive*, others would argue that a pro-life position is, in fact, consistent with other progressive positions (Conover 1988; Shield 2007). A similar problem arises when considering Feminists for Life, a pro-life feminist organization.

25. Groups like the Industrial Areas Foundation include religious and nonreligious progressives in broad networks of activism. Bread for the World is an ecumenical organization that focuses on hunger (Guth et al. 1995). The National Council of Churches is a coalition of religious bodies that endorses progressive politics.

26. Jesse Jackson, however, might be considered a Christian Left candidate in the 1980s. There have been no focused studies of his donors (but see Brown, Powell, and Wilcox 1995).

27. One observer invites us to "consider the attacks on the evils of monopoly, corrupt municipal government and slum housing; the concern for the welfare of the immigrant, the Indian, the Negro, and the indigent native-born; the new solicitude for children displayed in efforts to establish playgrounds, kindergartens, and juvenile courts, to promote progressive schools and visiting nurse's associations, and to secure passage of laws outlawing child labor and regulating the employment of women" (Smith 1960, p. 15).

28. For example, among the core of the Christian Right, 92 percent believe in an inerrant or literal Bible, and 91 percent think that Jesus is the only path to salvation.

29. For example, among the religious Left core, only 33 percent think that the Bible is inerrant or literally true, whereas only 45 percent believe that Jesus is the only path to salvation.

30. Moreover, although there is considerable support for congregational activism within white mainline Protestant churches, their members are also more likely to favor a high wall of separation between church and state (Olson 2007c).

REFERENCES

Aho, James Alfred. 1990. *The Politics of Righteousness: Idaho Christian Patriotism.* Seattle, Wash.: University of Washington Press.

Alpert, Rebecca T., ed. 2000. *Voices of the Religious Left: A Contemporary Sourcebook.* Philadelphia, Pa.: Temple University Press.

Apostolidis, Paul. 2000. *Stations of the Cross: Adorno and Christian Right Radio.* Durham N.C.: Duke University Press.

Baer, Denise L., and David A. Bositis. 1988. *Elite Cadres and Party Coalitions: Representing the Public in Party Politics.* New York: Greenwood Press.

Barkun, Michael. 1994. *Religion and the Racist Right: The Origins of the Christian Identity Movement.* Chapel Hill, N. C.: University of North Carolina Press.

Bates, Stephen. 1993. *Battleground: One Mother's Crusade, the Religious Right, and the Struggle for Control of Our Classrooms.* New York: Poseidon Press.

Bendyna, Mary E. 1994. "JustLife Action." In *Risky Business: PAC Decisionmaking in Congressional Elections*, ed. Robert Biersack, Paul S. Herrnson, and Clyde Wilcox, 195–202. Armonk, N.Y.: M. E. Sharpe.

Bendyna, Mary E. 2000. "The Catholic Ethic in American Politics: Evidence from Survey Research." Unpublished Doctoral Dissertation, Washington, D.C.: Georgetown University.

Bendyna, Mary E., and Clyde Wilcox. 1997. "The Christian Right Old and New: A Comparison of the Moral Majority and the Christian Coalition." In Corwin E. Smidt and James M. Penning (eds.) *Sojourners in the Wilderness, the Christian Right in Comparative Perspective.* Lanham, MD: Rowman & Littlefield.

Bendyna, Mary, John C. Green, Mark J. Rozell, and Clyde Wilcox. 2000. "Catholics and the Christian Right: A View from Four States." *Journal for the Scientific Study of Religion* 39: 321–332.

Bendyna, Mary E. R. S. M., John C. Green, Mark J. Rozell, and Clyde Wilcox. 2001. "Uneasy Alliance: Conservative Catholics and the Christian Right." *Sociology of Religion* 62: 51–64.

Berkowitz, Laura, and John C. Green. 1997. "Charting the Coalition: The Local Chapters of the Ohio Christian Coalition." In Corwin E. Smidt and James M. Penning (eds.) *Sojourners in the Wilderness: The Christian Right in Comparative Perspective.* Lanham, MD: Rowman & Littlefield.

Boston, Robert. 2000. *Close Encounters with the Religious Right: Journeys into the Twilight Zone of Religion and Politics.* Amherst, N.Y.: Prometheus.

Brown, Clifford W., Lynda W. Powell, and Clyde Wilcox. 1995. *Serious Money: Fundraising and Contributing in Presidential Nomination Campaigns.* New York: Cambridge University Press.

Brown, Steven P. 2004. *Trumping Religion: The New Christian Right, the Free Speech Clause, and the Courts.* Tuscaloosa, Ala.: University of Alabama Press.

Bruce, John M. 1995. "Texas: The Emergence of the Christian Right." In *God at the Grassroots: The Christian Right in the 1994 Elections,* ed. Mark J. Rozell and Clyde Wilcox, 109–132, Lanham, Md.: Rowman & Littlefield.

Bruce, Steve. 1988. *The Rise and Fall of the New Christian Right.* Oxford: Clarendon Press.

Buell, Emmett, and Lee Sigelman. 1985. "An Army That Meets Every Sunday? Popular Support for the Moral Majority in 1980." *Social Science Quarterly* 66: 426–434.

Campbell, David E. 2006. "Religious 'Threat' in Contemporary Presidential Elections." *Journal of Politics* 68: 104–115.

Cleary, Edward L., and Allen D. Hertzke. 2006. *Representing God at the Statehouse: Religion and Politics in the American States.* Lanham, Md.: Rowman & Littlefield.

Conover, Pamela Johnston. 1988. "Feminists and the Gender Gap." *The Journal of Politics* 50: 985–1010.

Conover, Pamela Johnston, and Virginia Gray. 1983. *Feminism and the New Right: Conflict over the American Family.* New York: Praeger.

Cook, Elizabeth Adell. 1989. "Measuring Feminist Consciousness." *Women & Politics* 9: 71–88.

Deckman, Melissa M. 2004. *School Board Battles: The Christian Right in Local Politics,* Washington, D.C.: Georgetown University Press.

Djupe, Paul A., and Christopher P. Gilbert. 2003. *The Prophetic Pulpit: Clergy, Churches, and Communities in American Politics.* Lanham, Md.: Rowman & Littlefield.

Elms, Alan. 1969. "Psychological Factors in Right-Wing Extremism." In *The American Right Wing,* ed. Robert Schoenberger, 143–163, New York: Holt, Rinehart and Winston.

Francia, Peter L. 2003. *The Financiers of Congressional Elections: Investors, Ideologues, and Intimates.* New York: Columbia University Press.

Fried, Amy. 1988. "Abortion as Symbolic Politics: An Investigation of a Belief System." *Social Science Quarterly* 69: 137–154.

Friedland, Michael B. 1998. *Lift up Your Voice Like a Trumpet: White Clergy and the Civil Rights and Anti-War Movements, 1954–1973,* Chapel Hill, N.C.: University of North Carolina Press.

Furniss, Norman. 1963. *The Fundamentalist Controversy, 1918–1931.* Hamden, CT: Archon Books.

Gilbert, Christopher P., and David A. Peterson. 1995. "Minnesota: Christians and Quistians in the GOP." In *God at the Grassroots: The Christian Right in the 1994 Elections,* ed. Mark J. Rozell and Clyde Wilcox, 169–190, Lanham, Md.: Rowman & Littlefield.

Gormley, William T., and Helen Cymrot. 2006. "The Strategic Choices of Child Advocacy Groups." *Nonprofit and Voluntary Sector Quarterly* 35: 102–122.

Green, John C. 1996. "A Look at the 'Invisible Army': Pat Robertson's 1988 Activist Corps." In *Religion and the Culture Wars: Dispatches from the Front*. ed. John C. Green, James L. Guth, Corwin E. Smidt, and Lyman A. Kellstedt, 44–61. Lanham, Md.: Rowman & Littlefield.

Green, John C., and Nathan S. Bigelow. 2005. "The Christian Right Goes to Washington: Social Movement Resources and the Legislative Process." In *The Interest Group Connection: Electioneering, Lobbying, and Policymaking in Washington*. 2nd ed., ed. Paul S. Herrnson, Ronald G. Shaiko, and Clyde Wilcox, 189–211. Washington, D.C.: CQ Press.

Green, John C., and James L. Guth. 1988. "The Christian Right in the Republican Party: The Case of Pat Robertson's Supporters." *The Journal of Politics* 50: 150–165.

Green, John C., James L. Guth, and Kevin Hill. 1993. "Faith and Election: The Christian Right in Congressional Campaigns 1978–1988." *The Journal of Politics* 55: 80–91.

Green, John C., James L. Guth, Lyman A. Kellstedt, and Corwin E. Smidt. 1994. "Uncivil Challenges? Support for Civil Liberties among Religious Activists." *The Journal of Political Science* 22: 25–49.

Green, John C., James L. Guth, and Clyde Wilcox. 1998. "Less Than Conquerors: The Christian Right in State Republican Parties." In *Social Movements and American Political Institutions*, ed. Anne N. Costain and Andrew S. McFarland, 117–135. Lanham, Md.: Rowman & Littlefield.

Green, John C., Mark J. Rozell, and Clyde Wilcox. 2001. "Social Movements and Party Politics: The Case of the Christian Right." *Journal for the Scientific Study of Religion* 40: 413–426.

Green, John C., Mark J. Rozell, and Clyde Wilcox. 2003. *The Christian Right in American Politics: Marching to the Millennium*. Washington, D.C.: Georgetown University Press.

Green, John C., Mark J. Rozell, and Clyde Wilcox. 2006. *The Values Campaign?: The Christian Right and the 2004 Elections*. Washington, D.C.: Georgetown University Press.

Gusfield, Joseph R. 1963. *Symbolic Crusade: Status Politics and the American Temperance Movement*. Urbana, Ill.: University of Illinois Press.

Guth, James L. 1983a. "The New Christian Right." In *The New Christian Right: Mobilization and Legitimation*, ed. Robert C. Liebman and Robert Wuthnow, 31–49. New York: Aldine Publishing.

Guth, James L. 1983b. "The Politics of Preachers: Southern Baptist Ministers and Christian Right Activism." In *New Christian Politics*, ed. David C. Bromley and Anson Shupe, 235–250. Macon, Ga.: Mercer University Press.

Guth, James L., and John C. Green. 1991. "An Ideology of Rights: Support for Civil Liberties among Political Activists." *Political Behavior* 13: 321–344.

Guth, James L., John C. Green, Lyman A. Kellstedt, and Corwin E. Smidt. 1995. "Onward Christian Soldiers: Religious Activist Groups in American Politics." In *Interest Group Politics*. 4th ed., ed. Burdette A. Loomis and Allan J. Cigler, 55–76. Washington, D.C.: CQ Press.

Guth, James L., Lyman A. Kellstedt, John C. Green, and Corwin E. Smidt. 2007. "Getting the Spirit? Religion and Partisan Mobilization in the 2004 Elections." In *Interest Group Politics*. 7th ed., ed. Allan Cigler and Burdett Loomis, 157–181. Washington, D.C.: CQ Press.

Guth, James L., and Oran P. Smith. 1997. "South Carolina Christian Right: Just Part of the Family Now?" In *God at the Grassroots 1996: The Christian Right in the 1996 Elections*, ed. Mark J. Rozell and Clyde Wilcox, 15–32. Lanham, Md.: Rowman & Littlefield.

Hacker, Hans J. 2005. *The Culture of Conservative Christian Litigation.* Lanham, Md.: Rowman & Littlefield.

Hadden, Jeffrey K. 1970. "Clergy Involvement in Civil Rights." *Annals of the American Academy of Political and Social Science* 387: 118–127.

Hall, Charles F. 1997. "The Christian Left: Who Are They and How Are They Different from the Christian Right?" *Review of Religious Research* 39: 27–45.

Harris, Fredrick C. 1999. *Something Within: Religion in African-American Activism.* New York: Oxford University Press.

Hedges, Chris. 2006. *American Fascists: The Christian Right and the War on America.* New York: Free Press.

Hertzke, Allen D. 1993. *Echoes of Discontent: Jesse Jackson, Pat Robertson, and the Resurgence of Populism.* Washington, D.C.: CQ Press.

Hofstadter, Richard. 1965. *The Paranoid Style in American Politics: And Other Essays.* New York: Knopf.

Hout, Michael, and Claude S. Fisher. 2002. "Why More Americans Have No Religious Preference: Politics and Generations." *American Sociological Review* 67: 165–190.

Jacobson, Gary C. 1999. "The Effect of the AFL-CIO's 'Voter Education' Campaigns on the 1996 House Elections." *The Journal of Politics* 61: 185–194.

Jelen, Ted G. 1991. *The Political Mobilization of Religious Beliefs.* New York: Praeger.

Jelen, Ted G. 1992. "Political Christianity: A Contextual Analysis." *American Journal of Political Science* 36: 692–714.

Jelen, Ted G. 1993a. "The Political Consequences of Religious Group Attitudes." *The Journal of Politics* 55: 178–190.

Jelen, Ted G. 1993b. *The Political World of the Clergy.* New York: Praeger.

Johnson, Stephen D., and Joseph B. Tamney. 1984. "Support for the Moral Majority: A Test of a Model." *Journal for the Scientific Study of Religion* 23: 183–196.

Kaplan, Esther. 2004. *With God on Their Side: How Christian Fundamentalists Trampled Science, Policy, and Democracy in George W. Bush's White House.* New York: The New Press.

Kazin, Michael. 2006. *A Godly Hero: The Life of William Jennings Bryan.* New York: Knopf.

Kellstedt, Lyman, 1988. "The Falwell Issue Agenda: Sources of Support among White Protestant Evangelicals," In *Research in the Social Scientific Study of Religion*, ed. Monty Lynn and David Moberg, 109–132. Westport, Conn.: JAI Press.

Kellstedt, Lyman A., Corwin E. Smidt, John C. Green, and James L. Guth. 2007. "A Gentle Stream or a 'River Glorious'? The Religious Left in the 2004 Election." In *A Matter of Faith: Religion in the 2004 Presidential Election*, ed. David E. Campbell, 232–258. Washington, D.C.: Brookings.

Kelly, James R. 1999. "Sociology and Public Theology: A Case Study of Pro-Choice/Pro-Life Common Ground." *Sociology of Religion* 60: 99–124.

Kintz, Linda, and Julia Lesage. 1998. *Media, Culture, and the Religious Right.* Minneapolis, Minn.: University of Minnesota Press.

Klein, Ethel. 1984. *Gender Politics: From Consciousness to Mass Politics.* Cambridge: Harvard University Press.

Layman, Geoffrey C. 1997. "Religion and Political Behavior in the United States: The Impact of Beliefs, Affiliations, and Commitment from 1980 to 1994." *The Public Opinion Quarterly* 61: 288–316.

Layman, Geoffrey. 2001. *The Great Divide: Religious and Cultural Conflict in American Party Politics.* New York: Columbia University Press.

Layman, Geoffrey C., and Thomas M. Carsey. 2002. "Party Polarization and 'Conflict Extension' in the American Electorate." *American Journal of Political Science* 46: 786–802.

Leege, David C. 1992. "Coalitions, Cues, Strategic Politics, and the Staying Power of the Religious Right, or Why Political Scientists Ought to Pay Attention to Cultural Politics." *PS: Political Science and Politics* 25: 198–204.

Leege, David C., Kenneth D. Wald, Brian S. Krueger, and Paul D. Mueller. 2002. *The Politics of Cultural Differences: Social Change and Voter Mobilization Strategies in the Post-New Deal Period.* Princeton, N.J.: Princeton University Press.

Liebman, Robert C. 1983. "Mobilizing the Moral Majority." In *The New Christian Right: Mobilization and Legitimation,* ed. Robert C. Liebman and Robert Wuthnow, 50–74. New York: Aldine Publishing.

Liebman, Robert C., and Robert Wuthnow. 1983. *The New Christian Right: Mobilization and Legitimation.* New York: Aldine.

Lienesch, Michael. 1993. *Redeeming America: Piety and Politics in the New Christian Right.* Chapel Hill, N.C.: University of North Carolina Press.

Lindsay, D. Michael. 2007. *Faith in the Halls of Power: How Evangelicals Joined the American Elite.* New York: Oxford University Press.

Lorentzen, Louise. 1980. "Evangelical Life Style Concerns Expressed as Political Action." *Sociological Analysis* 41: 144–154.

Lunch, William M. 1995. "Oregon: Identity Politics in the Northeast." In *God at the Grassroots: The Christian Right in the 1994 Election,* ed. Mark J. Rozell and Clyde Wilcox, 227–252. Lanham, Md.: Rowman & Littlefield.

Marsden, George M. 2006. *Fundamentalism and American Culture,* New York: Oxford University Press.

Martin, William. 1996. *With God on Our Side: The Rise of the Religious Right in America,* New York: Broadway Books.

Marty, Martin. 1999. "Who Is the Religious Left?" *Sightings,* April 30, 1999.

Marwell, Gerald, and N. J. Demerath III. 2003. "'Secularization' By Any Other Name." *American Sociological Review* 68: 314–316.

McAdam, Doug. 1999. *Political Processes and the Development of Black Insurgency, 1930–1970,* Chicago, Ill.: University of Chicago Press.

Miller, Arthur H., Patricia Gurin, Gerald Gurin, and Oksana Malanchuk, 1981. "Group Consciousness and Political Participation." *American Journal of Political Science* 3: 494–511.

Mitchell, Joshua. 2007. "Religion Is Not a Preference." *Journal of Politics* 69: 349–360.

Moen, Matthew C. 1989. *The Christian Right and Congress.* Tuscaloosa, Ala.: University of Alabama Press.

Monson, J. Quinn, and J. Baxter Oliphant. 2007. "Microtargeting and the Instrumental Mobilization of Religious Conservatives." In *A Matter of Faith: Religion in the 2004 Presidential Election,* ed. David E. Campbell, 95–119. Washington, D.C.: Brookings.

Mueller, Carol McClurg. 1992. "Building Social Movement Theory." In *Frontiers in Social Movement Theory,* ed. Aldon D. Morris and Carol McClurg Mueller, 3–27. New Haven, Conn.: Yale University Press.

Oldfield, Duane M. 1996. *The Right and the Righteous: The Christian Right Confronts the Republican Party,* Lanham, Md.: Rowman & Littlefield.

Olson, Laura R. 2006. "Mapping the Protestant Left at the Elite Level: Interest Groups and Social Movement Organizations." Presented at the annual meeting of the Society for the Scientific Study of Religion, Portland, Oregon, October.

Olson, Laura R. 2007a. "Characterizing the Protestant Left at the Mass Level." Presented at the annual meeting of the Southern Political Science Association, New Orleans, Louisiana, January.

Olson, Laura R. 2007b. "Is There a Protestant Left on the Ground? Grassroots Issues and Ideologies." Presented at the annual meeting of the Midwest Political Science Association, Chicago, Illinois, April.

Olson, Laura R. 2007c. "Whither the Religious Left? Religiopolitical Progressivism in Twenty-First Century America." In *From Pews to Polling Places: Faith and Politics in the American Religious Mosaic*, ed. J. Matthew Wilson, 53–80. Washington D.C.: Georgetown University Press.

Owen, Dennis E., Kenneth D. Wald, and Samuel S. Hill. 1991. "Authoritarian or Authority-Minded? The Cognitive Commitments of Fundamentalists and the Christian Right." *Religion and American Culture* 1: 73–100.

Ribuffo, Leo P. 1983. *The Old Christian Right: The Protestant Far Right from the Great Depression to the Cold War*, Philadelphia, Pa.: Temple University Press.

Robinson, Carin. 2006. "From Every Tribe and Nation? Blacks and the Christian Right." *Social Science Quarterly* 87: 591–601.

Robinson, Carin. 2008. "Doctrine, Discussion and Disagreement: Evangelical and Catholics Together in American Politics." Unpublished doctoral dissertation, Washington, D.C.: Georgetown University.

Robinson, Carin, and Clyde Wilcox. 2005. "Sowing on Rocky Soil: The Christian Right and College Students." Presented at the *In University of Maryland Symposium on Citizen Mobilization in Education.*

Roelofs, H. Mark. 1988. "Liberation Theology: The Recovery of Biblical Radicalism." *The American Political Science Review* 82: 549–566.

Rohter, Ira. 1969. "Social Psychological Determinants of Radical Rightism." In *The American Right Wing*, ed. Robert Schoenberger, 193–238. New York: Holt, Rinehart and Winston.

Rosenblum, Nancy. 1998. *Membership and Morals: The Personal Uses of Pluralism in America*, Princeton, NJ: Princeton University Press.

Rozell, Mark J. 2002. "The Christian Right in the 2000 GOP Presidential Campaign." In *Piety, Politics, and Pluralism: Religion, the Courts, and the 2000 Election*, ed. Mary C. Segers, 57–74, Lanham, Md.: Rowman & Littlefield.

Rozell, Mark J., and Clyde Wilcox. 1995. *God at the Grass Roots: The Christian Right in the 1994 Elections*, Lanham, Md.: Rowman & Littlefield.

Rozell, Mark J., and Clyde Wilcox. 1996. *Second Coming: The New Christian Right in Virginia Politics*, Baltimore, Md.: Johns Hopkins University Press.

Schwartz, Mildred A. 2006. *Party Movements in the United States and Canada: Strategies of Persistence*, Lanham, Md.: Rowman & Littlefield Publishers.

Shaw, Todd C., and Eric L. McDaniel. 2007. "'Whosoever Will': Black Theology, Homosexuality, and the Black Political Church." *National Political Science Review* 11: 137–155.

Shields, Jon A. 2007. "Between Passion and Deliberation: The Christian Right and Democratic Ideals." *Political Science Quarterly* 12: 89–113.

Sigelman, Lee. 1991. "'If You Prick Us, Do We Not Bleed? If You Tickle Us, Do We Not Laugh?' Jews and Pocketbook Voting." *Journal of Politics* 53: 977–992.

Sigelman, Lee, and Stanley Presser. 1988. "Measuring Public Support for the New Christian Right: The Perils of Point Estimation." *The Public Opinion Quarterly* 52: 325–337.

Simpson, John. 1984. "Support for the Moral Majority and Its Sociomoral Platform." In
    New Christian Politics, ed. David Bromley and Anson Shupe, 65–68. Macon, Ga.:
    Mercer University Press.
Smidt, Corwin. 1988a. "Evangelicals within Contemporary American Politics:
    Differentiating between Fundamentalist and Non-Fundamentalist Evangelicals." *The
    Western Political Quarterly* 41: 601–620.
Smidt, Corwin E. 1988b. "The Mobilization of Evangelical Voters in 1980: An Initial Test of
    Several Hypotheses." *Southeastern Political Review* 16: 3–33.
Smidt, Corwin E. 1989. "'Praise the Lord' Politics: A Comparative Analysis of the Social
    Characteristics and Political Views of American Evangelical and Charismatic
    Christians." *Sociological Analysis* 50: 53–72.
Smidt, Corwin E. 2007. "Evangelical and Mainline Protestants at the Turn of the
    Millennium: Taking Stock and Looking Forward." In *From Pews to Polling Places: Faith
    and Politics in the American Religious Mosaic*, ed. J. Matthew Wilson, 29–54,
    Washington, D.C.: Georgetown University Press.
Smidt, Corwin E., and James M. Penning. 1991. "Religious Self-Identifications and Support
    for Robertson: An Analysis of Delegates to the 1988 Michigan Republican State
    Convention." *Review of Religious Research* 32: 321–336.
Smith, Timothy L. 1960. "Historic Waves of Religious Interest in America." *Annals of the
    American Academy of Political and Social Science* 332: 9–19.
Smith, Rogers. Forthcoming. "An Almost Christian Nation: Constitutional Consequences
    of the Rise of Christian Conservatism." In *Evangelicals and American Democracy,
    vol. 1: Religion and Society*, ed. Steven Brint and Jean Reith Schroedel. New York: Russell
    Sage Foundation Press.
Tamney, Joseph, and Stephen Johnson. 1988. "Explaining Support for the Moral Majority."
    Sociological Forum 3: 234–255.
Tarrow, Sidney. 1994. *Power in Movement: Social Movements, Collective Action, and Politics*,
    New York: Cambridge University Press.
Thomas, Sue, and Clyde Wilcox. 1992. "Religion and Feminist Attitudes among African-
    American Women: A View from the Nation's Capitol." *Women & Politics* 12: 19–40.
Tinder, Glenn E. 1989. *The Political Meaning of Christianity: An Interpretation*, Baton Rouge,
    La.: Louisiana State University Press.
Wald, Kenneth D., and Allison Calhoun-Brown. 2007. *Religion and Politics in the United
    States*. 5th ed. Lanham, Md.: Rowman & Littlefield.
Wald, Kenneth D., Dennis E. Owen, and Samuel S. Hill, Jr. 1989. "Evangelical Politics and
    Status Issues." *Journal for the Scientific Study of Religion* 28: 1–16.
Wald, Kenneth D., Adam L. Silverman, and Kevin Fridy. 2005. "Making Sense of Religion in
    Political Life." *Annual Review of Political Science* 8: 121–143.
Warren, Mark E. 1999. *Democracy and Trust*, Cambridge: Cambridge University Press.
Warren, Mark E. 2001. *Democracy and Association*, Princeton, N.J.: Princeton University
    Press.
Warren, Mark R. 2001. *Dry Bones Rattling: Community Building to Revitalize American
    Democracy*, Princeton, N.J.: Princeton University Press.
Wilcox, Clyde. 1986. "Evangelicals and Fundamentalists in the New Christian Right:
    Religious Differences in the Ohio Moral Majority." *Journal for the Scientific Study of
    Religion* 25: 355–363.
Wilcox, Clyde. 1987a. "America's Radical Right Revisited. A Comparison of the Activists
    in Christian Right Organizations from the 1960s and the 1980s." *Sociological Analysis*
    48: 46–57.

Wilcox, Clyde. 1987b. "Popular Backing for the Old Christian Right: Explaining Support for the Christian Anti-Communism Crusade." *Journal of Social History* 21: 117–132.

Wilcox, Clyde. 1987c. "Popular Support for the Moral Majority in 1980: A Second Look." *Social Science Quarterly* 68: 157–167.

Wilcox, Clyde. 1988. "Political Action Committees of the New Christian Right: A Longitudinal Analysis." *Journal for the Scientific Study of Religion* 27: 60–71.

Wilcox, Clyde. 1989. "Evangelicals and the Moral Majority." *Journal for the Scientific Study of Religion* 28: 400–414.

Wilcox, Clyde. 1990. "Blacks and the New Christian Right: Support for the Moral Majority and Pat Robertson among Washington, D.C. Blacks." *Review of Religious Research* 32: 43–55.

Wilcox, Clyde. 1991. "The New Christian Right and the Mobilization of the Evangelicals." In *Religion and Political Behavior in the United States*, ed. Ted G. Jelen, 139–156. New York: Praeger.

Wilcox, Clyde. 1992a. *God's Warriors: The Christian Right in Twentieth Century America*, Baltimore, Md.: Johns Hopkins University Press.

Wilcox, Clyde. 1992b. "Religion and the Preacher Vote in the South: Sources of Support for Jackson and Robertson in Southern Primaries." *Sociological Analysis* 53: 323–332.

Wilcox, Clyde. 2007. "Radical Dreams and Political Realities: Religion and Social Movements in the United States." In *Faith Based Radicalism: Christianity, Islam, and Judaism between Constructive Activism and Destructive Fanaticism*, ed. Christiane Timmerman, Dirk Hutesbaut, Sara Mels, Walter Nonneman, and Walter Van Herek, 233–254. New York: Peter Lang.

Wilcox, Clyde. Forthcoming. "Of Movements and Metaphors: The Co-Evolution of the Christian Right and the GOP." In *Evangelicals and American Democracy, vol. 1: Religion and Society*, ed. Steven Brint and Jean Reith Schroedel. New York: Russell Sage Foundation Press.

Wilcox, Clyde, Matthew DeBell, and Lee Sigelman. 1999. "The Second Coming of the New Christian Right: Patterns of Popular Support in 1984 and 1996." *Social Science Quarterly* 80: 181–192.

Wilcox, Clyde, and Leopoldo Gomez. 1990. "The Christian Right and the Pro-Life Movement: An Analysis of the Sources of Political Support." *Review of Religious Research* 31: 380–389.

Wilcox, Clyde, and Carin Larson. 2006. *Onward Christian Soldiers: The Christian Right in American Politics*, 3rd edition. Boulder, Colo.: Westview.

Wilcox, Clyde, Ted G. Jelen, and Sharon Linzey. 1995. "Rethinking the Reasonableness of the Religious Right." *Review of Religious Research* 36: 263–276.

Wilcox, Clyde, Mark J. Rozell, and Roland Gunn. 1996. "Religious Coalitions in the New Christian Right." *Social Science Quarterly* 77: 543–559.

Wilcox, W. Bradford. Forthcoming. "How Focused on the Family? Christian Conservatives, the Family, and Sexuality." In *Evangelicals and American Democracy, vol. 1: Religion and Society*, ed. Steven Brint and Jean Reith Schroedel. New York: Russell Sage Foundation Press.

Witko, Christopher. 2009. "Understanding Party-Organized Interest Relationships." *Polity Online*, http://www.palgrave-journals.com/polity/journal/vaop/ncurrent/pdf/p01200830a.pdf

Wolfinger, Raymond, Barbara Kaye Wolfinger, Kenneth Prewitt, and Sheilah Rosenhack. 1964. "America's Radical Right: Politics and Ideology." In *Ideology and Discontent*, ed. David Apter, 262–293, New York: Free Press.

Wood, Richard L. 2002. *Faith in Action: Religion, Race, and Democratic Organizing in America*, Chicago, Ill.: University of Chicago Press.

Wuthnow, Robert, and John Hyde Evans. 2002. *The Quiet Hand of God: Faith-Based Activism and the Public Role of Mainline Protestantism*, Berkeley, Calif.: University of California Press.

Zwier, Robert. 1982. *Born-Again Politics: The New Christian Right in America*, Downers Grove, Ill.: InterVarsity Press.

C H A P T E R 1 1

....

RELIGIOUS INTEREST GROUPS IN AMERICAN POLITICS

....

ALLEN HERTZKE

ALTHOUGH religious interest groups vary widely in organizational style, ideology, and focus, collectively they have engaged in the full range of political activities—lobbying legislatures and executive branch officials, mobilizing voters, molding public opinion, and litigating in the courts. This chapter will concentrate on organized efforts to shape public policy through legislative and executive lobbying, with some analysis of social movement mobilization. Other entries will examine religious voting behavior and judicial rulings, so I will generally skip these topics even though it must be noted in passing that the judiciary (Ivers 1992; den Dulk and Pickerill 2003; Hoover and den Dulk 2004) and elections (Guth, Kellstedt, Smidt, and Green 1998; Green 2007) are also targets of some groups. One advantage of my focus is that in contrast to the relatively narrow (although admittedly growing) band of religious groups that attempt to influence elections or shape judicial rulings, a much broader array of groups lobby at the national and, increasingly, state and local levels.

From the colonial era to the founding of the republic, religious interests have organized to petition government. Among the most crucial instances were pitched battles over state establishments and free expression, especially in the wake of independence. In Virginia, for example, Baptist groups and other dissenters lobbied for passage of Thomas Jefferson's statute of religious freedom in 1786, which helped set the stage for congressional passage of the First Amendment in 1789.

As the nation grew, church groups were periodically drawn into organized lobbying campaigns, from battles over Sunday mail delivery and dueling to the more momentous issues of Indian removal and slavery (Hofrenning 1998). After the Civil War, reports of rampant corruption in Indian agencies led churches to petition the administration of U. S. Grant for reform, which led to his policy of granting contracts to different denominations to operate government-funded programs on reservations. By far some of the most formidable church-based activism in American history involved the prohibition movement, with the legendary Anti-Saloon League gaining passage of the 18th Amendment in 1919, banning the sale of alcoholic beverages throughout the nation (Gusfield 1963; Odegard 1966; Szymanski 2003). Religious groups were also intensely involved in initiatives of the populist and progressive movements.

On the eve of World War II, selective service legislation sparked intense efforts by pacifist church denominations and mainline Protestant allies to provide generous conscientious objector provisions exempting those opposed to war from military service. These successful efforts demonstrated the potential clout of small churches with strong moral claims (Ebersole 1953, chap. 1). Indeed, in this and other instances, religious groups have often enjoyed greater success securing their religious rights through congressional lobbying than litigation (Fisher 2002).

In more recent times, black churches, especially organized by the Southern Christian Leadership Conference, mobilized the massive campaign for civil rights legislation (McAdam 1985), joined by groups of Jews, Catholics, and mainline Protestants. Central to the success of the landmark Civil Rights Act of 1964 was an orchestrated "Midwest strategy," which relied on bringing delegations of mainline Protestant clergy to Washington to lobby moderate Republicans—the crucial swing members of Congress (Findlay 1993). Buoyed by the success of civil rights protests, veterans in the black churches went on to lead the successful legislative campaign against apartheid in South Africa (Nnorom 2005).

For most of the nation's history, religious interest group activity was episodic, not institutionalized. With the 20th century, however, we see the increasing formation of permanent national offices (and, in a number of cases, state ones) by diverse religious groups. Among the most notable were the Methodists, who established a Washington office in 1916 and then erected the stately United Methodist Building across the street from the capitol in 1923. Initially established to serve as the nerve center for prohibition forces, it has become the hub of liberal Protestant lobbying today. Methodists were followed by the National Catholic Welfare Conference, precursor to the U.S. Catholic Conference, which set up its Washington shop in 1919. Others followed suit. Jewish groups formed to battle antisemitism; Quakers and Mennonites, to secure conscientious objector status in war; African American religionists, to secure civil rights; Baptists, to "watch the Catholics"; and evangelicals, to protect their broadcast ministries, among other reasons (Hertzke 1988).

From the start, leaders of religious interest groups have generally eschewed the term *lobbying* (with its unsavory connotations) and to this day often speak of themselves as *advocates*. On the issue of nomenclature, however, scholars continue to use the terms *lobbyists* or *lobbying*—without implying anything untoward about the enterprise—to depict the efforts by groups to shape legislative and executive decisions.

Some religious groups do hire actual registered lobbyists (and thus forfeit tax-exempt status). Most, however, operate as nonprofit tax-exempt organizations that, under Section 501(c)3 of the Internal Revenue Code, cannot devote a "substantial" part of their time and resources to actual lobbying (which is no problem for large organizations with multiple activities) and cannot endorse candidates or engage in partisan campaigning. Of course, church-based electoral mobilization also occurs, but often under the guise of voter education campaigns that attempt to circumvent Internal Revenue Service (IRS) guidelines. Both IRS and lobby registration guidelines are "sufficiently vague" that most groups can and do "legally avoid registration" (Weber 1982).

INTEREST GROUPS AND POLITICAL SCIENCE

Interest groups occupy an important position within the American political process, because they serve as one form of "intermediary" agents that exist between the mass public and elected officials. Interest groups are central to the political process in that they articulate policy concerns and lobby for those concerns. They differ from the mass public in that the latter tends to have only episodic interest in the day-to-day workings of government, so in their intermediary role, interest groups attempt to inform, and at times mobilize, the public. At the same time, interest groups have a vested interest in raising policy concerns for governmental consideration, and, as a result, they also inform and "pressure" elected officials. Elected officials, on the other hand, are concerned "about the electoral consequences of their acts" (Carmines and Stimson 1989, p. 108). As a result, elected officials tend to favor change only when they see it to be in their electoral interest. Hence, interest groups are the central "change agents" in American politics, pushing both the mass public and elected officials to back their positions.[1]

The religious interest group studies surveyed in this chapter anchor their work in broader political science theories of interest group formation, incentives to participation, lobby strategies, representation, and power. As we will see, such scholarship intersects this mainstream political science in a number of intriguing ways. So before delving into the religious terrain, it is instructive to summarize themes in the general interest group literature.

A central focus of scholarship on interest groups concerns their origins and maintenance (Walker 1983). David Truman's work (1951), which inaugurated modern interest group inquiry, suggested that disturbances in the economic or social spheres spark people to form interest groups that address their concerns and grievances. Interest groups then contest each other in a policy-making process characterized by compromise and accommodation (Dahl 1961). This essentially pluralist interpretation was challenged by Schattschneider (1960), who argued that an elite bias characterized the "pressure system," because poorer Americans lacked groups to represent them. From early on, consequently, the debate over group formation was intimately tied to the issue of representation: Are some voices not heard? What does this bode for democratic governance?

This linkage emerged most sharply with Mancur Olson's work (1965) on the collective action dilemma, which attacked Truman's underlying assumption that aggrieved citizens naturally form groups to represent their interests. Because people gain regardless of whether they contribute to a group seeking some collective benefit, Olson (1965) argued, it is rational for them to be "free riders." This temptation is greatest for the very constituencies—the poor and diffuse—who have the most to gain by government action. Thus, the interest group universe will be heavily skewed in favor of those with the greatest resources or the easiest means of group formation.

Olson's work (1965) sparked extensive inquiry into the ways groups may overcome the free rider problem. Salisbury (1969) proposed an exchange theory in which entrepreneurial group leaders offer some material, solidary, or expressive benefits to prospective members in exchange for their contribution. However, his later research showed the dominance of institutions that do not face the same maintenance problems as membership-based interest groups (Salisbury 1969). Thus, his work and that of others did not fundamentally challenge the sobering portrait of the pressure system—one dominated by well-heeled institutions (Salisbury 1984), moneyed interests (Hall and Wayman 1990), groups focused on narrow niche issues (Browne 1990), and professional occupations "at the expense of the poor, minorities, and diffuse, hard-to-organize constituencies" (Berry 1984, p. 66). The mobilization tilt toward the well-to-do and the well-educated remains a dominant strand of interest group findings (Baumgartner and Leech 1998, p. 169).

To be sure, a body of contrary scholarship contests or qualifies this elite theory, producing what has been described as a "neopluralist" perspective on organized interests (Lowery and Gray 2004). Neopluralists find the system more pluralistic than Olson predicted because patrons and foundations often back the work of public interest lobbies (Walker 1983; Nownes 1995; Imig and Berry 1996), rendering less problematic the free-rider problem. Relatively low startup costs and the spread of education and affluence also buoy the work of public-interest entrepreneurs (Nownes and Neeley 1996a). Moreover, purposive incentives, especially when vital interests or values are threatened, can be powerful enough to induce people to join a citizen lobby despite the free rider temptation (King and Walker 1992). And a flowering of liberal citizen groups on the eve of the new century led Berry (1999) to qualify his own earlier pessimism. Finally, even well-heeled lobbies operate in an environment of uncertainty and opposition, and ever-shifting contexts provide opportunities for citizen groups to make a difference (Lowery and Gray 2004).

This neopluralist perspective, however, does not dismiss enduring biases embedded in the lobby system. As Lowery and Gray (2004, p. 424) note, there are "glaring holes in the pluralist universe." More trenchant is the critique of public interest lobbies by Theda Skocpol (2003), who argues that the new generation of "checkbook" citizen organizations reflect the purposive values of mostly white upper middle-class individuals or patrons rather than the actual economic needs of the less well off (a prospect alluded to earlier by Nownes and Neeley [1996b]). A different kind of elite bias, in other words, remains a feature of the pressure system.

Oddly, interest group scholarship largely ignores religious organizations—the very groups that may have the motives and means of articulating the needs and aspirations of less elite Americans. To be sure, certain dynamics of religious advocacy conform to patterns found in the broader lobby universe. As we would expect, membership groups are more fragile than church institutions (Salisbury 1984) and depend on entrepreneurial leaders to form and stay afloat, just as exchange theory suggests (Salisbury 1969; Cigler 1991). However, unique features enable religious groups to enhance the genuine pluralism and representativeness of the lobby system. Religious interest groups, for example, can help represent less advantaged members of society by overcoming the free-rider problem through *transcendent* appeals, a possibility to which Olson (1965, p. 160) himself alluded. Moreover, the social capital generated in churches can uniquely aid in the formation of groups and social movements that represent less elite Americans (Wood 2002). Religious groups thus deserve more attention by mainstream political science.

INSTITUTIONAL GROWTH OF NATIONAL RELIGIOUS INTEREST GROUPS

The institutional growth of national religious interest groups can be charted by successive studies. By mid century, when Luke Eugene Ebersole (1951) published the first major account of church lobbying, there were some 16 groups with permanent Washington offices. With the advocacy explosion beginning during the 1960s (Berry 1984), the number and diversity of religious lobbies grew substantially (Adams 1970). Moreover, as federal spending and regulation reach into more areas of American life, religious interest groups have continued to proliferate, drawn by the magnetic force of Washington politics. By the mid 1990s, Weber and Jones (1994) documented more than a hundred religious organizations that attempted to shape national policy, most with permanent Washington offices. Today the figure is much higher, because, in addition to groups with permanent offices in Washington, many more religious interests, such as church colleges and hospitals, periodically petition the government by sending delegations to the nation's capital or by hiring lobbying firms on their behalf (Henriques and Lehren 2007). This kind of lobbying is aided by the revolution in travel and communication that provides access for more groups to the political and policy processes (an intriguing line of research would be the impact of the Internet on religious lobbying). Most recently, researchers at *The New York Times* identified some 413 religious institutions that lobbied Congress in 2005 (Henriques, personal communication, July 26, 2007). Groups have also proliferated at the state and local levels.

This growth means that the dizzying pluralism of American religion is increasingly represented in national politics, with constituencies feeding on each other. Because liberal Jews had Washington offices, the Orthodox felt the need to do the same; as mainline Lutherans operated in the center, their evangelical brethren from the Missouri Synod felt the need to articulate their alternative concerns, and so forth. Thus, today, a wide variety of religious advocates maintain permanent Washington offices. From competing Muslim groups to Tibetan Buddhists, Southern Baptists to Chinese Fulong Gong members, liberal Catholics to traditionalists, Iranian Bahais to persecuted Christians abroad, faith-based women's groups to ethnoreligious minorities, we see how diverse religious interests vie for influence in the political system. Religious groups, in other words, widen the genuine pluralism of the lobby system.

With the exception of such issues as tax exemption or earmarks, the agenda of religious groups is not focused on pecuniary self-interest so characteristic of the highly advantaged business lobbies (Baumgartner and Leech 1999). Thus, in the language of interest group scholarship, religious interest groups mostly seek "purposive" aims (Clark and Wilson 1961) rather than material self-interest. However, who or what do religious advocates actually represent? Member opinions? Religious values or traditions? Church hierarchies? The voiceless? What coalitions form, and are they permanent or shifting? And how effective are they? These are among the questions that have occupied contemporary scholars.

Representation

The first question has been the most enduring concern of scholars. Taking cues from political science scholarship about the potential oligarchical tendencies of group leadership (summarized by Hertzke 1988, pp. 14–15), scholars have probed the relationship between leaders and members. Ebersole (1951) suggested that in many cases religious lobbyists promoted causes favored by church leaders rather than the views of lay members, a theme echoed by Adams (1970) and Hero (1973). The gap between religious lobbyists and the laity took on more significance in focused studies of mainline Protestant organizations, the most numerous and prominent of religious lobbies during the 1960s and 1970s. Scholars found religious leaders, shaped by the civil rights and antiwar movements of the 1960s, significantly more liberal than denominational members. Quinley (1974) termed such leaders "prophetic clergy," because they see themselves operating out of the prophetic biblical tradition of speaking truth to power or representing the voiceless of society. The problem, as Hadden (1969) depicted it in an evocative book titled *The Gathering Storm in the Churches*, is that this prophetic lobbying produces an enormous gap between the very liberal Washington advocates and their much more moderate or conservative laity, a gap that not only could undermine the effectiveness of the lobbies, but calls into question their legitimacy.

While exploring this gap, Reichley (1985) systematically compared the views and stances of mainline lobbyists with public opinion data broken down by denomination. He found that although large majorities of Episcopalians, Methodists, Presbyterians, Lutherans, and American Baptists voted for Ronald Reagan in 1980, their lobbyists were universally critical of the Republican administration and sympathetic with the Democratic opposition. To explain this gap, Reichley (1985) argued that a "managerial revolution" had occurred in the mainline churches, in which those clergy and laity who populated the social ministries of the churches—and attended national conventions and passed policy resolutions—constituted an activist minority of liberals in the denominations, whereas moderates and conservatives tended to eschew political engagement.

Later studies both confirmed and refined this assessment. The continuing liberalism of mainline lobbies came out in their pacifist response to the Gulf War of 1991 (Murphy 1993). However, in addition to political ideology, mainline Protestant lobbies do represent theological traditions (as interpreted by denominational leaders) within the denomination (Kraus 2007; Tipton 2007). A large survey of mainline clergy, moreover, suggested that their varying support for national lobbies was dependent on their own politics and views about the general direction of the denomination (Djupe, Olson, and Gilbert 2005).

This brings us to *Representing God in Washington* (Hertzke 1988), which surveyed the activities of the full range of religious lobbies at the time—mainline Protestants, Catholics, Jews, evangelicals, and fundamentalists. Guided by previous studies, this work explored the theme of representation. Based on interviews of religious advocates, it found that who or what they represented varied from issue to issue and group to group. At times, certain groups (especially the mainline Protestants but also Jews and Catholics) operated in a prophetic mode representing the disadvantaged or "voiceless," including those from abroad. At other times, group leaders (especially Catholics and Jews) represented longstanding religious traditions. And, at still other times, lobbyists reflected lay sentiment (especially those dependent on actual member contributions, which included some evangelical and Christian fundamentalist groups). Finally, at some point, all defended institutional interests (tax exemptions, religious freedom, and so forth).

To gain insight into the collective impact of this complex portrait, Hertzke (1988) compared lay opinion on different issues with the lobby stands of religious lobbyists. What he found offered a qualification to earlier depictions of leaders being out of touch with members. Lobbyists were most effective on issues for which lay sentiment was either supportive or undefined, or for which they had information valuable to the legislative process (conditions at soup kitchens, the impact of foreign policy on the poor abroad, effects on church ministries). When lobbyists strayed too far from clear lay opinion, on the other hand, they tended to be discounted by members of Congress or got checked by opposing groups. In other words, the *context* of action determined how and when religious groups successfully advanced their issues. Moreover, the enormous pluralism and intense competition among religious groups, along with the need to generate grassroots pressure for effectiveness, further serve to mitigate the oligarchic tendencies in group leadership. Hertzke (1988) thus concluded that *collectively* the pluralist religious community in Washington acted as a modest counterweight to the elite bias of the "pressure system" so vividly depicted by Schattschneider (1960) and others, because the diverse groups did articulate public concerns or values not represented by the dominant self-interested lobbies. In sum, religious lobbying has broadened representation in Washington.

Another key dynamic explored by Hertzke (1988) was the filtering of group demands through the Madisonian system of checks and balances. Over time, many groups learn to adapt to the congressional norms of compromise and consensus building. Indeed, most use secular language in making their case (Bailey 2002). So although religious lobbyists seek to influence the system, they are themselves shaped by it.

A later systematic study by Hofrenning (1995a) questioned how much religious lobbies actually do adapt to congressional norms. Returning to the theme of "prophetic politics," Hofrenning (1995a) argued, that in contrast to narrow self-interested lobbies, religious advocates sought more sweeping ends— nothing less than a fundamental reordering of societal values and structures. From the religious Right rolled a stringent jeremiad against moral collapse; from the religious Left streamed a critique of broad societal injustice. Although poles apart ideologically, religious lobbyists from across the spectrum share a prophetic disillusionment with the state of society. Because of this, Hofrenning (1995a) argued that religious lobbyists struggle with a poignant dilemma: Should they aim at "faithfulness" or success? At witnessing or winning? Because many do not fully adapt to the incremental norms of the congressional system, Hofrenning (1995a) saw religious lobbyists as not attending well to the details of "insider" lobbying, choosing "outsider" strategies of grassroots mobilization instead. Hertzke (1988) also argued that at least some religious advocates were either reluctant or ill equipped to engage in the "detail work" so central to the policy process. Another study found that religious groups are more likely to engage in demonstrating or boycotting than their secular counterparts (Guth, Green, Kellstedt, and Smidt 1995).

Inattention to detail work, however, is more true of some religious lobbies than others, and varies from issue to issue. Jewish groups are legendary for their strategic approach to insider lobbying, and other groups do sometimes engage in the "microprocess"—based on their specialized information, expertise, or keen interest. Nonetheless, the tension remains one with which religious leaders continue to grapple.

The Religious Right

The most important change from the earliest studies of religious interest groups to later ones was the rise of the New Religious Right, especially from the 1980s onward. The emergence of this new force spawned a veritable cottage industry of journalistic and often alarmist accounts. Focused scholarly studies, however, provided a more balanced picture of its manifestation in national politics, particularly its impact on Washington lobbying. Moen (1989) provided a systematic and measured analysis of the origins of the movement, particularly the profound sense of threat from excesses of the counterculture, the breakdown of the family, and secularization of influential institutions of society. He also chronicled the daunting task of translating such sweeping concerns into operational congressional strategies, finding that leaders decided to concentrate on a few issues of great salience or broad symbolic appeal and then mounted massive mobilization campaigns.

To assess the strengths and limitations of the Christian Right, Moen (1989) anchored his study in agenda-setting literature. He found that, although actual policy victories on the Hill were modest, the Christian Right did shape the congressional agenda, keeping liberal forces on the defensive, thereby deflecting initiatives contrary to their interests. However, the congressional system had a way of filtering the demands of the movement into more palatable outcomes. A good example was the campaign for a school prayer amendment in the 1980s. Popular with the public, but contrary to the weight of constitutional scholarship, it failed to obtain the two-thirds congressional vote necessary to move on to the next phase in the states. In the wake of that defeat, however, Congress passed the Equal Access Act of 1984, a more modest and broadly supported measure. The law stipulated that if public high schools provided space before, during, or after school for noncurricular-related student clubs, it could not deny the same space to religiously oriented clubs (Hertzke 1988). Thus, although the Christian Right set the agenda with its school prayer mobilization—in a sense signaling to Congress that something had to be done about "secular" public schools—it did not determine the outcome, which was ultimately so carefully crafted that it gained support of religious lobbies across the spectrum.

Moen (1989) ended his book during one of the low points of the movement and thus expressed skepticism about its staying power. Later studies, however, showed that it was here to stay, despite periodic announcements of its death. If the moral majority went defunct, there was the Christian Coalition to pick up the mantle; when the Christian Coalition foundered, the Family Research Council moved into the breach. Because discontent with the state of society remains, there will be Christian Right interest groups at all levels of society. Moreover, as Nazworth (2006) has shown, Christian Right groups enjoy infusions of new energy by continued social movement mobilization. In addition, the dense network of evangelical parachurch organizations provides a source of political activists for politicians seeking to mobilize the citizenry around traditional moral issues.

This relates to the theme of *Onward Christian Soldiers?: The Religious Right in American Politics*, now in its third edition (Wilcox and Larson 2006). This work grounds the contemporary religious Right in its historical context as the fourth (although most sophisticated) manifestation in a century of mobilization by conservative religionists. The authors find that a stable 10 percent to 15 percent of the population forms the core constituency of the movement, with a wider group of supporters on particular issues like abortion or gay marriage. It must be stressed that, although the Christian Right draws most of its support from the evangelical population, not all evangelicals are sympathetic with the aims, rhetoric, or tactics of the movement. The political vigor of the movement, in turn, waxes and wanes with changing circumstances, leadership, and opportunity structures, and is rife with theological factions, leadership rivalries, and strategic disputes.

Evangelicalism thrives in the free marketplace of American religion (Finke and Stark 1992; Stark and Finke 2000), producing a plethora of entrepreneurial leaders, a vital resource in interest group formation and maintenance (Salisbury 1969; Nownes and Neeley 1996a). Moreover, as Robert Putnam (2000, p. 162) observed, American evangelicals have built "the largest, best organized grassroots" social movement networks of the last quarter century. Thus, groups like the Family Research Council, Concerned Women for America, Focus on the Family, and the Traditional Values Coalition draw upon the resources of a host of conservative Protestant denominations and the extensive network of nondenominational mega-churches (Kellstedt and Green 2003), local activist groups, alternative schools, Christian colleges, parachurch organizations, broadcast ministries, and publishing houses. Lobby activity is thus melded into the multifarious social movement activities of institutional development, electoral mobilization, litigation, media campaigns, and demonstrations.

Like black church organizations, but unlike most other religious interest groups, Christian Right groups focus heavily on electoral mobilization, and some have even formed PACs to help finance campaigns (Wilcox 1988), a rarity among religious lobbies. From the Moral Majority to the Christian Coalition, groups have engaged in massive voter mobilization initiatives so successfully that a definable Christian conservative voting bloc has become an important part of the Republican electorate (Green, Guth, Smidt, and Kellstedt 1996; Guth, Kellstedt, Smidt, and Green 2006; Green 2007; Kellstedt, Green, Smidt, and Guth 2007). The paradox, as Wilcox and Larson (2006, p. 182) note, is that the Christian Right has been "the most successful social movement in influencing elections and party politics over the past century," but, on its core agenda, "the least successful in influencing policy and culture." The structure of American national government, with its numerous veto points, plus the countermobilization produced by threatened opponents, ensures that most victories will be modest and incremental.

Christian Right groups have also turned to the local level, fighting intense battles over school curricula, evolution, sex education, public expressions of faith, and religious symbols in public places. The best account of this local arena is Melissa Deckman's study (2004) of school board battles. Her central finding is that, despite a few celebrated cases of the "capture" of school boards by Christian Right activists, local mobilization has yielded mixed results. Relying on a major survey of school board candidates and in-depth case studies, Deckman (2004) explored the characteristics and impact of Christian conservative school board candidates. She found that Christian Right candidates are indeed motivated by religious and moral motivations, but that they run similar campaigns and enjoy no greater electoral success than other candidates. Most important, she found that Christian Right board members were less successful in enacting extreme or controversial policies (such as teaching creationism) than when they pursued goals that enjoyed broader public resonance, such as back-to-basics curricula (like phonics), better discipline, improved test scores, and character education. As in the national arena, local Christian Right political engagement results in modest gains, and mostly on issues that enjoy some general public backing.

Organizational Dynamics

One of the key findings of scholarship about religious interest groups is that they vary greatly in organizational structure and internal dynamics. A good point of departure is research by Zwier (1994), who found that religious groups cluster into three distinct types: church-based groups, individual membership groups, and coalition groups.

Zwier (1994) found that church or denominational-based groups commonly shared a number of characteristics. They were established initially to monitor government actions; only later did they become actively engaged in policy advocacy. They also generally have a longer history than membership groups. Crucially, they are directed by religious hierarchies often not headquartered in Washington. Moreover, because "political activity is not the primary mission of the churches" religious advocates must compete for "attention and resources within organizations dedicated to other priorities" (Zwier 1994, p. 98). Finally, they are often staffed not by Washington insiders or experienced political operatives, but by church officials who have risen through the ranks of their denominations.

Individual membership groups, in contrast, were formed explicitly to make an impact on public policy, and in many cases the Washington office is the headquarters of the group. They commonly arrived later to the nation's capital than denominational organizations and, unlike church groups, members normally join for overt political purposes. These groups vary greatly in size, from those with relatively small memberships, such as Network, made up principally of Catholic nuns, to some Christian conservative organizations that may have hundreds of thousands of contributors.

A key distinction between denominationally based groups and membership ones is the issue of accountability. Denominational groups, especially those representing mainline Protestantism, are accountable not to lay members or even pastors, but to church boards or hierarchies, and they are guided by policy resolutions passed by general church meetings. Membership groups, because they rely on direct contributions to stay afloat, are more accountable to members who can easily exit if unsatisfied (Hirschman 1970). Thus, leaders of the two types operate under different organizational constraints that shape their activities.

This categorical division cuts across religious communities. Evangelicals, for example, are represented by denominations (such as the Southern Baptist Convention, Assemblies of God, or the Lutheran Missouri Synod) and membership organizations (such as Prison Fellowship or Concerned Women for America). The National Association of Evangelicals, in turn, is a broad coalition of denominations and independent member congregations. And some groups, such as the liberal Sojourners ministry of Jim Wallis, defy easy categorization. Sojourners seeks to shape public opinion through its magazine, book tours by Wallis (2006), Internet communication, and rallies. During summer 2007, it even achieved the coup of hosting a debate by the Democratic presidential candidates that focused on peacemaking and poverty, its key concerns.

In contrast to the contention that religious groups are small (Zwier 1991), there are exceptions, as Weber and Jones (1994) document. The U.S. Catholic Conference, the policy arm of the Bishops Conference, runs an extensive operation with policy specialists and lobbyists on a range of domestic and international issues. And the legendary American Israel Political Affairs Committee sports one of the most sophisticated and extensive operations in Washington. Similarly, some denominational offices are indeed staffed by political veterans, not just "church bureaucrats." A notable example is Rabbi David Saperstein of the Religious Action Center for Reform Judaism, a highly regarded political professional with three decades of lobbying experience.

Beyond Zwier's categorization (1994), there are a number of other types of religious organizations. A host of professional associations articulate their policy concerns in Washington (and state capitals). Large associations of Catholic hospitals and parochial schools, for example, maintain policy arms to promote their keen interests in health and education policy, a finding in concert with general scholarship about the prominence of institutions in the lobby world (Salisbury 1984). In addition, a growing number of nonprofit social service groups have policy arms or associations, which is especially important as they become recipients of government funding, whereas NGOs increasingly lobby on international issues.

The NGOs, in particular, reflect an intriguing development. Diverse religious communities for years have maintained huge and highly regarded international relief and development agencies, such as Catholic Relief Services, Lutheran World Relief, World Vision, and Church World Service. With networks on the ground in some of the most forbidding places on earth, these NGOs gain unique insight into U.S. military, trade, or aid policies, which they share in testimony before Congress or meetings with executive agencies. Because of the large footprint of the U.S. government on the global stage, NGO leaders have become aware of how small changes in U.S. foreign policy can have huge impacts that magnify their own charitable efforts. Thus, they have a natural incentive to lobby for such changes.

Moreover, as Monsma (2001) has shown, the U.S. government increasingly contracts with NGOs to deliver famine relief, provide refugee services, or undertake development projects. Thus the budgets of religious NGOs contain sizable federal dollars, creating a powerful motivation for political advocacy. In some cases, religious NGOs are headquartered in the greater Washington, DC, metropolitan area; in other cases, they have established Washington offices for public policy advocacy.

Also rising in prominence are faith-based think tanks that generate policy ideas, such as the Ethics and Public Policy Center and the Center for Religious Freedom, along with a plethora of religious foundations and patrons that fund public advocacy. These have become important players in the public policy system, both in Washington and in some statehouses. Although general interest group scholarship has acknowledged the important role of think tanks, foundations, and their patrons (Walker 1983), to date religious counterparts have not received systematic scholarly attention, suggesting a fruitful new line of research.

One of the crucial questions in the literature on national religious groups is the linkage to local laity and clergy. Here we see a stark contrast between the liberal mainline Protestant and conservative evangelical groups. As Olson (2002) documents, there are small action networks of laity and pastors within mainline Protestant denominations, whereas their national offices work in relative isolation from local clergy. This does not mean that local pastors oppose the national offices; indeed, many local pastors approve of their denomination maintaining a Washington office and provide a kind of tacit support for its political witness. Rather, local pastors are heavily engaged in local social ministries, like food banks or community development projects that draw them into local political issues. As a result, Washington lobbyists and local pastors operate largely in "separate spheres." Olson (2002) concludes that the Washington offices of mainline groups could do more to provide information about their activities to local pastors, something the clergy say they want.

In contrast, evangelical Protestant denominations maintain closer ties to local churches and pastors. In part, this is because of a closer concordance on issues of concern to both national and local leaders. However, it also flows from the rich social networks linking national lobbying to local churches. When the national office of the Southern Baptist Convention wants to mobilize its member churches, for example, it can rely on denominational publications, direct mail lists of all affiliated churches, and radio broadcasts to get the word out.

A key difference, therefore, is the capacity to mobilize members. Because mainline Protestant leaders tend to be less entrepreneurial than their evangelical cousins, they are not as successful in building a grassroots following. Yet potential followers are out there. One study found that the constituency for liberal Christian interest groups is higher than group size would suggest (Stenger 2005), indicating latent potential. Interestingly, it has taken a liberal entrepreneurial evangelical, Jim Wallis (2006), to help activate that latent constituency.

A key dynamic of religious lobbying is the vital work of coalition building. Groups realize that coalitions are essential to magnify their voices. At the national and state levels we see contending progressive and traditionalist coalitions, often permanently formalized by steering bodies. However, these durable coalitions do not set in stone the relationships among religious interest groups, and "strange bedfellow" coalitions are not uncommon. On Israel, for example, liberal Protestant groups part company with their Jewish counterparts in staking out a critical posture toward Israeli policies that they see as unjust in the treatment of Palestinians. Fundamentalist and evangelical Protestants, on the other hand, have become increasingly supportive of Israel, both because of a theology that sees the formation of Israel as providential, and because it represents a bulwark against what they see as the same militant Islamist forces arrayed against the United States. In turn, the broadening agenda of the National Association of Evangelicals (2004), which encompasses concern for poverty, human rights, and the environment, has created new allies for causes normally the domain of liberals.

Often religious groups check each other, especially on contentious "culture war" issues like abortion or gay rights. However, the religious community can be formidable when groups across the ideological spectrum get together. For example, in 1990, a Supreme Court decision in *Employment Division v. Smith* (494 U.S. 872 1990) narrowed grounds for religious free exercise claims. In response, a virtual unanimity of religious groups coalesced to lobby Congress for legislation restoring language that government had to show a "compelling interest" before burdening religious freedom, sparking a decade-long battle between Congress and the Supreme Court over the contours of free exercise of religion (den Dulk and Pickerill 2003). Groups that normally fight like cats and dogs over school prayer, abortion, and gay rights found themselves lobbying side by side in this struggle (Fowler, Hertzke, Olson, and den Dulk 2004). These strange bedfellow relationships, in turn, helped facilitate broad religious alliances on global human rights issues (Hertzke 2004).[2]

Pluralism

As noted, one of the defining characteristics of the religious group universe is its pluralism. Not only are diverse faith traditions represented, but groups vary greatly by theological interpretation, ideology, size, resources, organizational structure, issue focus, and motivations. To grasp the texture of this pluralism, it is helpful to think of the interest group community as made up of a number of broad families, each with inner diversity. We see this manifested in a major initiative funded by the Pew Charitable Trusts that sought to inventory the civic activities of six different religious communities. The result of this initiative is a set of books on mainline Protestants (Wuthnow and Evans 2002), evangelicals (Cromartie 2003), Catholics (Steinfels 2004a, b), Jews (Mittleman, Sarna, and Licht 2002), Muslims (Bukhari, Nyang, Ahmad, and Esposito 2004), African American churches (Smith 2003, 2004; Smith and Harris 2005), and Hispanic religionists (Espinosa, Elizondo, and Miranda 2005). Although many of the contributions delve into the theological, philosophical, or social bases for political witness, what emerges is a portrait of enormous pluralism within these diverse communities, and a multiplicity of interest group forms and expressions.

Take Jews as an example. Although Jews are renowned for their liberalism and strong support for Israel, diversity nonetheless exists. There are Jewish groups that represent the faith, whether Orthodox (Agudath Israel and Orthodox Union) or Reform (the Union of American Hebrew Congregations). There are membership groups (the American Jewish Committee, the American Jewish Congress, Anti-defamation League of B'nai B'rith), women's groups (Hadassah and the National Council of Jewish Women), and single-issue groups (like the American Israel Political Affairs Committee). Moreover, policy disagreements do emerge. Groups representing Orthodox Jews, for example, part company with their Reform counterparts over aid to parochial schools, faith-based partnerships with government, and abortion rights. Tensions have also erupted over support for specific Israeli policies (Breger 2002).

Or consider Muslims. Relative newcomers to public advocacy, they nonetheless burst with an ever-growing number of diverse and sometimes competing groups (Bukhari et al. 2004). There are Washington-based Muslim groups, such as the Council for American Islamic Relations and the Muslim American Society, and there are national associations like the Islamic Society of North America. Some Washington groups, such as the Muslim PAC, serve the lobby arm of organizations based elsewhere. Moreover, there are groups (like the Islamic Supreme Council of America, the American Islamic Forum for Democracy, and the American Islamic Congress) that criticize the purported Islamist sympathies or foreign funding of other groups, such as the Council for American Islamic Relations or the Muslim American Society (Hertzke forthcoming 2009).

Among mainline Protestants, the picture that emerges qualifies earlier critiques of the gap between leaders and lay members. Although diverse ideologically, the mainline faithful have become less Republican during the past three decades and now often support the general aims (if not specific policies) of their leaders in fighting poverty and protecting the environment (Wuthnow 2002). Because support is greater for local initiatives than federal ones, mainline congregations continue to supply locally what Putnam (2000) termed "bridging social capital."

Pluralism within the Catholic world flows in part from the pronounced split between traditionalists and progressives. This is often manifested in the degree of emphasis different groups place on the pro-life cause versus the social justice agenda (Heyer 2006, chap. 4). Pro-life parishioners, however, tend to be the most supportive of church lobby groups (Welch, Leege, and Woodberry 1998). However, there still remains a sector of the church that genuinely blends both impulses—one of the distinctive features of Catholic activism.

It should be noted in passing that within all of these broad families, activist women's groups give voice to the often predominant female participation within many congregations, adding another layer to the religious quilt. Pluralism is also enhanced by the fact that individual congregations themselves function as lobbies (Beyerlein and Chaves 2003).

The Growing Global Agenda

From the beginning of the republic, national religious interest groups have focused periodically on international relations and foreign affairs (Ribuffo 2001). Mainline Protestant groups, for example, were pivotal in pressing for the UN's Universal Declaration for Human Rights of 1948 (Nurser 2005), and most groups since then have been drawn into contentious foreign policy issues—from the Vietnam War to Central American clashes in the 1980s to the current war on terrorism. However, globalization—the process by which people around the world are increasingly interlinked through commerce, travel, and communication—has heightened international awareness and increased international engagement by virtually all national religious interest groups.

We see this for specific groups. Jews lobby for Israel, Muslims for Palestinian rights, and Buddhists on behalf of their beleaguered counterparts in Tibet. We see it for specific issues, as religious lobbies have weighed in on the Iraq war, trade policy, and tactics in the war on terrorism.

Nowhere has this global engagement manifested itself so vigorously as on campaigns for religious freedom and human rights abroad. Beginning in the mid 1990s, a movement of unlikely religious allies burst unexpectedly onto the international scene—a faith-based quest to advance human rights through the machinery of American foreign policy. Activated by concern for religious persecution abroad, religious groups across the theological spectrum fought for passage of the International Religious Freedom Act of 1998. This legislation established a permanent office in the state department to report on the status of religious freedom in every country on earth, and required that actions be taken by the U.S. government against those countries that egregiously persecute religious believers.

Galvanized by that legislative success, coalition leaders mounted successful campaigns to enact laws on human trafficking, peace in Sudan, and human rights in North Korea. Collectively, these statutes built a new architecture for the promotion of human rights in American foreign policy. As argued in *Freeing God's Children* (Hertzke 2004), the movement is filling a void in human rights advocacy, raising issues previously slighted by secular groups, the foreign policy establishment, and the prestige press.

Central to this movement were American evangelicals, heretofore associated with domestic skirmishes in the culture wars, but increasingly engaged in international humanitarian and human rights causes. This engagement facilitated unlikely alliances, as evangelicals provided crucial grassroots muscle for causes backed by a wide array of religious groups. In varying campaigns, evangelical leaders teamed up with liberal Jewish groups, the Catholic Church, Episcopal leaders, Tibetan Buddhists, Iranian Bahai's, secular human rights groups, feminists, labor unions, and the Congressional Black Caucus (Hertzke 2004).

Driving the new engagement by evangelicals and other Christian groups is the tectonic shift of the globe's Christian population to the developing world, a momentous trend captured by the work of Phillip Jenkins (2002). While in 1900 80 percent of

Christians lived in greater Europe and North America, by 2000 at least 60 percent of all Christians hailed from Asia, Africa, and Latin America. Thus, many American denominations are now smaller arms of larger global ministries. Given population trends, this shift to the global south will accelerate, with the Christian message particularly appealing among populations vulnerable to internal strife and the disruptions of globalization (Jenkins 2006). Many Christian congregations abroad thus are nested amidst poverty, violence, exploitation, and persecution.

The expansion of global communications, travel, and international development networks ensure that many American believers increasingly hear about, and identify with, fellow Christians living amid persecution and hardship. And they also learn about the afflictions visited on the world's vulnerable, heightening the potential that they will back efforts to ameliorate their suffering. For the evangelical world, this means that the social networks built out of domestic social concerns are being put in service of human rights and justice concerns normally associated with progressive politics—a striking development indeed. Ironically, it took the prodding and buoying by leaders outside the evangelical community to help stitch together evangelical elites in common strategies for international human rights (Hertzke 2004, chap. 5).

However, the story of globalization is broader than even this notable movement. Growing and diverse immigrant populations in America, often organized through religious communities, have been drawn into foreign policy on behalf of their counterparts abroad. And humanitarian concerns increasingly receive attention of global religious communities. In 2000, religious groups joined secular organizations and celebrities like Bono in the "Year of Jubilee" campaign for global debt relief. In the United States, the effort focused on gaining a large congressional appropriation to help write off debts burdening poor countries. This successful campaign was led by the lobbyist for the Episcopal church, Tom Hart, who heard from his Anglican counterparts in Africa and elsewhere of how debts incurred by former dictators sap development efforts. He and other religious group leaders have since moved on to campaigns for increased AIDS funding and international development assistance.

RELIGIOUS INTERESTS AND THE STATES

Another notable development is how religious interest groups increasingly lobby state governments—a focus driven in part by the new federalism that devolves more policy-making authority to the states. Because the stakes are high, diverse religious groups now battle in statehouses over abortion, same-sex marriage, education policy, health care, social welfare spending, the death penalty, the environment, immigration, and state budget priorities.

Focused studies of this phenomenon have tended to concentrate on the activities of either the Catholic church or the Christian Right. Byrnes and Segers

(1992), for example, looked at Catholic group agitation on abortion, whereas Green, Rozell, and Wilcox (2003) examined the variable fortunes of Christian Right groups in different states. Specific studies document efforts by conservative Christian groups to defend home schools against state regulation (Bates 1991) or to fight gay marriage (Damore, Jelen, and Bowers 2007).

One of the most systematic and theoretical studies is Yamane's book (2005) on the advocacy of state Catholic conferences. Challenging aspects of secularization theory, Yamane (2005) shows how state Catholic conferences, directed by state bishops, are well entrenched in state politics, articulating a distinctive political vision anchored in Catholic social teaching. Guided by the doctrine of the "dignity of the human person," for example, Catholic lobbyists act as advocates on behalf of those they see as uniquely vulnerable—the poor, the uninsured, undocumented immigrants, laborers, prisoners, and the unborn. Similarly, Catholic lobbying is anchored in church social teaching on "subsidiarity"—the doctrine that the state should support, not supplant, the subsidiary institutions of society, such as the family or community. Under this doctrine, the church fights for various educational choice policies that provide access for parents to schools that embody their religious values. Thus, as another book argued, the Catholic church offers a "distinctive voice" in public advocacy (Steinfels 2004b), forming alliances across the political spectrum depending on the issue. Moreover, in contrast to accounts at the federal level, Yamane (2005) finds that the lobbyists for these Catholic conferences effectively engage "in the details" of legislative work—the day-to-day "sausage making" that produces tangible policy change. More important, he found that this Catholic lobby presence mostly recovered from the "long lent" of 2002, when priest sex abuse scandals rocked the American church.

In contrast to these focused studies, *Representing God at the Statehouse*, edited by Cleary and Hertzke (2006), provides the first attempt to survey the full range of religious interest group activism in the states. The diverse state-level case studies in this work offer a number of collective insights. First, religious advocacy is distinct from the professional and economic lobbies that tend to dominate pressure politics at the statehouses. Religious advocates are not hired guns who wine and dine legislators or who make PAC contributions to campaigns; rather, they rely on moral appeals and tend to exhibit intense commitment to their causes—commitment that flows from faith imperatives as they understand them.

Instead of narrow self-interest, religious interest groups articulate broad moral visions rooted in their respective church traditions and teachings. Representing so-called "postmaterialist" values, we hear religious advocates saying that their faith "demands that they defend morality, fight for the common good, promote social justice, protect the weak, and contribute to the well-being of all members of society." Although conservative and liberal religious coalitions sometimes compete with each other, collectively they do represent values that transcend those advanced by typical lobbies: "From family policy to gambling, abortion to euthanasia, homelessness to child poverty, sentencing guidelines to treatment of prisoners, religious advocates interject faith-based arguments into the grubby world of state lobbying" (den Dulk and Hertzke 2006, p. 226).

Second, because states vary greatly in culture, party competition, or legislative professionalism, we see a wide variability in the groups that operate in different statehouses, as well as in their relative effectiveness. Political and cultural contexts matter. Professional legislatures with extensive staffs, as in California and Michigan, tend to provide more access points for religious lobbyists, whereas part-time legislatures that meet infrequently, as in Virginia, tend to blunt the efficacy of religious appeals. And as Elazar (1984) suggested, the political culture of a state shapes the fortunes of different religious communities. Thus, in some states the Christian Right maintains a robust presence, partly as a result of intense election mobilization; in others, it barely registers. In some states, mainline Protestant councils operate effectively; in other states, black church groups are active. Jewish group engagement varies widely from state to state. And so it goes.

Echoing Yamane (2005), *Representing God at the Statehouse* (Cleary and Hertzke 2006) found active and well-developed Catholic lobbies in all the statehouses surveyed, indicating a notable reach into state-level politics. The institutional vitality of the church—with state Catholic conferences that parallel the federal structure of American government, along with a host of schools, hospitals, charitable agencies, and religious orders—ensures a robust presence in state politics. And, like Steinfels (2004a, b), this work finds Catholic lobbying defying neat Right/Left characterization: "Catholic lobbyists join with conservative evangelicals on abortion, gay marriage, educational vouchers, and public displays of religion, but turn around to back liberal Protestants and Jews on social welfare issues, food stamps, homelessness, the death penalty," crime, immigration, job training, and health care for the poor (den Dulk and Hertzke 2006, p. 239).

LOCAL COMMUNITY ORGANIZING
AND RELIGIOUS GROUPS

Religious congregations and communities are intimately woven into the fabric of local social life in America. They run a plethora of food banks, youth enterprises, after-school programs, anticrime efforts, substance abuse projects, and community improvement initiatives (Kellstedt and Green 2003). Indeed, in distressed communities the local churches are often havens of stability and succor. We see this with the work of John Perkins, an African American pastor in Mississippi, and the national Christian Community Development Association he helped to found (Perkins 1993, 1995). The emphasis of his ministry was to induce church leaders to live among the poor and help marshal their resources for community betterment. This puts them in touch with how political structures can inhibit or buoy their ministries and leads periodically to initiatives aimed at making government work for the less powerful members of society.

If community development focuses on the marshaling of resources of a community for the betterment of its citizens (Owens 2003), community organizing seeks to marshal those resources for more overt and sweeping political change. Faith-based community organizing traces its roots to the work of Saul Alinsky (1971), whose initiatives involved creating organizations to force local governments to be responsive to the needs of poor and working-class citizens. Alinsky (1971) created an institute (the Industrial Areas Foundation) to train leaders in the techniques of community organizing—identifying local leaders, building organizations, specifying problems, and developing tactics to attack them. The idea is to employ the strategic use of creative protests by massed citizens to create a dynamic tension that forces government officials to take desired actions.

Alinsky–style organizations often used local churches as one of their key bases of organization, but as Richard Wood (2002, appendix II) recounts, these efforts reflected a "parasitic relationship" rather than a true symbiotic one; faith communities were treated only as useful instruments for organizing. A crucial change occurred with the transformation of the Pacific Institute for Community Organization, headquartered in Oakland, California. After achieving only modest success, organization leaders began to develop true partnerships with local churches and pastors, and the effort flourished. It grew from a few projects in California to a national network with some thousand participating churches in 150 cities and towns, and local protests mobilized thousands of citizens on occasions, rather than the smaller numbers that had been the case previously. The Pacific Institute for Community Organization and other similar organizations represent the blossoming of a faith-based movement to make democracy work for citizens often bereft of effective representation.

Faith-based community organizing works primarily to make city and county governments more responsive to neglected neighborhoods. As Wood (2002) demonstrates, successful initiatives have involved enhancement of city services, eyesore removal, improved local schools, changes in policing, and infrastructure development, among many others.

And as citizens became empowered and more informed about political issues, local groups have identified state issues that impinge on their neighborhoods. This has led coalitions of federations to mount periodic statewide lobbying campaigns. As Wood (2002, p. 1) shows, these have resulted in some dramatic political impacts. For example, after 3000 neighborhood representatives "converged on the State Capitol in Sacramento, California" in 2000 to lobby for better health care for the uninsured, the state government appropriated an additional $50 million that year for community health clinics and $130 million the next year for broader health coverage (Wood 2002, pp. 1–3). This demonstration of the power of community organization has been corroborated by a separate investigation (Cleary 2006), and similar demonstrations have been mounted in other states.

Wood's (2002) account details the complex factors that lead to successful faith-based organizing, but he also notes its limitations. Some issues are too controversial for churches to tackle and are avoided. Moreover, local or statewide organizing cannot overcome the flows of capital out of inner cities as a result of globalization. Still, because of their roots in vulnerable neighborhoods and their efforts at outreach, local churches have proved themselves valuable allies in challenging political structures to meet the needs of less affluent citizens. The theoretical import of this phenomenon is that community organizing creates new social capital, replenishing what Putnam (2000) so famously showed had declined in America.

Among the constituencies that have most keenly sought to gain group power through community organizing are Hispanics and African Americans. Hispanic churches were crucial building blocks of the United Farm Workers movement, and a pioneering community organization, COPS of San Antonio, was based in Hispanic churches. Moreover, such leaders as Cesar Chavez often drew upon popular religious symbols, such as Our Lady of Guadalupe or the passion of Christ, to mobilize and buoy followers and build organizations (Leon 2005; Lloyd-Moffett 2005). The legacy of such efforts is that, today, a growing number of church-based organizations, both Catholic and Protestant, seek to empower Hispanics (Espinosa, Elizondo, and Miranda 2005).

In turn, in many inner cities, black churches form the core of civil society, where people gather, learn civic skills, and develop social capital necessary for group action (Calhoun-Brown 2003). Black church networks thus serve as a principal means by which African American citizens organize to demand better treatment by city or county governments. Indeed, in cities like Atlanta, Chicago, Detroit, Boston, New York, Cleveland, Buffalo, and Miami, individual congregations or ministerial associations act as pressure groups, making them "part and parcel of the nation's urban political landscape" (Smith and Harris 2005, p. ix). In some cases, this results in dramatic outcomes. In Boston during the 1990s, for example, a coalition of inner city pastors formed a partnership with the police department to attack the problem of youth violence. With an emphasis on community policing, church leaders and police invited gang members to forums at which they were presented with both a carrot (help with school or jobs) and a stick (strict enforcement of the law to get violent youth off the streets). This resulted in the so-called Boston miracle, in which murder rates plummeted and working relations between the police and community residents improved substantially (Winship 2004). To be sure, the promise of public policy influence by black churches has not always been fulfilled, a fact lamented by sympathetic scholars (Smith 2004).

POLICY IMPACT

To make an impact on policy, good lobbyists seek elite access, such as a fair hearing from legislators, White House officials, executive branch agencies, governors, or mayors. If religious lobbyists are seasoned and skilled, access comes easier than if they are inexperienced. Constituency backing also plays a role in whether an official listens to a religious group. Nationally, members of Congress and White House officials provide widely different access to religious lobbyists based on their own religious worldviews (Hertzke 1989), a finding not surprising in light of the work of Benson and Williams (1982) on the different religious types of representatives. The same dynamic operates at the state level (Yamane 1999; Yamane and Oldmixon 2006).

The challenge of assessing the actual power or impact of lobbying has bedeviled the general field of interest group scholarship, which has produced mixed or contradictory results (Smith 1995; Baumgartner and Leech 1998). The difficulty lies in isolating lobbying from the myriad and subtle variables impinging on the policy process. Thus, scholars have found it hard to posit plausible counterfactuals— alternative scenarios of what *would have happened* without interest group lobbying.

The same problem confounds the study of religious interest groups, although at least some studies at the federal, state, and local levels do document particular instances when religious lobbies appeared to have had a policy impact. For example, at the national level, the Christian Right successfully blocked passage of the Equal Rights Amendment and has succeeded in barring federal funding for abortions while gaining a recent federal law against so-called partial-birth abortion. At the state level, it has been most successful in mobilizing ballot initiatives barring gay marriage and gaining some modest restrictions on abortion. Religious progressives, through groups like Bread for the World (Cohn, Barkan, and Whitaker 1993), appear to have gained increased funding for antihunger programs. The religious Left was also an important part of the 1980s nuclear freeze movement (Imig and Meyer 1993) and the coalition that blocked Reagan–era attempts to fund counterrevolutionaries (or *contras*) against the Sandinista government of Nicaragua (Hertzke 1988). A number of the Pew-funded inventories of activism by diverse religious communities also point to particular instances of apparent policy impact. And, as noted, coalitions have successfully gained international debt relief and increased AIDS funding, and they have erected a permanent infrastructure for the promotion of human rights in American foreign policy (Hertzke 2004).

On the crucial issue of budgeting, whether at the federal or state levels, religious lobbyists historically have fought broad ideological battles over fiscal priorities in spending and taxation. Although groups point to instances in which they have helped shape budget priorities, it is especially difficult here to disentangle the diverse forces at play in the politics of government budgeting.

In contrast to other lobbies, religious groups have historically eschewed the politics of pork barrel spending. However, as national "earmarks" by individual members of Congress have mushroomed into a multibillion dollar enterprise, religious interests have been enticed into seeking funding for special projects, in some cases hiring professional lobby firms to gain funding—a relatively new phenomenon. As a major *New York Times* study has found (Henriques and Lehren 2007), during the past two decades Congress approved nearly 900 earmarks for religious entities (like small church colleges or hospitals), perhaps a dubious form of impact, with the vast majority of those earmarks coming in the 109th and 110th

Congresses. Some lobby firms now specialize in working with the religious community in obtaining earmarks, a practice that many of the well-established religious groups find troubling because they do not wish to be associated with such nakedly self-interested lobbying. Publicity about such practices has resulted in some groups reevaluating their use.

Although examples of impact emerge in specific studies of religious groups, a weak link in the literature is *systematic* analysis of policy impact. Instead, much scholarship focuses on the *activities* of religious interest groups, with only episodic or imputed impacts on policy. Given the diverse forces that impinge on the complex policy process, it is not surprising that scholars cannot precisely isolate the impact of religious lobbying. However, few have attempted in a systematic way to assess the policy influence of religious groups (an exception at the state level, however, is Yamane and Oldmixon [2006]).

At the national level, such research might involve a two-pronged strategy: broad systematic efforts and focused ethnographic studies. One fruitful strategy would involve interviewing policy makers in Congress, the White House, and executive agencies to gain their assessment of when and how much religious groups have shaped the agenda or achieved policy goals. Systematic efforts might also involve examining the match between the stated objectives of religious groups and the outcomes of the policy process in Washington. Equally valuable, intensive and multiyear ethnographic research would tease out tangible instances of impact. This kind of research, of course, requires unusual access and time not available to all scholars.

If measuring impact at the national level is difficult, the sheer number of venues at the state and local levels makes broad systematic study a daunting enterprise. As noted, we do have books of case studies that point to some instances of modest impact in particular states by religious interest groups. In addition to more systematic analyses of legislative roll call votes (Yamane and Oldmixon 2006), studies should focus on agenda setting and committee deliberations (Baumgartner and Leech 1998), along with detailed case studies, which could then be synthesized to provide a cumulative portrait of policy influence.

At the local level we have the valuable case studies presented by Djupe and Olson (2007), which do show tangible governmental outcomes from engagement by religious interests on such varied issues as gambling, health care, homelessness, race relations, and urban development. With respect to local educational policy, Deckman (2004) provides a pioneering inquiry into the impact of Christian Right influence on school boards.

Another model investigation of local impact is Wood's account (2002) of community organizing efforts. What makes his research notable is that he combined several years of intensive participant observation research in Oakland—providing rich ethnographic detail on the ways religiously empowered citizens gained tangible results from city government—and then linked that narrative to a wider examination of the impact of initiatives elsewhere. Because the church-based community organizing in Oakland operated through the same national umbrella group that sponsored initiatives in multiple cities, Wood (2002) was able to draw theoretical insights about how religious groups can serve to overcome democratic deficits and rebuild social capital among poor and working-class people.

The goal in research at all levels should be to advance a cumulative literature, "an ensemble of related findings," that addresses vital questions of democratic representation (Baumgartner and Leech 1998, p. 188). This can best be achieved by a blend of systematic studies with theoretically informed ethnographic research.

CONCLUSIONS

As suggested by this review, the collective activities of religious interest groups contribute to a more authentic neopluralism than we see in general interest group scholarship, an important finding for democratic theory. Religious organizations represent far-reaching or intangible concerns and can articulate the needs of less influential citizens at home and—through appeals to social justice—the voiceless abroad (Hodge 2007a, b). This is not surprising because, as noted, church membership is one of the principal means by which nonelite citizens coalesce for civic engagement (Putnam 2000), learn civic skills (Verba, Schlozman, and Brady 1995), and internalize humanitarian impulses. Because they are a mass phenomenon, congregational-based groups sometimes force the system to pay attention to populist discontent (Hertzke 1993). Religious conservatives, for example, succeeded in articulating widely felt, but diffuse, concerns about family breakdown, the coarsening of the culture, and the secularization of powerful institutions. In turn, religious liberals have been most successful when they tapped into the humanitarian impulse to tackle hunger, poverty, and disease. Without the collective power and legitimacy of religious organizations, it is hard to imagine the American government acting to reduce hunger, relieve debt burdens on impoverished peoples, end the trafficking of women and children into slavery, or to pour billions into the fight against AIDS in Africa. It is also hard to conceive some local governments responding to neglected citizens (or even undocumented workers) without church-based mobilization. Religious groups, in short, leaven the pressure system, making it better reflect public needs and, at times, the best impulses of the citizenry.

The most important finding to emerge from an examination of religious groups, therefore, is that their collective endeavors enhance the representativeness of the American political system. This finding has largely been missed by general interest group scholars, who tend to give short shrift to religious interests. Indeed, the religious scholarship reviewed in this chapter is absent in major summaries of the state of the interest group field (Baumgartner and Leech 1998; Lowery and Gray 2004). This may reflect a broader deficiency in political science. As Wald and Wilcox suggest (2006), the inattentiveness toward religion by mainstream political science is attributable to both sides: Secular political scientists find the complexity of religion a stumbling block, whereas scholars of religion and politics fail to tie their efforts to the theoretical work of leading scholars. Although this latter critique appears less apt for studies of religious interest groups, which generally do attempt to connect their work with general interest group theories (see especially, Hofrenning 1995b), certainly more could be done on this score by scholars of faith-based lobbies. And perhaps religious group researchers should attempt to ensure that the products of their inquiry get into the hands of leading scholars of interest groups. Both the field of religious interest groups, and political science in general, will be all the richer as a result.

NOTES

1. Political parties are also important intermediary institutions, but they tend to concentrate on winning elections and keeping segments of their electoral coalition together. Thus, parties tend to be the most active during elections and when the government is being organized, whereas interest groups tend to "predominate during the period between elections, when public policy is being formulated and implemented" (Walker 1991, p. 22).

2. Textbooks can be a useful gauge of how scholars synthesize material and literature on organizational dynamics. In a widely used textbook, Wald and Calhoun-Brown (2007, chap. 5) provide an extended discussion of the complex process by which religious interests become manifested in organized activism. They focus on appeals by elites to group identity, theological worldviews, and institutional interests. Another text (Fowler et al. 2004, chap. 5) catalogs the strategies of effective lobbying and then analyzes fortunes of the diverse groups that ply their trade in Washington. These different foci reflect two sides of a single equation. Wald and Calhoun-Brown (2007) examine group formation whereas Fowler et al. (2004) look at what groups do once they are formed. Another text (Corbett and Corbett 1999) emphasizes both the pluralism of religious groups and their tendency to cluster into a liberal "peace and justice" alliance and a conservative "traditional values" coalition.

REFERENCES

Adams, James Luther. 1970. *The Growing Church Lobby in Washington.* Grand Rapids, Mich.: Eerdmans.

Alinksy, Saul. 1971. *Rules for Radicals: A Practical Primer for Realistic Radicals.* New York: Random House.

Bailey, Michael E. 2002. "The Wisdom of Serpents: Why Religious Groups Use Secular Language." *Journal of Church and State* 44 (2): 249–269.

Bates, Vernon L. 1991. "Lobbying for the Lord: The New Christian Right Home-Schooling Movement and Grassroots Lobbying." *Review of Religious Research* 33: 3–17.

Baumgarter, Frank R., and Beth L. Leech. 1998. *Basic Interests: The Importance of Groups in Politics and in Political Science*. Princeton, N.J.: Princeton University Press.

Baumgartner, Frank R., and Beth L. Leech. 1999. "Business Advantage in the Washington Lobbying Community." Presented at the annual meeting of the Midwest Political Science Association, Chicago, Ill. April 15–17.

Benson, Peter C., and Dorothy L. Williams. 1982. *Religion on Capitol Hill: Myths and Realities*. San Francisco, Calif.: Harper and Row. [Reprinted 1986. New York: Oxford University Press.]

Berry, Jeffrey. 1984. *The Interest Group Society*. Boston, Mass.: Little, Brown.

Berry, Jeffrey. 1999. *The New Liberalism: The Rising Power of Citizen Groups*. Washington, D.C.: Brookings Institution Press.

Beyerlein, Kraig, and Mark Chaves. 2003. "The Political Activities of Congregations in the United States." *Journal for the Scientific Study of Religion* 42 (2): 229–246.

Breger, Marshall J. 2002. "Jewish Activism in the Washington 'Square': An Analysis and Prognosis." In *Jews and the American Public Square*, ed. Alan Mittleman, Jonathan D. Sarna, and Robert Licht, 53–186. Lanham, Md.: Rowman & Littlefield.

Browne, William P. 1990. "Organized Interests and Their Issue Niches: A Search for Pluralism in a Policy Domain." *Journal of Politics* 52: 477–509.

Bukhari, Zahid H., Sulayman S. Nyang, Mumtaz Ahmad, and John L. Esposito. 2004. *Muslims' Place in the American Public Square*. Walnut Creek, Calif.: AltaMira Press.

Byrnes, Timothy, and Mary C. Segers. 1992. *The Catholic Church and the Politics of Abortion*. Boulder, Colo.: Westview Press.

Calhoun-Brown, Allison. 2003. "What a Fellowship: Civil Society, African American Churches, and Public Life." In *New Day Begun: African American Churches and Civic Culture in Post-Civil Rights America*, ed. R. Drew Smith, 39–57. Durham, N.C.: Duke University Press.

Carmines, Edward G., and James A. Stimson. 1989. *Issue Evolution: Race and the Transformation of American Politics*. Princeton, N.J.: Princeton University Press.

Cigler, Allen J. 1991. "Interest Groups: A Subfield in Search of an Identity." In *Political Science: Looking to the Future*. Vol. 4., ed. William Crotty, 99–135. Evanston, Ill.: Northwestern University Press.

Clark, Peter B., and James Q. Wilson. 1961. "Incentive Systems: A Theory of Organizations." *Administrative Science Quarterly* 6: 129–166.

Cleary, Edward L. 2006. "The Lively World of California's Religion and Politics." In *Representing God at the Statehouse*, ed. Edward L. Cleary and Allen D. Hertzke, 201–224. Lanham, Md.: Rowman & Littlefield.

Cleary, Edward L., and Allen D. Hertzke, eds. 2006. *Representing God at the Statehouse: Religion and Politics in the American States*. Lanham, Md.: Rowman & Littlefield.

Cohn, Steven F., Steven E. Barkan, and William H. Whitaker. 1993. "Activists against Hunger: Membership Characteristics of a National Social Movement Organization." *Sociological Forum* 8: 113–131.

Corbett, Michael, and Julia Mitchell Corbett. 1999. *Politics and Religion in the United States*. New York: Garland Publishing.

Cromartie, Michael. 2003. *A Public Faith: Evangelicals and Civic Engagement*. Lanham, Md.: Rowman & Littlefield.

Dahl, Robert A. 1961. *Who Governs?* New Haven, Conn.: Yale University Press.

Damore, David F., Ted G. Jelen, and Michael W. Bowers. 2007. "Sweet Land of Liberty: The Gay Marriage Amendment in Nevada." In *Religious Interests in Community Conflict*, ed. Paul A. Djupe and Laura R. Olson, 51–71. Waco, Texas: Baylor University Press.

Deckman, Melissa M. 2004. *School Board Battles: The Christian Right in Local Politics*. Washington D.C.: Georgetown University Press.

den Dulk, Kevin R., and J. Mitchell Pickerill. 2003. "Bridging the Lawmaking Process: Organized Interests, Court–Congress Interaction, and Church–State Relations." *Polity* 35: 419–440.

den Dulk, Kevin R., and Allen D. Hertzke. 2006. "Conclusion: Themes in Religious Advocacy." In *Representing God at the Statehouse*, ed. Edward L. Cleary and Allen D. Hertzke, 225–239. Lanham, Md.: Rowman & Littlefield.

Djupe, Paul A., and Laura R. Olson, eds. 2007. *Religious Interests in Community Conflict*. Waco, Texas: Baylor University Press.

Djupe, Paul A., Laura R. Olson, and Christopher P. Gilbert. 2005. "Sources of Support for Denominational Lobbying in Washington." *Review of Religious Research* 47 (1): 86–99.

Ebersole, Luke. 1951. *Church Lobbying in the Nation's Capital*. New York: Macmillian.

Espinosa, Gaston, Virgilio Elizondo, and Jesse Miranda, eds. 2005. *Latino Religious and Civic Activism in the United States*. New York: Oxford University Press.

Elazar, Daniel J. 1984. *American Federalism: A View from the States*. 3rd ed. New York: Harper and Row.

Findlay, James. F. 1993. *Church People in the Struggle: The National Council of Churches and the Black Freedom Movement, 1950–1970*. New York: Oxford University Press.

Finke, Roger, and Rodney Stark. 1992. *The Churching of America, 1776–1990: Winners and Losers in Our Religious Economy*. New Brunswick, N.J.: Rutgers University Press.

Fisher, Louis. 2002. *Religious Liberty in America: Political Safeguards*. Lawrence, Kans.: University of Kansas Press.

Fowler, Robert Booth, Allen D. Hertzke, Laura R. Olson, and Kevin den Dulk. 2004. *Religion and Politics in America*. Boulder, Colo.: Westview Press.

Green, John C. 2007. *The Faith Factor: How Religion Influences American Elections*. Westport, Conn.: Praeger.

Green, John C., James L. Guth, Corwin E. Smidt, and Lyman A. Kellstedt, eds. 1996. *Religion and the Culture Wars: Dispatches from the Front*. Lanham, Md.: Rowman & Littlefield.

Green, John C., Mark J. Rozell, and Clyde Wilcox, eds. 2003. *The Christian Right in American Politics: Marching to the Millennium*. Washington D.C.: Georgetown University Press.

Gusfield, Joseph. 1963. *Symbolic Crusade*, Urbana, Ill.: University of Illinois Press.

Guth, James L., John C. Green, Lyman A. Kellstedt, and Corwin E. Smidt. 1995. "Onward Christian Soldiers: Religious Activist Groups in American Politics." In *Interest Group Politics*. 4th ed., ed. Allan J. Cigler and Burdett A. Loomis, 55–76. Washington D.C.: Congressional Quarterly Press.

Guth, James L., Lyman A. Kellstedt, Corwin E. Smidt, and John Green. 1998. "Thunder on the Right? Religious Interest Group Mobilization in the 1996 Election." In *Interest Group Politics*. 5th ed., ed. Allan J. Cigler and Burdett A. Loomis, 162–192. Washington D.C.: Congressional Quarterly Press.

Guth, James L., Lyman A. Kellstedt, Corwin E. Smidt, and John C. Green. 2006. "Religious Influences in the 2004 Presidential Election." *Presidential Studies Quarterly* 26: 223–242.

Hadden, Jeffrey K. 1969. *The Gathering Storm in the Churches*. Garden City, N.Y.: Doubleday.

Hall, Richard L., and Frank W. Wayman. 1990. "Buying Time: Moneyed Interests and the Mobilization of Bias in Congressional Committees." *American Political Science Review* 84: 797–820.

Henriques, Diana B., and Andrew W. Lehren. 2007. "Religious Groups Reap Federal Aid for Pet Projects." *The New York Times*, May 13.

Hero, Alfred O., Jr. 1973. *American Religious Groups View Foreign Policy: Trends in Rank-and-File Opinion, 1937–1969*. Durham, N.C.: Duke University Press.

Hertzke, Allen D. 1988. *Representing God in Washington: The Role of Religious Lobbies in the American Polity*. Knoxville, Tenn.: University of Tennessee Press.

Hertzke, Allen D. 1989. "Faith and Access: Religious Constituencies and the Washington Elites." In *Religion and Political Behavior in the United States*, ed. Ted G. Jelen, pp. 259–274. New York: Praeger.

Hertzke, Allen D. 1993. *Echoes of Discontent: Jesse Jackson, Pat Robertson, and the Resurgence of Populism*. Washington, D.C.: Congressional Quarterly.

Hertzke, Allen D. 2004. *Freeing God's Children: The Unlikely Alliance for Global Human Rights*. Lanham, Md.: Rowman & Littlefield.

Hertzke, Allen D. Forthcoming. 2009. "American Muslim Exceptionalism." In *On the Borders of Civilizations*, ed. Stig Jarle Hansen. London: C. Hurst.

Heyer, Kristin E. 2006. *Prophetic and Public: The Social Witness of U.S. Catholicism*. Washington, D.C.: Georgetown University Press.

Hirschman, Albert O. 1970. *Exit, Voice, and Loyalty*. Cambridge, Mass.: Harvard University Press.

Hodge, David R. 2007a. "Advocating for Persecuted People of Faith: A Social Justice Imperative." *Families in Society* 88: 255–262.

Hodge, David R. 2007b. "Social Justice and People of Faith: A Transnational Perspective." *Social Work* 52: 139–148.

Hofrenning, Daniel J. B. 1995a. *In Washington But Not of It: The Prophetic Politics of Religious Lobbyists*. Philadelphia, Pa.: Temple University Press.

Hofrenning, Daniel J. B. 1995b. "Into the Public Square: Explaining the Origins of Religious Interest Groups." *Social Science Journal* 32 (1): 35–49.

Hofrenning, Daniel J. B. 1998. "Lobbying, Religious." In *The Encyclopedia of Politics and Religion*, ed. Robert Wuthnow Vol. II, 480–484. Washington D.C.: Congressional Quarterly.

Hoover, Dennis R., and Kevin R. den Dulk. 2004. "Christian Conservatives Go to Court: Religion and Legal Mobilization in the United States and Canada." *International Political Science Review* 25 (1): 9–34.

Imig, Douglas R., and Jeffrey M. Berry. 1996. "Patrons and Entrepreneurs." *Political Research Quarterly* 49: 147–154.

Imig, Douglas R., and David S. Meyer. 1993. "Political Opportunity and Peace and Justice Advocacy in the 1980s: A Tale of Two Sectors." *Social Science Quarterly* 74: 750–770.

Ivers, Greg. 1992. "Religious Organizations as Constitutional Litigants." *Polity* 25: 243–266.

Jenkins, Philip. 2002. *The Next Christendom: The Coming of Global Christianity*. New York: Oxford University Press.

Jenkins, Philip. 2006. *The New Faces of Christianity: Believing the Bible in the Global South*. New York: Oxford University Press.

Kellstedt, Lyman A., and John C. Green. 2003. "The Politics of the Willow Creek Association Pastors." *Journal for the Scientific Study of Religion* 42: 547–561.

Kellstedt, Lyman A., John C. Green, Corwin E. Smidt, and James L. Guth. 2007. "Faith Transformed: Religion and American Politics from FDR to GW Bush." In *Religion and American Politics: From the Colonial Period to the Present.* 2nd ed., ed. Mark A. Noll and Luke E. Harlow, 269–295. New York: Oxford University Press.

King, David C., and Jack L. Walker. 1992. The Provision of Benefits by Interest Groups in the United States." *Journal of Politics* 54: 394–426.

Kraus, Rachel. 2007. "Laity, Institution, Theology, or Politics? Protestant, Catholic, and Jewish Washington Offices' Agenda Setting." *Sociology of Religion* 68: 67–81.

Leon, Luis D. 2005. "Cesar Chavez and Mexican American Civil Religion." In *Latino Religious and Civic Activism in the United States,* ed. Gaston Espinosa, Virgilio Elizondo, and Jesse Miranda, 53–64. New York: Oxford University Press.

Lloyd-Moffett. 2005. "The Mysticism and Social Action of Cesar Chavez." In *Latino Religious and Civic Activism in the United States,* ed. Gaston Espinosa, Virgilio Elizondo, and Jesse Miranda, 35–51. New York: Oxford University Press.

Lowery, David, and Virginia Gray. 2004. "A Neopluralist Perspective on Research on Organized Interests." *Political Research Quarterly* 57: 163–175.

McAdam, Doug. 1985. *Political Process and the Development of Black Insurgency, 1930–1970.* Chicago, Ill.: University of Chicago Press.

Mittleman, Alan, Jonathan D. Sarna, and Robert Licht. 2002. *Jews and the American Public Square.* Lanham, Md.: Rowman & Littlefield.

Moen, Matthew. 1989. *The Christian Right and Congress.* Tuscaloosa, Ala.: University of Alabama Press.

Monsma, Stephen V. 2001. "Faith-based NGOs and the Government Embrace." In *The Influence of Faith: Religious Groups & U.S. Foreign Policy,* ed. Elliott Abrams, 203–219. Lanham, Md.: Rowman & Littlefield.

Murphy, Andrew R. 1993. "The Mainline Churches and Political Activism: The Continuing Impact of the Persian-Gulf War." *Soundings* 76: 525–549.

National Association of Evangelicals. 2004. *For the Health of the Nation: An Evangelical Call to Civic Responsibility.* Washington D.C.: National Association of Evangelicals.

Nazworth, Napp. 2006. "Institutionalization of the Christian Right." Ph.D. diss., University of Florida.

Nnorom, Columba Aham. 2005. "African American Churches and the Evolution of Antiapartheid Activism." In *Long March Ahead: African American Churches and Public Policy in Post-Civil Rights America,* ed. R. Drew Smith, 193–215. Durham, N.C.: Duke University Press.

Nownes, Anthony. 1995. "The Other Exchange: Public Interest Groups, Patrons, and Benefits." *Social Science Quarterly* 76: 381–401.

Nownes, Anthony, and Grant Neeley. 1996a. "Public Interest Group Entrepreneurship and Theories of Group Mobilization." *Political Research Quarterly* 49: 119–146.

Nownes, Anthony, and Grant Neeley. 1996b. "Toward an Explanation for Public Interest Group Formation and Proliferation: 'Seed Money,' Disturbances, Entrepreneurship, and Patronage." *Policy Studies Journal* 24 (1): 74–92.

Nurser, John. 2005. *For All Peoples and All Nations: Christian Churches and Human Rights.* Washington D.C.: Georgetown University Press.

Odegard, Peter. 1966. *Pressure Politics: The Story of the Anti-Saloon League.* New York: Octagon Books.

Olson, Laura R. 2002. "Mainline Protestant Washington Offices and the Political Lives of Clergy." In *The Quiet Hand of God: Faith-Based Activism and the Public Role of Mainline Protestantism*, eds. Robert Wuthnow and John H. Evans, 54–79. Berkeley, Calif.: University of California Press.

Olson, Mancur. 1965. *The Logic of Collective Action*. Cambridge, Mass.: Harvard University Press.

Owens, Michael Leo. 2003. "Doing Something in Jesus' Name: Black Churches and Community Development Corporations." In *New Day Begun*, ed. R. Drew Smith, 215–247. Durham, N.C.: Duke University Press.

Perkins, John M. 1993. *Beyond Charity: The Call to Christian Community Development*. Grand Rapids, Mich.: Baker Books.

Perkins, John M., ed. 1995. *Restoring At-Risk Communities*. Grand Rapids, Mich.: Baker Books.

Putnam, Robert D. 2000. *Bowling Alone: The Collapse and Revival of American Community*. New York: Simon and Schuster.

Quinley, Harold E. 1974. *The Prophetic Clergy*. New York: Wiley.

Reichley, A. James. 1985. *Religion in American Public Life*. Washington D.C.: Brookings Institution Press.

Ribuffo, Leo P. 2001. "Religion in the History of U.S. Foreign Policy." In *The Influence of Faith: Religious Groups & U.S. Foreign Policy*, ed. Elliott Abrams, 1–27. Lanham, Md.: Rowman & Littlefield.

Salisbury, Robert H. 1969. "An Exchange Theory of Interest Groups." *Midwest Journal of Political Science* 13: 1–32.

Salisbury, Robert H. 1984. "Interest Representation: The Dominance of Institutions." *American Political Science Review* 78: 64–76.

Schattschneider, E. E. 1960. *The Semisovereign People*. New York: Holt, Rinehart, and Winston.

Skocpol, Theda. 2003. *Diminished Democracy: From Membership to Management in American Civic Life*. Norman, Okla.: University of Oklahoma Press.

Smith, R. Drew, ed. 2003. *New Day Begun: African American Churches and Civic Culture in Post-Civil Rights America*. Durham, N.C.: Duke University Press.

Smith, R. Drew, ed. 2004. *Long March Ahead: African American Churches and Public Policy in Post-Civil Rights America*. Durham, N.C.: Duke University Press.

Smith, R. Drew, and Fredrick C. Harris. 2005. *Black Churches and Local Politics: Clergy Influence, Organizational Partnerships, and Civic Empowerment*. Lanham, Md.: Rowman & Littlefield.

Smith, Richard A. 1995. "Interest Group Influence in the U.S. Congress." *Legislative Studies Quarterly* 20: 89–139.

Steinfels, Margaret O'Brien. 2004a. *American Catholics, American Culture: Tradition and Existence*. Vol. 2. Lanham, Md.: Rowman & Littlefield.

Steinfels, Margaret O'Brien. 2004b. *American Catholics and Civic Engagement: A Distinctive Voice*. Vol. 1. Lanham, Md.: Rowman & Littlefield.

Stenger, Katie E. 2005. "The Underrepresentation of Liberal Christians: Mobilization Strategies of Religious Interest Groups." *Social Science Journal* 42: 391–403.

Szymanski, Ann-Marie. 2003. *Pathways to Prohibition*. Durham, N.C.: Duke University Press.

Tipton, Steven M. 2007. *Pulpit Politics: Methodists and Mainline Churches in the Moral Argument of Public Life*. Chicago, Ill.: University of Chicago Press.

Truman, David B. 1951. *The Governmental Process*. New York: Knopf.

Verba, Sidney, Kay Lehman Schlozman, and Henry E. Brady. 1995. *Voice and Equality: Civic Voluntarism in American Politics.* Cambridge, Mass.: Harvard University Press.

Wald, Kenneth D., and Allison Calhoun-Brown. 2007. *Religion and Politics in the United States.* 5th ed. Lanham, Md.: Rowman & Littlefield.

Wald, Kenneth D., and Clyde Wilcox. 2006. "Getting Religion: Has Political Science Rediscovered the Faith Factor?" *American Political Science Review* 100: 523–529.

Wallis, Jim. 2006. *God's Politics: Why the Right Gets It Wrong and the Left Doesn't Get It.* New York: HarperOne.

Walker, Jack L., Jr. 1983. "The Origins and Maintenance of Interest Groups in America." *American Political Science Review* 77: 390–406.

Walker, Jack L., Jr. 1991. *Mobilizing Interest Groups in America: Patrons, Professions, and Social Movements.* Ann Arbor, Mich.: University of Michigan Press.

Weber, Paul. 1982. "Examining the Religious Lobbies." *This World* 1: 97–107.

Weber, Paul, and W. Landis Jones. 1994. *U.S. Religious Interest Groups: Institutional Profiles.* Westport, Conn.: Greenwood.

Welch, Michael R., David C. Leege, and Robert Woodberry. 1998. "Pro-life Catholics and Support for Lobbying by Religious Organizations." *Social Science Quarterly* 79: 649–663.

Wilcox, Clyde. 1988. "Political-Action Committees of the Christian Right: A Longitudinal Analysis." *Journal for the Scientific Study of Religion* 27: 60–71.

Wilcox, Clyde, and Carin Larson. 2006. *Onward Christian Soldiers?: The Religious Right in American Politics.* 3rd ed. Boulder, Colo.: Westview Press.

Winship, Christopher. 2004. "End of a Miracle? Crime, Faith, and Partnership in Boston in the 1990s." In *Long March Ahead: African American Churches and Public Policy in Post-Civil Rights America*, ed. R. Drew Smith, 171–192. Durham, N.C.: Duke University Press.

Wood, Richard L. 2002. *Faith in Action: Religion, Race, and Democratic Organizing in America.* Chicago, Ill.: University of Chicago Press.

Wuthnow, Robert. 2002. "Beyond Quiet Influence? Possibilities for the Protestant Mainline." In *The Quiet Hand of God: Faith-Based Activism and the Public Role of Mainline Protestantism*, ed. Robert Wuthnow and John H. Evans, 381–402. Berkeley, Calif.: University of California Press.

Wuthnow, Robert, and John H. Evans, eds. 2002. *The Quiet Hand of God: Faith-Based Activism and the Public Role of Mainline Protestantism.* Berkeley, Calif.: University of California Press.

Yamane, David. 1999. "Faith and Access: Personal Religiosity and Religious Group Advocacy in a State Legislature." *Journal for the Scientific Study of Religion* 38: 543–550.

Yamane, David. 2005. *The Catholic Church in State Politics: Negotiating Prophetic Demands and Political Realities.* Lanham, Md.: Rowman & Littlefield.

Yamane, David, and Elizabeth A. Oldmixon. 2006. "Religion in the Legislative Arena: Affiliation, Salience, Advocacy, and Public Policy." *Legislative Studies Quarterly* 21: 433–460.

Zwier, Robert. 1991. "The Power and Potential of Religious Interest Groups." *Journal of Church and State* 33: 271–285.

Zwier, Robert. 1994. "An Organizational Perspective on Religious Interest Groups." In *Christian Political Activism at the Crossroads*, ed. Williams R. Stevenson, Jr, 95–119. Lanham, Md.: University Press of America.

CHAPTER 12

RELIGION, PARTIES, AND VOTING BEHAVIOR: A POLITICAL EXPLANATION OF RELIGIOUS INFLUENCE

JOHN MICHAEL McTAGUE
AND GEOFFREY C. LAYMAN

The president got re-elected by dividing the country along fault lines of fear, intolerance, ignorance and religious rule . . . . [President George] W. [Bush] ran a jihad in America so he can fight one in Iraq—drawing a devoted flock of evangelicals, or "values voters," as they call themselves, to the polls by opposing abortion, suffocating stem cell research, and supporting a constitutional amendment against gay marriage.

—*New York Times* columnist Maureen Dowd,
November 4, 2004

> The wagers of this war on Christmas are a cabal of secularists,
> so-called humanists, trial lawyers, cultural relativists, and lib-
> eral, guilt-wracked Christians . . . [who] vote for John Kerry,
> Ted Kennedy, and Barney Frank.
>
> —*Fox News* personality John Gibson, quoted in
> Goldberg (2005)

The prominent role that religion plays in shaping voting decisions, party alignments, and electoral outcomes is today widely acknowledged by observers of
American politics. Popular accounts often characterize elections as contests between two distinct groups of citizens: religious "values" voters who are the most
loyal and important constituency of the Republican Party and secular, nonreligious
voters who comprise the base of the Democratic Party. As exemplified by the
inflammatory quotes at the beginning of this chapter, the popular press depicts
this pattern as the result of a broader "culture war" pitting "God's warriors" against
the champions of secular humanism. Despite the appeal of such a simplistic
storyline, social scientists have shown that the impact of religion on American
politics is far more complex and subtle. Thus, the primary task now for political
scientists is not to demonstrate that religion matters politically, but to identify
carefully *how*, *why*, and *when* religion influences American party politics and
electoral behavior.

Fortunately, scholarly understanding of the relationship between religion and
political behavior has increased, particularly during the past two decades as political scientists have "rediscovered" (Leege and Kellstedt 1993) the importance of
religion to American politics. Thanks to the extant literature, we know quite a bit
about the *what* in the relationship between religion and American political behavior (What about religion becomes connected to politics? What are the relevant
religious groups in American politics?).

We know less, however, about *how*, *why*, and *when* religion matters politically.
Religion's connection to partisan politics is not inevitable. The existence of religious cleavages in American society does not necessarily mean that these divides
will become partisan and electoral cleavages. For that to happen, the religious
fissures must be made politically relevant by political actors, circumstances, and
issues. Thus, identifying the political factors that produce such partisan and
electoral divides is crucial to understanding how religion matters for party politics
and voting behavior, why it matters, and when it is likely to matter most.

To that end, we offer a framework for understanding the links between religion
and partisan politics that emphasizes the major political parties and the interactions between their component parts. Those components, as famously identified by
Key (1964) are the *parties in the electorate*, the coalitions of citizens who identify
with the parties and support their candidates; the *party organizations*, the institutional structure of the parties and their bases of activist volunteers; and the *parties
in government*, those elected officials who serve under the party label. We argue that

the religious divisions between the parties in the electorate can be understood only in the context of how strategic political actors in the parties' organizations and coalitions in government frame the world of politics in a way that makes religion salient to electoral choice. We begin by presenting the puzzle: how religion's relationship to politics and voting behavior has changed during the past 40 years. We then try to solve the puzzle of why that change has occurred and when new religious divisions between the parties' electoral coalitions are most likely to take shape by focusing on the dynamic relationship between the three parts of the American party system. After that, we discuss caveats, challenges, and alternatives to our framework, and suggest paths for future research.

PRESENTING THE PUZZLE: RELIGION AND THE PARTIES IN THE ELECTORATE SINCE THE 1960S

As Smidt, Kellstedt, and Guth explain in the first chapter of this volume, there are two dominant perspectives in the literature on the link between religion and politics: the *ethnoreligious* model and the *theological restructuring* model. The ethnoreligious approach views religion primarily as a social group phenomenon, stressing religious belonging, which is closely associated with other group-level cultural factors such as ethnicity, race, and region. The role of religious beliefs and behaviors is principally to reinforce religious traditions, creating unique sets of distinctive values among adherents. The resulting cohesion within and distinctiveness between religious traditions makes those traditions building blocs in politics (e.g., McCormick 1986; Kleppner 1987).

Ethnoreligious divisions dominated political alliances through the middle of the 20th century, with Catholics, Jews, black Protestants, and southern Protestants tending to support the Democratic Party, and northern Protestants forming the backbone of the Republican coalition (Berelson, Lazarsfeld, and McPhee 1954; Sundquist 1983; Green 2007). However, as the social differences between Protestants, Catholics, and Jews declined during the post-World War II period, the political divide between these faith traditions gave way to a new cleavage within them.

According to the theological restructuring, or "culture wars," perspective,[1] this new religious divide is defined not by religious belonging, but by beliefs and behaviors, and pits individuals who subscribe to traditionalist religious beliefs and engage in traditional religious practices against those who hold modernist beliefs and have limited involvement in traditional forms of worship (Wuthnow 1988, 1989; Hunter 1991, 1994; White 2003). According to James Davison Hunter (1991), the "culture wars" between traditionalist and modernist religious groups—with secular individuals typically siding with the modernists—arise from their incompatible moral philosophies. Although the religiously orthodox camp is committed to transcendent and fixed sources of moral authority, religious progressives and seculars tend to adhere to a more fluid conception in which moral authority is defined relative to an individual's own judgment, historical context, and human progress.

Applied to politics, the new cleavage makes the former divisions between religious traditions "virtually irrelevant" (Hunter 1991), as the orthodox members of all major faith traditions join together against similarly unified religious progressives and their secular allies. The staunch conservatism of religious traditionalists—especially on moral issues such as abortion and gay rights, but, according to Hunter (1991), on a host of other issues as well—makes the Republican Party a natural political home for them. The moral and political liberalism of religious modernists and seculars attracts them to the Democratic Party.

As we discuss later, a number of scholars have raised serious questions about the culture wars thesis, particularly the expectation of growing societal polarization along orthodox–progressive religious and cultural lines (e.g., DiMaggio, Evans, and Bryson 1996; Wolfe 1998; Fiorina, Abrams, and Pope 2006). However, other researchers find that the orthodox–progressive divide is relevant for political behavior, attitudes on some political issues, and the composition of the Republican and Democratic electoral coalitions (Wuthnow 1989; Green, Guth, Smidt, and Kellstedt 1996; Kohut, Green, Keeter, and Toth 2000; Layman 2001; Guth, Green, Smidt, and Kellstedt 2006; Layman and Green 2006; Green 2007; Green, Kellstedt, Smidt, and Guth 2007).

At the same time, this and other research suggests that, far from being "virtually irrelevant," religious tradition remains important for contemporary partisanship and voting behavior. White Protestants continue to be somewhat more Republican than Catholics and both of those groups remain much more Republican than black Protestants and Jews (Kohut et al. 2000; Layman 2001; Leege, Wald, Krueger, and Mueller 2002; Green 2007; Green et al. 2007). Religious belonging also conditions the political impact of religious beliefs and behaviors, with the political divide between traditionalists and modernists varying in size and, in some instances, direction across faith traditions (Mockabee, Monson, and Grant 2001; Layman and Green 2006).

This suggests that the connection between religion and political behavior has changed markedly. However, rather than a cleavage based on religious beliefs and behaviors replacing the old cleavage based on religious belonging, the religious–political landscape is now defined by a mix of the old and new—as Smidt, Kellstedt, and Guth contend, by belonging, believing, and behaving. We turn now to an empirical evaluation of the degree to which the relationship between religion and partisan political orientations has shifted during the past four decades.

An Empirical Investigation

To assess the degree to which the relationship between religion and partisan support has shifted from one defined primarily by ethnoreligious differences to one structured by the fault lines of the culture wars perspective or by the interaction of belonging, believing, and behaving, we compare the effect of religious tradition and religious traditionalism on the presidential vote and party identification during the 1960s with that during the 2000s.[2] We pooled data from the 1964 and 1968 American National Election Studies (ANES) surveys and from the 2000 and 2004 ANES surveys, and estimated statistical models of partisanship and the vote in which the independent variables were religious tradition,[3] view of the Bible,[4] worship attendance,[5] and a set of demographic controls.[6] Table 12.1 shows the predictions from these models.[7]

The religious divisions that existed in political orientations during the 1960s were almost entirely ethnoreligious ones. There were clear differences between religious traditions in both presidential voting behavior and party loyalties, with the familiar fault lines between Protestants, Catholics, and Jews quite apparent. Both evangelical and mainline Protestants were markedly more Republican than Catholics and seculars, and all of these groups exhibited greater GOP support than did black Protestants and Jews.

Meanwhile, there is virtually no evidence of traditionalist–modernist political differences within faith traditions during the 1960s. In none of the major Christian traditions were religious traditionalists more likely than modernists to vote Republican or identify with the GOP. The only statistically significant difference was in the party attachments of Catholics, where, in keeping with ethnoreligious politics, traditionalists were more likely than modernists to adhere to the established loyalties of their faith and to identify themselves as Democrats.

In contrast, there is clear evidence of culture wars divisions in the political orientations of evangelical Protestants, mainline Protestants, and Catholics during the 2000s. In all three traditions, individuals with orthodox views of scripture and high levels of worship attendance are substantially and significantly more likely than their modernist and less committed counterparts to vote Republican by the 2000s. There also is a substantial and statistically significant traditionalist–modernist divide in party identification among evangelicals and mainliners. The gap in Catholic partisanship is more modest, but still statistically significant. As recent research demonstrates (Kellstedt, Green, Smidt, and Guth 2007), the traditionalist–modernist cleavage did not begin to take shape in the electorate until the 1980s, and, even then, only among evangelicals. For Catholics and mainline Protestants, the emergence of the traditionalist–modernist divide only became apparent with the elections of the 1990s (Kellstedt et al. 2007).

Contemporary political behavior, however, is not defined entirely by the traditionalist–modernist divide, because there remain noticeable discrepancies in vote choice and party ties between religious traditions. Evangelical Protestants now are more Republican than mainliners in both vote choice and party identification, and both groups are a bit more supportive of the GOP than are Catholics and seculars. All these groups are much more likely than black Protestants and Jews to vote for and identify with the GOP. Moreover, the pro-Republican influence of religious traditionalism is not uniform across faith traditions, as black Protestant traditionalists are no more likely than their modernist counterparts to support the GOP.

Table 12.1 Religious Tradition, Religious Traditionalism, and Political Orientation during the 1960s and the 2000s

	1960s			2000s		
	Modernist	Centrist	Traditionalist	Modernist	Centrist	Traditionalist
Presidential vote*						
Evangelical Protestant	.51	.52	.52	.55	.68	.79‡
Mainline Protestant	.56	.55	.55	.37	.53	.68‡
Black Protestant	.05	.02	.01	.04	.07	.10
Catholic	.29	.29	.28	.36	.48	.59‡
Jewish	—	.04	—	—	.06	—
Secular	—	.37	—	.41	.41	—
Party identification†						
Evangelical Protestant	.39	.41	.44	.49	.57	.64‡
Mainline Protestant	.41	.44	.46	.43	.51	.59‡
Black Protestant	.22	.21	.20	.23	.22	.20
Catholic	.35	.29	.24‡	.42	.45	.49§
Jewish	—	.17	—	—	.18	—
Secular	—	.37	—	—	.42	—

Entries are predictions from logit and regression models controlling for education, income, southern residence, age, gender, and union membership. Worship attendance and view of the Bible are set to the mean values for each tradition for the predictions for "centrists," at one standard deviation below their tradition means for the predictions for "modernists," and at one standard deviation above the tradition mean for the predictions for "traditionalists."

*Predicted probability of voting Republican.

†Predicted value on a scale ranging from zero for strong Democrat to one for strong Republican.

‡Predicted difference between traditionalists and modernists in the tradition is significant at $P < .001$.

§Predicted difference between traditionalists and modernists in the tradition is significant at $P < .05$.

Source: 1964, 1968, 2000, and 2004 National Election Studies.

In short, there has been both continuity and change in the connection between religion and political behavior during the past 40 years. Religious beliefs and behaviors, once irrelevant to party affiliation and vote choice, now create deep political fissures within faith traditions. However, noticeable differences remain in both the central political tendencies of religious traditions and the size of the traditionalist–modernist gap across traditions.

To assess further the changes over time in the partisan orientations of major religious groups, we show in figures 12.1 and 12.2 the percentages of frequent and infrequent church attenders within the three predominantly white Christian traditions and of seculars identifying themselves as Democrats, independents, and Republicans during the past five decades.[8] As past research (Layman 2001) indicates, there has been a clear realignment in the party ties of frequently attending evangelical Protestants. Predominantly Democratic during the 1960s, committed evangelicals began to abandon the Democrats in the 1970s, became increasingly loyal to the Republican Party during the 1980s and 1990s, and now heavily identify with the GOP in the 2000s. More important, Kellstedt (1989) and Campbell (2002) show that a key contributor to this realignment has been the especially substantial growth in Republicanism among young evangelicals first coming into the electorate.

Clearly suggesting that the evangelical realignment has been based in the traditionalist religious orientations of committed evangelicals is that such a clear partisan shift has not yet taken shape among their less committed brethren. Infrequently attending evangelicals were not as attached to the Democratic Party during the 1970s, '80s, and '90s as they were during the 1960s, but still were more likely to identify as Democrats than as Republicans. Spurred possibly by the presidency and policies of fellow evangelical George W. Bush (Layman and Hussey 2007), this group has shifted, in the 2000s, to being more Republican than Democratic. However, a plurality of less committed evangelicals continues to identify as independents.

The partisan shift among frequently attending Catholics has been nearly as impressive as that among churchgoing evangelicals. Overwhelmingly Democratic during the 1960s, committed Catholics are now as likely to identify with the Republicans as with the Democrats. Although devout Catholics have not yet clearly aligned themselves with the GOP, the increase in Republican attachment and the decrease in Democratic ties within this group have been on par with those of their evangelical counterparts.[9] Thus, the growth of a traditionalist–modernist gap in American party politics has been accompanied by extensive migrations of committed Catholics and evangelicals out of the Democratic fold and into the confines of the GOP.

Less devout Catholics have joined their committed counterparts in the category of partisan "free agents." These Catholics have become only slightly more likely to identify with the GOP than previously, but their Democratic ties clearly have weakened over time.

In contrast to those for evangelicals and Catholics, what is noteworthy about the patterns of party loyalties among mainline Protestants and seculars is their lack of change. Popular accounts often suggest that the increasing presence of

Evangelical Protestants

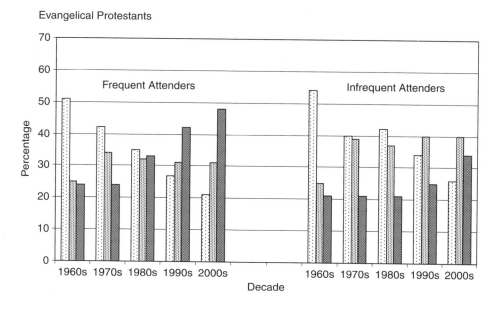

Catholics

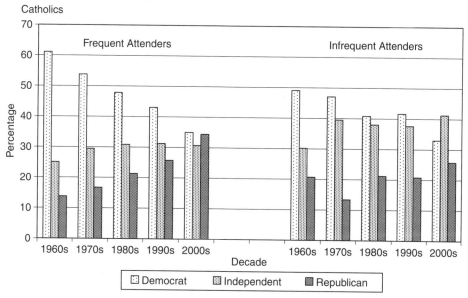

Figure 12.1 Party identification of evangelical Protestants and Catholics by worship attendance and decade. Source: 1960–2004 National Election Studies.

traditionalist evangelicals in the Republican fold has alienated mainliners, once the religious backbone of the Republican coalition, from the party. A scholarly account by Hout and Fischer (2002) argues that the increasing identification of the highly religious with the GOP has contributed to the increase in religious "nones." However, there is no evidence of such a change in the party ties of committed mainliners. A clear plurality of frequently attending mainline Protestants has

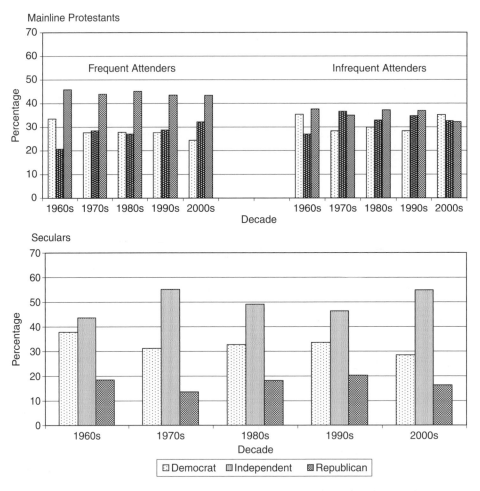

Figure 12.2 Party identification of mainline Protestants and seculars by worship attendance and decade. Source: 1960–2004 National Election Studies.

identified with the GOP during each of the past five decades, and the percentage of
Republicans in this group has not declined at all. There also is little sign of a shift in
the party loyalties of infrequently attending mainliners.

Given the growing secularism of Democratic activists (discussed later) and the
parallels between the staunch cultural liberalism of seculars (Jelen, chapter 8, this
volume) and that of the Democratic Party, it would not be unreasonable to expect a
growth in the Democratic attachments of seculars in the mass electorate. Such a
growth, however, has not occurred. Paralleling their lack of religious affiliation,
seculars tend to steer clear of party affiliation. A plurality of seculars has identified
as independent during every decade since the 1960s, and that plurality has become
a majority during the 2000s.

RELIGIOUS CLEAVAGES IN PARTY
COALITIONS: A POLITICAL EXPLANATION

Our analyses provide clues about how religion is related to party identification and voting behavior and how that relationship has changed over time. What it does not tell us, however, is why the religious cleavage between the parties in the electorate has changed from one based almost entirely on religious belonging to one based on both religious belonging and the traditionalism of religious beliefs and behaviors, and when this new religious divide in political behavior is likely to be most apparent.

Answering those questions, we argue, requires not just understanding the nature of divisions within American religion, but also understanding the nature of party politics and how particular religious divisions interact with the characteristics of the parties and the political actors operating within them. Like other "structural" cleavages—factors such as race, ethnicity, and language that differentiate social groups on something other than purely political grounds—religion only becomes relevant for citizens' party loyalties and voting decisions if it is connected to political issues on which the parties and their candidates and officeholders take distinct positions (Sundquist 1983; Carsey 2000; Layman 2001; Leege et al. 2002). In fact, a good deal of research suggests that even strictly political, issue-based cleavages only affect partisan change and become relevant for electoral choice if the parties promote and stake out distinct ground on the issues—if they provide citizens with a clear choice (Campbell, Converse, Miller, and Stokes 1960; Brody and Page 1972; MacDonald and Rabinowitz 1987; Layman and Carsey 2002a, b). The parties are likely to move to such distinct ground only if the issues further the strategic objectives of party politicians and attract the attention of citizen activists who may pursue their goals within the parties (Riker 1982; Carmines and Stimson 1989; Layman 2001; Leege et al. 2002).

In figure 12.3, we present our framework for explaining how such factors might translate a religious cleavage in American society (step 1) into a cleavage between the parties in the electorate. What follows is an explanation of this model and how the development of a traditionalist–modernist cleavage led to changes in the Republican and Democratic mass coalitions.[10]

Religion and Political Issues

Because political parties typically do not take positions on issues of religious doctrine or proper liturgical practice, societal cleavages based in such matters must be connected to subjects on which the parties can and do take stands—namely, issues of public policy—to become manifest in the parties' electoral coalitions (step 2 in fig. 12.3). Most policy issues, however, have little or no bearing on party identification or voting behavior, even if they meet the necessary

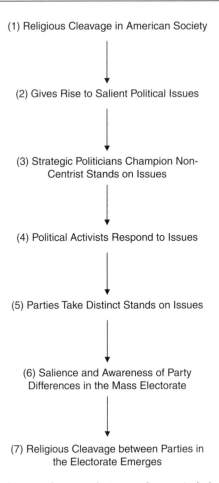

Figure 12.3 Explaining religious cleavages between the parties' electoral coalitions.

condition of being matters on which the parties and their candidates differ (Campbell et al. 1960; Carmines and Stimson 1989).

To shape or reshape patterns of party identification or voting behavior, political issues must capture the attention of the mass electorate and produce deeply held positions in a large number of people (Campbell et al. 1960; Schattschneider 1960; Brody and Page 1972; Sundquist 1983; Carmines and Stimson 1989; Leege et al. 2002). Most Americans pay relatively little attention to politics and possess firm positions on a limited number of policy issues (Converse 1964; Delli Carpini and Keeter 1996). Thus, the issues that can attract enough attention from and produce enough enthusiasm among the citizenry to exert a noticeable aggregate-level impact on partisan political orientations typically are those that Carmines and Stimson (1980, 1989) label "easy" issues: highly emotional matters that can be responded to at a "gut" level without a substantial base of factual knowledge or contextual understanding. Putting it somewhat differently, Sundquist (1983) argues that the issues that are most likely to produce partisan transformations are those that have a strong moral component: issues that are viewed by citizens in good-versus-evil terms.[11] Furthermore, if political issues and the social divisions related to them are to reshape the parties' coalitions in a significant way, they must be ones that cut across the existing lines of partisan cleavage (Sundquist 1983; Carmines and Stimson 1989). If they cleave the electorate in a way that is similar to the issues and sociodemographic factors underlying the extant party coalitions, then they may shape voting behavior and perhaps even alter the party loyalties of some individuals, but they are unlikely to produce a noticeable transformation in the ideological and social basis of the parties in the electorate.

A large part of the reason why the traditionalist–modernist divide in American religion has come to reconfigure the parties' electoral coalitions is that it is closely related to a set of issues that meets both of these criteria. Religious traditionalism is connected to attitudes in a number of different policy domains, but it is most closely associated with views on the so-called "moral" and "cultural" issues: issues such as abortion, homosexual rights, and prayer in the public schools that center on the role of traditional morality in American society and the government's responsibility to protect that role (Hunter 1991; Cook, Jelen, and Wilcox 1992; Layman 2001; Guth et al. 2006; Layman and Green 2006). These are subjects that clearly fit the mold of "easy" issues, containing a strong moral element and arousing intense emotions and deeply held views among large numbers of people (Hunter 1991, 1994; Mouw and Sobel 2001; Brewer 2003; Jelen and Wilcox 2003). They are made even easier by the dualistic, highly emotional, and symbol-laden way in which they tend to be presented to the public (Hunter 1991, 1994; Frank 2004).

Cultural issues and the traditionalist–modernist religious divide with which they are associated also clearly intersect the lines of party cleavage that were established during the New Deal era of the 1930s and existed for decades thereafter. They cut across not only the divide between faith traditions that undergirded the party coalitions through at least the 1950s, but also the class-based party cleavage associated with the social welfare issues of the New Deal. Lower status citizens, long Democratic and supportive of the party's social welfare liberalism, tend to be traditionally religious and hold conservative views on cultural issues. Their upper status counterparts generally support the Republican Party and its conservative stands on economic and social welfare concerns, but tend to be less attracted to traditional religion and cultural conservatism (Ladd 1975; Layman 2001).

Religion, Cultural Issues, and Strategic Politicians

The cultural issues that arose during the 1960s and 1970s clearly had the potential to reshape fundamentally the parties' coalitions and tie the traditionalist–modernist religious divide to partisanship and electoral choice. However, even if a set of political issues reflects moral divisions in society, arouses strong emotions in large parts of the populace, and cuts across the existing lines of party division, they are unlikely to exert a significant impact on mass party identification and voting behavior unless the parties take distinct stands on them. That, we argue, is probable only if the issues appeal to the strategic incentives of some set of party politicians—if some party leaders, candidates, or politicians see a potential for the new issues to enhance their political positions (step 3 in fig. 12.3).

However, is it not inevitable that a deep-seated societal division over powerful political issues will come to be reflected in party politics? After all, James Sundquist (1983, p. 328), in his seminal statement on American party change, asserts that "when a society polarizes, so do the parties." We contend that this is not necessarily so. Sundquist (1983) also tells us that the instinct of established leaders of the two major parties is typically to "straddle" powerful new cross-cutting issues—to cling to the center and avoid staking out clear positions on one side or the other of the issues (see also Carmines and Stimson 1989; Carmines 1991). Party elites, of course, follow this centrist impulse because powerful cross-cutting issues have the potential to tear apart their electoral coalitions and threaten their political positions.

At that point, the job of pushing the parties to polarized positions on new issues falls to political activists, who Carmines and Stimson refer to as the "dynamic element" in the partisan change process (Carmines and Stimson 1989; Carmines 1991). The decentralized American political parties, with their participatory nominating processes, are highly vulnerable to groups of activists, with agendas on one side or the other of particular political issues, becoming involved in the parties and, through their participation in party decision making, forcing them toward extreme policy positions. In fact, a number of scholars have shown that the importance of activists to the parties' nomination processes and prospects of electoral victory are what prevents the parties and their candidates from converging to the ideological center (Aranson and Ordeshook 1972; Aldrich 1995; Schofield and Miller 2007). Indeed, it is the very openness of the American parties to influence by zealous activists that leads Sundquist (1983) to his conclusion about the inevitable link between societal and partisan polarization.

However, the openness of the American party system to new groups of activists does not necessarily mean that those groups will choose to pursue their policy agendas through one of the two major parties. They have a range of other options. They may focus on interest group politics, decide to form their own political party, or may ally themselves with a third party. In the case of religion-based groups, they may choose an additional option—to forego politics altogether and concentrate on changing hearts and minds on political issues through religious testimony, education, and evangelism. This is something that some prominent evangelicals and conservative Catholics recently have called for (Thomas and Dobson 1999; Weyrich 1999). Even if activist groups are determined to pursue their policy targets through major party politics, they, of course, have a choice between the two parties.

Given this range of alternatives, it is unlikely that a set of activists motivated by their positions on a new issue agenda will choose to become involved in a particular major party without some evidence that the party either currently represents or eventually will support their views. Such evidence is likely to come from some set of politicians within the party championing the group's issue positions, and, for that to happen, party politicians must have strategic reasons to champion those issue stands.

Such strategic incentives are likely to arise from either losing politically or facing the prospect of political loss (Schattschneider 1960; Riker 1982; Carmines and Stimson 1989; Layman 2001). Because powerful new issues that cut across the existing lines of party cleavage have the potential to disrupt fundamentally the current political equilibrium, taking a clear stand on one side or the other of them carries considerable risk. It may splinter the base of support of your political opponents, but it also may shatter your own support base. Thus, candidates, elected officials, and party leaders who are relatively advantaged by existing political circumstances are likely to avoid such actions like the plague (Carmines 1991). However, political "losers"—politicians who are disadvantaged by the current state of party politics or who face the prospect of likely political defeat—have less to lose and should be more willing to take such a risk.

Although the most obvious candidates to be strategic political losers are the members of the current minority party (Riker 1982; Carmines and Stimson 1989; Leege et al. 2002), political losers exist in both parties (Layman 2001). Even in the majority party, there are minority factions that are at a disadvantage in the battles over party nominations, party leadership, and the party's policy stands. Both parties also have candidates for party nominations whose support from the party's traditional base or dominant faction is weaker than that of other candidates. All of these political losers may view new issue agendas as the vehicle through which they can become political winners and thus may have strategic incentives to champion one side or the other on the issues.

Layman (2001) points to two key sets of strategic politicians in the emergence of cultural issues and the traditionalist–modernist religious divide in party politics. In keeping with the idea that political losers may exist in intraparty, as well as interparty, competition, Layman (2001) contends that it was the majority Democratic Party, spurred by the strategic impulses of its 1972 presidential nominee George McGovern, that first moved away from the cultural center by staking out liberal ground on issues such as abortion and the legalization of marijuana. McGovern was clearly associated with the proreform elements of the Democratic Party and had little support from the party's traditional urban, blue collar, and union base. Needing to attract a new set of activists into Democratic politics to be a viable candidate for the party's presidential nomination in 1972, McGovern turned to cultural liberalism as a better way to appeal to the young, secular activists to whom his opposition to the Vietnam War already was attractive (e.g., White 1973).

On the Republican side, conservative operatives such as Paul Weyrich and Richard Viguerie not only helped to attract Christian Right organizations into GOP politics, but also were instrumental in the formation of these groups, encouraging and convincing evangelical leaders such as Jerry Falwell and Pat Robertson to form organizations directed at the political mobilization of evangelical Christians (Reichley 1987; Oldfield 1996). Conservative Republican strategists were in search of new constituencies to help them overcome both the moderate Republicans' dominance of intraparty politics and the Democrats' advantage in interparty competition, and the Christian Right was potentially helpful on both fronts. The evangelical constituency represented a large and highly motivated group of activists that might be counted on to support conservative policy stands and conservative candidates within the GOP. The Christian Right's conservative stands on cultural issues had the potential to attract traditionally Democratic constituencies into the Republican electoral coalition (Oldfield 1996; Layman 2001).

Our framework, like much of the literature on partisan issue change, focuses on the strategic incentives of party politicians. However, Oldfield's (1996) discussion of the relationship between the Christian Right and the Republican Party adds an important twist by pointing out that activist groups also make strategic calculations about the courses of action most likely to further their political interests. That supports the idea that an activist group's becoming involved in a party depends on party politicians reaching out to the group or endorsing its policy positions. It also suggests that, once drawn into a party, the group will choose strategically between various options for persuading the party and its leaders to support its agenda.

In the case of the Christian Right, Oldfield argues that in choosing between what Hirschmann (1970) calls "*Exit, Voice, and Loyalty,*" the most fruitful course for securing Republican support for cultural conservatism was through proving their loyalty to the party and then exercising their voice within it. For several reasons—a political culture within the GOP that places a premium on party unity and is wary of group-based demands (Freeman 1986), the quixotic nature of third-party efforts in American politics, and the emerging strength of cultural liberalism within the Democratic Party—attempts to gain GOP support for the Christian Right agenda by threatening to leave the party (exit) would have been counterproductive. Thus, evangelical activists and their leaders wisely chose to demonstrate their loyalty to the party and to work within the GOP nomination and decision-making processes to move the party toward their preferred positions. So, the fact that evangelical leaders, activists, and voters have become fiercely loyal to the GOP and highly influential within the party may be due just as much to the strategic calculations of Christian Right leaders and activists as it is to those of Republican politicians.

Party Activists and Partisan Religious and Cultural Polarization

As we have noted, party activists exercise considerable influence over party nominations, party platforms, and a party's general election hopes. Thus, if activists with noncentrist views on a set of issues become involved in and influential within the two parties (step 4 in fig. 12.3), they may well push the parties toward polarized positions on those issues (step 5 in fig. 12.3). With regard to the traditionalist–modernist religious and cultural divide, it appears that the first step has occurred: A number of scholars point to sharp differences between the religious orientations and cultural attitudes of Democratic and Republican activists (Guth and Green 1986, 1987; Green and Guth 1988; Guth and Green 1989; Green, Guth, and Fraser 1991; Smidt and Penning 1991; Baker and Steed 1992; Layman 1999; Clark 2004).

To assess the degree to which this divide between party activists has grown over time, we examine the religious orientations of Republican and Democratic National Convention delegates using the 2000 and 2004 Convention Delegate Studies (CDS).[12] Table 12.2 shows the religious profiles of various delegate cohorts— defined by the year in which respondents were first national convention delegates—in both parties in terms of both religious tradition and,[13] in the three largest traditions, level of religious traditionalism.[14]

Table 12.2 reveals both important changes over time in the religious characteristics of Republican and Democratic delegates and sharp religious differences between the two parties' activist bases. The key development is the marked increase over time in the representation of traditionalist evangelicals among Republican activists and of seculars among active Democrats. In the delegate cohorts of the 1980s and years prior, traditionalist evangelicals made up a noticeable, but relatively modest, segment of the GOP activist base as clear pluralities of Republican delegates came from the ranks of traditionalist and centrist mainline Protestants. However, evangelical traditionalists markedly increased their presence in the GOP during the 1990s and 2000s and are now the numerically dominant religious group among Republican activists.

In the Democratic activist base, seculars were a noticeable presence among first-time delegates in 1984 and in earlier years.[15] Secular representation was somewhat greater in the 1988 cohort and remained at a similar level among first-time delegates during the 1990s and 2000s. In 2004, however, the presence of seculars among first-time Democratic delegates grew substantially, making secular delegates a plurality of the party's activist base.

The ascendance of traditionalist evangelicals among Republican delegates and of seculars in Democratic delegations has accentuated a broader and apparently longstanding traditionalist–modernist cleavage between active Republicans and Democrats. First of all, the percentage of all evangelicals among Republicans nearly doubles or more than doubles the same percentage among Democrats in all cohorts, whereas the percentage of seculars among Democrats doubles that among Republicans in all the cohorts except for 1984. Meanwhile, in all the delegate cohorts, there are much higher percentages of Jews and members of liberal nontraditional faiths—two groups with highly modernist religious and cultural tendencies—among Democrats than among Republicans. Finally, there are substantial percentages of mainline Protestants and Catholics in all the cohorts for both parties. However, in most cohorts, a plurality of Republican mainliners and Catholics hold traditionalist religious beliefs, practices, and identifications,

Table 12.2 Religious Orientations of Republican and Democratic National Convention Delegates by Delegate Cohort (in percentages)

Party, Religious Tradition, and Religious Traditionalism	First Year as a Delegate						
	Pre-1984	1984	1988	1992	1996	2000	2004
Republicans							
Evangelical							
Protestants	11.4	9.8	15.2	22.0	28.8	24.5	25.8
Traditionalist	5.0	4.9	4.0	3.0	4.2	2.8	1.8
Centrist	—	—	—	—	—	—	—
Modernist	*						
Mainline Protestants							
Traditionalist	20.7	27.9	24.2	16.1	22.9	17.5	8.6
Centrist	27.1	14.8	22.2	20.3	12.7	16.7	21.6
Modernist	0.7	—	1.0	2.1	—	1.4	1.4
Catholics							
Traditionalist	19.3	19.7	16.2	14.4	11.9	13.9	12.2
Centrist	6.4	6.6	4.0	7.2	5.9	8.0	11.7
Modernist	1.4	—	—	—	0.9	0.7	1.4
Black Protestants	—	—	1.0	0.9	2.5	1.7	5.3
Eastern Orthodox	0.7	3.3	—	0.9	0.9	0.2	0.5
Conservative nontraditional	0.7	3.3	2.0	4.2	3.4	2.8	3.6
Liberal nontraditional	—	—	1.0	0.9	—	0.7	0.9
Jewish	2.9	1.6	5.1	1.7	2.5	1.4	1.8
Other faiths	—	—	—	—	—	0.5	0.9
Secular	3.6	11.5	4.0	6.4	3.4	7.2	2.7
Democrats							
Evangelical Protestants							
Traditionalist	3.9	2.3	5.7	4.7	4.2	4.5	1.0
Centrist	4.7	3.9	5.1	4.1	2.8	4.1	1.8
Modernist	0.4	0.8	—	0.4	0.5	0.2	1.0
Mainline Protestants							
Traditionalist	3.0	3.9	4.5	2.8	5.1	4.3	2.3
Centrist	14.1	20.2	15.9	16.8	18.6	15.0	20.2
Modernist	3.9	1.6	3.8	3.9	2.8	2.5	3.0
Catholics							
Traditionalist	7.3	7.0	5.1	5.5	4.2	4.7	5.1
Centrist	18.4	15.5	19.1	18.0	17.7	18.4	13.6
Modernist	5.6	4.7	3.2	4.9	6.5	2.7	2.5

Black Protestants	8.1	17.1	10.2	5.3	7.4	8.5	6.3
Eastern Orthodox	—	1.6	—	1.6	1.4	0.5	0.5
Conservative nontraditional	0.9	0.8	—	0.6	0.5	1.0	1.0
Liberal nontraditional	6.8	3.9	6.4	7.3	3.7	9.3	4.0
Jewish	12.4	7.0	6.4	7.7	7.4	8.0	9.6
Other faiths	0.9	—	0.6	0.8	1.9	1.8	3.3
Secular	9.8	10.1	14.0	15.6	15.4	14.4	24.9

*Indicates that no delegates fell into this category in a particular year.
Source: 2000 and 2004 Convention Delegate Studies.

whereas the Democrats in those traditions are more likely to have centrist or modernist religious orientations.

The polarization of Democratic and Republican activists along religious lines is closely related not just to party differences on cultural issues, but to an overall ideological and policy polarization among active partisans. In table 12.3, we demonstrate that by showing the mean attitudes of 2000 national convention delegates in various religious groups on cultural issues, social welfare issues, racial issues, and federal defense spending, as well as on liberal–conservative ideological identification.[16] Not surprisingly, Republican delegates are much more conservative than Democrats in every issue domain and in ideology, and the ideological divisions between Republicans and Democrats in the same religious category also are considerable. Less substantial, but still important, are the intraparty differences between religious groups. On virtually every measure, the traditionalist members of the largest faith traditions are at least slightly more conservative than their centrist and modernist counterparts within both parties. These gaps are largest on cultural issues, but are present in each policy domain and in ideology.

Moreover, the ascendant religious groups among Republicans and Democrats are clearly positioned at the ideological extremes of their parties. Traditionalist evangelical Protestants in the GOP are the most conservative Republican group on every measure, whereas seculars are one of the most liberal Democratic groups in every category.[17] Partisan religious polarization and the ideological polarization of party activists definitely have gone hand in hand.

Religious and Cultural Polarization in Party Platforms and the Parties in Government

The religious and cultural polarization of the Democratic and Republican activist bases should be associated with a growing divide between the two parties' positions on cultural issues, and there is clear evidence that the distance between the parties'

Table 12.3 Policy Attitudes and Ideology of 2000 National Convention Delegates by Religious Tradition and Religious Traditionalism

	Cultural Issues	Social Welfare Issues	Racial Issues	Defense Spending	Ideological Identification
Republicans					
Evangelical Protestants					
Traditionalist	.87	.80	.81	.86	.85
Centrist	.68	.75	.77	.83	.71
Mainline Protestants					
Traditionalist	.73	.73	.76	.83	.73
Centrist	.60	.70	.72	.79	.64
Catholics					
Traditionalist	.77	.72	.72	.83	.74
Centrist	.61	.71	.71	.79	.65
Conservative nontraditional	.72	.73	.73	.76	.75
Jewish	.58	.69	.73	.72	.71
Secular	.57	.70	.79	.80	.66
Democrats					
Evangelical Protestants					
Traditionalist	.42	.31	.46	.56	.41
Centrist	.30	.25	.48	.50	.33
Mainline Protestants					
Traditionalist	.35	.32	.44	.60	.41
Centrist	.22	.26	.39	.47	.32
Modernist	.15	.19	.36	.43	.24
Catholics					
Traditionalist	.48	.33	.45	.59	.45
Centrist	.28	.27	.39	.48	.34
Modernist	.17	.27	.37	.44	.25
Black Protestants	.32	.29	.20	.45	.33
Liberal nontraditional	.13	.20	.31	.38	.23
Jewish	.09	.23	.33	.45	.26
Other faiths	.23	.27	.34	.43	.33
Secular	.14	.20	.31	.34	.21

Entries are mean values on scales ranging from zero for most liberal to one for most conservative.
Source: 2000 Convention Delegate Study.

cultural stands has increased over time. Layman (2001) finds increasing differences in the statements on cultural issues contained in party platforms, and shows that the roll call votes of Democratic and Republican members of Congress on cultural issues have diverged over time (see also Adams 1997).

Of course, the policy positions taken by representatives, senators, and other members of the parties in government are not determined solely by the attitudes and orientations of party activists or of their constituents. A number of studies find that legislators' personal religious orientations influence their behavior above and beyond the effects of their party affiliations and the religious orientations of their constituents (Benson and Williams 1982; Green and Guth 1991; Fastnow, Grant, and Rudolph 1999; Yamane 1999; Guth and Kellstedt 2005; Oldmixon 2005). Thus, it is important to know the degree to which members of the parties in government differ not just in their policy positions, but also in their religious characteristics. To that end, Guth (2007; see also Guth and Kellstedt 2005) examines the religious affiliations, beliefs, and behaviors of U.S. House members and finds sharp differences between Democrats and Republicans as well as a strong influence of the "Three Bs" on representatives' cultural, economic, and foreign policy positions. Meanwhile, McTague and Pearson-Merkowitz (2006) find change between 1976 and 2004 in the religious affiliations of Democratic and Republican senators—particularly a declining presence of evangelicals among Democratic senators and an increasing representation of evangelicals among Republicans—and show that such change has been associated with the growth in the Senate of party polarization on cultural issues.

These findings suggest that the religious realignment of party activists may have spurred not just a change in the cultural issue positions of the parties in government, but also in the religious profiles of the types of people that seek office under the parties' labels. This may mean that the cultural polarization of the parties becomes increasingly entrenched, with "true believers" staffed in both the party organizations and the parties in government.

Mass Awareness, Salience, and the Religious Cleavage in Partisan Orientations

Most accounts of the partisan change process view the development of new cleavages between the parties in the electorate as a response to the polarization of the parties' elites along the lines of that cleavage and its related issues (Sundquist 1983; MacDonald and Rabinowitz 1987; Carmines and Stimson 1989). However, elite-level partisan differences do not necessarily lead to similar differences at the mass level. In order for that to happen, research on the relationship between issue attitudes and partisan political orientations points to two requirements (step 6 in fig. 12.3): Citizens must become aware that the parties have staked out different stands on the issues, and they must find the issues to be salient (Campbell et al. 1960; Brody and Page 1972; Carmines and Stimson 1989; Carsey and Layman 2006).

In order for individuals to cast votes on the basis of a set of issues or to rearrange their party loyalties in response to those issues, they obviously must see the parties and their candidates as giving them a choice on the issues—as having distinct positions.[18] However, simple awareness of partisan differences on issues is not enough to inspire citizens to structure their voting decisions, much less their party identifications, on the basis of those issues. Individuals must also care about the issues and feel differently about the parties and candidates because of their differences on the issues. In fact, Carsey and Layman (2006) find that if individuals are simply aware of party differences on an issue, but do not find the issue to be particularly salient, they are much more likely to reshape their attitude on the issue on the basis of their partisanship than to reshape their partisanship as a result of their attitude about an issue.

In the case of cultural issues, levels of awareness of party differences in the mass electorate have increased dramatically during the past three decades (Layman 2001; Layman and Carsey 2002a), and, even though cultural issues remain far less salient to the electorate than economic issues, their salience also has grown markedly over time (Layman 2001). Thus, the reason why the increase in religious and cultural polarization between the parties' activists, platforms, and elected officials has translated into a growing traditionalist–modernist religious divide between the parties in the electorate (step 7 in fig. 12.3) is, we argue, that those developments have led the electorate to care more about and become more aware of party differences on cultural issues. This has encouraged more citizens to connect their cultural attitudes and thus their levels of religious traditionalism to their party ties and voting decisions. Furthermore, once the traditionalist–modernist divide has restructured the electorate into opposing partisan camps, it is possible that, consistent with Hunter's (1991) predictions, the implications of theological restructuring can extend the political conflict to a broader set of issues than those that originally defined the debate (Layman and Carsey 2002a). Indeed, there is new evidence that the traditionalist–modernist divide has implications not just for cultural issues, but also economic and foreign policy attitudes (Guth et al. 2006).

Although this argument is about aggregate-level partisan change, we can gain some leverage on it with individual-level data. We can do so because even though awareness of party differences on cultural issues and the salience of those issues are increasing, both, of course, vary across individuals: Some citizens care more about abortion, gay rights, and other cultural issues than others, and some individuals are more likely to be aware of the parties' stands on cultural matters than others. If our argument is correct, then the impact of religious traditionalism on voting decisions and party ties should be greatest when individuals find cultural issues to be salient and to recognize party differences in them.

To determine whether this is the case, we use data from the 2000 and 2004 ANES surveys to replicate an analysis performed by Layman and Green (2006) with 1996 ANES data. In table 12.4, we show the impact of religious traditionalism on a measure of "party alignment" by the salience of abortion to evangelical Protestants,

Table 12.4 The Impact of Religious Traditionalism on Party Alignment by the Salience of and Awareness of Party Differences on Abortion

Effect (Slope) of Religious Traditionalism	Salience of Abortion and Awareness of Party Differences on Abortion			
	Not Salient/ Not Aware	Not Salient/ Aware	Salient/Not Aware	Salient/ Aware
Evangelical Protestants	.04	.18	.12	.50*
	(.05)	(.12)	(.20)	(.22)
Mainline Protestants	.13	.42	.14	.48*
	(.09)	(.30)	(.14)	(.07)
Catholics	−.01	.11	−.09*	.34*
	(.01)	(.15)	(.02)	(.02)

The entries are the unstandardized slope coefficients on religious traditionalism for each religious tradition from regression models of the party alignment index, ranging from most Democratic to most Republican. Robust standard errors are in parentheses.
*$P < .05$.
Source: 2000 and 2004 National Election Studies (pooled).

mainline Protestants, and Catholics, and whether the individuals in those traditions are aware of partisan differences on the abortion issue.[19]

Table 12.4 clearly shows the importance of awareness and salience for the connection of traditionalist–modernist religious orientations to partisan orientations. When respondents either do not find abortion to be salient or are unaware of party differences on abortion, or both, the effect of religious traditionalism on party alignment is statistically significant in only one instance. In that case— among Catholics who find abortion to be salient but are not aware of party differences on abortion—its effect is negative: Traditionalists are less Republican than modernists. However, when abortion is salient to citizens and they are aware of partisan differences on the issue, the impact of religious traditionalism meets the expectations of the culture wars thesis. Religious traditionalists are substantially and significantly more supportive of the GOP and its candidates than are the modernist members of the same faith traditions.

This suggests that the key factor in determining the degree to which a traditionalist–modernist cleavage is apparent in voting behavior and party identification is politics. Variance across individuals in the salience of cultural issues and awareness of party differences on them reflects not only the traits of individuals— for example, their political attentiveness and their religious convictions—but also disparities across political contexts. When parties and candidates clearly diverge on cultural matters and emphasize those subjects in their campaigns, citizens should be more aware of party differences on cultural issues, should find those issues to be more salient, and thus should be more likely to connect their traditionalist– modernist religious orientations to their political behavior. When religious and cultural differences between the parties and candidates are smaller and cultural issues receive less attention in campaigns, citizens should be less likely to recognize and care about the parties' stands on cultural subjects, and the traditionalist–modernist divide between the parties in the electorate should be more muted.[20]

ALTERNATIVE AND DISSENTING APPROACHES

A number of scholars offer perspectives on religion, party politics, and political behavior that differ from our framework in some way. In this section, we discuss these alternative and dissenting perspectives and the degree to which they can be reconciled with our framework. We first take up the idea that religion is connected to political orientations less through attitudes on policy issues and more through group affect and identification, and we discuss how both mechanisms link the traditionalist–modernist divide to party politics and electoral behavior. Second, we discuss how our approach fits with research that seeks to expand the study of cultural conflict in American politics beyond religion and a limited set of "moral issues" to include nonreligious social cleavages and a broader set of issues and political approaches that may be deemed "cultural." Third, we discuss the possibility that rather than being too narrow, the "Three Bs" approach is actually too broad and aggregated, largely ignoring the influence of local religious contexts on individual political orientations, and thus failing to provide a full understanding of the political impact of religion. Finally, we assess the possibility that the degree of religious and cultural polarization in American society is far less than the culture wars perspective suggests and that we, therefore, have exaggerated the importance of the traditionalist–modernist divide for American party politics and voting behavior.

One potential criticism of our account is that it focuses too much on attitudes toward policy issues and not enough on identification with and affect toward religious and social groups. A number of scholars point to group identities and affective group attachments as critical in linking religious orientations not only to partisan and electoral choice, but also to issue attitudes themselves (Smidt 1988; Wilcox 1990; Smidt and Penning 1991; Wilcox, Jelen, and Leege 1993; Miller and Shanks 1996; Leege et al. 2002; Layman and Hussey 2007). Jelen (1991, 1993), for example, finds that religious identifications and affective evaluations of both religious groups and groups involved in cultural political conflict help to connect religious beliefs to policy attitudes, party identification, and voting behavior. Bolce and De Maio (1999a, b, 2007) and Campbell (2006), meanwhile, highlight the political power of negative evaluations of and perceptions of threat from groups with cultural proclivities different from one's own. Bolce and De Maio (1999a, b, 2007) find that negative evaluations of Christian fundamentalists are widespread in American society—particularly among its liberal, more secular, and better educated elements—and that this antipathy toward fundamentalists is significantly linked to support for the Democratic Party and its candidates. Focusing on the other side of the cultural divide, Campbell (2006) posits that the threat of political and social influence by seculars motivates evangelicals to vote Republican, and finds that evangelical republicanism is greatest in areas where seculars are most prevalent.

This perspective on religion's connection to political behavior is supported by research showing that Americans are more likely to view politics through the lens of group-based evaluations than on the basis of ideological and policy orientations (Campbell et al. 1960; Converse 1964; Conover and Feldman 1981; Brady and Sniderman 1985) and that party identification is based on and changes in response to citizens' social group images of the parties (Miller, Wlezien, and Hildreth 1991; Green, Palmquist, and Schickler 2002). Thus, incorporating group identifications and evaluations into our framework undoubtedly would enhance our ability to explain how citizens' religious orientations are coupled with their party attachments and voting decisions.

However, the importance of group-based orientations does not diminish the significance of policy issues in translating religious cleavages into electoral and partisan cleavages. It is only through issues that groups become associated with political parties in the first place. Party politicians take positions on issues of importance to a group and group leaders, and activists become more closely associated with the party with stands that are most appealing to the group's sensibilities. When that connection is established by issues, the ordinary members of the group may come to support the party principally because they see it as being associated with their group or because they sense an association between the other party and groups that they dislike. However, if not for the synergy between the issue positions of the parties and those of particular groups, then such group associations or images would never take shape.

In the case of the traditionalist–modernist divide between the parties in the electorate, its most immediate source may well be evangelicals and other religious traditionalists voting Republican because they see the GOP as the party of "good Christians" and the Democrats as the party of "atheists, homosexuals, and radical feminists," and seculars and religious progressives voting Democratic because they see the GOP as standing with "intolerant fundamentalists." However, if not for the Republican Party taking conservative positions on cultural issues and the Democratic Party staking out liberal cultural stands, then those group images never would have formed. In sum, issue orientations precede group images, although both likely are crucial to connecting religious orientations to party ties and electoral choice.

Another potential shortcoming to our approach is that its conceptualization and operationalization of cultural conflict in American politics is too narrow. In recent research, several scholars suggest that most of the work on "culture wars" in party politics and political behavior is too focused on religion and a limited set of "moral" issues such as abortion, gay rights, and school prayer. They contend that a more complete understanding of cultural conflict and its political implications requires a more expansive conceptual definition and empirical assessments of a wider range of relevant variables (Leege et al. 2002; Weisberg 2005; Barker and

Tinnick 2006; Hetherington and Weiler 2009; Mockabee 2007). As Mockabee (2007, p. 223) notes, this new strand of research seeks "to develop a conceptualization of 'cultural' that is sufficiently broad to pay adequate attention to non-religious aspects of cultural conflict."

The nonreligious factor on which Mockabee (2007) and other scholars (Barker and Tinnick 2006; Hetherington and Weiler 2009) focus is closely related to the idea of an "authoritarian" personality that has a long and storied history in political psychology research (Adorno, Frenkel-Brunswik, Levinson, and Sanford 1950; Altemeyer 1981; Stenner 2005). Recently operationalized through a battery of ANES questions about desirable qualities in children, this variable is conceptualized as either "competing visions of parenting values" (Lakoff 2002; Barker and Tinnick 2006), "authority-mindedness" (Mockabee 2007), or simply authoritarianism (Hetherington and Weiler 2009). In all cases, it is taken to represent an underlying orientation toward authority, and is shown to have a powerful effect on political attitudes and behavior.

Because the research on the political impact of authoritarian orientations is in a relatively nascent stage of development, a number of important questions—several of which we point to in other work (Layman, McTague, Person-Merkowitz, and Spivey 2007)—remain about the operationalization of its central concept, its explanatory power relative to other conceptual definitions of cultural conflict, and the way in which it is connected to politics. However, the question that may be most relevant for the discussion here concerns the degree to which the divide between authoritarians and nonauthoritarians is related to the traditionalist–modernist religious cleavage. Although the recent research tends to treat the two cleavages as separate and distinct, Mockabee (2007) does point to the authoritarianism variable as a potential indicator of Hunter's (1991) proposed chasm over moral authority, and there is a relatively strong empirical relationship between religious traditionalism and authoritarian inclinations.[21] Thus, rather than competing with the traditionalist–modernist cleavage to shape citizens' party ties and voting decisions, orientations toward authority may well help to tie religious traditionalism and modernism to political behavior. Of course, our framework suggests that orientations toward authority may not become central to mass party identification and vote choice until the parties stake out definitive ground on them.

Pointing both to the political importance of groups and the need to define cultural conflict more broadly is the recent work by Leege, Wald, Krueger, and Mueller (2002). They agree fundamentally with our contention that the translation of cultural differences into political differences is a political process. However, their perspective is broader than ours in a number of ways. They see the groups involved in cultural political conflict as extending well beyond competing religious groups to include racial groups, social classes, genders, and residents of different geographic regions. They also envision cultural politics as "*any political controversy that turns on conflicts about social values, norms, and symbolic community boundaries*" (Leege et al. 2002, p. 27; emphasis in original), and thus focus not just on moral and cultural issues, but also on racial issues, issues of social welfare and taxation, and military and defense issues. However, an even more fundamental difference is that Leege et al. (2002, pp. 27–28; emphasis in original) suggest that *"cultural politics is less a set of issues than a style of argumentation that invokes fundamental social values and emphasizes group differences."* Thus, for these scholars, "the politics of cultural differences" is the process through which political parties and the strategic politicians within them work to exploit these group differences for political gain. Parties and politicians use cultural appeals not only to influence the party loyalties and voting decisions of social groups, but also to shape the size and character of the electorate by mobilizing sympathetic groups and demobilizing groups typically allied with the opposition party.

Some aspects of this approach do give us pause. For example, if all political subjects can be framed as cultural issues by invoking core values and pointing to group differences, and, as other scholars suggest, all politicians have incentives to emphasize the "easy," emotional aspects of their issue positions and to connect them to fundamental values, then where does regular politics begin and cultural politics end? Leege et al. (2002, p. 27) admirably anticipate this potential difficulty and seek to delimit their concept. However, further research comparing the electoral impact of campaigns that emphasize similar sets of issues but that frame those issues in more or less "cultural" ways—and move the empirical focus from the national level to the state and local levels, where such variation is more likely to take shape—might be necessary to establish with certainty the boundary between "normal" and cultural politics. Another concern we have about this perspective and others that seek to broaden the definition of cultural politics well beyond religion is that it runs the risk of masking the unique ability of religion and religious values to motivate political attitudes and behavior.

However, the contributions of the framework by Leege et al. (2002) far outweigh its potential problems, in our view. Although it is important for scholars to determine and explain the unique political influence of religion, understanding the degree to which religion's impact on politics truly is distinctive is difficult without a framework that places religion within its larger social and political context, and compares its political influence with that of other sociodemographic orientations. Meanwhile, the work of Leege et al. (2002) helps to expand our understanding of religion's connection to politics both by reminding us that religion is related to orientations on a range of political issues besides just the cultural issues (see also Mockabee 2007; and Wilson, chapter 7, this volume; Guth, chapter 9, this volume), and that the political importance of religion and other social and cultural orientations lies not just in their relationship to voting decisions, but also in their effect on whether citizens cast ballots in the first place. It is the task of future research to situate appropriately the political impact of the Three Bs of religion within a broader context of cultural politics, as implied by the approach of Leege et al. (2002), but also to remain focused on the unique influence of religion on political attitudes and behavior.

Finally, the most positive aspect of the perspective by Leege et al. (2002) may be that it properly puts the emphasis on the politics of cultural politics. Theories of moral and cultural divisions in American politics—for example, Hunter's (1991) culture wars theory and especially Lakoff's (2002) theory of "moral politics"— sometimes imply that the translation of these cleavages into partisan political cleavages is, through the sheer power of the moral or cultural divide, more or less inevitable. Political scientists too often are willing to go along and assume or search for a natural or "apolitical" connection between social, cultural, or ideological orientations and political behavior. However, Leege et al. (2002, p. 11) are exactly right to not be "satisfied with a theory that puts politicization in a black box, drawing a straight line, for example, from religion to culture to politics," and to remind scholars that the connection between cultural conflict on the one hand and party coalitions and voting behavior on the other hand is structured by inherently political incentives, actions, and processes.

Although the work of Leege et al. (2002) and other scholars implies that our framework may be too narrow, another school of thought suggests that it may be too broad. This research is critical of what it considers to be the overly aggregated nature of approaches to the political influence of religion such as the culture wars and Three Bs perspectives, and calls for greater attention to the contextual effects of clerical and congregational influence in connecting religion to political behavior. It points to the wide diversity of local religious communities and suggests that national sampling and categorization of religious adherents into broad categories of belonging, believing, and behaving not only may be marred by conceptual and measurement error, but also may mask important variation that takes shape across individual congregations and religious communities. Within the social context of a particular congregation, individuals develop important tools for civic engagement and are likely to receive political cues from either their fellow parishioners or their clergy (Wald, Owen, and Hill 1988, 1990; Jelen 1992; Gilbert 1993; Huckfeldt, Plutzer, and Sprague 1993; Verba, Schlozman, and Brady 1995; Guth, Green, Smidt, and Kellstedt 1997; Harris 1999; Crawford and Olson 2001; Djupe and Gilbert 2002, 2003, 2006). Thus, to understand the nature of religion's influence on political behavior, this work suggests that we must observe the connections between religion and politics that take shape in local religious communities.

Research on the influence of congregational context and clerical cues on individuals' political orientations provides rich insights into the nature of social networks within churches and the role of clergy in informing and reinforcing the religious beliefs and political attitudes of congregants. Thus, it helps to explain how and why such broad religious characteristics such as tradition membership, religious doctrine, and religious practice influence political behavior. Moreover, because it provides a much more intimate view than research based on national-level surveys of variation in the types of messages individuals receive, the types of religious activities they engage in, and the types of social interactions they experience, this work helps us to understand when and why individuals who are similarly placed within broad religious categories may exhibit different patterns of political behavior.

Of course, a drawback of this type of research is that the cost and difficulty of obtaining data on clerical messages and activities, congregational social networks, and the religious and political orientations of a substantial number of individuals within particular congregations necessarily tends to limit its empirical focus to particular religious denominations, particular congregations, or particular regions or locales. As a result, contextual research may yield results and conclusions that are unrepresentative of the more general relationship between religion and politics. Thus, a fruitful line of future research may be to include relatively comprehensive batteries of questions about congregational political context and clerical political cues—in other words—more, and more specific, questions than the handful of religious cueing questions included in some recent ANES surveys—within large-scale national surveys. Of course, recording respondents' impressions of the political leanings of their clergy and fellow congregants is not an adequate substitute for direct observation of those variables. However, such efforts might allow researchers to incorporate some of the strength of the contextual approach with the ability of national sample surveys to assess the political behavior of people of faith across a wide swath of the religious landscape.

A final shortcoming of our framework simply may be that we overstate the magnitude and importance of the traditionalist–modernist religious cleavage in American mass politics. This is the perspective of a number of scholars who offer empirical assessments of the degree to which American society and politics are divided along religious and cultural lines, focusing especially on Hunter's (1991, 1994) claim of a deep-rooted culture war with overarching political importance. Rather than a society that is divided into highly unified orthodox and progressive camps, fixated on moral and cultural concerns, and irrevocably polarized on those issues, these researchers find that most Americans tend to occupy centrist ground in both their religious orientations and cultural attitudes, that "bread-and-butter" economic issues tend to take precedence over cultural issues for most citizens, and that religious traditionalists and modernists are hardly monotonic in their political attitudes and orientations (Davis and Robinson 1996a, b; DiMaggio, Evans, and Bryson 1996; Davis and Robinson 1997; Demerath and Yang 1997; Smith, Emerson, Gallagher, Kennedy, and Sikkink 1997; Wolfe 1998; Evans, Bryson, and DiMaggio 2001; Baker 2005; Fiorina, Abrams, and Pope 2006). Most of this research does not explicitly connect the lack of evidence for a culture war to conclusions about the political importance of the traditionalist–modernist religious divide. However, the clear implication is that it has been overstated.

We agree that Hunter's (1991) argument and most popular accounts of the culture wars exaggerate the degree to which ordinary Americans are polarized along religious and cultural lines. We also concur that the idea of two highly unified religious and cultural "teams" in American society and politics greatly oversimplifies the complex reality of American religion and politics. It underestimates the importance of religious tradition in giving rise to various forms of religious traditionalism and modernism, and in conditioning their political impact. It also underestimates the importance of politics in selectively connecting religious traditionalism and modernism to certain types of political attitudes and behaviors.

However, we also suspect that the critics of the culture wars thesis have themselves underestimated the importance of politics by assuming that the lack of an increase in societal polarization along religious and cultural lines means that religious and cultural orientations have not become more important for American political behavior. The parties in the electorate have become more divided along traditionalist–modernist religious lines not because American religion has become more segregated into traditionalist and modernist camps or because American society has become more polarized on cultural issues, but because the parties and their candidates have placed more emphasis on cultural issues, taken distinct stands on them, and thus made the existing divide between religious traditionalists and modernists increasingly relevant for partisan ties and electoral choice. In short, political polarization along the lines of a social cleavage can occur even in the absence of increased social polarization on that cleavage.

Conclusion

We have presented a political explanation for the influence of religion on American party politics and voting behavior. During the past several decades, the ethno-religious cleavage that structured the parties' electoral coalitions for nearly a century has been overlaid by a new religious divide that spans religious traditions to pit the traditionalist members of the major faith groups against their modernist counterparts. This shift to a partisan religious divide based on believing, behaving, and belonging has been rooted in an explicitly political set of developments. The traditionalist–modernist divide is closely related to views on moral and cultural political issues such as abortion, gay rights, and religion in the public square that arouse intense emotions in large numbers of citizens. Strategic party politicians have taken clear stands on one side or the other of these issues to cultivate new bases of support. Political activists have responded to the appeals of strategic politicians by becoming involved in party politics and pushing the parties, their candidates, and elected officials toward polarized stands on cultural subjects. The polarization of the parties' activists, elites, and policy positions along religious and cultural lines has made the mass electorate increasingly aware of partisan differences on cultural issues. This alteration in public perceptions of the two parties has encouraged individuals to connect their traditionalist–modernist religious orientations to their party affiliations and voting decisions, and thus produced a Republican electoral coalition that is clearly more traditionally religious than is the Democratic Party in the electorate.

Although this framework provides a useful model for understanding how religious cleavages in American society are translated into partisan cleavages in American politics, there is plenty of work left to be done in uncovering the *who, what, when, why,* and *how* of the relationship between religion, party politics, and voting behavior in the United States. One phenomenon that clearly demands further research by students of religion and politics is the discrepancy between the cultural liberalism of seculars and the strong presence of seculars in the Democratic activist base on the one hand, and the continuing party detachment of the bulk of secular citizens on the other. The explanation for seculars' independence from party ties simply may be their independence from religious affiliations and resulting lack of clear social identity. However, the fact is that we have very little empirical traction on which to base our conclusions about the effect of secularism on political behavior. For example, although scholars may take advantage of extensive batteries of questions in surveys such as the ANES or the General Social Survey to classify members of religious traditions and to examine their religious beliefs and practices, seculars typically are identified simply as individuals who claim no religious affiliation. This, however, may be quite inadequate, as Hout and Fischer (2002) show that a large number of religious "nones" are actually "unchurched believers" who may not claim membership in a particular religious denomination, but who hold conventional Judeo-Christian beliefs, and other scholars note that individuals claiming a religious affiliation actually may be "closet" seculars (Kellstedt, Green, Guth, and Smidt 1996). Thus, it may require a more extensive set of inquiries about secular beliefs and practices to separate those who truly are nonreligious from believers who simply lack religious affiliation, and it may reveal that the truly secular actually have become more attached to the Democratic Party.[22]

Second, we have left one important question—*where?*—unanswered in this chapter. The importance of campaign context both in our own framework and in the discussion by Leege et al. (2002) of how normal politics is translated into "cultural politics" begs for further research in subnational settings. In such settings, variation in campaign context, partisan alignments, and the distribution of sociodemographic orientations exists and may be linked to variation in the extent to which moral issues and religious cleavages are relevant to electoral campaigns and vote choice. Specifically, the notion that the salience of moral issues is malleable based on the strategic incentives offered to particular campaigns in particular electoral settings is worthy of further rigorous testing. Are places with substantial populations of both seculars and "conservative" Christians (e.g., Oregon) more susceptible to cultural conflict than places with largely homogeneous religious populations (e.g., Mississippi)? How does variation in the salience of religious cleavages in subnational electorates then feed back to the salience of religious cleavages in presidential elections that are contested on a state-by-state basis?

Third, there remain questions in the literature about the degree to which religious orientations are connected to political behavior through attitudes on policy issues or through group affect and identity, and about whether the political influence of religion takes shape through a limited set of "cultural" issues or through a broader range of policy topics. We know that the answer to these questions is that it depends on the individual—their religious orientations, social experiences, and levels of political and religious attentiveness. However, the religion and politics literature does not yet have a satisfactory way of classifying individuals on this basis. It strikes us that a suggestion made nearly two decades ago, but, as far as we know, not yet taken up by scholars, might be very helpful in this regard. Guth, Jelen, Kellstedt, Smidt, and Wald (1988, pp. 388–389) called for a measure of "level of religious sophistication," akin to the "levels of [political] conceptualization" developed by Campbell et al. (1960), that would classify individuals according to the degree to which they are well versed in the theological tenets of their religious traditions and understand how those tenets apply to political issues. Some individuals might be like the "ideologues" of Campbell et al. (1960), being quite knowledgeable about the theology of their faith and its relevance for a wide range of policy matters. Others might be more like the "near ideologues," having a clear understanding of the connection between religious doctrine and their views on a narrow set of "moral" issues. Other religious people might fit better into the "group benefits" category, relying primarily on religious identification and affect toward religious and cultural "in-groups" and "out-groups" to make political judgments. Still others might best be classified as having "no issue content" to their religious or political behavior.

Finally, recent work by scholars interested in authoritarianism, or parenting values, demonstrates clearly that religion is not alone as an important source of conflict over moral issues. However, there is still a great deal of work to be done in terms of assessing the comparative explanatory power of religion compared with other sources of guidance for "values" voters. For instance, it remains to be seen whether the authority-based cleavage is as influential as religion in restructuring the electoral bases of the parties, and only rigorous longitudinal assessments of authoritarianism's impact on political behavior can resolve that uncertainty.

Moreover, the framework we have provided suggests that in order for any cleavage to become relevant to mass partisanship and voting behavior, there have to be strategic incentives for political entrepreneurs to promote the issues associated with that cleavage, the issues have to be powerful enough to arouse the attention and passions of the mass electorate, and the parties' elites and activists need to become clearly divided along the lines of the cleavage and its related issues. It remains to be seen if this is occurring with regard to an authority-based cleavage. However, this chapter and the expansive body of work we have discussed in it clearly demonstrate that such a process has taken shape for the traditionalist–modernist cleavage in American religion.

NOTES

1. We interchangeably refer to the *theological restructuring* perspective as the *culture wars model* and the *traditionalist–modernist* cleavage during the course of the chapter.

2. The fact that the ANES surveys in both 1964 and 1968 included a question about the authority of scripture—a key measure of religious believing (Jelen 1989; Kellstedt and

Smidt 1993; Green 2007) and a topic that would disappear from the ANES series until 1980—allows for this comparison.

3. Our models included dummy variables for the five largest religious traditions (evangelical Protestants, mainline Protestants, black Protestants, Catholics, and Jews) and for seculars. We assigned religious affiliations to these traditions following the recent literature (e.g., Kellstedt and Green 1993; Green et al. 2007) (see Layman and Green [2006] for details on coding religious traditions with recent ANES data). The list of religious affiliations in the ANES surveys was not nearly as detailed in the 1960s as it is in the 2000s. We attempted to make the coding of religious traditions as similar as possible across the two eras (see Layman and Hussey [2007, p. 185] for further details).

4. The Bible question in the 2000s includes three response options: "the Bible is a book written by men and is not the Word of God," "the Bible is the Word of God but not everything in it should be taken literally, word for word," and "the Bible is the actual Word of God and is to be taken literally, word for word." However, during the 1960s, respondents were given four response options: "the Bible was written by men who lived so long ago that it is worth very little today," "the Bible is a good book because it was written by wise men but God had nothing to do with it," "the Bible was written by men inspired by God but it contains some human errors," and "the Bible is God's Word and all it says is true." To make our measures of scriptural views comparable across the two eras, we combined the first two options in the 1960s into a single category.

5. The worship attendance variable in the 1960s surveys included four categories (never, seldom, often, regular), whereas the 2000s variable contains six categories (never, a few times a year, once or twice a month, almost every week, every week, and more than once a week). To make the attendance variables comparable for the two periods, we combine the last three categories of worship attendance in the 2000s into a single category of "regular" attendance (e.g., Layman and Hussey 2007), resulting in four-category attendance scales for both periods.

6. The demographic variables were education, income, southern residence, gender, age, and union membership.

7. To capture variation across religious traditions on the impact of worship attendance and view of the Bible, our logit models of the presidential vote and regression models of party identification (ranging from zero for strong Democrat to one for strong Republican) included interactions between each of the religious tradition dummy variables, and both attendance and Bible view. The predicted probability of voting Republican, predicted party identification, and level of statistical significance of the difference in predictions between religious traditionalists and religious modernists were computed using the CLARIFY program (King, Tomz, and Wittenberg 2000) while holding all the control variables constant at their sample means. To compute the prediction for religious modernists, centrists, and traditionalists within each faith tradition, we set the values of worship attendance and view of the Bible at their means for the tradition for centrists, at one standard deviation below their tradition means for modernists, and at one standard deviation above their tradition means for traditionalists. Because of the small numbers of Jews in the surveys and the lack of variation in worship attendance among seculars, we only show the predictions among centrists for these two groups.

8. We pooled the ANES surveys from both midterm election years (except for 1962, when the ANES did not include a detailed coding of religious affiliations) and presidential years for each decade to compute these percentages. Classified as frequent church attenders are those respondents in the "regular" attendance category prior to 1970 and those attending worship services "almost every week" or more often in the ANES from 1970

through 2004. All other attendance categories (see note 5) are classified as infrequent attenders.

9. Among frequently attending evangelicals, there was a decline of 29.6 percentage points in Democratic identification and an increase of 23.4 percentage points in Republican identification from the 1960s to the 2000s. Among committed Catholics, the decline in Democratic identification was 26.1 percentage points and the increase in Republican identification was 20.5 percentage points.

10. A similar and more thoroughly explicated version of this framework is provided by Layman (2001). Our presentation and discussion of the model is abbreviated here because of space limitations. As a case in point, the flow of causality in the process illustrated in figure 12.3 is almost certainly not unidirectional. For example, a positive response by activists to some strategic politicians championing ideologically extreme stands on particular issues (step 4) is likely to feed back and make it more likely that other strategic politicians in the parties will stake out such positions (step 3). Similarly, the parties taking distinct stands on the issues (step 5) may produce further responses by activists with noncentrist positions on them (step 4). We do not discuss such feedback loops to expedite the presentation of our framework.

11. It is no doubt true that political candidates and leaders make even the most technical and abstract issues relevant for party ties and political choice by framing them in "easy" terms and imbuing them with moral significance. William Jennings Bryan's portrayal of late-19th-century monetary policy as a "Cross of Gold," and the success of contemporary Republican politicians in framing taxes as a moral and cultural issue (Leege et al. 2002) are cases in point. At the same time, certain issues simply are inherently "easier" than others; regardless of how they are framed, issues such as capital punishment and affirmative action are more likely to spur mass attention and passions than are issues like agricultural subsidies and regulatory takings.

12. Both the 2000 and 2004 CDS were surveys of delegates to the two parties' national conventions that were designed to be continuations of the series of CDS surveys conducted from 1972 through 1992 by Warren E. Miller and others (e.g., Miller and Jennings 1986). The 2000 CDS, conducted by Thomas Carsey, John Green, Richard Herrera, and Geoffrey Layman, was a mail survey sent to all of the delegates to both parties' national conventions in 2000 as well as to all of the respondents to the 1992 CDS. The 2004 CDS, conducted by Green, Herrera, Layman, and Rosalyn Cooperman, combined data from an online survey of Democratic and Republican delegates to the 2004 national conventions with data from a follow-up mail survey of GOP delegates conducted to increase the Republican sample size.

13. The religious characteristics of all the cohorts that first attended national conventions in 2000 or earlier are taken from the 2000 CDS. We examine differences across delegate cohorts with only the 2000 and 2004 CDS surveys rather than with the full series of CDS surveys because the 2000 and 2004 CDS included far more extensive batteries of religious questions and gauged religious affiliation very differently than did the earlier surveys (relying on an open-ended question about religious preference rather than the rather limited set of response options that appeared in earlier CDS surveys). In addition to the major Judeo-Christian traditions, we also show the percentage of convention delegates belonging to smaller traditions such as the Eastern Orthodox faiths, conservative nontraditional faiths such as Mormons, liberal nontraditional religions such as Unitarians, and other (non-Judeo-Christian) religions.

14. To form categories of religious traditionalism, we first collapsed the indicators of view of the Bible, worship attendance, and religious identification into scales ranging from

one to three. The Bible question in the CDS surveys had four response options: (1) The actual word of God, to be taken literally, word for word; (2) The inspired word of God, with no errors but not to be taken literally; (3) The inspired word of God, but it contains human errors; and (4) A good book but not the word of God. We classified the fourth option as modernist, the third as centrist, and the first two as traditionalist. For worship attendance, we classified those respondents who "never" or "seldom" attend as modernist, those who attend "a few times a year" or "once or twice a month" as centrist, and those who attend "once a week" or "more than once a week" as traditionalist. For religious identification, we classified those respondents identifying themselves as "liberal/progressive Christian," "ethical humanist," or "liberal/progressive Catholic" as modernist; those identifying as "mainline Christian" as centrist; and those identifying as "fundamentalist Christian," "evangelical Christian," "charismatic/Pentecostal Christian," "born-again Christian," "conservative/traditional Christian," or "conservative/traditional Catholic" as traditionalist. When respondents had mixed religious identifications (e.g., evangelical Christian and liberal/progressive Christian), we classified their religious identification based on the general pattern of their identifications (e.g., a respondent with an equal number of traditionalist and modernist identifications would have been coded as having a centrist religious identification).

We then took each respondent's mean value on all of those three items on which he or she had nonmissing values. Finally, we classified all respondents with values at or rounding to one as "modernists," those with values at or rounding to two as "centrists," and those with values at or rounding to three as "traditionalists." Because the CDS surveys measured religious affiliation differently than the ANES and because we use a somewhat different set of religious variables to classify respondents' levels of religious traditionalism than we did for our analysis of ANES data, readers should be cautious in comparing our results for party activists to those for the mass electorate.

15. Using the CDS surveys from 1972 through 1992, Layman (2001) shows a high level of secularism among 1972 Democratic delegates, but much smaller percentages of seculars at the 1976 and 1980 Democratic conventions.

16. We only show the mean values of religious groups for which there are at least 15 observations on every variable. Attitudes toward cultural, social welfare, and racial issues are the scores from factor analyses of multiple issue positions. These include cultural issues such as abortion, homosexual rights in jobs, school prayer, and parental consent for abortion; social welfare issues such as government services and spending, government providing health insurance, and federal spending on welfare and on programs to assist the unemployed; and racial issues such as government responsibility to help blacks and preferential hiring of racial minorities. All the issue attitudes and ideological identification range from zero for most liberal to one for most conservative.

17. The differences between the mean values of traditionalist evangelical Republicans and all other Republicans, and between the mean values of secular Democrats and all other Democrats are statistically significant ($P < .01$) on every variable.

18. As Carmines and Stimson (1989) note, party activists, in their roles as grassroots-level opinion leaders, are key to the communication of elite-level issue differences to the mass electorate. As the composition of the parties' activist bases change, citizens who pay relatively little attention to elite-level politics may infer that the parties' policy positions have changed simply by observing changes in the behavior and party support of the politically active and attentive individuals in their communities or social circles.

19. Religious traditionalism is the score from a factor analysis of view of the Bible, worship attendance, the amount of guidance received from religion, and frequency of prayer.

Party alignment is the combination of party identification, two-party presidential vote, and the comparative feeling thermometer ratings of each party's presidential candidate. To gauge the impact of religious traditionalism on party alignment across religious traditions, we estimated regression models in which the independent variables were dummy variables for the five largest religious traditions and seculars, the religious traditionalism measure, and interactions between each of the tradition dummies and traditionalism, as well as demographic control variables and a dummy variable for 2004 respondents. The respondents coded as finding abortion to be salient are those who answered "very important" or "extremely important" on a question about the importance of abortion. The respondents coded as being aware of party differences on abortion are those who placed both parties' presidential candidates on the ANES abortion scale and assigned the Republican candidate a value that was more pro-life than that assigned to the Democratic candidate.

20. Of course, the degree to which parties and candidates are polarized on and put emphasis on cultural issues varies not just over time, but also—in fact, primarily—across states and localities (e.g., Green, Rozell, and Wilcox 2003). This means that the impact of religious traditionalism should vary noticeably across states and local areas, depending on the level of partisan religious and cultural polarization, and the amount of attention devoted to cultural subjects in political campaigns. In fact, Layman (2001) finds that the impact of religious traditionalism on voting behavior and party identification is largest in states in which party elites and activists are most polarized along religious lines.

21. For example, the correlation between an authoritarianism variable developed from the child qualities questions in the 2004 ANES and the view of the Bible variable is .44.

22. In fact, Green et al. (2007) find that making finer distinctions among religiously unaffiliated citizens provides greater leverage on the political behavior of this group. They distinguish between unaffiliated believers, who lack a religious affiliation but hold some conventional religious beliefs; seculars, who tend to lack religious beliefs or associated behaviors or identifications; and those unaffiliated people who identify themselves as atheists or agnostics. Although all three groups tend to vote for and identify with the Democratic Party, unaffiliated believers are noticeably more Republican than atheists and agnostics, with seculars falling in the middle.

REFERENCES

Adams, Greg D. 1997. "Abortion: Evidence of Issue Evolution." *American Journal of Political Science* 41: 718–737.

Adorno, Theodor W., Else Frenkel-Brunswik, Daniel J. Levinson, and R. Nevitt Sanford. 1950. *The Authoritarian Personality.* New York: W. W. Norton.

Aldrich, John H. 1995. *Why Parties? The Origin and Transformation of Political Parties in America.* Chicago, Ill.: The University of Chicago Press.

Altemeyer, Robert. 1981. *Right-Wing Authoritarianism.* Winnipeg: University of Manitoba Press.

Aranson, Peter H., and Peter C. Ordeshook. 1972. "Spatial Strategies for Sequential Elections." In *Probability Models of Collective Decision Making*, ed. Richard G. Niemi and Herbert F. Weisberg, 298–331. Columbus, Ohio: Charles E. Merrill.

Baker, Tod A., and Robert P. Steed. 1992. "Party Activists, Southern Religion, and Culture Wars: An Analysis of Precinct Party Activists in Eleven Southern States." Presented at the annual meeting of the Southern Political Science Association, Atlanta, Georgia, November.

Baker, Wayne. 2005. *America's Crisis of Values: Reality and Perception.* Princeton, N.J.: Princeton University Press.

Barker, David C., and James D. Tinnick, III. 2006. "Competing Visions of Parental Roles and Ideological Constraint." *American Political Science Review* 100: 249–263.

Benson, Peter L., and Dorothy L. Williams. 1982. *Religion on Capitol Hill: Myths and Realities.* San Francisco, Calif.: Harper & Row.

Berelson, Bernard R., Paul R. Lazarsfeld, and William N. McPhee. 1954. *Voting: A Study of Opinion Formation in a Presidential Campaign.* Chicago, Ill.: University of Chicago Press.

Bolce, Louis, and Gerald De Maio. 1999a. "Religious Outlook, Culture War Politics, and Antipathy toward Christian Fundamentalists." *Public Opinion Quarterly* 63: 29–61.

Bolce, Louis, and Gerald De Maio. 1999b. "The Anti-Christian Fundamentalist Factor in Contemporary American Politics." *Public Opinion Quarterly* 63: 508–542.

Bolce, Louis, and Gerald De Maio. 2007. "Secularists, Antifundamentalists, and the New Religious Divide in the American Electorate." In *From Pews to Polling Places: Faith and Politics in the American Religious Mosaic,* ed. J. Matthew Wilson, 251–276. Washington, D.C.: Georgetown University Press.

Brady, Henry E., and Paul M. Sniderman. 1985. "Attitude Attribution: A Group Basis for Political Reasoning." *American Political Science Review* 79: 1061–1078.

Brewer, Paul R. 2003. "The Shifting Foundations of Public Opinion about Gay Rights." *Journal of Politics* 65: 1208–1220.

Brody, Richard A., and Benjamin I. Page. 1972. "Comment: The Assessment of Policy Voting." *American Political Science Review* 66: 450–458.

Campbell, Angus, Philip E. Converse, Warren E. Miller, and Donald E. Stokes. 1960. *The American Voter.* Chicago, Ill.: The University of Chicago Press.

Campbell, David E. 2002. "The Young and the Realigning: A Test of the Socialization Theory of Realignment." *The Public Opinion Quarterly* 66: 209–234.

Campbell, David E. 2006. "Religious 'Threat' in Contemporary Presidential Elections." *Journal of Politics* 68: 104–115.

Carmines, Edward G. 1991. "The Logic of Party Alignments." *Journal of Theoretical Politics* 3: 65–80.

Carmines, Edward G., and James A. Stimson. 1980. "The Two Faces of Issue Voting." *American Political Science Review* 74: 78–91.

Carmines, Edward G., and James A. Stimson. 1989. *Issue Evolution: Race and the Transformation of American Politics.* Princeton, N.J.: Princeton University Press.

Carsey, Thomas M. 2000. *Campaign Dynamics: The Race for Governor.* Ann Arbor, Mich.: University of Michigan Press.

Carsey, Thomas M., and Geoffrey C. Layman. 2006. "Changing Sides or Changing Minds? Party Identification and Policy Preferences in the American Electorate." *American Journal of Political Science* 50: 464–477.

Clark, John A. 2004. "Religion: Culture Wars in the New South." In *Southern Political Party Activists: Patterns of Conflict and Change, 1991–2001,* ed. John A. Clark and Charles L. Prysby, 13–28. Lexington, Ky.: University Press of Kentucky.

Conover, Pamela Johnston, and Stanley Feldman. 1981. "The Origins and Meaning of Liberal/Conservative Self-Identifications." *American Journal of Political Science* 25: 617–645.

Converse, Philip E. 1964. "The Nature of Belief Systems in Mass Publics." In *Ideology and Discontent*, ed. David E. Apter, 206–261. New York: Free Press.

Cook, Elizabeth, Ted Jelen, and Clyde Wilcox. 1992. *Between Two Absolutes: American Public Opinion and the Politics of Abortion*. Boulder, Colo.: Greenwood.

Crawford, Sue E. S., and Laura R. Olson, eds. 2001. *Christian Clergy in American Politics*. Baltimore, Md.: Johns Hopkins University Press.

Davis, Nancy J., and Robert V. Robinson. 1996a. "Are the Rumors of War Exaggerated? Religious Orthodoxy and Moral Progressivism in America." *American Journal of Sociology* 102: 756–787.

Davis, Nancy J., and Robert V. Robinson. 1996b. "Religious Orthodoxy in American Society: The Myth of a Monolithic Camp." *Journal for the Scientific Study of Religion* 35: 229–245.

Davis, Nancy J., and Robert V. Robinson. 1997. "A War for America's Soul? The American Religious Landscape." In *Cultural Wars in American Politics: Critical Reviews of a Popular Myth*, ed. Rhys H. Williams, 39–62. New York: De Gruyter.

Delli Carpini, Michael X., and Scott Keeter. 1996. *What Americans Know about Politics and Why It Matters*. New Haven, Conn.: Yale University Press.

Demerath, N. J., III, and Yonghe Yang. 1997. "What American Culture War? A View from the Trenches as Opposed to the Command Posts and the Press Corps." In *Cultural Wars in American Politics: Critical Reviews of a Popular Myth*, ed. Rhys H. Williams, 17–38. New York: De Gruyter.

DiMaggio, Paul, John Evans, and Bethany Bryson. 1996. "Have Americans' Social Attitudes Become More Polarized?" *American Journal of Sociology* 102: 690–755.

Djupe, Paul A., and Christopher P. Gilbert. 2002. "The Political Voice of Clergy." *Journal of Politics* 64: 596–609.

Djupe, Paul A., and Christopher P. Gilbert. 2003. *The Prophetic Pulpit: Clergy, Churches, and Communities in American Politics*. Lanham, Md.: Rowman & Littlefield.

Djupe, Paul A., and Christopher P. Gilbert. 2006. "The Resourceful Believer: Generating Civic Skills in Church." *Journal of Politics* 68: 116–127.

Dowd, Maureen. 2004. "The Red Zone." *New York Times*, November 4, p. 25.

Evans, John H., Bethany Bryson, and Paul DiMaggio. 2001. "Opinion Polarization: Important Contributions, Necessary Limitations." *American Journal of Sociology* 106: 944–959.

Fastnow, Chris, J. Tobin Grant, and Thomas J. Rudolf. 1999. "Holy Roll Calls: Religious Tradition and Voting Behavior in the U.S. House." *Social Science Quarterly* 80: 687–701.

Fiorina, Morris P., Samuel J. Abrams, and Jeremy C. Pope. 2006. *Culture War? The Myth of a Polarized America*. 2nd ed. New York: Pearson Longman.

Frank, Thomas. 2004. *What's the Matter with Kansas?* New York: Metropolitan Books.

Freeman, Jo. 1986. "The Political Culture of Democrats and Republicans." *Political Science Quarterly* 101 (3): 327–344.

Gilbert, Christopher P. 1993. *The Impact of Churches on Political Behavior: An Empirical Study*. Westport, Conn.: Greenwood.

Goldberg, Michelle. 2005. "How the Secular Humanist Grinch Didn't Steal Christmas." http://dir.salon.com/story/news/feature/2005/11/21/christmas/index.html.

Green, Donald P., Bradley Palmquist, and Eric Schickler. 2002. *Partisan Hearts and Minds*. New Haven, Conn.: Yale University Press.

Green, John C. 2007. *The Faith Factor: How Religion Influences American Elections*. Westport, Conn.: Praeger.

Green, John C., and James L. Guth. 1988. "The Christian Right in the Republican Party: The Case of Pat Robertson's Supporters." *Journal of Politics* 50: 150–165.

Green, John C., and James L. Guth. 1991. "Religion, Representatives, and Roll Calls." *Legislative Studies Quarterly* 16: 571–584.

Green, John C., James L. Guth, and Cleveland R. Fraser. 1991. "Apostles and Apostates? Religion and Politics among Party Activists." In *The Bible and the Ballot Box: Religion and Politics in the 1988 Election*, ed. James L. Guth and John C. Green, 113–136. Boulder, Colo.: Westview Press.

Green, John C., James L. Guth, Corwin E. Smidt, and Lyman A. Kellstedt. 1996. *Religion and the Culture Wars.* Lanham, Md.: Rowman and Littlefield.

Green, John C., Lyman A. Kellstedt, Corwin E. Smidt, and James L. Guth. 2007. "How the Faithful Voted: Religious Communities and the Presidential Vote." In *A Matter of Faith: Religion in the 2004 Presidential Election*, ed. David E. Campbell, 15–36. Washington, D.C.: Brookings Institution Press.

Green, John C., Mark J. Rozell, and Clyde Wilcox, eds. 2003. *The Christian Right in American Politics: Marching to the Millennium.* Washington, D.C.: Georgetown University Press.

Guth, James L. 2007. "Religion and Roll Calls: Religious Influences on the U.S. House of Representatives, 1997–2002." Presented at the annual meeting of the American Political Science Association, Chicago, Illinois, August 30–September 2.

Guth, James L., and John C. Green. 1986. "Faith and Politics: Religion and Ideology among Political Contributors." *American Politics Quarterly* 14 (3): 186–199.

Guth, James L., and John C. Green. 1987. "The Moralizing Minority: Christian Right Support among Political Contributors." *Social Science Quarterly* 68: 598–610.

Guth, James L., and John C. Green. 1989. "God and the GOP: Religion Among GOP Activists." In *Religion and Political Behavior in the United States*, ed. Ted G. Jelen, 223–242. New York: Praeger.

Guth, James L., John C. Green, Corwin E. Smidt, and Lyman A. Kellstedt. 1997. *The Bully Pulpit: The Politics of Protestant Clergy.* Lawrence, Kans.: University Press of Kansas.

Guth, James L., John C. Green, Corwin E. Smidt, and Lyman A. Kellstedt. 2006. "Religious Influences in the 2004 Presidential Election." *Presidential Studies Quarterly* 26: 223–242.

Guth, James L., Ted G. Jelen, Lyman A. Kellstedt, Corwin E. Smidt, and Kenneth D. Wald. 1988. "The Politics of Religion in America: Issues for Investigation." *American Politics Quarterly* 16: 357–397.

Guth, James L., and Lyman A. Kellstedt. 2005. "The Confessional Congress: Religion and Legislative Behavior." Presented at the annual meeting of the Midwest Political Science Association, Chicago, Illinois, April 7–10.

Harris, Frederick C. 1999. *Something Within: Religion in African-American Political Activism.* New York: Oxford University Press.

Hetherington, Marc J., and Jonathan Weiler. 2009. *Divided We Stand: Polarization, Authoritarianism, and the Contemporary Political Divide.* New York: Cambridge University Press.

Hirschmann, Albert O. 1970. *Exit, Voice, and Loyalty.* Cambridge, Mass.: Harvard University Press.

Hout, Michael, and Claude S. Fischer. 2002. "Why More Americans Have No Religious Preference: Politics and Generations." *American Sociological Review* 67: 165–190.

Huckfeldt, Robert, Eric Plutzer, and John Sprague. 1993. "Alternative Contexts of Political Behavior: Churches, Neighborhoods, and Individuals." *Journal of Politics* 55: 365–381.

Hunter, James Davison. 1991. *Culture Wars: The Struggle to Define America.* New York: Basic Books.

Hunter, James Davison. 1994. *Before the Shooting Begins: Searching for Democracy in America's Culture War.* New York: Macmillan.

Jelen, Ted. G. 1989. "Biblical Literalism and Inerrancy: Does the Difference Make a Difference?" *Sociological Analysis* 49: 421–429.

Jelen, Ted G. 1991. *The Political Mobilization of Religious Beliefs.* Westport, Conn.: Praeger.

Jelen, Ted. 1992. "Political Christianity: A Contextual Analysis." *American Journal of Political Science* 36: 692–714.

Jelen, Ted G. 1993. "The Political Consequences of Religious Group Attitudes." *Journal of Politics* 55: 178–190.

Jelen, Ted G., and Clyde Wilcox. 2003. "Causes and Consequences of Public Attitudes towards Abortion: A Review and Research Agenda." *Political Research Quarterly* 56: 489–500.

Kellstedt, Lyman A. 1989. "Evangelicals and Political Realignment." In *Contemporary Evangelical Political Involvement: An Analysis and Assessment,* ed. Corwin E. Smidt, 99–117. Lanham, Md.: University Press of America.

Kellstedt, Lyman A., and John C. Green. 1993. "Knowing God's Many People: Denominational Preference and Political Behavior." In *Rediscovering the Religious Factor in American Politics,* ed. David C. Leege and Lyman A. Kellstedt, 53–71. Armonk, N.Y.: M. E. Sharpe.

Kellstedt, Lyman A., John C. Green, James L. Guth, and Corwin E. Smidt. 1996. "Grasping the Essentials: The Social Embodiment of Religion and Political Behavior." In *Religion and the Culture Wars,* ed. John C. Green, James L. Guth, Corwin E. Smidt, and Lyman A. Kellstedt, 174–192. Lanham, Md.: Rowman & Littlefield.

Kellstedt, Lyman A., John C. Green, Corwin E. Smidt, and James L. Guth. 2007. "Faith Transformed: Religion and American Politics from F.D.R. to G.W. Bush." In *Religion and American Politics: From the Colonial Period to the Present.* 2nd ed., ed. Mark A. Noll and Luke E. Harlow, 269–295. New York: Oxford University Press.

Kellstedt, Lyman A., and Corwin E. Smidt. 1993. "Doctrinal Beliefs and Political Behavior: Views of the Bible." In *Rediscovering the Religious Factor in American Politics,* ed. David C. Leege and Lyman A. Kellstedt, 177–198. Armonk, N.Y.: M. E. Sharpe.

Key, V. O., Jr. 1964. *Politics, Parties, and Pressure Groups.* 5th ed. New York: T. Y. Crowell.

King, Gary, Michael Tomz, and Jason Wittenberg. 2000. "Making the Most of Statistical Analyses: Improving Interpretation and Presentation." *American Journal of Political Science* 44: 341–355.

Kleppner, Paul. 1987. *Continuity and Change in Electoral Politics, 1893–1928.* New York: Greenwood Press.

Kohut, Andrew, John C. Green, Scott Keeter, and Robert C. Toth. 2000. *The Diminishing Divide: Religion's Changing Role in American Politics.* Washington, D.C.: Brookings.

Ladd, Everett Carll, Jr., with Charles D. Hadley. 1975. *Transformations of the American Party System.* New York: W. W. Norton.

Lakoff, George. 2002. *Moral Politics: How Liberals and Conservative Think.* Chicago, Ill.: University of Chicago Press.

Layman, Geoffrey C. 1999. "Culture Wars in the American Party System: Religious and Cultural Change among Partisan Activists Since 1972." *American Politics Quarterly* 27 (1): 89–121.

Layman, Geoffrey C. 2001. *The Great Divide: Religious and Cultural Conflict in American Party Politics.* New York: Columbia University Press.

Layman, Geoffrey C., and Thomas M. Carsey. 2002a. "Party Polarization and 'Conflict Extension' in the American Electorate." *American Journal of Political Science* 46: 786–802.

Layman, Geoffrey C., and Thomas M. Carsey. 2002b. "Party Polarization and Party Structuring of Policy Attitudes: A Comparison of Three NES Panel Studies." *Political Behavior* 24: 199–236.

Layman, Geoffrey C., and John C. Green. 2006. "Wars and Rumours of War: The Contexts of Cultural Conflict in American Political Behaviour." *British Journal of Political Science* 36: 61–89.

Layman, Geoffrey C., and Laura S. Hussey. 2007. "George W. Bush and the Evangelicals: Religious Commitment and Partisan Change among Evangelical Protestants, 1960–2004." In *A Matter of Faith: Religion in the 2004 Presidential Election*, ed. David E. Campbell, 180–198. Washington, D.C.: Brookings Institution Press.

Layman, Geoffrey C., John Michael McTague, Shanna Pearson-Merkowitz, and Michael Spivey. 2007. "Family Values Revisited." Presented at the annual meeting of the Southern Political Science Association, New Orleans, Louisiana, January 3–7.

Leege, David C., and Lyman A. Kellstedt, eds. 1993. *Rediscovering the Religious Factor in American Politics*. Armonk, N.Y.: M. E. Sharpe.

Leege, David C., Kenneth D. Wald, Brian S. Krueger, and Paul D. Mueller. 2002. *The Politics of Cultural Differences: Social Change and Voter Mobilization Strategies in the Post-New Deal Period*. Princeton, N.J.: Princeton University Press.

MacDonald, Stuart Elaine, and George Rabinowitz. 1987. "The Dynamics of Structural Realignment." *American Political Science Review* 81: 775–796.

McCormick, Richard L. 1986. *Party, Period, and Public Policy*. New York: Oxford University Press.

McTague, John Michael, and Shanna Pearson-Merkowitz. 2006. "Voting from the Pew: The Effect of Senators' Religious Affiliations on Cultural Issues Votes, 1976–2004." Presented at the annual meeting of the Midwest Political Science Association, Chicago, Illinois, April 20–23.

Miller, Arthur H., Christopher Wlezien, and Anne Hildreth. 1991. "A Reference Group Theory of Partisan Coalitions." *Journal of Politics* 53: 1134–1149.

Miller, Warren E., and M. Kent Jennings. 1986. *Parties in Transition: A Longitudinal Study of Party Elites and Party Supporters*. New York: Sage.

Miller, Warren E., and J. Merrill Shanks. 1996. *The New American Voter*. Cambridge, Mass.: Harvard University Press.

Mockabee, Stephen T. 2007. "A Question of Authority: Religion and Cultural Conflict in the 2004 Election." *Political Behavior* 29: 221–248.

Mockabee, Stephen T., Joseph Quin Monson, and J. Tobin Grant. 2001. "Measuring Religious Commitment among Catholics and Protestants: A New Approach." *Journal for the Scientific Study of Religion* 40: 675–690.

Mouw, Ted, and Michael E. Sobel. 2001. "Culture Wars and Opinion Polarization: The Case of Abortion." *American Journal of Sociology* 106: 913–943.

Oldfield, Duane M. 1996. *The Right and the Righteous: The Christian Right Confronts the Republican Party*. Lanham, Md.: Rowman & Littlefield.

Oldmixon, Elizabeth Anne. 2005. *Uncompromising Positions: God, Sex, and the U.S. House of Representatives*. Washington, D.C.: Georgetown University Press.

Reichley, A. James. 1987. "The Evangelical and Fundamentalist Revolt." In *Piety and Politics: Evangelicals and Fundamentalists Confront the World*, ed. Richard John Neuhaus and Michael Cromrartie, 69–95. Washington, D.C.: Ethics and Public Policy Center.

Riker, William H. 1982. *Liberalism against Populism*. San Francisco, Calif.: Freeman.

Schattschneider, E. E. 1960. *The Semisovereign People: A Realist's View of Democracy in America*. New York: Holt, Rinehart, and Winston.

Schofield, Norman, and Gary Miller. 2007. "Elections and Activist Coalitions in the United States." *American Journal of Political Science* 51: 518–531.

Smidt, Corwin. 1988. "Evangelicals within Contemporary American Politics: Differentiating between Fundamentalist and Non-Fundamentalist Evangelicals." *Western Political Quarterly* 41: 601–620.

Smidt, Corwin E., and James M. Penning. 1991. "Religious Self-Identifications and Support for Robertson: An Analysis of Delegates to the 1988 Michigan Republican State Convention." *Review of Religious Research* 32: 321–36.

Smith, Christian, Michael Emerson, Sally Gallagher, Paul Kennedy, and David Sikkink. 1997. "The Myth of Culture Wars: The Case of American Protestantism." In *Cultural Wars in American Politics: Critical Reviews of a Popular Myth*, ed. Rhys H. Williams, 175–195. New York: De Gruyter.

Stenner, Karen. 2005. *The Authoritarian Dynamic*. New York: Cambridge University Press.

Sundquist, James L. 1983. *Dynamics of the Party System: Alignment and Realignment of Political Parties in the United States*. Washington, D.C.: The Brookings Institution.

Thomas, Cal, and Ed Dobson. 1999. *Blinded By Might: Can the Religious Right Save America?* Grand Rapids, Mich.: Zondervan.

Verba, Sidney, Kay Lehman Scholzman, and Henry E. Brady. 1995. *Voice and Equality: Civic Voluntarism in American Politics*. Cambridge, Mass.: Harvard University Press.

Wald, Kenneth D., Dennis E. Owen, Samuel S. Hill, Jr. 1988. "Churches as Political Communities." *American Political Science Review* 82: 531–548.

Wald, Kenneth D., Dennis E. Owen, and Samuel S. Hill, Jr. 1990. "Political Cohesion in Churches." *Journal of Politics* 52: 197–215.

Weisberg, Herbert F. 2005. "The Structure and Effects of Moral Predispositions in Contemporary American Politics." *The Journal of Politics* 67: 646–668.

Weyrich, Paul M. 1999. "Separate and Free." *Washington Post* March 7, B7.

White, John Kenneth. 2003. *The Values Divide*. New York: Chatham House.

White, Theodore H. 1973. *The Making of the President, 1972*. New York: Atheneum.

Wilcox, Clyde. 1990. "Religion and Politics Among White Evangelicals: The Impact of Religious Variables on Political Attitudes." *Review of Religious Research* 32: 27–42.

Wilcox, Clyde, Ted G. Jelen, and David C. Leege. 1993. "Religious Group Identifications: Toward a Cognitive Theory of Religious Mobilization." In *Rediscovering the Religious Factor in American Politics*, ed. David C. Leege and Lyman A. Kellstedt, 72–99. Armonk, N.Y.: M. E. Sharpe.

Wolfe, Alan. 1998. *One Nation, After All: What Middle-Class Americans Really Think About: God, Country, Family, Racism, Welfare, Immigration, Homosexuality, Work, the Right, the Left, and Each Other*. New York: Viking.

Wuthnow, Robert. 1988. *The Restructuring of American Religion*. Princeton, N.J.: Princeton University Press.

Wuthnow, Robert. 1989. *The Struggle for America's Soul: Evangelicals, Liberals, and Secularism*. Grand Rapids, Mich.: Eerdmans.

Yamane, David. 1999. "Faith and Access: Personal Religiosity and Religious Group Advocacy in a State Legislature." *Journal for the Scientific Study of Religion* 38: 543–550.

CHAPTER 13

....

CLERGY AND AMERICAN POLITICS

....

LAURA R. OLSON

NOTWITHSTANDING two centuries of official church–state separation, clergy have played important political roles throughout the entirety of American history. Rev. John Witherspoon of New Jersey was a signer of the Declaration of Independence and Rev. Abraham Baldwin of Georgia was among the framers of the U.S. Constitution. African American clergy, most notably Rev. Dr. Martin Luther King, Jr., drove the civil rights movement, which was arguably the most successful social movement in American history. Countless other clergy—from those with famous names to those acting nearly invisibly—have made their mark on American politics by leading and opposing social movements, articulating their views on a vast array of issues and candidates, and shaping the political views of their congregations.

Clergy have the capacity to affect political change through their own actions and by setting a tone for the many millions of Americans who belong to their congregations. Moreover, the United States' tremendous religious diversity means that clergy representing every imaginable religious tradition—and, by extension, political persuasion—can bring their views to bear on American politics. American political culture carries heavy religious–moral overtones, which places clergy (who are by definition in the business of defining and promoting morality) in a unique position to exercise moral suasion when they have sufficient interest, motivation, and opportunity.

However, clergy do not become involved in politics without taking some risks. Alexis de Tocqueville (1840 [1969]) explains that 19th-century American clergy exercised substantial political power—in part because they took great care to *avoid* explicit affiliations with political parties. Today's clergy risk loss of livelihood or legitimacy if their congregations perceive them as excessively or inappropriately political. Clergy's first priorities are religious, not political, in nature. They must maintain and tend to their flocks before all else, necessarily leaving political activity as a secondary pursuit (see Crawford 1995). All clergy must reconcile the institutional rules and expectations of the congregations and broader religious traditions they serve with their own goals and preferences when they decide whether to engage in political activity. Some clergy reject the idea of translating their religious authority into political authority, whereas others choose to partake in a wide array of political endeavors. What factors explain these choices? The existing literature on clergy and politics offers two broad sets of variables that explain whether and how clergy take political action: (1) their own theological orientations as well as their own religious traditions' theological teachings and traditions, and (2) the broader contexts within which they work.

This chapter is designed to explore the central currents in the literature on clergy and politics. I begin by charting a brief historical map of scholarship on clergy and politics to date. Next I explore the question of whether clergy are paradigmatic of other politically relevant social elites. To understand the range of political opportunities available to clergy, I consider how we might categorize the politically relevant activities in which they engage. I then discuss the specific ways in which the existing literature helps us understand whether and why clergy become politically active. Finally, I conclude by reinforcing other scholars' call for further research on the extent to which clergy's political action is consequential.

A Brief Overview of Scholarship on Clergy and Politics

Leadership is a concept of enduring importance in both political science and sociology because both disciplines concern themselves with the study of social structures and their ramifications for people's everyday lives. Without some form of leadership, of course, no complex social structure could exist over the long term. Therefore, both political scientists and sociologists maintain a keen and necessary interest in the concept of leadership, including the forms it takes, the effects it has on other individuals, and the changes that leaders can and do bring to social structures themselves. Organized religion is no different from any other complex social structure in its need for leadership. By its very nature, religion is dependent on leadership of the divine variety. It is logical, then, that virtually all of organized religion worldwide features identifiable leadership structures of one variety or another. It stands to reason as well that religious leaders might be called upon—or feel personally called—to offer moral guidance to the broader societies in which they live and work. As a result, clergy often find themselves touching the hem of politics.

Recognizing these facts, scholars have worked for more than four decades to understand the nature and significance of clergy's political orientations and involvement in the United States. After the publication of several path-breaking seminal studies (e.g., Hadden 1969; Stark, Foster, Glock, and Quinley 1971; Quinley 1974), the clergy-and-politics field lay largely dormant until the 1990s. During the relatively recent past, however, scholars' interest in the political roles of religious leaders has experienced tremendous renewal. Although research on clergy and politics could stand to be connected even more fully to broader scholarship on political leadership, many significant strides have been made in our understanding of how and why clergy might become involved in politics, around which issues and principles, and to what effect.

The first systematic studies of clergy and politics were driven by scholars' fascination with clergy's involvement in the civil rights movement. These studies emphasized the ideological and theological radicalization of a "new breed" (Cox 1967; Garrett 1973) of liberal, activist clergy. Ernest Campbell and Thomas Pettigrew (1959) argued that it was essential for clergy who wished to participate in the movement toward racial integration in Little Rock, Arkansas, during the 1950s not only to be committed personally to the civil rights cause, but also to have the support of their congregations. Again emphasizing the importance of congregational support, Jeffrey Hadden (1969) documented the emergence of a widespread "clergy–laity gap" that began to separate ideologically liberal clergy from their more moderate-to-conservative congregations during the mid 20th century. Harold Quinley (1974) contended that the prominence of clergy's leadership during the civil rights era actually was an aberration that would soon pass away, whereas Benton Johnson (1966, 1967) examined Oregon clergy, establishing that theological liberalism went hand-in-hand with both ideological liberalism and Democratic partisanship. Rodney Stark et al. (1971) added the related observation that conservative clergy largely shunned politics because of their "otherworldly" theology (see also Koller and Retzer 1980). Instead of connecting conservative theology to conservative ideology (and, notably, support for the Republican Party), conservative clergy were relatively apolitical until the 1980s (see Guth, Green, Smidt, Kellstedt, and Poloma 1997). Finally, Aldon Morris (1984) offered a sweeping view of the role of African American clergy in the development of the early civil rights movement.

Taken together, these studies were driven primarily by a desire to understand two factors: (1) the theological and political liberalization of (primarily) mainline Protestant clergy, and (2) the mobilizing role clergy played around one central historical event (the civil rights movement). No large-scale theory-building effort regarding clergy's potential as political leaders in general was mounted. Therefore, early scholarship on clergy and politics is limited both by its narrow focus on a certain "breed" of clergy and by the time-bound nature of its focus on the civil rights era. Nonetheless, these early studies made significant strides in elucidating the connections between clergy's theological orientations and their personal ideological, partisan, and issue positions.

However, the emergence of the religious Right during the 1980s led scholars to reevaluate the emphasis placed on liberal clergy in the first wave of research. Suddenly, conservative clergy were at the forefront of American politics whereas liberals were seemingly fading to the margins. This sea change led to broader theorization regarding the role of theology (Guth 1983, 1984; Beatty and Walter 1989; Jelen 1993; Guth 1996; Guth et al. 1997, 2001b; Smidt 2004) and contextual factors (Jelen 1993; Olson 2000; Crawford and Olson 2001; Djupe and Gilbert 2002, 2003; Djupe, Olson, and Gilbert 2005, 2006; Olson, Crawford, and Deckman 2005) in shaping clergy's political inclinations. As a whole, this newer body of work has shed substantial light on the question of how clergy approach politics, thanks largely to measurement innovation and methodological pluralism.

A significant pioneer in the second wave of research on clergy and politics was James Guth. For nearly three decades, Guth (1983, 1984, 1996, 2001b) has collected survey data on Southern Baptist clergy, which paved the way for his broader *oeuvre* of work on clergy and politics with several collaborators (Guth et al. 1997; Guth, Green, Smidt, and Poloma 1991), culminating most recently in the 2001 Cooperative Clergy Study, which involved nearly 30 scholars studying clergy in more than 20 American religious traditions (Smidt 2004).

Guth and colleagues argue that theology and its political by-product, "social theology," play central roles in shaping clergy's personal political orientations, and therefore the nature and purpose of clergy's political activism. Social theology is defined as "beliefs connecting theology to public affairs" (Guth et al. 1997, p. 8) and is posited to act as an intervening variable connecting theology to clergy's political attitudes and views on the general appropriateness of clerical political activism. Guth et al. (1997) identify two general social theological orientations among Protestant clergy: the "social justice" orientation and the "moral reform" orientation. Clergy who espouse the social justice agenda reflect 1960s-style ideological liberalism, emphasizing issues of injustice and poverty; they are found primarily in mainline Protestant denominations. Clergy who embrace the moral reform agenda, who are most likely to be evangelical Protestants, are concerned primarily with sociomoral issues such as abortion and homosexuality, and take uniformly conservative positions on them (Guth et al. 1997; Smidt 2004). Theoretically speaking, Guth et al. (1997) argue that Protestant clergy cleave in two general political directions based primarily, although not exclusively, on the *religious* contexts within which they work. Meanwhile, their most important empirical contribution lies in the sheer quantity of survey data they have collected throughout several decades of scholarship.

A parallel body of recent scholarship explores the extent to which contextual factors beyond the context of religious tradition and denomination shape clergy's political orientations. Several qualitative studies have illustrated how local contexts shape the circumstances under which clergy make political choices (Jelen 1993;

Olson 2000; Cavendish 2001). These studies are limited by the questions of generalizability, but offer far more ethnographic detail than can be captured through survey research. Scholars also have worked to establish the broader theoretical relevance of extrareligious contextual factors in clergy's political calculi. The work of Paul Djupe (Djupe and Gilbert 2002, 2003) is particularly significant in this regard, as he ably draws on the political context literature (e.g., Huckfeldt and Sprague 1987) to argue systematically that clergy's political orientations are shaped primarily by the ways in which they "respond to the political and social environments in which they live and work" (Djupe and Gilbert 2002, p. 599). Although no one study of clergy and politics may be called definitive, the cumulative effect of recent research is impressive both in its breadth and depth. Qualitative case studies enhance the broad understanding we gain from survey research. This methodological pluralism also has contributed to recent theoretical innovation about clergy and their place in American politics (see especially Djupe and Gilbert [2006]).

THE POLITICAL RELEVANCE OF CLERGY

A key challenge facing scholars who study clergy and politics is the question of whether clergy can exert anything more than a tangential influence on the political and policy processes. Why bother to study clergy if they have little, if any, effect on the political process?

In many ways, clergy are paradigmatic nongovernmental social leaders insofar as political participation is not their primary responsibility (Crawford, Olson, and Deckman 2001). Clergy may, or may not, find politics relevant to their work. But is it really fair to say that clergy are just like elites in other professions? Clergy do share characteristics with other professionals who find themselves involved in politics as a result of their primary occupation. As is the case with other socially visible professionals, clergy not only have the potential to be mobilized for politics themselves, but they also have a hand in the mobilization of others. Like professionals in other fields, clergy are limited in what they can do politically by their job responsibilities.

Yet, in many ways, clergy stand apart from other professionals. They differ from other groups of professionals because their "industry" is, in an important sense, not of this world. Because clergy are professional arbiters of values and absolute truths, their pronouncements on what is right and wrong may indeed place them in a unique position to shape American political debates compared with, say, lawyers, physicians, or college professors.

In addition, clergy have an especially high degree of legitimacy when they speak out on issues that fall under the "morality politics" rubric (Tatalovich and Daynes 1998; Hunter 1991; Meier 1994; Wald, Button, and Rienzo 2001; Olson,

Guth, and Guth 2003; Penning and Storteboom 2007). Indeed, American political discourse increasingly is being cast in moral (if not explicitly religious) terms. The issues discussed in such terms now range beyond abortion and homosexuality to include matters that extend from taxes to immigration to the environment. James Davison Hunter (1991) has argued that the most significant political and social divisions in the United States are based on assumptions about the source of moral authority, which has created a schism between people with socially conservative beliefs and those with progressive beliefs (but see Fiorina 2005). Although there is ample reason to question whether the "culture wars" division really has replaced older divisions in public opinion and politics in the United States (see, for example, DiMaggio, Evans, and Bryson 1996), it is indisputably true that public debates about moral and cultural matters have been keen. And clergy, as leaders in a social structure that exists explicitly for spiritual and moral guidance, have great legitimacy in such debates.

Also, more than half of all Americans say they attend religious services at least once a month. Even if this figure is inflated, as some scholars have argued (Hadaway, Marler, and Chaves 1993), American clergy are in a position to provide political cues grounded in unbending and unshakeable beliefs about the divine and the eternal to a large and diverse array of citizens on a weekly basis. The same could not be said of professionals in any other walk of life, with the possible exception of a small handful of journalists and college professors.

Therefore, even though many American clergy may choose to avoid the political arena altogether (Olson 2000), it is an undeniable fact that a sizable number of their counterparts do aspire to shape political debates, public policy, and electoral outcomes. Arriving at a definitive conclusion regarding whether clergy are similar to or different from other groups of professionals may not be as crucial as it is to create a consensus among political scientists that clergy *must* be acknowledged as potentially powerful opinion leaders, agents of political socialization, and political organizers.

What Do Clergy Do in the Political Realm?

What exactly do clergy *do* if and when they become involved in the political realm?[1] What sorts of activities might they define as political? First and foremost, clergy have the capacity to shape public opinion on political issues. Because they preside over congregations, clergy have ample opportunity to provide political cues for often large and often trusting audiences on a regular basis. For the most part, clergy appear to use these opportunities to discuss politics at least on occasion, and their cues do not always fall on deaf ears. Some clergy also choose to participate directly in the political and policy processes. Several noted political officials and candidates themselves have been ordained clergy, such as Rev. Jesse Jackson, Rev. Pat Robertson, Rev. Mike Huckabee, and several members of the U.S. Congress. Clergy also have the ability to mobilize themselves and others for organized and sustained political action. The civil rights movement would nearly have been inconceivable were it not for the political involvement of clergy (Morris 1984).

Generally speaking, clergy bring religious thought and experiences to bear on policy discussions; work in citywide coalitions to address poverty, racism, and violence; develop partnerships with social service agencies; and foster nongovernmental efforts to provide social services or community development. Some of these activities, such as protesting or speaking on behalf of candidates or issues, place clergy in the middle of contentious debates about who should run the government and what it should do. Other activities, such as participating in government-sponsored coalitions or partnering with government to provide social services, allow clergy to have a far subtler political impact. These illustrations show that the range of actions clergy might choose to take in the political realm is rather wide.

Theoretical Grounding

In their classic work on political participation, Sidney Verba and Norman Nie (1972, p. 2) define the concept as "those activities by private citizens that are more or less directly aimed at influencing the selection of governmental personnel and/ or the actions they take." Steven Rosenstone and John Mark Hansen (1993, p. 4) define political participation even more broadly: it is "action directed explicitly toward influencing the distribution of social goods and social values." Beyond these general definitions, scholars have drawn distinctions between conventional and unconventional participation (Barnes and Kaase 1979), and between symbolic and instrumental participation (Edelman 1971). Activities as varied as voting, working for candidates and political parties, writing to public officials, demonstrating, and even rioting have been included in lists of participatory actions.

In their later work, Verba, Schlozman, and Brady (1995) emphasize that individuals (and, logically, groups) who participate in politics must possess three crucial resources: time, money, and civic skills. Religious organizations are a significant repository of these crucial political resources (Verba et al. 1995; Putnam 2000; Djupe and Grant 2001; Djupe and Gilbert 2006), particularly civic skills, which Verba and colleagues define as "the communications and organizational skills that facilitate effective participation" (Brady, Verba, and Schlozman 1995, p. 271). To some extent, all clergy possess the resources of which Verba and colleagues speak; taken together, these resources represent substantial potential energy for political participation as part of their official roles as clergy. The degree to which pastors choose to deploy these resources in the pursuit of political goals defines their orientations to the political realm (see also Olson 2000).

Verba, Schlozman, Brady, and Nie (1993, pp. 486–487) also have distinguished between "skill-producing churches" and "politically mobilizing churches." Each type of church (or synagogue, mosque, ashram, and so on) is thought to enhance a congregation's potential for political participation, albeit in a different way. Skill-producing churches provide people with opportunities to practice civic skills in ways that need not be explicitly political (such as organizing a rummage sale). Politically mobilizing churches expose their congregations directly to political messages or activity. Certainly clergy play a role in determining whether a given congregation will place greater emphasis on skill production or political mobilization—at least to the extent that clergy can shape their congregations' cultures (see Hougland and Wood 1979; Becker 1999). It is therefore especially important to understand the nature and extent of the political activity in which clergy engage on behalf of the groups they serve (their congregations, the neighborhoods surrounding their churches, and the broader religious traditions to which they belong). Clergy may espouse clear personal political beliefs or be active in politics on their own as private citizens, but if they do not bring their politics directly to bear on their congregations, they are not acting as political leaders on behalf of, or even in reference to, those whom they lead.

The Nature of Clergy's Political Involvement

Previous research (Olson et al. 2005) emphasizes that the political activities in which clergy engage range from those commonly seen as political to those often viewed as social service activities. Although some activities might be contained within one's congregation, they might also transpire in or be directed toward the world outside the congregation. It is fair to say that clergy's political activities nearly always seek to influence collective decision making, resource distribution, or enforcement of values beyond the membership of their congregations. To make sense of the broad range of possible political activities available to clergy, we must examine two separable dimensions: *where* clergy act and *how* clergy act. Both dimensions are, of course, constrained both by various aspects of religious tradition (Stark et al. 1971; Guth et al. 1997) and by additional contextual factors unique to each clergyperson's work situation (Olson 2000; Djupe and Gilbert 2002, 2003).

In considering *where* clergy act, we must distinguish between activities conducted within the congregation (and, one would think, designed primarily to influence the political attitudes and behaviors of congregation members) and activities that directly involve clergy in politics outside of their congregations. Roughly speaking, Guth et al. (1997) label the first type of action "cue giving" and the second, "direct action." Cue-giving activities rely on clergy's use of their teaching and leadership authority *inside* their congregations, whereas direct action finds clergy acting to influence resource distribution or enforcement of values *outside* of the congregational context.[2]

In thinking about *how* clergy act, my colleagues and I have posited four broad categories of action: electoral activities, advocacy, partnership, and gap filling (see Crawford 1995; Crawford et al. 2001; Olson et al. 2005). *Electoral* activities (such as campaigning, running for office, or contributing money to candidates) are intended to affect the selection of the individuals who will make government decisions. *Advocacy* (such as protesting, contacting political officials, or forming congregational study groups on issues) is designed to influence government officials or shape public opinion. Such action sometimes takes place via the ministerial associations found in most American cities and towns (see Niles 2007). *Partnership* activities involve working with a government entity to address some problem or provide some service (such as working on a community policing task force or being a member of a mayoral task force on race relations). Finally, *gap filling* involves working to offer social services that government does not adequately provide, such as serving meals to the hungry in soup kitchens.

These two organizing concepts (where clergy act and how clergy act) may be married together to yield a general typology of the range and scope of political activities available to clergy. Drawing upon existing empirical work on clergy and politics (Guth et al. 1997; Crawford et al. 2001; Smidt 2004; Olson et al. 2005), table 13.1 offers the skeleton of such a typology. The table shows that clergy may avail themselves of an extremely wide variety of politically relevant activities. They can (and do) pick and choose between the two poles of exercising a relatively "quiet" influence (Wuthnow and Evans 2002) and offering visionary prophetic leadership. Of course, it is important to remember that some clergy also opt for total political disengagement.

Why Clergy Choose Political Action

American clergy are confronted with a variety of opportunities to engage in action[3] that might be deemed politically relevant. On what basis do they choose among these opportunities? The literature on clergy and politics has taken two complementary approaches to answering this question. Both revolve around the notion of political context. "Contextual theories of politics build on the argument that individual political preference is not a simple function of individual characteristics alone, but rather the complex product of an individual's own characteristics in combination with the characteristics and predispositions of other surrounding individuals" (Huckfeldt, Plutzer, and Sprague 1993, p. 366). Scholars have argued that the religious contexts within which clergy work play a significant role in shaping their political preferences, priorities, and strategies. More recently, scholars have argued that contextual factors beyond religious tradition and theology also affect clergy's political choices.

The Significance of Religious Context

Because religion constitutes clergy's explicit enterprise, it is natural that theology and religious worldview would influence their political orientations. Previous studies outline the ways in which theology and religious worldviews influence the clergy's political ideology, partisanship, attitudes about issues, and orientations toward political activism (e.g., Johnson 1966, 1967; Hadden 1969; Stark et al. 1971; Quinley 1974; Roozen, McKinney, and Carroll 1984; Guth et al. 1997; Johnson 1998). Guth et al. (1997) do an especially effective job of showing that different social theologies[4] are tied to different theological orientations and that these social theologies are differentially distributed across religious denominations and traditions. Social theology is largely learned in seminary (Carroll, Wheeler, Aleshire, and Marler 1997; Guth 2001a) and later brought to bear upon congregations. Guth et al.

Table 13.1 A Typology of Clergy's Political Activities

	Inside the Congregation	Outside the Congregation
Electoral activities	• Urging congregation members to vote • Distributing voter guides to congregation • Inviting candidates to speak to congregation • Holding preelection forums • Endorsing a candidate from the pulpit	• Running for public office • Endorsing or contributing to a candidate or political party • Registering voters in the community • Displaying a campaign button, bumper sticker, or yard sign
Advocacy	• Preaching about a contentious issue • Organizing congregational letter-writing campaigns • Spearheading congregational study groups or action groups around contentious issues • Sponsoring a congregational crisis pregnancy center • Signing or circulating a petition • Organizing a boycott of a product or service	• Taking a public stand on an issue or policy • Participating in a rally, protest march, or civil disobedience • Working to solve social problems with a local ministerial association • Writing a letter to the editor or op-ed column
Partnership	• Offering congregation-based social service delivery programs	• Being appointed to a local task force or commission • Joining a civic organization or ministerial association
Gap filling	• Sponsoring congregational soup kitchens, food pantries, clothing banks, homeless shelters, health care clinics, and so forth	• Joining interfaith programs designed to feed, clothe, shelter, and otherwise care for disadvantaged persons

Source: Adapted from Crawford et al. (2001), Guth et al. (1997), Olson et al. (2005), and Smidt (2004).

(1997) contrast the different social theologies found within evangelical and main-line Protestantism, but their theory would extend beyond Protestantism, as partic-ular sociopolitical meaning also derives from being Catholic, Jewish, or Muslim in the United States. Thus, religious leaders operate within distinctive *religious* contexts that may lead them to emphasize certain issues over others and incline them toward certain modes of political activity.

Religious context shapes the scope of political strategies available to clergy. For example, some religious traditions are ecumenical, meaning that they usually welcome the chance to work side by side with people of other faiths, whereas other religious groups are particularistic, rendering them skeptical of people who espouse different theological orientations. Clergy in religious traditions that espouse ecumenism have an easier time justifying the coalition building that today's politics often requires, whereas leaders within particularistic traditions often must go it alone politically.

Different religious worldviews can influence the resources clergy are able to bring to political action as well as their potential effectiveness in mobilizing their congregations (Jelen 2001). Clergy who work in religious traditions that confer the authority to speak "the truth" upon their clergy (more orthodox traditions) are more likely to feel that they can also speak "the truth" about politics. Clergy in more progressive traditions, on the other hand, may be more likely to assume that their roles in both politics and religious teaching should focus on raising questions and providing guidance, but not giving final and unyielding answers.[5] These opposing views of religious authority (Wuthnow 1988) have divergent implications for clergy who seek ways to challenge people in the pews to democratic participation. Clergy from "the truth" perspective should find it much easier to make direct and explicit calls for participation on a political issue than would be the case for clergy from the "questioning" tradition.

Mainline Protestant clergy face unique constraints as a result of the "clergy–laity gap." On the one hand, several generations of mainline Protestant clergy have been interested and involved in politics (playing nationally visible roles in the civil rights movement, the nuclear freeze movement, and the sanctuary movement [Hertzke 1988; Findlay 1993; Smith 1996; Friedland 1998]). Mainline Protestant theology demands that its clergy and laity will be involved in "this world" by working to ameliorate poverty and eliminate injustice (Niebuhr 1951). This view would seem to compel political action outside the congregation. Not all mainline clergy, however, find it easy—or even possible—to involve themselves in prophetic politics. Relatively few mainline laity wholeheartedly endorse the liberal political ideology that often accompanies mainline theology, and which clergy learn in seminary (Carroll et al. 1997; Guth et al. 1997). Consequently, since at least the 1960s, dividing lines have been drawn between many mainline clergy and the moderate-to-conservative people in their pews.[6] Therefore, in recent years, mainline Protestant clergy's political and social outreach increasingly has come to focus on addressing problems quietly on the local level (Wuthnow and Evans 2002).[7]

Evangelical Protestant clergy have made news during the past three decades because of their involvement in and support for the religious Right political movement (see Wilcox and Larson 2006). However, it might be tempting at this point to forget that evangelical clergy historically eschewed politics before the 1980s. Through most of the 20th century, evangelical leaders viewed politics as a realm tainted by sin that was best kept at arm's length. The emergence of the religious Right during the 1980s led to a gradual but fundamental shift in this attitude of political avoidance among clergy. Today, many (but by no means all) evangelical clergy prioritize—and take conservative stands on—sociomoral issues such as abortion and homosexuality, especially inside their congregations (Smidt 2004). Evangelical clergy benefit from the fact that their tradition's conservative theology creates a context that confers a good deal of legitimacy upon them as authoritative speakers and leaders. They face far fewer challenges than their mainline Protestant counterparts when it comes time to "rally the troops" for political action, because evangelical laity may be more accustomed to accepting their clergy's teachings than are mainline Protestant laity.[8] Moreover, conservative theology allows for clear stands to be taken on the nature of "right" and "wrong." This theological context gives evangelical clergy an added advantage when they articulate morally absolutist positions on issues such as abortion: Unlike mainline Protestants, most evangelicals are accustomed to receiving clear definitions of what is "right" and what is "wrong."

African American Protestant clergy have made history as community leaders, particularly during the civil rights era (Morris 1984; Lincoln and Mamiya 1990; Harris 1999), but their political influence continues to this day (Harris 1999; Smith 2003, 2005; Smith and Harris 2005). It is fair to say that African American clergy founded the civil rights movement and led one of its most influential social movement organizations: the Southern Christian Leadership Conference (Morris 1984). It is also a widely accepted norm that African American clergy should invite politicians to speak from their pulpits and at times endorse candidates; such behavior falls outside acceptable bounds in other religious traditions in the United States. Black clergy have long enjoyed tremendous support and legitimacy both inside and outside their congregations, in part because for many years the ministry was one of the few routes available to elite status for African Americans. It is within this context that African American clergy are encouraged, and perhaps even expected, to act as community leaders beyond the walls of their churches.

Catholic clergy also exercise political influence in the United States. Changes wrought by the Second Vatican Council (1962–1965) created a new context for American Catholic clergy within which they enjoy expanded opportunities to exercise political leadership (Byrnes 1991, 2001). Catholic clergy played key roles in the civil rights and antiwar movements of the 20th century (Friedland 1998). More recently, in the run up to each presidential election, the U.S. Conference of Catholic Bishops has released an official statement on "election-year issues." In 2004, some Catholic clergy made news for their public refusal to administer the Holy Eucharist to Catholic politicians who support abortion rights (Allen 2004). The broad American political context may constitute the most significant barrier for Catholic clergy who wish to exercise a political voice. The Catholic church's position on abortion would warrant an alliance with the Republican Party, but its positions on a host of other social and economic issues resonate better with the agenda of the Democratic Party. Perhaps as a result, Jelen (2004) finds that individual priests today are relatively unlikely to engage in political activism, but it is still the case that Catholic clergy make their mark on American politics, particularly via the statements and pastoral letters issued by the U.S. Conference of Catholic Bishops.

Finally, there is a great paucity of research on the extent to which *non-Christian* clergy take part in American politics. Jewish rabbis hold a range of theological and political viewpoints, even with regard to the state of Israel and the question of peace in the Middle East (Sokhey and Djupe 2003, 2006). Muslims have only recently begun to organize politically, particularly in an effort to combat anti-Muslim biases that have grown all the more prevalent since the events of 9/11. What role imams play in American politics, however, is an open question.

The Significance of Broader Contexts

To be sure, religious context affects the choices clergy make about engaging in political activity. However, a range of nonecclesiastical variables also must be considered in studies of clergy and politics. Studies of such broader contextual variables comprise an important and growing thread of the clergy-and-politics literature. The nonecclesiastical contexts scholars emphasize most frequently include political context, congregational context, neighborhood context, and personal context.

American political culture leaves clergy mostly free from government regulation. It allows religion to maintain a strong yet detached social presence (see Neuhaus 1984; Fowler 1989). This *political* context heightens clergy's ability to act as public citizens and political educators in the United States. Current tax law restricts party-oriented activity by religious institutions that wish to maintain their tax-exempt status. Churches and other religious organizations have had, on occasion, their tax-exempt status challenged as a result of excessive partisan activity. This legal context provides a concrete reason for clergy to steer clear of electoral activities and focus instead on advocacy, partnership, and gap-filling activities. Moreover, many religious traditions have long applied strong normative pressure against explicitly partisan talk by clergy, which reinforces the pressure on clergy to choose issue-oriented (as opposed to party-oriented) strategies. Clergy in religious traditions with political views that fit naturally with the agenda of a major political party (such as evangelical Protestantism or black Protestantism) are more likely to be mobilized for politics—and to have success in their efforts to encourage citizens to participate in elections and other political actions. So, although a great deal of research has documented the fact that theology plays a significant role in structuring clergy's partisan attitudes (Johnson 1966, 1967; Hadden 1969; Quinley 1974; Guth et al. 1997; Smidt 2004), clergy themselves are quite constrained in the extent to which they are able to communicate their electoral preferences to their congregations.

The specifics of local politics also structure the opportunities available to clergy wishing to become involved in politics (Olson et al. 2005). One of the surest paths to political involvement is to be asked by someone else to become involved. Recruitment plays a powerful role in political mobilization generally speaking, so the same should be true for busy clergy. If an interest group, ministerial association, or other organization intentionally recruits clergy to take part in political action, the opportunity is placed at their feet. Many such organizations have found it fruitful to target clergy for mobilization around a wide range of causes during the past several decades. The dynamics of local politics undoubtedly influence the sorts of political tasks that clergy might be recruited to undertake as well as the opportunities that clergy seeking political outlets might encounter. More research is needed on how clergy are mobilized by outside organizations.

Congregational context also affects clergy's political orientations. Each congregation constitutes a unique microcontext featuring long-entrenched norms and assumptions about "who we are" and "how we do things here" (Becker 1999). Some congregations are explicitly political, whereas others eschew politics entirely. Some congregations are uniformly liberal or conservative, whereas others are mixed ideologically. Some congregations take part in many social service activities, whereas others focus primarily on religious endeavors (Cnaan 1999, 2002; Chaves 2004; Ammerman 2005).[9] Congregations can shape people's thinking about a full range of matters, including politics (Wald, Owen, and Hill 1988, 1990; Gilbert 1993; Huckfeldt et al. 1993; Welch, Leege, Wald, and Kellstedt 1993).

Clergy must mold themselves to fit the context created by their congregations or risk losing their legitimacy. In fact, Djupe and Gilbert (2003) liken the political relationship between clergy and their congregations to the representative–constituent relationship. Like elected officials, sometimes they must keep their views under wraps and suppress any desire to take political action around them. In the competitive religious marketplace that characterizes the United States today (Finke and Stark 1992), clergy may seek to carve out distinctive niches for their congregation. This may lead them either to shun politics altogether or to become involved in political activities that may not reflect their personal political priorities (Olson et al. 2005). However, it could also create a positive impetus for clergy to become involved in political action, because some people are attracted to churches that articulate clear political priorities and offer opportunities for political involvement (Becker 1999; Wellman 1999; Olson 2002).

A congregation's *neighborhood* context may also shape its clergy's orientations to the political world. It is a well-established fact that people with more resources (especially education and income) are more likely to participate in politics (see Verba and Nie 1972). Although personal socioeconomic differences have not been shown to have a great effect on clergy's political orientations, the socioeconomic conditions of the neighborhoods in which their congregations are situated do matter. In economically depressed neighborhoods, clergy often feel compelled to tackle poverty and its accompanying social problems either on their own or through coalitions run by grassroots organizations such as the Industrial Areas Foundation (Olson 2000; Warren 2001). Indeed, clergy who work in low-income neighborhoods tend to participate in local politics more than do those in neighborhoods of higher socioeconomic status (Olson 2000; Crawford and Olson 2001; see also Roozen et al. 1984). These higher rates of participation by clergy in low-income neighborhoods appear to be explained by a mix of self-selection into such neighborhoods and the leadership vacuum that often exists in such neighborhoods (Crawford and Olson 2001).

Clergy whose churches are located in impoverished neighborhoods may have more immediate incentives to become involved in politics than those who work in settings where there are higher per capita incomes, lower unemployment rates, and fewer people living below the poverty level (Olson 2000). They are likely to encounter people who struggle to survive on a daily basis, so their congregations may be called upon to provide more social services than would be the case for congregations in higher income neighborhoods. And they may serve parishioners who also have more basic grievances against the political establishment. As a result, a capable and motivated elite (like a clergyperson) may have an easier time creating political consensus and raising group members' political consciousness for political purposes.

Finally, aspects of the *personal* contexts that constitute individual leaders' everyday lives play significant roles in their political decisions. In recent years a growing number of women have been entering the ministry and rabbinate in the United States (Zikmund, Lummis, and Chang 1998), and much speculation is afoot about the future impact of female clergy, especially within mainline Protestantism. Gender represents an important personal context that influences clergy's decisions about when, whether, and how to participate in politics, because it is an important factor in accounting for differences in roles chosen by clergy. Olson et al. (2005) report that female clergy's minority status influences the nature of the political issues that matter most to them, as well as their choices about whether to act on these concerns. Female clergy also display a heightened awareness of discrimination issues because of their awareness of gender discrimination in their own profession (see also Olson, Crawford, and Guth 2000; Deckman, Crawford, Olson, and Green 2003).[10]

An even more significant personal context for clergy in the United States undoubtedly is race. Clergy's approaches to politics have differed dramatically along racial lines. African American clergy historically have been more comfortable translating their religious authority into political authority than have their colleagues from other racial and ethnic groups. Their political work takes place both inside and outside their congregations and spans the gamut of electoral, advocacy, partnership, and gap-filling activities. Many scholars have illustrated how the history of discrimination against African Americans has influenced black clergy's religious worldviews and political orientations (e.g., Lincoln and Mamiya 1990; Harris 1999; McDaniel 2004a, b; Smith and Harris 2005).

LOOKING TO THE FUTURE

American clergy face a wide variety of demands on their time and energy. They must balance these demands in ways that maximize their ability to meet the externally defined expectations of their position and allow them to achieve their

own personal and professional goals. It is crucial that clergy present their preferences to their congregations in such a way as to rally support for their goals
(Campbell and Pettigrew 1959; Djupe and Gilbert 2002, 2003). If they are able to
rally the troops—or at least prevent them from mutinying—clergy can and do
encounter plenty of opportunities to influence American politics. Moreover, there
is no reason to think that clergy's political relevance will diminish in the near
future. We must continue to study clergy and their political orientations using both
national surveys and more in-depth qualitative studies. After all, in the Internet
age, drawing a sample of denominational clergy is quite straightforward. The
websites of many denominations provide lists of clergy (and often their contact
information), which gives scholars access to treasure troves of potential data.

Future research also must go beyond the study of clergy themselves to assess
the effectiveness of clergy's attempts to influence politics. Jelen (2001) has argued
that both the amount and consequence of political activity by clergy are both
variables and thus difficult subjects for broad theorization. Guth (2001a, p. 41)
echoes Jelen: "The most obdurate problem is discovering the consequences of
[clergy's political] activity. . . . Assessing influence has always been notoriously
risky. . . . Clergy influence is especially difficult to gauge, given the great variety of
targets and the multiple possibilities for impact."

To begin to theorize about and measure the consequences of religiopolitical
leadership, scholars must answer three questions: (1) What defines effectiveness?
(2) Are we concerned primarily with political effectiveness inside the congregation
or outside of it? (3) Whom are leaders trying to influence: congregation members,
media, other clergy or leaders, policy makers? Future research should include data
collected from the targets of clergy's political action, especially congregation
members and policy makers. To what extent do they respond to clergy's pronouncements and mobilization efforts?

There are many possible metrics of political effectiveness, but perhaps the most
appropriate of these for clergy is the extent to which they are able to shape the
political views of their congregation members. Jelen (2001) notes four possible
ways in which clergy might shape their congregation members' political orientations. First, they may try to reinforce members' preexisting beliefs and issue
positions—perhaps the most straightforward of Jelen's four propositions. We
might hypothesize that clergy who serve politically homogeneous congregations
would have a substantial advantage in this regard, especially because the congregation often serves as an important locus of political socialization (Wald, Owen, and
Hill 1988, 1990; Gilbert 1993). Second, clergy might endeavor to show members how
and why certain political views are rooted in religious values and understandings,
consequently raising members' prioritization of such views. Some clergy would
argue that working to connect religious values to political values actually is a
requirement of their position; mainline Protestants, for example, often speak of
"holding the Bible in one hand and the newspaper in the other." Third, clergy may
attempt to mobilize congregation members to act on their political beliefs in a
wide variety of ways, ranging from letter writing to organized protest activity.

Finally, clergy may work to change the political views of members of their congregations, which certainly would be the most difficult political consequence to bring about. Changing people's minds about politics, after all, is often a tricky business, especially for clergy (Djupe and Gilbert 2003). Doing so is made even trickier by the widespread assumption among Americans that church and state should be kept separate. To answer these questions, we need much more research on how congregation members perceive and respond to their clergy in the context of politics.

Meanwhile, the consequences of political action cannot be examined in a vacuum, apart from the consequences of clergy's other actions. A clergyperson who provides sufficient spiritual, educational, social, or psychological benefits to congregation members often will have the latitude to act on more controversial political matters with less retribution from the congregation (Djupe 2001). Moreover, Guth (2001a) clearly articulates the need for a greater scholarly understanding of how long-term socialization and outside mobilization efforts might affect clergy's political effectiveness. Future research must emphasize the measurement and evaluation of clergy's political effectiveness.

Clergy have been visible and powerful political actors at various times throughout American history. At other times they have remained largely silent. The matters about which they choose to advocate are as diverse as American religion is pluralistic. Regardless of whether they make headlines, clergy reach millions of Americans each week. Likewise, regardless of whether their words are explicitly political, the messages they convey in their sermons, teachings, and informal conversations shape the ways Americans think about how to order their lives together in the religious, social, and political realms. Even though all clergy in the United States work within a political context that grants them great freedom to act politically, tremendous diversity characterizes the contexts within which they live and work.

NOTES

1. Prior questions related to what factors shape the political orientations of clergy and what factors lead to clergy political activism will be addressed. Of course, these issues are also of importance politically, but limitations of space incline me to pass over these prior questions in this review.

2. Corwin Smidt (2004) has also noted that a clergyperson may choose to take political action in fulfillment of three separable roles: (1) as an individual, (2) as the leader of a particular congregation, and (3) as a religious professional, broadly construed.

3. Again, it is true that a prior question is why clergy choose the particular agenda they do and whether these choices are linked to political action. However, because this review focuses primarily on political *action* rather than attitudes or orientations, these prior questions are not reviewed here.

4. Such social theologies can be viewed, in large part, to constitute religiously informed ideologies.

5. However, it may well be that the issue of which clergy are most likely to offer "final and unyielding answers" varies less by the particular theological perspective advanced by the clergy than the particular political issue under question. In other words, were one to examine issues related to race, war, and perhaps even the environment, clergy from more liberal progressive traditions may be just as likely, if not more likely, to offer "final and unyielding answers" on such matters.

6. Based on data gathered through the 2001 Cooperative Clergy Study (Smidt 2004), the extent to which mainline Protestant clergy perceive differences between their political perspectives and those of their congregations has diminished during the past decade, at least when one compares the reports of pastors across the same mainline Protestant denominations in 1989 (Guth et al. 1997) with comparable reports in 2001 (data not shown).

7. This may also be a function of changing theological orientations within mainline Protestant denominations, because there has been an increase between 1989 and 2001 in the proportion of pastors in mainline Protestant denominations who express more historically orthodox positions on theological matters (see Smidt 2004, chap. 23).

8. On the other hand, contrary to popular impressions, there was actually a decline in the level of political activities reported by evangelical Protestant clergy between the 1989 and 2001 elections (see Smidt 2004, chap. 23).

9. A great deal of attention has been given recently to the social services provided by congregations. Assessments vary regarding the proportion of congregations that provide such services, with Chaves' (2004) national congregational study revealing that nearly 60 percent of congregations do so, whereas Cnaan (2006) find that the overwhelming majority of congregations provide some kind of social service (92 percent).

10. The data from the 2001 Cooperative Clergy Survey reveal that female clergy are more likely than their male counterparts to indicate that they are more liberal politically than the congregations they serve.

REFERENCES

Allen, Charlotte. 2004. "For Catholic Politicians, A Hard Line." *The Washington Post* April 11, B1.

Ammerman, Nancy T. 2005. *Pillars of Faith: American Congregations and their Partners.* Berkeley, Calif.: University of California Press.

Barnes, Samuel H., and Max Kaase. 1979. *Political Action.* Beverly Hills, Calif.: Sage.

Beatty, Kathleen Murphy, and Oliver Walter. 1989. "A Group Theory of Religion and Politics: The Clergy as Group Leaders." *Western Political Quarterly* 42: 129–146.

Becker, Penny Edgell. 1999. *Congregations in Conflict: Cultural Models of Local Religious Life.* New York: Cambridge University Press.

Brady, Henry E., Sidney Verba, and Kay Lehman Schlozman. 1995. "Beyond SES: A Resource Model of Political Participation." *American Political Science Review* 89: 271–294.

Byrnes, Timothy A. 1991. *Catholic Bishops in American Politics.* Princeton, N.J.: Princeton University Press.

Byrnes, Timothy A. 2001. "American Church or Church in America? The Politics of Catholic Bishops in Comparative Perspective." In *Christian Clergy in American Politics*, ed. Sue E. S. Crawford and Laura R. Olson, 120–138. Baltimore, Md.: Johns Hopkins University Press.

Campbell, Ernest Q., and Thomas F. Pettigrew. 1959. *Christians in Racial Crisis: A Study of Little Rock's Ministry*. Washington, D.C.: Public Affairs Press.

Carroll, Jackson W., Barbara G. Wheeler, Daniel O. Aleshire, and Penny Long Marler. 1997. *Being There: Culture and Formation in Two Theological Schools*. New York: Oxford University Press.

Cavendish, James C. 2001. "To March or Not to March: Clergy Mobilization Strategies and Grassroots Antidrug Activism." In *Christian Clergy in American Politics*, ed. Sue E. S. Crawford and Laura R. Olson, 203–223. Baltimore, Md.: Johns Hopkins University Press.

Chaves, Mark. 2004. *Congregations in America*. Cambridge, Mass.: Harvard University Press.

Cnaan, Ram A. 1999. *The Newer Deal: Social Work and Religion in Partnership*. New York: Columbia University Press.

Cnaan, Ram A. 2002. *The Invisible Caring Hand: American Congregations and the Provision of Welfare*. New York: New York University Press.

Cnaan, Ram A., with Stephanie C. Boddie, Charlene C. McGrew, and Jennifer Kang. 2006. *The Other Philadelphia Story: How Local Congregations Support Quality of Life in Urban America*. Philadelphia, Pa.: University of Pennsylvania Press.

Cox, Harvey. 1967. "The 'New Breed' in American Churches: Sources of Social Activism in American Religion." *Daedalus* 96: 135–150.

Crawford, Sue E. S. 1995. "Clergy at Work in the Secular City." Ph.D. diss., Indiana University.

Crawford, Sue E. S., and Laura R. Olson. 2001. "Clergy as Political Actors in Urban Contexts." In *Christian Clergy in American Politics*, ed. Sue E. S. Crawford and Laura R. Olson, 104–119. Baltimore, Md.: Johns Hopkins University Press.

Crawford, Sue E. S., Laura R. Olson, and Melissa M. Deckman. 2001. "Understanding the Mobilization of Professionals." *Nonprofit and Voluntary Sector Quarterly* 30: 321–350.

Deckman, Melissa M., Sue E. S. Crawford, Laura R. Olson, and John C. Green. 2003. "Clergy and the Politics of Gender: Women and Political Opportunity in Mainline Protestant Churches." *Journal for the Scientific Study of Religion* 42: 621–632.

de Tocqueville, Alexis. [1840] 1945. *Democracy in America*, ed. Francis Bowen and Phillips Bradley. New York: Knopf.

DiMaggio, Paul J., John H. Evans, and Bethany Bryson. 1996. "Have Americans' Social Attitudes Become More Polarized?" *American Journal of Sociology* 102: 690–755.

Djupe, Paul A. 2001. "Cardinal O'Connor and His Constituents: Differential Benefits and Public Evaluations." In *Christian Clergy in American Politics*, ed. Sue E. S. Crawford and Laura R. Olson, 188–202. Baltimore, Md.: Johns Hopkins University Press.

Djupe, Paul A., and Christopher P. Gilbert. 2002. "The Political Voice of Clergy." *Journal of Politics* 64: 596–609.

Djupe, Paul A., and Christopher P. Gilbert. 2003. *The Prophetic Pulpit: Clergy, Churches, and Communities in American Politics*. Lanham, Md.: Rowman & Littlefield.

Djupe, Paul A., and Christopher P. Gilbert. 2006. "The Resourceful Believer: Generating Civic Skills in Church." *Journal of Politics* 68: 116–127.

Djupe, Paul A., and J. Tobin Grant. 2001. "Religious Institutions and Political Participation in America." *Journal for the Scientific Study of Religion* 40: 303–314.

Djupe, Paul A., Laura R. Olson, and Christopher P. Gilbert. 2005. "Sources of Support for Denominational Lobbying in Washington." *Review of Religious Research* 47: 86–99.

Djupe, Paul A., Laura R. Olson, and Christopher P. Gilbert. 2006. "Whether to Adopt Statements on Homosexuality in Two Denominations." *Journal for the Scientific Study of Religion* 45: 609–621.

Edelman, Murray. 1971. *Politics as Symbolic Action*. New York: Academic Press.

Findlay, James F., Jr. 1993. *Church People in the Struggle: The National Council of Churches and the Black Freedom Movement, 1950–1970*. New York: Oxford University Press.

Finke, Roger, and Rodney Stark. 1992. *The Churching of America, 1776–1990: Winners and Losers in Our Religious Economy*. New Brunswick, N.J.: Rutgers University Press.

Fiorina, Morris P. 2005. *Culture War? The Myth of a Polarized America*. New York: Pearson Longman.

Fowler, Robert Booth. 1989. *Unconventional Partners: Religion and Liberal Culture in the United States*. Grand Rapids, Mich.: Eerdmans.

Friedland, Michael B. 1998. *Lift up Your Voice Like a Trumpet: White Clergy and the Civil Rights and Antiwar Movements, 1954–1973*. Chapel Hill, N.C.: University of North Carolina Press.

Garrett, William R. 1973. "Politicized Clergy: A Sociological Interpretation of the 'New Breed.'" *Journal for the Scientific Study of Religion* 12: 384–399.

Gilbert, Christopher P. 1993. *The Impact of Churches on Political Behavior: An Empirical Study*. Westport, Conn.: Greenwood.

Guth, James L. 1983. "Southern Baptist Clergy: Vanguard of the Christian Right?" In *The New Christian Right: Mobilization and Legitimation*, ed. Robert C. Liebman and Robert Wuthnow, 117–130. Hawthorne, N.Y.: Aldine Publishing Company.

Guth, James L. 1984. "The Politics of Preachers: Southern Baptist Ministers and Christian Right Activism." In *New Christian Politics*, ed. David G. Bromley and Anson Shupe, 235–249. Macon, Ga.: Mercer University Press.

Guth, James L. 1996. "The Bully Pulpit: Southern Baptist Clergy and Political Activism, 1980–92." In *Religion and the Culture Wars: Dispatches from the Front*, ed. John C. Green, James L. Guth, Corwin E. Smidt, and Lyman A. Kellstedt, 146–173. Lanham, Md.: Rowman and Littlefield.

Guth, James L. 2001a. "Reflections on the Status of Research on Clergy in Politics." In *Christian Clergy in American Politics*, ed. Sue E. S. Crawford and Laura R. Olson, 30–43. Baltimore, Md.: Johns Hopkins University Press.

Guth, James L. 2001b. "The Mobilization of a Religious Elite: Political Activism among Southern Baptist Clergy in 1996." In *Christian Clergy in American Politics*, ed. Sue E. S. Crawford and Laura R. Olson, 139–156. Baltimore, Md.: Johns Hopkins University Press.

Guth, James L., John C. Green, Corwin E. Smidt, Lyman A. Kellstedt, and Margaret M. Poloma. 1997. *The Bully Pulpit: The Politics of Protestant Clergy*. Lawrence, Kans.: University Press of Kansas.

Guth, James L., John C. Green, Corwin E. Smidt, and Margaret M. Poloma. 1991. "Pulpits and Politics: The Protestant Clergy in the 1988 Election." In *The Bible and the Ballot Box: Religion and Politics in the 1988 Election*, ed. James L. Guth and John C. Green, 73–93. Boulder, Colo.: Westview Press.

Hadaway, C. Kirk, Penny Long Marler, and Mark Chaves. 1993. "What the Polls Don't Show: A Closer Look at U.S. Church Attendance." *American Sociological Review* 58: 741–752.

Hadden, Jeffrey K. 1969. *The Gathering Storm in the Churches.* Garden City, N.Y.: Doubleday.

Harris, Fredrick C. 1999. *Something Within: Religion in African-American Political Activism.* New York: Oxford University Press.

Hertzke, Allen D. 1988. *Representing God in Washington: The Role of Religious Lobbies in the American Polity.* Knoxville, Tenn.: University of Tennessee Press.

Hougland, James G., and James R. Wood. 1979. "Determinants of Organizational Control in Local Churches." *Journal for the Scientific Study of Religion* 18: 132–145.

Huckfeldt, Robert, Eric Plutzer, and John Sprague. 1993. "Alternative Contexts of Political Behavior: Churches, Neighborhoods, and Individuals." *Journal of Politics* 55: 365–381.

Huckfeldt, Robert, and John Sprague. 1987. "Networks in Context: The Social Flow of Political Information." *American Political Science Review* 81: 1197–1216.

Hunter, James Davison. 1991. *Culture Wars: The Struggle to Define America.* New York: Basic Books.

Jelen, Ted G. 1993. *The Political World of the Clergy.* Westport, Conn.: Praeger.

Jelen, Ted G. 2001. "Notes for a Theory of Clergy as Political Leaders." In *Christian Clergy in American Politics,* ed. Sue E. S. Crawford and Laura R. Olson, 15–29. Baltimore, Md.: Johns Hopkins University Press.

Jelen, Ted G. 2004. "Roman Catholic Priests." In *Pulpit and Politics: Clergy in American Politics at the Advent of the Millennium,* ed. Corwin E. Smidt, 235–246. Waco, Texas: Baylor University Press.

Johnson, Benton. 1966. "Theology and Party Preference among Protestant Clergymen." *American Sociological Review* 31: 200–208.

Johnson, Benton. 1967. "Theology and the Position of Pastors on Public Issues." *American Sociological Review* 32: 433–442.

Johnson, Benton. 1998. "Theology and the Position of Pastors on Social Issues: Continuity and Change since the 1960s." *Review of Religious Research* 39: 293–308.

Koller, Norman B., and Joseph D. Retzer. 1980. "The Sounds of Silence Revisited." *Sociological Analysis* 41: 155–161.

Lincoln, C. Eric, and Lawrence H. Mamiya. 1990. *The Black Church in the African American Experience.* Durham, N.C.: Duke University Press.

McDaniel, Eric. 2004a. "African Methodist Episcopal Church." In *Pulpit and Politics,* ed. Corwin Smidt, 247–258. Waco, Texas: Baylor University Press.

McDaniel, Eric. 2004b. "Church of God in Christ." In *Pulpit and Politics,* ed. Corwin Smidt, 259–271. Waco, Texas: Baylor University Press.

Meier, Kenneth J. 1994. *The Politics of Sin.* Armonk, N.Y.: M. E. Sharpe.

Morris, Aldon D. 1984. *The Origins of the Civil Rights Movement: Black Communities Organizing for Change.* New York: Free Press.

Neuhaus, Richard John. 1984. *The Naked Public Square.* Grand Rapids, Mich.: Eerdmans.

Niebuhr, H. Richard. 1951. *Christ and Culture.* New York: Harper and Row.

Niles, Franklyn C. 2007. "Unity in the Face of the Faceless: Clergy Opposition to the Ku Klux Klan in Northwest Arkansas." In *Religious Interests in Community Conflict,* ed. Paul A. Djupe and Laura R. Olson, 229–250. Waco, Texas: Baylor University Press.

Olson, Laura R. 2000. *Filled with Spirit and Power: Protestant Clergy in Politics.* Albany, N.Y.: State University of New York Press.

Olson, Laura R. 2002. "Mainline Protestant Washington Offices and the Political Lives of Clergy." In *The Quiet Hand of God: Faith-Based Activism and the Public Role of Mainline Protestantism*, ed. Robert Wuthnow and John H. Evans, 54–79. Berkeley, Calif.: University of California Press.

Olson, Laura R., Sue E. S. Crawford, and Melissa M. Deckman. 2005. *Women with a Mission: Religion, Gender, and the Politics of Women Clergy*. Tuscaloosa, Ala.: University of Alabama Press.

Olson, Laura R., Sue E. S. Crawford, and James L. Guth. 2000. "Changing Issue Agendas of Women Clergy." *Journal for the Scientific Study of Religion* 39: 140–153.

Olson, Laura R., Karen V. Guth, and James L. Guth. 2003. "The Lotto and the Lord: Religious Influences on the Adoption of a Lottery in South Carolina." *Sociology of Religion* 64: 87–110.

Penning, James M., and Andrew Storteboom. 2007. "God and Gaming: Community Conflict over a Proposed Indian Casino in West Michigan." In *Religious Interests in Community Conflict*, ed. Paul A. Djupe and Laura R. Olson, 17–49. Waco, Texas: Baylor University Press.

Putnam, Robert D. 2000. *Bowling Alone: The Collapse and Revival of American Community*. New York: Simon and Schuster.

Quinley, Harold E. 1974. *The Prophetic Clergy: Social Activism among Protestant Ministers*. New York: Wiley.

Roozen, David A., William McKinley, and Jackson W. Carroll. 1984. *Varieties of Religious Presence: Mission in Public Life*. New York: Pilgrim.

Rosenstone, Steven J., and John Mark Hansen. 1993. *Mobilization, Participation, and Democracy in America*. New York: Macmillan.

Smidt, Corwin E., ed. 2004. *Pulpit and Politics: Clergy in American Politics at the Advent of the Millennium*. Waco, Texas: Baylor University Press.

Smith, Christian. 1996. *Resisting Reagan: The U.S. Central America Peace Movement*. Chicago, Ill.: University of Chicago Press.

Smith, R. Drew, ed. 2003. *New Day Begun: African American Churches and Civic Culture in Post-Civil Rights America*. Durham, N.C.: Duke University Press.

Smith, R. Drew, ed. 2005. *Black Churches and Local Politics: Clergy Influence, Organizational Partnerships, and Civic Empowerment*. Durham, N.C.: Duke University Press.

Smith, R. Drew, and Fredrick C. Harris, eds. 2005. *Black Churches and Local Politics: Clergy Influence, Organizational Partnerships, and Civic Empowerment*. Lanham, Md.: Rowman and Littlefield.

Sokhey, Anand E., and Paul A. Djupe. 2004. "American Rabbis." In *Pulpit and Politics: Clergy in American Politics at the Advent of the Millennium*, ed. Corwin E. Smidt, 223–234. Waco, Texas: Baylor University Press.

Sokhey, Anand E., and Paul A. Djupe. 2006. "Rabbi Engagement with the Peace Process in the Middle East." *Social Science Quarterly* 87: 903–923.

Stark, Rodney, Bruce D. Foster, Charles Y. Glock, and Harold E. Quinley. 1971. *Wayward Shepherds: Prejudice and the Protestant Clergy*. New York: Harper and Row.

Tatalovich, Raymond, and Byron Daynes, ed. 1998. *Moral Controversies in American Politics: Cases in Social Regulatory Policy*. Armonk, N.Y.: M. E. Sharpe.

Verba, Sidney, and Norman H. Nie. 1972. *Participation in America: Political Democracy and Social Equality*. Chicago, Ill.: University of Chicago Press.

Verba, Sidney, Kay Lehman Schlozman, and Henry E. Brady. 1995. *Voice and Equality: Civic Voluntarism in American Politics*. Cambridge, Mass.: Harvard University Press.

Verba, Sidney, Kay Lehman Schlozman, Henry Brady, and Norman H. Nie. 1993. "Race, Ethnicity, and Political Resources: Participation in the United States." *British Journal of Political Science* 23: 453–497.

Wald, Kenneth D., James W. Button, and Barbara A. Rienzo. 2001. "Morality Politics vs. Political Economy: The Place of School-Based Health Centers." *Social Science Quarterly* 82: 221–234.

Wald, Kenneth D., Dennis E. Owen, and Samuel S. Hill. 1988. "Churches as Political Communities." *American Political Science Review* 82: 531–548.

Wald, Kenneth D., Dennis E. Owen, and Samuel S. Hill. 1990. "Political Cohesion in Churches." *Journal of Politics* 52: 197–215.

Warren, Mark R. 2001. *Dry Bones Rattling: Community Building to Revitalize American Democracy.* Princeton, N.J.: Princeton University Press.

Welch, Michael R., David C. Leege, Kenneth D. Wald, and Lyman A. Kellstedt. 1993. "Are the Sheep Hearing the Shepherds? Cue Perceptions, Congregational Responses, and Political Communication Processes." In *Rediscovering the Religious Factor in American Politics*, ed. David C. Leege and Lyman A. Kellstedt, 235–254. Armonk, N.Y.: M. E. Sharpe.

Wellman, James K. 1999. *The Gold Coast Church and the Ghetto: Christ and Culture in Mainline Protestantism.* Urbana, Ill.: University of Illinois Press.

Wilcox, Clyde, and Carin Larson. 2006. *Onward Christian Soldiers: The Religious Right in American Politics.* 3rd ed. Boulder, Colo.: Westview Press.

Wuthnow, Robert. 1988. *The Restructuring of American Religion: Society and Faith since World War II.* Princeton, N.J.: Princeton University Press.

Wuthnow, Robert, and John H. Evans, ed. 2002. *The Quiet Hand of God: Faith-Based Activism and the Public Role of Mainline Protestantism.* Berkeley, Calif.: University of California Press.

Zikmund, Barbara Brown, Adair T. Lummis, and Patricia Mei Yin Chang. 1998. *Clergy Women: An Uphill Calling.* Louisville, Ky.: Westminster John Knox.

CHAPTER 14

RELIGION AND AMERICAN POLITICAL PARTICIPATION

PETER W. WIELHOUWER

THERE is much that we know about the political behavior of the American electorate, and much that we do not. The most common act of political participation among Americans is casting a ballot for a presidential candidate, with nearly three in five eligible Americans typically doing so every four years.[1] Voter turnout rates vary considerably between elections and across subsets of the American electorate. Relatively high turnout rates characterized American elections following the emergence of the mass political parties in the 1830s, through the progressive reforms of the early 20th century. After those reforms, which eliminated much widespread voter fraud, and after women were given the right to vote, turnout in presidential elections dropped significantly; fraud had artificially inflated vote totals, and many women initially chose not to exercise their newly granted right. The civil rights movement lowered voting barriers for African Americans, eventually reversing historic turnout disparities between the South and the rest of the nation. Turnout increased between the 1940s and 1950s, peaked in 1960, and declined slightly to about 55 percent in 1972, where it remained fairly consistent until the 2004 election. In comparison, other forms of political participation occur less frequently. Contacts with governmental officials, a relatively common American practice, still tends to be more sporadic and concentrated among citizens with high socioeconomic status, mobilized subsets of the polity, and people with a variety of individual political concerns. On the other hand, engagement in campaign activities tends to be the province of a relative few highly committed citizens, averaging perhaps 10 percent per year. Although making campaign contributions was historically an activity largely limited to so-called fat cats, by 2008 changes in campaign finance laws and aggressive efforts by candidates and the political parties brought millions of Americans into the fray. Political protests and demonstrations vary greatly in size, from individuals or small groups seeking to disrupt political meetings to large-scale marches in major cities, including the nation's capitol.

Political scientists have developed numerous explanations to account for political participation. Some explanations are internal to the individual, others involve external efforts by "outsiders" to mobilize the polity, and still others are legal or institutional, emphasizing the "rules of the game" of political engagement. In organizing the factors that shape political engagement, social scientists generally fall under several schools of thought (see Brooks, Manza, and Bolzendahl 2003). This chapter discusses these approaches to explaining political participation and examines how religion relates to each. First, the various ways that political participation has been classified are briefly reviewed. Then the focus shifts to a discussion of major research orientations on political engagement, how religion relates to each, and to the findings that have emerged through these different approaches. Along the way, the chapter raises possibilities for future research.

THE CONCEPT OF POLITICAL PARTICIPATION

Engagement in public life is not limited to political participation, because citizens need not necessarily address collective problems through governmental institutions. *Political participation* is a particular form of public behavior—one that seeks to influence "the selection of governmental personnel and/or the actions they take," whereas *civic participation* reflects "publicly spirited collective action" not directly guided "by some desire to shape public policy" (Campbell 2004, p. 7). Some analysts see civic engagement as essentially apolitical and distinctive in nature (e.g., Theiss-Morse and Hibbing 2005), but others argue that civic participation and political participation are related (Macedo et al. 2005, pp. 6–7; see also Zukin, Keeter, Anderson, Jenkins, and Delli Carpini 2006).

Clearly, individuals can participate in public life at varying levels and in different ways. Recognizing this, Zukin et al. (2006) created a fourfold typology of public engagement based on differences in the types and levels of engagement. *Electoral specialists* focus on campaigns and elections, whereas *civic specialists* participate more heavily in civic, rather than political, activities. *Dual activists* are highly involved in both civic and political activities, whereas the *disengaged* report little activity in either domain. The debate over what kinds of civic activity are actually political is ongoing, but social scientists are "increasingly accepting the notion that civic behavior is politically relevant" even if such behavior is not explicitly political (Jenkins, Andolina, Keeter, and Zukin 2003, p. 3). This chapter, however, will limit its focus explicitly to political participation, leaving the growing literature on civic participation to another occasion.

Throughout the years, scholars have classified the forms of political participation and the individuals engaged in them in a variety of ways. Verba and Nie (1972) divided political participation into *electoral* and *nonelectoral* activity, with the former including voting and other campaign activities whereas the latter encompassed *communal activity* (e.g., working with a group to address local problems) and citizen-initiated *particularized contacts*, which can occur at any level of government. These scholars' primary focus was thus on the *content* of activity. On the other hand, Milbrath and Goel (1977) categorized citizens by their *level* of activity, as *active, passive supportive*, or *apathetic*. Apathetics undertake no activities or "patriotic inputs" into the political system, passive supportives regularly vote and express patriotism by flying the flag or attending parades, whereas active citizens are much more engaged and can be differentiated by their preference for either unconventional or conventional modes of participation.[2] Later, Barnes and Kaase (1979) classified participants in five categories—*inactives, conformists, reformists, activists*, and *protesters*—using both *content* and *levels* of activity. More recently, Claggett and Pollack (2006) expanded the typology of Verba and Nie (1972), showing that *contributing* to candidates and parties is a distinct mode apart from *campaigning*, as are *political discussions* and simply joining organized groups. Thus, political participation as a concept is not limited to electoral activity. However, because of space limitations this chapter focuses only on religion's influence on voting turnout and other forms of campaign activism at the individual level.

Major Research Orientations

How do we account for political participation? Researchers have coalesced around several prevailing theories that explain why some citizens participate and others do not.[3] The first approach focuses on socioeconomic status, a model often associated with the early work of Sidney Verba and his colleagues (e.g., Verba and Nie 1972; Verba, Nie, and Kim 1978). In this approach, educational attainment, occupational status, and income serve to differentiate citizens, because higher education, professional and managerial occupations, and higher income are associated with greater political involvement. Other demographic traits have also been linked to variation in participation rates. For example, differences among ethnicities exist and have changed dramatically over time. African American political involvement was, for many years, much lower than that of white Americans, both for economic and legal reasons, but blacks have now nearly reached parity, especially when controlling for socioeconomic status. Latino participation is lower, *ceteris paribus*, than that of whites or blacks, but Asian American participation tends to be comparable. Differences also exist between first- and second-generation immigrants, with the latter more active than their parents. Other demographic factors have been linked to greater participation: Men tend to be more involved than women, married than single, the middle aged than youth, and residents outside the South more than their southern counterparts.

A second theoretical orientation emphasizes the sociopsychological correlates of political engagement and participation, such as group identification and orientations to the political system. Research in this approach reveals that higher rates of involvement are evident among those psychologically engaged in politics (e.g., those who pay attention to campaign stories in the media, care about election outcomes, believe participation makes a difference, and trust the political system). Likewise, partisanship has a major impact (the stronger one's party identification, the greater the propensity for participation), as do strong ideological commitments (which often produce higher participation but can occasionally produce alienation from the moderation of the American two-party system). A growing literature suggests that political activity among minority groups is associated with belief in the "linked fate" of community members, reflecting in-group and out-group orientations, and research has revealed that the black church has often fostered political efficacy, group identification, and a sense of the obligation to work for political change—all psychological resources that black Americans can bring to bear in the political arena.

A third account of political participation, the civic volunteerism model, extends and merges the socioeconomic and sociopsychological approaches (e.g., Verba, Schlozman, and Brady 1995). Here, political participation is seen as a function of the combination of resources, skills, and orientations, with each factor working to increase the likelihood of involvement. In fact, these three factors are interwoven: Socioeconomic resources foster psychological engagement in politics and together the two factors provide opportunities for political recruitment and the practice of civic skills (Verba et al. 1995, p. 20).

Another school of thought focuses on the structural contexts of political participation. The political, legal, social, and economic contexts of citizens can have a dramatic influence on political participation. For decades, southern states maintained legal barriers, such as grandfather clauses, poll taxes, literacy tests, and the white primary to prevent African Americans from voting. As these barriers came down, participation by black southerners increased dramatically, as did that of poor whites. Extensive research has shown that restrictive registration laws influence registration rates and, thus, turnout. Cross-national analysis suggests that single-member districts with plurality decision rules produce less competition and lower turnout than do multiple-member districts and proportional representation. In addition, legislative redistricting often creates intentionally "safe" seats, which produce lower turnout than in competitive areas. Thus, the competitiveness of electoral districts (states, counties, cities, and election precincts) shape participation rates. Strong party districts (i.e., those that demonstrate regular support for candidates of one party) may get targeted for grassroots mobilization efforts to get out the vote or, conversely, they may be viewed as poor locales for investing scarce campaign resources. Swing districts may get targeted for political persuasion, and later for selective mobilization as election day approaches. Noncompetitive districts are less likely to witness campaign activities designed to mobilize voters than are "battleground" districts with hotly contested races. Finally, the demographic context of a district, such as ethnic heterogeneity, may also be associated with varying levels of political activity.

Models based on microeconomic approaches to analyzing politics provide some intellectual purchase in integrating the wide range of explanations for political participation. These approaches emphasize citizens' perceptions of party performance (past, present, and future), the transferable and nontransferable transaction costs of political participation, and estimates of the likely consequences of election results. Variations in perceived costs, benefits, and likely results of election outcomes explain why some people engage in participatory acts, whereas others remain disengaged from politics (see, for example, Downs 1957; Olson 1965; Fiorina 1981; Aldrich 1993; Alvarez 1997).

A final analytical approach to explaining participation incorporates mobilization models to integrate the approaches just discussed. From this perspective, individual participation is explained based on the interaction between citizens' personal traits and mobilization efforts by others. Efforts to mobilize citizens—including minorities—are more effective when the recruiters are part of a person's social network or are social acquaintances (e.g., Brady, Schlozman, and Verba 1999; Leighley 2001). Moreover, those who "are well integrated into their communities are substantially more likely to vote in national elections than those whose social networks are weaker," in part because homeowners, long-time residents, and churchgoers are more likely to be targeted by political parties in that they are easier to reach than "the footloose and fancy-free" (Rosenstone and Hansen 1993, pp. 166–167). Perceived benefits to be gained from the political process are incentives for mobilization efforts, and social conflict can be harnessed to motivate participation on behalf of parties, candidates, and interests (e.g., Leege, Wald, Krueger, and Mueller 2002).

RELIGION IN THE POLITICAL PARTICIPATION LITERATURE

The extent to which religion has been analyzed as a factor shaping political participation, as well as the way in which religion is viewed analytically, has changed over time. To understand the current state of research on religion and political participation, each of these changes will be reviewed briefly.

Historical Overview

Political behavior research of the 1940s and '50s focused more on the partisan decisions of voters than on whether citizens chose to participate in politics, or how. When early researchers used religion in their analyses, they painted with very broad strokes. The classic voting studies were rooted in sociology, emphasizing membership in broadly defined social groups (Lazarsfeld, Berelson, and Gaudet 1944; Berelson, Lazarsfeld, and McPhee 1954). Religious affiliations were thus classified simply as "Protestant, Roman Catholic, or Jewish." Although these groups differed markedly in vote choice, no efforts were made to link religion with turnout or other forms of electoral participation. Researchers at the University of Michigan also adopted the Protestant–Catholic–Jewish religious classification affiliation for the American National Election Studies (ANES), and they gave more attention to turnout and other forms of participation. Nevertheless, while the religious–vote choice linkage underwent considerable analysis, religious differences in participation itself were left unexamined (Campbell, Converse, Miller, and Stokes 1960).[4]

Religion received only slightly more attention in the classic study of political participation in the 1960s: Verba and Nie's (1972) *Participation in America.* Although they demonstrated the multidimensional nature of participation and used a socioeconomic status model to explain involvement, religion played only a minor role in their analysis. Using the familiar Protestant/Catholic distinction, they found Catholics to be somewhat more active than Protestants in voting, campaign activity, and contact with public officials (Verba and Nie 1972, pp. 97–101). These results, however, were noted in passing, and religious differences in participation were not explored in any depth.

Not only was the attention to religion minimal in early studies, but the research that existed often yielded conflicting findings. Lenski (1961), using data from a Detroit–area survey, found that regular church attenders were more likely to vote than those who attended less frequently; he also found that Protestants active in church life were more likely to contact public officials than inactive Protestants and Catholics. Milbrath and Goel (1977), using national survey data collected in 1956, reported findings broadly consistent with Lenski's. However, they discovered that church attendance was unrelated to participation in "gladiatorial" forms of activity, thereby raising the possibility that religion's effects may not be similar across all forms or modes of political activity.

By the 1970s, voting behavior specialists began to recognize the internally diverse nature of religious groups. For example, Nie, Verba, and Petrocik (1979, pp. 213–217, 382–383) compared high-, middle-, and low-status northern WASPs, southern WASPs, and Irish and Polish Catholics as components of major party coalitions. Nevertheless, though this scheme was used to examine vote choice, it was not incorporated in the analysis of turnout or participation rates. Several other studies, however, did report small differences in participation rates by denominational affiliation (e.g., Macaluso and Wanat 1979; Hougland and Christenson 1983).

One of the first studies to connect religious salience with political participation was Marsh and Kaase's (1979) comparative study of political participation in five countries. They found few differences between Protestant and Catholic participation in conventional activities, but noted that the nonaffiliated were much more active in protest activity. This led them to postulate political participation as a function of "religiosity," which influenced the propensity for conventional and unconventional participation. Still, most research during this period failed to examine the role of religion in shaping political participation, and when examined, such analyses generally lacked sophistication in assessing the unique contributions of religion and its consequences for political activity.

During the late 1970s and early 1980s, several studies indicated that church attendance increased voter turnout (e.g., Macaluso and Wanat 1979; Hougland and Christenson 1983).[5] Later, Peterson (1990) developed a "spillover" model, suggesting that involvement in a local church is likely to be related to greater political activity (in other words, behavior in one milieu begets behavior in another). Using a small survey ($n = 112$), he tested the theory and found that both high church attendance and feelings that participation in church decisions had a direct impact on "civic orientations," which in turn increased political participation (Peterson 1990, p. 15). Secondary analysis of ANES data revealed that "people who attend church every week are 15.1 percent more likely to vote in presidential elections and 10.2 percent more likely to vote in midterm years than people who never attend religious services" (Rosenstone and Hansen 1993, p. 158). Yet, even if church attendance is directly related to the likelihood of voting, it might not necessarily increase participation in other modes of activity, such as working in a campaign, making campaign donations, or engaging in political persuasion (Hougland and Christenson 1983; Rosenstone and Hansen 1993, p. 159).

It was not until the 1980s and '90s that research on religion and political behavior came into maturity. The 1989 ANES pilot study led to changes in ANES surveys that gave religious measures a more prominent place. The research on this pilot study led to publication of *Rediscovering the Religious Factor in American Politics* (Leege and Kellstedt 1993), in which the concept of religious tradition was clarified, and emphasis given to its precise measurement. Although the focus of this work was on religious measurement, voter turnout and political participation were examined throughout (Leege and Kellstedt 1993; but see specifically Leege and Kellstedt 1993, pp. 112, 129–130, 150, 205, 259, 280–297). Finally, the research by Verba et al. (1995, pp. 282–283) found that civic skills developed in churches via active involvement in church activity (e.g., acting in some type of leadership role, serving on committees, and so on) were linked to higher rates of political activity, confirming the spillover effect discussed earlier.

Analytical Approaches

Broadly speaking, the way in which religion relates to political engagement may be viewed as a function of factors either internal or external to the individual. Four distinct approaches have emerged on religion's role as an internal factor in shaping political participation: (1) sociological approaches emphasizing religious affiliation, (2) sociopsychological approaches stressing religious beliefs, (3) social integration approaches focusing on religious behavior, and (4) economic approaches. With regard to external factors, political participation may be viewed as a function of political mobilization, as parties and interest groups attempt to generate greater involvement among the like-minded.[6] Religious institutions, leaders, and organizations simply represent another potential source of mobilization. Despite these distinctions, these approaches are inextricably intertwined, and they are distinguished here simply to organize how social scientists have used religion to understand differences in the rates and kinds of political participation exhibited by American citizens.[7]

Sociological Approaches Focusing on Religious Belonging

Religious group membership is a potentially relevant variable in relation to political participation, based on the assumption that individuals within specific social groups display common perspectives and share common interests. Although differences exist in the political participation of those affiliated with different denominations (e.g., Kellstedt and Green 1993), such differences in political behavior are best examined in terms of affiliation with a religious tradition (e.g., Kellstedt, Green, Guth, and Smidt 1996, pp. 182–186).[8] Some attention has been given to how political participation varies by religious tradition, but most scholarly attention has been given to linkages between religious tradition and attitudes on political issues (e.g., abortion) or vote choice. Nevertheless, most research findings suggest that Jews and mainline Protestants exhibit the highest levels of voter turnout, followed by Roman Catholics and evangelical Protestants, whereas black Protestants, Latinos (both Protestant and Catholic), and the religiously unaffiliated are less likely to vote (e.g., Kellstedt, Green, Guth, and Smidt 1994; Smidt, Green, Kellstedt, and Guth 2007).

What accounts for such differences? Certainly, variations in resources (e.g., the socioeconomic status model) may account for some disparities, but other factors are often at work as well. Congregations are important locales where political communication occurs, and exhibit different "political cultures" and communication patterns depending on religious tradition. Churches are often conceptualized as communities within which people in general agreement with certain theological principles can interact (or fellowship) with one another (Wald, Owen, and Hill 1988; Huckfeldt, Plutzer, and Sprague 1993), and which serve as agents of socialization, passing on their respective values and behavioral expectations (e.g., Ellison 1993; Wielhouwer 2004). As the most visible and formal leaders of churches, clergy have multiple opportunities to influence the political ideas and behavior of their congregations, and, at the very least, clergy tend to encourage voting (see Jelen 1993; Guth, Green, Smidt, Kellstedt, and Poloma 1997; Olson 2000; Smidt 2004; Olson, chapter 13, this volume).

In a groundbreaking data collection, Chaves and colleagues (Beyerlein and Chaves 2003) documented the political activities of congregations.[9] They found that congregations (1) varied considerably in the extent of their political activities; (2) when engaged, often specialized in particular modes of political activity; and (3) that such specialization varied by religious tradition. Evangelical congregations specialized in distributing voter guides; Roman Catholic congregations were more likely to organize groups, demonstrate, or lobby public officials; black Protestant congregations more typically brought political candidates into their church to speak and worked to get people registered to vote; and mainline Protestants did not specialize, but exhibited "a distinctively mainline way of engaging in politics" (Beyerlein and Chaves 2003, p. 241).

Sociopsychological Approaches Focusing on Religious Believing

Do religious beliefs affect political participation? The concept of *believing* as an approach to studying religion in social science emphasizes the internal, psychological role of beliefs and their effects on the adoption of political attitudes or behavior. Regardless of the object of examination, this approach views religion predominantly as an internal motivator and sees the individual primarily in isolation from his or her particular social context.

In sociopsychological approaches, people view the world around them from within a framework or worldview that helps them interpret events, political messages, governmental politics and actions, and the behavior of other individuals and groups. For example, the early literature demonstrated that "racial consciousness" increased the likelihood of participation on the part of African Americans (Verba and Nie 1972, p. 158). Although a variety of studies have examined the role of religious beliefs in shaping political behavior (e.g., candidate vote choice), examinations of the role of religious beliefs in fostering political participation are relatively rare. There are analysts who suggest that religious beliefs stressing "otherworldly" orientations might discourage political participation (Quinley 1974), but with the exception of some research on this issue among African Americans (see Harris [1994] for a review), there has been little rigorous analysis of this possibility (Regnerus and Smith 1998). Still other scholars claim that "macrobeliefs" orienting people toward "general world concerns" encourage political participation (Driskell, Embry, and Lyon 2008).

Social Integration Approaches Focusing on Religious Behavior

Although there is a paucity of research on how religious beliefs influence political participation, numerous studies have examined the influence of religious involvement on political participation (e.g., Macaluso and Wanat 1979; Hougland and Christianson 1983; Leege, Wald, and Kellstedt 1993; Tate 1993, pp. 95–103; Wald, Kellstedt, and Leege 1993; Layman 1997). Three approaches characterize explanations for this phenomenon. The first essentially extends group- or congregation-based arguments, suggesting that the kinds of people who engage in one form of social involvement, such as church attendance, are also likely to engage in other forms of social involvement, such as voting and campaign activism (e.g., Maccoby 1958; Olsen 1972; Jones-Correa and Leal 2001). Rosenstone and Hansen (1993), for example, included frequency of church attendance as a measure of social involvement and found that the more frequently people attended church, the greater their probability of voting in presidential and midterm elections. Teixiera (1992) attributed declines in turnout between 1960 and 1988 to dropping church attendance during that period. These studies, however, assess aggregate relationships and do not directly consider the impact of religiosity as an aspect of one's personal makeup.

The second approach views faith as a resource for social engagement; the more one is exposed to the social environment of churches with their concomitant messages about social and political matters, the more one is equipped to participate in politics (e.g., Wilcox and Gomez 1990; Cassell 1999; Harris 1999). This includes the view that churches are centers for electoral mobilization. Accordingly, people who are well integrated into their congregations will become targets for mobilization efforts by campaigns, political parties, and interest groups (Guth, Kellstedt, Green, and Smidt 2002). Using pooled ANES data from 1956 to 1988, Rosenstone and Hansen (1993) found, for example, that frequent church attendance increased the probability of contact by a political party during the campaign. Wielhouwer (2003) found that this relationship existed only for the probability of a general party contact and Republican contact in the 1980s and '90s, and for Democratic contacts from the 1970s onward (see also Gershtenson 2003). Church attendance also increased the likelihood of being targeted for voter registration and get-out-the-vote drives.

Analyses of African American churches are a well-developed example of integrating group-based and resource approaches to connecting religion and political behavior. America's black churches have long histories of political engagement and have served as a critical training ground for development of political skills, especially for women and blue collar men (e.g., Frazier [1963] 1974; Githens and Prestage 1977; Harmon-Martin 1994; Darling 1998). Black religious commitment and socialization are critical sociopsychological resources that can be linked to other concepts important to the study of minority politics—for example, racial identity and race consciousness (Allen, Dawson, and Brown 1989; Demo and Hughes 1990; Brown and Wolford 1994; Reese and Brown 1995) and political attitudes and behavior (Dawson, Brown, and Allen 1990; Wilcox and Gomez 1990; Calhoun-Brown 1998; Harris 1999; Alex-Assensoh and Assensoh 2001). The political activism of black congregations is a function of their internal social capital resources, including clergy characteristics (Langley and Kahnweiler 2003; Brown 2006). Moreover, black churches that provide political information and structure opportunities for mobilization increase the political participation of members (Tate 1993; Calhoun-Brown 1996; Brown and Brown 2003).[10]

Finally, a third approach to connecting religious behavior with political behavior integrates the first two approaches, observing that church congregations are social communities in which frequency of church attendance reflects integration into those communities. Research has shown that religious communities are important venues within which political conversations take place and political participation is encouraged (e.g., Wald, Owen, and Hill 1988, 1990; Huckfeldt, Plutzer, and Sprague 1993; Harris 1994). More fully integrated individuals are more likely to be engaged in the organizational aspects of their congregations, and thereby get recruited for tasks that help them develop civic skills that can be readily applied in the civic arena (e.g., Lipset [1960] 1981). In fact, churches have come to be viewed as more than mere organizations that socialize their members to expectations about politics; they are now often seen as funnels for social resources that members—especially active members—can apply to political participation, and, in so doing, make congregations crucibles of democratic skills. In much the same way that higher education acclimates people to the bureaucratic experiences in the voter registration process (Wolfinger and Rosenstone 1980), church life, with its organizational meetings in which people may speak in public, serves to equip people for political engagement (Smidt 1999, 2003). Verba et al. (1995), in particular, show that participation is strongly correlated with civic skills developed within social institutions, such as the workplace, political and nonpolitical organizations, and churches.

The kinds of civic skills that churches provide engaged members include attending meetings where decisions get made, planning meetings, writing letters, and making speeches or presentations. People active in religious institutions acquire and exercise these skills just as frequently as people involved in other social organizations; but, unlike other social institutions in which the exercise of civic skills is often structured by social class, ethnicity, or gender, the practicing of skills within churches is more evenly distributed (Verba et al. 1995, pp. 312–325).[11] Moreover, the most influential religious-based predictor of political behavior is not mere membership in a church, but the exercise of civic skills there (Brady, Verba, and Schlozman 1995). Nevertheless, there are opportunity costs to participating in politics: There may be a tradeoff between applying one's civic skills to political matters and to other areas of life. Thus, political participation is a function of people's relative priorities of religious and political activism, and the decision to apply those skills in respective arenas (Djupe and Grant 2001).

Belonging, Believing, Behaving, and Political Participation

The maturation of the religion and politics literature has provided an improved set of categories for comparing and analyzing religious subgroups in the American electorate. This provided a foundation for an even more finely tuned classification of religious groups according to adherents' commitment to traditionalistic or modernistic interpretations of scripture and personal devotional practices (e.g., Kellstedt and Smidt 1993). Research beginning in the 1990s, studies based on the National Surveys of Religion and Politics (NSRP), began to operationalize these concepts by subdividing mainline Protestants, evangelical Protestants, and Roman Catholics into traditionalists, centrists, and modernists (e.g., Guth, Kellstedt, Smidt, and Green 2006, p. 227). Here the emphasis with regard to such differentiation within religious traditions has been largely, although not exclusively, on religious *beliefs*.[12]

In table 14.1, we compare the older, simplistic approach to categorizing religious groups with more finely tuned categorizations, enabling us to assess the improved analytical purchase of the evolved religious conceptual frameworks. The table examines voter turnout rates between 1992 and 2004, comparing the common belonging categories, belonging–behaving combinations, and composite belonging–behaving–believing measures.

The top half of table 14.1 uses ANES data, separating mainline Protestants, evangelical Protestants, Roman Catholics, black Protestants, Jewish respondents, and atheists/nonbelievers.[13] (A useful baseline for comparisons is the "Total" row, which reflects the overall turnout rate of ANES respondents in each year examined.) Table 14.1 shows, first of all, that even using the coarsest religious belonging categories reveals substantial differences in reported turnout. In each year, Jewish respondents exhibit the highest turnout. Among Christians, mainline Protestants consistently have the highest rate, followed by Roman Catholics. Evangelical

Table 14.1 Reported Voter Turnout, 1992 to 2004, by Belonging, Believing, and Behaving Categories

Belonging and Behaving Categories	1992, %	1996, %	2000, %	2004, %
Belonging and Behaving Categories (NES)				
Mainline Protestants (all)	81.0	78.1	79.9	78.2
Regular attenders	86.0	85.0	84.5	83.3
Infrequent attenders	77.1	72.3	73.0	71.4
Evangelical Protestans (all)	70.3	70.6	69.4	77.0
Regular attenders	74.4	77.2	77.5	82.6
Infrequent attenders	59.4	55.1	52.3	65.2
Roman Catholics (all)	81.0	77.2	79.3	75.1
Regular attenders	84.8	83.4	85.0	77.8
Infrequent attenders	75.1	66.2	71.6	73.3
African American Protestants	67.6	67.3	71.8	75.2
Jewish	97.4	92.0	87.9	96.0
Atheist, agnostic, none, nonbelievers	65.2	56.9	61.6	75.7
Total	75.1	72.9	73.3	76.4
Belonging, Behaving, and Believing Categories (NSRP)				
Mainline Protestants				
Traditionalist	75.6	67.0	62.8	77.8
Centrist	62.2	58.5	50.8	70.6
Modernist	60.5	54.0	54.3	55.6
Nominal	60.5	61.5	63.8	76.4
Evangelical Protestants				
Traditionalist	65.9	63.7	64.7	70.8
Centrist	46.8	45.3	47.6	56.3
Modernist	56.7	40.0	42.7	61.8
Nominal	40.0	39.7	44.3	69.0
Roman Catholics				
Traditionalist	75.0	62.3	63.8	77.6
Centrist	72.4	57.1	59.1	68.4
Modernist	55.5	57.1	56.3	54.8
Nominal	55.8	46.9	39.4	63.9
African American Protestants	40.9	56.9	53.9	50.4
Latino Protestants	36.8	50.0	38.5	49.3
Latino Catholics	36.6	47.6	36.3	43.1
Seculars	37.0	40.2	46.3	52.6
Atheists	65.5	52.7	70.3	71.8
Total	54.6	51.9	54.3	60.8

Sources: National Election Studies Cumulative Data File, 1948–2004; National Surveys of Religion and Politics, 1992–2004 (obtained from volume editors; see also Green, Kellstedt, Smidt, and Guth [2007]).

Protestants tend to have a somewhat lower than average turnout, although this difference vanished in 2004. Note that any classification combining mainline and evangelical Protestants would mask an average 10 percent difference in turnout rates between the two traditions in these years. African American Protestants had the lowest turnout of these religious groups, although in 2000 and 2004 they were very close to the overall rates. Those without religious affiliation (ANES respondents classifying themselves as atheists, agnostics, or reporting no religious affiliation) tend to have the lowest turnout rates of all, except in 2004.

The top part of table 14.1 also divides each of the largest religious subgroups into two subsets based on the frequency of their church attendance, permitting us to compare differences in religious group belonging and one aspect of religious behavior. *Regular attenders* are those who report attending church at least once a month, whereas *infrequent attenders* report that they rarely or never attend church. Within each tradition, those attending religious services infrequently have lower turnout than their regularly attending counterparts. For mainline Protestants and Catholics, the turnout of infrequent attenders tracks fairly closely with the overall ANES rates. Mainline regular attenders vote more than their infrequent counterparts, and these differences increased between the first two and last two elections, whereas differences between the two Catholic groups declined during the same time period. Frequent evangelical attenders vote at a rate slightly higher than average, but infrequent evangelicals vote like the religiously unattached, substantially below the ANES average. The nonmonotonicity of each of the three large Christian groups demonstrates the inadequacy of the simple group-based analysis that still characterizes much research that purports to "control for" religious affiliation in multivariate analyses.

The bottom half of table 14.1 displays turnout rates from the 1992 to 2004 NSRP, which permit division of the major religious groups into the traditionalist, centrist, and modernist categories, as well as into black Protestant, Latino Protestant, Latino Catholic, and religiously unattached ("secular") and atheist respondents.[14] (The NSRP surveys use a "corrected" turnout measure based on past turnout rates of the respondent as well as such things as interest in the campaign and political knowledge to deal with the overreporting of turnout that typically occurs in surveys.) Although substantial variations exist within each subgroup over time, as a general rule traditionalist mainline Protestants, evangelicals, and Roman Catholics all have higher turnout than their counterparts; nominal and modernist Catholics and evangelicals tend to have lower turnout (there are exceptions, of course). Black Protestants had a substantially lower turnout than average in 1992 and 2004, but are comparable in 1996 and 2000. Latinos, whether Protestant or Catholic, generally have the lowest turnout among all the religiously defined groups. Finally, secular persons have substantially lower turnout rates than nearly all the religious subgroups except for Latinos, whereas atheists are somewhat more likely to vote than the average citizen.[15]

The remaining question, of course, is which dimensions of religion produce higher participation rates? Is affiliation, religious beliefs, or religious involvement most influential? In a full model of the 2000 NSRP data, Guth, Green, Kellstedt, and Smidt (2002) found that religious tradition variables were reduced to insignificance after education, income, age, and gender were introduced as controls. Orthodox beliefs had a mild discouraging effect on participation, whereas religious involvement encouraged political engagement, as did religious mobilization efforts (discussed later). Whether these results will be confirmed for other elections and in other surveys is an important question for future analysis.

Economic Models

A final, though largely neglected, approach in the study of religion and political participation is the resource approach. Although related to other perspectives, this view often makes most sense in the context of economic models of political behavior because it sees religious membership and beliefs as psychological and practical resources for engaging in politics. Because these models often emphasize the costs of political participation, political resources become integral to coping with these costs. In the religion and politics literature, faith is a politically relevant resource, and churches equip members with civic skills that can be applied in the political arena.

Economic models of politics are prominent in the scholarly literature on political participation, but they have, as yet, received little attention from the religion and politics subfield. Economic models emphasize the policy incentives people have for engaging in political action. In contrast to religious group theories that emphasize intergroup dynamics, believing models that emphasize theological orientations and cognitive processing, or church-based approaches that emphasize integration into religious communities, economic models focus on a citizen's desire to obtain favorable policy outcomes from government.

Religious beliefs have long been an important motivation for attempting to influence public policy. The abolition and temperance movements, for example, gained traction largely as a result of Christian political activism. Similarly in the 19th century, evangelicals engaged in a massive letter-writing campaign to prevent the ejection of Cherokees from Georgia (West 1996); today, the antiabortion movement remains a predominantly religious one. Based on the theological differences between faith traditions and the resulting priorities placed on governmental versus personal or congregational solutions for social problems, careful analysis of religious groups using economic models might be useful in analyzing the intersection of individual and collective faith, religious institutions, public policy preferences, and political processes.

Although some issues of theological concern may not be directly related to the more fiscally based orientation of traditional economic models of voting (e.g., Downs 1957), these models are applicable to issues beyond social welfare. Lowry (1998), for example, examines state religious populations and their relationship to membership in civic groups advocating preservationist and private stewardship approaches to environmental policy. Economic models also emphasize the relationship between the perceived policy benefits of election outcomes and the costs associated with participation. Within this context, the transaction costs of political engagement may not vary based upon religious belief or belonging, but other religious variables such as faith more broadly, church membership, and religious involvement are recognized as civic resources that permit people to cope with participation costs (e.g., Brady et al. 1995; Verba et al. 1995). Churches are also efficient means for communicating campaign messages and mobilizing political participation, thus linking transaction cost mitigation with policy outcomes.

Spatial preference theories are another important set of economic approaches to analyzing policy incentives for participation that could be applied to religious subgroups (core texts include Downs [1957], Buchanan and Tullock [1962], Enelow and Hinich [1984], Mueller [1989], and Morton [2006]). In this approach, individuals are seen as holding preferences that can be arrayed along ideological issue spaces. Individuals then see the selection of government officials, whose policy promises and positions can also be arrayed along issue spaces, as means to achieving those preferences (e.g., Hinich and Munger 1994; but see Stokes 1963).

Comparative placement of oneself, candidates, and political parties forms a basis for estimating policy outcomes, an important component in a voter's "calculus." Large differences in placement between voters and candidates may push people to participate, whereas minimal or equivalent differences may suggest abstention (e.g., Rabinowitz and MacDonald 1989; MacDonald, Listhaug, and Rabinowitz 1991; Plane and Gershteson 2004). Real-world examples of political actors thinking along these lines are numerous. For example, in October 2007, James Dobson, a prominent conservative Christian leader, described a resolution considered at a meeting of conservative Christian leaders, writing:

> After two hours of deliberation, we voted on a resolution that can be summarized as follows: If neither of the two major political parties nominates an individual who pledges himself or herself to the sanctity of human life, we will join others in voting for a minor-party candidate. Those agreeing with the proposition were invited to stand. The result was almost unanimous. (Dobson 2007, A29)

In this instance, pro-choice Republican candidates were seen as too ideologically distant from the leaders' preferences, leading them to threaten defection or abstention. Although the resolution described was not binding, it would send a signal to those looking for a message about how they should be thinking about their vote choices. It is worth noting that Dobson made much the same threat in 1998 (see Thomas and Dobson 1999, chap. 9). Spatial approaches may thus provide a useful framework for considering differences in participation among religious traditions. By analyzing differences in ideological and issue attitudes, comparing those with candidate and party ideologies and issue placements, and then correlating those placements with political participation, researchers may fruitfully assess the policy reasons for differences in religious groups' electoral turnout.

Another aspect of economic models of political behavior emphasizes the likelihood of an individual participating in the political process as a function of the costs of political participation in relationship to perceived policy benefits of different election outcomes. The idea of costs associated with information collation and evaluation has been especially important in the political science literature. As elaborated by Downs (1957), and adapted by others (such as Riker and Ordeshook 1968, and Aldrich 1993), the typical "rational choice" voter model suggests that even if people perceive large policy differences between candidates or political parties, the probability that their vote will affect the outcome (even subjectively), combined with the costs of voting, will so decrease the value of participation that many will abstain (for a review of the arguments and evidence, see Whitely [1995]). Voters bear unavoidable costs of participation[16] and avoidable information costs, including computational costs of assessing the candidates' and parties' respective policies (Downs 1957, chap. 11–12; Carmines and Kuklinski 1990; see also Wielhouwer 1999). (The latter costs are avoidable because eligibility to vote is not contingent on how well informed one is.) As discussed earlier, churches can be a resource for information acquisition and serve as crucibles for developing civic skills useful in politics.

ELECTIONEERING AND MOBILIZATION

Political practitioners, in the quest for victory, grasp the potential associated with tapping into the group-based orientations and resources of religious groups. Election campaigns often provide the catalyst for sociopolitical groups' engagement in politics. This is true of both religious groups and those opposed to religion's influence in the public square. We have already examined differences in religious individuals' political activities, now we will examine group-based electioneering and mobilization.

Political parties and interest groups often coordinate activities, hoping to win elections by first influencing public opinion, and then by shaping the actual composition of the voting public. Because members of religious groups often have internally coherent worldviews and belong to cohesive local organizations that lend themselves naturally to mobilization, modern campaigns frequently attempt to communicate with, and activate, these voting segments. Even "independent" mobilization efforts are often not nonpartisan in their goals, as most focus on (that is, *target*) their own members or like-minded people so that the group's contribution to the electoral success of a particular party or candidate is increased. For example, in one campaign manual geared toward "traditional values" activists, organizers are told "the task of [your campaign's] voter registration chairperson is to register all the potential voters who will vote for your candidate. You can be sure your opponents are registering those who are likely to vote for them" (Phillips 1990, p. 153). This should make clear that persuasion and mobilization can be very closely related. An interest group tries to persuade members that one candidate is preferable to another so they will show up at the polls and vote for the preferred candidate.

Campaign Strategy and Tactics

Campaign practitioners organize campaigns using two broad conceptual frameworks: *strategy* and *tactics*. Strategic thinking involves matching the ultimate ends of the campaign (winning the election) to the conditions (e.g., name recognition, political context, and initial resource levels) at the outset of the campaign (see, for example, Burton and Shea [2003]). Tactics are the specific methods used to implement a campaign strategy, maximizing the probability that the campaign will attain its strategic objective—namely, winning the election by producing a larger voting bloc. Thus, the tactic of voter persuasion through direct mail is associated with convincing voters "on the fence" that the candidate bears consideration; voter mobilization through church-based get-out-the-vote drives is associated with making sure that supporters make it to the polls. The 2004 Bush–Cheney campaign, for example, divided the electorate into dozens of "microtargeting segments," including several related to religious beliefs, for highly targeted communications (Sosnick, Dowd, and Fournier 2006; see also Monson and Oliphant 2007).

The logic of social group targeting hinges on the longstanding observation that elections are fundamentally a group activity (Lazarsfeld et al. 1944; Berelson et al. 1954; see also Stanley, Bianco, and Niemi 1986; Erikson, Lancaster, and Romero 1989; Stanley and Niemi 1999). Campaign strategies, messages, and tactics explicitly or implicitly involve existing (and prior) aspects of group politics, sometimes playing on group conflict, perceptions, prejudices, and fears. As Leege et al. (2002, p. 7) note, "The propensity for party coalitions to represent group conflicts is a durable feature of American politics." The process by which group-based conflicts are incorporated into campaign strategies and messages is complex, although it includes salient ethnic, cultural, and denominational tendencies (e.g., Fowler, Hertzke, and Olson 1999, chap. 3; Glaeser and Ward 2006).

The contours of these cultural conflicts go directly to fundamental differences between the worldviews of religious groups, especially over the proper role of government on issues of economic justice, human rights, war and peace, and even the stability of society as a whole (Leege et al. 2002). Conflicts grounded in changing notions of morality and the consequences for traditional concepts of marriage and family have emerged as American culture has moved from a largely Christian moral consensus on social issues toward the contemporary postmodern era. New definitions of culturally acceptable social relationships were fostered at the elite level as a cohort of highly educated professionals, including college and university professors, rejected the old order (Bloom 1987). As other cultural opinion leaders perceived threats to the traditional Judeo-Christian order, some citizens began to organize in response, often engaging in state, local, and congressional elections (see, for example, the state-based analyses in Green, Rozell, and Wilcox [2000, 2003] and Rozell and Wilcox [1995, 1997]). In short, "[t]he open challenges to traditional values and widespread perception of the disintegration of the social order may have provided the necessary conditions that encouraged countermobilization" (Leege et al. 2002, p. 37; see also McVeigh and Sikkink 2001; Campbell 2006).

Rozell and Wilcox (1996) observe that Christian Right leaders started out with some naive perceptions about politics, but eventually developed a more sophisticated grasp of what it took to engage successfully in the political process. Early efforts were characterized by idealism and policy purism that often degenerated into name calling and fear mongering. Godwin (1988), for example, demonstrated that the direct mail and telemarketing used by religious and conservative organizations during the 1980s explicitly tried to evoke fears about the potential loss of cherished values. Partisan campaign strategists, ever aware of these trends, frequently incorporated such virulent rhetoric into their campaign messages—often literally demonizing their political opponents, as "hatred is a convenient instrument for mobilizing a community for defense" (Hoffer 1951, p. 101). Nevertheless, by the 1990s, many religious and political leaders had taken a more pragmatic approach, although tensions between the purists and pragmatists remained.[17] Preexisting electoral coalitions and personal political predispositions manifest themselves in cultural politics *qua* election campaigns, either as efforts to mobilize elements of one political coalition or to demobilize elements of the opposing coalition (Leege et al. 2002).[18]

Partisan Targeting

Central to the narrative of political mobilization is personal contact, long a staple of retail and grassroots politics. Both survey and experimental research has confirmed that personal contacts are one of the most effective means to elicit participation, and political parties routinely use face-to-face and telephone contacts to persuade and mobilize voters (e.g., Gosnell 1926, 1927; Eldersveld and Dodge 1954; Eldersveld 1956; Huckfeldt and Sprague 1992; Wielhouwer and Lockerbie 1994; Gerber and Green 2000a, b, 2001; McClurg 2004). The efficacy of contacts varies substantially by method, locale, the partisan character of the election, and electorally relevant groups (see, for example, Green and Gerber [2004, 2005]). Taking into account a host of individual and contextual factors, the people most likely to be contacted are those already predisposed to participate (namely, those who have high socioeconomic status, are registered to vote, and are socially connected to their communities) and to vote for the party's candidates. In other words, Democrats mainly contact Democratic-oriented groups, whereas Republicans focus on Republican-oriented groups (Rosenstone and Hansen 1993; Gershtenson 2003; Wielhouwer 2003; Panagopolous and Wielhouwer 2008). For example, in 2004 the Bush team made the mobilization of the evangelical Protestants a high priority, while Democrats undertook similar efforts among black Protestants; after all, houses of worship provide a natural venue for organizing people for many purposes, including politics.

Table 14.2 shows the rates at which religious subgroups were personally contacted by party workers during the 2000 and 2004 elections. These two years witnessed the highest levels of personal contact by political parties since the ANES introduced this item in 1956, with nearly 45 percent receiving some contact from one or both major parties (Wielhouwer 2006). In 2000, 22 percent reported contact by Democrats, 25 percent by Republicans, and about 12 percent by both parties. Looking at the subgroups that deviate most from the average, some interesting patterns emerge. In 2000, the Democrats contacted Jewish and regular-attending Catholic respondents most frequently, whereas in 2004 they focused on Jewish respondents, regularly attending mainline Protestants, and infrequent Catholics.

Table 14.2 Political Party Contacting (measured as a percentage), 2000 and 2004: Belonging and Behaving Categories

Belonging and Behaving Categories (NES data)	2000 Contacted by			2004 Contacted by		
	Democratic Party	GOP	Both	Democratic Party	GOP	Both
Mainline Protestants (all)	25.2	35.2	16.7	35.2	43.8	23.5
Regular attenders	25.9	38.2	16.6	42.6	54.2	27.5
Infrequent attenders	24.3	31.1	16.9	25.3	30.1	15.3
Evangelical Protestants (all)	17.7	21.3	9.1	28.7	27.7	16.6
Regular attenders	19.2	24.7	10.2	28.1	31.1	18.1
Infrequent attenders	14.6	14.0	6.7	29.4	19.7	12.9
Roman Catholics (all)	26.8	28.2	15.9	35.2	27.9	18.1
Regular attenders	30.9	31.7	17.9	34.4	27.6	17.0
Infrequent attenders	21.2	23.4	13.0	36.7	28.8	19.9
African American Protestants	15.4	10.7	9.4	21.5	10.7	7.6
Jews	38.4	11.4	8.2	55.7	16.1	16.1
Atheists, agnostics, none	16.7	17.7	8.7	25.9	19.2	11.2
Total	21.9	24.8	12.2	31.4	28.1	16.8

Sources: National Election Studies Cumulative Data File, 2000–2004.

In 2000, the GOP contacted mainline Protestants and regularly attending Catholics most often; whereas in 2004, regularly attending mainline Protestants were the target. Consistent with general mobilization patterns (e.g., Tate 1993; Wielhouwer 2000; Leighley 2001), the groups least likely to receive GOP contacts were black Protestants, Jews, atheists, and infrequently attending evangelical Protestants.

The third column in each year shows contacts of people by *both* major political parties. Although the strategy of contacting one's own is effective for reinforcement and mobilization, presumably groups targeted by both parties are viewed as the objects of persuasion. In 2000, such groups included mainline Protestants and regularly attending Catholics, but in 2004 only one group substantially exceeded the average contact rates: regularly attending mainline Protestants. In general, we see a church attendance "gap," with some changes occurring between the two election years, such as the increase in both parties' attention to regularly attending mainline Protestants.

Religious Recruitment into Political Participation

Beyond mobilization by political parties, many religious interest groups engage in the political process and distribute information to the electorate to influence politics and policy (e.g., Wilcox and Sigelman 2001). Whether this is a method of affecting cultural change via the political arena (Leege et al. 2002) or of reducing costs of political participation as in economic models of political behavior, the intent is to persuade or mobilize the electorate through both independent and coordinated means. As discussed earlier, congregational life produces social capital and permits the building of personal communication networks that are associated with political participation. Analyzing 1996–2004 presidential elections, Guth and colleagues (Guth, Kellstedt, Green, and Smidt 1998, 2002, 2007) have documented the extent of religious contacting, showing that a great deal of political engagement occurs at church. They found, for example, that moral or religious interest groups are active and cover the full breadth of the liberal–conservative political continuum. In addition, groups vary considerably in the kinds of information they distribute, with different groups within religious traditions distributing different kinds of information. For example, in 2000 the Roman Catholic National Council of Catholic Bishops stressed antiabortion rights issues as "the key to 'faithful' Catholic voting," whereas in 2004 conservative core issues relating to human life and traditional marriage were treated equally with other kinds of social justice issues such as the minimum wage (Guth et al. 2002, p. 164; 2007, p. 159). Meanwhile, unofficial Roman Catholic groups ranged across the ideological spectrum.

Table 14.3 abstracts NSRP data (from Guth et al. 2002, 2007) to get a sense of congregation-based information distribution and mobilization during the 2000 and 2004 election campaigns. The items presented here measured respondents' reports regarding whether they had been contacted by a moral or religious group, whether their clergy or other church leaders urged the congregation to vote, whether they encountered voter guides at church, and a summary measure of the percent of respondents who reported at least one church-based political contact each election year.[19]

The groups exposed to the highest amounts of religiopolitical content were traditionalists of all three stripes and African American Protestants. These groups were not exceptional in terms of contacts by moral or religious interest groups, but all had high rates of church leaders who urged them to vote, as well as very high rates of overall church political contacts—even compared with half of all Americans in each election year who report at least one such contact. The use of voter guides still constitutes a relatively important, although declining, form of political information distribution for traditionalist evangelicals and black Protestants, and for traditionalist Catholics (in 2000). The groups least likely to report church-based political contacts were all three groups of modernists and, to a lesser extent, centrist mainline Protestants. It is clear that churches continue to be, at least for some traditions, particularly important venues through which political contacts are made and participation encouraged (see also Brewer, Kersh, and Peterson 2003).

The effects of partisan campaign contacts described earlier are well documented: People personally contacted by campaigns are significantly more likely to become politically active, even after taking into account their participation predispositions. They are more likely to vote, to campaign, and to contribute financially to campaigns (Rosenstone and Hansen 1993; Wielhouwer and Lockerbie 1994). Verba et al. (1995) found that (1) about half of those asked to work for a campaign do so, and (2) about a

Table 14.3 Church-Based Contacting (measured as a percentage), 2000 and 2004: Belonging, Behaving, and Believing Categories

Belonging, Behaving, and Believing Categories (NSRP data)	Interest Group Contact	Leaders Urge to Vote	Voter Guides in Church	At Least one Church Contact
2000				
Mainline Protestants (all)	6	27	7	42
Traditionalists	8	42	13	63
Centrists	5	23	8	38
Modernists	5	23	1	29
Evangelical Protestants (all)	10	35	18	56
Traditionalists	19	55	25	80
Centrists	4	23	12	41
Modernists	8	14	4	28
Roman Catholics (all)	11	37	12	51
Traditionalists	11	63	29	71
Centrists	13	38	10	54
Modernists	6	22	6	36
African American Protestants	4	50	27	68
Total	7	31	13	47
2004				
Mainline Protestants (all)	12	28	4	48
Traditionalists	14	42	6	64
Centrists	12	24	2	46
Modernists	11	20	5	38
Evangelical Protestants (all)	22	45	11	65
Traditionalists	31	61	17	83
Centrists	13	31	6	51
Modernists	15	26	4	44
Roman Catholics (all)	19	40	10	59
Traditionalists	22	55	13	75
Centrists	17	39	10	60
Modernists	18	24	7	44
African American Protestants	19	49	21	69
Total	15	32	9	50

Sources: National Election Studies Cumulative Data File, 2000–2004; National Surveys of Religion and Politics, 2000–2004 (abstracted from Guth et al. [2002a, 2007]).

quarter of those who are asked to contribute financially make a contribution. The success of requests for political participation frequently hinges upon who does the asking, with personal acquaintance playing a key role—as most recruitment efforts come from personal acquaintances and other people who are acquaintances of acquaintances (Lazarsfeld et al. 1944; Berelson et al. 1954; Verba et al. 1995).

What do the NSRP data tell us about the effects of the religious and church-based contacts on political participation? In general, personal conversations about elections at churches produce significantly higher voter turnout rates across evangelical Protestant, mainline Protestant, and Roman Catholic traditions; traditionalist subgroups had their turnout increased to a greater extent than centrists or modernists, but the effects of religious contacts on turnout were greatest among mainline Protestants. The importance of personal networks reinforces earlier research (e.g., Wald, Owen, and Hill 1988; Huckfeldt and Sprague 1991, 1992; Kenny 1992; Huckfeldt, Plutzer, and Sprague 1993) (for application to African American churchgoers see McKenzie [2004]). In short, whether a church member will be exposed to religious messages with persuasive or mobilization content is a function of the leadership context and civic skills development approach of the congregation. Immersion in a congregation where politics is a topic discussed openly thus appears to be a baptism into political activism.

CONCLUSION

Political scientists, sociologists, and economists have studied the relationship between religion and American political participation in a variety of contexts and from several conceptual perspectives. This chapter has organized these perspectives and findings by differentiating between internal and external perspectives. Four broad but overlapping approaches, which build upon and reinforce one another, were distinguished within the internal approach. Sociological, sociopsychological, and behavioral approaches all acknowledge a central role for group membership, but emphasize different aspects of group dynamics and group-based information processing and resource generation. Economic models, with their explicit emphasis on perceptions of beneficial policy outcomes and cost–benefit calculations have been a major part of the political science literature for the past 40 years, although they have yet to be applied extensively to religious groups' interaction with the political realm. Finally, in terms of external perspectives, political mobilization models emphasize the strategic and competitive nature of the American political scene.

Scholars have examined factors shaping political participation from a variety of perspectives, but social scientists have been slow to examine the role of religion within these various explanations of political participation. The limited research that has been done has largely examined the religious affiliations and practices of individuals, attempting to link them to political activity. Possibly the most important finding of this research has been the importance of high levels of religious practices, particularly church attendance, in predicting political participation in the mass public.

Given the paucity of research on the links of religion to political participation, there is much work yet to be done. For example, in-depth studies of churches from a variety of religious traditions could explore the efforts, if any, within the congregational context that serve to encourage participation and to see whether mobilization of the congregants takes place. In 2004, we know that there was variation in the number of secular and religious contacts by religious traditions (Guth et al. 2007), but we do not have a "thick" description of the mechanisms of mobilization and the factors that account for variation from one local church to another. Since numerous scholars have shown the value of examining contextual effects and their application to political behavior, it is time to turn more extensively to these models to understand better the "participatory contexts" in the local church.

Second, prior research (Layman 2001; Guth et al. 2006) has shown the importance of religious beliefs in models of vote choice, but the evidence is less clear about the linkage of such beliefs to vote turnout and other forms of political activity. Future research should examine these linkages. As noted previously, scholarship has demonstrated the importance of leadership practices in the local church as a resource for political participation, but more research is needed to understand this finding more thoroughly, in the context of religious tradition, congregational context, and incentives for political involvement.

Central to much of the research on political participation are concepts related to perceptions of the political arena and political outcomes, especially retrospective and prospective evaluations of the economy, but theoretical and empirical linkages in religious contexts remain undeveloped. Thus, even though the intersection of religion and Americans' political behavior extends to the colonial period, the subfield is still wide open for studies linking religious beliefs, belonging, and behavior to activities in the public square.

NOTES

1. Although there is some controversy about how to measure aggregate voter turnout, I choose to use estimates based on the Voting Eligible Population as opposed to the traditional measure of Voting Age Population, which tends to understate turnout by including millions of persons ineligible to vote in state and federal elections (see McDonald and Popkin 2001).

2. Milbrath and Goel (1977) specify that unconventional modes include people engaging in protest activities or civil disobedience, whereas conventional modes include community activists, party and campaign workers, contact specialists (those who primarily contact elected officials), and those who consume or engage in basic forms of political communication.

3. References for this section would be legion, and we refer the reader to standard texts in the field. Excellent beginnings include Abramson, Aldrich, and Rohde's (2007) biennial series, most recently, *Change and Continuity in the 2006 Elections;* Flanigan and Zingale (2006), and Conway (2000).

4. Meanwhile, some sociological research began to note that Protestants, Roman Catholics, and Jews were not monolithic in political preferences. Lipset ([1960] 1981), for example, documented economic divisions within religious groups both in the United States and western Europe during the 1950s. He noted partisan preference differences among French Roman Catholic voters who were practicing, nonpracticing, and indifferent; and among Catholics, Protestants, and people with no religion. In the Netherlands, he found substantial differences among Catholics, moderate Protestants, and Calvinists, including differences between adherents who attended church and those who did not (Lipset [1960] 1981, pp. 255–260). He also noted that, along with unions, churches were important contexts for political training and the acquisition of political skills (Lipset [1960] 1981, pp. 398–399).

5. Other research, however, suggested that, at least for some people, participation in church activities might decrease the likelihood of political participation (Madron, Nelsen, and Yokley 1974).

6. These models of mobilization strategies often blend elements of the previous approaches just introduced. When researchers examine religious people's behavior as a function of their memberships in rather diffuse groups with common interests, analyses will largely resemble the sociological approach. However, as like-minded individuals consciously organize themselves into more discrete groups, and then work to involve others in the political process through mobilization or lobbying, those activities begin to resemble the traditional acts of interest groups in pluralist political analysis. The involvement of individuals in group activities is viewed as a joint function of sociological, sociopsychological, and incentive-centered motivations, whereas formal groups attempt to mobilize still greater numbers of like-minded, but perhaps formally unattached, people. The motivation of the formal group is policy influence (either through lobbying governmental officials or influencing election outcomes), which may or may not be shared by the people being mobilized. The strategies of parties and interest groups to increase political participation rates selectively involve cost mitigation via distribution of campaign information and other campaign communication efforts designed to make citizens aware of the perceived policy and social changes that will result from different election outcomes.

7. Conceptualizing religious "affiliation" is not standardized. Sometimes broad religious traditions are used, other times scholars choose to focus on denominational affiliation, whereas analyses of the influence of religious belonging have also considered how social roles, friendship patterns, residential patterns, or church activities shape political participation (e.g., Gilbert 1991; Alex-Assensoh and Assensoh 2001). One's theoretical focus strongly influences one's analytical approach.

8. Wald (2003), for example, emphasizes the interaction of creed (belief), institutions (belonging), and institutional or policy incentives for political engagement.

9. Such activities included informing worshipers about political opportunities, having church groups participating in marches or demonstrations or discussing politics, conducting voter registration drives, sponsoring political speakers, engaging in lobbying of elected officials, and displaying election voter guides. More than 40 percent of congregations engaged in at least one activity.

10. McDaniel and McClerking (2005) note, however, that African Americans predisposed to participate in politics often seek out and join political churches.

11. However, Verba et al. (1995) do note that such exercise of skills in church was more common among Protestants than Roman Catholics.

12. There is evidence that biennial studies of voting behavior have made use of the new NES religious measures with attention paid to affiliation, beliefs, and practices

(compare with Abramson, Aldrich, and Rohde 2003, pp. 80–81). In addition, the work of David Leege et al. (1993; 2002, pp. 232–233) has demonstrated the importance of these measures in coming to grips with vote turnout or, to use their terminology, "vote yield." In addition, this work has used the ANES religious measures in investigations of "demobilization" of the electorate.

13. One immediate concern is the notable (and well-documented) inflation of the reported vote in surveys, shown by the basic math of the number of votes cast in an election divided by the voting age population, or by the voting eligible population (for a comparison of these two measures see McDonald and Popkin [2001]). On overreporting, see Abramson and Claggett (1989, 1991); Anderson and Silver (1986); and Silver, Anderson, and Abramson (1986). On misreporting and overreporting of vote choices, see Atkeson (1999), Gronke (1992), and Wright (1992, 1993). And, on the relationship between frequency of church attendance and vote overreporting, see Bernstein, Chadha, and Montjoy (2001).

14. For a discussion of these groups and their contributions to the Republican and Democratic presidential vote coalitions, see Green, Kellstedt, Smidt, and Guth (2007) and Guth et al. (2006).

15. Voting is not the only form of political participation, of course, because myriad opportunities present themselves during election years for citizens to engage actively in things political. Space precludes a detailed discussion of religious differences in many forms of political behavior.

16. These unavoidable costs entail the fact that people must invest the actual time to go to vote or acquire an absentee ballot, and so on (see Rosenstone and Wolfinger 1978; Teixeira 1992; Hill and Leighley 1993).

17. However, one enduring legacy of the religious conflict-based campaigns of the 1980s (e.g., those of Jesse Jackson and Pat Robertson) was the integration of church-based networks into viable political operations (see, for example, Hertzke [1993]).

18. Often, this may be a function of efforts to transform public and private images of the political parties and their leaders (e.g., Philpot 2007). It should be noted, however, that research on the effects of campaign activities almost never produces direct evidence of demobilization; evidence is either null or positive.

19. This last measure also includes other forms of church religious contacts, including having a discussion about politics in church, whether their clergy or leadership endorsed a candidate, whether the church facilitated voter registration, and whether information on parties or candidates was made available at church.

REFERENCES

Abramson, Paul R., John H. Aldrich, and David W. Rohde. 2003. *Change and Continuity in the 2000 and 2002 Elections.* Washington, D.C.: CQ Press.

Abramson, Paul R., John H. Aldrich, and David Rohde. 2007. *Change and Continuity in the 2006 Elections.* Washington, D.C.: CQ Press.

Abramson, Paul R., and William Claggett. 1989. "Race-Related Differences in Self-Reported and Validated Turnout in 1986." *Journal of Politics* 51: 397–408.

Abramson, Paul R., and William Claggett. 1991. "Racial Differences in Self-Reported and Validated Turnout in the 1988 Presidential Election." *Journal of Politics* 53: 86–197.

Abramson, Paul R., John H. Aldrich, and David W. Rohde. 2003. *Change and Continuity in the 2000 and 2002 Elections.* Washington, D.C.: CQ Press.

Abramson, Paul R., John H. Aldrich, and David W. Rohde. 2007. *Change and Continuity in the 2004 and 2006 Elections.* Washington, D.C.: CQ Press.

Aldrich, John H. 1993. "Rational Choice and Turnout." *American Journal of Political Science* 37: 246–278.

Alex-Assensoh, Yvette, and A. B. Assensoh. 2001. "Inner-City Contexts, Church Attendance, and African-American Political Participation." *Journal of Politics* 63: 886–901.

Allen, Richard L., Michael C. Dawson, and Ronald E. Brown. 1989. "A Schema-Based Approach to Modeling an African-American Racial Belief System." *American Political Science Review* 83 (2): 421–441.

Alvarez, R. Michael. 1997. *Information & Elections.* Rev. ed. Ann Arbor, Mich.: University of Michigan Press.

Anderson, Barbara A., and Brian D. Silver. 1986. "Measurement and Mismeasurement of the Validity of the Self-Reported Vote." *American Journal of Political Science* 30: 771–785.

Atkeson, Lonna Rae. 1999 "'Sure, I Voted for the Winner!' Overreport of the Primary Vote for the Party Nominee in the National Election Studies." *Political Behavior* 21 (3): 197–215.

Barnes, Samuel H., and Max Kaase, eds. 1979. *Political Action: Mass Participation in Five Western Democracies.* Beverly Hills, Calif.: Sage.

Berelson, Bernard R., Paul F. Lazarsfeld, and William N. McPhee. 1954. *Voting: A Study of Opinion Formation in a Presidential Campaign.* Chicago, Ill.: University of Chicago Press.

Bernstein, Robert, Anita Chadha, and Robert Montjoy. 2001. "Overreporting Voting: Why It Happens and Why It Matters." *Public Opinion Quarterly* 65: 22–44.

Beyerlein, Kraig, and Mark Chaves. 2003. "The Political Activities of Religious Congregations in the United States." *Journal for the Scientific Study of Religion* 42: 229–246.

Bloom, Alan. 1987. *The Closing of the American Mind.* New York: Simon and Schuster.

Brady, Henry E., Kay L. Schlozman, and Sidney Verba. 1999. "Prospecting for Participants: Rational Expectations and the Recruitment of Political Activists." *American Political Science Review,* 93: 153–168.

Brady, Henry E., Sidney Verba, and Kay Lehman Schlozman. 1995. "Beyond Socioeconomic Status: A Resource Model of Participation." *American Political Science Review* 89: 271–294.

Brewer, Mark D., Rogan Kersh, and R. Eric Petersen. 2003. "Assessing Conventional Wisdom about Religion and Politics: A Preliminary View from the Pews." *Journal for the Scientific Study of Religion* 42: 125–136.

Brooks, Clem, Jeff Manza, and Catherine Bolzendahl. 2003. "Voting Behavior and Political Sociology: Theories, Debates, and Future Directions." *Research in Political Sociology* 12: 137–173.

Brown, Khari R. 2006. "Racial Differences in Congregation-Based Political Activism." *Social Forces* 84: 1581–1604.

Brown, Khari R., and Ronald E. Brown. 2003. "Faith and Works: Church-Based Social Capital Resources and African American Political Activism." *Social Forces* 82: 617–641.

Brown, Ronald E., and Monica L. Wolford. 1994. "Religious Resources and African-American Political Action." *National Political Science Review* 4: 30–48.

Buchanan, James M., and Gordon Tullock. 1962. *The Calculus of Consent: Logical Foundations of Constitutional Democracy.* Ann Arbor, Mich.: University of Michigan Press.

Burton, Michael John, and Daniel M. Shea. 2003. *Campaign Mode: Strategic Vision in Congressional Elections.* Lanham, Md.: Rowman and Littlefield.

Calhoun-Brown, Allison. 1996. "African American Churches and Political Mobilization: The Psychological Impact of Organizational Resources." *Journal of Politics* 58 (4): 935–953.

Calhoun-Brown, Allison. 1998. "While Marching to Zion: Otherworldliness and Racial Empowerment in the Black Community." *Journal for the Scientific Study of Religion* 37: 427–439.

Campbell, Angus, Philip E. Converse, Warren E. Miller, and Donald E. Stokes. 1960. *The American Voter.* New York: Wiley.

Campbell, David. 2004. "Community Heterogeneity and Participation." Presented at the annual meeting of the American Political Science Association, Chicago, Ill., September 2–5.

Campbell, David E. 2006. "Religious 'Threat' in Contemporary Presidential Elections." *The Journal of Politics* 68: 104–115.

Carmines, Edward G., and James Kuklinski. 1990. "Incentives, Opportunities, and the Logic of Public Opinion in American Political Representation." In *Information and Democratic Processes*, ed. John A. Ferejohn and James H. Kuklinski, 240–268. Chicago, Ill.: University of Illinois Press.

Cassel, Carol A. 1999. "Voluntary Associations, Churches, and Social Participation Theories of Turnout." *Social Science Quarterly* 80: 504–517.

Claggett, William, and Philip H. Pollock, III. 2006. "The Modes of Participation Revisited, 1980–2004." *Political Research Quarterly* 59: 593–600.

Conway, M. Margaret. 2000. *Political Participation in the United States.* 3rd ed. Washington, D.C.: CQ Press.

Darling, Marsha J. 1998. "African-American Women in State Elective Office in the South." In *Women and Elective Office: Past, Present and Future*, ed. Sue Thomas and Clyde Wilcox, pp. 150–162. New York: Oxford University Press.

Dawson, Michael C., Ronald E. Brown, and Richard L. Allen. 1990. "Racial Belief Systems, Religious Guidance, and African-American Political Participation." *National Political Science Review* 2: 22–44.

Demo, David H., and Michael Hughes. 1990. "Socialization and Racial Identity among Black Americans." *Social Psychology Quarterly* 53 (4): 364–374.

Djupe, Paul A., and J. Tobin Grant. 2001. "Religious Institutions and Political Participation in America." *Journal for the Scientific Study of Religion* 40: 303–314.

Dobson, James C. 2007. "The Values Test." *The New York Times*: October 4, A29.

Downs, Anthony. 1957. *An Economic Theory of Democracy.* New York: Addison Wesley Longman.

Driskell, Robyn, Elizabeth Embry, and Larry Lyon. 2008. "Faith and Politics: The Influence of Religious Beliefs on Political Participation." *Social Science Quarterly* 89: 294–314.

Eldersveld, Samuel J. 1956. "Experimental Propaganda Techniques and Voting Behavior." *American Political Science Review* 50: 154–165.

Eldersveld, Samuel J., and Richard W. Dodge. 1954. "Personal Contact or Mail Propaganda? An Experiment in Voting Turnout and Attitude Change." In *Public Opinion and Propaganda: A Book of Readings*, ed. Daniel Katz, Dorwin Cartwright, Samuel Eldersveld, and Alfred M. Lee, 532–542. New York: Dryden.

Ellison, Christopher G. 1993. "Religious Involvement and Self-Perception among Black Americans." *Social Forces* 71 (4): 1027–1055.

Enelow, James M., and Melvin J. Hinich. 1984. *The Spatial Theory of Voting: An Introduction.* New York: Cambridge University Press.

Erikson, Robert S., Thomas D. Lancaster, and David W. Romero. 1989. "Group Components of the Presidential Vote." *Journal of Politics* 51: 337–346.

Fiorina, Morris P. 1981. *Retrospective Voting in American National Elections*. New Haven, Conn.: Yale University Press.

Flanigan, William H., and Nancy H. Zingale. 2006. *Political Behavior of the American Electorate*. 11th ed. Washington, D.C.: CQ Press.

Fowler, Robert B., Allen D. Hertzke, and Laura R. Olson. 1999. *Religion and Politics in America: Faith, Culture, and Strategic Choices*. Boulder, Colo.: Westview Press.

Frazier, E. Franklin. [1963] 1974. *The Negro Church in America*. New York: Schocken.

Gerber, Alan S., and Donald P. Green. 2000a. "The Effect of a Nonpartisan Get-out-the-Vote Drive: An Experimental Study of Leafletting." *Journal of Politics* 62: 846–857.

Gerber, Alan S., and Donald P. Green. 2000b. "The Effects of Canvassing, Telephone Calls, and Direct Mail on Voter Turnout: A Field Experiment." *American Political Science Review* 94: 653–663.

Gerber, Alan S., and Donald P. Green. 2001. "Do Phone Calls Increase Voter Turnout? A Field Experiment." *Public Opinion Quarterly* 65: 75–85.

Gershtenson, Joseph. 2003. "Mobilization Strategies of the Democrats and Republicans, 1956–2000." *Political Research Quarterly* 56 (3): 293–308.

Gilbert, Christopher. 1991. "Religion, Neighborhood Environments and Partisan Behavior: A Contextual Analysis." *Political Geography Quarterly* 10 (2): 110–131.

Githens, Marianne, and Jewell Prestage, eds. 1977. *A Portrait of Marginality: The Political Behavior of American Women*. New York: McKay.

Glaeser, Edward L., and Bryce A. Ward. 2006. "Myths and Realities of American Political Geography." *Journal of Economic Perspectives* 20 (2): 119–144.

Godwin, R. Kenneth. 1988. *One Billion Dollars of Influence: The Direct Marketing of Politics*. Chatham, N.J.: Chatham House.

Gosnell, Harold F. 1926. "An Experiment in the Stimulation of Voting." *American Political Science Review* 20: 869–874.

Gosnell, Harold F. 1927. *Getting Out the Vote: An Experiment in the Stimulation of Voting*. Chicago, Ill.: University of Chicago Press.

Green, Donald P., and Alan S. Gerber. 2004. *Get out the Vote! How to Increase Voter Turnout*. Washington, D.C.: Brookings Institution.

Green, Donald P., and Alan S. Gerber, eds. 2005. "Recent Advances in the Science of Voter Mobilization." *The Annals of the American Academy of Political and Social Sciences* 601: 6–9.

Green, John C., Lyman A. Kellstedt, Corwin E. Smidt, and James L. Guth. 2007. "How the Faithful Voted: Religious Communities and the Presidential Vote." In *A Matter of Faith: Religion in the 2004 Presidential Election*, ed. David E. Campbell, 15–36. Washington, D.C.: Brookings Institution.

Green, John C., Mark J. Rozell, and Clyde Wilcox. 2000. *Prayers in the Precincts: The Christian Right in the 1994 Elections*. Washington, D.C.: Georgetown University Press.

Green, John C., Mark J. Rozell, and Clyde Wilcox. 2003. *The Christian Right in American Politics: Marching to the Millennium*. Washington, D.C.: Georgetown University Press.

Gronke, Paul. 1992. "Overreporting the Vote in the 1988 Senate Election Study: A Response to Wright." *Legislative Studies Quarterly* 17: 113–129.

Guth, James L., John C. Green, Lyman A. Kellstedt, and Corwin E. Smidt. 2002b. "Religion and Political Participation." Presented at the annual meeting of the American Political Science Association, Boston, Mass: August 29–September 1.

Guth, James L., John C. Green, Corwin E. Smidt, Lyman A. Kellstedt, and Margaret M. Poloma. 1997. *The Bully Pulpit*. Lawrence, Kans.: University Press of Kansas.

Guth, James L., Lyman A. Kellstedt, John C. Green, and Corwin E. Smidt. 1998. "Thunder on the Right? Religious Interest Group Mobilization in the 1996 Election." In *Interest Group Politics*. 5th ed., ed. Allan J. Cigler and Burdett A. Loomis, 169–192. Washington, D.C.: CQ Press.

Guth, James L., Lyman A. Kellstedt, John C. Green, and Corwin E. Smidt. 2002. "A Distant Thunder? Religious Mobilization in the 2000 Elections." In *Interest Group Politics*. 6th ed., ed. Allan J. Cigler and Burdett A. Loomis, 161–184. Washington, D.C.: CQ Press.

Guth, James L., Lyman A. Kellstedt, John C. Green, and Corwin E. Smidt. 2007. "Getting the Spirit: Religious and Partisan Mobilization in the 2004 Elections." In *Interest Group Politics*. 7th ed., ed. Allan J. Cigler and Burdett A. Loomis, 157–181. Washington, D.C.: CQ Press.

Guth, James L., Lyman A. Kellstedt, Corwin E. Smidt, and John C Green. 2006. "Religious Influences in the 2004 Presidential Election." *Presidential Studies Quarterly* 36 (2): 223–242.

Harmon-Martin, Shiela F. 1994. "Black Women in Politics: A Research Note." In *Black Politics and Black Political Behavior: A Linkage Analysis*, ed. Hanes Walton, Jr., pp. 209–217. Westport, Conn.: Praeger.

Harris, Frederick C. 1994. "Something Within: Religion as a Mobilizer of African-American Political Activism." *Journal of Politics* 56 (1): 42–68.

Harris, Frederick C. 1999. *Something Within: Religion in African-American Political Activism*. New York: Oxford University Press.

Hertzke, Allen D. 1993. *Echoes of Discontent: Jesse Jackson, Pat Robertson, and the Resurgence of Populism*. Washington, D.C.: CQ Press.

Hill, Kim Q., and Jan E. Leighley. 1993. "Party Ideology, Organization, and Competitiveness as Mobilizing Forces in Gubernatorial Elections." *American Journal of Political Science* 37: 1158–1178.

Hinich, Melfin J., and Michael Munger. 1994. *Ideology and the Theory of Political Choice*. Ann Arbor, Mich.: University of Michigan Press.

Hoffer Eric. 1951. *The True Believer*. New York: Time.

Hougland, James G., and James A. Christenson. 1983. "Religion and Politics: The Relationship of Religious Participation to Political Efficacy and Involvement." *Sociology and Social Research* 67 (4): 405–420.

Huckfeldt, Robert, Eric Plutzer, and John Sprague. 1993. "Alternative Contexts of Political Behavior: Churches, Neighborhoods, and Individuals." *Journal of Politics* 55: 365–381.

Huckfeldt, Robert, and John Sprague. 1991. "Discussant Effects on Vote Choice: Intimacy, Structure, and Interdependence." *Journal of Politics* 53: 122–158.

Huckfeldt, Robert, and John Sprague. 1992. "Political Parties and Electoral Mobilization: Political Structure, Social Structure, and the Party Canvass." *American Political Science Review* 86: 70–86.

Jelen, Ted G. 1993. *The Political World of the Clergy*. Westport, Conn.: Praeger.

Jenkins, Krista, Molly Andolina, Scott Keeter, and Cliff Zukin. 2003. "Is Civic Behavior Political? Exploring the Multidimensional Nature of Political Participation." Presented at the annual meeting of the Midwest Political Science Association, Chicago, Illinois, April 3–6.

Jones-Correa, Michael A., and David L. Leal. 2001. "Political Participation: Does Religion Matter?" *Political Research Quarterly* 54 (4): 751–770.

Kellstedt, Lyman A., and John C. Green. 1993. "Knowing God's Many People: Denominational Preference and Political Behavior." In *Rediscovering the Religious Factor in American Politics*, ed. David C. Leege and Lyman A. Kellstedt, 53–71. Armonk, N.Y.: M. E. Sharpe.

Kellstedt, Lyman A., John C. Green, James L. Guth, and Corwin E. Smidt. 1994. "Religious Voting Blocs in the 1992 Election: The Year of the Evangelical?" *Sociology of Religion* 55: 307–326.

Kellstedt, Lyman A., John C. Green, James L. Guth, and Corwin E. Smidt. 1996. "Grasping the Essentials: The Social Embodiment of Religion and Political Behavior." In *Religion and the Culture Wars: Dispatches from the Front*, ed. John C. Green, James L. Guth, Corwin E. Smidt, and Lyman A. Kellstedt, 174–192. Lanham, Md.: Rowman and Littlefield.

Kellstedt, Lyman A., and Corwin E. Smidt. 1993. "Doctrinal Beliefs and Political Behavior: Views of the Bible." In *Rediscovering the Religious Factor in American Politics*, ed. David C. Leege and Lyman A. Kellstedt, pp. 177–198. Armonk, N.Y.: M. E. Sharpe.

Kenny, Christopher B. 1992. "Political Participation and Effects from the Social Environment." *American Journal of Political Science* 32: 259–267.

Langley, W. Mary, and William M. Kahnweiler. 2003. "The Role of Pastoral Leadership in the Sociopolitically Active African American Church." *Organization Development Journal* 21 (2): 43–51.

Layman, Geoffrey C. 1997. "Religion and Political Behavior in the United States: The Impact of Beliefs, Affiliations, and Commitment from 1980 to 1994." *Public Opinion Quarterly* 61: 288–316.

Layman, Geoffrey. 2001. *Religious and Cultural Conflict in American Party Politics*. New York: Columbia University Press.

Lazarsfeld, Paul F., Bernard Berelson, and Hazel Gaudet. 1944. *The People's Choice: How the Voter Makes up His Mind in a Presidential Campaign*. New York: Duell, Sloan and Pearce.

Leege, David C., and Lyman A. Kellstedt. 1993. *Rediscovering the Religious Factor in American Politics*. Armonk, N.Y.: M. E. Sharpe.

Leege, David C., Kenneth D. Wald, and Lyman A. Kellstedt. 1993. "The Public Dimension of Private Devotionalism." In *Rediscovering the Religious Factor in American Politics*, ed. David C. Leege and Lyman A. Kellstedt, 139–156. Armonk, N.Y.: M. E. Sharpe.

Leege, David C., Kenneth D. Wald, Brian S. Krueger, and Paul D. Mueller. 2002. *The Politics of Cultural Differences: Social Change and Voter Mobilization Strategies in the Post-New Deal Period*. Princeton, N.J.: Princeton University Press.

Leighley, Jan E. 2001. *Strength in Numbers: The Political Mobilization of Racial and Ethnic Minorities*. Princeton, N.J.: Princeton University Press.

Lenski, Gerhard. 1961. *The Religious Factor*. Garden City, N.Y.: Doubleday.

Lipset, Semour M. [1960] 1981. *Political Man: The Social Bases of Politics*. Exp. ed. Baltimore, Md.: Johns Hopkins University Press.

Lowry, Robert C. 1998. "Religion and the Demand for Membership in Environmental Citizen Groups." *Public Choice* 94: 223–240.

Macaluso, Theodore F., and John Wanat. 1979. "Voting Turnout and Religiosity." *Polity* 12: 158–169.

Maccoby, Herbert. 1958. "The Differential Political Activity of Participants in a Voluntary Association." *American Sociological Review* 23: 524–532.

MacDonald, Stuart E., Ola Listhaug, and George Rabinowitz. 1991. "Issues and Party Support in Multiparty Systems." *American Political Science Review* 85: 1107–1132.

Macedo, Stephen, et al. 2005. *Democracy at Risk: How Political Choices Undermine Citizen Participation, and What We Can Do About It.* Washington, D.C.: Brookings Institution Press.

Madron, Thomas W. M., Hart M. Nelsen, and Raytha L. Yokley. 1974. "Religion as a Determinant of Militancy and Participation among Black Americans." *American Behavioral Scientist* 17: 783–796.

Marsh, Alan, and Max Kaase. 1979. "Background of Political Action." In *Political Action: Mass Participation in Five Western Democracies*, ed. Samuel H. Barnes and Max Kaase, pp. 97–136. Beverly Hills, Calif.: Sage.

McClurg, Scott D. 2004. "Indirect Mobilization: The Social Consequences of Party Contacts in an Election Campaign." *American Politics Research* 32: 406–443.

McDaniel, Eric L., and Harwood K. McClerking. 2005. "Who Belongs? Understanding How Socioeconomic Stratification Shapes the Characteristics of Black Political Church Members." *National Political Science Review* 10: 15–28.

McDonald, Michael P., and Samuel L. Popkin. 2001. "The Myth of the Vanishing Voter." *The American Political Science Review* 95: 963–974.

McKenzie, Brian D. 2004. "Religious Social Networks, Indirect Mobilization, and African-American Political Participation." *Political Research Quarterly* 57: 621–632.

McVeigh, Rory, and David Sikkink. 2001. "God, Politics, and Protest: Religious Beliefs and the Legitimation of Contentious Tactics." *Social Forces* 79: 1425–1458.

Milbrath, Lester W., and M. L. Goel. 1977. *Political Participation.* 2nd ed. Chicago, Ill.: Rand McNally.

Monson, J. Quin, and J. Baxter Oliphant. 2007. "Microtargeting and the Instrumental Mobilization of Religious Conservatives." In *A Matter of Faith: Religion in the 2004 Presidential Election*, ed. David E. Campbell, 95–119. Washington, D.C.: Brookings Institution.

Morton, Rebecca B. 2006. *Analyzing Elections.* New York: Norton.

Mueller, Dennis C. 1989. *Public Choice II.* New York: Cambridge University Press.

Nie, Norman H., Sidney Verba, and John R. Petrocik. 1979. *The Changing American Voter.* Enl. ed. Cambridge, Mass.: Harvard University Press.

Olsen, Marvin E. 1972. "Social Participation and Voting Turnout: A Multivariate Analysis." *American Sociological Review* 37: 317–333.

Olson, Laura R. 2000. *Filled with Spirit and Power.* Albany, N.Y.: State University of New York Press.

Olson, Mancur. 1965. *The Logic of Collective Action: Public Goods and the Theory of Groups.* Cambridge, Mass.: Harvard University Press.

Panagopolous, Costas, and Peter W. Wielhouwer. 2008. "The Ground War 2000–2004: Strategic Targeting in Grassroots Campaigns." *Presidential Studies Quarterly* 38 (2): 347–362.

Peterson, Steven. 1990. *Political Behavior: Patterns in Everyday Life.* Newbury Park, Calif.: Sage.

Phillips, Charles R. 1990. *The Blue Book for Grassroots Politics.* Nashville, Tenn.: Oliver Nelson.

Philpot, Tasha S. 2007. *Race, Republicans, and the Return of the Party of Lincoln.* Ann Arbor, Mich.: University of Michigan Press.

Plane, Dennis L., and Joseph Gershtenson. 2004. "Candidates' Ideological Locations, Abstention, and Turnout in U.S. Midterm Senate Elections." *Political Behavior* 26: 69–93.

Quinley, Harold E. 1974. *The Prophetic Clergy: Social Activism among Protestant Ministers.* New York: Wiley.

Rabinowitz, George, and Stuart E. MacDonald. 1989. "A Directional Theory of Issue Voting." *American Political Science Review* 83 (1): 93–121.

Reese, Laura A., and Ronald E. Brown. 1995. "The Effects of Religious Messages on Racial Identity and System Blame." *Journal of Politics* 57 (1): 24–43.

Regnerus, Mark D., and Christian Smith. 1998. "Selective Deprivatization among American Religious Traditions: The Reversal of the Great Reversal." *Social Forces,* 76: 1347–1372.

Riker, William H., and Peter C. Ordeshook. 1968. "A Theory of the Calculus of Voting." *American Political Science Review* 62: 25–42.

Rosenstone, Steven J., and John M. Hansen. 1993. *Mobilization, Participation, and Democracy in America.* New York: MacMillan.

Rosenstone, Steven J., and Raymond E. Wolfinger. 1978. "The Effect of Voter Registration Laws on Voter Turnout." *American Political Science Review* 72: 22–45.

Rozell, Mark J., and Clyde Wilcox. 1995. *God at the Grassroots: The Christian Right in the 1994 Elections.* New York: Rowman & Littlefield.

Rozell, Mark J., and Clyde Wilcox. 1996. "Second Coming: The Strategies of the New Christian Right." *Political Science Quarterly* 111 (2): 271–294.

Rozell, Mark J., and Clyde Wilcox. 1997. *God at the Grassroots: The Christian Right in the 1996 Elections.* New York: Rowman & Littlefield.

Silver, Brian D., Barbara A. Anderson, and Paul R. Abramson. 1986. "Who Overreports Voting?" *The American Political Science Review* 80: 613–624.

Smidt, Corwin E. 1999. "Religion and Civic Engagement: A Comparative Analysis." *Annals of the American Academy of Political and Social Science* 565: 176–192.

Smidt, Corwin E. 2003. *Religion as Social Capital: Producing the Common Good.* Waco, Texas: Baylor University Press.

Smidt, Corwin E. 2004. *Pulpit and Politics: Clergy in American Politics at the Advent of the Millennium.* Waco, Texas: Baylor University Press.

Smidt, Corwin E., John C. Green, Lyman Kellstedt, and James L. Guth. 2007. " 'What Does the Lord Require?' Evangelicals and the 2004 Presidential Vote." In *Religion and the Bush Presidency,* ed. Mark J. Rozell and Gleaves Whitney, 31–47. New York: Palgrave Macmillan.

Sosnick, Douglas B., Matthew J. Dowd, and Ron Fournier. 2006. *Applebee's America: How Successful Political, Business, and Religious Leaders Connect with the New American Community.* New York: Simon and Schuster.

Stanley, Harold W., Wiliam T. Bianco, and Richard G. Niemi. 1986. "Partisanship and Group Support over Time: A Multivariate Analysis." *American Political Science Review* 80 (3): 969–976.

Stanley, Harold W., and Richard G. Niemi. 1999. "Party Coalitions in Transition: Partisanship and Group Support, 1952–96." In *Reelection 1996,* ed. Herbert F. Weisberg and Janet Box-Steffensmeier, 220–240. New York: Chatham House.

Stokes, Donald. 1963. "Spatial Models of Party Competition." *American Political Science Review* 57: 368–377.

Tate, Katherine. 1993. *From Protest to Politics: The New Black Voters in American Elections.* Cambridge, Mass.: Harvard University Press.

Teixeira, Ruy A. 1992. *The Disappearing American Voter.* Washington, D.C.: Brookings Institution.

Theiss-Morse, Elizabeth, and John R. Hibbing. 2005. "Citizenship and Civic Engagement." *Annual Review of Political Science* 8: 227–249.

Thomas, Cal, and Ed Dobson. 1999. *Blinded by Might: Can the Religious Right Save America?* New York: Harper Collins/Zondervan.

Verba, Sidney, and Norman Nie. 1972. *Participation in America.* Chicago, Ill.: University of Chicago Press.

Verba, Sidney, Norman Nie, and Jae-on Kim. 1978. *Participation and Political Equality.* New York: Cambridge University Press.

Verba, Sidney, Kay L. Schlozman, and Henry E. Brady. 1995. *Voice and Equality: Civic Volunteerism in American Politics.* Cambridge, Mass.: Harvard University Press.

Wald, Kenneth D. 2003. *Religion and Politics in the United States.* Washington, D.C.: CQ Press.

Wald, Kenneth D., Lyman A. Kellstedt, and David C. Leege. 1993. "Church Involvement and Political Behavior." In *Rediscovering the Religious Factor in American Politics,* ed. David C. Leege and Lyman A. Kellstedt, pp. 121–138. Armonk, N.Y.: M. E. Sharpe.

Wald, Kenneth D., Dennis E. Owen, and Samuel S. Hill, Jr. 1988. "Churches as Political Communities." *American Political Science Review* 82: 531–548.

Wald, Kenneth D., Dennis E. Owen, and Samuel S. Hill, Jr.. 1990. "Political Cohesion in Churches." *Journal of Politics* 52: 197–215.

West, John G. 1996. *The Politics of Revelation & Reason: Religion & Civic Life in the New Nation.* Lawrence, Kans.: University Press of Kansas.

Whiteley, Paul F. 1995. "Rational Choice and Political Participation: Evaluating the Debate." *Political Research Quarterly* 48: 211–234.

Wielhouwer, Peter W. 1999. "The Mobilization of Campaign Activists by the Party Canvass." *American Politics Quarterly* 27: 177–200.

Wielhouwer, Peter W. 2000. "Releasing the Fetters: Parties and the Mobilization of the African-American Electorate." *Journal of Politics* 62: 206–222.

Wielhouwer, Peter W. 2003. "In Search of Lincoln's Perfect List: Targeting in Grassroots Campaigns." *American Politics Research* 31: 632–669.

Wielhouwer, Peter W. 2004. "The Impact of Church Activities and Socialization on African-American Religious Commitment." *Social Science Quarterly* 85: 767–792.

Wielhouwer, Peter W. 2006. "Grassroots Mobilization." In *The Electoral Challenge: Theory Meets Practice,* ed. Stephen Craig, pp. 163–182. Washington, D.C.: CQ Press.

Wielhouwer, Peter W., and Brad Lockerbie. 1994. "Party Contacting and Political Participation, 1952–1990." *American Journal of Political Science* 38: 211–229.

Wilcox, Clyde, and Leopoldo Gomez. 1990. "Religion, Group Identification, and Politics among American Blacks." *Sociological Analysis* 51: 271–285.

Wilcox, Clyde, and Lee Sigelman. 2001. "Political Mobilization in the Pews: Religious Contacting and Electoral Turnout." *Social Science Quarterly* 82 (3): 524–535.

Wolfinger, Raymond E., and Steven J. Rosenstone. 1980. *Who Votes?* New Haven, Conn.: Yale University Press.

Wright, Gerald C. 1992. "Reported Versus Actual Vote: There Is a Difference and It Matters." *Legislative Studies Quarterly* 17: 131–142.

Wright, Gerald C. 1993. "Errors in Measuring Vote Choice in the National Election Studies, 1952–88." *American Journal of Political Science* 37: 291–316.

Zukin, Cliff, Scott Keeter, Molly Anderson, Krista Jenkins, and Michael Delli Carpini. 2006. *A New Engagement? Political Participation, Civic Life, and the Changing American Citizen.* New York: Oxford University Press.

CHAPTER 15

RELIGION AND POLITICAL TOLERANCE IN THE UNITED STATES: A REVIEW AND EVALUATION

MARIE A. EISENSTEIN

To a casual observer, it might seem that in every generation religion invades the public square. However, religion is always in the public square because it never left; it is merely "rediscovered" periodically by new observers. In the United States, the separation of church and state does not create a separation of religion and politics. The first is institutional whereas the second is behavioral, and it is counterintuitive to think that religious individuals "can, in any meaningful way, divorce themselves from their beliefs when behaving as a political actor" (Eisenstein 2005, p. 5). Thus, religion remains, as it has for generations, an important component in the study of American politics.

Any study or discussion of religion and politics must, of necessity, include political tolerance. Political tolerance is an important issue central to the maintenance of democratic institutions, especially in pluralistic societies such as the United States. Both pundits and scholars often assume that strong religious views produce intolerance. This chapter examines this assumption through an in-depth analysis of scholarly literature on political tolerance. Because of the importance of both religion and tolerance for democratic politics, we might expect to find a *clearly* designated body of academic research that spells out the linkages between the two. This is not the case. Instead, there is a divided literature—a "mainstream" political tolerance literature, mainly within political science, and a body of research on political tolerance by religion specialists in both political science and sociology.[1] These research traditions are like the proverbial ships passing in the night, each largely unaware of the other.

Any examination of the relationship between religion and political tolerance needs to incorporate key concepts and measures from both traditions. Religion specialists understand the many dimensions of religion, such as affiliation, beliefs, and practices (see chapter 1 in this volume), but mainstream scholars have not systematically used these distinct facets of religion in their research. Religion specialists, on the other hand, have neglected three influences on tolerance that mainstream scholars have emphasized: personal insecurity, commitment to democratic values, and threat perceptions (compare with Finkel, Sigelman, and Humphries [1999]; Sullivan and Transue [1999]; and Gibson [2006, 2007] for reviews of the mainstream research).

This chapter highlights both research traditions and examines recent efforts to bridge the two. In the first section, I start with political tolerance, its definition and its measurement. Then I bring together the two literatures, making note of advances within the religion literature vis-à-vis those within the mainstream political tolerance literature. Last, I focus on directions for future research.

DEFINING AND MEASURING
POLITICAL TOLERANCE

Understanding what political tolerance is, and what it is not, is central to any assessment of how religion and tolerance intersect. As Sullivan, Piereson, and Marcus (1982) note, political tolerance is a difficult concept and is often confused with others such as prejudice, norms of democracy, religious toleration, and open-mindedness, or is even used interchangeably with these. Political tolerance, as defined by mainstream scholars, has a very specific meaning: It is about *actions* not attitudes (compare with Murphy [1997] for an excellent discussion of this point). It is not synonymous with agreement with a set of particular issue positions, where disagreement implies intolerance. Rather, it "implies a willingness to 'put up with' those things one rejects or opposes. Politically, it implies a willingness to permit the expression of ideas or interests one opposes. In a narrower sense, tolerance is closely associated with the idea of procedural fairness" (Sullivan et al. 1982, p. 2). As long as one is willing to apply the "rules of the game" equally, even to groups one opposes, one is tolerant.

Like Sullivan et al., Nunn, Crockett, and Williams (1978, p. 12) argue that "[t]olerance is a straightforward attitude that allows people to have freedom of expression even though one may feel that their ideas are incorrect or even immoral." Thus, tolerance should not be equated with acceptance. "Acceptance is to agree with or condone the opinions, values, and behavior of others who are perhaps initially different from oneself" (Nunn et al. 1978, p. 12). Individuals cannot be tolerant of ideas or groups that they agree with, nor of those to which they are indifferent. In sum, political tolerance allows those with whom you disagree to enjoy their civil liberties. As Marcus, Sullivan, Theiss-Morse, and Stevens (1995, p. 3) state, "[p]olitical tolerance requires that democratic citizens and leaders secure the full political rights of expression and political participation of groups they find objectionable."

In addition, political intolerance is not the same as prejudice; an individual may harbor prejudice toward a group but be tolerant of their actions. According to Sullivan et al. (1982, p. 4), "[w]e sometimes say a person without prejudice is very tolerant, while those who are prejudiced are necessarily intolerant. Yet this need not be so. The prejudiced person may in fact be tolerant, if he understands his prejudices and proceeds to permit the expression of those things toward which he is prejudiced." Nunn et al. (1978, p. 11) agree: "One may hold to prejudices and still be willing to let other people have their opinions and beliefs. Or one may even have a relatively benign attitude toward a people of a particular ethnic background and yet frequently violate others' civil liberties." In general, prejudice is a negative value judgment of an individual or group based upon a stereotyped generalization. In contrast, political tolerance depends on the *actions* one takes in relationship to such judgment—prejudiced or not—to ideas, groups, or persons one opposes.

In earlier research, tolerance was often defined as acceptance of abstract norms of democratic procedure (McClosky 1964). In the abstract, most Americans—90 percent—believe in free speech for all (McClosky and Brill 1983), but when asked to apply this general principle to a disliked group, their willingness to extend free speech drops below 50 percent. As McClosky and Brill (1983) show, questions about abstract principles, rather than concrete applications of general principles, overestimate political tolerance. Moreover, support for abstract democratic norms has proved more useful as a predictor of political tolerance rather than as a *definition* of it (Sullivan et al. 1982; Marcus, Sullivan, Theiss-Morse, and Wood 1995).

Measuring Political Tolerance

The research on political tolerance began with sociologist Samuel Stouffer's (1955) classic *Communism, Conformity, and Civil Liberties*. Stouffer asked respondents if they were willing to extend civil liberties to Communists, socialists, and atheists (e.g., allow them to give a speech in their community, teach in a college or university, or allow their book in the public library). These "Stouffer" action items were adopted in 1972 by the General Social Survey (GSS); in 1976, the GSS modified the "objects" of tolerance, dropping socialists but adding racists, militarists, and homosexuals. This included ideological groups from both Left and Right, in lieu of the exclusively Left groups (Communists, socialists, and atheists) used previously.

Political scientist John Sullivan and his colleagues (Sullivan, Piereson, and Marcus 1979; Sullivan et al. 1982) criticized both the original Stouffer items and the revised GSS versions. They complained that all respondents were asked to make tolerance judgments, including those without a strong dislike of the groups specified. Those sympathetic to the objects of tolerance should naturally be more willing to extend civil liberties to them, but this does not make these individuals more tolerant. Sullivan, Piereson, and Marcus (1982) argued that tolerance questions should be asked only about groups that the respondent dislikes. They also contended that the Stouffer/GSS items did not separate group effects from action effects. Any adequate assessment must disentangle tolerance toward a group from tolerance toward the actions taken by that group. Thus, asking about willingness to tolerate a speech by a Communist taps not only attitudes toward the action (i.e., speaking), but also attitudes toward Communists. Finally, Sullivan et al. (1982) argued that the target groups included in the Stouffer/GSS items were insufficient in number and diversity.

To correct these problems, Sullivan et al. (1982) used a "content-controlled" measure (alternatively, a "least-liked" measure). Respondents selected their most disliked group from a list of "extremist" groups, from both the ideological Left and Right, as well as some that did not fall on the Left–Right continuum. If the individuals' most disliked group was not listed, they were asked to name that group. Next, they were asked to respond to six statements about "a range of peaceful activities in which members of that group might participate or about steps the government might take against that group" to measure political tolerance (Sullivan et al. 1982, p. 61). Table 15.1 presents these individual items; each statement has a five-point scale ranging from strongly agree (1 point) to strongly disagree (5 points).

Although some scholars challenged the "least-liked" or content-controlled method (e.g., Mueller 1988; Gibson 1992; Weissberg 1998), these objections have not been compelling enough to abandon the approach. Indeed, one early critic, James Gibson (1986, 1989, 1992a), has modified his position. After using both GSS and "least-liked" approaches, he concluded that the two were equally effective, but

Table 15.1 Content-Controlled Political Tolerance Scale Items

1. Members of the (*subject-selected least-liked group*) should be banned from being president of the United States.
2. Members of the (*least-liked group*) should be allowed to teach in public schools.
3. The (*least-liked group*) should be outlawed.
4. Members of the (*least-liked group*) should be allowed to make a speech in this city.
5. The (*least-liked group*) should have their phones tapped by our government.
6. The (*least-liked group*) should be allowed to hold public rallies in our city.

has utilized the latter in his own research (e.g., Gibson and Gouws 2000). Nonetheless, he identifies the measurement of intolerance as one of five "enigmas" of tolerance research that need further consideration (Gibson 2006, p. 27–28). Those researching the links between religion and political tolerance will need to stay alert to new measurement developments (compare with Mondak and Sanders 2003).[2]

RELIGION AND POLITICAL TOLERANCE: THE TWO BODIES OF LITERATURE

From the very beginning, studies of American attitudes toward civil liberties (i.e., political tolerance) included some consideration of religion. Indeed, Stouffer's (1955) *Communism, Conformity, and Civil Liberties* found that both religious behavior and religious affiliation influenced political tolerance. Regular church attenders were less tolerant than those attending irregularly or not at all, and southern Protestants were more intolerant than both their northern brethren and Roman Catholics, who in turn were less tolerant than the small subsample of Jews (Stouffer 1955, pp. 142–143). And although Stouffer (1955) found that "civic leaders" were consistently more tolerant than the mass public, religious factors worked in the same fashion among both groups. These results held up under controls for other variables.

In a later comprehensive study using GSS data, Nunn et al. (1978, p. 122) found that "Americans who are most committed to religious institutions are typically among the most ethnocentric—the least willing to extend the benefit of the doubt." Using the same items as Stouffer (1955), Nunn et al. (1978) found that tolerance had increased dramatically since the 1950s. Nevertheless, the relationship between religious variables and tolerance remained consistent. High church attendance encouraged intolerance, and although Protestants and Catholics had similar levels of tolerance, Jews were more tolerant than either, and the nonreligious were most tolerant of all. Like Stouffer (1955), Nunn et al. (1978) questioned community leaders and found them more tolerant than the mass sample, but religious variables worked similarly for both. In addition to gauging the influence of religious behavior and belonging, Nunn et al. (1978) also considered the impact of religious belief, such as belief in God and the devil. They concluded that political intolerance was linked to belief in the devil, most strongly among the less educated and the less affluent. They surmised that such belief leads to intolerance, because "nonconformity" is viewed as the work of the devil.

In contrast to Stouffer (1955) and Nunn et al. (1978), Sullivan et al. (1982) gave only brief attention to religion in their groundbreaking work. They found a substantial bivariate difference between those with a denominational attachment and those with none; the nonreligious were far more likely to fall into the "more tolerant" category than were Protestants, Catholics, and Jews. Although the differences between Protestant denominations proved small, Baptists exhibited less political tolerance than Presbyterians, Episcopalians, Methodists, or Lutherans (Sullivan et al. 1982, p. 138). On the whole, when utilizing their content-controlled measure, Sullivan et al. (1982) found few differences in tolerance among Protestants, Catholics, and Jews, in contrast to the findings by Stouffer (1955). They concluded that religion was important insofar as one had a denominational attachment rather than none, but that the particular denomination was of little consequence (Sullivan et al. 1982, p. 139). Like the earlier work of Stouffer (1955) and Nunn et al. (1978), Sullivan et al. (1982) used crude measures of denominational affiliation and made no effort to aggregate denominational families (e.g., Baptist, Lutheran, and so forth) into religious traditions (e.g., evangelical, mainline). Nor did they consider religious behavior or commitment.

In a final multivariate analysis, Sullivan et al. (1982) made perhaps their most important finding concerning religion: It had no independent influence on tolerance. "Secular detachment" (a three-point index of "Baptist," "other religion," and "no religion") had no direct influence on either political tolerance or norms of democracy, and only a small impact on psychological security (Sullivan et al. 1982, p. 222). The finding is important in that support for "norms of democracy" and "psychological security" are key predictors of political tolerance (Finkel et al. 1999; Sullivan and Transue 1999; Gibson 2006, 2007). In sum, the early research by Sullivan et al. (1982), the gold standard for tolerance scholars, assessed only the impact of religious belonging—using very crude measures—and left out of the analysis any measures of religious belief and behavior.

Shortly after this research was published, McClosky and Brill (1983) reported one of the most comprehensive analyses of political tolerance in America. Like Stouffer (1955) and Nunn et al. (1978), they used both mass and elite samples, and like much of the scholarly work preceding them, they concluded that religion had a negative influence on political tolerance. Although they explicitly recognized several dimensions of religion, they ended up using rather crude affiliation and belief measures. Regarding religious affiliation, they found that Jews, Episcopalians, and those with no religious affiliation were most supportive of civil liberties, whereas Baptists scored lowest (McClosky and Brill 1983, pp. 404–405). McCloskey and Brill (1983, p. 406) also used a variable called "religiosity," defined as "strength of religious conviction...the degree to which respondents value and rely upon religious beliefs and modes of explanation." This measure is better described as a combination of religious salience and traditional religious belief (conflating two separate dimensions of religion), with specific items varying from sample to sample (McClosky and Brill 1983, p. 406). In all three of their data sets (McClosky and Brill 1983, pp. 406–411), increased "religiosity" reduced support for civil liberties, even controlling for education. In general, the relationship between both religious belonging (or affiliation) and religious belief ("religiosity") and political tolerance was similar in both elite and mass samples, although once again elites were more tolerant than the mass public. Thus, McClosky and Brill (1983) strongly suggested the importance of religion for political tolerance, but they did not engage in extensive multivariate analysis, their measures of religious affiliation and belief were less than ideal, and they ignored religious behavior.

If we overlook measurement problems and summarize the political tolerance scholarship from Stouffer (1955) through McClosky and Brill (1983), we would conclude that religion has a negative effect on political tolerance. This conclusion would have to be held lightly, however, for religion was not a central independent variable in any of the studies cited so far, and it was measured without much care. As suggested by Peffley, Knigge, and Hurwitz (2001, p. 380), mainstream studies investigating the impact of religion on political tolerance are the exception, and not the rule.[3]

Why has mainstream political tolerance scholarship neglected religion? First, religion is but one of the sociodemographic variables that have received attention. Others, like education, have attracted more interest, because the relationships between higher education and tolerance have been robust. In addition, religion is one of the most difficult sociodemographic variables to conceptualize and measure (compare with chapter 1 in this volume; see also Wald and Wilcox 2006). Indeed, some investigators almost literally gave up on undertaking a sophisticated analysis of religion because of its complexity (see, for example, McClosky and Brill 1983, p. 403). And all the sociodemographic variables took a back seat to the three variables that emerged as key predictors of tolerance: psychological insecurity, commitment to democratic values, and threat perceptions. These predictors are captured in figure 15.1 in what can be labeled the *standard model of political tolerance* (compare with Gibson 2006).

Much of the best political science scholarship since Sullivan et al. (1982) has been preoccupied with better conceptualization and measurement of these three key predictors (Marcus et al. 1995; Peffley et al. 2001; Hurwitz and Mondak 2002; Mondak and Sanders 2003; Davis and Silver 2004). This scholarship has taken several different, but often overlapping, directions: in-depth examination of personality factors (Marcus et al. 1995; Stenner 2005), the role of threat perceptions (Gibson and Gouws 2003; Davis and Silver 2004), experimental designs (Marcus et al. 1995; Gibson 1998), methodological research (Gibson 1992; Mondak and Sanders 2003), and comparative analysis of tolerance in the United States and other countries (among the scores of publications, compare with Sullivan, Shamir, Walsh, and Roberts 1985; Gibson and Duch 1993; Sullivan, Walsh, Shamir, Barnum, and Gibson 1993; Gibson 2002, 2004). Clearly, political tolerance scholars had other fish to fry. Religion was not on their radar screens.[4]

Figure 15.1 Standard model of political tolerance

Religion Scholars and Political Tolerance

Political tolerance has also been investigated by religion specialists, mainly in political science and sociology. Indeed, the number of studies in this genre is quite large. Robert Postic (2007, p. 84) located 112 full-length articles on tolerance after a thorough web search, many of them outside of the "mainstream." Table 15.2 includes selections from the research by religion specialists. The chart includes the authors, the year the study was published, data sources, the religious measures used by the authors, and findings on the relationships between religion and tolerance.

Like the studies of mainstream scholars, work by religion specialists usually finds some link between religion and intolerance; but, surprisingly, most do not sort out which aspects of religion produce intolerant attitudes.[5] Is it religious affiliation, religious beliefs, religious practices, or some combination of the three that leads to intolerance? The results of the research of the religion specialists are unclear in this regard. Many early studies are also characterized by limited multivariate analysis, although this is not as true of more recent research. However, even when sophisticated multivariate analysis is conducted, it is often done with measures of religion that do not take advantage of the possibilities within the data sets employed.

The earliest work on the willingness to grant civil liberties to unpopular or disliked groups emphasized the differences between the mass public and activist or elite groups (Stouffer 1955; Prothro and Grigg 1960; McClosky 1964; Nunn et al. 1978; McClosky and Brill 1983), with the latter much more "tolerant" in their responses. Most studies cited in table 15.2 focus on the mass public because the GSS data are from the populace at large. There are a few exceptions when both elite and mass data are explored with similar results to the earlier studies (e.g., Jelen and Wilcox 1990). In addition, there have been a few studies of activist groups that do not allow for easy comparisons with the mass public—of PAC contributors (Guth and Green 1991) and religious activists (Green et al. 1994),[6] but these are the exceptions. As scholarship proceeds, further efforts should be made to explore the links between religion and intolerance among elites and activists as well as in the mass public.

Although the traditional political tolerance literature has tended to ignore religion, or to give it short shrift, the work by religion scholars also has difficulties. In particular, it fails to include the key determinants of political tolerance, identified by "mainstream" scholars. If measures of personal insecurity, threat perceptions, and commitment to democratic values are not included in the analysis, it makes it difficult to assess the independent effects of religion on intolerance. However, if the analysis is done on data without these key "predictor" variables, there is little that can be done about it.

Table 15.2 suggests a number of additional conclusions. First, note the dependence on the GSS for both measures of political tolerance and measures of religion in the vast majority of studies. This approach has the virtue of allowing longitudinal analysis with the same measures. If, however, either tolerance or religion measures are flawed, the testing of theory is limited. This suggests taking a careful look at both tolerance *and* religion measures in the GSS.

Table 15.2 Overview of Political Tolerance Research by Religion–Politics Specialists

Author, Year	Data Source	Religious Measures	Findings on Tolerance
Lenski, 1962	Detroit-area study 1959	Affiliation (Protestant, Catholic, Jewish, black Protestant).	Middle-class white Protestants most tolerant, then Jews, Catholics, and black Protestants. No religious differences among working-class whites.
Whitt and Nelsen, 1975	Detroit-area study 1959; southern Appalachian study	Biblical inerrancy. Adventism—world coming to an end soon plus God punishes and rewards in next life. Moral traditionalism—drinking, gambling, and so forth—is wrong.	"Biblicism," "Adventism," and moral traditionalism linked to intolerance of atheists, but only the last holds up in multivariate analysis. Study of native-born white Protestants only.
Filsinger, 1976	GSS 1973	Affiliation (Protestant, Catholic, Jewish, none), church attendance.	Intolerance of atheists related to high church attendance and Protestant affiliation.
Corbett, 1978	Muncie, Indiana survey	Literal bible; belief in miracles.	"Fundamentalists" intolerant.
Steiber, 1980	Detroit-area study 1958 and 1971	Affiliation (Protestant, Catholic, Jewish). Piety—importance of God in making decisions.	White Protestants more tolerant than blacks and Catholics, but personal piety linked to intolerance.
Corbett, 1982	GSS 1977	Affiliation (Protestant, Catholic, Jewish, other, none), salience, church attendance.	Protestants most intolerant, followed by Catholics, Jews, and unaffiliated. High salience and attendance also related to intolerance.
Jelen, 1982	GSS 1972–1978	"Irreligious," "fundamentalist," "nonfundamentalist" based on crude denominational affiliation.	Irreligious most tolerant, then nonfundamentalists. Fundamentalists least tolerant, even with controls.
Smidt and Penning, 1982	GSS 1974, 1977, 1980	Church attendance.	Ideological conservatives more intolerant than liberals. High church attendance increases intolerance for the latter only.
Beatty and Walter, 1984	GSS 1976–1980	First study to provide an in-depth denominational breakdown.	Conservative Protestant denominations most intolerant. Some liberal Protestant denominations as tolerant as Jews and seculars.

(continued)

Table 15.2 Continued

Author, Year	Data Source	Religious Measures	Findings on Tolerance
Hunter, 1987	Evangelical colleges and seminaries. Public university. GSS 1982	Civil liberties scale for students has only one "political" item. Orthodoxy index, affiliation.	Evangelicals less tolerant than nonevangelicals in GSS. Young and college-educated evangelicals more tolerant than others. Public university students more tolerant than evangelical students.
Roof and McKinney, 1987	GSS 1972–1984	Affiliation: conservative, moderate, liberal Protestant.	Conservative Protestants most intolerant.
Bobo and Licari, 1989	GSS 1984	Affiliation: Protestant, Catholic, Jewish.	Education the focus, but in multivariate analysis religious affiliation had no impact on tolerance.
Jelen and Wilcox, 1990	GSS 1972–1987	Affiliation: evangelical and mainline Protestant, Catholic, Jewish, none.	Whites only: Tolerant responses vary by religious traditions, by target group, and content. Education controls: All Christian groups more intolerant when education issues the content of tolerance questions.
Wilcox and Jelen, 1990	GSS 1972–1988, Nunn 1973 survey	Nunn: Evangelical Protestant, other Protestant, Catholic, Jewish, none. Multi-item doctrinal orthodoxy. GSS affiliation: evangelical, fundamentalist, Pentecostal, other Protestant, Catholic, Jewish, none.	Whites only: Evangelicals and doctrinal orthodox most intolerant in Nunn survey. In GSS, evangelicals most intolerant even after controls; fundamentalists and Pentecostals most intolerant.
Guth and Green, 1991	Contributors to 60 PACs	Denominational orthodoxy ranging from fundamentalist–charismatics to none. Salience.	Fundamentalists, charismatics, and high religious salience most intolerant.
Ellison and Musick, 1993	GSS 1988	Fundamentalist Protestant by affiliation, attendance, theological conservatism scale with Bible, other theological items, and salience.	Fundamentalist Protestants and high attenders intolerant, but both are washed out by the effects of "theological conservatism."
Gay and Ellison, 1993	GSS 1985, 1987, 1988	Detailed denominational categories plus denomination families plus GSS FUND*.	Jews and no religious preference category most tolerant. "Conservative" Protestants, including southern Baptists, most intolerant. Moderate and liberal Protestants in between the groups.

Green, Guth, Kellstedt, and Smidt, 1994	Religious activist groups	Affiliation; orthodox and fundamentalist beliefs.	"Fundamentalists" most intolerant. Fundamentalism variable washed out impact of other religion items.
Davis, 1995	GSS 1987 and Gibson	GSS FUND* measure.	Religious fundamentalism related to intolerance for whites but not blacks.
Golebiowska, 1995	GSS 1988	Affiliation, church attendance.	Low religiosity directly related to "modern" values and indirectly related to intolerance.
Tamney and Johnson, 1997	Muncie, Indiana survey	Conservative versus mainline affiliation, fundamentalism index, attendance.	Tolerance questions on book banning only. Fundamentalism predicts intolerance for "conservative" Protestants.
Karpov, 1999	Stouffer items plus GSS 1972–1993	Attendance.	Tolerance of communists and atheists decreased with high attendance.
Smith, 2000	GSS 1996	Affiliation, religious self-identification items.	Self-identified evangelicals and fundamentalists, as well as "conservative" Protestants more intolerant.
Loftus, 2001	GSS 1973–1998	Affiliation, prayer in school, Bible measure.	"Fundamentalist" Protestants intolerant toward homosexuals.
Reimer and Park, 2001	GSS 1972–1998 whites only	Affiliation, attendance.	"Conservative" Protestants most intolerant. All whites becoming more tolerant. High attenders intolerant.
Karpov, 2002	GSS 1991, 1998; survey in Poland	Affiliation, beliefs, religious practices.	Evangelical orthodoxy (inerrancy of the Bible and born again) and theological orientations (positive about church and religious organizations have too little power) linked to intolerance.
Penning and Smidt, 2002	Evangelical college students, like Hunter (1984)	Affiliation, orthodoxy, fundamentalism, moral traditionalism, civic gospel.	Strong links from orthodoxy to fundamentalism to moral traditionalism to tolerance, but almost no direct tie. Tolerance items different from GSS.

(continued)

Table 15.2 Continued

Author, Year	Data Source	Religious Measures	Findings on Tolerance
Burdette, Ellison, and Hill, 2005	GSS 1988, limited use of GSS 2002	Affiliation with a mainline versus conservative Protestant distinction, Bible item, attendance.	Conservative Protestants less tolerant of homosexuals, mediated by attendance, views of Bible, and a few other "nonreligious" variables.
Tuntiya, 2005	GSS 2000	Affiliation using FUND.* Bible, attendance, prayer.	Affiliation not related after controls. Bible item related to intolerance. Attendance and prayer not significantly related to intolerance.
Hunsberger and Jackson, 2005	College students	Intrinsic versus extrinsic religion.	A key article for reviewing the social psychological studies of prejudice and tolerance.
Moore and Ovadia, 2006	GSS 1976–2000	Religious tradition, religious data by primary sampling unit.	Intolerance greater among evangelical Protestants where percentage of the evangelical population is highest.
Mason and Feldman, 2007	GSS 1988, 1998	"Fundamentalist" beliefs: Bible plus others. Affiliation using FUND.* High religiosity: attendance, prayer, strong preference.	Fundamentalist beliefs associated with intolerance. Highly religious do not tend toward intolerance.
Postic, 2007	GSS 2000–2004	Effort to use affiliation, belief, and practice items in multivariate analysis.	Religious affiliation has no independent effect on intolerance except for evangelicals when homosexuals are the group examined. Bible beliefs and high church attendance are related to intolerance.

Beginning in the 1990s, the General Social Surveys included a created variable FUND in their data files which divided respondents into the three categories of fundamentalists, moderates, and liberals based simply on their affiliation with particular religious denominations.

The introductory statement to the tolerance questions is as follows: "There are always some people whose ideas are considered bad or dangerous by other people." Note that the statement assumes that there are "bad or dangerous" people out there. This might encourage respondents to give intolerant answers. An alternative would simply have been to ask respondents whether they felt there are groups that are dangerous or a threat to the society, and, if so, to name the group or groups. In addition, a follow-up question (or questions) could ask about the "degree" of threat perceived by the respondent. Then tolerance questions could be asked about such a group (or groups).

The GSS then asks if atheists, socialists,[7] racists, Communists, militarists, and homosexuals[8] should be allowed to make a speech, allowed to teach in a college or university, or have their books removed from the public library. Five of the groups have been the focus of the three tolerance questions through most of the time period covered by GSS surveys (atheists, Communists, and homosexuals on the Left; racists and militarists on the Right). Typically, tolerance (or intolerance) scores are computed ranging from 0 to 15 points for each year of study (five groups times three tolerance items), with these scores serving as the key dependent variable in the analysis. At times, the analysis may focus on tolerance for a particular group, such as atheists or homosexuals, but this is not the common practice.

As noted earlier, mainstream political tolerance scholars have been critical of the groups listed by the GSS, arguing that the respondent should be able to select his or her "least-liked" group before being asked the tolerance items. Others have argued that perceptions of which groups are threatening changes, and therefore the groups listed should change. For example, when Stouffer (1955) asked tolerance questions about Communists in the 1950s, the party was perceived as a real threat; but few people today would regard it as such. Sullivan et al. (1982) listed the Symbionese Liberation Army as a "least-liked" group; it would be absurd to ask about the Symbionese Liberation Army today. However, the GSS is unlikely to change their listing of the five "bad or dangerous" groups for reasons of comparability over time. Nevertheless, arguably, it is preferable to ask whether the respondent perceives groups as threats to the society, and, if so, to name the groups. As for the tolerance items, lots of other possible questions come to mind apart from the GSS triad. The Sullivan items in table 15.1 are a good place to start. In fact, the more tolerance items posed, the greater the likelihood that a respondent will elicit an "intolerant" response.

As table 15.2 implies, there is a lack of consensus on how religion should be conceptualized, with, in most cases, minimal attention given to the issue. Rarely are measures of affiliation, beliefs, and practices all utilized in studies, despite the fact that they are available in GSS surveys. Often, religious classifications use crude categories of Protestant, Catholic, Jewish, other, and none, although the wide variety of denominations within Protestantism suggests the need for some sort of scheme to classify Protestants. Such schemes have been developed (Green, Guth, Smidt, and Kellstedt 1996; Steensland, Park, Regnerus, Robinson, Wilcox, and Woodberry 2000) that allow scholars to focus on the important distinction between evangelical, mainline, and black Protestants. In addition, the GSS has quite detailed codes for Protestant groups (see the variables DENOM and OTHER) that permit the application of these schemes.

In addition, scholars have often failed to use the belief questions in the GSS. An item that asks about belief in life after death has appeared in almost every survey since 1972, whereas a Bible item has been asked since 1984, as have measures concerned with conceptions of God. Two items concerning the sinful nature or inherent "goodness" of human beings were also added at about that time. In addition, in certain years (1988 and 1998) detailed religion modules included all kinds of religious belief measures. Scholars may find many of these items to be less than ideal, but they do allow for an examination of this important dimension of religion.

Religious practice or religious behavior items in the GSS are rarely all utilized by scholars as well. The church attendance measure would be the exception to this generalization. Frequency of prayer has been asked since 1984, whereas other behavior measures have appeared on occasion. In addition, religious identification or religious movement measures (identification as a "fundamentalist," for example) appeared for the first time in the GSS in 1996. A born-again identification item has been asked on occasion, whereas a religious salience measure has been part of GSS questionnaires almost from the start of the series. In documenting the plethora of religious measures, the point is simply this: Scholars who use the GSS to look at the links between religion and tolerance need to take full advantage of what the surveys have to offer, and, for the most part, the studies noted in table 15.2 have not done this.

In sum, religion scholars have reached similar conclusions to mainstream tolerance researchers: Religion is linked to intolerance. The former have been heavily dependent on the GSS with three consequences: (1) almost unanimous examination of tolerance in the mass public, and not among activists or elites; (2) failure to include the key political and psychological variables that mainstream tolerance scholars have found to be the best predictors of tolerance; and (3) failure to incorporate all the religion measures available in the GSS.

Most "mainstream" political tolerance scholars shy away from the GSS. The most plausible reason for this is that key predictors of tolerance are not included in GSS questionnaires.[9] Clearly, the "hotspot" in political tolerance research is not with exploring the impact of religion (or any other sociodemographic variable) on tolerance judgments. The result, as noted earlier, is that the work of mainstream tolerance scholars and religion scholars tends to be done in isolation from one another.

Efforts to Bring the Two Literatures Together

Two scholars have made serious efforts to bridge the gap between the two strands of literature: Beverly Gaddy and Marie Eisenstein. Gaddy (2003) argues:

> Nearly a half-century of research has confirmed that religious belief is indeed associated with intolerance.... In fact few, even among the religiously committed themselves, have challenged this linkage between religion and intolerance.... Actually there has been little comprehensive empirical examination of the relationship of religion to tolerance, and almost none using content-controlled measures. (p. 160)

Gaddy (1998, 2003) challenged the evidence supporting the link between religion and intolerance using a merged data set from the 1987 GSS and James Gibson's 1987 study, *Freedom and Tolerance in the United States*.[10] The study was unique in that it included an innovative effort to tap "disliked" groups (individuals selected up to 4 from a list of 13), six tolerance questions were asked rather than the three in the standard GSS survey, and questions were included involving "political and psychological traits that are significant predictors of tolerance . . . (support for democratic norms, perceptions of threat, dogmatism, self-esteem, and traditionalism)" (Gaddy 2003, p. 180). In addition, the Gibson data (1987 *Freedom and Tolerance* study) allowed for comparisons between the "least-liked" approach of Sullivan et al. (1982) and the usual GSS effort. Gaddy (2003) also developed a measure of religious commitment that went beyond the religious measures used previously by most scholars. All of these things allowed her to reexamine the relationships between religious variables and political tolerance.

Her findings stand in stark contrast to the previous literature.[11] First, she found that "orthodox" believers did not differ from other respondents in their selection of most disliked groups (Gaddy 2003, p. 174). Second, she found that believers and seculars did not "vary in their willingness to tolerate their least-liked group" (Gaddy 2003, p. 174). There were simply no appreciable differences between the two groups in mean tolerance scores. Finally, using the "least-liked" approach, Gaddy (2003) proceeded to examine the political, psychological, and demographic predictors of political tolerance vis-à-vis the religious variables. She concluded: "[R]eligion is not related to tolerance. This is partly because the religiously committed and orthodox vary from the non-orthodox and nonbelievers only in their social and demographic characteristics, and not in the political and psychological characteristics that are actually the sources of political tolerance" (Gaddy 2003, p. 177).

More important, when assessing the links between political tolerance and demographic variables (such as education, income, age, gender, and so on), as well as with ideology, no significant relationships were found, as there were when GSS political tolerance measures were used. Gaddy (2003, p. 177) attributed the latter findings to weaknesses in the GSS questionnaire—"poor measures of religion which inadequately captured religious belief and commitment." Although Gaddy (2003) did find differences between the orthodox and religiously committed and less orthodox religionists in terms of demographic variables, she demonstrated that the relationships between religion and intolerance were merely an artifact of the relationship between religion and those key demographic variables.

In addition, the religiously committed and orthodox believers did not differ from others in their psychological and political predispositions. After multivariate controls, these latter measures affected tolerance attitudes, washing out any impact of the bivariate relationships between religion and tolerance commonly found in the research of most of the religion scholars cited earlier in this chapter. Gaddy (2003) concluded:

> In sum, religious belief and religious commitment are unrelated to political tolerance. . . . Religion does not contribute to tolerance attitudes and, for the most part, is

not associated with characteristics that do contribute to tolerance attitudes, at least when tolerance is defined so as to require opposition or dislike. (p. 182)

Despite her findings, her research is rarely cited, although it challenges both the mainstream political tolerance literature and the work of religion scholars.

Following in Gaddy's footsteps, Eisenstein (2003, 2006b, 2008) reexamined the relationship between religion and political tolerance. Her research used a least-liked political tolerance measure, presenting respondents with two sets of four groups. From each set, respondents identified one group as their most disliked, resulting in two most-disliked groups. From those two groups, the most disliked was then chosen. In addition, an opportunity was given to each respondent to identify any group that they disliked more than the one previously chosen.

Eisenstein's (2006b, 2008) research also utilized measures of doctrinal ortho-doxy, religious tradition, as well as religious commitment in the model, and it also incorporated all the important political and psychological predictors from main-stream political tolerance scholarship. She concluded that "increased religious commitment did not directly lead to decreased levels of political tolerance; and doctrinal orthodoxy did not directly lead to decreased political tolerance" (2006b, p. 342). In fact, religious commitment had a direct and positive impact on political tolerance, whereas doctrinal orthodoxy had a statistically insignificant influence (Eisenstein 2006b, p. 338). These findings remained after controlling for religious tradition. The results were similar to those of Gaddy (2003).

In addition, using qualitative analysis of focus groups, Eisenstein (2008, chap. 3) concluded that the content of each focus group discussion demonstrated a commit-ment to liberal democratic politics on the part of evangelical, mainline, and black Protestants, as well as Roman Catholics. Members of these four different religious traditions had all been socialized into an acceptance of and a preference for a liberal democratic form of government. Eisenstein (2008, chap. 4) also designed a survey-based experiment to examine the linkage between religion, political tolerance, and issue attitudes. Because of the general conservative issue attitude position of evan-gelical Protestants, and the links found by numerous scholars between evangelical religion and intolerance, Eisenstein (2008, chap. 4) focused on the hot-button issues of abortion, stem cell research, and same-sex marriage. For each of these issue topics, respondents were asked whether their opposition to abortion, stem cell research, and same-sex marriage was based on either a social opposition (e.g., it is bad for society), a moral opposition (e.g., it is immoral), or a neutral opposition. Whatever the source of opposition, it made no difference in mean political tolerance levels.

There were limitations, however, to her research. First, the sample size was small (601 respondents) and from a single county in Indiana. Furthermore, the key predictors of political tolerance were measured by less than an ideal number of indicators. Finally, although religious tradition and religious commitment were measured in greater depth, doctrinal orthodoxy was tapped by a single biblical literalism item. Nonetheless, standard survey research, focus groups, and a survey-based experimental design all confirmed that there was no causal relationship between religion and intolerance.

FUTURE RESEARCH CONSIDERATIONS

It may seem unusual to suggest a return to the 1987 GSS–Gibson data set for further research, but that is, arguably, an appropriate starting point. Despite the strengths of Gaddy's (2003) research, it left some issues unresolved. Ideally, analysis of the effects of religion on tolerance attitudes would have a better set of religious measures than Gibson brought to the table in his 1987 *Freedom and Tolerance* survey. The measurement of religious tradition in GSS surveys has been controversial. Steensland et al. (2000) proposed a coding scheme to capture the religious affiliations of GSS respondents; however, only a few religion scholars (e.g., Moore and Ovadia 2006; Postic 2007) have attempted to use this method. Meanwhile, no mainstream political tolerance scholars have done so. The approach by Steensland et al. (2000) would allow scholars to examine the bivariate relationships between religious traditions (evangelical, mainline, and black Protestant, for example) and tolerance, and to create "dummy" variables for these religious traditions for multivariate analysis. Second, the Gaddy (2003) research used a measure of "religious commitment," but without the key ingredient in this concept: religious beliefs (Stark and Glock 1968). The term *commitment* implies beliefs. As noted earlier, the GSS contain a number of possible belief measures.[12] Ideally, using the 1987 *Freedom and Tolerance* survey Gibson data, one could examine the bivariate relationships between each of these religious measures, including church attendance, prayer, and a religious salience item (used by Gaddy (2003) in her religious commitment measure), and the individual tolerance questions, and for each GSS tolerance group as well as for each of the groups named in the least-liked approach that Gibson included in his 1987 *Freedom and Tolerance* study. So, do the Gaddy (2003) findings hold up under a more thorough test of the impact of religious variables? Then, ideally, a contemporary study could attempt a similar analysis in the 21st century. Such a study would incorporate the best work of mainstream political tolerance scholars as well as the best measures of religion. It might also include measures of intrinsic and extrinsic religion, dear to the hearts of the psychologists of religion (Hunsberger and Jackson 2005).[13]

Such a research effort should be done for elites and activists as well to determine whether tolerance findings are similar for each. We need to determine whether the traditional elite versus mass public findings with regard to tolerance have changed. And the groups to which tolerance questions are directed may need to be changed. To the point, Bolce and De Maio (1999a, b) have demonstrated that there is an extreme level of antagonism and antipathy against Christian fundamentalists, particularly among the highly educated and secular. Moreover, they have argued that "[f]rom the perspective of some in the media, Christian fundamentalists are the Christian Right, a political movement whose views on abortion, school prayer, and homosexuality they perceive as intolerant, extreme, and anti-pluralistic. . . ." (Bolce and De Maio 1999b, pp. 509–510).

Alongside these undertakings, there should be a serious reconsideration of the widespread view that religion, inherently, leads to intolerance. "There has also not been, in my estimation, satisfactory theory developed as to *why* the religiously committed should be more intolerant than other citizens" (Gaddy 2003, p. 160; emphasis in original). Although Gaddy (2003) acknowledges that churches may explicitly link religious values and policy on issues like abortion, for example, tolerance learning is more likely done in schools. As a result, little difference in tolerance judgments might be expected between strong religionists and others. Kraynak (2001, p. 1) reaches a similar conclusion via a different line of reasoning. He argues that within the American Christian community, there is widespread agreement that "the form of government most compatible with the Christian religion is democracy." Democracy is a God–ordained style of governance that is to be preferred above other types of governance. If he is correct that those within current American religious culture welcome "modern liberal democracy as a friend and an ally, even though they may criticize some of its features as misguided or downright immoral" (Kraynak 2001, p. 167), then there is no reason to conclude that there is a natural link between religion and intolerance.

Further support for Kraynak's argument (2001) comes from the work of Alan Wolfe (2003, p. 255) who wrote: "Religious believers blend into the modern American landscape. They increasingly live in suburbs, send their children to four-year liberal-arts colleges, work in professional capacities, enjoy contemporary music, shop in malls, raise confused and uncertain children, and relate primarily to other people with whom they share common interests."

Wolfe (2003, p. 248) makes the case that religion in America has gone through dramatic changes including "a palpable increase in religious toleration that extends to non-Christians." Yet, as he indicates, these changes have been hardly noticed in the public arena:

> Somehow the news about the transformation of American religion has not been transmitted, at least to a significant number of intellectuals who write about the subject. As they advocate one position or another about the proper role of faith in American public life, it is as if Jonathan Edwards is still preaching and his congregation is still quaking in fear. (Wolfe 2003, p. 249)

Can the changes in tolerance that Wolfe discusses be fully documented?

In conclusion, this chapter has argued that mainstream political tolerance literature has pursued one course, whereas scholars interested in the links between religion and tolerance have pursued another. The former has followed the course of "normal science," with research building on the work of predecessors. *Political Tolerance and American Democracy* by Sullivan et al. (1982) is more than a quarter century old and yet still dominates the field in a manner similar to Key's (1949) *Southern Politics* or *The American Voter* by Campbell, Converse, Miller, and Stokes (1960). Meanwhile, religion scholars have also examined political tolerance, buoyed on by the presence of readily available GSS data. In the near future, the two strands of literature should come together in a manner consistent with the suggestions made in this chapter.

NOTES

1. Psychologists of religion have developed a "cottage industry" based on the intrinsic–extrinsic distinction developed by Allport and Ross (1967). See a summary of this work in Hunsberger and Jackson (2005). Intrinsic religion focuses on the personal dynamics of religion (my faith permeates all aspects of my life), whereas extrinsic religion emphasizes the social benefits of the faith. This line of research has been used in studies of prejudice, but has rarely been used in political tolerance studies (for an exception, see Eisenstein [2004, 2006a]).

2. Weissberg (1998, p. 77) makes the following observation about the content-controlled method: "Recall that the choice of groups and activities deserving acceptance is privately made by the researcher . . . . Boundaries are authoritatively, privately, and quietly decided prior to the research, not openly discussed within the questionnaire." For an in-depth review and assessment of efforts to measure both commitment to democratic values and political tolerance, see Finkel et al. (1999).

3. In fact, a recent publication continues the practice of failing to examine the impact of religion (Gibson 2008). In this particular study, Gibson (2008) compared changes in levels of intolerance from Stouffer (1955) through 2005, when he conducted his study. Gibson (2008) does provide an updated list of "least-liked" groups by including "radical Muslims," "Christian fundamentalists," and abortion opponents and proponents. In brief, he concludes that the perception of constraints on individual freedom has increased since 1954, whereas intolerance itself has decreased. No sociodemographic variables are included in his analysis.

4. None of the major reviews of the tolerance literature (Finkel et al. 1999; Sullivan and Transue 1999; Gibson 2007) focused on the role of religion. This situation may be changing. At this writing, James Gibson is preparing an essay on "Religion and Tolerance" for a task force on religion and democracy in the United States. The task force was set up by The American Political Science Association (http://www.apsanet.org/section_684.cfm). As the citations in this section make clear, Gibson has been a leading scholar of political tolerance for a quarter century, and in preliminary analysis for the paper for the task force, Gibson finds that "religiosity," a composite of a number of religious measures, has a modest impact on intolerance (Gibson forthcoming).

5. Ellison and Musick (1993) show that the links between "fundamentalist" Protestantism (a measure of affiliation that more properly should be labeled "evangelical" Protestantism) and high church attendance and intolerance are washed out by "conservative" theology in an insightful use of the 1988 GSS.

6. Green et al. (1994, p. 43) conclude: "We can now summarize the impact of religion on tolerance. Fundamentalists are indeed less supportive of civil liberties than other religious activists, though not perhaps as severely intolerant as some observers suppose. Their special worldview reduces support for civil liberties directly, but it also helps generate a higher level of perceived threat, an aggressive distrust of the political process, and intense concern about moral decay, all of which reduce tolerance." "Fundamentalism" is measured by an index of biblical literalism, "born-again" experience, fundamentalist self-identification, belief in the "rapture" of the church, a premillennial view of scripture, and belief in the second coming of Jesus Christ, among other items (Green et al. 1994, pp. 35–36). "Fundamentalism" is differentiated from "orthodoxy" in which the latter is measured by items "such as salvation only through Jesus Christ, that He was fully God and fully man, and the historicity of the Virgin Birth and Resurrection" (Green et al.

1994, p. 36). The study also had separate measures for religious tradition and religious behavior. In multivariate analyses, however, only their "fundamentalism" variable demonstrated significant relationships with intolerance; it also demonstrated a negative relationship to threat perception.

7. This category or group was asked only until 1974.

8. The question asked about "a man who admits he is a homosexual."

9. Undoubtedly, this results from the work of Sullivan et al. (1979, 1982), who first made the argument that psychological and political variables were the most proximate influences on political tolerance.

10. The same respondents were interviewed for both data sets, thus enabling the two data files to be combined.

11. Gaddy (2003) used religious tradition as a proxy for orthodoxy. Furthermore, she developed a religious commitment variable by combining four separate dimensions: affiliation or belonging (e.g., did the respondent report a religious affiliation or not), level of religious salience, level of church attendance, and frequency of prayer. By combining the answers to all four of these dimensions, she created a scale of low to high commitment.

12. Essentially, Gaddy (2003) included measures for religious belonging and religious behavior, but she did not include a measure of religious belief. Thus, a central component of religion was excluded from the analysis.

13. Gaddy (1998, 2003) also suggested that examining the relationship between extrinsic and intrinsic religion (developed within the psychology of religion), and political tolerance would be a fruitful avenue of research. Those with an intrinsic religious orientation will be more likely to exhibit political tolerance than those with an extrinsic religious orientation. Although the religionist literature has historically demonstrated that religion leads to political intolerance, psychologists of religion have disagreed, although the disagreement has only recently been examined explicitly. Eisenstein (2004, 2006a) explicitly studied the linkages between extrinsic and intrinsic religious orientation to political tolerance, and her research was not able to demonstrate empirically the theoretical link predicted by the psychology of religion literature.

REFERENCES

Allport, Gordon W., and J.M. Ross. 1967. "Personal Religious Orientation and Prejudice." *Journal of Personality and Social Psychology* 5: 432–443.

Beatty, Kathleen Murphy, and Oliver Walter. 1984. "Religious Preference and Practice: Reevaluating Their Impact on Political Tolerance." *Public Opinion Quarterly* 48: 318–329.

Bobo, Larry, and Frederick C. Licari. 1989. "Education and Political Tolerance. *Public Opinion Quarterly* 53: 285–308.

Bolce, Louis, and Gerald De Maio. 1999a "Religious Outlook, Culture War Politics, and Antipathy toward Christian Fundamentalists." *Public Opinion Quarterly* 63: 29–61.

Bolce, Louis, and Gerald De Maio. 1999b. "The Anti-Christian Fundamentalist Factor in Contemporary Politics." *Public Opinion Quarterly* 63: 508–542.

Burdette, Amy M., Christopher G. Ellison, and Terrence D. Hill. 2005. "Conservative
    Protestantism and Tolerance toward Homosexuals: An Examination of Potential
    Mechanisms." *Sociological Inquiry* 75: 177–196.
Campbell, Angus, Phillip Converse, Warren Miller, and Donald Stokes. 1960. *The American
    Voter*. New York: Wiley.
Corbett, Michael. 1978. "Tolerance, Religion, and Personality." Presented at the annual
    meeting of the Southern Political Science Association, Atlanta, Georgia.
Corbett, Michael. 1982. *Political Tolerance in America*. New York: Longman.
Crick, Bernard. 1973. *Political Theory and Practice*. New York: Basic Books.
Davis, Darren W. 1995. "Exploring Black Political Intolerance." *Political Behavior* 17: 1–22.
Davis, Darren W., and Brian D. Silver. 2004. "Civil Liberties vs. Security: Public Opinion in the
    Context of the Terrorist Attacks on America." *American Journal of Political Science* 48: 28–46.
Eisenstein, Marie A. 2003. "Political (In)tolerance, Dogmatism, and Doctrinal Orthodoxy:
    Understanding the Determinants of Political Tolerance." *Journal of the Indiana
    Academy of the Social Sciences* 7: 44–56.
Eisenstein, Marie A. 2004. "Religion, Tolerance, and Democracy: Re-thinking the Role
    of Religion." Unpublished Ph.D diss., Purdue University.
Eisenstein, Marie A. 2005. "Religion, Values and Freedom of Speech in Public Places."
    Public Administration Times 28: 5 (8).
Eisenstein, Marie A. 2006a. "Religious Motivation vs. Traditional Religiousness: Bridging
    the Gap between Religion and Politics and the Psychology of Religion."
    Interdisciplinary Journal of Research on Religion 2, article 2. www.religjournal.com.
Eisenstein, Marie A. 2006b. "Rethinking the Relationship between Religion and Political
    Tolerance in the US." *Political Behavior* 28: 327–348.
Eisenstein, Marie A. 2008. *Religion and the Politics of Tolerance: How Christianity Builds
    Democracy*. Waco, Texas: Baylor University Press.
Ellison, Christopher G., and Marc A. Musick. 1993. "Southern Intolerance: A Fundamentalist
    Effect?" *Social Forces* 72: 379–398.
Filsinger, Erik. 1976. "Tolerance of Non-Believers: A Cross-Tabular and Log-Linear
    Analysis of Some Religious Correlates." *Review of Religious Research* 17: 232–240.
Finkel, Steven E., Lee Sigelman, and Stan Humphries. 1999. "Democratic Values and
    Political Tolerance. In *Measures of Political Attitudes,* ed. John P. Robinson, Phillip
    R. Shaver, and Lawrence S. Wrightsman, 203–296. San Diego, Calif.: Academic Press.
Gaddy, Beverly. 1998. "Faith, Truth, and Tolerance: Religion and Political Tolerance in
    the United States." Unpublished Ph.D diss., University of Nebraska. [Written under
    the name Beverly G. Busch.]
Gaddy, Beverly. 2003. "Faith, Tolerance, and Civil Society." In *Faith, Morality, and Civil
    Society,* ed. Dale McConkey and Peter Augustine Lawler, 159–195. Lanham, Md.
    Lexington Books.
Gay, David A., and Christopher G. Ellison. 1993. "Religious Subcultures and Political
    Tolerance: Do Denominations Still Matter?" *Review of Religious Research* 34: 311–332.
Gibson, James L. 1986. "Pluralistic Intolerance in America." *American Politics Quarterly*
    14: 267–293.
Gibson, James L. 1989. "The Structure of Attitudinal Tolerance in the United States."
    British Journal of Political Science 19: 562–570.
Gibson, James L. 1992. "Alternative Measures of Political Tolerance: Must Tolerance be
    'Least-Liked'?" *American Journal of Political Science* 36 (2): 560–577.
Gibson, James L. 1998. "A Sober Second Thought: An Experiment in Persuading Russians
    to Tolerate." *American Journal of Political Science* 42 (July): 819–850.

Gibson, James L. 2002. "Becoming Tolerant? Short-Term Changes in Russian Political Culture." *British Journal of Political Science* 32 (2): 309–334.

Gibson, James L. 2004. *Overcoming Apartheid: Can Truth Reconcile a Divided Nation?* New York: Russell Sage Foundation.

Gibson, James L. 2006. "Enigmas of Intolerance: Fifty Years after Stouffer's Communism, Conformity, and Civil Liberties. *Perspectives on Politics* 4: 21–34.

Gibson, James L. 2007. "Political Intolerance in the Context of Democratic Theory." In *The Oxford Handbook of Political Behavior*, ed. Russell J. Dalton and Hans-Dieter Klingemann, 323–341. New York: Oxford University Press.

Gibson, James L. 2008. "Intolerance and Political Repression in the United States: A Half Century after McCarthyism." *American Journal of Political Science* 52: 96–108.

Gibson, James L. Forthcoming. "The Political Consequences of Religiosity: Does Religion Always Cause Intolerance?" American Political Science Association—Task Force on Religion and Democracy in the United States.

Gibson, James L., and Raymond M. Duch. 1993. "Political Intolerance in the USSR: The Distribution and Etiology of Mass Opinion." *Comparative Political Studies* 26: 286–329.

Gibson, James L., and Amanda Gouws. 2000. "Social Identities and Political Intolerance: Linkages within the South African Mass Public." *American Journal of Political Science* 44: 278–292.

Gibson, James L., and Amanda Gouws. 2003. *Overcoming Intolerance in South Africa: Experiments in Democratic Persuasion.* New York: Cambridge University Press.

Golebiowska, Ewa A. 1995. "Individual Value Priorities, Education, and Political Tolerance." *Political Behavior* 17: 23–48.

Green, John C., James L. Guth, Lyman A. Kellstedt, and Corwin E. Smidt. 1994. "Uncivil Challenges? Support for Civil Liberties among Religious Activists." *The Journal of Political Science* 22: 25–49.

Green, John C., James L. Guth, Corwin E. Smidt, and Lyman A. Kellstedt. 1996. *Religion and the Culture Wars.* Lanham, Md.: Rowman & Littlefield.

Guth, James L., and John C. Green. 1991. "An Ideology of Rights: Support for Civil Liberties among Political Activists." *Political Behavior* 13: 321–344.

Hunsberger, Bruce, and Lynne M. Jackson. 2005. "Religion, Meaning, and Prejudice." *Journal of Social Issues* 61: 807–826.

Hunter, James Davison. 1987. *Evangelicalism: The Coming Generation.* Chicago, Ill.: University of Chicago Press.

Hurwitz, Jon, and Jeffrey J. Mondak. 2002. "Democratic Principles, Discrimination and Political Intolerance." *British Journal of Political Science* 32: 93–118.

Jelen, Ted G. 1982. "Sources of Political Intolerance: The Case of the American South." In *Contemporary Southern Political Attitudes*, ed. Laurence W. Moreland, Tod A. Baker, and Robert P. Steed, 73–91. New York: Praeger.

Jelen, Ted. G., and Clyde Wilcox. 1990. "Denominational Preference and the Dimensions of Political Tolerance." *Sociological Analysis* 51: 69–80.

Karpov, Vyacheslav. 1999. "Political Tolerance in Poland and the United States." *Social Forces* 77: 1525–1549.

Karpov, Vyacheslav. 2002. "Religiosity and Tolerance in the United States and Poland." *Journal for the Scientific Study of Religion* 41: 267–288.

Key, V.O. Jr. 1949. *Southern Politics in State and Nation.* Knoxville, Tenn.: University of Tennessee Press.

Kraynak, Robert P. 2001. *Christian Faith and Modern Democracy: God and Politics in the Fallen World.* Notre Dame, Ind.: University of Notre Dame Press.

Lenski, Gerhard 1962. *The Religious Factor.* Garden City, N.Y.: Doubleday.

Loftus, Jeni. 2001. "America's Liberalization in Attitudes toward Homosexuality, 1973 to 1988." *American Sociological Review* 66: 762–788.

Marcus, George E., John L. Sullivan, Elizabeth Theiss-Morse, and Daniel Stevens. 2005. "The Emotional Foundations of Political Cognition: The Impact of Extrinsic Anxiety on the Formation of Political Tolerance Judgments." *Political Psychology* 26: 949–963.

Marcus, George E., John L. Sullivan, Elizabeth Theiss-Morse, and Sandra L. Wood. 1995. *With Malice toward Some: How People Make Civil Liberties Judgments.* Cambridge: Cambridge University Press.

Mason, Lilliana, and Stanley Feldman. 2007. "Religion, Fundamentalism, and Intolerance among Protestant Christian Americans." Presented at the annual meeting of the Midwest Political Science Association, Chicago, Illinois, April 12–15.

McClosky, Herbert. 1964. "Consensus and Ideology in American Politics." *American Political Science Review* 58: 361–382.

McClosky, Herbert, and Alida Brill. 1983. *Dimensions of Tolerance.* New York: Sage.

Mondak, Jeffrey J., and Mitchell S. Sanders. 2003. "Tolerance and Intolerance, 1976–1998." *American Journal of Political Science* 47: 492–502.

Moore, Laura M., and Seth Ovadia. 2006. "Accounting for Spatial Variance in Tolerance: The Effects of Education and Religion." *Social Forces* 85: 2205–2222.

Mueller, John. 1988. "Trends in Political Tolerance." *Public Opinion Quarterly* 52: 1–25.

Murphy, Andrew. 1997. "Tolerance, Toleration, and the Liberal Tradition." *Polity* 29: 593–623.

Nunn, Clyde Z., Harry J. Crockett, Jr., and J. Allen Williams, Jr. 1978. *Tolerance for Nonconformity.* San Francisco, Calif.: Jossey-Bass.

Peffley, Mark, Pia Knigge, and Jon Hurwitz. 2001. "A Multiple Values Model of Political Tolerance." *Political Research Quarterly* 54: 379–406.

Penning, James M., and Corwin E. Smidt 2002. *Evangelicalism: The Next Generation.* Grand Rapids, Mich.: Baker Academic.

Postic, Robert K. 2007. "Political Tolerance: The Effects of Religion and Religiosity." Unpublished Ph.D. diss., Wayne State University.

Prothro, James W., and Charles M. Grigg. 1960. "Fundamental Principles of Democracy: Bases of Agreement and Disagreement." *Journal of Politics* 22: 276–294.

Reimer, Sam, and Jerry Z. Park. 2001. "Tolerant (In)civility? A Longitudinal Analysis of White Conservative Protestants' Willingness to Grant Civil Liberties." *Journal for the Scientific Study of Religion* 40: 735–745.

Roof, Wade Clark, and William McKinney. 1987. *American Mainline Religion.* New Brunswick, N.J.: Rutgers University Press.

Smidt, Corwin E., and James M. Penning. 1982. "Religious Commitment, Political Conservatism, and Political and Social Tolerance in the United States: A Longitudinal Analysis." *Sociological Analysis* 43: 231–246.

Smith, Christian. 2000. *Christian America? What Evangelicals Really Want.* Berkeley, Calif.: University of California Press.

Stark, Rodney, and Charles Glock. 1968. *American Piety.* Berkeley, Calif.: University of California Press.

Steensland, Brian, Jerry Z. Park, Mark D. Regnerus, Lynn D. Robinson, W. Bradford Wilcox, and Robert D. Woodberry. 2000. "The Measure of American Religion: toward Improving the State of the Art." *Social Forces* 79: 291–318.

Steiber, Steven R. 1980. "The Influence of the Religious Factor on Civil and Sacred Tolerance, 1958–1971. *Social Forces* 58: 811–832.

Stenner, Karen. 2005. *The Authoritarian Dynamic.* New York: Cambridge University Press.

Stouffer, Samuel A. [1955] 1992. *Communism, Conformity & Civil Liberties: A Cross-Section of the Nation Speaks Its Mind.* New Brunswick, N.J.: Transaction Publishers.

Sullivan, John L., James Piereson, and George E. Marcus. 1979. "An Alternative Conceptualization of Political Tolerance: Illusory Increases, 1950's–1970's." *American Political Science Review* 73: 233–249.

Sullivan, John L., James Piereson, and George E. Marcus. 1982. *Political Tolerance and American Democracy.* Chicago, Ill.: University of Chicago Press.

Sullivan, John L., Michal Shamir, Patrick Walsh, and Nigel S. Roberts. 1985. *Political Tolerance in Context: Support for Unpopular Minorities in Israel, New Zealand, and the United States.* Boulder, Colo.: Westview Press.

Sullivan, John L., and John E. Transue. 1999. "The Psychological Underpinnings of Democracy: A Selective Review of Research on Political Tolerance, Interpersonal Trust, and Social Capital." *Annual Review of Psychology* 50: 625–650.

Sullivan, John L., Pat Walsh, Michal Shamir, David G. Barnum, and James L. Gibson. 1993. "Why Politicians Are More Tolerant: Selective Recruitment and Socialization among Political Elites in Britain, Israel, New Zealand, and the United States." *British Journal of Political Science* 23: 51–76.

Tamney, Joseph B., and Stephen D. Johnson. 1997. "Christianity and Public Book Burning." *Review of Religious Research* 38: 263–271.

Tuntiya, Nana. 2005. "Fundamentalist Religious Affiliation and Support for Civil Liberties: A Critical Reexamination." *Sociological Inquiry* 75: 153–176.

Wald, Kenneth D., and Clyde Wilcox. 2006. "Getting Religion: Has Political Science Rediscovered the Faith Factor?" *American Political Science Review* 100: 523–529.

Weissberg, Robert. 1998. *Political Tolerance: Balancing Community and Diversity.* Thousand Oaks, Calif.: Sage Publications.

Whitt, Hugh P., and Hart M. Nelsen. 1975. "Residence, Moral Traditionalism, and Tolerance of Atheists." *Social Forces* 54: 328–340.

Wilcox, Clyde, and Ted G. Jelen. 1990. "Evangelicals and Political Tolerance." *American Politics Quarterly* 18: 25–46.

Wolfe, Alan. 2003. *The Transformation of American Religion: How We Actually Live Our Faith.* New York: Free Press.

CHAPTER 16

RELIGION AND POLITICS AND THE MEDIA

C. DANIELLE VINSON

IN 1999, Jerry Falwell garnered considerable media coverage of his suggestions that Tinky Winky, a character on a PBS children's program, showed signs of being gay. The story received attention in many national news outlets, and the coverage ranged from amusement to mocking and disdain for Falwell. Although it would be easy to dismiss the Falwell versus Tinky Winky episode as merely a colorful and entertaining blip in the media's coverage of religious figures, Falwell's decision to take on Tinky Winky and the subsequent media coverage it generated illustrate many of the issues that arise when media, religion, and politics intersect.[1]

The incident began when Falwell used his own religious media to raise an important social and political issue, an increasingly common practice among religious leaders or groups, especially on the Right. The story was then picked up by the mainstream media. Although some trivialized it (by putting it in features or style sections of the paper and by treating it humorously), others gave voice to gay rights advocates offended by Falwell, while largely ignoring those voices who agreed with Falwell on the larger issue of homosexuality, if not the particulars of Tinky Winky. Both story lines lend validity to complaints by some religious groups, particularly on the Right, that the media are biased against religion (or at least do not cover it seriously).

It is clear that religion and religious leaders are often newsworthy in the context of American politics, but what do we really know about how they are covered by mainstream media? Is coverage biased against religion generally or certain religious denominations or traditions specifically, as many on the religious and political Right claim? Is coverage of religion and politics sensationalized or trivialized? Why is religion and politics covered the way it is? And how do religious media fit into the information environment? What political content do they cover, and how do religious leaders or groups use this alternative media? And what effects, if any, does coverage of religion and politics have on political behavior and attitudes? These are the questions that will guide the following discussion as we look at the existing research on religion and politics and the media. After examining the key findings in the field, I will evaluate the existing research and identify potential directions for future research.

Two major tracks are evident in the scholarship on religion and politics and the media. The first focuses on how mainstream media cover the intersection of religion and politics. Most scholars find a trend toward religion being covered as hard news, as a part of larger stories on politics or public issues. This kind of coverage has prompted accusations of media bias against religion or certain religious traditions, though the evidence of bias is somewhat mixed. The second major branch of the existing research examines how religious leaders and groups have tried to use the media—both mainstream and alternative religious media— for political purposes. These scholars find that political content of religious media and the messages of religious leaders and groups has increased over time. We will explore these findings in more detail in the following sections.

RELIGION BECOMES HARD NEWS

Serious coverage of religion by the media is a relatively new phenomenon (Hoover 1998). Traditionally, religion was considered a marginal beat, reflecting the conventional wisdom "that religion was not a serious object of press scrutiny; that it deserved limited and compartmentalized treatment; that the journalists that covered it were less professional," and that readers were not very interested (Hoover 1998, p. 4). As long as most of society viewed religion as a private matter, the media were content to avoid controversy and not to cover it unless necessary, and then to do so with deference to religious institutions and to relegate it to religion pages (Hoover 2002, p. 79).

During the late 1970s and early '80s, a series of events changed the nature of the media's coverage, expanding it beyond the religion pages into the A section of the papers with the politics and hard news. Three events, according to Hoover (1998), were important in this transformation. First, with the election of Jimmy Carter, a self-proclaimed born-again Christian, to the presidency, the media became interested in the potential political power of evangelical Christians. Second, Carter's election coincided with the rise of religious broadcasting and televangelists who were increasingly willing to venture into the realm of politics. And, finally, the Iran hostage crisis and its connection to Islamic fundamentalists added an international dimension to the coverage of religion.

As a result of these events, religion coverage has become more mainstream. Buddenbaum (1990) offers evidence of this through her excellent content analysis of network news. For one constructed month from 1976, 1981, and 1986, she analyzed religion stories broadly defined to include not only mentions of religion, religious institutions, or religious persons, but also stories that use religious language or show "a religious person, institution, or symbol . . . in a way that suggests the story would tell the average viewer something about religion" (Buddenbaum 1990, pp. 251–252). She found that most religion news is not primarily about religion but that it covers religion in the context of politics and disputes involving religious factions. Close to half the coverage dealt with foreign affairs like conflicts in the Middle East and Northern Ireland. She also found that religion was treated like hard news in most coverage. Reflecting common news values, the focus of these religion stories was mostly on conflict and violence, as well as a few human interest stories.

It is common now to see religion covered as part of a variety of political contexts. Hoover (1998, p. 208) mentions the frequency of stories about the political activism of religious organizations, noting that as religious groups and individuals have become "more active in attempting to prosecute their [political] agendas in the mediated public sphere," the media often see them more as a "pressure group" than a religious institution that would traditionally have warranted deferential coverage. Indeed, no presidential campaign would be complete these days without some media coverage of the mobilization of religious groups, particularly on the Right, and the impact of their religious beliefs on their voting decisions (see, for example, Vinson and Guth 2009).

Campaigns offer additional avenues for hard news coverage of religion. In most campaigns since 1976, the press has engaged in some coverage of the candidates' religious beliefs. During the 1980s, coverage moved away from religious institutions and shifted toward stories on the individual religious spirituality of presidents and candidates (Hoover 2002, p. 81). This was certainly true during the 2004 campaign, although the media were more explicit in exploring the link between the candidates' faith and their policy positions than Hoover (2002) had observed earlier (Vinson and Guth 2009). In addition, journalists now give heed to the religious rhetoric of candidates (Muirhead, Rosenblum, Schlozman, and Shen 2006; Vinson and Guth 2009).

Religion has also become a common feature in coverage of certain policy areas, especially those linked to the culture war. Some of this occurs in the context of political campaigns, as was true in 2004 when stem cell research, abortion, and gay marriage all found their way into the campaign coverage (Vinson and Guth 2009). However, religion in policy debates is not limited to the campaigns. End-of-life controversies like the Terry Schiavo case in Florida or physician-assisted suicide legislation in Oregon and its subsequent Supreme Court case have attracted the involvement of religious activists who, in turn, were covered in the press (Miller and Niven 2007).

And sometimes religious institutions or leaders do or say something on their own that merits coverage under the media's standards of newsworthiness. David Koresh and his Branch Davidian followers engaged in a standoff with federal agents in Waco, Texas, in 1993 that drew substantial media interest. The Revs. Pat Robertson, Jesse Jackson, and Al Sharpton all garnered significant media attention when they decided to run for president, although former Baptist pastor and Arkansas governor Mike Huckabee discovered in 2007 that being a pastor is no guarantee of early coverage in a presidential bid. And Falwell's publicly expressed concerns about Tinky Winky's impact on children is one in a long line of provocative statements by religious leaders on social and political issues that have attracted media attention.

Antireligion Bias in the Press?

From this brief discussion, it is clear that today religion news is a regular part of hard news and has to meet standards of newsworthiness. As such, it is no longer covered just by the religion editor and, consequently, religion is treated less deferentially than it was during the first half of the 20th century (Hoover 1998, pp. 24–28). As religion finds itself covered like hard news, the inevitable question of bias in coverage arises. Whether the media are biased against religion or specific religious groups is an undercurrent in nearly all the existing research—theoretical and empirical—on how media cover religion. We will begin with the theoretical debate.

On one side are those who believe that religion has been pushed out of the public square, a development that is reflected in media coverage that is, at best, skeptical or even cynical about religion and that, at worst, is antireligious. Stephen Carter's (1993) book *The Culture of Disbelief* typifies this line of thinking. Carter (1993) asserts that American society does not want religion in the public square. Society does not mind if people believe in God and the supernatural, but "you really ought to keep it to yourself" (Carter 1993, p. 25). According to Carter (1993, p. 49), there was an increasing trend during the 1990s toward attacking the religious commitment of religious activists—that is, raising concerns about what motivates them or their use of religious language—rather than criticizing their position or cause. Carter (1993) offers the example of those who complained about the 1992 Republican convention's "God talk" rather than the actual positions Republicans were taking on such issues as prayer in the schools. And he offers anecdotal evidence that candidates who appear to take their religion seriously are viewed with suspicion in the media, citing most notably the coverage Pat Robertson received during his run for the Republican presidential nomination in 1988 (Carter 1993, p. 59). Schultze (2003, pp. 30–31) adds some nuance to this debate, saying that all people, even Christians, can participate in public life—but only if they are not overtly religious: "Faith commitments are relegated to private space so that anyone who enters the public square with a religious interest is likely to be discussed as a fanatic or criticized as an interloper." From the assertion that religion has been banished from the public sphere emerges the claim that the media are secular if not blatantly hostile to religion.

On the other side of the theoretical debate are those who do not see the media as biased against religion or even as secular. Mark Silk (1995, p. xii) articulates this position, claiming the "media present religion from a religious rather than secular point of view." He (Silk 1995, p. 55) explains that the media cover religion in a cultural context that includes religion's own culture of exposing wrong. To illustrate this, Silk identifies five *topoi* or story lines that commonly appear in coverage of religion: (1) good works, what churches are or should be doing; (2) tolerance, the virtue of tolerance and vice of intolerance; (3) hypocrisy, seen in coverage of preachers caught in scandal (or, we might add, politicians who have affairs even while campaigning on a platform of family values); (4) false prophesy, concerns about particular religious beliefs such as polygamy or the Branch Davidians in Waco; and (5) inclusion, often seen in coverage of members of minority religions in the United States and their similarity to ordinary Americans.

Silk (1995, p. 57) claims the media are predisposed to view religion as good and are critical when religion is misused, contending that those who complain about media's coverage of religion are not seeing the big picture, but only what offends them. They fail to see the positive press coverage of religion "as reflecting any point of view . . . because it is a point of view they share" (Silk 1995, p. 141).

Although Silk's (1995) argument that the media are not secular or particularly biased against religion is not tested empirically, possible media bias against religion is a recurring theme throughout empirical studies of media coverage of religion and politics. In her content analysis of network news, Buddenbaum (1990, p. 258) finds that coverage was fair to the extent that no religious group that was the subject of more than three stories was covered completely favorably or unfavorably. However, she notes several other aspects of coverage that leave the press open to charges of bias. Not all religions were covered equally or even representatively. Catholics were mentioned most often and most consistently across the years of her study whereas mainline Protestants and evangelicals were barely noticed (Buddenbaum 1990, pp. 255–256). Neither was coverage representative in the types of stories reported; instead, the majority focused on conflict, and many were sensational. Finally, Buddenbaum (1990, p. 259) points out that while most stories included multiple perspectives, a quarter may have appeared biased against religion by giving a secular spokesperson or reporter the last word. Many of the possible sources of bias that Buddenbaum (1990) identifies are picked up and elaborated on in studies that focus on more specific political contexts in which religion is covered.

Related to, but distinct from, the issue of media bias is the matter of religious stereotyping. Many religious groups complain that the media stereotype them in their coverage. And there is at least some evidence to suggest that three different kinds of religious stereotyping occur—namely, (1) that members of a religious group are all alike, (2) that religious people are extremists, and (3) that religious people are relatively uneducated, particularly those in the religious Right.

Dionne (2006) sees evidence of the first stereotype in press coverage of the 2004 election. He notes that the press attributed Bush's victory to the turnout of the religious Right, although Bush's gains actually came from moderates and the less religious among whom Kerry did not do as well as he needed to do. Thus, to some extent the media failed to portray the complexity of religion and the diversity evident within religious groups by implicitly suggesting in their coverage that all Christians were conservative (Dionne 2006, p. 199).

At other times, coverage of religion fosters a stereotype that religious people or groups are extremists. Muirhead et al. (2006, pp. 226–227) note that in an effort to fuel the idea of a culture war there is a tendency to interview the extremists from both sides of the divide (i.e., ardent secularists and religious traditionalists), thereby leaving out the moderate religious groups found in the middle. And other coverage of religion can easily be framed in such a fashion (e.g., conflict between the Israelis and Palestinians or coverage of Islamic terrorists).

The final stereotype that bothers critics of the media is the portrayal of religious people, especially on the Right, as uneducated and irrational. Vinson and Guth (2009) found evidence of this during the 2004 presidential campaign as the press compared the impact of Bush's irrational faith on policies, including the Iraq war and stem cell research, with Kerry's rational intellectual approach to policy making. Schultze (2003, p. 282) offers another more subtle example: With headlines like the *Grand Rapids (Michigan) Press*' "Religious Right Shaped by Reason," the media reported a study that found religious Right voters made rational voting decisions by choosing candidates who agreed with them. According to Schultze (2003), the fact that the press deemed this newsworthy reveals the media's implicit assumption that religious people—at least those on the Right—are not rational.

Besides stereotyping, another reason for allegations of press bias against religion may be negative portrayals of certain religious groups. Although little research on coverage of specific religious groups or traditions in the context of politics exists, a couple of studies suggest that some groups, especially minority religions may have a valid concern. For example, in a qualitative study on media coverage of the siege at the Branch Davidian complex in Waco, Texas, in 1993, Richardson (1995) offers evidence that the media marginalize cults or new religions and that coverage is often anticult. In the Waco case, the media referred to the Branch Davidians as a cult and reported federal agents' statements that frequently demonized the group's leader, David Koresh. Furthermore, when the media sought "expert" sources on cults, they often turned to groups like the Cult Awareness Network, which helps people who want to leave cults. Although Richardson (1995, p. 163) acknowledges that journalists were not allowed access to the Branch Davidians, which certainly limited coverage, he says the media's willingness to portray the group on the government's terms without humanizing members or taking their religious beliefs seriously made the Davidians "unworthy victims" who elicited little sympathy from the public, thus making it possible for the government to end the siege as it did.

Likewise, Muslims are another minority religious group that has frequently received coverage in the context of foreign and domestic politics in recent years, and evidence suggests it may have been largely negative in nature. In a well-crafted study involving content analysis of local and national news before and after the terrorist attacks on 9/11, Nacos and Torres-Reyna (2007) look at how media cover Muslims and the extent to which coverage was stereotypical or negative. They find, as have others, that the media are not always precise in their use of religious labels, often using Muslim and Arab interchangeably. Prior to 9/11, they found coverage to be quite negative and stereotypical. It focused on conflict and the ties between Muslims and terrorists. Common in the coverage were stories about campaign controversies in which a candidate for office was criticized for receiving campaign contributions or endorsements from Muslim groups or individuals who were later accused of having links to terrorists. Somewhat surprisingly, coverage of Muslims immediately after 9/11 was more positive, centering on concerns about curbing the civil liberties of Muslim Americans. In this coverage, Muslims were given more of a chance to speak for themselves as sources in the stories. However, some of these improvements in coverage were short-lived. A year after 9/11, there continued to be more Muslim sources used in coverage, but the positive stories had declined, replaced by more negative accounts (Nacos and Torres-Reyna 2007, pp. 29–30).

This particular study is a good illustration of the complexities in assessing the media's portrayal of a religious group within a political context. Coverage is affected by different events involving the group, some of which are positive and some of which are negative. If the events involving a particular group are consistently negative, then is such negative coverage necessarily evidence of bias or is it simply a reflection of reality? Also, a religion's practitioners in the United States may be covered differently than its practitioners in other parts of the world, or no distinctions may be made—either of which may have an impact on the favorability of coverage. Nacos and Torres-Reyna (2007) also found that gender mattered at least in the message of the visuals used in the news. Muslim men were usually depicted negatively whereas Muslim women were shown in neutral or sympathetic ways.

One group that has traditionally been unhappy with its media coverage has been the religious Right. Their dissatisfaction is related to a broader dissatisfaction among those who believe there is an overall bias against conservatism—political and religious—in the elite mainstream media. Although research on political bias in the media more generally has been mixed at best,[2] there is surprisingly little systematic research on the media's portrayal of the religious Right and whether that coverage is fair. Most of what we suspect is simply based on anecdotal evidence or is the by-product of studies on other topics. For example, in *The Culture of Disbelief,* Carter (1993) claims that candidates who appear to take their religion seriously are viewed suspiciously by the media, but only with regard to those candidates they do not like (usually those on the Right). He provides two examples. The first is drawn from the 1992 presidential election in which news reports characterized George H. W. Bush's speeches to religious organizations as "pandering," whereas Bill Clinton's speeches to religious groups were described as "shrewd" (Carter 1993,

p. 59). The second is the contrasting coverage that the Revs. Jesse Jackson and Pat Robertson received in their attempts to gain their respective parties' nominations for president in 1988. Garry Wills (1990, p. 63) corroborates Carter's impression. His own recollection was that coverage of Jackson was largely secular, a feat that required ignoring Jackson's religious language, whereas coverage of Robertson always focused on his religion. Wills (1990) notes that the press simply failed to notice the religious similarities between the two candidates. Vinson and Moore (2007) found a similar, if more subtle, example in national media coverage of the 2000 Republican presidential primary in South Carolina: George W. Bush endured much scrutiny and criticism for his visit to Bob Jones University and his campaign to win the votes of the religious Right, but the national press ignored John McCain's own quiet efforts to court the Bob Jones crowd even though reporters actually witnessed or knew about such efforts.

In 2004, the religion of both presidential candidates was an important topic, but concern about how the candidates' beliefs would influence their policies was raised only in conjunction with Bush (Vinson and Guth 2009). The press worried openly about Bush's "faith-based" presidency, with at least one pundit critiquing Bush's choice of devotional readings (Wright 2004). Yet, even when Kerry declared that the Bible would influence him, journalists reported the statement without elaboration or analysis. The press extended this discrepancy in coverage to the voter mobilization efforts of churches on both sides of the 2004 campaign. Democratic campaign activities in black churches were reported as routine whereas Republican efforts through evangelical groups were called into question (Vinson and Guth 2009). In all these cases, the religious beliefs, statements, and strategies of the candidate closest to the political Right were scrutinized more closely in the press than those of the more moderate or liberal candidates.

In addition, qualitative research shows that the Christian Right is often portrayed as being both effective in mobilizing and influencing elections or policy but is covered in a way that suggests its concerns challenge or threaten society's norms of freedom of religion, speech, and press (Buddenbaum 1990). Adding to this evidence, a content analysis of newspaper coverage from around the country between 1980 and 2000 by Kerr and Moy (2002) found a somewhat negative portrayal of fundamentalist Christians as intolerant and too likely to push their views on society. These findings lend some credence to the claims by evangelicals and those in the religious Right that the press treats them differently and with more suspicion than other religious traditions or groups.

Still, we must be careful about drawing conclusions on the basis of a few examples and limited content analysis of specific campaigns or groups. Two other studies challenge the conventional wisdom about coverage of the religious Right. The first is a study by Miller and Niven (2007) that looked at news coverage of end-of-life issues in the congressional vote on the Terry Schiavo controversy and the Supreme Court case challenging Oregon's Death with Dignity Act. Although Miller and Niven (2007) found the overall tone of coverage to be negative, most coverage was balanced, and the religious activists—many of whom were on the Right—were portrayed more positively than negatively. Although the study does not offer much qualitative discussion of the context and reporting on the religious activists, it does suggest that coverage of the religious Right is not always negative.

The second study, conducted by Media Matters for America (2007), makes the bold claim that coverage of religion in politics "overrepresents some voices" in ways that are advantageous to conservatives, giving little room to religious leaders on the Left. After analyzing all of the stories in major newspapers and television newscasts from November 2004 through December 2006 that mentioned any of 20 major religious leaders (10 on the Right and 10 on the Left), the authors concluded that conservative voices received substantially more attention than liberal leaders.

There are a few methodological problems with this study. Most important, it leaves out so-called "celebrity" religious leaders who not only comment on events and issues, but also become the news. These include Jesse Jackson and Al Sharpton on the Left, and James Dobson, Pat Robertson, and Jerry Falwell on the Right. One could argue that regardless of whether these men sometimes make the news, they are still seen by the media as moral or religious voices for their respective sides of the debate; to leave them out is to neglect a significant source of commentary. Furthermore, excluding them skews the results as Sharpton's and Jackson's combined coverage exceeds that of the three conservative celebrities by almost 2000 mentions.

A second methodological concern is that there is no way of knowing the context in which the leaders were covered, because the focus of the analysis is simply on whether they were quoted or mentioned.[3] Without information about the substance of the articles, we do not know whether the religious leaders' comments were framed authoritatively or were challenged within the stories. For this reason, more coverage for conservatives might not necessarily mean advantageous coverage. These shortcomings notwithstanding, the study offers a path toward more systematic, objective, and measurable ways of evaluating media coverage of and potential bias against particular religious traditions, raising the possibility that the religious Right may not be as negatively treated by the press as conventional wisdom suggests.

Secular Reporters or Journalistic Culture?

Although there is little systematic data on how media cover religion and the extent to which antireligious bias really exists in the press, the thesis of media bias has gained sufficient currency for some scholars to explain why it exists. The explanations fall into two camps: (1) reporters are not religious and do not understand the complexities of religion, or (2) the secular nature of reporting is an inevitable consequence of journalistic standards and processes. We will look at the evidence for each of these.

Drawing on his own experience as a reporter in the 1988 election, Garry Wills (1990, p. 18) wrote that editors and reporters were not comfortable with religion and most were not practitioners of religion. Because religion writers were not regularly assigned to cover candidates on the campaign trail, even when preachers like Jesse Jackson and Pat Robertson were running, secular reporters were left to make sense of the mix of religion and politics in the campaign. Journalists' religiosity (or lack of it) has been the subject of almost as much debate as the partisanship of reporters. The study by Lichter, Rothman, and Lichter (1986) of elite journalists was an opening salvo on this issue. Surveying elite journalists in New York and Washington, DC, the authors found that half the reporters claimed no religious affiliation and 86 percent attended religious services seldom or never, thus raising the question of whether journalists with nominal religious ties could be expected to understand those of faith or even be aware of, interested in, or take seriously the religious aspects of newsworthy issues and events.

Some scholars took issue with the Lichter study, noting that it only looked at journalists in two cities and defined religiosity fairly narrowly. Therefore, a number of scholars and organizations have conducted their own surveys during the past 20 years with varying results. Studying a wider variety of journalists—religion reporters, investigative journalists, and generalists—across the country, Underwood and Stamm (2001) attempted to broaden the definition of religiosity beyond affiliation with a particular denomination or faith. They found that 72 percent of the journalists said religion or spirituality was important to them. This mirrored the results of a 1993 Freedom Forum survey of editors (reported in Underwood and Stamm [2001]). Most surveys since 1986 have found higher levels of church attendance and a greater willingness to claim a specific religious affiliation (see, for example, Rothman's research reported in Underwood and Stamm [2001]). Yet the large majority of reporters do not attend church very often, and Rothman and Black (1999) maintain that elite reporters continue to be less religious than other elites. And beyond simple measures of affiliation and church attendance, we have very little data about the religious beliefs and worldviews of media personnel.

The real problem is that this research has been unable to do more than allow us to speculate on the impact of reporters' relatively weak religious connections. Intuitively, the argument makes sense that people without strong religious ties will, at a minimum, not understand the complexities of religion and religious institutions and, at worst, will be hostile to them. However, we have done little to test this. In this sense, the concern about the secularism of reporters parallels that of the partisanship of reporters. Is it possible for a Democratic journalist to cover Republicans fairly? Is it possible for a secular reporter to cover religion fairly? The current research has offered few definitive answers largely because it has not taken the leap from describing the religious and partisan attitudes of journalists to studying the impact of those attitudes on their actual reporting. Underwood and Stamm (2001) move us a step closer to this by asking journalists to respond to a series of statements applying various religious values to journalistic practice. They find that even "religiously oriented journalists" are "cautious about endorsing explicitly religious values," suggesting personal beliefs may not have a major impact on reporting (Underwood and Stamm 2001, p. 780).

One growing body of literature provides a theoretical foundation to help us understand the finding by Underwood and Stamm (2001). It maintains that the culture of journalism—its values, standards, and processes—is much more important in shaping news about religion and politics and the secular direction of reporting than any individual reporter's personal beliefs would be. In his research, Hoover (2002) explains that religion creates some particular difficulties for the press. Historically, it has been viewed as a source of controversy, and its complexity poses a problem for reporters who may not be experts and who must use story formats that are often short and leave little room for extended explanations. Journalism also deals with the empirical, not the spiritual—a sort of "just-the-facts" mentality that emphasizes what is known and can be observed. Matters of faith and intangible spirituality are at odds with that mind-set and culture (Hoover 2002, p. 75ff). Coverage of religion is further complicated by the lack of a "consensual public language of religion" on which journalists can rely, which increases their discomfort with the subject (Hoover 1998, p. 210).

Given these challenges, the media have turned to the same professionalism and practices they use in covering other hard news, and it is that professionalism, some argue, that has pushed journalism in a secular direction (Schultze 2003, p. 266). In the interest of professionalism, the media often encourage distance from their subjects. Thus, the *Washington Post's* notice for a religion writer specified that "[t]he ideal candidate is not necessarily religious nor an expert in religion" (Schultze 2003, p. 276). Anyone can cover religion just as anyone can cover politics or sports, and indeed the media tend to cover all three in similar ways, focusing on facts and objective information. Schultze (2003, p. 277) refers to this as "informational fundamentalism," an intentional play on religious fundamentalism's strict and often unquestioning adherence to its doctrines and religious texts. This leads to reporting that may notice that a religious group has gained prominence or influence (for example, religious voters in 2000 or 2004) but cannot explain why the group has become active in politics or the theological beliefs that have pushed it in particular directions.

This concept of informational fundamentalism fits well with the theoretical work Cook (1998) has done on the media as a political institution. He details the institutional norms and processes that guide the decisions reporters and editors make in selecting and reporting the news. Cook (1998) notes that the practices and standards intended to make news objective (such as reporting facts, relying on sources, and looking for news in particular places) are the very factors that lead the media to favor certain issues, events, groups, and individuals over others in their coverage of politics. Schultze (2003, p. 287) similarly claims that this devotion to informational fundamentalism that demands neutrality and skepticism, particularly toward religion, inherently creates a "bias against religion" in journalism.

Hoover (2002) offers some specific examples of the consequences of the choices reporters make in the name of professionalism and journalistic standards. Treating religion as hard news requires religious leaders and groups to play by the media's rules in coverage. Therefore, if religious leaders or groups expect to speak for a particular group, their links to their constituencies must be validated with evidence, and those who cannot do that are dismissed. The media are more interested in general values than the particular values of a specific faith or sect, and religious groups that can frame their issues in those general terms are more likely to make the news. Finally, the media deal in rationality and things that can be verified. This means that the beliefs of some groups may be subject to suspicion in the press. Take, for example, the media's coverage of the Branch Davidians in Waco, Texas. Press coverage, in part reflecting the views of government agents and the public, failed to recognize that group members took their apocalyptic beliefs seriously regardless of how irrational they may have sounded to the press (Shupe and Hadden 1995; Hoover 1998, pp. 2–4).

We see additional evidence of this tendency in the 2004 presidential election. The press accepted John Kerry's assertions that he would follow the social justice dictates of the Bible to help the poor and work for justice; such claims were verifiable and not particularly mysterious (Vinson and Guth 2009). However, some journalists had real problems with Bush's claims of being led by his faith in God and sustained by prayer; as Maureen Dowd explained, Bush's reliance on faith "equates disagreeing with him [Bush] to disagreeing with Him" (Vinson and Guth 2009). The problem for reporters was that Bush's beliefs could not be easily validated empirically, leaving them quite skeptical and sometimes hostile to the intermingling of that kind of faith with politics. Intentional or not, the culture of journalism requires certain decisions about how religion is covered that may help account for the secularism or bias against religion and certain religious groups that some analysts see in the coverage.

Religion Uses the Media

To this point the chapter has focused on how mainstream media cover religion in the context of politics, but another track in the existing research is how religious leaders and groups use the media. There is no doubt that "in contemporary (media-saturated) public life, religious *people* and *institutions* have an incentive to engage in 'publicity'" (Hoover 1998, p. 10, emphasis in the original). They can do this in one of two ways: create their own alternative media or communicate through the mainstream press. Religious leaders, particularly those on the "theocratic Right," have done both (Berlet 1998). I will begin our discussion by looking at the alternative religious media, their purpose, content, and effects.

Religious media are not new in American society. Schultze (2003, p. 93) provides a detailed look at some of the many religious publications that began in the 1800s, and he notes that "the religious press was not just an organ for religious news but also a forum for religiously engaging the wider culture." Feeling excommunicated from the public square, religious leaders have fought back by creating their own media as a way to protect their own culture and foster "communities of resistance against mainstream culture" (Schultze 2003, pp. 28–31). Gross (1990, 231) contends that the creation of religious television was a direct response to concerns that mainstream media were pushing the philosophy and values of secular humanism; the religious Right could not control its image and agenda if it was mediated by the mainstream press, but the group could compete through its own media.

The alternative religious media have taken many forms, and the religious Right has been particularly adept at incorporating new technologies. Beginning primarily with print media in the forms of magazines and newsletters, the leaders of the religious Right have added radio and television. Popular examples include Pat Robertson's Christian Broadcast Network (CBN) that broadcasts Robertson's own *700 Club* and Dr. James Dobson's syndicated radio show *Focus on the Family*. However, the growth extends beyond specific Christian shows and Christian-owned stations and networks like Robertson's CBN or Salem Communications in radio. Today, the religious Right has entire synergistic networks of interrelated media that include television, radio (satellite and regular), magazines, fax alerts, and websites (Lesage 1998b). It is not uncommon for the host of a Christian television show to direct people to a website for additional information on a topic discussed in the show or to include promotions for other radio and television shows and advertising for Christian magazines, making it possible for audiences to receive information in whatever way individuals prefer. The willingness to embrace new technologies has also allowed religious groups to respond quickly to events and issues through the media. In 2004, for example, many religious websites popped up during the election. The Republican National Committee set up a site called kerrywrongforevangelicals.com, and Southern Baptists provided the website IVoteValues.com, with comparisons of the candidates and voter registration information (Denton 2005, p. 264).

Although the primary purpose of these alternative media is to communicate a religious message and evangelize, there is growing evidence that many of these media also include political messages. Schultze (2003, p. 117) found that some early religious magazines like *Christian Century* began, over time, to discuss many of the same kinds of issues discussed in the mainstream press, such as "foreign and domestic political affairs and social justice." However, a study of religious television programming in 1983 initially found mostly religious content and an emphasis on evangelism with little political content. In their excellent content analysis of the religious television programs most widely available to people across the country, Abelman and Neuendorf (1987) saw little focus on politics or political problems, but some attention to social issues. What political content they did find seemed to be concentrated in programs with a magazine-type format, and it was usually presented in a fairly neutral way, although if it was discussed with a particular perspective, it was usually conservative. However, given the increasing visibility of televangelists in the 1980s and the high-profile scandals involving some of them, the authors updated their research to determine whether these changes had affected content. Indeed, they found that in 1986 there was a noticeable increase in political themes among some televangelists, including Pat Robertson and Jerry Falwell (Abelman and Neuendorf 1987).

These findings have been confirmed and elaborated in more recent research. Noll (2002) has found that the subject matter in evangelical magazines has become more politicized, and Berlet (1998) has noted that the political content on Christian broadcast media has become overtly political. James Dobson frequently discusses public policy issues that affect families on his radio show (Lesage 1998b). Frankl (1998) explains that religious broadcasters like Pat Robertson offer information on current issues of interest to their viewers with "traditional moral values." And although their political appeals were at one time made in explicitly religious terms (Podesta and Kurtzke 1990, p. 208), Frankl (1998) finds that to bring more people into their efforts, religious leaders have moved beyond theology and doctrine to focus on broader Christian values. The shift toward political content has extended even to Christian entertainment. Robertson's entertainment-oriented Family Channel on cable has moved from saving souls to raising awareness of social and political issues like abortion (Frankl 1998, p. 177).

In addition to the increasing political content, Christian media emphasize action. Listeners and viewers are encouraged to contact members of Congress in response to the issues discussed on the shows (Frankl 1998). Christian radio, television, and print media often provide their audiences with advice on how to get involved to influence policy and elections (Ammerman 1998, p. 97; Lesage 1998b, p. 32).

Another development in the political content of Christian media is that it is increasingly presented in formats that resemble mainstream media, making the political messages more subtle than they would be if delivered through sermons and lectures. Robertson's *700 Club* follows CBN's own news show that looks just like regular news, with reporters covering stories from various locations, but it does contain a Christian perspective (Frankl 1998; Lesage 1998b). Meryem Ersoz (1998) offers an in-depth look at how one fairly typical Christian radio station has adopted a format that looks and sounds like that of an adult contemporary radio station, but with a decidedly "traditional family values" message. She describes a mix of music, short segments on practical issues like handling money, entertainment, and talk shows (some of which deal with political issues and encourage political action) that are not obviously different from secular radio. Schultze (2003, p. 34) also notes this trend and an increase in personality-driven radio formats on Christian radio. He explains that part of the purpose in mimicking secular radio and television formats is to attract a larger audience to religious media, although he worries that the secular formats will cause religious groups to lose their distinctiveness and be co-opted into the mainstream.

Given the increasing political content of religious media and the efforts to expand the audience, we might reasonably be curious about the effects of religious media. Although little systematic research has been done on this, a few notable studies suggest some evidence of religious media effects. Perhaps most obvious is the higher visibility of religious leaders in mainstream media. Pettey (1990, p. 202) claims that part of the media's willingness to cover the Moral Majority in the 1980s was Falwell's visibility, due in large part to his involvement with religious media.

Frankl (1998, p. 174) notes that religious broadcasters like Robertson have created an image of themselves in their own media as leaders in society's culture war, and that has carried through to mainstream media that turn to these leaders to comment on the culture war issues. High visibility combined with television or radio audiences in the millions allows these religious leaders to meet the media's requirement to validate their following, and thus their authority and credibility to speak for more than just themselves. The media then accept them into the circle of legitimate sources for news stories that have a moral dimension.

Research also suggests that religious media have enjoyed some success in mobilizing voters and political activists. Most of the audience for religious media tends to be religious and therefore more likely to share already the political positions and concerns raised by the shows' hosts (Abelman and Hoover 1990). They do not really need to be persuaded to accept the views of the program, but they may need to be encouraged to do something about those views. A number of studies claim that religious media were important in mobilizing the Moral Majority and evangelicals to get involved in politics in the 1970s and '80s (see, for example, Pettey 1990). Podesta and Kurtzke (1990, p. 213) credit televangelists for laying "the intellectual groundwork for 'religious right' interest groups and grassroots activists to defeat" policy makers critical of them.

Although much of this research is anecdotal, some surveys provide evidence of media effects on participation and attitudes. Gross (1990, p. 234) offers survey data to support this, noting that high levels of general television viewing are associated with lower levels of political activity, but frequent viewers of religious television are more likely to vote—possibly because religious television explicitly encourages ways to act on what viewers see. In one of the more sophisticated studies on the effects of religious media, Newman and Smith (2007) use survey data to investigate who used religious media for political cues in the 2000 election and what effect that use had on political attitudes and behavior. The authors found that nearly one fourth of respondents claimed to use religious media when making voting decisions, and those who did felt closer to the Republican candidates and were more likely to vote for the Republican candidates than those who did not rely on religious media, even when religious and political variables such as ideology, religious tradition, and political predispositions were controlled. Smidt, Kellstedt, Guth, and Green (2005) provide additional data to show that not only do religious traditions rely on religious and secular media to varying degrees—for example, evangelicals rely more on religious media than do mainline Protestants—but also that there are predictable distinctions within each religious tradition along the traditionalist–modernist divide. And the authors demonstrate that high reliance on religious media combined with low reliance on secular media was associated with voting for George W. Bush in 2004, but that media combination was also linked with lower voter turnout (Smidt et al. 2005, pp. 456–457). The anecdotal evidence and survey research combine to suggest that religious media produce political effects.

While creating their own alternative media, religious groups and religious leaders have not forgotten about the importance of mainstream media. As Cook

(1998) explains, news gathering is an interactive process among reporters, news makers, and the public. He describes a "negotiation of newsworthiness" in which reporters decide what to cover and whom to cover, and news makers decide what information to provide and how to shape it. Although Cook's focus is on political elites, Shupe and Hadden (1995) use a similar theoretical framework to illustrate what happens when news makers do not participate in this negotiation (whether by choice or by force). They note that in the siege of the Branch Davidian complex in Waco, government agents were able to interact freely with the media whereas the Branch Davidians' access to the press was blocked. Without this, their side of the story was largely unreported, and the media's reporting of the siege adopted the perspective of the government.

Religious leaders, particularly on the Right, seem well aware of the importance of trying to shape the mainstream media's news reporting by actively engaging reporters. Several studies have focused on their media relations efforts. Lesage (1998a) offers insight into the importance that the Christian Coalition places on media relations in her discussion of the group's training tapes, which offer practical advice on dealing with the press and provide rhetorical strategies for communicating based on standard advertising strategies. The tapes encourage local Christian Coalition chapters to put a communications staff together quickly, and they coach spokespersons to use catchy phrases, focus on only a few main points in an interview, and avoid too much analysis. The video emphasizes the importance of framing issues consistently and carefully, using terms like *pro-life* instead of *antiabortion*. The tactics are similar to what one would hear from any media consultant. Lesage (1998a) explains that the purpose behind the Christian Coalition's focus on media relations stems from its need to go beyond evangelicals to gain political influence. The organization needs to communicate with secular people and "to control its public rhetoric to capture the high ground rather than giving the press an occasion to describe it as driven by violence-prone crazies" associated with extremist conservative views (Lesage 1998a, p. 315).

Other scholars have noticed the religious Right's focus on framing the issues. Berlet (1998) highlights this and explains how the leaders on the Right work on the best way to frame the issues about which they are concerned first in their own religious media and then spread it to the mainstream media through interviews with reporters and their network of interest groups. He cites the example of antigay rights campaigns in the press, especially in Colorado in 1992, in which the religious Right cast the issue as homosexuals seeking "special rights or privileges" and explicitly rejected the notion that gay rights were an extension of the black civil rights movement. Schulze and Guilfoyle (1998) provide an in-depth look at the framing and tactics of the Colorado Family Values campaign to pass an amendment to prohibit giving homosexuals protected status in antidiscrimination laws in 1992.

It is evident in the scholarly research and in casual observation of the mainstream media that religious leaders and groups have become frequent participants in the negotiation of newsworthiness. Jesse Jackson, Al Sharpton, Pat Robertson, Jerry Falwell, James Dobson, and more recently Rick Warren have become familiar names far beyond their own religious denominations. It is not clear that they have always received the kind of media attention they wanted or have been effective in communicating their messages. Indeed, Falwell's experience related to the Tinky Winky incident suggests they are not always successful, which brings us back to how the media cover religion and the state of the existing research.

ASSESSING THE CURRENT STATE
OF THE FIELD AND GOING FORWARD

Although research on religion and politics in the media pursues important questions and themes, it has room for improvement in two major ways. First, it needs a methodological upgrade, and second, it needs to focus more attention on identifying and understanding the effects of mainstream and religious media's coverage of religion and politics, the impact of religious political messages, and the effects of religious leaders' media relations efforts. This section elaborates on these two concerns.

Too many of the existing studies make claims simply based on anecdotal or impressionistic evidence, or their findings are by-products of other research that is not particularly well equipped to answer the specific questions of interest to those wanting to know how media cover religion and politics. Only about one third of the studies cited in this chapter provided systematically gathered evidence to support their claims and draw conclusions.

Political communication research on media content and its effects has made enormous strides during the past 15 years, and almost none of those advances can be found in the literature on religion and politics. Content analysis has been made easier by the wealth of information (e.g., newspapers, television transcripts and even video, and political speeches) contained in computer databases and software designed to aid in content analysis. Yet, studies by Buddenbaum (1990) and Nacos and Torres-Reyna (2007) are notable because they are among the few that provide systematic content analysis that intentionally seeks to understand how media cover religion.

Surveys with relevant media questions are also increasingly available (see, for example, ANES and Pew Center for the People and the Press surveys), and although there are problems with many measures of religiosity and media use, the data that exist are underutilized. The work of Newman and Smith (2007) and Bolce and De Maio (2008) demonstrates the potential of these surveys to help link media content to political attitudes and behavior. Also missing from existing research are experimental methods. Incorporating these improved methods into the research would give scholars access to a wider range of data and allow them to explore questions about religion and politics and the media that have been difficult or even impossible to consider before.

One such question would be the effects of media coverage and religious communication on political behavior. This chapter has discussed a small and somewhat speculative body of literature on the effects of religious media, but Nacos and Torres-Reyna (2007) and Bolce and De Maio (2008) provide the only research we have found that explicitly tries to link mainstream media coverage of religion to public opinion or behavior. The media cover religion as part of politics. New research by Monson and Oliphant (2007) shows that parties and other groups are now using religious messages in their mailings and campaign communications in the new campaign strategy of microtargeting, and Domke and Coe (2007) have recently reported that presidents since 1980 use religious language more frequently than earlier presidents.

Domke (2004) has also argued that George W. Bush incorporated a religious fundamentalist worldview into his rhetoric on political events and issues after 9/11. Domke (2004) goes a step further to show that the media picked up many of Bush's fundamentalist themes, including a focus on good versus evil, urgency, and an enduring commitment and the universal gospel of freedom. Taken together, these developments suggest the political information environment is increasingly incorporating religious messages or perspectives.

The general literature on media effects would lead us to expect that this attention to religion would have an impact on the public, but there are good reasons to expect religious messages to be absorbed and processed differently than other kinds of political messages. Religion may be more personal for some people than politics and, thus, subject to different media effects. The existing scholarship on religion and politics has barely scratched the surface of this subject.

There is much that can be done to improve our understanding of how media, religion, and politics interact with each other. Above all, the research needs to focus on more systematic studies—both quantitative and qualitative—with a purpose of explicitly understanding how religion is covered as part of political stories and why it is covered as it is. The few studies, like Buddenbaum's (1990), that are based on content analysis and are intentionally designed to study media coverage of religion and politics need to be replicated with more recent coverage that takes into account the relatively recent developments of 24-hour news channels and the Internet. Future studies could focus on how the media cover religion in the context of hard news, much as Buddenbaum (1990) did, looking not only at the contexts in which religion is covered, but how it is framed and the religious sources used. This would add to our understanding of who speaks for religious groups and traditions in the media and would clarify the extent to which bias actually exists or what form it takes. Content analysis of the media's coverage of specific religious traditions or denominations would go a long way toward answering claims of bias in coverage. Such studies would need to go beyond simply determining the amount of coverage a group receives to the actual content of the coverage, and they would need to guard against the researchers' own selective perception through objective measures and careful "intercoder" reliability tests of subjective evaluations.

We can look to the political communications literature for examples of what this kind of research might look like. Hart, Jarvis, Jennings, and Smith-Howell

(2005) demonstrate the potential of extensive content analysis of a variety of media in their study of political key words. They examine how important political words—including *politics, government,* and *parties*—are used over time, the meanings or images associated with their use, and the implications of these conceptions. In the context of religion and politics, one might conduct a similar study using key words like *religious Right* or *Muslims,* or even a phrase like *separation of church and state.* Such studies could incorporate a wide range of media and be adapted for both long and short time frames.

A second study that would potentially translate well to a study of media coverage of religion and politics is Kellstedt's (2003) research on racial attitudes in the United States. He examines media coverage of race over nearly 45 years and illustrates how content analysis software can be used to help identify themes or values in the coverage. This kind of content analysis could be used to study coverage of religious groups and their involvement in politics or political issues such as abortion or prayer in the schools that have a moral or religious component and might allow us to see how successful religious leaders or groups have been in framing public issues. In addition, Kellstedt's (2003) research shows the potential for sophisticated statistical methods to link the ebb and flow of the various themes in coverage over time to shifts in public attitudes. Although this kind of longitudinal study of media effects may not yet be possible because of the lack of relevant survey data on attitudes toward religious groups or issues, it does offer a glimpse of what the future might look like for this field.

Beyond studying coverage of religion or religious groups in the press, analysis of specific issues or policy areas in which religious leaders and groups have been active might teach us more about the possible effects and effectiveness of religious groups' media relations efforts. One cannot help but wonder if the bias toward conservative religious leaders found in the study by Media Matters for America (2007) is not in part related to differences in media relations efforts of the religious Right and religious progressives. Given the religious Right's contention that the media are biased against conservatives and are moving in a secular direction, the Right's leaders may be more active in courting media coverage. Also, the Right's religious leaders may be more explicit in using religious language to talk about the issues with which they are most concerned than the Left's leaders, whose issues of concern (such as the environment or poverty) are less exclusively tied to religious arguments, causing the media to turn more readily to conservative religious leaders for a religious perspective on issues than liberal or progressive religious leaders. Comparisons of the language used by religious leaders in speaking about these issues in their own media and the language journalists use in reporting on them would help us understand the influence religious leaders have in shaping press coverage and public debates on policy.

Studies of religion and politics in the media also need to expand to include new media such as the websites of religious organizations and leaders that might contain political information and religious blogs. Political communications scholars are still grappling with how to study these new media, but there is some research that might provide a useful framework for studying the impact of religious websites and blogs on political participation and public debate (see, for example, Chadwick 2006). Johnson and Kaye (1998) used an online survey to try to ascertain the impact of Internet use on political attitudes and participation. One could envision a similar study that focuses on visitors to religious websites and blogs during the context of a campaign or even a national debate on a policy area such as stem cell research that has a moral or religious dimension.

Political communication research has identified a variety of media effects that would be worth exploring in the realm of religion and politics. I have already mentioned the possibility of religious leaders framing issues through their media coverage. What impact do religious leaders and religious media have on the agenda and framing of mainstream media? Do political elites or the public adopt these frames? Iyengar's (1991) classic experimental design for studying the impact of media frames could serve as a starting point for understanding the impact of religious framing of political issues.

Research might also look at the possible persuasive effects of media coverage on so-called moral issues. When religion is explicitly part of a story on an issue, are people more or less likely to change their minds? Again, experimental designs might prove beneficial. For example, Clinton and Lapinski (2004) used a web-based experiment to study the short- and long-term effects of negative advertising on participants in the 2000 presidential election. Such web-based studies may help overcome the potential limitations of more traditional in-person experiments and may expand the number of people who can participate in the experiment.

A final area of growing importance for the study of religion and politics in the media is the use of religious political messages by secular groups and political leaders. Monson and Oliphant (2007) note the increase of microtargeting as a campaign strategy. In microtargeting, parties, candidates, and interest groups can gather detailed demographic, political, and consumer information about citizens and then craft very specific messages to appeal to the concerns of narrow groups of voters, including religious voters. These targeted messages can go out across a variety of media—most commonly mailings, e-mail, or phone calls, but also as ads on specific radio or television programs. Monson and Oliphant (2007) found that parties, particularly the Republicans, were active in using religious messages in 2004. Given the success of microtargeting in helping to mobilize religious voters, we can expect this trend to continue in both parties. This provides an excellent opportunity for scholars to study the impact of secular groups and candidates using religious messages.

The intersection, and sometimes collision, of media, religion, and politics is an important aspect of American politics that has been seriously neglected by scholars. Religion and politics are inextricably linked in countless ways—from religion's impact on voters' decisions and the policy positions of elected officials to historical religious tensions that are the source of wars and conflict. Willingly or not, the media have become a central player in American politics; some would even say they are a political institution (Cook 1998). They decide what will be reported about politics and at the same time are used by political elites to communicate their messages to the public and each other. A better understanding of this interaction among the press and politics and religion is essential to understanding American politics.

NOTES

1. Under the headline "A 'Tubby' Ache for Jerry Falwell; Religious Right Leader Sees Gay Threat in Children's TV Character," the *Washington Post* reported that the Rev. Falwell had alerted parents in his magazine, *National Liberty Journal*, that Tinky Winky, one of the characters on the PBS children's show *Teletubbies*, showed signs of being gay (Rosin 1999, p. C1). According to Falwell, "The character, whose voice is obviously that of a boy, has been found carrying a red purse . . . . He is purple—the gay pride color; and his antenna is shaped like a triangle—the gay pride symbol" (Rosin 1999, p. C1). Rosin (1999) noted that Falwell forgot to mention Tinky Winky's penchant for wearing a tutu and dancing to "technobabble." An article in the *Atlanta Journal Constitution* (Kloer 1999) reported that Falwell was "late to the party" and somewhat slack as a cultural watchdog given that Tinky Winky's sexual orientation had been widely discussed in British newspapers for nearly two years. Many of the articles included dismissive quotes from those opposed to Falwell: "'Jerry Falwell's paranoia about gay people has reached a new and ludicrous high-water mark,' said . . . a spokesman for the Human Rights Campaign" (Rosin 1999, p. C1), and the chief executive officer of the company that licenses the show said, "The controversy is 'frankly stupid. I hope we get past it'" (Sparta 1999, p. 2D).

2. Miller and Niven (2007, p. 9) note that there is academic evidence supporting claims of liberal media bias, conservative media bias, and no bias. Graber (1989, pp. 102–103) explains some of the reasons why bias is so difficult to determine empirically.

3. The authors did exclude coverage of a scandal involving one of the leaders during the time studied, but beyond that we do not know what issues the leaders were commenting on and whether there were nonreligious sources providing commentary on the other side. It is possible that political rather than religious leaders on the Left were refuting the conservative religious leaders.

REFERENCES

Abelman, Robert, and Stewart M. Hoover, eds. 1990. *Religious Television: Controversies and Conclusions.* Norwood, N.J.: Ablex Publishing.

Abelman, Robert, and Kimberly Neuendorf. 1987. "Themes and Topics in Religious Television Programming." *Review of Religious Research* 29: 152–174.

Ammerman, Nancy T. 1998. "North American Protestant Fundamentalism." In *Media, Culture, and the Religious Right*, ed. Linda Kintz and Julia Lesage, 55–144. Minneapolis, Minn.: University of Minnesota Press.

Berlet, Chip. 1998. "Who Is Mediating the Storm? Right-Wing Alternative Information Networks." In *Media, Culture, and the Religious Right*, ed. Linda Kintz and Julia Lesage, 249–274. Minneapolis, Minn.: University of Minnesota Press.

Bolce, Louis, and Gerald De Maio. 2008. "A 'Prejudice' for the Thinking Classes: Media Exposure, Political Sophistication, and the Anti-Christian Fundamentalist." *American Politics Research* 36: 155–185.

Buddenbaum, Judith M. 1990. "Religion News Coverage in Commercial Network Newscasts." In *Religious Television: Controversies and Conclusions*, ed. Robert Abelman and Stewart M. Hoover, 249–264. Norwood, N.J.: Ablex Publishing.

Carter, Stephen L. 1993. *The Culture of Disbelief*. New York: Basic Books.

Chadwick, Andrew. 2006. *Internet Politics: States, Citizens, and New Communication Technologies*. New York: Oxford University Press.

Clinton, Joshua D., and John S. Lapinski. 2004. "'Targeted' Advertising and Voter Turnout: An Experimental Study of the 2000 Presidential Election." *The Journal of Politics* 66: 69–96.

Cook, Timothy. 1998. *Governing With The News*. Chicago, Ill.: University of Chicago Press.

Denton, Robert E., Jr. 2005. "Religion, Evangelicals, and Moral Issues in the 2004 Presidential Campaign." In *The 2004 Presidential Campaign: A Communication Perspective*, ed. Robert E. Denton, Jr., 255–282. Lanham, Md.: Rowman & Littlefield.

Dionne, E. J. 2006. "Polarized by God." In *Red and Blue Nation?*, ed. Pietro S. Nivola and David W. Brady, 175–205. Washington, D.C.: Brookings Institution Press/Hoover Institution.

Domke, David S. 2004. *God Willing? Political Fundamentalism in the White House, the "War on Terror," and the Echoing Press*. Ann Arbor, Mich.: Pluto Press.

Domke, David S., and Kevin M. Coe. 2007. *The God Strategy: How Religion Became a Political Weapon in America*. New York: Oxford University Press.

Ersoz, Meryem. 1998. "Gimme That Old-Time Religion in a Postmodern Age: Semiotics of Christian Radio." In *Media, Culture, and the Religious Right*, ed. Linda Kintz and Julia Lesage, 211–226. Minneapolis, Minn.: University of Minnesota Press.

Frankl, Razelle. 1998. "Transformation of Televangelism: Repackaging Christian Family Values." In *Media, Culture, and the Religious Right*, ed. Linda Kintz and Julia Lesage, 163–190. Minneapolis, Minn.: University of Minnesota Press.

Graber, Doris A. 1989. *Mass Media and American Politics*. 3rd ed. Washington, D.C.: CQ Press.

Gross, Larry. 1990. "Religion, Television, and Politics: The Right Bank of the Mainstream." In *Religious Television: Controversies and Conclusions*, ed. Robert Abelman and Stewart M. Hoover, 227–236. Norwood, N.J.: Ablex Publishing.

Hart, Roderick P., Sharon E. Jarvis, William P. Jennings, and Deborah Smith-Howell. 2005. *Political Keywords: Using Language that Uses Us*. New York: Oxford University Press.

Hoover, Stewart M. 1998. *Religion in the News: Faith and Journalism in American Public Discourse*. Thousand Oaks, Calif.: Sage Publications.

Hoover, Stewart M. 2002. "Religion, Politics, and the Media." In *Religion, Politics, and the American Experience*, ed. Edith L. Blumhofer, 72–85. Tuscaloosa, Ala.: University of Alabama Press.

Iyengar, Shanto. 1991. *Is Anyone Responsible? How Television Frames Political Issues*. Chicago, Ill.: University of Chicago Press.

Johnson, Thomas J., and Barbara K. Kaye. 1998. "A Vehicle for Engagement or a Haven for the Disaffected? Internet Use, Political Alienation, and Voter Participation." In

Engaging the Public: How Government and the Media Can Reinvigorate American Democracy, ed. Thomas J. Johnson, Carol E. Hays, and Scott P. Hays, 123–135. Lanham, Md.: Rowman & Littlefield.

Kellstedt, Paul M. 2003. *The Mass Media and the Dynamics of American Racial Attitudes.* New York: Cambridge University Press.

Kerr, Peter A., and Patricia Moy. 2002. "Newspaper Coverage of Fundamentalist Christians 1980–2000." *Journalism and Mass Communication Quarterly* 79: 54–72.

Kloer, Phil. 1999. "Falwell Comes Late to Teletubby Psychobabble." *Atlanta Journal Constitution*, February 11, D14.

Lesage, Julia. 1998b. "Christian Media." In *Media, Culture, and the Religious Right*, ed. Linda Kintz and Julia Lesage, 21–50. Minneapolis, Minn.: University of Minnesota Press.

Lesage, Julia. 1998a. "Christian Coalition Leadership Training." In *Media, Culture, and the Religious Right*, ed. Linda Kintz and Julia Lesage, 295–326. Minneapolis, Minn.: University of Minnesota Press.

Lichter, S. Robert, Stanley Rothman, and Linda S. Lichter. 1986. *The Media Elite.* Bethesda, Md.: Adler & Adler.

Media Matters for America. 2007. "Left Behind: The Skewed Representation of Religion in Major News Media." www.mediamatters.org.

Miller, Kenneth W., and David Niven. 2007. "Whose Life Is It Anyway? Religion, Politics, and Process in Media Coverage of 'End of Life' Controversies." Presented at the annual meeting of the Midwest Political Science Association, Chicago, Illinois, April 12–15.

Monson, J. Quin, and J. Baxter Oliphant. 2007. "Microtargeting and the Instrumental Mobilization of Religious Conservatives." In *A Matter of Faith: Religion in the 2004 Presidential Election*, ed. David E. Campbell, 95–119. Washington, D.C.: Brookings Institution Press.

Muirhead, Russell, Nancy L. Rosenblum, Daniel Schlozman, and Francis X. Shen. 2006. "Religion in the 2004 Presidential Election." In *Divided States of America: The Slash and Burn Politics of the 2004 Presidential Election*, ed. Larry J. Sabato, 221–242. New York: Pearson Longman.

Nacos, Brigitte L., and Oscar Torres-Reyna. 2007. *Fueling Our Fears: Stereotyping, Media Coverage, and Public Opinion of Muslim Americans.* Lanham, Md.: Rowman & Littlefield.

Newman, Brian, and Mark Caleb Smith. 2007. "Fanning the Flames: Religious Media Consumption and American Politics." *American Politics Research* 35: 846–877.

Noll, Mark. 2002. "Evangelicals Past and Present." In *Religion, Politics, and the American Experience*, ed. Edith L. Blumhofer, 103–122. Tuscaloosa, Ala.: University of Alabama Press.

Pettey, Gary R. 1990. "Bibles, Ballots, and Beatific Vision: The Cycle of Religious Activism in the 1980s." In *Religious Television: Controversies and Conclusions*, ed. Robert Abelman and Stewart M. Hoover, 197–206. Norwood, N.J.: Ablex Publishing.

Podesta, Anthony T., and James S. Kurtzke. 1990. "Conflict Between the Electronic Church and State: The Religious Right's Crusade Against Pluralism." In *Religious Television: Controversies and Conclusions*, ed. Robert Abelman and Stewart M. Hoover, 207–226. Norwood, N.J.: Ablex Publishing.

Richardson, James L. 1995. "Manufacturing Consent about Koresh: A Structural Analysis of the Role of Media in the Waco Tragedy." In *Armageddon in Waco*, ed. Stuart A. Wright, 153–176. Chicago, Ill.: University of Chicago Press.

Rosin, Hanna. 1999. "A 'Tubby' Ache for Jerry Falwell; Religious Right Leader Sees Gay Threat in Children's TV Character." *Washington Post*, February 11, C1.

Rothman, Stanley, and Amy Black. 1999. "Elites Revisited: American Social and Political Leadership in the 1990s." *International Journal of Public Opinion Research* 11: 169–191.

Schultze, Quentin J. 2003. *Christianity and the Mass Media in America*. East Lansing, Mich.: Michigan State University Press.

Schulze, Laurie, and Frances Guilfoyle. 1998. "Facts Don't Hate; They Just Are." In *Media, Culture, and the Religious Right*, ed. Linda Kintz and Julia Lesage, 327–344. Minneapolis, Minn.: University of Minnesota Press.

Shupe, Anson, and Jeffrey K. Hadden. 1995. "Cops, News Copy, and Public Opinion: Legitimacy and the Social Construction of Evil in Waco." In *Armageddon in Waco*, ed. Stuart A. Wright, 177–204. Chicago, Ill.: University of Chicago Press.

Silk, Mark. 1995. *Unsecular Media: Making News of Religion in America*. Chicago, Ill.: University of Illinois Press.

Smidt, Corwin S., Lyman Kellstedt, James Guth, and John Green. 2005. "Religion and the 2004 Presidential Election." In *American Politics: Media and Elections*, ed. Tomasz Pludowski, 438–465. Turin: Adam Marszalek and Collegium Civitas Press.

Sparta, Christine. 1999. "Falwell: Teletubby Looks Way Too Gay for Kids' Well-being." *USA Today*, February 11, D2.

Underwood, Doug, and Keith Stamm. 2001. "Are Journalists Really Irreligious? A Multidimensional Analysis." *Journalism and Mass Communication Quarterly* 78: 771–786.

Vinson, C. Danielle, and James L. Guth. 2009. "Misunderestimating Religion in the 2004 Presidential Campaign." In *Blind Spot: When Journalists Get it Wrong*, ed. Paul Marshall, Lela Gilbert, and Roberta Green Ahmanson, 87–105. New York: Oxford University Press.

Vinson, C. Danielle, and William V. Moore. 2007. "Campaign Disconnect: Media Coverage of the 2000 Republican Presidential Primary in South Carolina." *Political Communication* 24: 393–413.

Wills, Garry. 1990. *Under God: Religion in American Politics*. New York: Simon and Schuster.

Wright, Robert. 2004. "Faith, Hope, and Clarity," *New York Times*, October 28, A29.

CHAPTER 17

....

RELIGION AND THE
U.S. PRESIDENCY

....

HAROLD F. BASS
AND MARK J. ROZELL

THE political science subfield of presidency research has seldom tapped the potentially rich arena of religion for insights into the institution. Perhaps the constitutional concept of separation of church and state explains why scholars have largely ignored the religion factor when studying the American presidency. Even recent best-selling biographies of presidents who were deeply religious and whose faith guided many of their decisions largely ignore the role that religion played in their lives and presidential administrations (Ambrose 1983–1984; Cannon 1991; McCullough 1992).

A lack of theoretical underpinnings of the impact of religion on the presidency makes any generalizations here very problematic. Indeed, if our chapter is to serve as a worthwhile contribution, it is as a call to the profession to take up seriously the study of the role of religion in the presidency, because research on the presidency can advance significantly with a deeper understanding of the role that religion has played in the lives and administrations of our chief executives.

To be sure, there is a significant literature on the religious beliefs and practices of certain presidents widely known to have been men of deep faith. And most recently, there has been an explosion of writings on the faith of former President George W. Bush (e.g., Mansfield 2003; Aikman 2004; Kaplan 2004; Kengor 2004a; Rozell and Whitney 2007b). In the modern era, presidents who have professed their faith openly and attracted political support by so doing—Jimmy Carter and Bush especially—have been the subjects of numerous analyses of the religion factor in their administrations. Yet what is significant is that the role of faith for many other presidents of deep religious convictions—including Truman, Eisenhower, and

Reagan—has not attracted much interest by political scientists and biographers. Indeed, leading accounts of these presidents tended either to ignore religion or characterized them wrongly as nonreligious men who merely used rhetorical appeals to faith for politically calculated reasons.

Presidential scholars customarily divide their attention between individual presidents and the institution of the presidency. Our consideration of religion and the presidency begins with a focus on individualistic perspectives, and then it shifts to a more institutional one. We begin by examining the important, but often neglected and misunderstood, role of religion in selected presidencies to underscore the point of our analysis (Rozell and Whitney 2007a).

PRESIDENTS AND RELIGION

Historian Gary Scott Smith (2005, 2007) is one of the few scholars doing serious analysis of the role of religion on the presidency. As Smith (2005, p. 6) correctly states in his recent book on presidents and religion: "Even though thousands of volumes have been written about America's presidents, we do not know much about the precise nature of their faith or how it affected their performance and policies." Thus, Smith's (2005) sweeping account of the history of religion and the presidency is a necessary resource for political scientists seeking a stronger grounding in this area.

Smith (2007) also has written in detail on the faith of George Washington, illustrating that the whole topic of religion and the presidency has been one of contention and misunderstanding from the origins of the republic. To some extent, the debate over Washington's religiosity has been driven by efforts to advance partisan agendas. Just as scholars historically have turned to the founding generation for guidance, advocates of contemporary causes invoke the founders for the legitimacy of their positions.

According to Smith (2007), some contend that Washington was a man of robust, orthodox Christian faith. Others maintain that Washington was a Deist or a Unitarian who attended church to satisfy social expectations and to assure pious Americans that their leader was devout. Smith (2007), however, contends that Washington actually was a theistic rationalist; he adopted a hybrid system of thought combining Christianity, natural religion, and rationalism. More important, Washington never attracted the condemnation that Thomas Jefferson received from opponents for being insufficiently devout or even an atheist: "The fact that Washington believed in a God who watched over and protected America seemed to be enough for most citizens" (Smith 2007, p. 23). Smith (2007) maintains that religion was not for Washington merely some means or cue to assure Americans, because the country's founding father became more committed to his faith during difficult periods in his life (e.g., while leading the Continental Army and later the new nation). Thus, to ignore Washington's faith is to miss an important part of his leadership and legacy.

No president has had a more profound and lasting impact on American thinking about the proper role of religion in government than Thomas Jefferson, who famously articulated the concept of "a wall of separation between church and state" (Buckley 2007, p. 40). Large bodies of scholarship and judicial opinions have taken Jefferson's famous phrase to advocate the strict separationist view. However, religion scholar Thomas J. Buckley (2007) and constitutional law scholar Daniel Dreisbach (2002) have shown that this statement from Jefferson's 1802 letter to the Danbury Baptist Association has often been taken out of context to mean that the third president had advocated a separation that was absolute. Their examinations of Jefferson's presidency tell a different story, one in which religion played an important role. Jefferson's presidential addresses, private correspondences, and the public papers of his administration reveal that the third president contributed significantly to the development of American civil religion, more so than any of his contemporaries (Buckley 2007, p. 41).

Furthermore, and most fascinating from a contemporary standpoint, Jefferson directed government funds to support the work of Christian missionary groups to "civilize" and to convert Native Americans. As one example, Buckley (2007, p. 47) reports, "with his approval, the federal government encouraged a Presbyterian Minister's work among the Cherokees by appropriating several hundred dollars to found what was designed as a Christian school to teach religion along with other subjects." Common portrayals of the George W. Bush administration's faith-based initiative characterize this endeavor as without historical precedent. Thus, a clear understanding of religion's role in Jefferson's presidency puts the contemporary government program in a more accurate historical context.

Contrary to the conventional view of Jefferson, the principle of religious freedom guided the third president much more than the sentiment he had expressed to the Danbury Baptist Association. Buckley shows that the "wall of separation" comment has been taken out of context to justify an absolutist church–state separation not intended by Jefferson. Furthermore, Jefferson's "remarks . . . were out of character with the official face that he maintained as president not only toward religion but toward the churches" (Buckley 2007, p. 47).

Scholars have erroneously placed a number of modern presidents in the nonreligious category. For example, many historians perceived Harry Truman's publicly concealed religiosity as a lack of serious faith commitment (McCullough 1992; Ferrell 1994; Hamby 1995). However, political scientist Elizabeth Edwards Spalding (2007) has studied the importance of faith to President Harry Truman's foreign policy and she draws fascinating parallels to the George W. Bush presidency. Although widely regarded as one who cared little about religion, Truman, the second Baptist to serve in the White House, was a believer and someone who saw the Cold War as a clash between "the atheism of communist totalitarianism and the theism of the rest of the world" (Spalding 2007, p. 95). Thus, scholars who downplayed or ignored Truman's religiosity have missed a vital component of his foreign policy belief system.

Spalding (2007) maintains that we cannot properly understand the early Cold War era without an examination of Truman's religious faith. She reveals that Truman was deeply religious, but that he was often uncomfortable with overt displays of faith, and was skeptical of those who claimed that their own religion gave them a favored relationship with God. "To Truman, all Christians, even every revealed religion, could agree on the meaning as well as the value of the biblical precepts of the Ten Commandments and the Sermon on the Mount" (Spalding 2007, p. 99).

Truman reached out to religious groups to aid the West during the Cold War. Spalding (2007) explains that the president believed that because the battle of the Cold War was ultimately a moral as well as a strategic one, he needed to enlist the support of different religions to defeat communism. He purposefully gave a policy address at a Catholic college to showcase his desire to enlist the support of the church in combating communism and he made efforts to establish formal relations between the United States and the Vatican to further this effort. Truman also wrote a provocative statement to the president of the Baptist World Alliance: "To succeed in our quest for righteousness we must, in St. Paul's luminous phrase, put on the armor of God" (Spalding 2007, p. 103).

Although Truman supported an independent Jewish state in the Middle East to promote democracy and prevent the Soviet Union from gaining a foothold in the region, he also was motivated by a "moral commitment to the Jewish people" (Spalding 2007, p. 110). In response to criticism of his support for the state of Israel, Truman advocated a Jewish right to territory in Palestine preceding the atrocities of World War II and the plight of refugees. He recognized strategic interests in the Middle East as paramount, but he was also driven by a moral framework that told him to fulfill the mandate of God's chosen people (Merkley 2004).

Many scholars have characterized Dwight D. Eisenhower as perhaps the least religious of any modern president, but historian Jack Holl has carefully studied Eisenhower's religiosity and concluded that the president's biographers have mostly gotten the story wrong. An overriding theme in Eisenhower studies has been that, although he had had a strongly religious upbringing, Ike all but abandoned religious faith after entering West Point. As Holl (2007, p. 120) points out, "no one emphasizes the influence of Eisenhower's deeply ingrained religious beliefs on his public life and work." This finding is almost astonishing when placed against the backdrop of a close examination of Eisenhower's words and actions as president. Perhaps most tellingly, Eisenhower said a mere four years prior to being elected president: "I am the most intensely religious man I know" (Holl 2007, p. 119).

A part of the Eisenhower image as nonreligious derives from rhetoric that struck many observers as superficial, such as his famous remark in a December 1952 address to the Freedom Foundation: "Our form of government has no sense, unless it is grounded in a deeply felt religious faith, and I don't care what it is" (Holl 2007, p. 120). Eisenhower was open about his aversion to organized religion, but as Holl (2007) explains, we do not necessarily comprehend the full story of one's inner faith by examining the outward expressions. "Eisenhower had given deep thought to the meaning and function of prayer and had concluded that prayer was the central religious act of his personal faith and civil religion" (Holl 2007, p. 127). The outward signs also were there for a president who was the first to write his own inaugural prayer, who was baptized in the White House, who approved "one nation, under God" being added to the Pledge of Allegiance and "In God We Trust" to the U.S. currency, and who appointed a new office of special assistant for religion in his administration. Holl's research (2007, p. 133) reveals how Eisenhower drew on his private faith for solace and strength as he confronted the Cold War and was haunted by "nightmares of nuclear Armageddon."

Like Eisenhower, Ronald Reagan did not attend church while president and also seemed to harbor an aversion to organized religion. Reagan biographers characterized the man as mostly indifferent to religion, except to the extent that he could attract political support from religiously motivated voters who liked his conservative social issue positions (Cannon 1991; Morris 1999). This conventional view has held for years, although the one scholar to examine fully Reagan's religiosity has arrived at a completely opposite conclusion.

Political scientist Paul Kengor (2004b) carefully reviewed Reagan's private papers and letters, and interviewed many people close to the former president. He finds that Reagan was a deeply religious man. The neglect and misunderstanding of Reagan's religiosity "leaves an unbridgeable gap in our own understanding of Reagan and what made him tick, especially in the great calling of his political life: his cold war crusade against the Soviet Union" (Kengor 2007, p. 175). Like Truman, Reagan perceived the battle of the Cold War as not merely a strategic one, but a moral one against atheistic communism. For Reagan, "God had appointed the United States of America with a special role in a divine plan—a plan that the USSR spurned as much as it did the very concept of the existence of God" (Kengor 2007, p. 187).

Kengor (2007) shows that Reagan avoided church attendance as president largely out of security concerns. Reagan had regularly attended services prior to his presidency, and he resumed the practice after he left office. Thus, those who merely observed what appeared to be Reagan's outward indifference to religion while in office misunderstood his true sentiments. Yet, although the failure of Reagan's contemporaries to understand what could be found through careful primary research is understandable, the failure of major biographers to do so is puzzling. Kengor (2007, p. 187) speculates that the study of the religious side of presidents has not been a focus of academic inquiry, perhaps because of a largely secularized academic profession.

Interest in the role of religion nonetheless grew during the George W. Bush presidency. Unfortunately, because of its topical nature, much of the literature has a clear political slant. Nonetheless, there are academic studies that attempt to make sense of the role of religion in the Bush presidency (Guth 2004; Robinson and Wilcox 2007; Rozell and Whitney 2007b), and some in-depth analyses of the Bush administration's Office of Faith-Based Initiatives (Formicola, Segers, and Weber 2003; Black, Koopman, and Ryden 2004; Fauntroy 2007).

Part of the elevated interest in the role of religion in the Bush presidency is the result of the perception that Bush was unique in his openness about his faith and the belief that his policy agenda was driven significantly by his religiosity (Domke 2004). Although it is true that Bush was much less constrained about expressing his religiosity publicly than many past presidents, it is an exaggeration to claim that he stood unique in this regard among America's chief executives. In the modern era, for example, presidents such as Jimmy Carter and Bill Clinton have been at least as open about their faith as Bush, perhaps even more so. One study showed, surprising to many, that Bill Clinton invoked Christ in presidential speeches more often than Bush per number of years in office (Kengor 2004b, p. 2; see also Penning 2007, p. 210; compare with Domke and Coe 2007).

Finally, Bush's close relationship with the Christian Right fueled intense interest in the intersection of faith and the presidency during his tenure. Although partisan critics tagged Bush as beholden to that movement and to some of its extreme views, Guth (2004) shows that the former president maintained some distance from certain controversial leaders and positions of the Christian Right, and tried to build a broadly ecumenical base of support through various efforts to reach out to different groups, including Catholics, black Protestants, and Latino Protestants, as well as evangelical Protestants.

Whatever the reason for the neglect and misunderstanding of the religion factor to the U.S. presidency, some recent studies give hope that this area of research is ready to grow and fill in many gaps in our knowledge of our chief executives and what makes them tick. Furthermore, such a research agenda might profitably review and recast some "classics" in presidential scholarship.

For example, this heightened focus on religion among recent presidential biographers encourages reconsideration of the provocative, psychologically based evaluations of 20th-century presidents advanced by James David Barber (1992). Seeking to predict presidential performance, Barber (1992) developed an analytical framework that placed character, worldview, and style in the context of a power situation and a climate of expectations. He proposed a four-cell categorization scheme based on level of activity (active–passive) and perceived affect derived from that activity (positive–negative). He proceeded to locate 20th-century presidents in appropriate cells, based on evidence gleaned from presidential biographies. He went on to assert that this exercise has value in predicting the presidential performance of aspirants for the office. In Barber's (1992) account, religion loomed large as a formative factor for Woodrow Wilson and Jimmy Carter, but it was negligible for other 20th-century chief executives. Subsequent biographies noted herein document the significance of religion for several recent presidents, and provide an argument for reexamination and possible revision of Barber's (1992) assessments. In turn, the rising salience of religion in electoral behavior also suggests that other efforts to frame and understand presidential leadership within the broad context of the political climate (e.g., Barber 1980; Skrowronek 1997) merit a fresh look from presidential scholars attuned to the religious dimensions of both presidents and voters.

One challenge in studying the religion–presidency intersections is that indeed all presidents find it useful politically to connect religious themes at times to policy goals or to sustain political support. Evoking the symbols of the U.S. civil religion and using religious-based discourse are expected roles of all presidents, who occupy, in Theodore Roosevelt's memorable phrase, the bully pulpit. Indeed, this role has received substantial general and specific attention in the scholarly literature (see Gufstason 1970; Novak 1974; Fairbanks 1981, 1982; Dunn 1984; Pierard and Linder 1988; Calhoun 1993; Linder 1996; Warber and Olson 2006).

As studies of civil religion demonstrate, presidents have undertaken this role in different ways. Linder (1996, p. 735) describes Lincoln's role as "national prophet," Eisenhower's as "national pastor," and Reagan's as "high priest of civil religion." As Linder (1996, p. 735) explains, the first is the role of the president calling upon a nation to make sacrifices during crisis and "to repent of their corporate sins when their behavior falls short of the national ideals," the second role is a president providing "spiritual inspiration to the people by affirming American core values," whereas the third role is "affirming and celebrating nation" and reminding people of the "national mission."

Still, it is not always clear whether presidents evoking certain symbols or using religious rhetoric do so because they believe that they have to, or because it comes naturally to them. Kengor's (2004b) study of Reagan is particularly instructive because the conventional wisdom for years has been that the former president used symbols and words merely to please certain constituencies. Yet after interviewing many people closest to the former president, Kengor found the conventional wisdom was simply wrong. In his analysis, Reagan comes out as a president who comfortably evoked religious symbols and used religious language because of a deeply felt personal religiosity. For scholars studying religion and the presidency, this finding suggests that mere counts of religious-based words and phrases used by presidents in speeches have limited utility in explaining the religious foundation of influences on our chief executives.

In this regard, Linder (1996, p. 736) explains that although all presidents may play the role of identifying themselves with American civil religion, the effort comes more naturally for some because they are more "conversant with the language of faith." He identifies Bill Clinton as one of the modern presidents for whom discussing faith in public was easy because of his own religiosity. Again, this finding may be surprising to many, especially given the intense dislike of Clinton by religious traditionalists who were appalled by his personal behavior and suspicious of his use of religious symbols and rhetoric (Guth 2000). Thus, many of Clinton's outspoken detractors characterized him as a secular liberal pretending to be religious merely for reasons of political utility. Yet scholarly reviews of Clinton's faith showcase a man strongly influenced by his faith background, perhaps very conflicted about religious tenets, but still very steeped in the culture, traditions, and beliefs of his denomination, the Southern Baptist Convention (Linder 1996; Guth 2000; Penning 2007).

What is striking, perhaps, is the extent to which presidents and presidential aspirants of both political parties in the modern era eagerly invoke religious language and symbols. One study (Domke and Coe 2007) shows that since the 1980s, there has been a very significant upswing in references to religion and the deity in presidential addresses, as well as in the number of speeches that presidents have made before churches and religious organizations. Domke and Coe (2007) maintain that religion has become a "political weapon" in the hands of presidents and aspirants for the office, a trend that goes against the separationist preferences of some of the country's founders.

RELIGION AND THE INSTITUTIONAL PRESIDENCY

Presidential Selection, Staffing, and Policy Making

One commonplace way that scholars of the institutional presidency have confronted the topic of religion is through the pluralist lens of interest representation. This approach has figured prominently in considerations of presidential selection, staffing, and policy making. The pluralist perspective perceives politics as the arena in which groups organize and compete in efforts to translate their private interests into public policy, through electioneering and lobbying (see Truman 1951). Students of interest groups in the American political system observe that, although the presidency is rarely the primary focus of interest group activity, it is a significant one nevertheless. Interactions between presidents and pressure groups are clearly on the rise, owing to a heightened role for the president in domestic policy making and to the proliferation of interest groups (see Tichenor 2006).

Implicitly, the ethnoreligious perspective has dominated in considerations of religion in presidential selection, staffing, and policy making. However, the underlying assumptions of the religious restructuring model can occasionally be discerned in some more recent treatments that look beyond religious affiliation to the intensity of that commitment (see Brooks and Manza 1997; Green 2007a, b).

This array of scholarship typically considers religion in essentially secular fashion. It represents religion as a descriptive demographic category, addressed alongside such counterparts as socioeconomic status, race, ethnicity, region, age, and gender in shaping political behavior. Discussions of interest representation in electoral coalitions and presidential policy making via policy makers identify and include religious interests in the context of overlapping and competing entities.

As such, there has been scant attention given to the distinctive character of religion as a descriptive category (see Mitchell, 2007). This scholarly literature largely ignores what makes religious groups noteworthy and problematical, compared with their more numerous secular counterparts in the pluralist arena—

namely, their transcendent character. This feature arguably heightens their intensity of the commitment of religious groups and diminishes their willingness to compromise with and accommodate competing interests.

Those who seek to account for the increasing salience of religion in American politics should seek partial answers in structural developments in presidential selection and the presidential office. Modern party reforms of the presidential nomination process, establishing presidential primaries and participatory caucuses as normative, have provided religious interests with expanded opportunities for involvement in presidential selection.

Similarly, developments in recent decades in the establishment and expansion of the White House Office have provided new avenues and institutions for mutual interaction between the president and religious interests. Modern presidents and their staff assistants engage in systematic outreach to religious interests to draw them into, and maintain their presence within, the presidential electoral coalition. In turn, religious interests make known to the White House their expectations and demands with regard to nominations, appointments, policies, and priorities.

The presidential campaign paves the way for the accession of the winner to the presidency. Similarly, the place of religious interests in the campaign often foreshadows their subsequent contributions to presidential politics and policy making.

Presidential Selection

One prominent area of presidential studies that has routinely dealt with the topic of religion is that of presidential selection. Considerations here have addressed both the religious affiliations and commitments of presidential candidates and the status of religious interests in presidential electoral coalitions. Media coverage of presidential campaigns devotes increasing attention to these topics as well. Another arena less well represented is campaign communications. Fairbanks and Burke (1992) surveyed and assessed how liberal and conservative religious periodicals covered presidential campaigns between 1960 and 1988.

No Religious Tests?

Article VI of the Constitution stipulates that "no religious test shall ever be required as a qualification to any office or public trust under the United States." Nevertheless, the presidential selection process has evidenced some norms with regard to the religion of presidential aspirants. The most compelling is the clear expectation that the president be a person of faith. All our presidents to date have made this claim, at least nominally. A 2004 poll indicated that almost 60 percent of likely voters surveyed expressed the opinion that it is important that the president believe in God and be deeply religious (see Banks 2004).

Well into the 20th century, that faith was presumed to be Protestant Christianity, notwithstanding the presence of a handful of Unitarians in the White House. In the decade of the 1920s, Governor Al Smith of New York, a Democrat, became the first Roman Catholic to receive serious consideration for a major party's presidential nomination. After falling short in 1920 and 1924, he finally prevailed in 1928, but the fall campaign featured considerable anti-Catholicism and Smith suffered a decisive general-election defeat. Initial and enduring interpretations attributed the outcome in large measure to his religion (see White 1961, pp. 237–240), although subsequent scholarship has revised this conventional wisdom (see Silva 1962).

Three decades later, Senator John F. Kennedy's presidential prospects turned on whether his Catholicism would prove an insurmountable obstacle. The 1956 Bailey Memorandum, ostensibly authored by John Bailey, the Democratic Party chair in Connecticut, but actually prepared by Kennedy aide Theodore Sorenson, asserted that the shifting midcentury electoral landscape actually advantaged a Catholic candidate, who could mobilize increasing numbers of Catholic voters in key states (White 1961, pp. 240–243; Sorensen 1965, pp. 81–83).

During the course of the 1960 nomination contest, Kennedy delivered a key speech to an assembly of Protestant ministers in Houston, Texas, in which he assured them that his faith would not compromise his exercise of the powers and duties of the office of president (White 1961, pp. 391–393). This commitment to separate his private faith from his public responsibilities resonated well with midcentury American culture and society. In contrast, the contemporary cultural climate appears to embrace the expectation that personal faith will and should inform public policy positions.

Kennedy won the nomination convincingly, and the election narrowly, amid abiding concerns among Protestants. He remains the only Roman Catholic president to date, although the Democrats have subsequently nominated Catholics for vice president (Edmund Muskie in 1968, Sargent Shriver in 1972, and Geraldine Ferraro in 1984) and president (John Kerry in 2004). After Kennedy's election in 1960, the Republican Party nominated William E. Miller, a Roman Catholic, for vice president in 1964.

No person of Jewish faith has received a major party presidential nomination. Senator Barry Goldwater (Arizona), the 1964 Republican nominee, was of Jewish descent on his father's side, but he identified himself as an Episcopalian. Senator Joseph Lieberman (Connecticut), an Orthodox Jew, received the Democratic vice presidential nomination in 2000. In this instance, the effect on public opinion and electoral behavior appeared to be negligible (see Kane, Craig, and Wald 2004; Cohen 2005).

On three occasions during the past four decades, Mormons figured prominently in presidential contests. On the Republican side, Governor George Romney (Michigan) was a leading contender in 1968 for the nomination that went to Quaker Richard Nixon. Four decades later, Romney's son, Mitt, was a top-tier candidate. The elder Romney's faith was commonly noted, but it did not prove especially controversial in his pursuit of the party nomination (see White 1970, pp. 43–50, 65–75). Indeed, the fact that his parents were Mormon missionaries serving in Mexico when he was born seemed more intriguing, in light of the constitutional requirement that the president be a natural-born citizen, than did his religious affiliation per se (see Corwin, Chase, and Ducat 1978, p. 155, fn. 25). In contrast, his son's religious identity appears much more noteworthy and problematical, reflecting both the increasing salience of religion in American politics and significant changes in the nomination process that provide avenues to express religious sensitivities. In 1976, Representative Morris Udall (Arizona) contended for the Democratic nomination that went to Jimmy Carter. Far more media and public attention during the presidential primary season focused on Carter's evangelical background than on Udall's Mormonism.

Another recent development with regard to the religious backgrounds of presidential aspirants is the conspicuous presence of former clergy in the nominating contests of the Republican Party: Pat Robertson in 1988 and Mike Huckabee in 2008. Their emergence as credible candidates is clearly related to the increase of evangelical interests in the body politic in general and the Republican Party in particular. We will now address this development, in the broader context of religious interests within presidential electoral coalitions.

Electoral Coalitions

A second way that the topic of presidential selection embraces religion is with regard to the efforts by presidential aspirants to assemble coalitions of interests at both the nomination and general election stages (see Polsby and Wildavsky 2000, chap. 2). Religious interests occupy time-honored places in presidential nominating and electoral coalitions. This arena of scholarship unites presidential scholars with their political party counterparts. Although party coalitions transcend particular presidents, the presidential role of party leadership ensures that nominees are key players in their creation, maintenance, expansion, and deterioration. Sundquist (1983) argues for a party-centered presentation of the emergence and realignment of national party coalitions, whereas Skowronek (1997) advances a presidency-centered interpretation.

The preponderance of such attention has focused on the mass level—that is, the voters themselves. The advent and proliferation of sophisticated survey research, and scholarly reliance on it, has made this electoral behavior approach to religion and the presidency commonplace. As previously noted, this literature typically treats religion simply and as one of several descriptive categories, with little regard for nuance or distinctiveness. (For a conspicuous exception, see Guth, Kellstedt, Smidt, and Green [2006].)

Contests for the presidency have long featured the mobilization of voters based on religious affiliations. Traditionally identifying with the Democratic Party, Catholics and Jews provided stable electoral foundations for Democratic presidential nominees, whereas mainline Protestants did likewise for the Republicans. These identifications generally coincided with parallel socioeconomic ones, with the Republicans capturing the support of the more established elements of society and the Democrats the more marginal. Similarly, religious identities often correlated with regional and residential ones. For example, Democratic strongholds in the urban Northeast housed substantial numbers of Catholics and Jews. In turn, white Protestants in the solid South were part and parcel of the Democratic presidential coalition, based on longstanding regional foundations.

More recent developments have modified these traditional patterns, as parties, candidates, and campaigns have systematically sought to attract support from religiously rooted voters based on issues and ideologies. Democrats have claimed the enthusiastic support of African American Protestants with pro-civil rights commitments. Republicans have appealed to Jewish voters on the foreign policy front by advocating a strong pro-Israel stance. In addition, they have made inroads with some Catholic voters with their pro-life position on abortion. Moreover, upward class mobility has generally made the GOP more attractive to middle-class Catholics (see Prendergast 1999).

However, the most important development along these lines in recent decades has been the mobilization of evangelicals. Evangelicals were traditionally relatively disengaged from the electoral process. Alternative factors, notably class and region, better explained such partisan and presidential preferences as they manifested. For example, the traditional inclination of Southern Baptists to vote Democratic reflected a regional norm, reinforced by their lower middle-class location in southern society.

The decade of the 1970s saw dramatic changes in this pattern. Several factors contributed to the change. One was economic development, which moved evangelicals upward within the middle class. Another was the emergence of issues on the political agenda that enraged and engaged the evangelical community. These included controversial Supreme Court decisions prohibiting public prayer in public schools and restricting antiabortion legislation. More generally, cultural changes in the 1960s threatened the traditional values of evangelicals.

In 1976, a self-proclaimed evangelical successfully sought the Democratic presidential nomination and went on to win the general election. Jimmy Carter brought attention to this segment of the population and engaged it on his behalf as well. Four years later, frustrated by his policy stances, evangelicals deserted Carter's reelection bid to embrace the candidacy of Republican nominee Ronald Reagan. Since then, this constituency has been a vital component in the presidential coalitions assembled by Republican Party nominees (see Oldfield 1996a, b; Nesmith 1997).

Furthermore, the Republicans have benefited from an emerging religiosity gap, wherein those who say they are frequent church attenders, regardless of affiliation, are more likely to vote Republican than their infrequent counterparts (see Green 2007a, b). This finding calls attention to the emerging theological restructuring model for understanding the role of religion in American politics. In concert, these electoral shifts have proved generally significant during the post-New Deal era resurgence in Republican presidential fortunes, and particularly in explaining narrow Republican victories in the presidential contests in 2000 and 2004.

Another approach addresses interaction of two sets of elites: presidential strategists who seek to engage electoral support based on religion for their candidates and leaders of religious groups who aspire to be power brokers and king makers in delivering that support. Here again, scholars have generally approached these interactions utilizing the secular frameworks of pluralism and interest group liberalism.

Changes in the presidential nomination process featuring the expansion of primaries and participatory caucuses (Shafer 1983) afford interest groups new avenues for involvement in presidential selection. They establish new electoral opportunities to cast faith-based ballots in presidential contests. Furthermore, they encourage the development of channels of communications whereby presidential candidate organizations systematically gear up to reach out to such faith-based voters. In pursuit of the presidential nomination, aspirants must establish full-fledged campaign organizations that assign staff assistants to outreach efforts with interest group leaders and their electoral constituencies. Contemporary presidential nominating campaign organizations in both parties include staff assistants with liaison assignments to religious-based groups.

In the array of power brokers and king makers who attempt to influence voter preferences for presidential nominations, those who claim to speak for religious interests have become quite prominent in the councils of the Republican coalition. They have included the likes of the former Jerry Falwell (Moral Majority), Charles Colson (Prison Fellowship), Ralph Reed and Pat Robertson (Christian Coalition), James Dobson (Focus on the Family), Gary Bauer (American Values), and Richard Land (Southern Baptist Convention Ethics and Religious Liberty Commission).

Iowa's caucuses, since 1972 the opening salvo in the delegate selection contests for the national party conventions, have played a critical role in structuring the ensuing nomination campaigns. The Iowa caucuses have magnified opportunities for religious interests to influence campaign dynamics in a highly visible fashion, as they have consistently featured enthusiastic participation by social conservatives motivated by religion in what is frequently a multicandidate race. For example, Jimmy Carter's dark-horse candidacy was propelled by his strong showing of nearly 28 percent, leading the Democratic field of candidates. In 1988, Pat Robertson, head of the Christian Coalition, garnered almost 25 percent of the Republican vote, finishing in second place. In 2000, Allan Keyes and Gary Bauer, both appealing to the Christian conservatives in the electorate, got a combined 23 percent. And in 2008, Mike Huckabee, the leading choice of evangelical conservatives in the GOP, won the Iowa caucuses with 34 percent. The placement of the Iowa caucuses, and media publicity surrounding them, virtually guarantee that the early stages of the nomination contests will focus attention on the preferences of religiously motivated participants.

In a pluralist environment, interest groups may well be more successful in vetoing unacceptable initiatives than in advancing their own preferences. In the 2008 Republican presidential nomination contest, we saw the highly visible leaders of the religious interests within the GOP presidential coalition unsuccessful in anointing a putative nominee, but still insistent on stipulating who was an unacceptable choice in their eyes.

Perhaps these religiously motivated interests had their greatest influence that year on GOP nominee Senator John McCain's choice for a vice presidential running mate. Religious conservatives made known their disapproval and likely protests at the GOP national convention if McCain would have chosen a social moderate. McCain ultimately sought to shore up his support among religious conservatives with his choice of strong prolife Alaska Governor Sarah Palin. Yet although McCain may have succeeded in solidifying his backing from religious conservatives, the choice of Palin showcased the politically risky nature of this strategy, as opinion polls revealed throughout the campaign that the Palin selection overall had hurt the GOP ticket.

On the Democratic Party side in 2008, a different dynamic involving faith and electoral politics emerged. The nomination campaign of Senator Barack Obama almost was derailed by the public airing of an inflammatory sermon by the candidate's well-known pastor, Rev. Jeremiah Wright. Obama ultimately denounced his pastor's rhetoric and overcame the political storm on his way to the White House.

Presidential Staffing

A successful presidential campaign presents the incumbent with the challenge and opportunity to staff the administration. Key campaign organization aides typically follow the president into office, wherein they continue to labor on their leader's behalf. At issue for us is the extent to which religious interests mobilized in the presidential campaign receive recognition as the new administration prepares to conduct presidential politics and policy.

During the New Deal era, a period dominated by Democratic presidents Franklin D. Roosevelt and Harry Truman, the national party chair of the Democratic Party from 1928 until 1960 was always a Roman Catholic. After a postconvention interlude in 1960, the Democrats resumed this pattern under Presidents Kennedy and Johnson until 1969. This afforded symbolic representation to a key electoral constituency. Early on, it also provided substantial patronage opportunities, although these receded considerably over the decades.

More important, the creation of the executive office of the president in 1939, the cornerstone of which is the White House Office, has given presidents a location to house key assistants, many drawn from the campaign organization. Close at hand, they oversee the president's pursuit of political and policy objectives. Reflecting bureaucratic patterns, the White House Office has experienced dramatic growth in size, accompanied by division of labor and specialization (see Burke 2000; Patterson 2000).

In this organizational setting, attention to representation and cultivation of interest groups has been a presidential priority, and from the outset, religious interests have been routinely included (see Pika 1987–1988). Early on, President Truman identified a specific aide, David Niles, as his liaison with minorities, notably Catholics and Jews. His successors followed suit. Dwight Eisenhower enlisted Frederick Fox, a Congregationalist minister, as a presidential assistant to deal with volunteer groups in general and religious ones in particular. One of President Lyndon Johnson's top aides, Bill Moyers, had been a Southern Baptist seminarian a decade earlier. Presidents Richard Nixon and Gerald Ford institutionalized this relatively informal commitment to group representation. In 1974, Ford established the Office of Public Liaison within the White House Office. Henceforth, organized interests, including religious ones, have benefited from its presence, enjoying varying degrees of access and attention.

During the past three decades, the number and visibility of religious liaisons on White House staffs has heightened considerably. Channels of communication between the White House and religious constituencies occur primarily, but by no means exclusively, through the Office of Public Liaison. For example, in 1979, President Jimmy Carter, experiencing alienation from the evangelical community that had rallied to his 1976 presidential candidacy, brought Robert Maddox, a Southern Baptist pastor from his home state of Georgia, into the White House. Nominally a speechwriter, Maddox's real assignment was to communicate with and assuage the restive evangelicals, working with their leaders, as the reelection campaign neared.

Ronald Reagan assigned Morton Blackwell, a campaign aide who had dealt with the evangelicals, to the Office of Public Liaison in a parallel capacity. In his second term, he deployed Gary Bauer, who was and remains closely tied to the evangelical community as a domestic policy adviser. Vice President George H. W. Bush enlisted Doug Wead, an ordained Assemblies of God minister, to assist his 1988 presidential campaign in enlisting evangelical support, ably assisted by George W. Bush. Then, he brought Wead into the White House as a special assistant, where he continued these outreach efforts.

Bill Clinton continued this now-familiar pattern of designating a White House aide as liaison with the religious community. He located Flo McAtee in this capacity within the Office of Public Liaison. Beset by personal scandal, Clinton also brought prominent pastors to the White House to provide him with spiritual counsel (Guth 2000).

The George W. Bush White House featured extremely high-level opportunities for evangelical leaders to make their concerns known. The routine efforts of the Office of Public Liaison were handled primarily by Tim Goeglein. Another Office of Public Liaison staffer, Jerry Zeidman, provided outreach to the Jewish community. Furthermore, the Office of Political Affairs, under the supervision of Karl Rove, Deputy Chief of Staff, proved especially attentive to evangelical needs and interests. Finally, Michael Gerson, a key White House speechwriter and policy adviser, brought a strong evangelical background and orientation to his assignment.

The George W. Bush White House merits mention on another institutional front. On assuming office, the 43rd president fulfilled a campaign pledge and established by executive order the White House Office of Faith-Based and Community Initiatives. This office is charged with expanding the role of faith-based bodies in the delivery of social services through the provision of federal grants (see Formicola, Segers, and Weber 2003; Black, Koopman, and Ryden 2004; Fauntroy 2007). Comparable offices created in major executive departments provided yet another channel of communication between the administration and favored faith communities.

Finally, any discussion of modern presidents and their religious advisers has to make mention of the extraordinarily enduring role that Billy Graham has played during the post-World War II era. This prominent evangelist has enjoyed access and provided counsel to every president since Harry Truman (Gibbs and Duffy 2007).

These appointments and offices demonstrate the growing propensities of modern presidents to place on their White House staffs assistants who can communicate with religious constituencies in the electoral environment. From the president's perspective, these interactions are linked to reelection efforts, but they also pertain to policy initiatives.

Religious interests operate in reciprocal fashion. After successfully supporting a favored candidate for the presidential nomination and general election, leaders of religious interest groups seek to influence public policies. They do so by seeking the appointment of acceptable candidates for presidential nominations and appointments within the government (see Davidson, Kraus, and Morissey 2005). They also promote their policy agendas in both positive and negative fashions.

Perhaps the most neglected field for investigation with respect to presidential appointments is the extent to which cabinet and subcabinet appointments reflect the religious composition of the president's electoral constituencies. George W. Bush not only established White House channels of communication with religious constituencies, but he appointed executives from some of the GOP's key religious constituencies, such as his first-term Attorney-General John Ashcroft (Guth 2004). Although no systematic study has appeared, many reports claimed that evangelical Protestants, traditionalist Catholics, and members of other religious groups important to the Bush electoral coalition were quite numerous in second- and third-tier administration posts (Unger 2007).

Faith Foundations of Presidential Policy Agendas

Nineteenth-century presidents rarely advanced ambitious policy agendas. Typically, they deferred to Congress. There were some conspicuous exceptions, and religion occasionally loomed large as a foundation for them, as noted earlier with regard to Thomas Jefferson. Certainly, emancipation can be considered as such.

The progressive era coincided with and contributed to an expansion of presidential power in the political system. In turn, the reform agenda of the progressive movement was infused with social justice concerns advanced by Protestants and Catholics alike. For Protestants, it was the social gospel articulated by Walter Rauschenbusch in 1907 in *Christianity and the Social Crisis* (see Rauschenbush 2007). For Catholics, Leo XIII's papal encyclical *Rerum Novarum* (1891) heightened sensitivities to the plight of the working class in industrializing society and led to calls for responsive public policies.

Early 20th-century presidents Theodore Roosevelt and Woodrow Wilson associated themselves with these causes in their Square Deal and New Freedom agendas. Franklin Roosevelt did so as well with the New Deal (see Gustafson and Rosenberg

1989). Lyndon Johnson's Great Society, with its commitment to civil rights and the expansion of the welfare state, reflected these emphases as well (see Billington 1987). Bill Clinton's New Covenant was an effort to advance these themes at century's end.

The literature on interest groups makes clear that their efforts to influence the public policy agenda involve mobilization and countermobilization. Successes by one group encourage others to emulate them. In part in reaction to perceived excesses of Johnson's Great Society, the Christian Right emerged around 1980 as a major force in American politics (see Wilcox 1992).

A pro-life stance on the abortion issue has been at the forefront of the Christian Right's policy agenda. Freedom of religious expression, against claims that it fosters religious establishment, has been another priority. President Reagan and his Republican successors have rhetorically embraced this agenda. It has certainly figured into their judicial nominations. To date, it has not been advanced as far in the legislative process.

On the foreign policy front, presidential policy leadership is less constrained. During the post-World War II era, religious interests and convictions have undergirded several presidential policies. As previously noted, during the Cold War, U.S. presidents led the struggle against "godless" communism on behalf of religious believers. Consistent U.S. foreign policy support for Israel is rooted in the Judeo-Christian heritage of the West. The more recent terrorist threat emanating from militant Islam calls attention to that heritage and demands its defense as well. President Carter's commitment to human rights as a foundation for his foreign policy was an expression of his deeply held religious beliefs, as is the current President Bush's Freedom agenda.

Thus, one set of linkages between religion and the presidency can be identified through the pluralist lens of interest representation. Religious interests clearly occupy a seat at the table of presidential politics and policy. During recent decades, this position has been enhanced by profound organizational changes in presidential politics and policy making that broaden the avenues for influencing outcomes. These changes pertain to presidential nominations and elections, as well as to presidential staffing. Presidential campaign-based channels of communication carry over into the administrations, wherein presidential outreach efforts and reciprocal interest group lobbying explicitly represent religious interests. In concert, they have opened new avenues of access and interaction that have been noted by presidential scholars.

However, the treatment of religion in this body of scholarship has been ironically secular. Religion is typically conceived as one of many overlapping and competing factors shaping political behavior. Viewing religion through the lens of interest representation can misunderstand and misrepresent its avowedly transcendent character and claims. An important empirical question for presidential scholars is how effectively religious interest representatives in the arena of presidential politics and policy engage in the processes of negotiation, bargaining, compromise, and accommodation that the pluralist model presumes. Similarly, beset by cross-pressures in presidential primaries and general elections, do religiously driven voters reconcile competing interests in a fashion that differentiates them from voters in general?

CONCLUSION

This chapter has examined how scholars considering both individual presidents and the institutional presidency have dealt with the topic of religion. We have observed that mainstream presidential scholarship has not traditionally accorded it a great deal of specific interest. Furthermore, the handful of general treatments (see Richter and Dulce 1962, Alley 1972, Hutcheson 1988) has made little impact on the field.

However, we discern a dramatic uptick in recent decades. We attribute it in part to the willingness of some recent presidents to deal with their faith perspectives in an open fashion that both reflects and advances a cultural trend toward religiosity and that negates previous expectations of increased societal secularization. As such, we expect this heightened focus on the religious dimension of presidential personality to continue, and we encourage ongoing reexamination of previous presidents in hopes of unearthing new insights and understandings about how their religion affected their presidencies.

We note that considerations of American civil religion have routinely referenced the symbolic leadership role of the president. Looking forward, however, we wonder how growing religious pluralism in the United States will affect this traditional role.

In addition, we contend that longstanding opportunities for the expression of religiously rooted interests in presidential politics have been dramatically strengthened by institutional developments in recent decades pertaining to presidential nominations and the presidential office. We find that the standard theoretical framework for considering religion in this context—pluralistic interest representation—treats it in essentially secular fashion, devoting little attention to its distinctive features and qualities. More generally, we find that analytical frameworks appropriate for consideration of religion in presidential studies are largely lacking. This is troubling, given the numerous arenas in which it appears to have relevance. We trust that this chapter, and this volume, will stimulate creative ways and means to do so.

REFERENCES

Aikman, David. 2004. *A Man of Faith: The Spiritual Journey of George W. Bush.* Nashville, Tenn.: W Publishing Group.

Alley, Robert S. 1972. *So Help Me God: Religion and the Presidency, Wilson to Nixon.* Richmond, Va.: John Knox Press.

Ambrose, Stephen E. 1983–1984. *Eisenhower.* 2 Vols. New York: Simon and Schuster.

Banks, Adelle M. 2004. "Poll: Americans Want a 'Deeply Religious' Person as President." Pew Forum on Religion and Public Life, January 9. http://pewforum.org/news/display.php?NewsID=3012.

Barber, James D. 1980. *The Pulse of Politics: Electing Presidents in the Media Age.* New York: Norton.

Barber, James D. 1992. *The Presidential Character: Predicting Performance in the White House.* 4th ed. Englewood Cliffs, N.J.: Prentice Hall.

Billington, Monroe. 1987. "Lyndon B. Johnson: The Religion of a Politician." *Presidential Studies Quarterly* 17: 519–530.

Black, Amy, Douglas L. Koopman, and David K. Ryden. 2004. *Of Little Faith: The Politics of George W. Bush's Faith-Based Initiatives.* Washington, D.C.: Georgetown University Press.

Brooks, Clem, and Jeff Manza. 1997. "The Religious Factor in U.S. Presidential Elections, 1960–1992." *American Journal of Sociology* 103: 38–81.

Buckley, Thomas E. 2007. "Thomas Jefferson and the Myth of Separation." In *Religion and the American Presidency*, ed. Mark J. Rozell and Gleaves Whitney, 39–50. New York: Palgrave/MacMillan.

Burke, John P. 2000. *The Institutional Presidency: Organizing and Managing the White House from FDR to Clinton.* Baltimore, Md.: Johns Hopkins University Press.

Calhoun, Charles W. 1993. "Civil Religion and the Gilded Age Presidency: The Case of Benjamin Harrison." *Presidential Studies Quarterly* 23: 651–667.

Cannon, Lou. 1991. *President Reagan: The Role of a Lifetime.* New York: Simon and Schuster.

Cohen, Jeffrey E. 2005. "The Polls: Religion and the 2000 Presidential Election: Public Attitudes toward Joseph Lieberman." *Presidential Studies Quarterly* 35: 389–402.

Corwin, Edward S., Harold W. Chase, and Craig R. Ducat. 1978. *Edward S. Corwin's the Constitution and What It Means Today.* 14th ed. Princeton, N.J.: Princeton University Press.

Davidson, James D., Rachel Kraus, and Scott Morrissey. 2005. "Presidential Appointments and Religious Stratification in the United States, 1789–2003." *Journal for the Scientific Study of Religion* 44: 485–495.

Domke, David. 2004. *God Willing?: Political Fundamentalism in the White House, "The War on Terror," and the Echoing Press.* Ann Arbor, Mich.: University of Michigan Press.

Domke, David, and Kevin Coe. 2007. *The God Strategy: How Religion Became a Political Weapon in America.* New York: Oxford University Press.

Dreisbach, Daniel. 2002. *Thomas Jefferson and the Wall of Separation between Church and State.* New York: New York University Press.

Dunn, Charles W. 1984. "The Theological Dimensions of Presidential Leadership: A Classification Model." *Presidential Studies Quarterly* 14: 22–30.

Fairbanks, James David. 1981. "The Priestly Functions of the Presidency: A Discussion of the Literature on Civil Religion and Its Implications for the Study of Presidential Leadership." *Presidential Studies Quarterly* 11: 214–232.

Fairbanks, James David. 1982. "Religious Dimensions of Presidential Leadership: The Case of Dwight Eisenhower." *Presidential Studies Quarterly* 12: 260–267.

Fairbanks, James D., and John Francis Burke. 1992. "Religious Periodicals and Presidential Elections, 1960–1988." *Presidential Studies Quarterly* 22: 89–105.

Fauntroy, Michael K. 2007. "Buying Black Votes? The GOP's Faith-Based Initiative." In *Religion and the Bush Presidency*, ed. Mark J. Rozell and Gleaves Whitney, 177–196. New York: Palgrave/MacMillan.

Ferrell, Robert H. 1994. *Harry S. Truman: A Life.* Columbia, Mo.: University of Missouri Press.

Formicola, Jo Renee, Mary Segers, and Paul Weber. 2003. *Faith-Based Initiatives and the Bush Administration.* Lanham, Md.: Rowman & Littlefield.

Gibbs, Nancy, and Michael Duffy. 2007. *The Preacher and the Presidents: Billy Graham in the White House*. Nashville, Tenn.: Center Street.

Green, John C. 2007a. "Religion and the Presidential Vote: A Tale of Two Gaps." Pew Forum on Religion and Public Life, August 21. http://pewforum.org/docs/?DocID=240.

Green, John C. 2007b. *The Faith Factor: How Religion Influences American Elections*. Westport, Conn.: Praeger.

Gustafson, Merlin. 1970. "The Religious Role of the President." *Midwest Journal of Political Science* 14: 708–722.

Gustafson, Merlin, and Jerry Rosenberg. 1989. "The Faith of Franklin Roosevelt." *Presidential Studies Quarterly* 19: 559–566.

Guth, James L. 2000. "Clinton, Impeachment, and the Culture Wars." In *The Postmodern Presidency: Bill Clinton's Legacy in U.S. Politics*, ed. Steven E. Schier, 203–222. Pittsburgh, Pa.: University of Pittsburgh Press.

Guth, James L. 2004. "George W. Bush and Religious Politics." In *High Risk and Big Ambition: The Presidency of George W. Bush*, ed. Steven E. Schier, 117–144. Pittsburgh, Pa.: University of Pittsburgh Press.

Guth, James L., Lyman A. Kellstedt, Corwin E. Smidt, and John C. Green. 2006. "Religious Influences in the 2004 Presidential Election." *Presidential Studies Quarterly* 36: 223–242.

Hamby, Alonzo. 1995. *Man of the People: The Life of Harry S. Truman*. New York: Oxford University Press.

Holl, Jack. 2007. "Dwight D. Eisenhower: Civil Religion and the Cold War." In *Religion and the American Presidency*, ed. Mark J. Rozell and Gleaves Whitney, 119–138. New York: Palgrave/MacMillan.

Hutcheson, Richard G., Jr. 1988. *God in the White House: How Religion Has Changed The Modern Presidency*. New York: Collier Books.

Kane, James G., Stephen C. Craig, and Kenneth D. Wald. 2004. "Religion and Presidential Politics in Florida: A List Experiment," *Social Science Quarterly* 85: 281–293.

Kaplan, Esther. 2004. *With God on Their Side: How Christian Fundamentalists Trumped Science, Policy, and Democracy in George W. Bush's White House*. New York: New Press.

Kengor, Paul. 2004a. *God and George W. Bush*. New York: Regan Books.

Kengor, Paul. 2004b. *God and Ronald Reagan: A Spiritual Life*. New York: Regan Books.

Kengor, Paul. 2007. "Ronald Reagan's Faith and Attack on Soviet Communism." In *Religion and the American Presidency*, ed. Mark J. Rozell and Gleaves Whitney, 175–190. New York: Palgrave/MacMillan.

Linder, Robert. 1996. "Universal Pastor: Bill Clinton's Civil Religion." *Journal of Church and State* 38: 733–749.

Mansfield, Stephen. 2003. *The Faith of George W. Bush*. New York: Penguin Books.

McCullough, David. 1992. *Truman*. New York: Simon and Schuster.

Merkley, Paul Charles. 2004. *American Presidents, Religion, and Israel: The Heirs of Cyrus*. Westport, Conn.: Praeger Press.

Mitchell, Joshua. 2007. "Religion is Not a Preference." *Journal of Politics* 69: 351–362.

Morris, Edmund. 1999. *Dutch*. New York: Random House.

Nesmith, Bruce. 1997. "The New Republican Coalition: The Reagan Campaigns and White Evangelicals." *Review of Religious Research* 39: 80–83.

Novak, Michael. 1974. *Choosing Our King: Powerful Symbols in Presidential Politics*. New York: Macmillan.

Oldfield, Duane M. 1996a. "The Christian Right in the Presidential Nominating Process." In *In Pursuit of the White House: How We Choose Our Presidential Nominees*, ed. William G. Mayer, 254–279. Chatham, N.J.: Chatham House.

Oldfield, Duane M. 1996b. *The Right and the Righteous: The Christian Right Confronts the Republican Party*. New York: Rowman & Littlefield.

Patterson, Bradley H., Jr. 2000. *The White House Staff: Inside the West Wing and Beyond*. Washington, D.C.: Brookings Institution Press.

Penning, James. 2007. "The Religion of Bill Clinton." In *Religion and the American Presidency*, ed. Mark J. Rozell and Gleaves Whitney, 191–214. New York: Palgrave/MacMillan.

Pierard, Richard V., and Robert D. Linder. 1988. *Civil Religion and the Presidency*. Grand Rapids, Mich.: Zondervan.

Pika, Joseph A. 1987–1988. "Interest Groups in the White House under Roosevelt and Truman." *Political Science Quarterly* 102: 647–668.

Polsby, Nelson W., and Aaron Wildavsky. 2000. *Presidential Elections: Strategies and Structures in American Politics*. 10th ed. New York: Chatham House.

Prendergast, William B. 1999. *The Catholic Voter in American Politics*. Washington, D.C.: Georgetown University Press.

Rauschenbusch, Paul, ed. 2007. *Christianity and the Social Crisis in the 21st Century: The Classic That Woke Up the Church*. New York: HarperCollins.

Richter, Edward J., and Berton Dulce. 1962. *Religion and the Presidency: A Recurring American Problem*. New York. Macmillan.

Robinson, Carin, and Clyde Wilcox. 2007. "The Faith of George W. Bush: The Personal, Practical, and Political." In *Religion and the American Presidency*, ed. Mark J. Rozell and Gleaves Whitney, 215–238. New York: Palgrave/MacMillan.

Rozell, Mark J., and Gleaves Whitney, eds. 2007a. *Religion and the American Presidency*. New York: Palgrave Macmillan.

Rozell, Mark J., and Gleaves Whitney, eds. 2007b. *Religion and the Bush Presidency*. New York: Palgrave/MacMillan.

Shafer, Byron E. 1983. *Quiet Revolution: The Struggle for the Democratic Party and the Shaping of Post-Reform Politics*. New York: Russell Sage.

Silva, Ruth. 1962. *Rum, Religion, and Votes: 1928 Reexamined*. University Park, Pa.: The Pennsylvania State University Press.

Skowronek, Stephen. 1997. *The Politics Presidents Make: Leadership from John Adams to Bill Clinton*. Cambridge, Mass.: Belknap.

Smith, Gary Scott, 2005. *Faith and the Presidency*. New York: Oxford University Press.

Smith, Gary Scott. 2007. "The Faith of George Washington." In *Religion and the American Presidency*, ed. Mark J. Rozell and Gleaves Whitney, 9–38. New York: Palgrave/MacMillan.

Sorensen, Theodore. 1965. *Kennedy*. New York: Harper & Row.

Spalding, Elizabeth Edwards. 2007. " 'We Must Put on the Armor of God': Harry Truman and the Cold War." In *Religion and the American Presidency*, ed. Mark J. Rozell and Gleaves Whitney, 95–118. New York: Palgrave/MacMillan.

Sundquist, James L. 1983. *Dynamics of the Party System: Alignment and Realignment of Political Parties in the United States*. Rev. ed. Washington, D.C.: Brookings Institution Press.

Tichenor, Daniel J. 2006. "The Presidency and Interest Groups: Allies, Adversaries, and Policy Leadership." In *The Presidency and the Political System*. 8th ed., ed. Michael Nelson, 311–340. Washington, D.C.: CQ Press.

Truman, David B. 1951. *The Governmental Process: Political Interests and Public Opinion*. New York: Knopf.

Unger, Craig. 2007. *The Fall of the House of Bush.* New York: Scribner.

Warber, Adam, and Laura Olson. 2006. "Religion and the Public Presidency." Presented at the annual meeting of the American Political Science Association, Marriott, Loews, Philadelphia, and the Philadelphia Convention Center, Philadelphia, Pennsylvania, August 31.

White, Theodore H. 1961. *The Making of the President, 1960.* New York: Atheneum.

White, Theodore H. 1970. *The Making of the President, 1968.* New York: Pocket Books.

Wilcox, Clyde. 1992. *God's Warriors: The Christian Right in Twentieth-Century America.* Baltimore, Md.: Johns Hopkins University Press.

CHAPTER 18

RELIGION AND LEGISLATIVE POLITICS

ELIZABETH A. OLDMIXON

IN democratic societies, legislatures provide the institutional context for groups to deliberate on and make policy for entire communities. More than just representative bodies, legislatures are called on to recognize and resolve salient conflicts (Dodd 1993, pp. 418–419). As Alexis de Tocqueville famously observed, and as other authors in this volume note, religion has been a vital element of American society since the early republic. It is no surprise, then, that Congress and 50 state legislatures address many conflicts that directly implicate religion, such as civil rights, nuclear proliferation, the welfare state, abortion, school curricula, and gay rights. When such conflicts emerge, religious values and interests may shape legislative politics. Nevertheless, congressional scholarship has seldom focused on religion as an element of institutional politics. Theories of legislative decision making typically focus on "the usual suspects"—namely, party, constituency, ideology, interest group pressures, presidential lobbying, and staff input (Kingdon 1973). Of these, party, constituency, and ideology usually provide the most explanatory power.

Although congressional party unity does not match that in Westminster systems, partisanship still provides the most robust explanation for legislative behavior, capturing vital differences in members' values, preferences, and priorities. Because of these shared qualities, copartisans usually favor similar policies. And because congressional districts are usually drawn for partisan ends, copartisans often represent similar constituencies. Thus, intraparty homogeneity, coupled with interparty polarization, lays the groundwork for party voting and contributes to strong party leadership (Aldrich and Rohde 2005). Moreover, given their heavy workload, legislators need decision shortcuts and often look to copartisans for cues. Finally, as instruments of organization, parties also create incentives for loyalty. Still, the different voting records of Senators James Inhofe (R-OK) and Olympia Snowe (R-ME) remind us that partisanship does not explain everything on Capitol Hill.

Constituencies also influence legislative behavior. Indeed, whatever pressure party leaders, the president, or lobbyists might exert, classic and contemporary choice theoretical approaches assume that legislators are strategic actors who listen to constituents as a way to enhance job security. Such attention affects roll call voting, career calculations, agenda setting, and the distribution of power within the chambers (Fenno 1973; Kingdon 1973; Mayhew 1974; Dodd 1977; Rohde 1991; Arnold 1992; Aldrich 1995; Aldrich and Rohde 2005; Sulkin 2005). Certainly, strategic legislators balance several career goals and influences; they are more attentive to some constituents than others, and the "electoral connection" may or may not be linear. However, ultimately we assume electoral rationality and expect that constituents elect representatives who mirror their preferences on salient issues, and that legislators respond to constituents' preferences when they can discern them and when their jobs depend on it.

In addition to party and constituency preferences, legislators also bring their own values, experiences, and interests to legislative politics (Burden 2007). Ideology is sometimes used as a proxy for these personal factors, and is a powerful predictor of legislative behavior (Poole and Rosenthal 1997). Of course, this approach is at least partially circular: Scholars measure ideology using roll call votes—the very thing they are trying to predict. The resulting ideological scores place issues on a somewhat artificial Left–Right continuum and often fail to explain the variance on individual policies. Nor does this approach tell us much about how legislator preferences develop. Moreover, Burden (2007, p. 39) argues that in addition to "public ideology," personal traits provide legislators with "internal cues" that guide their behavior. Personal traits may not influence all votes and policy domains, but when there is ambiguity, or when legislators are unconstrained by constituents, they "may rely on introspective representation." In other words, they act on their own preferences, as informed by their values, interests, and experiences.

How does religion fit into the dynamic of legislative politics? It does so in two ways. First, as Burden (2007) argues, religion is a personal trait that informs a legislator's values. When policy issues implicate those values, legislators may bring their religious perspectives to bear on roll call voting or, especially, on prefloor activities such as cosponsorships, committee action, and speeches, all less constrained by partisanship. Second, when legislators respond to constituency preferences shaped and mobilized by religion, religious factors may again influence legislative behavior. Such influence is facilitated by electoral politics, as religion shapes opinion, partisanship, and electoral choices among voters (Layman 2001; Green 2004; Green, Smidt, Guth, and Kellstedt 2005). Party activists also divide along religious lines and may frame elections in ways that amplify religious differences (Layman 1999; Leege, Wald, Krueger, and Mueller 2002). And, not surprisingly, there are clear religious patterns to party affiliation in the U.S. House. Between 1997 and 2002, for example, most evangelicals, Latter-day Saints, and mainline Protestants were on the GOP side of the aisle, whereas seculars, Jews, black Protestants, and Latino Catholics were concentrated on the Democratic side (Guth 2007).

The rest of this chapter reviews existing religion and legislative studies, a limited but growing body of literature. One major challenge to scholarship here has been the conceptualization and measurement of religion, and that is where we begin. From there, the chapter summarizes and critiques the legislative behavior scholarship, discusses aggregate outputs, points to the role of organized religious interests, and suggests future directions for research.

THE CONCEPTUALIZATION
AND MEASUREMENT OF RELIGION

A major impediment to scholarship on religion and legislative politics is the thorny problem of conceptualizing and measuring religion. Too often legislative scholars use imperfect or oversimplified proxies to measure complex concepts and have not taken advantage of advances made, for example, in electoral and public opinion analysis. Using information easily available, scholars tend to measure religion with very broad categories of religious affiliation such as Catholic, Protestant, Jewish, Mormon (e.g., Richardson and Fox 1972) or of denominational families (Catholic, Lutheran, Baptist, Presbyterian, Methodist). In the same vein, constituency religion is often defined as the proportion of the population identifying with broad traditions or denominational families.

Measures based on such classifications have been of some use. They allow us to infer something about the religious institutions in which legislators participate, the beliefs to which they ascribe, and the community of believers to which they belong (Kellstedt and Green 1993; Wilcox, Jelen, and Leege 1993; Wald and Calhoun-Brown 2007). They encapsulate "differences in belief, practice, and commitment, even for individuals with minimal religiosity" (Kellstedt and Green 1993, p. 55). Sometimes, however, the earliest scholars adopted even blunter religious frameworks at the elite and constituency levels. For example, Fairbanks (1977) used the proportion of state populations classified as "conservative" Protestant and Catholic to predict state policy making. The term *conservative* included denominations that believed in biblical literalism, as identified by the National Council of Churches. Richardson and Fox (1972) focused on legislators' affiliation to predict legislative outputs, classifying them as Catholic, Protestant, Jewish, or Mormon.

Even with inadequate measures, both studies found interesting and significant results. They assumed that theological differences would produce political differences, and that these differences would have legislative implications. Accordingly, they tried to draw clear lines between religious traditions. However, these earlier denominational measures ignored theological nuance and the extent to which theological and historical circumstances intersect (as among black Protestants) to produce distinct traditions that have different policy implications. Thus, the Protestant–Catholic–Jewish framework might have captured differences between Christians and Jews, but not between black Pentecostals and white Southern Baptists. In the same way, if one measured ideology as a dichotomous variable, one would probably find significant differences between Charlie Rangel (D-NY) and Tom Delay (R-TX), but be incapable of making fine-grained distinctions between, say, John Sununu (R-NH) and James Inhofe (R-OK) or Joe Lieberman (I-CT) and Olympia Snowe (R-ME).

To be sure, measures based on religious tradition are more sophisticated than they used to be. Scholars increasingly break down "Protestants" on the basis of theology, history, and liturgy, into groups such as evangelical (including fundamentalists, Pentecostals, and charismatics), black, and mainline (Fastnow, Grant, and Rudolph 1999; Oldmixon and Calfano 2007). This is an important step, because it better captures differences in "belief, practice, and commitment." However, even use of fine-grained denominational categories can be problematic. In the first place, it is deceptively difficult to obtain accurate denominational information on legislators. Data are publicly available from various editions of *The Almanac of American Politics* (Barone and Cohen 2007) or *CQ's Politics in America* (Koszczuk and Angle 2007), but this information is often vague. For example, some legislators list themselves as "Baptist," a religious family, without specifying the particular denomination, such as the Southern Baptist Convention or American Baptist Churches USA. The former is an evangelical denomination, whereas the latter is mainline, yet those identifying as "Baptist" tend to be grouped as evangelical. Thus, even with the use of more detailed religious categories, the analysis can be predicated on inaccurate denominational assignments. Locating precise denominational affiliations can require a great deal of investigation. As a case in point, Guth (2007) visited campaign and congressional web pages, Project Vote Smart, and media sources to find more specific information on legislator affiliation, sometimes producing results at variance with an uncritical use of public data. Without accurate placement of legislators into religious categories, determining the impact of affiliation on policy choices may be problematic.

Second, even accurate denominational assignments to religious traditions do not necessarily reveal just what it is one is tapping. Is it the particular belief system that drives legislative behavior or simply identification with a social group? Denominational measures may fail to capture religious differences that transcend denomination; they tell us little about the public religiosity, religious worldviews, and private devotionalism of members. These are all issues of conceptualization. Measurement should be a function of *how* we expect religion to influence legislative politics. If we are interested in the effect of beliefs or social group identification, denomination may be a useful proxy, despite its imprecision. However, if we want to investigate other religious dimensions, such as religiosity or private devotionalism, denomination is inappropriate. The problem for congressional scholars is how to acquire such data. Just as accurate denominational information is difficult to procure, so, too, are measures of doctrinal orientation, devotionalism, religiosity, and the like. As a result, the kinds of questions we have answered about the relationship between religion and legislative politics have been limited.

Scholars wishing to move away from blunt denominational categories have had to be creative. Green and Guth (1991) and Oldmixon (2002) used the elite and constituency denominational measures to create indices of Protestant orthodoxy. Denominations were arrayed based on their level of Protestant orthodoxy, with Southern Baptists receiving high scores; the unchurched receiving low scores; and Catholics, Jews, and mainliners falling somewhere in between. Constituencies were weighted accordingly. The article by Green and Guth (1991) is particularly important, because it establishes a link between religion and legislative behavior across policy domains, and not just on issues such as abortion or school prayer. However, attempting to array all members of Congress, including Catholics and Jews, across a basically "Protestant" orthodoxy scale probably does not make much conceptual sense. (See chapter 1 in this volume for a discussion of this problem.)

Other scholars have eschewed denominationally based measures altogether. In their path-breaking work, *Religion on Capitol Hill,* Benson and Williams (1982, p. 12) define religion as "the cognitions (values, beliefs, thoughts), affect (feelings, attitudes), and behaviors involved in apprehending and responding to a reality (a supernatural being or beings, force, energy, principle, absolute consciousness) that is affirmed to exist." During interviews with a sample of U.S. Senate and House members, Benson and Williams developed scales to measure the importance of religion, theological perspectives, and other religious themes, For example, is religion meant to provide comfort or act as an impulse for change?

Based on 13 dimensions, Benson and Williams (1982) identified six religious types, which cross-cut denominations. They found that religion did affect congressional voting behavior, although its influence was more complex than common categorical measures would suggest. It was not so much denominational affiliation as one's view of religious reality that affected legislative behavior. For example, they identified "legalistic religionists" as holding an individualistic conception of religion rooted in Christian orthodoxy; conceiving of a strict, judging God; and valuing self-restraint. These legislators, in their analysis, embrace a conservative political orientation. On the other hand, "people-concerned religionists" are communal in approach to religion and view God as liberating rather than judging; they tend toward more liberal voting records. This work moves us away from popular false dichotomies that suggest that conservatives are animated by religion whereas liberals are not. The question is really not *whether* religion affects voting behavior, but rather *how* it affects behavior.

Benson and Williams (1982) conceptualize religion in a way that recognizes its complexity, and they develop measures accordingly. However, their particular approach is difficult to replicate, because extended elite interviews are difficult to secure, especially in the numbers required for this kind of analysis.[1] As a result, scholars typically default to denominational measures because they are useful and seemingly easy to procure. However, in so doing, they miss important vectors of religious influence of the sort that Benson and Williams (1982) captured. As we move forward, studies of legislative behavior need to address other sources of religious influence by borrowing from their general approach, if not their specific framework. Otherwise, we will continue to underspecify and misspecify our models, because it will be unclear just what aspect of religion is captured by denominational measures. A number of strategies show promise, such as interviewing state legislators and retired federal legislators (Yamane and Oldmixon 2006, Burden 2007), and using unobtrusive sources to garner information on religious activity and theological orientation (Guth and Kellstedt 2001; Guth 2007).

In another innovative approach, Burden (2007) supplements quantitative analysis of legislative behavior with interviews of retired legislators, designed to tease out the more personal influences on their decision making. Retired legislators are generally more accessible and open, and in many cases eager to talk. Burden's work is also notable because he analyzes activities that precede final votes: bill cosponsorships, committee action, and floor speeches. Legislators have the least personal agency in roll call voting, whereas prevote activities provide them with opportunities to shape legislation "upstream" and with more independence from party leaders and constituents. Scholars interested in the effect of religion on legislative behavior might well focus on these aspects of legislative behavior.

Turning our attention to the states is probably another useful exploratory strategy, especially because scholars are more likely to have access to state legislators than to members of Congress. Moreover, state legislatures address a broad array of policy conflicts to which religion is relevant. For example, Yamane and Oldmixon's (2006) study of the Wisconsin legislature found that the effects of denominational affiliation were mediated by religiosity. Like Benson and Williams (1982), their measures of religion were based on elite interviews, but with state legislators rather than national ones.

To develop measures of affiliation, religious activity, and theological orientation for members of Congress, Guth (2007, pp. 5–6) reviewed legislator campaign and congressional web pages, Project Vote Smart questionnaires, and various media sources and found "treasure troves of data on legislators' lives, their interaction with churches and religious organizations, and their personal religious 'constituencies.'" Not only do these measures show real innovation, they possess considerable analytical power, as Guth (2007) found a strong and statistically significant relationship between religious measures, including theological orientations, and legislative behavior across policy domains. Replicating Guth's (2007) measures in other legislatures may be challenging, but certainly not impossible.

RELIGION, MORALITY, AND
LEGISLATIVE BEHAVIOR

As noted earlier, legislative behavior is a function of both constituency and elite-level factors. Constituencies influence legislators because voters choose those who reflect their preferences, and legislators have an electoral incentive to be attentive to constituency demands, even if such pressure is only a matter of perception (Miller and Stokes 1963). Members' party and ideology also affect legislative behavior and, although these two phenomena are increasingly difficult to decouple (Poole and Rosenthal 1997; Binder 2003), their importance suggests that legislators have room to bring their own preferences and values to bear on policy making. It is in this context, then, that religion emerges as an aspect of both elite and constituency effects that may influence policy making across an array of issues.

Moral Issues

Scholars most often bring religion into the legislative arena as a function of morality or cultural politics—two related, but distinct, approaches. Application of morality policy theory is a policy domain-specific approach. Although there is no fixed list of morality policy issues, these issues typically involve the demand for "sin"—or at least what is perceived to be sin given a set of values (Meier 2001). Abortion, sex and sexuality, drugs, pornography, and alcohol all fall under this rubric. Because these issues are managed most often at the state level, much of morality politics research has focused on state legislatures, with some exceptions (Haider-Markel 2001; Burden 2007). Both the religious characteristics of legislators and of their constituencies might well influence decision making.

Practitioners of cultural theory may not identify a set of issues as essentially cultural per se. As Leege et al. (2002, pp. 27–28, emphasis in original) note, "*cultural politics is less a set of issues than a style of argumentation that invokes fundamental social values and emphasizes group differences.*" "*Cultural conflict,*" then, "*is simply argument . . . about how we should live*" (Leege et al. 2002, p. 26, emphasis in original). Stated differently, culture provides "a shared sense of how people ought to live their lives and what social relationships are compatible with that vision" (Oldmixon 2002, p. 775). Religion influences cultural politics to the extent that it informs who we are.

Whether one adopts morality policy or cultural language does not usually matter. The models derived from these theories overlap a great deal. Morality and cultural policies are both rooted in fundamental first principles, rather than instrumentalities, and they share some characteristics of so-called "easy issues" (Carmines and Stimson 1980; Mooney 2001). They are nontechnical, highly salient, and easy for elites and (crucially) nonelites alike to understand. Political conflicts involving these issues tend to be rooted in identity-based concerns, which are stoked when government tries to set policy on issues evoking those conflicts (Smith and Tatalovich 2003). These issues present unique difficulties for legislators because there is no consensus on the ends of policy, and making policy inevitably affirms one set of moral values over another.

Scholars adopt different approaches to explain the efficacy of religion in this domain. Hutcheson and Taylor (1973) argue that religion is a "cultural factor" that influences the political system as whole as well as policy outputs more specifically. They find that the size of each state's fundamentalist Protestant[2] population is negatively correlated with political system traits (such as party competition and voter participation), negatively correlated with state property tax levels, but positively correlated with student–teacher ratios.

In a complementary approach, Fairbanks (1977) argues that religion influences state policy making to the extent that issues engage religious concerns. He analyzes state policy making on alcohol and gambling, expecting that Protestantism will be associated with restrictive policies, attributable to its "emphasis on piety and asceticism" (Fairbanks 1977, p. 411). Using states as the units of analysis, he correlates the size of Catholic and conservative Protestant[3] populations with policy restrictiveness. He finds that restrictive gambling and alcohol policies are positively correlated with conservative Protestant membership, whereas restrictive alcohol policies are negatively correlated with Catholic affiliation. Although these early studies lay important groundwork in establishing the importance of religion in institutional politics, they did not consider legislators per se. Rather, religion is measured at the mass level and represents a factor exogenous to political institutions, although one that may exert pressure on policy makers.

Most morality politics research is focused on a few "usual suspects," often hot-button issues such as abortion and gay rights. Some of this work self-consciously adopts the morality/cultural approach (Tatalovich and Schier 1993; Haider-Markel 2001; Oldmixon 2005). However, Haider-Markel's (2001) analysis of U.S. House votes on gay issues from the 101st to the 104th Congress (1989–1996) is one of the first efforts to apply the morality politics framework to elite decision making. In modeling legislative behavior, he posits that both elite and constituency religion will influence decision making, because "morality politics is often organized around religious beliefs" (Haider-Markel 2001, p. 118).

Even after controlling for party and ideology, Haider-Markel (2001) finds that elite affiliation with a "religious conservative" denomination[4] and constituency opposition to gay rights diminishes support for a gay rights index based on roll call votes. He also analyzes separate votes on gays in the military, domestic partnerships, and school curricula. His findings indicate that although religious "conservatives" are less supportive of gays in the military than their colleagues, they are indistinguishable on the other two issues. This suggests that some gay issues are more salient than others to religious conservatives.

Oldmixon and Calfano (2007) revisit this question in an analysis of House voting on gay issues from 1993 to 2002. In their view, gay issues represent a cultural conflict between religious traditionalists and progressives. Legislator religion is measured using three categorical variables: Catholic, black Protestant, and white evangelical Protestant. Their analysis also provides a direct test of constituency religion, using the same categories developed for legislators.[5] Oldmixon and Calfano argue that, if gay issues are symbolic of a cultural rift, then legislators should be driven by a desire to affirm their culture and the culture of their constituents. Thus, religion as well as party and ideology are expected to influence legislator decision making. They find that evangelical Protestantism at the district level is significantly associated with traditionalism on gay issues (see also Campbell and Davidson 2000; Lewis and Edelson 2000). Although larger district populations of Catholics and black Protestants are also associated with opposition to gay rights, these associations are not consistently significant. Interestingly, at the elite level, members' affiliation as black Protestant and white evangelical does not add significantly to the influence of district religious composition, because these legislators are indistinguishable from their mainline and Jewish colleagues, when district religion is in the equation. Nevertheless, affiliation as a white Catholic still produces significantly less legislator support for gay rights in four of five congresses.[6] These findings suggest that legislator behavior is often the product of both district and member religious characteristics.

In a broader analysis, Oldmixon (2005) investigates legislator decision making on gay issues, reproductive policy, and school prayer. However, the main research question is not whether religion affects legislative voting, but how leaders build compromise and how legislative majorities are built when policy issues reflect a cultural cleavage exemplified by the importance of religion in the policy process. Nonetheless, her study includes analysis of roll call votes, cosponsorship behavior, as well as elite interviews of legislators and staff. She concludes that culturally significant issues do produce a different kind of legislative politics. In the view of legislators, these are issues on which people are polarized.

Oldmixon's (2005) models include both legislator religious affiliation[7] and the distribution of religious groups in congressional districts. Her analysis of cosponsorship and roll call voting reveals that Catholic legislators are more pro-life and more opposed to gay rights than their mainline, liberal Protestant, and Jewish colleagues, but are indistinguishable from these colleagues on school prayer. District Catholicism is significantly associated with pro-life and antigay rights roll call voting (although significance varies somewhat with regard to gay issues). White religious conservative and black Protestant legislators are generally indistinguishable from their colleagues on these issues, but district religious conservatism is significantly associated with antigay rights and pro-school prayer cosponsorships as well as pro-life and antigay rights roll call voting.

These results have a number of implications. First, legislators receive a great deal of pressure from constituents. Yet, most representatives indicate that, given the nature of these issues, they nevertheless vote on principle. Still, most legislators are hardly profiles in courage, because they believe that their preferences are consistent with those of their district. Second, the polarized nature of these issues makes compromise—a staple of the legislative process—difficult to achieve, but not impossible. Sometimes morality/cultural issues can be reframed so that legislators can switch votes without abandoning core principles. In a redistributive context, for example, money spent on contraception can be framed as a way to limit abortions.

Other analyses of elite behavior adopt different theoretical approaches. Guth (2007) investigates the influence of religion on ideological content of social voting more generally, as quantified by the *National Journal's* social issue index. The index captures voting on a variety of moral issues such as abortion and gay issues, and issues with strong moral implications such as judicial nominations. Focusing on members of the U.S. House from 1997 to 2002, legislator affiliation is measured by a full complement of dummy variables for Mormons, evangelical Protestants, mainline Protestants, black Protestants, white Catholics, Latino Catholics, Jews, seculars, and others. Constituency religion is measured using an analogous set of variables.

In addition to these rather precise measures of religious tradition, the analysis also includes measures of theological orientation and religious practice, leading to a classification of legislators as traditionalists, centrists, or modernists. Traditionalists "insist on an orthodox interpretation of their faith's beliefs, modernists seek to reinterpret those doctrines in accordance with modern science and culture, and centrists try to work out a middle position" (Guth 2007, p. 12). Classification is based on a legislator's own personal testimony, leadership in various religious groups, and specific congregation membership, among other indicators. Legislators' religious activity is captured by indicators such as regular church attendance or holding congregational leadership positions. Guth's (2007) findings indicate that affiliation has no direct impact on social issue liberalism for white evangelical and mainline Protestants and Anglo-Catholics, but does for black Protestants, Latino Catholics, Jews, and seculars. The member's own theological traditionalism and a higher proportion of evangelicals within the constituency exert a strong conservative pull on legislative behavior on social issues. This finding is important, because it suggests that affiliation is not an entirely adequate proxy for theological orientation or religious involvement when discerning the nexus between religion and legislative behavior.

Although conceding that a strictly denominational approach probably underestimates religion's importance, Burden (2007) investigates the influence of religious affiliation on legislative behavior. His theoretical framework delves into the importance of legislators' personal traits more generally. Religion, he suggests, is particularly relevant in the "murky" domain of morality issues that often pit conscience against partisanship, science, and technology (Burden 2007, p. 112). He studies three cases: the Religious Freedom Restoration Act of 1993, designed to protect the free exercise of religion; the Community Solutions Act of 2001, a Charitable Choice bill that (among other things) expanded government funding for religious providers of social services; and the Human Cloning Prohibition Act of 2001.

The Religious Freedom Restoration Act of 1993 passed overwhelmingly, so Burden's (2007) analysis focuses on cosponsorship. As noted previously, prefloor activities such as cosponsoring legislation are more proactive than roll call voting, and, in that sense, are better measures of personal commitment to a policy. Thus, Burden (2007) argues that personal traits are more likely to emerge at this stage. He finds that evangelical, mainline Protestant, and Roman Catholic legislators were less likely to cosponsor the Religious Freedom Restoration Act of 1993 than their black Protestant, Jewish, Mormon, and unaffiliated colleagues. However, these relationships varied by party, with Republican Protestants and Catholics more disinclined to cosponsor the bill than Democratic Protestants and Catholics. Burden (2007, p. 122) attributes these contrasts to the "differing compositions of adherents within the parties."

The effect of personal religious traits is magnified when analysis focuses on an even more "selective" behavior: speech making. Although Burden does not break down the analysis by party, he finds that mainline Protestant and Roman Catholic representatives, a majority of the House, were least likely to speak, "while the smallest groups (evangelicals, Jews, Mormons, and others)," who are more likely to feel threatened, "were most proactive" (Burden 2007, p. 122) and, as a result, more likely to support additional codification of religious liberty.

Burden's (2007) analysis of Charitable Choice legislation further reveals that the impact of personal traits such as religion may be diminished in the very partisan context of roll call voting, although still present at earlier stages. In this instance, religious affiliation had no direct impact on roll call voting, but analysis of cosponsorships indicates that Catholics, mainline Protestants, and evangelicals were more likely to cosponsor the bill than their colleagues. And, as in the case of the Religious Freedom Restoration Act of 1993, legislators from smaller religious traditions were, on the basis of perceived threat, more likely to be proactive than colleagues from larger traditions.

The Human Cloning Prohibition Act emerged in 2001 in the wake of conflict over embryonic stem cell research, and sought to ban the cloning of human embryos. On this bill, Jews and mainline Protestants were less supportive of such restrictions. Among Democrats, black Protestants were more supportive of the bill than colleagues from other religious traditions, whereas other religious variables were insignificant. However, religion seemed to matter more among Republicans, where Catholics (breaking with their church) and mainline Protestants were less likely to support the bill than copartisans of other faiths. Republicans led the effort to protect human life in this new domain, and thus personal religious traits were especially efficacious.

In an approach similar to Burden (2007), Highton and Rocca (2005) also stress the importance of the religious characteristics of legislators. They focus on voluntary position taking, examining abortion as a case study. They find that Catholic legislators representing pro-life districts are more likely to "position take" than their similarly situated non-Catholic colleagues. As districts become more pro-choice, the probability of position taking by Catholic legislators diminishes. Their results suggest that the personal preferences of legislators interact with district preferences to produce certain kinds of behavior. Constituency opinion can have either a constraining or enhancing effect, depending on the nature of legislators' preferences vis-à-vis their districts.

General Voting Patterns

The lion's share of the research on religion and legislative behavior is focused on so-called moral issues. And yet, if religion provides individuals with values, then surely those values are engaged across an array of issues—not just "moral" ones. Religious values may well speak to questions of war and use of force, nuclear proliferation, foreign policy, environmental protection, welfare, and the minimum wage.

A handful of studies have investigated the possibility that religion influences general legislative behavior. As noted earlier, Green and Guth (1991) used an indexed measure of district and elite religious conservatism to model the ideological content of roll call voting. Aligning denominations based on orthodoxy, legislators were scored with respect to their denomination's place on the alignment, and their constituencies were given orthodoxy scores based on the relative size of denominations within district boundaries. Green and Guth (1991) found that elite and district orthodoxy produce diminished liberalism among legislators. Although their operationalization of orthodoxy was critiqued earlier (and has been abandoned in more recent work [see, for example, Guth 2007]), the findings bolster the results discussed in the previous section. Religious conservatism, however it may be defined, is associated with political conservatism. This suggests that the influence of religion on legislative behavior is much wider than scholars have thought.

In the same vein, Fastnow et al. (1999) investigated the effect of religion on general legislative ideology, as tapped by Americans for Democratic Action scores from 1959 to 1994. In their own words, "[i]f religion is truly an important determinant of voting behavior, then it should show up in a general voting scale" (Fastnow et al. 1999, p. 691). After controlling for the usual suspects, they found that Catholics, black Protestants, and Jews were more liberal than their mainline Protestant colleagues, whereas Mormons and evangelicals were more conservative. Prior to the 1980s, however, Mormons were indistinguishable from their mainline and liberal Protestant colleagues. And, although Catholic legislators were more liberal overall, their behavior changed over time. In the 1960s, Catholic legislators were clearly more liberal than their mainline and liberal Protestant counterparts, but by the 1970s this pattern had diminished.

Yamane and Oldmixon (2006) adopted a different approach to estimating the effects of religion on ideological voting. They focused on the Wisconsin legislature and used structural equation modeling to map the effect of religion. The ideology measure was an index based on important roll call votes, with two dummy variables to measure legislator religion (Catholic and white evangelical Protestant). In addition to using religious tradition variables, they included a measure of religious saliency based on legislators' answers to questions dealing with church attendance, prayer, and the importance of religion. They found that their salience measure had a direct effect on legislative voting—with higher religious salience producing higher ideological conservatism. The effect of denominational affiliation, however, worked primarily through other variables. Evangelical Protestantism was negatively related to Democratic partisanship, and Democratic partisanship was negatively related to conservative roll call voting. However evangelicalism was positively related to religiosity—as was Catholic affiliation—and religiosity, then, was positively related to conservative voting. Thus, religion's influence is much more complicated than previous studies have shown, suggesting the need for path models to untangle the direct and indirect effects.

Guth (2007) also analyzed the influence of religion on general patterns of ideological voting by regressing DW-Nominate scores on elite religious tradition dummy variables, analogous constituency religious variables, measures of religious activism and theological orientation, as well as various control variables. Among the religious variables, theological orientation had the most robust impact on ideology, and the findings indicate that traditionalism is negatively associated with liberalism. Affiliation with certain religious traditions (Hispanic Catholics, Jews, seculars) was significantly associated with liberalism, whereas affiliation with other such traditions (evangelical Protestants, Mormons, white Catholics, and mainline Protestants) had no direct impact on ideology, indicating that it is members' "location on the theological scale that influences voting" (Guth 2007, p. 18). Having high proportions of evangelical Protestant constituents also produced conservative voting, whereas large proportions of black Protestants produced more liberal tendencies. When partisanship was controlled, however, the effect of constituency religion washed out, suggesting that its influence is "fully mediated by party preference of the faithful and their choice of representatives" (Guth 2007, p. 20). Religious activity had no direct impact on ideological voting.

Domestic Policy

Two studies have investigated the effect of religion on (nonmoral) domestic policy. Oldmixon and Hudson (2008) examined the influence of religion on social policy, which includes such issues such as immigration reform, the minimum wage, housing issues, and reconciliation legislation. They were particularly interested in the influence of Catholic religious affiliation, because Fastnow et al. (1999) found that ideology and religion tend to pull Catholic Democrats in different directions (their policy liberalism is at odds with church teaching on cultural issues). Oldmixon and Hudson (2008) investigated this dilemma from the perspective of Catholic Republicans, given that their policy conservatism is at odds with church teaching in the social domain. They found that with regard to roll call voting, Catholic Republicans tended to defect from church teachings. Their roll call analysis was complemented by a series of interviews in which Catholic Republican legislators explained their defection from church teaching by three different arguments: by distinguishing between their personal beliefs and their responsibilities as public officials; by arguing that, contrary to what the American episcopacy says, their position is consistent with church teaching; and/or by contending that their defections are on issues of prudential judgment.

Overall, Oldmixon and Hudson (2008) found that Catholics, Jews, and white evangelicals were more liberal on these issues than their mainline and liberal

Protestant colleagues. Although it was not the focus of the study, their finding with regard to white evangelicals was especially interesting. Scholars generally associate this group with ideological conservatism, yet when they controlled for ideology and partisanship, white evangelicals were found to be more than twice as likely as their mainline colleagues to support the Left-leaning tenants of Catholic social teaching. Perhaps this apparent anomaly reflects differences between religious affiliation and religious belief—in that Guth (2007) found that although affiliation has no direct impact on voting in this domain (in the fully specified model), theological traditionalism and district evangelicalism are strongly associated with conservative voting on these kinds of issues.

Another study of domestic policy focused on immigration. Fetzer (2006) analyzed the 2005 House vote on H.R. 4437, which would have criminalized not just illegal immigration but assistance to illegal aliens as well. The bill was opposed vociferously by the Catholic church; indeed, Cardinal Mahoney of Los Angeles instructed priests to disobey the law. Fetzer (2006) found that voting on this bill was largely a function of geography and district sociodemographics rather than religious factors. Republican legislators and southerners were more likely to support H.R. 4437 than their colleagues, whereas legislators from strongly Latino districts were less likely to support this bill. The effects of Catholic and Jewish affiliations among the legislators were insignificant.

Foreign Policy

Although scholars have identified religious dimensions to foreign policy attitudes at the mass level (Rothenberg and Newport 1984; Smidt 1987; Jelen 1994), only a handful of studies have investigated whether these patterns are reflected among legislators. Guth (2007) finds that legislator secularism and religious activity are positively related to foreign policy liberalism. Theological traditionalism and district evangelicalism, on the other hand, are negatively related.

Beyond that, many studies have investigated congressional policy making related to Israel. It is worth noting, however, that among foreign policy issues, the status of Israel is atypical, given its importance to Jewish voters and, increasingly, to many evangelicals. Thus, although Congress does not set specific U.S. policies toward Israel, it provides a venue in which Jews and other religious groups can push for symbolic shows of support. Both the Democratic and Republican parties have a long history of Zionism (Feuerweger 1979), but Trice (1977) found that Democratic senators were slightly more supportive of Israel than Republicans. Even so, partisanship explained little variation in support for Israel in the 1970s. Trice (1977) found the size of the Jewish constituency (the only religious variable included in his model) was related to support for Israel, but that its effect was minimal. Contemporary studies indicate that by the late 1990s, the effect of party appears to be unstable at best. Oldmixon, Rosenson, and Wald (2005) found that in the House, party influence changed from 1997 to 2002 as Republicans became more outspoken in support for Israel. In the Senate, Republicans were more supportive of Israel than Democrats from 1993 to 1998, but by 1999 the behavior of Republicans and Democrats became indistinguishable (Rosenson, Oldmixon, and Wald 2008).

The most consistent predictor of support for Israel among legislators has been Jewish identification (Garnham 1977; Trice 1977). In analyses of the House (Oldmixon et al. 2005) as well as the Senate (Rosenson et al. 2008), Jewish legislators and those legislators representing large Jewish constituencies were consistently and strongly supportive of Israel. Of course, identification as a Jew in these instances is more likely a reflection of social group identification than subscription to a set of beliefs.

On the other hand, scholars and pundits alike have typically attributed evangelical support of Israel to theology, rather than social group identification. Regardless of its conceptual underpinnings, the effects of affiliation with the evangelical tradition are a bit more confusing. Wald, Guth, Fraser, Green, Smidt, and Kellstedt (1997) found that evangelical affiliation did not necessarily predict greater support for Israel among members of Congress. In fact, when they examined voting on House appropriation bills in 1994 and 1995, they found that evangelical members of the House were *less* supportive than their fellow House Republicans of the foreign aid bill that included more than $2 billion annually for Israel. And, in analysis of House votes and cosponsorships, Oldmixon et al. (2005) found that both member evangelical affiliation and district evangelical population were insignificant between 1997 and 2000. In the 107th Congress (2001–2002), evangelical representatives emerged as strong supporters of Israel, although the effect of having large proportions of evangelical Protestant constituents remained insignificant. Catholic legislators were indistinguishable from their mainline and liberal Protestant colleagues, and although constituency Catholicism was positively related to support for Israel in the 106th Congress (1999–2000), it was otherwise insignificant.

In the Senate, evangelical senators were among Israel's strongest supporters from 1995 to 1996 and 1999 to 2002. A state's evangelical population, however, appeared generally unrelated to senatorial voting—except from 1997 to 2000, when it was negatively related to senatorial support for Israel. In the 103rd Congress (1993–1994), Catholic senators were less likely to support Israel than their mainline and liberal Protestant colleagues. Catholic affiliation was insignificant from 1995 to 2000, but in 2001 Catholic senators emerge as strongly supportive of Israel. The effect of state Catholic population was also insignificant from 1995 to 2000, but strongly positive in the 103rd (1993–1994) and 107th (2001–2002) Congresses (Rosenson et al. 2008).

Aggregate Outputs

A number of studies have analyzed the influence of religion on aggregate policy outputs. In such studies, religion is measured at the mass level and is thought to contribute indirectly to the policy process. Here, scholars conceive of religion as contributing to an opportunity structure in which moral reform may or may not thrive (Norrander and Wilcox 2001). In addition, religion may also provide ideological, personnel, and organization resources that can be mobilized for advocacy. In these studies, the units of analysis are usually states, with religion being operationalized as the percentage of the population falling within one or more religious categories. These studies provide an important snapshot of where and under what circumstances religious forces will engage legislative politics, although they leave legislative politics unexamined in "a black box."

Overall, these studies produce findings consistent with the legislative behavior studies examined earlier. Just as Catholic and evangelical constituencies are associated with conservative decision making by legislators, so, too, are such constituencies associated with conservative policy outputs (Berkman and O'Connor 1993; Meier and MacFarlane 1993; Mooney and Lee 1995; O'Connor and Berkman 1995). Because the leaders of the Roman Catholic Church and evangelical Protestant denominations typically embrace traditional moral values, sizeable Catholic and evangelical populations would suggest strong constituent support for moral traditionalism. Moreover, larger population numbers might suggest that such adherents may also be well organized. Not only do church communities provide a way for religious values to be taught and reinforced by fellow believers (Wald, Owen, and Hill 1988), but as organized bodies they may also facilitate political mobilization supporting those values (Calfano 2006).[8]

Conclusion

As evidenced by the studies reviewed in this chapter, the religion and legislative politics literature has focused primarily on legislative behavior. This literature straddles two subfields of political science: religion and politics, which often stresses mass behavior questions, and legislative studies, which focuses on power within the chamber, careerism, and procedures. The collective wisdom of this scholarship is that both the religious traits of members and constituency religious factors influence legislator decision making across an array of issues. In addition, policy analysts have found that community religious demographics influence aggregate policy outcomes and that organized interests regularly lobby Congress in support of policy that comports with their religious vision. These are important findings because they establish the importance and relevance of religion to legislative politics.

On a more substantive level, these findings repeatedly indicate that evangelical denominational affiliation is associated with political conservatism. However, if we are to demonstrate that religion influences legislative behavior over a spectrum, rather than a narrow range, of issues, it is vital to consider policy issues beyond abortion and gay marriage. From the perspective of morality policy specialists, such issues exemplify a certain kind of political disagreement and lend themselves to a distinct style of politics. But from the perspective of religion and politics specialists, there is nothing about such issues that make them inherently "religious" to the exclusion of other kinds of issues. For different communities of believers, religion may shape perspectives across a wide array of policy questions. In a sense, we have only examined the easiest, most obvious, intellectual targets, and we now need to put our theories to more rigorous tests. Some research has begun to do this, but much more is needed.

Second, we need to broaden our perspective beyond the roll call vote. Floor votes are only one (albeit very important) part of the legislative process. However, we know very little about the extent to which religion influences bill drafting or committee deliberations, whether at the national or state levels. Researching these questions will require access to testimony and deliberation, elite interviewing, and perhaps extensive content analysis (Oldmixon and Heaney 2007). Measuring these other activities is not as easy as examining roll call votes, but as Burden's (2007) work suggests, it is probably at least as important.

Finally, as we conceptualize and measure religion, we need to consider multiple vectors of religious influence. Using denominational measures is completely appropriate if we are positing a religious effect based on social group affiliation. The best practices in this regard use sophisticated measures of religion at the elite and constituency levels. Yet, total reliance on denominational affiliation misses the potential importance of religious beliefs and practices. The salience of religion to legislators is also potentially relevant. The evidence we do have strongly suggests that some—if not most—of the influence of religion on legislative politics transcends denominational affiliation. When salience, theological traditionalism, and worldview are taken into account, we find that the relationship between religion and legislative politics is pervasive, but also nuanced and complex. Although these aspects of religion are difficult to measure, the intellectual payoff may well be enormous. Certainly, they provide the greatest promise for both innovation and theoretical development.

NOTES

1. Moreover, such measures enhance thick description, but may be inaccessible to the larger scholarly community (Jelen 1998), whereas an honest accounting of the literature has to concede that even though denomination is a blunt instrument, it conveys important information.

2. To estimate the proportion of fundamentalist Protestants in each state, Hutcheson and Taylor (1973, p. 417) use the percentage of the population "affiliated with Protestant religious organizations which believe in the literal inspiration of the Bible," based on data reported by the National Council of Churches.

3. Fairbanks' (1977, p. 414) measure of "conservative Protestantism" is based on the percentage of each state's population belonging to Protestant denominations not associated with the National Council of Churches, although members of the

United Methodist Church were included given its historic role in the prohibition movement.

4. Haider-Markel's (2001) measure of "conservative Protestantism" includes "Protestant fundamentalists, Baptists, and those members simply stating Christian." He specifies the specific denominational affiliations classified as fundamentalist in endnote 9, among which Latter-day Saints are included (Haider-Markel 2001, p. 129). District-level religion is only indirectly included in the model as part of a composite measure of constituency opinion.

5. Oldmixon and Calfano (2007, p. 67) detail in endnote 11 the particular denominations classified as "conservative Protestants," following closely the manner specified by Kellstedt and Green (1993) for identifying evangelical Protestants, noting the grounds upon which Mormon legislators may be appropriately classified in this instance within the category, but why for other purposes it may inappropriate to do so.

6. These findings are also consistent with Oldmixon's (2002) and Tatalovich and Schier's (1993) work on reproductive policy.

7. In this analysis, "religious conservatives" included evangelicals and nontraditional conservatives such as Mormons and Christian Scientists.

8. In discussing the relationship between religion and legislative politics, this chapter has emphasized the importance of constituency and elite-level religious preferences. However, organized religious interests also influence legislative politics. This literature is not reviewed in this chapter, because it is largely addressed in chapter 11 of this volume.

REFERENCES

Aldrich, John H. 1995. *Why Parties? The Origins and Transformation of Political Parties in America*. Chicago, Ill.: University of Chicago Press.

Aldrich, John, and David Rohde. 2005. "Congressional Committees in the Partisan Era." In *Congress Reconsidered*, ed. Lawrence C. Dodd and Bruce I. Oppenheimer. Washington, D.C.: CQ Press, 249–270.

Arnold, R. Douglas. 1992. *The Logic of Congressional Action*. New Haven, Conn.: Yale University Press.

Barone, Michael and Richard E. Cohen. 2007. *Almanac of American Politics 2008*. Washington, D.C.: National Journal.

Benson, Peter, and Dorothy Williams. 1982. *Religion on Capitol Hill: Myths and Realities*. San Francisco, Calif.: Harper & Row.

Berkman, Michael B., and Robert E. O'Connor. 1993. "Do Women Legislators Matter? Female Legislators and State Abortion Policy." *American Politics Quarterly* 21 (1): 102–124.

Binder, Sarah A. 2003. *Stalemate: Causes and Consequences of Legislative Gridlock*. Washington, D.C.: Brookings Institution Press.

Burden, Barry C. 2007. *Personal Roots of Representation*. Princeton, N.J.: Princeton University Press.

Calfano, Brian R. 2006. "Of Denominations and Districts: Examining the Influence of 'Pro-life' Denominational Communities on State Representatives." *Journal of Church and State* 48 (1): 83–100.

Campbell, Colton, and Roger H. Davidson. 2000. "Gay and Lesbian Issues in the Legislative Arena." In *The Politics of Gay Rights*, ed. Craig A. Rimmerman, Kenneth D. Wald, and Clyde Wilcox, 347–376. Chicago, Ill.: University of Chicago Press.

Carmines, Edward G., and James A. Stimson. 1980. "The Two Faces of Issue Voting." *American Political Science Review* 74: 78–91.

Dodd, Lawrence C. 1977. "Congress and the Quest for Power." In *Congress Reconsidered.* 1st ed., ed. Lawrence C. Dodd and Bruce I. Oppenheimer, 269–307. New York: Praeger.

Dodd, Lawrence C. 1993. "Congress and the Politics of Renewal: Redressing the Crisis of Legitimation." In *Congress Reconsidered,* ed. Lawrence C. Dodd and Bruce I. Oppenheimer, 417–446. Washington, D.C.: CQ Press.

Fairbanks, David. 1977. "Religious Forces and 'Morality' Policies in the American States." *Western Political Quarterly* 30 (3): 411–417.

Fastnow, Chris, J. Tobin Grant, and Thomas J. Rudolph. 1999. "Holy Roll Calls: Religious Tradition and Voting Behavior in the U.S. House." *Social Science Quarterly* 80: 687–701.

Fenno, Richard F. 1973. *Congressmen in Committees.* Boston, Mass.: Little, Brown.

Fetzer, Joel S. 2006. "Why Did House Members Vote for H.R. 4437?" *International Migration Review* 40 (3): 698–706.

Feuerweger, Marvin C. 1979. *Congress and Israel: Foreign Aid Decision-Making in the House of Representatives, 1969–1976.* Westport, Conn.: Greenwood Press.

Garnham, David. 1977. "Factors Influencing Congressional Support for Israel during the 93rd Congress." *Jerusalem Journal of International Relations* 2: 23–45.

Green, John C. 2004. "American Religious Landscapes and Political Attitudes." Pew Forum on Religion and Public Life. http://pewforum.org/docs/index.php?DocID=55.

Green, John C., and James L. Guth. 1991. "Religion, Representatives and Roll Calls." *Legislative Studies Quarterly* 16: 571–584.

Green, John C., Corwin Smidt, James Guth, and Lyman Kellstedt. 2005. *The American Religious Landscape and the 2004 Presidential Vote: Increased Polarization.* Washington, D.C.: Pew Forum on Religion and Public Life.

Guth, James L. 2007. "Religion and Roll Calls: Religious Influences on the U.S. House of Representatives." Presented at the annual meeting of the American Political Science Association, Chicago, Illinois, August 30–September 2.

Guth, James L., and Lyman A. Kellstedt. 2001. "Religion and Congress." In *In God We Trust: Religion & American Political Life,* ed. Corwin E. Smidt, 213–233. Grand Rapids, Mich.: Baker Academic.

Haider-Markel, Donald. 2001. "Morality in Congress? Legislative Voting on Gay Issues." In *The Public Clash of Private Values: The Politics of Morality Policy,* ed. Christopher Z. Mooney, 115–129. Chatham: Chatham House Press.

Highton, Benjamin, and Michael S. Rocca. 2005. "Beyond the Roll-Call Arena: The Determinants of Position Taking in Congress." *Political Research Quarterly* 58 (2): 303–316.

Hutcheson, John D., and George A. Taylor. 1973. "Religious Variables, Political System Characteristics, and Policy Outputs in the American States." *American Journal of Political Science* 17 (2): 414–421.

Jelen, Ted G. 1994. "Religion and Foreign Policy Attitudes: Exploring the Effects of Denomination and Doctrine." *American Politics Quarterly* 22: 382–400.

Jelen, Ted G. 1998. "Research in Religion and Mass Political Behavior in the United States: Looking Both Ways after Two Decades of Scholarship." *American Politics Research* 26: 110–134.

Kellstedt, Lyman A., and John C. Green. 1993. "Knowing God's Many People: Denominational Preference and Political Behavior." In *Rediscovering the Religious*

Factor in American Politics, ed. David C. Leege and Lyman A. Kellstedt, 53–71. Armonk, N.Y.: M. E. Sharpe.

Kingdon, John W. 1973. Congressmen's Voting Decisions. Ann Arbor, Mich.: University of Michigan Press.

Koszczuk, Jackie and Martha Angle, eds. 2007. CQ's Politics in America 2008: The 110th Congress. Washington, D.C.: CQ Press.

Layman, Geoffrey C. 1999. "'Culture Wars' in the American Party System: Religious and Cultural Change among Partisan Activists since 1972." American Politics Quarterly 27: 89–121.

Layman, Geoffrey. 2001. The Great Divide: Religious and Cultural Conflict in American Party Politics. New York: Columbia University Press.

Leege, David C., Kenneth D. Wald, Brian S. Krueger, and Paul D. Mueller. 2002. The Politics of Cultural Differences: Social Change and Voter Mobilization in the Post-New Deal Period. Princeton, N.J.: Princeton University Press.

Lewis, Gregory B., and Jonathan L. Edelson. 2000. "DOMA and ENDA: Congress Votes on Gay Rights." In The Politics of Gay Rights, ed. Craig A. Rimmerman, Kenneth D. Wald, and Clyde Wilcox, 193–216. Chicago, Ill.: University of Chicago Press.

Mayhew, David. 1974. Congress: The Electoral Connection. New Haven, Conn.: Yale University Press.

Meier, Kenneth J. 2001. "Sex, Drugs, and Rock and Roll: A Theory of Morality Politics." In The Public Clash of Private Values: The Politics of Morality Policy, ed., Christopher Z. Mooney, 21–36. Chatham: Chatham House Publishers.

Meier, Kenneth J., and Deborah R. McFarlane. 1993. "The Politics of Funding Abortion." American Politics Quarterly 21: 81–101.

Miller, Warren E., and Donald E. Stokes. 1963. "Constituency Influence in Congress." American Political Science Review 57: 45–57.

Mooney, Christopher Z. 2001. "The Public Clash of Private Values: The Politics of Morality Policy." In The Public Clash of Private Values: The Politics of Morality Policy, ed., Christopher Z. Mooney, 3–18. Chatham: Chatham House Publishers.

Mooney, Christopher Z., and Mei-Hsien Lee. 1995. "Legislating Morality in the American States: The Case of Pre-Roe Abortion Regulation Reform." American Journal of Political Science 39 (3): 599–627.

Norrander, Barbara, and Clyde Wilcox. 2001. "Public Opinion and Policymaking in the States: The Case of Post-Roe Abortion Policy." In The Public Clash of Private Values: The Politics of Morality Policy, ed. Christopher Z. Mooney, 143–159. Chatham: Chatham House Publishers.

O'Connor, Robert, and Michael Berkman. 1995. "Religious Determinants of State Abortion Policy." Social Science Quarterly 76: 447–459.

Oldmixon, Elizabeth A. 2002. "Culture Wars in the Congressional Theater: How the U.S. House of Representatives Legislates Morality, 1993–1998." Social Science Quarterly 83: 775–788.

Oldmixon, Elizabeth A. 2005. Uncompromising Positions: God, Sex, and the U.S. House of Representatives. Washington, D.C.: Georgetown University Press.

Oldmixon, Elizabeth A., and Brian Calfano. 2007. "The Religious Dynamics of Decision Making on Gay Rights Issues in the U.S. House of Representatives, 1993–2002." The Journal for the Scientific Study of Religion 46: 55–70.

Oldmixon, Elizabeth A., and Michael Heaney. 2007. "Of Heaven or Earth? Religious Organizations and Rhetorical Strategies before Congressional Committees." Presented at the annual meeting of the American Political Science Association, Chicago, Illinois, August 30–September 2.

Oldmixon, Elizabeth A., and William Hudson. 2008. "Catholic Republicans and Conflicting Impulses in the 109th Congress." *Politics and Religion* 1 (1): 113–136.

Oldmixon, Elizabeth A., Beth Rosenson, and Kenneth D. Wald. 2005. "Conflict over Israel: The Role of Religion, Race, Party and Ideology in the U.S. House of Representatives, 1997–2002." *Terrorism and Political Violence* 17: 407–426.

Poole, Keith T., and Howard Rosenthal. 1997. *Congress: A Political–Economic History of Roll Call Voting.* New York: Oxford University Press.

Richardson, James, and Sandie Wrightman Fox. 1972. "Religious Affiliation as a Predictor of Voting Behavior in Abortion Reform Legislation." *Journal for the Scientific Study of Religion* 11: 347–359.

Rohde, David W. 1991. *Parties and Leaders in the Postreform House.* Chicago, Ill.: University of Chicago Press.

Rosenson, Beth, Elizabeth Oldmixon, and Kenneth Wald. 2008. "U.S. Senators' Support for Israel Examined Through Sponsorship/Co-Sponsorship Decisions, 1993–2002: The Influence of Elite and Constituent Factors." *Foreign Policy Analysis* 5: 73–91.

Rothenberg, Stuart, and Frank Newport. 1984. *The Evangelical Voter.* Washington, D.C.: The Free Congress Foundation.

Smidt, Corwin E. 1987. "Piety and Patriotism: Evangelicals and Foreign Policy." In *Religion and Politics: Is the Relationship Changing?,* ed. Thomas E. Scism, 90–99. Charleston, Ill.: Eastern Illinois University.

Smith, T. Alexander, and Raymond Tatalovich. 2003. *Cultures at War: Moral Conflicts in Western Democracies.* Orchard Park, N.Y.: Broadview Press.

Sulkin, Tracy. 2005. *Issue Politics in Congress.* New York: Cambridge University Press.

Tatalovich, Raymond, and David Schier. 1993. "The Persistence in Ideological Cleavage in Voting on Abortion Legislation in the House of Representatives, 1973–1988." *American Politics Quarterly* 21: 125–139.

Trice, Robert H. 1977. "Congress and the Arab–Israeli Conflict: Support for Israel in the U.S. Senate, 1970–1973." *Political Science Quarterly* 92: 443–463.

Wald, Kenneth D., and Allison Calhoun-Brown. 2007. *Religion and Politics in the United States.* Lanham, Md.: Rowman & Littlefield.

Wald, Kenneth D., James L. Guth, Cleveland R. Fraser, John H. Green, Corwin Smidt, and Lyman A. Kellstedt. 1997. "Reclaiming Zion: How American Religious Groups View the Middle East," In *U.S.–Israeli Relations at the Crossroads,* ed. Gabriel Sheffer, 147–168. London: Frank Cass.

Wald, Kenneth D., Dennis E. Owen, and Samuel S. Hill. 1988. "Churches as Political Communities." *American Political Science Review* 82: 531–548.

Wilcox, Clyde, Ted G. Jelen, and David C. Leege. 1993. "Religious Group Identifications: Toward a Cognitive Theory of Religious Mobilization." In *Rediscovering the Religious Factor in American Politics,* ed. David C. Leege and Lyman A. Kellstedt, 73–99. Armonk, N.Y.: M. E. Sharpe.

Yamane, David, and Elizabeth A. Oldmixon. 2006. "Religion in the Legislative Arena: Affiliation, Salience, Advocacy and Public Policy-Making." *Legislative Studies Quarterly* XXXI (3): 433–460.

CHAPTER 19

RELIGION AND JUDICIAL POLITICS

PAUL J. WAHLBECK

ON June 9, 2005, William H. Pryor, Jr. won Senate confirmation to a seat on the 11th Circuit Court of Appeals. This followed a heated battle over his and others' nominations to the federal courts. The controversy over President George W. Bush's judicial nominations, and delays in confirming several of them, led to a discussion of changing Senate rules governing filibusters on judicial nominations.[1] In the face of that controversy, a potent allegation was made by supporters of William Pryor: Senate Democrats were accused of discriminating against the religious views held by Catholic nominees to the bench (York 2003). These charges were leveled in newspaper advertisements that ran in Rhode Island and Maine (Dewar 2003b).[2] The ads, according to news accounts (Lewis 2003), showed a courthouse door with a sign declaring, "Catholics Need Not Apply." The text of the ads pronounced, "Some in the U.S. Senate are attacking Bill Pryor for having 'deeply held' Catholic beliefs to prevent him from becoming a federal judge. Don't they know the Constitution expressly prohibits religious tests for public office?" (Dewar 2003b, p. A3).

Democratic members of the Senate Judiciary Committee, including some Catholic senators, objected to this interjection of religion into the confirmation process. The nominee earlier tried to defuse the controversy surrounding his nomination by minimizing the impact of his religious and personal views on judging: "I have a record as [the Alabama] attorney general that is separate from my personal beliefs. I have demonstrated as attorney general that I am able to set aside my personal beliefs and follow the law, even when I strongly disagree with the law" (Allen 2003, p. A37). Of course, this begs the question of what role religion plays in judicial politics. To what extent do religious beliefs influence the nomination of federal judges? Does a judge's religion affect his or her decisions?

The controversy over William Pryor's nomination also extended to his presumptive behavior as an appellate court judge in religious cases. His decisions on religious freedom and the establishment of religion evoked fear, as a *Washington Post* (2003, p. A26) editorial put it, because he "is probably best known as a zealous advocate of relaxing the wall between church and state." The editorial elaborated: "He teamed up with one of Pat Robertson's organizations in a court effort to defend student-led prayer in public schools, and he has vocally defended Alabama's chief justice, who has insisted on displaying the Ten Commandments in state court facilities." So, in addition to the effect of a judge's religious beliefs, another facet of religion and judicial politics is the pattern of constitutional decisions related to religious freedom and establishment of religion: What motivates a judge's decisions in such cases? To what extent are these decisions faithfully implemented after a court renders a decision?

The political science literature has provided some answers to these questions, and this chapter reviews that research. Yet, with some notable exceptions, this literature is not on the cutting edge of social science theory or empirical practices. In the pages that follow, I will present an overview of the extant literature as background for formulating answers to these questions. After reviewing the theoretical and empirical research on matters of judicial selection, decision making, interest group activity in litigation, and the implementation of judicial decisions, I will discuss the literature that has investigated the role played by a judge's religious affiliations and cases pertaining to the Constitution's religious clauses. Along the way, I will suggest research topics that might prove fruitful in better understanding the role of religion in judicial politics and the Court's religion cases.

THE STUDY OF JUDICIAL POLITICS

The study of judicial politics is marked by two assumptions: courts are political institutions and judges are political actors. Undergirding these two assumptions is the view that judicial decisions constitute significant policy statements that affect the choices made by private citizens, government officials, and judges alike.[3] The Supreme Court's written opinion, as Segal and Spaeth (2002, p. 357) concede, "constitutes the core of the Court's policy-making process" by articulating legal principles that guide lower courts and others. These rules have potent effects on society by establishing expectations about what behavior is appropriate in a wide range of societal interactions and establishing the grounds for sanctioning violations of those expectations (Knight 1992). Not only do legal rules, contained in court opinions, provide private parties and organizations with information about future Court actions, thus influencing private behavior, they also may structure interactions that favor one interest over another; in other words, as a formal institutional rule, they determine distributional consequences (Hurst 1956, pp. 10–11; Knight 1992).

The role of the courts in resolving policy questions is not a recent development (see, for example, de Tocqueville [1835] 1956, p. 126; Holmes [1881] 1991, p. 1). Court decisions are laden with political significance, and judges' decisions on these important policy questions are influenced by their own views of good public policy. The role of courts in resolving policy issues and the factors influencing judicial decisions led Jack Peltason (1955, p. 1) to question whether it is "not then appropriate to describe the activity of judges in the same terms that are used to discuss legislators and administrators? . . . Furthermore, by describing the political role of the judges, analysis of the political process will be more complete."

The enterprise of understanding judicial behavior through this policy lens has occupied the attention of judicial scholars. Given the important role played by judges in judicial politics, scholars have examined the process by which judges are selected. This area of inquiry encompasses the selection of federal judges by the president (see, for example, Abraham 1992; Moraski and Shipan 1999; Nemacheck 2007b) and the confirmation of judges by the Senate (see, for example, Cameron, Cover, and Segal 1990; Binder and Maltzman 2002; Epstein, Lindstädt, Segal, and Westerland 2006). The study of judges, furthermore, extends to their decisions after they have been appointed, with a focus on the role of the judges' preferences or attitudes (see, for example, Segal and Spaeth 2002), the law (see, for example, Segal 1984; Johnson, Wahlbeck, and Spriggs 2006), and strategic calculations (see, for example, Murphy 1964; Epstein and Knight 1998; Maltzman, Spriggs, and Wahlbeck 2000). Judicial scholars also explore the choices and activities of other actors in court, especially the role of organized interests in litigation. These interest groups see the courts as another venue in their pursuit of their policy objectives (see, for example, Barker 1967; Hansford 2004). Finally, judicial scholars understand that the efficacy of a Supreme Court decision rests with those actors who will implement it in a myriad of situations. The impact of the Supreme Court on legal policy and society is dependent on the choices made by members of its supporting cast (see, for example, Tarr 1977; Rosenberg 1991).

RELIGION AND JUDICIAL APPOINTMENTS

What explains the selection of judges? "[W]hile there are many supposed criteria for the selection of a Justice," Sandra Day O'Connor recounted two years after her appointment to the Supreme Court, it "is probably a classic example of being the right person in the right spot at the right time. Stated simply, you must be lucky" (Abraham 1992, p. 7). Generally, as social scientists, judicial scholars hesitate to attribute something to luck or fortune, but seek out systematic explanations of political choices, like nominations. The accepted wisdom is that there are four factors that disproportionately influence a president's choice of Supreme Court justices: qualifications and ethical behavior, past personal or political loyalty, pursuit of political support, and policy compatibility (Abraham 1992). The importance of these factors underscores that presidents may use judicial appointments to fulfill different goals: goals on the president's policy agenda, partisan agenda, or personal agenda (Goldman 2006). Observers generally place religious considerations as a tactic in advancing the president's partisan or electoral agenda: "[A]ppointments could reward part of the core constituency or attempt to attract a religious group to join the party" (Goldman 2006, p. 195).

The electoral value of judicial nominations to a president's party prompted Schmidhauser (1959, p. 20) to state that although the courts are not representative institutions, "the pattern of judicial selection has tacitly recognized the coming of age politically of many, but not all, of the ethnic and religious groups in America." Generally, a group's coming of age politically is signaled by its growing size in the electorate and its increased presence in positions of authority (thereby establishing their credentials to hold other positions in government) (Gryski, Zuk, and Barrow 1994). The value of the former, growth in population size, is illustrated by the appointment of Joseph McKenna, a Catholic, to the Supreme Court in 1898. During the last two decades of the 19th century, the number of Catholics in the United States doubled as European Catholics immigrated to urban areas in the East and Midwest (Goldman 2006, p. 196). The Republican President William McKinley, who did not want to relinquish the growing number of Catholic voters to the Democratic Party but wanted to signal that Republicans welcomed Catholics, consequently appointed McKenna to the Supreme Court (Goldman 2006).

The partisan advantage derived from appointing a person of faith to the bench manifested itself in President Dwight Eisenhower's appointment of William Brennan, a Catholic Democrat, to the Supreme Court. The Eisenhower administration was keenly aware that nominating Catholics to the bench could help them woo "traditionally Democratic Roman Catholics to the Republican Party" (Goldman 1997, p. 116). Indeed, Eisenhower sought to nominate a Catholic to the Supreme Court to shore up his support among that group in the upcoming presidential election: "The president easily concurred in the encomiums and in the political wisdom of designating, especially in an election year, a Democrat who also happened to be a Roman Catholic. It might well avoid a return home to the Democratic nominee by the Eisenhower Democrats of 1952" (Abraham 1992, pp. 265–266).[4]

The second attribute of a group's political maturation, increased presence in positions of authority, has been evidenced in the appointment of Catholics to the federal bench by Presidents Reagan and Roosevelt. The Reagan administration did not necessarily give preference to Catholics because of their religion, according to Goldman (1997, p. 344), but rather "more Catholics had entered the potential pool from which Republican judicial nominees emerged, thus increasing the proportion of Catholics chosen." A similar dynamic apparently motivated President Franklin Roosevelt's selection of Catholic judges: "[A]t the district court level

Catholics were generously recognized, perhaps a reflection of the influence of Catholic participation in the ranks of the Democratic party and the prominence of Catholics at the head of local party organizations" (Goldman 1997, pp. 62–63).

Yet, the presence of a group in the pool of potential candidates may allow presidents to move beyond partisan or electoral agendas when appointing group members. As a party's policy goals attract adherents from a particular group, the president may satisfy policy and personal goals through nomination of group members; a person's appointment may often be notwithstanding his or her religious views (Schmidhauser 1959). Early in American history, path-breaking nominations were made without apparent regard to religion. Perry (1991, p. 23) concluded that the first Catholic justice on the Supreme Court, Roger Taney, owed his appointment to factors other than religion, especially "given [the] hostile and extreme anti-Catholic climate." Instead, she argues that Chief Justice Taney's "rise to the highest judicial position in the land proves the strength of other factors (namely, merit, politics, friendship, and geography)" (Perry 1991, p. 23). To some observers, religious background is shorthand for other politically relevant factors:

> Religious diversity in America has at its root a social basis as well as a doctrinal rationale. To some denominations attach factors of prestige and social status while others are viewed socially as "churches of the disinherited," of unpopular immigrant groups, or of ethnic groups which, because of color, have not been fully accepted. (Schmidhauser 1959, p. 21)

Future Research Directions on Religion and Judicial Selection

Research on religion and judicial selection could be developed further theoretically and empirically. Recent work on judicial selection articulates a theory grounded in the role of information (Nemacheck 2007b). After all, presidents make choices while facing uncertainty over a prospective nominee's future behavior on the bench. The motivating fact is that presidents cannot perfectly anticipate the decisions that their nominees will make as justices even though presidents see these appointees as marking a policy legacy influencing legal policy long after the president has left the Oval Office. Nemacheck (2007b) argues that the president can act strategically to lessen his uncertainty over a nominee: consideration of congressional endorsements of prospective nominees, use of the White House or Justice Department to enhance the reliability of information gathered, and choice of nominees who have a track record on a lower court or in public service.

What role does religion or religious beliefs play in the context of reducing a president's uncertainty over a prospective nominee? One might believe that a person's religious beliefs provide valuable information about his or her future performance on the bench. Observers and political leaders alike seem to believe that there is a correlation between religious beliefs and policy preferences. In 2005, when President Bush's Supreme Court nominee, Harriett Miers, was subjected to criticism from other conservatives, some supporters pointed to the fact that Miers was an evangelical Christian who attended "a very conservative church" as evidence that she would provide a reliable conservative vote (Nemacheck 2007a). If, indeed, a person's religious background provides valuable information about future behavior, an empirical question is whether presidents use that information. The more recent empirical research on judicial selection (see, for example, Yalof 1999; Nemacheck 2007b) makes use of information found in presidential papers, a source that could illuminate the president's use of information drawn from the potential nominee's religious affiliation.

The bulk of the literature on the role of religion in judicial selection discusses the role of representation: For electoral reasons, presidents select members of particular religious sects. Yet, the bulk of the evidence supporting these conclusions is qualitative. Although quantitative studies have been conducted to examine the selection of racial and ethnic minority judges (Gryski et al. 1994), the same methods have not been used to test the conventional wisdom surrounding the role of religious background. Yet, this approach could be applied fruitfully to understand more fully the role of religion in appointment politics. For instance, have presidents nominated members of particular religious traditions as that group has come to political maturity (e.g., share of voting public, size of a party's constituency base, number of individuals in the pool of qualified candidates)?

DECISION MAKING

The most common assumption surrounding judicial behavior is that justices make decisions that comport with their policy preferences. "Each member of the Court," argue Rohde and Spaeth (1976, p. 72), "has preferences concerning the policy questions faced by the Court, and when the justices make decisions they want the outcomes to approximate as nearly as possible those policy preferences." This assumption has been borne out with a wealth of evidence beginning with the work of C. Herman Pritchett (1948). More recently, Segal and Cover (1989) found a high correspondence between a justice's support for civil liberties and their measure of each justice's policy views.[5]

This perspective on judicial decision making was first conceptualized, following psychological theory, as a function of underlying values and attitudes (see, for example, Schubert 1965; Rohde and Spaeth 1976). The central premise was that a case presents stimuli that will trigger the justice's attitudes toward situations, or issue areas, and objects, or types of litigants. In more recent years, rational choice approaches supplanted the psychologically oriented attitudinal model. At the heart of rational choice theory is the assumption that decision makers choose alternatives that maximize the utility they derive from a choice (Elster 1986). How do political decision makers rank possible outcomes or form preferences for one outcome compared with another? Generally, political scientists argue that the principal motivating factor of political decision makers is policy. "A major goal of all justices," say Epstein and Knight (1998, p. 11), "is to see the law reflect their preferred policy positions, and they will take actions to advance this objective."

A competing explanation of judicial decision making is the legal model, which posits that judges are guided by the law when making decisions. Judges, according to this perspective, deductively reach decisions by applying legal rules or standards, whether derived from statutes, the Constitution, prior court decisions, or other authoritative sources, to the case facts presented to them. Segal (1984) provided an empirical test of the legal model using the Supreme Court's search and seizure decisions.[6] He identified the legal standards governing the Court's Fourth Amendment jurisprudence, including the role of a person's expectation of privacy in determining the reasonableness of a search. Then, with these legal standards identified, Segal (1984) proposed the use of case facts to determine whether the standard had been met. The legal fact model successfully explained Supreme Court decisions.

A third explanation of judicial behavior, which builds on principles central to the legal model and the attitudinal model, focuses on the strategic choices made by Supreme Court justices. Strategic decisions are those in which there is an interdependence of choice: The utility derived from a choice is conditioned on the decision of another actor. Two principal forms of strategic behavior have been identified in the literature: internal and external. With internal constraints, the benefits derived from a justice's decision are influenced by the choices made by that justice's colleagues (Epstein and Knight 1998; Maltzman et al. 2000). For instance, a Supreme Court majority opinion author cannot simply express his or her sincere preferences, but must accommodate the views of his or her colleagues as well, leading to bargaining over opinion content (see Wahlbeck, Spriggs, and Maltzman 1998; Maltzman et al. 2000). The external constraints are most frequently imposed by Congress. To write opinions that are efficacious in establishing or guiding legal policy, the Court must moderate its views to forestall Congress from passing legislation that would overturn its decisions (Spiller and Gely 1992; Meernik and Ignagni 1997).

The Role of Religion in Decision Making

Those scholars who examine the role of religion, along with other background characteristics, do not usually conceptualize its influence within a psychological or a rational decision-making framework, but from a sociological perspective. Social background theory "implies that the life experiences of individuals play a role in the formation of predispositions that in turn shape behavior" (Ulmer 1970, p. 585). The argument is that a person's religious affiliation might signal the person's experiences and thus their political socialization. Some scholars, however, have expressed reservations with a reliance on religious affiliation because it might be "too broad a variable encompassing a multitude of individual experiences and thus is affected by a host of intervening variables" (Goldman 1975, p. 498).

With this sociological perspective in view, a spate of research has examined the effect of judges' personal attributes, including religious affiliation. Vines (1964) investigated the decisions of federal district court judges in race relations cases in the South from 1954 to 1962. He found that orthodox Protestants who served as federal district court judges in the South comprised more than two thirds of all judges who were segregationists or moderates (Vines 1964, pp. 353–354).[7] In contrast, the integrationists were comprised of judges who did not list a religious affiliation (45.4 percent), Catholics (18.2 percent), and some orthodox Protestants (36.4 percent). Vines (1964) speculated that religious affiliation might have served as a proxy for whether the judge is part of the southern social structure, because southern society was Protestant and orthodox.

This finding is consistent with those of other scholars. Ulmer (1970) found that a Supreme Court justice's religious background (i.e., whether the justice was Catholic) affected his propensity to cast a dissenting vote: The six Catholic justices who served from the appointment of John Jay (in 1789) to Potter Stewart (in 1959) were more likely to be frequent dissenters than the 86 other justices. Ulmer's research (1973) also found a significant influence of three personal attributes (i.e., justice's age at appointment, federal administrative experience, and religious affiliation) on the justices' votes in criminal cases from 1947 to 1956.[8] Using stepwise regression, he found that religious affiliation explained an additional 21 percent of the voting variance over that explained by the other two variables. He went on to speculate that the causal link between religious affiliation and support for the government in criminal cases might be related to socioeconomic class. In particular, when Ulmer (1973) divided Protestant justices into "low-income" and "high-income" denominations, he found that justices who affiliate with the high-income Protestant denominations were more likely to support the government than those who affiliated with low-income denominations.[9]

Not all of the extant research on religious affiliations as a background characteristic has found support for its influence. Tate (1981) tackled the issue of whether the personal attributes of Supreme Court justices who sat on the Court between the 1946 and 1977 terms influenced their decisions in civil rights and liberties, and economic cases. He found that "religious affiliation adds little or nothing" to our understanding of Supreme Court justices' voting behavior (Tate 1981, p. 362). More specifically, although the justices' religious affiliation (i.e., Protestant or not) has the highest correlation with the justices' liberalism, it does not add to our understanding after other variables are included as controls.[10]

Similarly, Goldman (1966) found a limited impact of religious affiliations on appellate court decision making. He found a significant effect for a judge's religion in only one legal issue: Catholic judges were more likely than Protestants to vote liberally in fiscal cases (e.g., cases raising issues of taxation or eminent domain) (Goldman 1966, p. 381).[11] In a later study of appellate decisions from 1965 to 1971, Goldman (1975) found significant differences between Catholic and Protestant judges in cases implicating two issues: injured persons and economic liberalism.[12] In those cases, Catholic judges voted more liberally for the economic underdog than Protestant jurists. When he controlled for the judge's party affiliation, however, the impact of religion was diminished (Goldman 1975, p. 498). Only among Democratic judges did religious background wield a significant effect, with Democratic Catholics being more liberal than Democratic Protestants, but only in economic liberalism cases. There was no difference between Republican Protestants and Republican Catholics on any studied issue.

Marshall (1993), arguing that some appointments are symbolic, including the filling of the "Catholic seat" and the "Jewish seat" on the Supreme Court, questioned whether those justices provide policy representation for their group. To test this relationship, Marshall (1993) compared the expressed public opinion of a nationwide sample on issues raised in 107 cases. In particular, he compared each justice's vote from the 1967 to the 1988 Supreme Court terms with the attitudes expressed by Catholic and Jewish voters. He found that Catholic justices and non-Catholic justices agreed with the Catholic survey respondents at the same rate overall (57.0 percent).

This mix of findings suggests that the role of religion, like other sociological background characteristics, may be more nuanced. The key may be that the socialization provided by religion is connected to the particular experiences of the religious sect. In other words, the link between background characteristics, such as religion, and judicial behavior may be mediated by the issues considered by the courts. Scholars have begun to test the differential effects of socioeconomic traits on judges across issue areas. For instance, Songer, Davis, and Haire (1994a) examined the effects of gender on voting behavior in the federal appellate courts, finding that women's unique experiences shaped their views in related areas of the law, like discrimination claims.

A similar perspective, in which social background shapes attitudes on issues for which group members have had unique experiences that will set them apart, has been applied to religious affiliation. Songer and Tabrizi (1999) studied the decisions made by evangelical state supreme court judges in several types of cases (i.e., death penalty, gender discrimination, and obscenity) between 1970 and 1993. They expected that evangelical judges, as defined by their denominational affiliation, would be more conservative than state supreme court justices from other denominations or faiths. Songer and Tabrizi (1999) include in their analysis controls for several relevant factors: case facts to signal the unique traits of each case, judicial attitudes to capture the justices' preferences, changes in the U.S. Supreme Court to reflect doctrinal alterations, and contextual variables (i.e., whether the justice was a prosecutor, holds elective judicial office, and the state's ideology).

Songer and Tabrizi (1999) found support for their hypothesis: Evangelical state supreme court justices voted more conservatively than their colleagues.[13] More specifically, they found that evangelical justices were more prone to be "law and order" supporters, favoring the imposition of the death penalty more frequently than mainline Protestant justices and Jewish justices, and somewhat more frequently than Catholic justices. In cases of obscenity, which "often involve choices that most directly involve moral judgments that impinge on religious beliefs [and where evangelicals] tend to support traditional values that are hostile to toleration of even soft-core pornography," (Songer and Tabrizi 1999, p. 521), evangelical justices (as well as Catholic justices) again were more apt to exhibit conservative inclinations than their mainline Protestant brethren. Finally, in gender discrimination cases, where evangelicals frequently oppose abortion and the Equal Rights Amendment (ERA), and favor the maintenance of traditional gender distinctions, evangelical state supreme court justices are significantly more likely to vote in support of the conservative position.

The Law and Decision Making in Religious Cases

From the foregoing discussion of the role of religious attachment on decision making, one might erroneously conclude that the law does not play any role in guiding judicial decisions. Judges' religious background, as discussed in the previous section, tends to be examined independently of the effect of the law or strategic calculations. In contrast, studies of cases based on the First Amendment's religion clauses have incorporated legal and strategic considerations. In the paragraphs that follow, I will first discuss the role of the law and then the strategic calculations.

Two groups of scholars applied to religious cases Segal's (1984) approach to testing the legal model. Joseph Ignagni engaged in a similar exercise with Establishment Clause cases (Ignagni 1994a, b) and Free Exercise cases (Ignagni 1993). After discussing the relevant doctrinal developments to identify the key issues in this area of law, Ignagni (1994a, b) operationalized the legal principles governing Establishment Clause jurisprudence with seven variables, ranging from one that captures whether the sole or predominant purpose of the law is religious, whether the aid can be described as a general welfare service, whether the aid affected all groups equally, and whether the law required surveillance or inspection of religious institutions. He also included two variables that indicated whether there was a concurrent free exercise claim and whether the federal government supported an accommodationist decision.

Ignagni (1994a) found that three of the fact-based variables influenced the Court's decision: general government service, neutral policy, and extensive government surveillance of religious organizations. He (Ignagni 1994b) also found that individual justices, when casting votes on the Court's opinion, were more apt to support accommodation of religion when the law provided a general government service to a religious organization, neutrally applied to all groups, and did not require extensive government surveillance of the religious organization. In that study, Ignagni (1994b) controlled for the predilections of the justices, including their preferences on these policies, by incorporating variables marking the observations of individual justices. Justices William O. Douglas, William J. Brennan, Jr., and Thurgood Marshall were significantly less accommodationist than the excluded Justice John M. Harlan during the Burger Court; Chief Justice Burger and Justices Byron R. White and Lewis F. Powell were significantly more accommodationist than Harlan. Even after controlling for justices, Ignagni (1994b) finds support for fact-based legal variables.

Kritzer and Richards (2003) took this analysis of Establishment Clause cases a step further by examining change in jurisprudential regimes. They posited that there may be regimes, comprised of key precedents, that "structure the way in which the Supreme Court justices evaluate key elements of cases in arriving at decisions in a particular legal area" (Richards and Kritzer 2002, p. 308). More particularly, this seemingly suggests that the influence of key legal facts, including those explored by Ignagni, may change after the Court issues a decision that alters the legal doctrine.

The Supreme Court's decision in *Lemon v. Kurtzman* (1971) may have created a regime shift in Establishment Clause doctrine. Using the legal facts identified by Ignagni (1994a, b), Kritzer and Richards (2003) examined whether there was a discernible shift in the weight accorded to these legal facts after *Lemon*. Indeed, they found a significant change in the influence of two legal facts: the law was supported by historical practice (i.e., the practice has been in place at least 200 years) and the requirement for additional government monitoring of religious organizations. A third variable, general government service, fell just shy of conventional statistical significance. These findings bolstered their expectation that the law and legal doctrine can affect judicial decision making.

Strategic Explanations of the Supreme Court's Religion Cases

Although judicial scholars have not probed the effect of a chief justice's religious affiliation on his willingness to engage in strategic behavior or to lead the Court, Kobylka (1989) explored the leadership of Chief Justice Warren Burger in religious Establishment Clause cases. Kobylka (1989) concluded that Chief Justice Burger came close to altering Establishment Clause doctrine, but he failed when he was unable to hold the "middle" or median justice. Burger's influence over this policy domain waxed and waned. In two periods during Burger's tenure as chief (1969–1972 and 1978–1983 terms), he exercised influence on the Court, but was in dissent much of the time in two other periods (1973–1977 and 1984–1985 terms).

During the first period, he took the lead in reshaping doctrine to comport with his vision of good legal policy: In particular, Burger assigned the majority opinion to himself in five of the six Establishment Clause cases decided between 1969 and 1972. In these opinions, he paved the way for accommodationist policy—that is, the desire "to accommodate indirect state support for religious activities" (Kobylka 1989, p. 550). Standing in contrast to accommodationists, other justices held to a separatist view, opposing government support of religion. Burger's early success was seen in *Walz v. Tax Commission* (1970) when he created a new constitutional requirement—no excessive entanglement between church and state. He added to this doctrinal development in *Lemon v. Kurtzman* (1971) when he articulated a three-part test for assessing a challenged law: the law possesses a secular legislative purpose, the primary effect is not to advance or inhibit religion, and the law does not result in excessive government entanglement with religion. Although the Court in *Lemon* reached a separatist result, striking down the state aid to teachers in nonpublic schools, Burger was able to institutionalize further his accommodationist preference in the excessive entanglement prong of the *Lemon* test.

Despite these early successes, Burger was not able to fulfill his vision of remaking Establishment Clause policy. Burger lost three out of four battles over cases seeking to apply *Lemon* between 1973 and 1977 (Kobylka 1989, p. 555). The outcomes in these four cases rested with a coalition of three moderate justices (Stewart, Blackmun, and Powell), who upheld one parochaid law, invalidated a second, and partially supported and rejected two other laws. However, between 1978 and 1983, the Court decided eight cases, striking four laws as constitutionally flawed, even though these cases were so narrow that they did not advance doctrinal development (Kobylka 1989, p. 556). The more significant development was Justices Byron White's and William Rehnquist's adoption of the *Lemon* test to advance accommodationist objectives. As Kobylka (1989, p. 558) put it, "these decisions dulled *Lemon*'s separationist edge and brought it back with Burger's vision. Court watchers saw the 'wall of separation' to be crumbling." Yet, Burger's influence over policy development was not sustained in the final two years of his tenure as chief justice, as he found himself in the minority in the most important cases (Kobylka 1989, p. 559).

Kobylka (1989) argued that Burger's struggle with reorienting the Establishment Clause doctrine stemmed from his personal leadership capacity and the context that he faced on the bench and in the political environment. For instance, Burger's leadership strategies were not well developed, such as his "insensitivity in monopolizing majority and plurality opinions" (Kobylka 1989, p. 561). As his tenure as chief justice continued, he modified his tactics by diversifying his opinion assignments to other justices—White and Rehnquist—who were the most extreme justices in his coalition (Kobylka 1989, p. 562). He was also limited in his ability to establish an accommodationist jurisprudence by the composition of the Court. Burger enjoyed only a slim majority with the assured hostility of Justices Brennan, Marshall, Stevens, and Blackmun. Moreover, public officials passed legislation that ran counter to the Court's previous decisions: "With governments largely ignoring decisions with which they disagreed, and with the Solicitor General actively seeking the reversal of 'objectionable' precedents, the hesitancy of the centrist justices to go along with Burger, lest the Court be seen as caving in to overtly political pressures, may have been heightened" (Kobylka 1989, p. 562).

Future Research Directions on Religion and Judicial Decision Making

One challenge facing research into the influence of religion on decision making is to make it relevant to the dominant decision-making paradigm found in rational choice theories. The research of Songer and Tabrizi (1999), as well as Songer et al. (1994a), suggest a path by unraveling the causal pathway between religion (and other personal attributes) and decisions. Tate (1981, p. 364) offered speculation on whether personal attributes have direct or indirect effects on choices made by Supreme Court justices: The effect of social background (e.g., size of town of upbringing, educational prestige) and hereditary factors (e.g., birth region, age) are mediated by professional training and values. Put another way, personal attributes like religious beliefs can have a profound effect on the values held by an individual—or what one might call a person's preference structure. Those values or preferences then have a direct bearing on the choices that a person makes. Although judicial scholars have examined the influence of policy preferences on court decisions, we have not sought to understand systematically the formation of judicial preferences.[14] Undoubtedly, the structure of preferences is complex, informed by a range of factors like religious beliefs and personal experiences. Yet, with few exceptions (see Epstein, Hoekstra, Segal, and Spaeth 1998), judicial scholars take preferences as an exogenous variable without questioning its origins. It is long past time to seek a better understanding of the formation of judges' policy preferences and, perhaps, the role of religious beliefs in shaping those priorities.

A second challenge is found in the classification of the judge's religion. As Smidt, Kellstedt, and Guth outline in chapter 1 of this volume, current theory posits that both religious affiliation and religious beliefs, along with religious behavior, help to explain how religion shapes American politics. Yet, most of the scholarship discussed here classifies a judge's religion as strictly a function of their religious affiliation: Is the judge Protestant, Catholic, or Jewish? It has been unusual to categorize judges' religious attachments into more refined groups, even at the denominational level.[15] Scholarship has not begun to examine judges' religious traditions, which are denominational groupings, as Smidt, Kellstedt, and Guth define it, with similar beliefs and historical and organizational interrelations. Guth's work (2007) on the religious influence in the House of Representatives suggests research avenues for scholars interested in the effect of religion on judges. There, he used unobtrusive techniques, including public sources that reveal the person's local house of worship, personal roles in leadership, and even attendance habits. Similar techniques could be used to classify judicial religious views more accurately.

A third challenge facing decision-making studies is to appreciate fully the strategic considerations and how they have constrained decision making in religion cases. Although Kobylka's (1989) study is suggestive of the constraints faced by the chief justice as he sought to lead the Supreme Court, further work could be done to explore the dynamics of crafting opinions for the Court in religious cases. There have been interesting studies of the Court's internal deliberation in particular cases. Schwartz (1986), for example, used resources found in the retired justices' papers to examine the opinion-writing process in the Court's decision governing busing to advance school desegregation (*Swann v. Charlotte-Mecklenburg Board of Education* 1971). He (Schwartz 1986, p. 187) concluded that Burger's "lack of votes induced [him] to agree to rewrite and ultimately to issue a *Swann* opinion that the [other justices] were willing to accept. But the final opinion still was not as forthright as it would have been had it been written by [a supporter of busing]."

A similar story line might emerge from a study of the Establishment Clause cases: The chief justice, while pursuing his vision of good legal policy, is constrained by his colleagues from expressing his sincere preferences in the opinion. The justices' papers, for instance, reveal in *Lemon v. Kurtzman* (1971) that Justice Harlan objected to Burger's attempt to tie "the non-entanglement principle entirely to the Free Exercise clause," rather than viewing it as "deducible from the Establishment and Free Exercise clauses taken together" (Harlan 1971). Harlan (1971) directly asked Chief Justice Burger to omit a phrase in Burger's draft opinion that concluded that the programs in question created excessive entanglement "and thus conflict with the Free Exercise Clause." Indeed, the final, published version of the opinion broadens this conclusion to state that the government's entanglement results in a "conflict with the Religion Clauses" (*Swann* 1971, p. 620). Thus, one can surmise that Burger was unable to pursue his sincere policy preference unhindered by his colleagues' views.

INTEREST GROUPS IN LITIGATION

Judicial scholars, assuming that the courts are political institutions that influence public policy, have examined the role of interest groups in judicial decision making. This fascination with interest group participation in the courts extends back to Truman (1950) and Bentley (1908). American courts and judges, Truman (1950, p. 479) stated, "are endowed with power to make choices that are important in the lives and to the expectations of individuals and groups." Interest groups resort to litigation to achieve their policy goals: "Litigation, in this context, was not a technique of resolving private differences.... It is thus a form of political expression. Groups which find themselves unable to achieve their objectives through the ballot frequently turn to the courts" (Barker 1967, pp. 49–50).

There are two principal mechanisms by which interest groups seek to influence judicial decisions: case sponsorship and *amicus* filings. I will discuss each in turn. First, groups sponsor cases to control every facet of the litigation: encouraging and counseling plaintiffs, securing expert witnesses, commissioning research studies, preparing numerous briefs, and, of course, financing the litigation. Scholars have explored in-depth case studies of interest group-sponsored litigation campaigns to overturn laws through the courts (see, for example, Vose 1955). In a review of interest group participation during the first six years of the Rehnquist Court (1986–1991 terms), Epstein (1993) found that half of the "most important cases" were sponsored by groups (17 of 34 cases).

Manwaring (1962) conducted an extensive study to investigate the Jehovah's Witnesses' litigation campaign over flag-saluting ceremonies in the 1930s and 1940s. The Jehovah's Witnesses' movement inadvertently entered this controversy in the mid 1930s after they faced opposition in Nazi Germany by refusing to give the Nazi salute. After a 1935 speech by the national Jehovah's Witnesses leader, Joseph Franklin Rutherford, members of the movement applied to the American flag his admonition to not salute worldly leaders in the place of God. In particular, a third grader, Carleton Nicholls, refused to participate in his school's opening ceremonies during which students recited the pledge of allegiance. Rutherford, supporting Nicholls' actions, gave a radio address saying, "The Nichols [sic] lad . . . has made a wise choice, declaring himself for Jehovah God and his kingdom. . . . All who act wisely will do the same thing" (Manwaring 1962, p. 31). The Jehovah's Witnesses then challenged the disciplinary action against Nicholls in court, asking the court to force the school to reinstate the boy. This was the opening salvo in the battle over saluting the flag, which focused on the courts. The choice to pursue litigation was influenced by the group's "total helplessness in any other arena" (Manwaring 1962, p. 33): their small numbers, trivial political influence, and extreme unpopularity among the public. The organization did not sponsor all litigation over the flag salute, focusing their resources on a few cases (see Manwaring 1962, p. 84), but after they chose to move ahead with a case, they secured an attorney and took command of the action (Manwaring 1962, p. 85).

The second form of judicial activity in which interest groups regularly participate is *amicus* brief filings. *Amici curiae*, meaning friends of the court, were seen originally as a neutral source of relevant information that the parties did not supply (Krislov 1963). Yet, today, amici are seen as an advocate for their interests before the Court: "[T]he *amicus* has evolved from a neutral friendship to a partisan advocacy of specific positions" (Barker 1967, p. 53). Amici serve this role by providing the Court with factual data about the implications of relevant alternatives, the policy consequences of each choice, and identification of potential supporters or opponents (Barker 1967). In addition to providing useful, but novel, information, amici also serve to bolster the credibility of arguments already made by the parties (Spriggs and Wahlbeck 1997). Interest groups, as a whole, have participated as amici at an increasing rate during the past four decades. Owens and Epstein (2005) found that although for the first time a majority of Supreme Court cases enjoyed *amicus* support in 1971, participation increased sharply to more than 95 percent of cases in 2001.

Religious organizations similarly have turned increasingly to the courts to pursue their political goals.[16] Ivers (1992) examined religious organizations' use of the courts. His interviews with the leaders of religious organizations revealed they believe that litigation is a means of representing their interests "in the courts on legal issues that can have repercussions in their communities" (Ivers 1992, p. 248). These leaders regard their participation as important because they provide arguments that are otherwise unavailable to judges. Some suggested that their briefs can serve as a "moral stamp of approval" for a position and possibly a Court decision (Ivers 1992, p. 252). The arguments contained in their briefs, however, are not necessarily limited to religious perspectives. As one leader commented:

> We do speak from a traditional Catholic point of view, and we do view church–
> state litigation as a chance to educate the court to the interest of our faith

community, but in the context of the law. Legal advocacy that stresses the education and public policy arguments of an issue is better than one which relies on the
religious ingredients. (Ivers 1992, p. 249)

For instance, their briefs can communicate the agreement of different religious
traditions on an issue or the impact of a decision on religious communities.

In a movement parallel to that observed among secular conservative organizations (see Epstein 1985), Ivers (1992) reported that religious organizations' involvement in courts increased beginning around 1980. This growth is especially striking
when one examines participation in church–state litigation from 1969 to 1989 (Ivers
1992, p. 254). During the first decade of that period (1969–1979), religious organizations sponsored 4 of the 25 decided cases (16 percent) and filed *amicus* briefs in 16
of those cases (64 percent). Participation was sharply higher during the second
decade: Religious organizations sponsored 14 of the 39 cases (35.8 percent) and filed
amicus briefs in 36 cases (92.3 percent). One official commented to Ivers (1992,
p. 255) that "church–state litigation has become more plural, with more groups
making their voices heard, but also more confrontational." This growth was
attributed to the entrance of certain religious groups, such as the Christian Legal
Society, the Rutherford Institute, and Concerned Women for America, whereas
other groups widened their interests in church–state litigation.

Ivers (1990) found that not only is there an increasing number of religious
interests participating in church–state litigation, but the array of religious interests
is quite diverse. Once upon a time, church–state litigation was marked by
organized interests that supported the separation of church and state. The groups
that joined the fray in recent decades advocate the opposing, accommodationist
viewpoint. Ivers (1990, pp. 786–789) noted that divisions exist within religions.
Among Jewish groups, separatist views were once the predominant position, as
articulated by the American Jewish Committee and the Anti-Defamation League,
but they have been joined by accommodationist groups led by the Orthodox Jewish
group National Jewish Commission on Law and Public Affairs. In Protestant
circles, mainline denominations supported the separationist position, especially
the National Council of Churches of Christ in the United States (Pfeffer 1981, p. 92),
whereas most evangelicals and fundamentalists advocated an accommodationist
stance, as seen in 28 of the 30 related groups who filed *amicus* briefs.[17]

Future Research Directions on Interest Groups
in Litigation

The growth in participation by religious groups begs the question of why they
choose to submit *amicus* briefs. Hansford (2004) proposed that groups participate
in cases in which they have the greatest capacity to influence the resulting legal
policy. These opportunities tend to surface for groups, who provide policy makers
with information regarding different policy alternatives, when the justices are
relatively information poor. After all, justices may not fully appreciate or

understand the consequences of every policy alternative. Groups can assess the justices' need for information by observing whether the Court invites the solicitor general to file an *amicus* brief, the complexity of the underlying legal issues, or the relative inexperience of the parties' attorneys.[18]

Hansford (2004) collected data on the *amicus* activities of a random sample of 735 organized interests from all organized interests listed in directories (i.e., *Washington Representatives* and *Washington Information Directory*), regardless of their involvement in litigation. He found, as hypothesized, that groups are significantly more likely to file *amicus* briefs when the justices are operating in an information-poor environment. Groups are almost twice as likely to participate as amici when the Court asks the solicitor general to file a brief and when a case is legally complex. At the same time, groups are significantly more likely to file an *amicus* brief when the parties' attorneys lack experience.

The next logical step in understanding religious organizations' use of the courts is to examine the behavior of a broad sample of groups, including both religious organizations and secular organizations.[19] This would allow scholars to appreciate better whether religious organizations' decisions to participate are comparable with the choices made by other groups, as well as to reveal what influences their decisions to participate in court.

IMPLEMENTATION AND IMPACT

Alexander Hamilton wrote in the *Federalist Papers* that compared with other branches of the federal government, "the judiciary, from the nature of its functions, will always be the least dangerous to the political rights of the Constitution; because it will be least in a capacity to annoy or injure them" (Hamilton, Madison, and Jay [1788] 1961, p. 465). Although the executive branch possesses the sword and the legislative branch commands the purse and writes the rules, the courts have only judgment and "must ultimately depend upon the aid of the executive arm even for the efficacy of its judgments" (Hamilton et al. [1788] 1961, p. 465). The reliance of the courts on others to implement its rulings was vividly displayed when President Andrew Jackson reputedly reacted to the Court's decision supporting the Cherokees in a treaty dispute (*Worcester v. Georgia* 1832): "John Marshall has made his decision. Now let him enforce it" (Provine 2005, 313).

There is certainly some truth to these assertions of the Court's reliance on others to implement or enforce its decisions. Indeed, the courts are reliant on a multitude of actors to implement their decisions. Canon and Johnson (1999) describe four distinct populations who influence the efficacy of the Court's decision: the interpreting population, the implementation population, the consumer population, and the secondary population. The interpreting population consists of judges and other officials who are charged with interpreting the meaning of court decisions. The implementing population includes officials who apply the rules articulated by the Court to persons subject to their authority. The consuming population is comprised of those individuals who are directly affected by the policies enunciated in the Court's opinions. The secondary population is a residual category of implementers, including state legislators, interest groups, the media, and the public. The efficacy of legal policy espoused in a Court decision depends on the response of these implementing populations; if it faces concerted opposition, the efficacy of the Court's policy will be limited.

Two studies, in particular, have examined the implementation of the Supreme Court's decisions concerning the role of religion in the public schools. The first study (Sorauf 1959; see also Sorauf 1976) investigated the impact of the Court's decision in *Zorach v. Clauson* (1952), which validated a release-time program in New York City during which school children were released during school hours to receive religious instruction away from the school. This decision came just four years after the Court in *McCollum v. Board of Education* (1948) struck an Illinois release-time program held inside the school building.

This study reveals the actors who played a role in determining the efficacy of the Court's Establishment Clause decisions. Although participation in release-time programs dropped following *McCollum*, enrollments grew modestly after *Zorach*: Participation in New York state release-time programs increased from 225,000 in the year *Zorach* was decided to 450,000 four years later in 1956 (Sorauf 1959, p. 782). This growth in release-time programs came despite no new legislation in any state and the silence of states' attorneys general (Sorauf 1959, p. 783)—members of the implementing and secondary populations, respectively. Of course, because non-compliance with *McCollum* was running rampant, it was not necessary to enact new laws and counsel school boards or districts on the permissibility of release-time programs. School boards and parents were all too happy to comply.

The expansion of release-time programs only tells part of the tale. Members of the interpreting and implementing populations used the Court's *Zorach* decision to support other religious programs in the schools. In light of Justice William Douglas's comment in *Zorach* that Americans "are a religious people whose institutions presuppose a Supreme Being" (*Zorach* 1952, p. 313), the New York Board of Regents recommended the injection of moral and spiritual values into the public school curricula (Sorauf 1959, p. 787). Some courts relied on *Zorach* to justify Bible reading in public schools or the recitation of the Lord's Prayer (Sorauf 1959, p. 788). Sorauf (1959, p. 789) concluded that "the impact of *Zorach* beyond the bounds of the facts it decided and the rules it enunciated illustrates how Supreme Court precedents, as soon as they leave judicial hands, enter another realm of policy-making and become symbols in political debate and deliberation."

The second piece of research (Birkby 1966) studied the impact of the Supreme Court's ruling in *Abington School District v. Schempp* (1963), which held that school boards may not require Bible readings and the recitation of the Lord's Prayer at the beginning of the school day. In particular, Birkby (1966) examined compliance with this ruling in school districts across Tennessee, where a state law enacted in 1915 required school teachers to read to their classes a selection from the Bible at the opening of each school day.

The state commissioner of education, reported Birkby (1966, p. 307), commented that "it was permissible to read the Bible in public schools despite *Schempp* but he left the final decision to local school officials." To study the compliance of local school boards with the Court's decision, Birkby (1966) surveyed school superintendents, school board chairs, and members to ascertain the district current and past policy on devotions. In particular, he was interested in testing the relationship of compliance with factors like urbanization of the school district, religious pluralism in the district, opposition expressed toward the school's devotional exercises, and the socioeconomic characteristics of the local school board.

The majority of responding school districts (70 out of 121, 57.9 percent) did not conform their policy to that required by the Supreme Court, but continued to follow the extant state law requiring Bible reading in schools (Birkby 1966, p. 308). Although the balance of school districts made some policy changes, only one reported eliminating all Bible reading and devotions in their schools. The changes that were reported in most school districts entailed making participation voluntary and giving teachers—members of the consuming population—discretion to hold devotions. Birkby (1966, p. 312) characterizes these changes as procedural changes, making Bible reading or participation voluntary, rather than a substantive policy change: "[T]here has been little change in fact." Perhaps because there was so little substantive change, Birkby (1966) found no statistical relationship between changes following the Court's *Schempp* decision and his hypothesized factors.

Why did the implementers fail to implement the Court's decision faithfully? Comments made in response to Birkby's survey questions suggest that policy change, albeit procedural, was a function of the policy maker's perception of the Court's role, his or her beliefs about the importance of the challenged programs, the perceived views of his or her constituency, and the policy maker's view of his or her role (Birkby 1966, p. 314). For instance, the policy maker's preference for devotional activities in public schools was dispositive. Birkby (1966, p. 315) quotes school board members from districts that did not change, including one person who said, "I thought the Bible should be read and prayer held on account this was the only time some of our students ever had any spiritual guidance." These decision makers were also influenced by the expected response of the community if changes were or were not made. One board member said, "We thought public opinion would want us to comply with Federal Law" (Birkby 1966, p. 316). Birkby's (1966) findings are consistent with the literature on Supreme Court impact (see, for example, Bond and Johnson 1982).[20]

Studies of implementation, especially those examining the decisions of lower court judges, have recently used a principal–agent theoretical framework. This relationship is when "one party (the principal) delegates work to another (the agent), who performs that work" (Eisenhardt 1989, p. 58; quoted in Brent 1999,

p. 237). Principal–agent relationships assume that there is an information asymmetry where the agent holds an information advantage over the principal. This allows the agent either to shirk on his responsibility to the principal, pursuing his own policy preferences, or to serve the principal's interests faithfully (Songer, Segal, and Cameron 1994b; Haire, Lindquist, and Songer 2003). The principal can overcome this informational disadvantage through a number of mechanisms: careful appointment of the agent, structuring incentives to encourage faithful service, and monitoring the agent's behavior. The principal–agent framework, with some adaptation, can shed light on the relationship between higher courts and inferior courts. Although Supreme Court justices do not play a formal role in the selection of lower court judges, they can and do monitor the lower court decisions. If a lower court has not faithfully implemented its decision, the Supreme Court can reverse the lower court decisions, imposing a reputational cost on those judges (but see Klein and Hume 2003).[21] Indeed, research has found that federal appellate court judges are responsive to changes in the policy articulated by the Supreme Court, although they still find opportunity to pursue their own policy preferences (Songer et al. 1994b).

Brent (1999) applied this theoretical framework to cases arising under the Free Exercise Clause of the Constitution. Indeed, he extended the framework to ask how federal appellate courts would behave when confronting a scenario in which they served two principals: the Supreme Court and Congress. Brent (1999) made creative use of the quasi-experiment created by the Supreme Court's decision in *Employment Division, Department of Human Resources v. Smith* (1990), where the Court changed its reliance on strict scrutiny in examining alleged infringement of religious freedom, ruling instead that governments are not under a constitutional obligation to accommodate a person's religious practices (Brent 1999, p. 239). A few years later, Congress created the judicial dilemma by passing the Religious Freedom Restoration Act to overturn the Court's decision. At that point, the lower courts faced multiple agents who directed them to reach different decisions. Four years later, the Supreme Court ended this dilemma by ruling the Act as unconstitutional (*City of Boerne v. Flores* 1997).

Given this history, there are four periods in time: (1) pre-*Smith*, (2) post-*Smith* and pre-Act, (3) post-Act and pre-*Flores*, and (4) post-*Flores*. Brent (1999) found a significant difference in the winning percentage enjoyed by religious claimants in the appellate courts during the second interval between *Smith* and passage of the Act (where mainstream religions lost 75.9 percent of its cases) and the third period after passage of the Act (when mainstream religions lost only 50 percent of its cases).[22] However, this relationship does not withstand a multivariate analysis with case facts and political variables. When controlling for these variables, Brent (1999) finds that the appellate courts were not responsive to their congressional principals. The appellate courts were less supportive of religious liberty claims after the Supreme Court's *Smith* decision, and the Act did not have any appreciable effect on their support for religious claims. Thus, one might conclude, lower courts have a single principal—the Supreme Court of the United States.

Future Research Directions on Implementation and Impact

The direction of research in this domain is promising, adopting as it has the principal–agent perspective. One limitation, however, is that the research has studied the implementation or impact of a few cases, raising the question of generalizability. There are many cases that could be studied to determine when and under what conditions the public and political elites have complied with the Court's decisions. For instance, one could study the implementation of *Zorach v. Clauson* (1952). At this juncture, the decision upholding release-time programs has not been overturned by the Supreme Court, although its validity has been questioned in one federal district court decision and distinguished in 16 other decisions. There are many other decisions that could be studied to probe the generalizability of our understanding of implementation and impact.

CONCLUSION

Most of the judicial politics literature that addresses the influence of a judge's religious background on his or her behavior or that delves into the courts' religious decisions is rather dated. Despite substantial theoretical and empirical advances in the study of law and courts during the past two decades, very little work on religion and the courts has incorporated those advances. This suggests that scholars should work to bring up-to-date our understanding of religion and judicial politics. As I hope the foregoing discussion makes clear, research is needed to develop the theoretical and empirical approaches to the standard set of questions that interest judicial scholars.

Kritzer and Richards (2003) stand as an example of the type of work that could be productive. They developed a general approach to the study of law's influence of judicial decision making, focusing on the impact of jurisprudential regime shifts on the legal model (see Richards and Kritzer 2002). They found in their *American Political Science Review* article (Richards and Kritzer 2002) that the impact of legal facts shifted after the Court rendered paradigmatic changes in the law. They subsequently applied their framework to the Supreme Court's Establishment Clause cases, finding a similar jurisprudential regime shift after *Lemon v. Kurtzman* (1971) (see Kritzer and Richards 2003).

In a sense, I am encouraging normal science that tests extensions of the extant theory to a different set of observations—religious liberty cases and judges' religious background. Yet, I believe there is potential to make substantial break-throughs in our understanding of judicial behavior by studying religion and the courts. Most notably, although some judicial scholars recognize that preferences are endogenous (Epstein et al. 1998), we have not begun to grapple with the causal mechanism underlying preference formation or change. To date, we have seen that religious background and beliefs affect judicial choices in some areas of the law, but we do not understand the role that religious beliefs play in the formation of preferences held by judges. A study that illuminates the causal mechanism underlying preference formation, and perhaps the role of religion in shaping a person's worldview and preference structure, could make a lasting mark in our understanding of judicial behavior.

In short, there is much work in religion and judicial politics that could be fruitful in shedding light on judicial behavior. It is time to integrate religion once again into the study of judicial politics.

NOTES

1. William Pryor's confirmation was stymied in 2003 by a filibuster led by Democratic senators. An effort at cloture, requiring 60 votes, was defeated on July 31, 2003, by a vote of 53 to 44 in favor of ending the debate (Dewar 2003a). President Bush then issued a recess appointment to Pryor in February 2004, seating him on the appellate tribunal (Allen 2004). At the beginning of the next congressional session on February 14, 2005, President Bush renominated him for a seat on the 11th Circuit Court of Appeals.

2. The advertisements were sponsored by the Committee for Justice, a group founded to win support for judicial nominees, and the Ave Maria List, a group seeking to elect pro-life candidates to Congress.

3. Judicial policy making is not limited to the U.S. Supreme Court, although many justices have stated that their organizational purpose is to "confine its attention to those cases that were important to the development and coherence of the federal law," rather than correcting errors made by lower courts (White 1982, p. 349). Trial courts can engage in policy making, as well (see, for example, McIntosh 1990; Mather 1995).

4. As Abraham (1992) notes, there had not been a Catholic justice on the Supreme Court since the death of Justice Frank Murphy in 1949. It was hoped that this would accentuate the effect of nominating a Catholic to the Supreme Court.

5. Segal and Cover (1989) found that the pairwise correlation between a justice's ideology and his or her subsequent voting behavior is as high as 80 percent for justices nominated between 1953 and 1987.

6. Although Segal (1984, p. 892) grounded this model in legal standards, discussing at length the constitutional requirements and judicial interpretations, he included the caveat that "such a model is not necessarily inconsistent with policy preferences." Segal and Spaeth (2002, p. 319) argue that "facts obviously affect the decisions of the Supreme Court, but on that point the attitudinal model does not differ from the legal model. The models differ in that proponents of the legal model conjoin facts with legalistic considerations . . . , while proponents of the attitudinal model describe the justices' votes as an expression of the fact situations applied to their personal policy preferences."

7. Vines (1964) does not describe how he defines Orthodox Protestant or the source of information on judges' religious affiliation.

8. Ulmer (1973) does not claim that these three variables comprise a complete theory of decision making on the Court. He argues that socialization patterns, like those evidenced by these three variables, determine attitudinal structure, which in turn influences votes.

9. More specifically, six of the eight justices who affiliate with high-income denominations supported the government more than half of the time and up to 75 percent of the time. In contrast, two of the three justices who affiliate with low-income denominations supported the government less than a third of the time (Ulmer 1973, p. 628). Ulmer (1973) does not define "high-income" and "low-income" denominations, but Schmidhauser (1959, p. 22) does: Episcopalian, Presbyterian, French Calvinist, Congregational, and Unitarian were deemed "high social status religious affiliations," whereas Methodist, Baptist, Christian (Disciples of Christ), Lutheran, and Dutch Reformed were classified as "low social status religious affiliations."

10. Tate (1981, p. 362) found that a justice's liberalism in civil liberty cases could be explained best by the justice's party affiliation, whether the justice was nominated by President Harry Truman, and the justice's prosecutorial experience.

11. The other issue areas studied by Goldman (1966) were criminal, civil liberties, government regulation, labor, and private economic cases.

12. In this study, Goldman (1975) examined cases raising a number of different issues, including criminal procedure, civil liberties, labor, private economic, government fiscal, and injured persons.

13. Blakeman and Greco (2004), in contrast, did not find that federal district court judges who were mainline Protestant, Catholic, or Jewish voted differently than other judges in religious speech cases.

14. Many judicial biographies admittedly seek to shed light on the views held by individual jurists by exploring the person's unique background and life experiences.

15. One exception is Yarnold (2000), who identified judges' religious denomination, including Methodist, Presbyterian, Baptist, Christian, Protestant, Episcopalian, Catholic, Lutheran, Jewish, Disciples of Christ, and Church of Christ. In her study of federal appellate court decisions in religious liberty cases, she only found Baptist and Catholic judges are more likely to rule in a pro-religion direction than other judges.

16. den Dulk and Pickerill (2003) went beyond the study of religious groups' participation in courts by proposing an "interinstitutional conception of legal mobilization." Examining church–state cases, they found that groups do not limit themselves to a single institution, but can provide valuable information to both justices and members of Congress.

17. Pfeffer (1981) examined the groups that are active in church–state litigation, as well as the particular issues that interest them. O'Connor and Ivers (1988) and McIntosh (1985) examined litigation over the teaching of creationism in public schools.

18. Hansford (2004) also hypothesized that organized interests that are reliant on mass membership will be more likely to participate in cases that will be visible to their membership or prospective members. He found empirical support for this hypothesis.

19. Hoover and den Dulk (2004) explored the use of courts by religious organizations in the United States and Canada, making use of data drawn from court records and interviews. They posited that the use of courts is a function of resource mobilization, political opportunity structures, and religious worldviews. Their study, however, is limited to religious groups' litigation over education, abortion, and the right to die.

20. Bond and Johnson (1982) found that organizational preferences, economic incentives and disincentives, and organizational norms affected the impact of *Roe v. Wade* (1973) on hospital policies.

21. Following the U.S. Supreme Court's decision in *In re R.M.J.* (1982), a judge from the overturned Missouri Supreme Court wrote to Justice Lewis Powell to express his feelings on being reversed: "I did not understand, and even resented, the tone of your opinion and your evidenced distaste for a presumed dereliction on the part of the majority of the

Missouri Supreme Court. . . . Of course, the fact that the Court on which I have sat for nearly eighteen years was publicly ridiculed in your Court galls me" (Donnelly 1983, p. 1).

    22. Wybraniec and Finke (2001) made a similar finding in their study of court decisions on religion from 1981 to 1996.

REFERENCES

Abington School District v. Schempp. 1963. 374 U.S. 203.

Abraham, Henry J. 1992. *Justices & Presidents: A Political History of Appointments to the Supreme Court.* New York: Oxford University Press.

Allen, Mike. 2003. "Judicial Nominee Admits Mistake; Pryor Regrets 'Octogenarian' Comment." *Washington Post* June 12, A37.

Allen, Mike. 2004. "Bush Again Bypasses Senate to Seat Judge." *Washington Post* February 21, A1.

Barker, Lucius J. 1967. "Third Parties in Litigation: A Systemic View of the Judicial Function." *Journal of Politics* 29: 41–69.

Bentley, Arthur F. 1908. *The Process of Government.* Chicago, Ill.: University of Chicago Press.

Binder, Sarah A., and Forrest Maltzman. 2002. "Senatorial Delay in Confirming Federal Judges, 1947–1998." *American Journal of Political Science* 46: 190–199.

Birkby, Robert H. 1966. "The Supreme Court and the Bible Belt: Tennessee Reaction to the 'Schempp' Decision." *Midwest Journal of Political Science* 10: 304–319.

Blakeman, John C., and Donald E. Greco. 2004. "Federal District Court Decision Making in Public Forum and Religious Speech Cases, 1973–2001." *Journal for the Scientific Study of Religion* 43: 439–449.

Bond, Jon R., and Charles A. Johnson. 1982. "Implementing a Permissive Policy: Hospital Abortion Services after *Roe v. Wade.*" *American Journal of Political Science* 26: 1–24.

Brent, James C. 1999. "An Agent and Two Principals: U.S. Court of Appeals Responses to *Employment Division, Department of Human Resources v. Smith* and the Religious Freedom Restoration Act." *American Politics Quarterly* 27: 236–266.

Cameron, Charles, Albert Cover, and Jeffrey A. Segal. 1990. "Senate Voting on Supreme Court Nominees." *American Political Science Review* 84: 413–524.

Canon, Bradley C., and Charles A. Johnson. 1999. *Judicial Policies: Implementation and Impact.* 2nd ed. Washington, D.C.: CQ Press.

City of Boerne v. Flores. 1997. 521 U.S. 507.

den Dulk, Kevin R., and J. Mitchell Pickerill. 2003. "Bridging the Lawmaking Process: Organized Interests, Court-Congress Interaction, and Church-State Relations." *Polity* 35: 419–440.

de Tocqueville, Alexis. [1835] 1956. *Democracy in America,* ed. Richard D. Heffner. New York: Mentor Book.

Dewar, Helen. 2003a. "Appeals Court Nominee Again Blocked; Senate Action Renews Angry Exchanges Over Charges of Anti-Catholic Bias." *Washington Post* August 1, A2.

Dewar, Helen. 2003b. "In New Ads, Judicial Battle Is a Matter of Faith." *Washington Post* July 22, A3.

Donnelly, Robert T. 1983. Letter to Lewis F. Powell, Jr., April 21. Available in the personal papers of Lewis F. Powell, Jr., Washington and Lee University.

Eisenhardt, Kathleen M. 1989. "Agency Theory: An Assessment and Review." *Academy of Management Review* 14: 57–74.

Elster, Jon, ed. 1986. *Rational Choice*. New York: New York University Press.

Employment Division, Department of Human Resources v. Smith. 1990. 494 U.S. 872.

Epstein, Lee. 1985. *Conservatives in Court*. Knoxville, Tenn.: University of Tennessee Press.

Epstein, Lee. 1993. "Interest Group Litigation During the Rehnquist Court Era." *Journal of Law & Politics* 9: 639–717.

Epstein, Lee, Valerie Hoekstra, Jeffrey A. Segal, and Harold J. Spaeth. 1998. "Do Political Preferences Change? A Longitudinal Study of U.S. Supreme Court Justices." *Journal of Politics* 60: 801–818.

Epstein, Lee, and Jack Knight. 1998. *The Choices Justices Make*. Washington, D.C.: CQ Press.

Epstein, Lee, René Lindstädt, Jeffrey A. Segal, and Chad Westerland. 2006. "The Changing Dynamics of Senate Voting on Supreme Court Nominees." *Journal of Politics* 68: 296–307.

Goldman, Sheldon. 1966. "Voting Behavior on the United States Courts of Appeals, 1961–1964." *American Political Science Review* 60: 374–383.

Goldman, Sheldon. 1975. "Voting Behavior on the United States Courts of Appeals Revisited." *American Political Science Review* 69: 491–506.

Goldman, Sheldon. 1997. *Picking Federal Judges: Lower Court Selection from Roosevelt through Reagan*. New Haven, Conn.: Yale University Press.

Goldman, Sheldon. 2006. "The Politics of Appointing Catholics to the Federal Courts." *University of St. Thomas Law Journal* 4: 193–220.

Gryski, Gerard S., Gary Zuk, and Deborah J. Barrow. 1994. "A Bench that Looks Like America? Representation of African Americans and Latinos on the Federal Courts." *Journal of Politics* 56: 1076–1086.

Guth, James L. 2007. "Religion and Roll Calls: Religious Influences on the U.S. House of Representatives, 1997–2002." Presented at the annual meeting of the American Political Science Association, Chicago, Illinois, August 30–September 2.

Haire, Susan B., Stefanie A. Lindquist, and Donald R. Songer. 2003. "Appellate Court Supervision in the Federal Judiciary: A Hierarchical Perspective." *Law & Society Review* 37: 143–168.

Hamilton, Alexander, James Madison, and John Jay. [1788] 1961. *The Federalist Papers*, ed. Clinton Rossiter. New York: Mentor.

Hansford, Thomas G. 2004. "Information Provision, Organizational Constraints, and the Decision to Submit an Amicus Curiae Brief in a U.S. Supreme Court Case." *Political Research Quarterly* 57: 219–230.

Harlan, John M. 1971. Letter to Chief Justice Warren E. Burger, June 22. Available in the personal papers of Harry A. Blackmun, Library of Congress.

Holmes, Oliver Wendell, Jr. [1881] 1991. *The Common Law*. New York: Dover.

Hoover, Dennis R., and Kevin R. den Dulk. 2004. "Christian Conservatives Go to Court: Religion and Legal Mobilization in the United States and Canada." *International Political Science Review* 25 (1): 9–34.

Hurst, James Willard. 1956. *Law and the Conditions of Freedom in the Nineteenth-Century United States*. Madison, Wisc.: University of Wisconsin Press.

Ignagni, Joseph A. 1993. "U.S. Supreme Court Decision-Making and the Free Exercise Clause." *Review of Politics* 55: 511–529.

Ignagni, Joseph A. 1994a. "Explaining and Predicting Supreme Court Decision Making: The Burger Court's Establishment Clause Decisions." *Journal of Church and State* 36: 301–327.

Ignagni, Joseph A. 1994b. "Supreme Court Decision Making: An Individual–Level Analysis of the Establishment Clause Cases during the Burger and Rehnquist Court Years." *American Review of Politics* 15: 21–42.

In re R. M. J. 1982. 455 U.S. 191.

Ivers, Gregg. 1990. "Organized Religion and the Supreme Court." *Journal of Church and State* 32: 775–793.

Ivers, Gregg. 1992. "Religious Organizations as Constitutional Litigants." *Polity* 25: 243–266.

Johnson, Timothy R., Paul J. Wahlbeck, and James F. Spriggs, II. 2006. "The Influence of Oral Arguments on the U.S. Supreme Court." *American Political Science Review* 100: 99–113.

Klein, David E., and Robert J. Hume. 2003. "Fear of Reversal as an Explanation of Lower Court Compliance." *Law & Society Review* 37: 579–606.

Knight, Jack. 1992. *Institutions and Social Conflict*. New York: Cambridge University Press.

Kobylka, Joseph F. 1989. "Leadership on the Supreme Court of the United States: Chief Justice Burger and the Establishment Clause." *Western Political Quarterly* 42: 545–568.

Krislov, Samuel. 1963. "The Amicus Brief: From Friendship to Advocacy." *Yale Law Journal* 72: 694–721.

Kritzer, Herbert M., and Mark J. Richards. 2003. "Jurisprudential Regimes and Supreme Court Decisionmaking: The *Lemon* Regime and Establishment Clause Cases." *Law & Society Review* 37: 827–840.

Lemon v. Kurtzman. 1971. 403 U.S. 602.

Lewis, Neil A. 2003. "Judicial Nominee Advances Amid Dispute Over Religion." *New York Times* July 24, A17.

Maltzman, Forrest, James F. Spriggs, II, and Paul J. Wahlbeck. 2000. *Crafting Law on the Supreme Court: The Collegial Game*. New York: Cambridge University Press.

Manwaring, David R. 1962. *Render Unto Caesar: The Flag-Salute Controversy*. Chicago, Ill.: University of Chicago Press.

Marshall, Thomas R. 1993. "Symbolic versus Policy Representation on the U.S. Supreme Court." *Journal of Politics* 55: 140–150.

Mather, Lynn. 1995. "The Fired Football Coach (Or, How Trial Courts Make Policy)." In *Contemplating Courts*, ed. Lee Epstein, 170–202. Washington, D.C.: CQ Press.

McCollum v. Board of Education. 1948. 333 U.S. 203.

McIntosh, Wayne V. 1985. "Litigating Scientific Creationism, or 'Scopes' II, III, ..." *Law & Policy* 7: 375–394.

McIntosh, Wayne V. 1990. *The Appeal of Civil Law: A Political–Economic Analysis of Litigation*. Urbana, Ill.: University of Illinois Press.

Meernik, James, and Joseph Ignagni. 1997. "Judicial Review and Coordinate Construction of the Constitution." *American Journal of Political Science* 41: 447–467.

Moraski, Bryon J., and Charles R. Shipan. 1999. "The Politics of Supreme Court Nominations: A Theory of Institutional Constraints and Choices." *American Journal of Political Science* 43: 1069–1095.

Murphy, Walter J. 1964. *Elements of Judicial Strategy*. Chicago, Ill.: University of Chicago Press.

Nemacheck, Christine L. 2007a. "Have Faith in Your Nominee? The Role of Candidate Religious Beliefs in Judicial Selection Politics." Presented at the annual meeting of the Southern Political Science Association, New Orleans, Louisiana, January 4–7.

Nemacheck, Christine L. 2007b. *Strategic Selection: Presidential Nomination of Supreme Court Justices form Herbert Hoover through George W. Bush*. Charlottesville, Va.: University of Virginia Press.

O'Connor, Karen, and Gregg Ivers. 1988. "Creationism, Evolution and the Courts." *PS: Political Science and Politics* 21: 10–17.

Owens, Ryan J., and Lee Epstein. 2005. "Amici Curiae during the Rehnquist Years." *Judicature* 89: 127–132.

Peltason, Jack W. 1955. *Federal Courts in the Political Process.* Garden City, N.Y.: Doubleday.

Perry, Barbara A. 1991. *A "Representative" Supreme Court?* New York: Greenwood.

Pfeffer, Leo. 1981. "Amici in Church-State Litigation." *Law and Contemporary Problems* 44: 83–110.

Pritchett, C. Herman. 1948. *The Roosevelt Court: A Study in Judicial Politics and Values 1937–1947.* New York: MacMillan.

Provine, Doris Marie. 2005. "Judicial Activism and American Democracy." In *The Judicial Branch*, ed. Kermit L. Hall and Kevin T. McGuire, 313–340. New York: Oxford University Press.

Richards, Mark J., and Herbert M. Kritzer. 2002. "Jurisprudential Regimes in Supreme Court Decision Making." *American Political Science Review* 96: 305–320.

Roe v. Wade. 1973. 410 U.S. 113.

Rohde, David W., and Harold J. Spaeth. 1976. *Supreme Court Decision Making.* San Francisco, Calif.: W. H. Freeman.

Rosenberg, Gerald. 1991. *The Hollow Hope.* Chicago, Ill.: University of Chicago Press.

Schmidhauser, John R. 1959. "The Justices of the Supreme Court: A Collective Portrait." *Midwest Journal of Political Science* 3: 1–57.

Schubert, Glendon. 1965. *The Judicial Mind: The Attitudes and Ideologies of Supreme Court Justices 1946–1963.* Evanston, Ill.: Northwestern University Press.

Schwartz, Bernard. 1986. *Swann's Way: The School Busing Case and the Supreme Court.* New York: Oxford University Press.

Segal, Jeffrey. 1984. "Predicting Supreme Court Decisions Probabilistically: The Search and Seizure Cases." *American Political Science Review* 78: 891–900.

Segal, Jeffrey A., and Albert Cover. 1989. "Ideological Values and the Votes of U.S. Supreme Court Justices." *American Political Science Review* 83: 557–565.

Segal, Jeffrey A., and Harold J. Spaeth. 2002. *The Supreme Court and the Attitudinal Model Revisited.* New York: Cambridge University Press.

Songer, Donald R., Sue Davis, and Susan Haire. 1994a. "A Reappraisal of Diversification in the Federal Courts: Gender Effects in the Courts of Appeals." *Journal of Politics* 56: 425–439.

Songer, Donald R., Jeffrey A. Segal, and Charles M. Cameron. 1994b. "The Hierarchy of Justice: Testing a Principal–Agent Model of Supreme Court–Circuit Court Interactions." *American Journal of Political Science* 38: 673–696.

Songer, Donald R., and Susan J. Tabrizi. 1999. "The Religious Right in Court: The Decision Making of Christian Evangelicals in State Supreme Courts." *Journal of Politics* 61: 507–526.

Sorauf, Frank J. 1959. "*Zorach v. Clauson*: The Impact of a Supreme Court Decision." *American Political Science Review* 53: 777–791.

Sorauf, Frank J. 1976. *The Wall of Separation: The Constitutional Politics of Church and State.* Princeton, N.J.: Princeton University Press.

Spiller, Pablo T., and Rafael Gely. 1992. "Congressional Control or Judicial Independence: The Determinants of U.S. Supreme Court Labor-Relations Decisions, 1949–1988." *Rand Journal of Economics* 23: 463–492.

Spriggs, James F., II, and Paul J. Wahlbeck. 1997. "Amicus Curiae and the Role of Information at the Supreme Court." *Political Research Quarterly* 50: 365–386.

Swann v. Charlotte-Mecklenburg Board of Education. 1971. 402 U.S. 1.

Tarr, G. Alan. 1977. *Judicial Impact and State Supreme Courts.* Lexington, Mass. Lexington Books.

Tate, C. Neal. 1981. "Personal Attribute Models of the Voting Behavior of U.S. Supreme Court Justices." *American Political Science Review* 75: 355–367.

Truman, David. 1950. *The Governmental Process.* New York: Alfred A. Knopf.

Ulmer, S. Sidney. 1970. "Dissent Behavior and the Social Background of Supreme Court Justices." *Journal of Politics* 32: 580–598.

Ulmer, S. Sidney. 1973. "Social Background as an Indicator to the Votes of Supreme Court Justices in Criminal Cases: 1947–1956 Terms." *American Journal of Political Science* 17: 622–630.

Vines, Kenneth N. 1964. "Federal District Judges and Race Relations Cases in the South." *Journal of Politics* 26: 337–357.

Vose, Clement E. 1955. "NAACP Strategy in the Covenant Cases." *Western Reserve Law Review* 6: 101–145.

Wahlbeck, Paul J., James F. Spriggs, II, and Forrest Maltzman. 1998. "Marshalling the Court: Bargaining and Accommodation on the United States Supreme Court." *American Journal of Political Science* 42: 294–315.

Walz v. Tax Commission. 1970. 397 U.S. 664.

Washington Post. 2003. "Unfit to Judge." April 11, A26.

White, Byron R. 1982. "The Work of the Supreme Court: A Nuts and Bolts Description." *New York State Bar Journal* 54: 346–349, 383–386.

Worcester v. Georgia. 1832. 31 U.S. 515.

Wybraniec, John, and Roger Finke. 2001. "Religious Regulation and the Courts: The Judiciary's Changing Role in Protecting Minority Religions from Majoritarian Rule." *Journal for the Scientific Study of Religion* 40: 427–444.

Yalof, David Alistair. 1999. *Pursuit of Justices: Presidential Politics and the Selection of Supreme Court Nominees.* Chicago, Ill.: University of Chicago Press.

Yarnold, Barbara M. 2000. "Did Circuit Courts of Appeals Judges Overcome Their Own Religions in Cases Involving Religious Liberties? 1970–1990." *Review of Religious Research* 42: 79–86.

York, Byron. 2003. "Catholics Need Not Apply?" *National Review Online* July 30. http://www.nationalreview.com/york/york073003.asp (accessed January 9, 2009).

Zorach v. Clauson. 1952. 343 U.S. 306.

CHAPTER 20

....

RELIGION AND AMERICAN PUBLIC POLICY: MORALITY POLICIES AND BEYOND

....

DOUGLAS L. KOOPMAN

THERE are many roads and even more roadside distractions in any review of religion and American public policy. Summarizing such research is fraught with peril. Which public policy issues are "religious" and which are not? Should traditional constitutional issues of church and state be included? Or should the focus be on "morality policy" issues like abortion and gay rights? Or, alternatively, should the chapter concentrate on "social justice" issues like concern for the poor; or should issues of "war and peace," world poverty, AIDS, or even international freedom abroad be examined?

Second, any effort to examine the role of religion in public policy formation raises the issue of how to distinguish between religious and "moral" claims. Many individuals bring moral claims to the policy process—many on the basis of a religious faith, but others from foundations avowedly not religious. Moreover, as all legislation imposes one set of values on society as opposed to another, do not all public policies, in that sense, legislate morality and constitute a politics of "morality?"

Although this chapter will touch on some of the questions just mentioned, it cannot cover them all. Rather, given the confines of one chapter, it will follow one narrow road, closing off other useful paths, trying to limit distracting scenery along even this road. The focus will be largely on the "morality policy" literature, because it is that research that examines the role of religion in some depth. However, even within this relatively narrow framework, the discussion is further limited in two other ways. First, attention is limited to policy *outcomes,* and, second, it focuses only on those policies in which religious individuals and organizations tend to be involved because they believe their faith requires it. This is an admittedly narrow search, because these morality policies are only a small subset of policies that engage religious individuals and groups in the policy-making process. What are the fundamental assumptions of this approach and its basic hypotheses? And, even within this relatively narrow confine, how has that literature contributed to theories of public policy more generally or even broadened the study of public policy to include substantive areas previously ignored? And are there other topics, not yet examined, that fit under the morality policy rubric?

The first portion of this chapter outlines the history as well as the character-istics of morality policies. Next, the chapter examines research related to specific public policies that fall within the morality politics classification and evaluates the relative fit of such policies within the morality politics rubric. The third section of the chapter addresses additional public policy issues with religious dimensions. And, finally, the chapter concludes with suggestions for future research.

THE STUDY OF PUBLIC POLICY

Approaches to the Study of Public Policy

Because there are thousands of different policies enacted by national, state, and local governments, scholars have developed several approaches to analyze them more capably. One relatively common approach is to differentiate between and among various types of public policy according to "their effect on society and the relationships among those involved in policy formation" (Anderson 2006, p. 11). This approach typically divides public policy into three broad categories: (1) distributive policies that involve allocation of services or benefits to particular segments of the population, (2) regulatory policies that impose restrictions or limitations on the behavior of individuals or groups, and (3) redistributive policies that involve deliberate efforts by the government to shift the allocation of resources and wealth from the "haves" to the "have nots."

A second approach focuses on the "stages" of policy making—formation, implementation, and evaluation. Although some criticize these divisions as overly rigid (Cochran, Mayer, Carr, and Cayer 2006, p. 7), such categories are frequently used as a heuristic device to isolate and focus attention on these particular aspects of policy making.

Finally, analysts have examined public policy making in terms of specific substantive areas. In fact, most major texts in the field typically divide the subject matter into chapters on the policy process and chapters on major public policies. In terms of the latter, the focus tends to be on broad areas of policy like health, environment, and defense.[1]

The Emergence of "Morality Policy" as a Field of Study

Although moral issues have been evident within American politics since the founding, the use of the terms *morality politics* and *morality policies* by social scientists is, in fact, quite recent. These terms rise out of earlier studies of "symbolic" and "value" politics (Gusfield 1963; Edelman 1964). When policy analysts contrast these concepts with their opposites—"material" and "substantive"—one almost detects disappointment, if not disdain, that such types of policies even emerge in American politics. The argument is that "symbolic" politics do not reflect the appropriate "stuff" of politics; groups should not conflict over "symbols," but instead over "tangible" considerations. The groups that promote such values and symbols are typically described as threatened, choosing to enter the policy process out of anxiety over their status and identity as opposed to engaging politics in a more rational and appropriate desire to receive a greater share of economic goods. Gusfield (1963), for example, presents prohibition as a clash between conservative Protestantism and Catholicism over cultural supremacy, an advantage that would apparently be conveyed by victory or defeat on this symbolic issue.

Accordingly, alcohol laws have long been interpreted by researchers to reflect status disputes and religious differences. Fairbanks (1977), for example, reviewed various state enactments regarding liquor and gambling laws (as well as academic studies of them), and he found that the religious composition of the state had greater explanatory power than economic indicators in accounting for whether states chose to relax prohibition era alcohol laws. States in which conservative religious values still dominated tended to retain liquor restrictions, whereas the repeal of more restrictive alcohol laws occurred in those states in which the religious doctrines upon which the laws were originally based were "no longer widely held" (Fairbanks 1977, p. 417).[2]

But just how should one label these noneconomic policy issues in a disciplinary subfield that had focused on economic policies largely negotiated quietly by experts, interest groups, and elected officials in incremental bargaining? Symbolic and status issues were a category of policy issues that seemed to operate under different rules—and a category of issues that, starting in the 1960s, seemed to be proliferating. As a result, scholars began writing about a "moral" category of public policy issues. Tatalovich and Daynes (1988), for example, initially labeled them *social* regulatory policies, in apparent contrast to *economic* regulatory policies.

Their list of such policies included abortion, the death penalty, gay rights, and pornography, along with several others.[3] Later, Tatalovich, Smith and Bobic (1994, 3) characterized these public policy issues as "essentially noneconomic" issues that seek to "generate emotional support for deeply held values," contending that these issues were not easily explained by the dominant policy theories based upon individual economic or economic class interests. These issues involve first principles, not mere profit or prudential calculations, even though prior research largely suggested that they seemed to reflect concerns about social status anxiety or economic uncertainty by the various identified groups.

However, it was Meier (1994, 1999) who popularized, if not coined, the term *morality politics,* cleverly labeling it as "the politics of sin." He argues that morality policies reflect the way in which core social values interact with the policy of the state, because they embody disputes over the values and behaviors that are endorsed or rejected by the government (Meier 1999, p. 681). Thus, morality policy would appear to be a subtype of redistributive policy, although with one important difference: Morality policies redistribute "values," whereas redistributive policies redistribute "economic" rewards. Nevertheless, despite these differences, both involve zero-sum games, with the policy outcomes clearly signifying the "winners" and "losers" in the process.

To understand why morality policy constitutes a distinct class of public policy, it is necessary to specify what scholars have argued are its defining characteristics (e.g., Tatalovich and Daynes 1988; Nice 1992; Meier 1994; Mooney and Lee 1995; Haider-Markel and Meier 1996). As noted earlier, morality policy involves "debate over first principles," in which at least one side portrays the issue as one of morality or sin and uses moral arguments in its policy advocacy.[4] Thus, at the center of morality policy debate is conflict over fundamental values about which no consensus exists among members of society.

Several other characteristics flow from this defining quality (Mooney 2001, pp. 7–8). The first is its perceived simplicity, involving "easy issues" (Carmines and Stimson 1980). Because the debate is about first principles, and not instrumental values, almost anyone can legitimately claim to be well informed. Second, because the morality policy debate is characterized by conflicts over first principles, the issues are usually highly salient to the general public (Mooney and Lee 1995; Haider-Markel and Meier 1996). A third characteristic flows from the second—namely, that morality politics is characterized by high levels of citizen participation (Carmines and Stimson 1980; Haider-Markel 1999). Fourth, in morality politics, compromise is difficult to achieve, unlike in other policy arenas.[5] And, finally, in cash-strapped governmental settings, such policies require little expenditure or bureaucratic time and attention in that they do not transfer economic assets.

Morality policies hold a special attraction to ambitious politicians who seek to benefit from appeals to the electorate. However, ambition is not the only reason why politicians may latch on to morality issues; many are forced to respond to public opinion out of self-preservation (Mooney 2001). Because of their salience, elected officials who wish to retain their positions will likely adopt positions on such issues that reflect constituency attitudes. Furthermore, although the typical drivers of economic regulatory policy are linked to sociological variables like income and urbanization, those that drive morality policy are either religious factors (e.g., the dominant religious traditions in a state or district) or "political" factors such as tight electoral and partisan competition (Mooney 2001).[6]

Mooney (2000) has linked morality politics to federal court decisions. Historically, the Reserved Powers Clause in the 10th Amendment had been interpreted to reserve decision making on many morality politics issues to the states (the so-called "police power"). This left room for "policy heterogeneity" across states and regions, because morality policies varied as a result of differences in public opinion within the states (Mooney 2000, p. 172). However, various Supreme Court rulings in the period after World War II served to "nationalize" some morality issues, setting guidelines that ran counter to many widely accepted policies at the state and local levels. This situation created opportunities for state-level policy entrepreneurs that encouraged a perpetual state of intense, unstable, and visible politics in many states. As Mooney (2000) summarizes:

> Federal government intervention in [moral politics] in the past 30 years is in no small part responsible for the high level of active morality policy making throughout the United States.... and there is no indication that this pattern will change in the near future.... [W]e will undoubtedly see continued acrimonious, divisive, and irreconcilable morality-policy activity in the U.S. states and communities for the foreseeable future. (p. 188)

Once federal courts have "nationalized" an issue, there is little likelihood that decision-making authority will be returned to the states.

Analytically, the study of morality policy takes a middle ground between classifications based on substantive topics (e.g., health policy, defense policy, environmental policy) and those based on types of policy outcomes (e.g., regulatory, distributive, and redistributive policies). The former is used in many textbooks, but does not prove to be very helpful theoretically, whereas the latter has more theoretical richness but poses challenges in empirical application (Mooney 2001, p. 6). Moreover, as noted earlier, most theories of policy making are derived from the study of economic or material matters—namely, the distribution and redistribution of wealth and the regulation of business activity. However, issues related to "moral conflict are not easily assimilated into theories and models based upon economic and class interests" (Tatalovich et al. 1994, p. 2), and conventional explanatory variables related to analyses of economic policy (e.g., incrementalism, the impact of socioeconomic and political factors on state policy adoption, and the power of interest groups) may be far less important in shaping morality policies. Thus, the study of morality policy "seeks to expand and test the generalizability of our understanding of policy making by identifying whether or not, and in what ways, morality policy politics differs from that of nonmorality policy" (Mooney 2001, p. 7).

Specific Public Policies

Having outlined the defining characteristics of morality politics, we are now in a position to review studies that have examined various public policies within the morality policies framework. As will become evident in this review, few issues of public policy are "purely" moral in their outline and process. Sometimes policy disputes appear to involve a clash of fundamental values, but the actual policy debate itself may be much more narrowly focused. At other times, policy proposals initially embody the characteristics of morality politics, but then circumstances change so that the issue no longer fits the morality policy genre. And, sometimes morality policies get linked to other policies and begin to operate in much the same way as traditional economic policies. Despite these caveats, the specific policy issues discussed in this section of the chapter typically are examined within the morality policy framework.

Abortion

For decades, abortion has been a public policy controversy, particularly so after *Roe v. Wade* was decided in 1973. A substantial number of studies (e.g., Cook, Jelen, and Wilcox 1992; Craig and O'Brien 1993; Goggin 1993; O'Connor 1996; McFarland and Meier 2001) have examined the varied policy responses to the Supreme Court's abortion decisions. Nevertheless, despite what appears to be a natural fit within the category of morality policies, most issues related to abortion are not pure examples of the genre. Meier and McFarland (1993, p. 85) note, for example, that, although it may exhibit many of the characteristics of morality politics, "abortion funding policy is not a pure morality issue." Certainly the matter exhibits some of the major characteristics of morality politics: It is highly salient to a significant share of the public, and both sides in the debate frequently choose to provide simple value-based arguments to the public.[7] In addition, Meier and McFarland (1993, p. 86) note that abortion debates are "made to order" for ambitious politicians. Nevertheless, one important characteristic prevents abortion policy from being completely reflective of "moral politics." Given that the fundamental constitutional right of abortion has been established in *Roe*, policy debates on abortion are now much more often redistributive in nature (e.g., whether there should be public funding of abortions for low-income pregnant women). Still, some post-*Roe* conflicts appear to be about "first principles": Should parents and spouses be notified? Should information on the status of the fetus be shared with the mother? And, should alternatives to abortion be presented to the mother for consideration?

Mooney and Lee (1995) studied the state-by-state progress of abortion law reform (prior to *Roe*), with reform defined as state policies that moved in a more pro-choice direction. They did this to determine whether adoption of more pro-choice abortion policies in that period reflected morality politics characteristics. They found that such adoptions were not always a good fit with the characteristics of morality politics. Instead, debates generally reflected more typical social learning processes that drive policy diffusion[8] and reinvention patterns found in other types of policy adoption[9] more than they did morality politics. However, certain religious variables (e.g., the combined percentage of Catholics and "fundamentalist" Protestant Christians[10] within the state) strongly affected reform outcomes.[11]

The *Roe v. Wade* decision is generally seen as a pivotal point with regard to the issue. Norrander and Wilcox (1999) examined post-*Roe* abortion politics—abortion regulation, government funding specifically, and parental consent laws. Again, they found that abortion debates often conformed to the expectations of morality politics—but sometimes they did not, because much depended on the particular circumstances. However, they did find that the percentage of Catholic adherents in the state correlated, as expected, with more abortion regulation and less government funding for the procedure.

Gay Rights and Related Issues

A fair amount of scholarly attention has also been given to political issues related to the gay community (e.g., Adam 1987; Colby and Baker 1988; Haider-Merkel and Meier 1996; Button, Rienzo, and Wald 1997; Haider-Markel and Meier 2003). Colby and Baker (1988) studied state-level policy responses to the AIDS crisis in its early years between 1981 and 1987. They (Colby and Baker 1988, p. 128) conjectured that states with more conservative political cultures, "particularly when this conservatism is expressed and reinforced by a dominant fundamentalist religious community,"[12] would predict opposition to the adoption of AIDS policies. Their measurement of the state's political culture was based simply on how the state's congressional delegations voted on socially conservative issues as measured by the *National Journal* scores. They found that states with more conservative political cultures spent less on AIDS education, prevention, and treatment programs.

Other studies have focused on gay issues at the local government level. Local gay antidiscrimination ordinances were examined by Wald, Button, and Rienzo (1996), who compared communities that had such ordinances with those that did not. Their analysis suggested that the greater public presence of morally traditional religious groups[13] was related to more conservative decision making in regard to such ordinances.[14] Similarly, Haider-Markel and Meier (1996), working directly in the morality politics tradition, studied gay rights policy in Colorado and Oregon, focusing on a variety of local antidiscrimination issues in education, housing, employment, as well as on public statewide ballot initiatives. Their analysis revealed that these "quieter" local antidiscrimination issues generally followed an interest group model of resolution,[15] whereas the more highly salient statewide initiatives (which passed in Colorado and failed in Oregon) were explained better by the morality politics model. These findings were subsequently reaffirmed in a study of Wisconsin's antidiscrimination statute in regard to gays and lesbians (Heider-Markel and Meier 2003). That analysis suggested "if the scope of the conflict over gay and lesbian civic rights is limited, an interest group politics model best explains state policies for lesbians and gays," but when the issue becomes salient to the broader public and "the scope of the conflict is expanded to the electoral arena, the pattern of politics is best explained by a morality politics model" (Haider-Markel and Meier 2003, p. 686).

Finally, at the national level, Haider-Markel (1999) examined votes on gay rights initiatives by members of the U.S. House, finding the denominational affiliation of individual legislators shaped voting on such issues in the 101st through 104th Congress, with legislators affiliated with conservative religious denominations[16] less likely to support pro-gay positions on roll call votes. These findings reflected earlier results (Haider-Markel and Meier 1996) that "morality politics factors seem to have more influence on legislative voting behavior when the salience of the issue is high, and interest groups appear to have more influence when issue salience is low" (Haider-Markel 1999, p. 745). Interestingly, however, Haider-Markel (1999) noted that morality issues can actually embody two different types of politics—(1) "sin politics," where one side of an issue has successfully defined the issue solely in terms of sin, making it politically impossible for opponents to be "for" sin; and (2) "morality politics" issues in which "opposing coalitions" use a variety of arguments, including value arguments. However, in the latter case, it appears that the process looks a lot like more typical redistributive politics. Initially, organized interests spend most of their time arguing over frames of reference, although over time the relevance of the morality facet of the issues diminishes. As it lessens, issues become more likely to be resolved in incremental and prudential ways (Haider-Markel 1999, p. 746).

End-of-Life Issues

Physician-assisted suicide, living wills, and right-to-die issues have faced state and federal legislatures for some time and have been studied by scholars (e.g., Glick 1992; Smith 1993; Hoefler and Kamoie 1994). Clearly, these issues are classic examples of morality policy issues in that fundamental values (e.g., the worth of human life in unusual circumstances) are involved. Nevertheless, despite their presumed fit within that framework, the processes and outcomes related to these end-of-life issues only partially appear to reflect the attributes of morality politics. Hoefler (1994, p. 163), for example, asserts: "The diversity in legislative acts is attributable to the important role played by the Roman Catholic Church in state legislative politics" at the interest group and elite levels. And when Glick and Hutchinson (1999, p. 751) examined physician-assisted suicide laws, they found that their content was affected by the strength of the Catholic lobby and, only to a lesser extent, their portrayal in the mass media—suggesting only a partial fit with the characteristics of morality policy. End-of-life issues have a clear religious dimension, and thus a moral one, but these particular issues seem to play out in more conventional ways without the high public salience of classic morality policies.

Gambling

Gambling and state lotteries may also arouse moral concerns. Lindaman (2007) has found that local government decisions on gambling policy proposals follow many of the characteristics of morality policy. In fact, gambling is condemned by some religious groups, and many others oppose it because of alleged links to prostitution, drinking, smoking, and the like. As result, it is not surprising that a variety of religious variables have been found to be related to the support of and opposition to gambling policy proposals. Berry and Berry (1990, p. 406), for example, have found that the "likelihood of a lottery adoption decreases as the share of state's population adhering to fundamentalist religions increases."[17] Olson, Guth, and Guth (2003) examined surveys of voters in a 2000 South Carolina lottery referendum, and, because their questionnaire contained a variety of religious questions, they were able to tease out the impact of a number of religious factors on support for or opposition to the referendum. They found that the political salience of religion had a major impact: Those who saw their faith as relevant to their political choices were more likely to vote against the lottery. Likewise, they found that those who were affiliated with the evangelical Protestant tradition were more likely than members of other religious traditions to be opposed to the lottery.

However, many states that allow gambling and lotteries have tied their establishment to dedicated revenue requirements to fund various popular state programs (e.g., education spending). This linkage of moral issues to popular activities changes the nature of policy debates. Pierce and Miller (1999) examined factors that shaped the adoption (or rejection) of general gambling laws compared with those that shaped the adoption of gambling laws when such laws tied gambling revenue to popular state functions. They (Pierce and Miller 1999, p. 700) found that the relative size of fundamentalist faith adherents in a state[18] was a significant factor discouraging general fund lottery adoptions, but was insignificant in terms of whether education fund lotteries were adopted. As a result, Pierce and Miller (1999, p. 702) concluded that researchers "need to appreciate the variation *within* the general category of morality policy," because such variation is linked to how the choice is framed, and whether and how the moral policy is linked to other issues.

Sex Education Policy

Sex education policy in public schools has also been examined within the morality policy framework. In the 1996 welfare reform law, the federal government provided $50 million each year to the states during the course of five years to promote abstinence-only sex education. This policy—a change in a conservative direction from previous reproductive health education—was passed by the newly elected Republican congresses of the late 1990s and was signed by Democratic president Bill Clinton. However, when this issue became more publicized and likely more salient to the mass public, the strictures of the legislation were loosened in the administrative interpretation and implementation phases, because the directly affected interest groups found more friendly audiences in the federal bureaucracy and state governments to make implementation more lenient than Congress had expected (Vergari 2000).

Wald, Button, and Rienzo (2001) examined school-based health centers and the level of reproductive health care services provided to adolescents. Building on previous research (Sharp 1999), they noted that innovative morality policies are likely to be shaped by both cultural values and governmental structures. In their analysis, they found that both cultural and socioeconomic factors were involved in the type and distribution of such services. The local culture had some small effect on public policy implementation, but the distribution of the centers followed the lines one would expect from standard socioeconomic factors, especially local-needs assessments. As a result, morality politics seemed only marginally evident.

Thus, although such studies reveal that the factors shaping sex education policies differ from those shaping policies outside the category of morality policy, it is also true that morality policy issues are really much less distinctive than is commonly imagined. As Wald et al. (2001, p. 230) state: "[C]ultural factors do not completely supplant other considerations but rather are supplemented by economic, political, and racial predictors."

Death Penalty

Capital punishment for certain crimes has a clear moral dimension, because it involves the power of the state to take a human life as an ultimate form of punishment and deterrence. Given its long history as a public policy controversy, the death penalty has also been the subject of many scholarly treatments (e.g., Bedau 1967; Berns 1979). The death penalty debate fits a major morality policy criterion in that it is a conflict of first principles (Mooney and Lee 1999a). And, when the debate over capital punishment stays fixed on first principles, the characteristics of morality policy prevail. However, when the debate moves to more narrow issues, then more typical policy learning and incremental policy change typically occur. Consequently, Mooney and Lee (1999a, p. 778) note that, for death penalty debates at least, "the distinction between morality policy and nonmorality policy certainly is not objective, but resides in the issue definitions and arguments that support a given policy debate."

In the case of capital punishment, it is possible for opponents to "chip away" at its practice. Thus, opponents who argue for small and incremental limitations on the practice, rather than its outright ban, are more likely to be successful. However, when the death penalty is directly challenged, some characteristics of morality policy emerge, particularly strict adherence to public opinion over elite policy learning (Mooney and Lee 1999b, p. 90). Mooney and Lee (2000, p. 234) also find that, when opinion on a morality policy is closely divided, lawmakers pay close attention to public opinion, but when opinion is one-sided, elites are more influential. They conclude that with regard to morality policy debates:

[P]olicy makers will respond to public opinion when that opinion is clear and communicated to them, whether because of a democratic impulse or out of electoral fear. But in the absence of clear and strong signals from the public, policy makers will resort to whatever guidance they can get, which is usually from political elites who send clear and strong signals even when the general public does not. (Mooney and Lee 2000, p. 235)

Morality Policy as an Analytical Tool

Scholars of morality policy have focused on a rather narrow band of issues, primarily those "moral" issues that have dominated media coverage. The link that these studies make to religion is understandable, because religious groups and religiously backed moral claims are common in debates on such matters as abortion, gay rights, the death penalty, and gambling.

And, as noted earlier, morality politics exhibits certain distinct characteristics. It is characterized by controversies over deeply held values that are easily grasped by the public—not disputes over "mere" economic matters. Public accessibility suggests that these issues do not need expert commentary or elite framing, both of which cloud the issues and make the choices relative. Practitioners in morality policies tend to argue their issue positions in terms of clear right and wrong, morally unambiguous, language. Morality policy outcomes involve official "signaling" of approved and disapproved behaviors, and thus those groups with identities that are connected to those particular behaviors. In morality politics, characteristics common to other policy areas—interest group resolution, "policy learning" by individuals and state officials from others, gradualism, and incrementalism— are quite uncommon. Public appeals on moral issues typically have a religious coloration. Such issues generally invite public participation and comment, and there is evidence that "direct democracy" plays more of a role in morality, than in other, policy decisions.[19]

However, few issues, if any, are purely and always moral. Outside of a very few "pure" morality policies (e.g., possibly the teaching of creationism), the morality policy model serves more as a useful analytical tool than a fully descriptive snapshot of reality. Even for morality policy scholars, different issues "fit" differently. None fit perfectly, and some "morph" into more traditional policy dynamics later on. As has been noted, even scholars working within the morality policy framework have concluded that moralization is subject to particular contexts and linkages; reality is simply more complex.

In the end, the scholarship on morality policies reveals various strengths and limitations. Its strengths include making comparisons and distinctions. Indeed, morality politics starts with Lowi's (1964) notion that "politics follows policies," and that moral policies lead to a new kind of moral politics. The most useful contribution is the point that moral policies in pure form do not fit the typical, and otherwise quite useful, models of public policy analysis.

Because the two major American political parties broadly agree on democratic capitalism, the cleavages and contests between them are likely to be based increasingly on noneconomic or moral issues. That these grievances are natural seems to be the case, resulting from the nature of American culture, our political structures, and the federalization of many policy issues. And, issues considered to be merely symbolic in the 1970s have developed into major bones of contention, leading to the establishment of a field of study labeled *morality policy*.

Nevertheless, some of the limitations of the morality policy framework have become more evident over time. First, some specific issues within this framework have been studied more than others. Of course, this is not an inherent problem to the approach, but it does limit our ability to assess how well the framework may be applied to a breadth of political issues. A more substantial problem is that few political matters and public policies are "purely" moral in their outline and process. Sometimes policy disputes appear to be a clash of moralities, sometimes policy proposals lose their moral qualities over extended periods of time, and sometimes that happens quickly as they get linked to other policies, soon operating in much the same way as traditional economic policies.

Second, most of the morality policy literature has focused on the formation of policy, typically in legislative bodies, but it has given much less attention to the process of implementation. Although there are exceptions to this generalization (e.g., Meier 1999), the fact remains that more research is needed to investigate the difficulties of implementing morality policy outcomes and whether the implementation of morality policy differs in systematic ways from the implementation of other kinds of public policies. Meier argues (2001, p. 27) that "sin" policies are difficult to implement, and, as a result, are doomed to failure, but little effort has been made thus far to assess this contention.

Third, as noted earlier, when religious variables are used in explanations, they are often conceptualized and measured in an unclear manner. Terms like *fundamentalist* tend to be used indiscriminately, with little attention given to the conceptual and measurement advances made in the religion and politics literature. Burden (2007) shows the importance of religion in the analysis of legislative outcomes that goes beyond what is generally found in most morality politics research. Rather than simply focusing on the religious characteristics of states and districts, he demonstrates that the "personal" characteristics of legislators, like religion, are often central in cosponsorships and floor debate as well as in final votes.

Last, the morality politics framework does not capture all the ways in which religious individuals, groups, and values come to shape public policy. A variety of other policy issues have been advanced by religious groups, but such issues do not fall so neatly within the morality politics framework. As an example of another public policy clearly related to religion, but falling largely outside the morality politics framework, we will discuss the proposal to fund faith-based initiatives, because a considerable amount of scholarly literature has emerged that addresses this matter.

Faith-Based Initiatives

The Charitable Choice provision of the Welfare Reform Act of 1996, signed by President Clinton, specifies that when the government chooses to partner with community groups in addressing social welfare needs, no private agency should be excluded from consideration simply because of its religious character. The specific nature of the program, rather than the agency, is to serve as the basis of assessment. All programs, whether religious or secular, should be evaluated on the basis of how well they train the unemployed, care for children, or heal drug addicts. If a program is "successful," it deserves funding consideration regardless of whether the agency is religious or secular.

The faith-based and community initiative program championed by President Bush went beyond the earlier Charitable Choice provision. First, the new Charitable Choice policy sought to boost charitable giving to religious and other organizations by allowing taxpayers to receive a tax credit for their contributions to nonprofit organizations (Burden 2007, p. 124). Second, the proposed policy sought to expand governmental funding for religious groups by allowing them to compete for governmental funding, without necessarily restricting their religious activities (Bartkowski and Regis 2001, p. 3; Burden 2007, p. 124). This new Charitable Choice legislation was introduced in the House in early 2001.

The legislation reveals how the framing of issues can have important consequences for the success or failure of policies, as avowed "friends" of policy proposals do not always frame issues in ways that are likely to achieve legislative success. The faith-based initiative could have been framed in a variety of ways: as a constitutional question involving whether religious agencies can receive public funds, as an issue of social service effectiveness, or as support for racial and ethnic minorities, given that African American and Latino churches were in the forefront of efforts to provide social services. Or, more broadly, the issue could have been framed as an effort to combat poverty in both urban and rural areas. In fact, the faith-based initiative became mired in partisan politics. Final vote on The Community Solutions Act of 2001 "fell almost perfectly along party lines, passing 233 to 198," (Burden 2007, p. 125), as only 19 members voted differently from their fellow partisans. Still, despite such partisanship, "religious attachments became increasingly important predictors of legislative behavior as the locus of study moved from roll call votes to bill sponsorship" (Burden 2007, p. 129).

A fair number of scholarly analyses of the faith-based initiative have been conducted (e.g., Bane, Coffin, and Thiemann 2000; Dionne and Chen 2001; Wineburg 2001; Black, Koopman, and Ryden 2004; Wuthnow 2006). These studies document the intense political firestorm in Congress around the initiative when the Bush administration first introduced it in 2001, and, at times, even scholarship on narrower aspects of the initiative (e.g., its relative effectiveness, or its constitutionality) reflects the choosing of ideological sides.

As noted earlier, many of the religious providers eligible for federal support under Charitable Choice provisions are operated by racial and ethnic minorities in urban areas. This suggests that the faith-based initiative could have been framed in traditional affirmative action terms by politicians on the progressive side of the political spectrum (by including these new groups in the government benefits which are now distributed to a more established, but less diverse, clientele). Or it could have been framed as support for "programs that work" to alleviate difficult societal problems. However, the politics played out quite differently, with conservatives attempting to appeal to racial and ethnic minorities, particularly in urban cores. This attempt failed.

In scholarly analyses, the racial implications of the initiative were generally emphasized, but doubts were expressed about the capability of these new providers to replace or supplement significantly the current social safety net (Chaves 1999; Chaves and Tsitsos 2001). And when the Bush administration's appeals to racial and ethnic minorities were assessed, they were seen as half hearted and insincere (see, for example, Wineburg 2007).

The main research on faith-based policy initiatives has focused, however, on two other matters—the relative effectiveness of the proposed new providers and the constitutional implications of their more direct participation in public funding for meeting social needs. With regard to the first issue, studies of the effectiveness of faith-based social services are many (Johnson 2002; Fisher and Stelter 2006; Grettenberger, Bartkowski, and Smith 2006; Wuthnow 2006; Boddie and Cnaan 2007). Analysts have tried to assess whether overtly religious social services are superior to secular providers, the mainstays of state-supported social service delivery. One general finding is that committed service providers—committed to their jobs, to the treatment protocols of their program, and to the program recipients—generate better outcomes regardless of whether the provider is religious or secular.[20]

However, nearly all early assessment studies reached the conclusion that the government knew very little about the effectiveness of its funding partners. Certainly the government requires these partners to have trained professionals certified by the relevant guild delivering the particular services they provide as well as sufficient budget and accounting procedures in place to track the specified use of public dollars. However, information about whether the programs produce the desired outcomes is notoriously spotty. Thus, in this regard, the faith-based debate over effectiveness has exposed a significant policy evaluation problem.

Constitutional studies are also common. First Amendment religion cases handed down by the Supreme Court during the latter half of the 20th century were often inconsistent in their interpretation and application of the establishment clause. *Lemon v. Kurtzman* (1971) attempted to provide some guidance on these matters, but it set ambiguous standards for interpreting the Establishment Clause—secular purpose, primary effect, and excessive entanglement—that led the court to "accommodate" religion at times (*Lynch v. Donnelly, Marsh v.Chambers, Mueller v. Allen*) and to prohibit aid to religion at others (*Grand Rapids School District v. Ball, Aquilar v. Felton*). All these cases were decided within a three-year period during the mid 1980s, making it unclear how the court would react when new issues arose related to providing "aid" to religion in general or to faith-based service providers in particular. And, although *Lemon* still remains the law of the land, what constitutes "secular purpose," "primary effect," and "excessive" entanglement tends to be in the "eye of the beholder," a fairly subjective standard prone to shifting assessments within different contexts and across time.

The current scholarship reflects the ambiguity of the current situation (Lupu and Tuttle 2004; Ryden and Polet 2005, Lupu and Tuttle 2006), with some arguing for the constitutionality of Charitable Choice (Esbeck 1997; Esbeck, Carlson-Theis, and Sider 2004; Esbeck 2006) and others arguing against it (Stern 2001). In the final analysis, however, the issue is not whether government should partner with religious organizations (Catholic and Methodist hospitals, and Catholic and Lutheran social services have long received federal dollars in their provision of social services, even prior to the passage of the Charitable Choice provisions of the Welfare Reform Act of 1996); rather, the important questions relate to "when and how such partnering should occur, with which organizations, and under what circumstances" (Kennedy 2005, p. 51).

Clearly the issue of faith-based initiatives does not fit the morality policy framework very well. Elites and interest groups seem to be the most heavily involved, whereas the mass public does not seem nearly as engaged as the morality policy framework would expect (see the following analysis). This appears to be an issue on which cues are taken more from party, than religious, leaders—despite the fact that faith-based initiatives involve a clash of first principles related to the extent to which there should be a "high wall" or "low wall" separating church and state.

Table 20.1 examines the links between religious affiliation and strength of partisanship and attitudes toward Charitable Choice, (with comparisons made

Table 20.1 Support for Morality-Related Policies by Religious Tradition

Religious Tradition	Charitable Choice				Abortion			
	2000		2004		2000		2004	
Protestant	Agree	Disagree	Agree	Disagree	Life	Choice	Life	Choice
Evangelical	42	42	59	27	65	34	70	30
Mainline	37	43	46	37	38	61	35	65
Latino Protestant	62	21	63	25	47	51	63	34
Black Protestant	63	10	62	23	46	53	54	45
Catholic								
Anglo	45	38	51	36	47	52	48	52
Latino	56	28	59	23	50	49	56	44
Jewish	28	48	39	57	16	82	16	84
Unaffiliated	36	45	36	49	29	69	27	72
All	43	39	50	35	46	53	48	51
Strength of Party								
Strong Republican	37	46	58	26	66	33	70	30
Strong Democrat	53	34	49	38	36	63	39	61

Source: 2000 and 2004 National Surveys of Religion and Politics.

with abortion attitudes) using data from the Third (2000) and Fourth (2004) National Survey of Religion and Politics. The groups most supportive of public funding in 2000 were religious minorities—particularly, black Protestants, Latino Protestants, and Latino Catholics, all groups that stood to benefit from the program. Those affiliated with the larger religious traditions (i.e., evangelical Protestants, mainline Protestants, and Anglo Roman Catholics) were fairly evenly divided, whereas Jews and the unaffiliated stood largely opposed. The nation as a whole was fairly evenly divided on the issue, but leaned in the direction of supporting the initiative. Strong Republicans, however, stood opposed to such funding in 2000, whereas strong Democrats favored it, perhaps reflecting the fact that the Clinton administration had backed the initiative and the support for such legislation among minority religious groups (other than Jews).

Attitudes were more favorable in 2004 than they were in 2000. Those affiliated with the three largest religious traditions (white evangelical and mainline Protestants and Anglo Catholics) moved to support such public funding between 2000 and 2004, whereas minorities continued to favor, and Jews and the unaffiliated continued to oppose. However, in a partisan Congress polarized after the controversy of the 2000 presidential election, the faith-based initiative became framed more in partisan terms, than in terms of effectiveness, which contributed to its rather quick failure—at least as legislation. The partisan split in Congress appears to have moved strong Republicans from opposition in 2000 to support in 2004, whereas strong Democrats moved slightly in the opposite direction between the 2000 and 2004 presidential campaigns.

Finally, attitudes on abortion are presented in table 20.1 as a contrast to perspectives on Charitable Choice. The former fit the morality policy literature much better than the latter. This is evident in several ways. Relatively few Americans fail to adopt some kind of position on abortion, and the religious and partisan polarization on this issue is much greater than on faith-based initiatives. Finally, given such polarization of attitudes, it is not surprising that one detects relatively little shifting in positions on the abortion issue between 2000 and 2004,[21] whereas Charitable Choice tends to be largely "off the radar screen" for most members of the mass public. Accordingly, legislators are not under the same constituent pressures on such matters as they would be in any policy vote related to abortion. As a result, shifts in public opinion on these kinds of issues are more likely to transpire and be related to elite-driven efforts than any shifts related to first principles.

CONCLUSION

This chapter concludes with several reflective comments on morality policies and also makes some suggestions for future research in this field of study. First, it should be evident that most morality policy studies treat moral issues very narrowly. The approach itself relies in some sense on its distinction between social and economic issues, with an early characterization of its subject matter as "social regulatory" policy as opposed to economic regulatory policy. But on closer inspection this distinction falls apart. Certainly, economic policy can involve moral concerns. Any fair reading of the Jewish and Christian, or even Islamic, scriptures shows a healthy interest, if not preoccupation, with issues of economic justice. Throughout these texts, there are clear evaluations of political and social authorities, and these almost always include economic and material factors.

Second, within the morality politics literature, religious variables are not conceptualized or operationalized in any sophisticated manner. Many studies utilize rather crude categories of religious groups—frequently discussing religion in terms of the proportion of religious adherents who are designated fundamentalist, or in terms of the proportion who are Roman Catholics. The latter may not be problematic, but the former certainly is. No effort is made to differentiate adherents of different religious traditions based on appropriate classification schemes (Kellstedt, Green, Guth, and Smidt 1996; Steensland et al. 2000; and appendix A of chapter 1 in this volume). Certainly, to some extent, operational measures suffer from inevitable data limitations on religious variables. Affiliation data may be available for the electorate at the county and state levels, but even such data require careful assignment to their proper religious category and greater attention to nuances related to religious designations (e.g., how the analyst chooses to differentiate a fundamentalist, from an evangelical, denomination).

Third, hardly any effort is made to try to connect the specific religious components of the moral claims to a selected policy. Instead, one gets the impression that a religious connection makes intuitive sense, but just why there should be linkages between the two is addressed very generally, if at all. Simply finding a connection between "the proportion of fundamentalist Protestants" within a state and a policy outcome provides little explanation regarding whether it is affiliation, beliefs, or religious practices that are affecting the result. In defense of the literature, however, in many instances data may only be available on the aggregate religious characteristics of the relevant population.

Finally, the morality politics literature tends to see the influence of religion on the formation of public policy only in terms of legislation that reflects differences over first principles, and then primarily in terms of the religious composition of the electorate (e.g., the proportion of fundamentalist Protestants). However, Burden (2007) has recently made a strong claim for the importance of the religious characteristics of legislators in efforts to explain policy outcomes. His analysis reveals that religion's impact on public policy formation can extend beyond roll call votes to sponsorship of bills and debates on the floor of Congress. What is less clear is whether these religious factors have similar effects within legislative processes at the state level. Still, given these patterns at the national level, to what extent then are state responses to morality politics legislation a function of the particular religious culture of the state or the distinctive religious characteristics of state legislators themselves? Affiliation data for state policy makers may not be available, and religious beliefs and practices of these decision makers may be even more difficult to obtain. Nevertheless, if religion is going to be a useful variable in the morality politics literature, and in public policy analysis more broadly, then attention to these analytical and measurement concerns is essential.

Assuming that these issues can be addressed, the question then becomes a matter of what kinds of theoretical issues might be examined. The remainder of this chapter seeks to point scholars in such directions. First, many articles in the morality policy literature examine issues that appeared to be "moral," but upon closer inspection became "de-moralized" in significant ways. Some studies suggest system fatigue about moral policies—in that elected officials or interest groups begin to frame or resolve issues in more traditional ways. Is there, therefore, some kind of secular demoralization that may operate even in relationship to the most intense moral issues? Do the traditional policy types—redistributive, distributive, and regulatory—eventually impose their will on even the most purely moral issues if these issues persist on engaging the policy process? Does the policy system "tire" of the moralization of a particular issue or does "system learning" take place so that eventually these issues revert to other issue types? Or do the once-intense citizen groups themselves tire of the process? Conversely, does the cycle also work in the other direction? In other words, can some issues start out as traditional economic issues and then become moral matters? Anecdotal evidence suggests they do, as the political Left seems to be picking up moralizing language on the budget and environmental issues. If transitions in and out of moralization exist, then how do they stop, start, and develop?

Second, when one reviews the literature on morality policies, one is struck by how many issues have little hope of achieving the outcomes they purportedly desire—to be enacted into law and affect enough behavioral change to be a social regulatory "success." For many issues, efforts to pass morality policies persist despite repeated failures to accomplish their policy goals. This raises the question of whether individuals and groups may advance morality policies not necessarily to succeed in passing such legislation, but to lose—not so much to create a majority coalition of friends, but to identify a collection of enemies; not so much to achieve policy success, but to mark social decline. Persistent failure suggests that success might not be an important goal. It may be that groups enter the moral politics debate, or advance issues as moral, not to redefine government policy, but to reinforce their "otherness" from mainstream values or to generate financial support for their particular organizational structures. Groups from the far Right or Left, or outside such easy continua, could enter the moral politics field more intent on reinforcing their separateness and self-viewed superiority than actually believing the state would sanction their position. They could do this to reinforce a self-identity of being "not of this world," to retain influence within one political party at the expense of losing a public majority, or to solidify their identity as being more progressive than mainstream politics can handle. Further research that connects perpetually failing morality policies more closely to the goals of their promoters would be a useful addition to the literature.

In actual practice, however, morality politics issues such as abortion, gay rights, or capital punishment policies may exhibit considerable complexity, comparable with policies outside the morality politics domain. Nevertheless, two key characteristics of morality politics are its tendency to cast such issues as "easy issues" related to first principles and its proclivity to follow the values and opinions of the masses in decision making. Consequently, if there is a growth in morality poli*cies*—policies that are presented as simple moral choices—then does that suggest a decline in representative government, where elected legislators seek to resolve issues according to mutually acceptable, fair, and open procedures? Growth of morality poli*cies* could well reflect a decline in republican government and its emphasis on procedural fairness and thoughtful representation bargaining. Representative government has served to protect minorities and prevent majority tyranny, and to the extent morality policies chip away at representation, values related to representative government are threatened.

During the past several decades, moral issues of religious coloration have moved from the periphery to the center of American political discourse. Moral arguments are now invading discussions ranging from the federal budget to the fuel efficiency standards for automobiles. Major party candidates for the presidency and many other offices now often talk about their religious faith and religion both during campaigns and while in office. And what is the effect on the public policy agenda? Does increased religious expression by politicians expand the morality politics agenda? Or is this the first sign that morality policies have run their course and the public is again seeking more moral politicians and fewer moral issues?

NOTES

1. This rather unsettled nature of religion and public policy may be one reason why undergraduate public policy textbooks typically avoid religious matters in their content and discussion. Usually, the first half of these introductory textbooks discusses public policy in general, whereas the second half is generally divided into large topical public policy categories. Most textbooks usually start the second half with chapters on fiscal and budget policy, and then move to large social programs such as welfare, retirement, and health care. Next come chapters on the environment and energy, and typically one or two chapters on foreign and military policy end the book. A few exceptions (e.g., Peters 2006) might touch on "morality politics" in a chapter on "cultural" issues, in which issues as abortion, gay rights, and church–state separation might be addressed. But, generally, the undergraduate public policy student seems unlikely to encounter much discussion of the interaction between religion and public policy, an unfortunate limitation given the persistence of religious belief in the nation and the increasing presence of religious rhetoric and groups in the public square and the policy-making world.

2. Fairbanks (1977) actually examines several different religious variables in his analysis. One measure was the proportion of a state belonging to any Protestant

denomination, another was the percentage of each state's population belonging to Protestant denominations not associated with the National Council of Churches— although members of the United Methodist Church were included given its historic role in the prohibition movement (a measure of conservative Protestantism), and a third was a fundamentalism index. Of the three Protestant measures, the measure with the strongest relationship to liquor and gambling was the conservative Protestantism measure (Fairbanks 1977, p. 414).

3. Johnson and Meier (1990) studied what has long been referred to colloquially as "sin" taxes—levies on alcohol, tobacco, gambling or lotteries, and similar projects, investigating both where they are enacted and whether they actually reduce the consumption of "sin." They isolated two aggregate-level religious "belonging" variables—the percentage of Catholic population and percentage of Protestant fundamentalists. Both religious variables usually were tied to the incidence of public policies regarding gambling, lotteries, state liquor control boards, and tax rates on alcohol and cigarettes. Consequently, they suggested that state morality policies result from competition of citizens groups, especially those self-identified as religious. They also found that sin taxes actually did little to reduce the consumption of the "sin" being taxed, suggesting dissonance between the publicly proclaimed demand for reducing such sinful behavior and the actual demand for the freedom to engage in that sin by the same public.

4. Mooney (2001) argues that this characterization could fit economic policy areas if at least one side perceived the issue as involving first principles of right and wrong.

5. Although Meier (2001) is pessimistic about making and enforcing moral policies, he does suggest one possible means out of this dilemma is through the reframing of issues in ways that work with established policy-making procedures within the political branches of government. Such a reframing could entail presenting the debate as a more ambiguous clash of different, although widely held, values (e.g., abortion as a clash between the preservation of life and the privacy and freedom rights of a pregnant female). If core values clash, although policy still needs to be made, perhaps a more typical policy process might transpire. Another potential reframing could be to link a "sin" issue to a public good (such as linking state allowance or sponsorship of gambling to higher funding for popular functions such as education), converting moral politics into more redistributive politics.

6. In addition to Mooney, Raymond Tatalovich has been a major contributor to the study of morality policies. He and Byron Daynes published a widely used edited volume in the field (Tatalovich and Daynes 1988). Their first 1988 edition was published as *Social Regulatory Policy*, but by the third, 2005, edition, the title had changed to *Moral Controversies in American Politics* (Tatalovich and Daynes 2005). The usual issues— abortion, death penalty, gay rights, pornography—are in each. Other issues—animal rights, English as an official language, school prayer, gun control, and hate crimes—fall in and out of editions, but the core remains.

7. These value-based arguments consist of the fetus' right to life on the one side, and the woman's right to privacy and self-determination on the other—despite some of the complexities related to the issue.

8. This contention posits that state policy makers seek shortcuts to rational decision making. One important such shortcut may be to draw on the policy formulations adopted by nearby states, and "follow the local leader," as opposed to the policies of states located much farther away. Not only do states within a region tend to share greater similarities (economically, geographically, and demographically), but their physical

proximity also serves to breed familiarity—enabling legislators and citizens to analogize more easily to states nearby than far away (see Mooney and Lee 1995, p. 605).

9. This expectation is based on the notion that, with regard to policy innovation, one or two states may try a new policy, whereas other states in the region wait to see how such a policy works before adopting it (or a modified policy) themselves.

10. In classifying "fundamentalist Protestants," Mooney and Lee (1993) adopted the approach used by Meier and McFarlane (1993). Using Glenmary data (Bradley, Green, Jones, Lyon, and McNeil 1992), they utilized the level of membership in the following denominations to reflect the proportion of fundamentalist Protestants found in that particular state: Churches of God, Church of the Latter-day Saints, Churches of Christ, Church of the Nazarene, Mennonite, Conservative Baptist Association, Missouri and Wisconsin Synod Lutherans, Pentecostal Free Will Baptist, Pentecostal Holiness, the Salvation Army, Seventh-Day Adventist, and the Southern Baptist Convention. All but the Church of Latter-day Saints would fit an "evangelical" label (see appendix A in chapter 1 of this volume).

11. O'Connor and Berkman (1995), found much the same for the same time period, with religious variables (percentage of Catholics and percentage of "fundamentalist" Protestants) affecting abortion policy, and with broad public activity and issue simplification not always being evident.

12. Clearly, there is uncertainty as to what the authors mean by "fundamentalist religious community." They do not attempt to measure the variable, focusing instead on the "political culture" of the state.

13. The words "morally traditional religious groups" were used in the abstract of the article, although not in the text itself. In the article, the focus on was on "communal protest" to the gay rights campaign that was rooted in religious groups "marked by the moral orthodoxy that is empirically associated with negative attitudes about gays and gay rights" (Wald et al. 1996, p. 1162). To measure the concentration of churches with socially traditionalist orientations, the authors first used denominations identified by Meier and Johnson (1990, 426, n. 6). They then added denominations with at least 100,000 adherents if those denominations had been classified as fundamentalist/evangelical by both Smith (1990) and Kellstedt (1989). Finally, they added the Presbyterian Church in America based on its formal statement regarding homosexuality (Wald et al. 1996, fn. 5).

14. Population size of the community was the single largest factor differentiating cities and counties with gay rights ordinances/policies and those without them. In addition, the analysis revealed that the political opportunity structure of the locality, along with the presence of "morally traditional religious groups," were the two other factors that served to shape the likelihood of the presence or absence of such policies.

15. The contrast between an "interest group model" and a "morality politics model" is based on the fact that "in morality politics little information on the issue is needed for participation," as the issue itself is generally highly salient for the individuals involved. It may be the case that interest groups will still be active with regard to matters of morality politics, but "their prime resource (information) is not needed, giving them relatively less influence over the outcome" (Haider-Markel and Meier 2003, p. 673). As a result, interest groups "are likely to try to limit broader involved in the formulation of policy, or in Schattschneider's (1960) terms, limit the scope of conflict" (Haider-Markel and Meier 2003, p. 673). When the scope of conflict is widened, different factors become important in the shaping of public policy than when the scope of conflict is much narrower.

16. According to Haider-Markel (1999, p. 747, n. 9), "conservative religion affiliation included Protestant Fundamentalists, Baptists, and those members simply stating Christian." The Protestant fundamentalist category included those legislators with

affiliations to the Church of God, Latter-day Saints, Church of Christ, Church of the Nazarene, Mennonites, Conservative Baptist Association, Missouri Synod Lutherans, Pentecostal Free Will Baptists, Pentecostal Holiness, Salvation Army, and Seventh-Day Adventist denominations.

17. Berry and Berry (1990) report that they used Glenmary data (Bradley, Green, Jones, Lyon, and McNeil 1992) to estimate the size of the state's population adhering to a "fundamentalist religion," but they do not provide details as to which specific denominations reported in the Glenmary data were classified as falling within that category.

18. Pierce and Miller (1999) cite sources used to assign denominations to the "fundamentalist sect," but do not report just what denominations are so assigned. The proportion of state residents belonging to a fundamentalist sect was estimated through the use of Glenmary data (Bradley, Green, Jones, Lyon, and McNeil 1992).

19. It is also quite likely that morality policies are debated more often, and more publicly, in America than elsewhere.

20. However, although the evidence is sketchy, it appears that higher levels of commitment are more evident within overtly religious groups than within governmental agencies (Unruh and Sider 2005; Wuthnow 2006). Nevertheless, even if this is the case, a broader research question remains—namely, under what particular circumstances (e.g., in terms of what programs, with what clientele, dealing with what human needs, and within what social or religious contexts) do overtly religious social services achieve outcomes better than, or at least comparable with, the outcomes of other types of providers? Answers to these questions call for quasi-experimental designs of the type that have not been used in prior evaluations.

21. There was, however, some shifting of attitudes among Latino Protestants and black Protestants in a more pro-life direction between 2000 and 2004. Although this shift may reflect real change in positions, it may also be a function of the relatively small sample numbers found with regard to these two categories—more so for Latino, than black, Protestants.

REFERENCES

Adam, Barry D. 1987. *The Rise of a Gay and Lesbian Movement.* Boston, Mass.: Twayne.
Anderson, James. 2006. *Public Policymaking,* 6th ed. Boston, Mass.: Houghton Mifflin.
Aquilar v. Felton. 1985. 473 U.S. 402.
Bane, Mary Jo, Brent Coffin, and Ronald Thiemann, eds. 2000. *Who Will Provide: The Changing Role of Religion in American Welfare.* Boulder, Colo.: Westview Press.
Bartkowski, John, and Helen Regis. 2001. *Charitable Choices: Religion, Race, and Poverty in the Post-Welfare Era.* New York: New York University Press.
Bedau, Hugo. 1967. *The Death Penalty in America.* Garden City, N.J.: Anchor.
Berns, Walter. 1979. *For Capital Punishment: Crime and the Morality of the Death Penalty.* New York: Basic Books.
Berry, Frances S. and William D. Berry. 1990. "State Lottery Adoptions as Policy Innovations: An Event History Analysis." *American Political Science Review* 84 (2): 395–416.
Black, Amy E., Douglas L. Koopman, and David K. Ryden. 2004. *Of Little Faith: The Politics of George W. Bush's Faith-Based Initiatives.* Washington, D.C.: Georgetown University Press.

Boddie, Stephanie C., and Ram A. Cnaan. 2007. *Faith-Based Social Services: Measures, Assessments, and Effectiveness.* Binghamton, N.Y.: Haworth.

Bradley, Martin, Norman Green, Dale Jones, Mac Lyon, and Lou McNeil. 1992.*Churches and Church Membership in the United States 1990.* Atlanta, GA: Glenmary Research Center.

Burden, Barry. 2007. *Personal Roots of Representation.* Princeton, N.J.: Princeton University Press.

Button, James W., Barbara A. Rienzo, and Kenneth Wald. 1997. *Private Lives, Public Conflicts: Battles over Gay Rights in American Communities.* Washington, D.C.: CQ Press.

Carmines, Edward G., and James A. Stimson. 1989. *Issue Evolution: Race and the Transformation of American Politics.* Princeton, N.J.: Princeton University Press.

Chaves, Mark. 1999. "Religious Congregations and Welfare Reform: Who Will Take Advantage of 'Charitable Choice'?" *American Sociological Review* 64: 836–846.

Chaves, Mark, and William Tsitsos. 2001. "Congregations and Social Services: What They Do, How They Do It, and with Whom." *Nonprofit and Voluntary Sector Quarterly* 30 (4): 660–683.

Cochran, Clarke E., Lawrence C. Mayer, T.R. Carr, and N. Joseph Cayer. 2006. *American Public Policy: An Introduction,* 8th edition: Thomson Wadsworth.

Colby, David C., and David G. Baker. 1988. "State Policy Responses to the AIDS Epidemic." *Publius* 18: 113–130.

Cook, Elizabeth Adell, Ted G. Jelen, and Clyde Wilcox. 1992. *Between Two Absolutes: Public Opinion and the Politics of Abortion.* Boulder, Colo.: Westview Press.

Craig, Barbara H., and David M. O'Brien. 1993. *Abortion and American Politics.* Chatham, N.J.: Chatham House.

Dionne, E. J., and Ming Su Chen. 2001. *Sacred Places, Civic Purposes: Should Government Help Faith-Based Charity?* Washington, D.C.: Brookings Institution Press.

Edelman, Murray. 1964. *The Symbolic Uses of Politics.* Urbana, Ill.: University of Illinois Press.

Esbeck, Carl H. 1997. "A Constitutional Case for Governmental Cooperation with Faith-Based Social Service Providers." *Emory Law Journal* 46: 1–42.

Esbeck, Carl. 2006. "'Play in the Joints between the Religion Clauses' and Other Supreme Court Catachreses." *Hoftra Law Review* 34: 1331–1336.

Esbeck, Carl H., Stanley Carlson-Thies, and Ron Sider. 2004. *The Freedom of Faith-Based Organizations to Staff on a Religious Basis.* Washington, D.C.: Center for Public Justice.

Fairbanks, J. David. 1977. "Religious Forces and 'Morality' Policies in the American States." *Western Political Quarterly* 30: 411–417.

Fischer, Robert L., and Judson D. Stelter. 2006. "Testing Faith: Improving the Evidence Base On Faith-Based Human Services." *Journal of Religion & Spirituality in Social Work* 25 (3–4): 105–122.

Glick, Henry R. 1992. *The Right to Die: Policy Innovation and Its Consequences.* New York: Columbia University Press.

Glick, Henry R., and Amy Hutchinson. 1999. "The Rising Agenda of Physician-Assisted Suicide: Explaining the Growth and Content of Morality Policy." *Policy Studies Journal* 27 (4): 750–765.

Goggin, M., ed. 1993. *Understanding the New Politics of Abortion.* Newbury Park, Calif.: Sage Publications.

Grand Rapids School District v. Ball. 1985. 473 U.S. 373.

Grettenberger, Susan, John Bartkowski, and Steven R. Smith. 2006. "Evaluating the Effectiveness of Faith-Based Welfare Agencies: Methodological Challenges and Possibilities." *Journal of Religion & Spirituality in Social Work* 25 (3–4): 223–240.

Gusfield, Joseph. 1963. *Symbolic Crusade.* Urbana, Ill.: University of Illinois Press.

Haider-Markel, Donald P. 1999. "Morality Policy and Individual-Level Political Behavior. The Case of Legislative Voting on Lesbian and Gay Issues." *Policy Studies Journal* 27 (4): 735–749.

Haider-Markel, Donald P., and Kenneth J. Meier. 1996. "The Politics of Gay and Lesbian Rights: Expanding the Scope of Conflict." *The Journal of Politics* 58: 332–349.

Haider-Markel, Donald P., and Kenneth J. Meier. 2003. "Legislative Victory, Electoral Uncertainty: Explaining Outcomes on the Battles over Lesbian and Gay Civil Rights." *Review of Policy Research* 20 (4): 671–690.

Hoefler, James M. 1994. "Diffusion and Diversity: Federalism and the Right to Die in the Fifty States." *Publius* 24: 153–170.

Hoefler, James M., and Brian Kamoie. 1994. *Deathright: Culture, Medicine, Politics, and the Right to Die.* Boulder, Colo.: Westview Press.

Johnson, Byron. R. 2002. *Objective Hope—Assessing the Effectiveness of Faith-Based Organizations: A Review of the Literature.* Philadelphia, Pa.: Center for Religion and Urban Civil Society, University of Pennsylvania.

Johnson, Cathy M., and Kenneth J. Meier. 1990. "The Wages of Sin: Taxing America's Legal Vices." *Western Political Quarterly* 43: 577–595.

Kellstedt, Lyman. A. "Evangelical Religion and Political Behavior: A Validation Effort." Paper presented at the annual meeting of the Society for the Scientific Study of Religion, Octobr, Salt Lake City, Utah.

Kellstedt, Lyman A., John C. Green, James L. Guth, and Corwin E. Smidt. 1996. "Grasping the Essentials: The Social Embodiment of Religion and Political Behavior." In *Religion and the Culture Wars,* ed. John C. Green, James L. Guth, Corwin E. Smidt, and Lyman A. Kellstedt, 174–192. Lanham, Md.: Rowman & Littlefield.

Kennedy, Sheila. 2005. "Religion, Rehabilitation, and the Criminal Justice System." In *Sanctioning Religion: Politics, Law, and Faith-Based Public Services,* ed. David Ryden and Jeffrey Polet, 39–52. Boulder, Colo.: Lynne Rienner Publishers.

Lemon v. Kurtzman. 1971. 403 U.S. 602.

Lindaman, Kara L. 2007. "Place Your Bet on Politics: Local Governments Roll the Dice." *Politics & Policy* 35 (2): 274–297.

Lowi, Theodore. 1964. "American Business,Public Policy, Case Studies, and Political Thoery." World Politics 16: 677–715.

Lupu, Ira C., and Robert W. Tuttle. 2004. *Partnerships between Government and Faith-Based Organizations: The State of the Law—2004. Roundtable on Religion and Social Welfare Policy.* Albany, N.Y.: Rockefeller Institute of Government.

Lupa, Ira C. and Robert W. Tuttle. 2006. *The State of the Law 2006: Legal Developments Affecting Government Partnerships with Faith-Based Organizations.* Washington, D.C. Roundtable on Religion and Social Policy.

Lynch v. Donnelly. 1984. 465 U.S. 668.

Marsh v. Chambers. 1983. 463 U.S. 783.

McFarland, Deborah R., and Kenneth J. Meier. 2001. *The Politics of Fertility Control: Family Planning and Abortion Policies in the American States.* Chatham, N.J.: Chatham House.

Meier, Kenneth J. 1994. *The Politics of Sin: Drugs, Alcohol, and Public Policy.* Armonk, N.Y.: M. E. Sharpe.

Meier, Kenneth J. 1999. "Drugs, Sex, Rock, and Roll: A Theory of Morality Politics." *Policy Studies Journal* 27 (4): 681–695.

Meier, Kenneth J. 2001. "Drugs, Sex, Rock, and Roll: A Theory of Morality Politics." In *The Public Clash of Private Values,* ed. Christopher Mooney, 21–36. New York: Chatham House Publishers.

Meier, Kenneth J. and Cathy Johnson. 1990. "The Politics of Demon Run: Regulating Alcohol and Its Deleterious Consequences." *American Politics Quarterly* 18: 404–429.

Meier, Kenneth J., and Deborah R. McFarland. 1993. "The Politics of Funding Abortion: State Responses to the Political Environment." *American Politics Quarterly* 21 (1): 81–101.

Mooney, Christopher Z. 2001. "The Public Clash of Private Values." In *The Public Clash of Private Values: The Politics of Morality Policy*, ed. Christopher Z. Money, 3–18. New York: Chatham House Publishers.

Mooney, Christopher Z. 2000. "The Decline of Federalism and the Rise of Morality-Policy Conflict in the United States." *Publius* 30: 171–188.

Mooney, Christopher Z., and Mei-Hsien Lee. 1995. "Legislative Morality in the American States: The Case of Pre-*Roe* Abortion Regulation Reform." *American Journal of Political Science* 39: 599–627.

Mooney, Christopher Z., and Mie-Hsien Lee. 1999a. "Morality Policy Reinvention: State Death Penalties." *Annals of the American Academy of Political and Social Science* 566: 80–92.

Mooney, Christopher Z., and Mie-Hsien Lee. 1999b. "The Temporal Diffusion of Morality Policy: The Case of Death Penalty Legislation in the American States." *Policy Studies Journal* 27 (4): 766–792.

Mooney, Christopher Z., and Mie-Hsien Lee. 2000. "The Influence of Values on Consensus and Contentious Morality Policy: U.S. Death Penalty Reform, 1956–82." *Journal of Politics* 62: 223–239.

Mueller v. Allen. 1983. 463 U.S. 388.

Nice, David C. 1992. "The States and the Death Penalty." *Western Political Quarterly* 45 (4): 1037–1048.

Norrander, Barbara, and Clyde Wilcox. 1999. "Public Opinion and Policymaking in the States: The Case of Post-*Roe* Abortion Policy." *Policy Studies Journal* 27 (4): 707–722.

O'Connor, Karen. 1996. *No Neutral Ground: Abortion Politics in an Age of Absolutes*. Boulder, Colo.: Westview Press.

O'Connor, Robert E., and Michael B. Berkman. 1995. "Religious Determinants of State Abortion Policy." *Social Science Quarterly* 76: 447–459.

Olson, Laura R., Karen V. Guth, and James L. Guth. 2003. "The Lotto and the Lord: Religious Influences on the Adoption of a Lottery in South Carolina." *Sociology of Religion* 64: 87–110.

Peters, B. Guy. 2006. *American Public Policy: Promise and Performance*. 7th ed. Washington, D.C.: CQ Press.

Pierce, Patrick A., and Donald E. Miller. 1999. "Variations in the Diffusion of State Lottery Adoptions: How Revenue Dedication Changes Morality Politics." *Policy Studies Journal* 27 (4): 696–706.

Roe v. Wade. 1973. 410 U.S. 113.

Ryden, David, and Jeffrey Polet. 2005. *Sanctioning Religion: Politics, Law, and Faith-Based Public Services*. Boulder, Colo.: Lynne Rienner Publishers.

Schattschneider, E.E. 1960. *The Semi-Sovereign People: A Realist's View of Democracy in America*. New York: Holt, Rinehart and Winston.

Sharp, Elaine B., ed. 1999. *Culture Wars and Local Politics*. Lawrence, Kans.: University of Kansas Press.

Smith, Cheryl K. 1993. "What About Legalized Assisted Suicide?" *Issues in Law and Medicine* 8: 503–519.

Smith, Tom. 1990. "Classifying Protestant Denominations." *Review of Religious Research* 31: 225–245.

Steensland, Brian, Jerry Park, Mark Regnerus, Lynn Robinson, W. Bradford Wilcox, and Robert Woodberry. 2000. "The Measure of American Religion." *Social Forces* 79 (1): 291–318.

Stern, Mark D. 2001. "Charitable Choice: The Law as it is and May be." In *Can Charitable Choice Work?*, ed. Adnrew Walsh, 157–177. Hartford, Conn.: The Leanard E. Greenberg Center for the Study of Religion in Public Life.

Tatalovich, Raymond, T. Alexander Smith, and Michael P. Bobic. 1994. "Moral Conflict and the Policy Process." *Policy Currents* 4 (4): 1, 3–6.

Tatalovich, Raymond, and Byron W. Daynes, eds. 1988. *Social Regulatory Policy.* Boulder, Colo.: Westview Press.

Tatalovich, Raymond, and Byron W. Daynes, eds. 2005. *Moral Controversies in American Politics.* 3rd ed. Armonk, N.Y.: M. E. Sharpe.

Unruh, Heidi Rolland, and Ronald J. Sider. 2005. *Saving Souls, Serving Society: Understanding the Faith Factor in Church-Based Social Ministry.* New York: Oxford University Press.

Vergari, Sandra. 2000. "Morality Politics and Educational Policy: The Abstinence-Only Sex Education Grant." *Educational Policy* 14 (2): 290–310.

Wald, Kenneth D., James W. Button, and Barbara A. Rienzo. 1996. "The Politics of Gay Rights in American Communities: Explaining Antidiscrimination Ordinances and Politics." *American Journal of Political Science* 40 (4): 1152–1178.

Wald, Kenneth D., James W. Button, and Barbara A. Rienzo. 2001. "Morality Politics vs. Political Economy: The Case of School-Based Health Centers." *Social Science Quarterly* 82 (2): 221–234.

Wineburg, Robert. 2001. *A Limited Partnership: The Politics of Religion, Welfare, and Social Service.* New York: Columbia University Press.

Wineburg, Robert 2007. *Faith-Based Inefficiency: The Follies of Bush's Initiatives.* Westport, Conn.: Praeger Press.

Wuthnow, Robert. 2006. *Saving America?: Faith-Based Services and the Future of Civil Society.* Princeton, N.J.: Princeton University Press.

INDEX

·····················